Why Do You Need this New Edition?

If you're wondering why you should buy this new edition of *Social Work Practice*, here are some good reasons!

● Part I from previous editions has been condensed into two chapters and a chapter on **Diversity Competence** has been added (Chapter 3).

● Chapter 3 develops the concept of **diversity competent practice**–the application of cultural competence to all diverse populations–which encourages students to assume a learning role and develop an approach that is consistent with the norms and expectations of the population that is being served. Diversity competent practice is infused throughout the text.

● A revised Chapter (10) on Direct Practice Actions demonstrates how the Johnson/Yanca model can be used as a framework for any social work intervention. Sections have been added on the use of **Brief and Solution Focused Models, Person Centered Theory, Task Centered Models, Narrative Approaches, Afrocentric Approach, Feminist Practice, and Practice with People Who Are Gay or Lesbian**.

● **Actions to change organizations and communities** have been added to a revised chapter on Indirect Practice Actions (Chapter 11).

Social Work Practice

Social Work Practice

A Generalist Approach

TENTH EDITION

Louise C. Johnson

University of South Dakota

Stephen J. Yanca

Saginaw Valley State University

Allyn & Bacon

Boston   Columbus   Indianapolis   New York   San Francisco   Upper Saddle River
Amsterdam   Cape Town   Dubai   London   Madrid   Milan   Munich   Paris   Montreal   Toronto
Delhi   Mexico City   Sao Paulo   Sydney   Hong Kong   Seoul   Singapore   Taipei   Tokyo

Editor: *Patricia Quinlin*
Editorial Assistant: *Carly Czech*
Marketing Manager: *Wendy Albert*
Marketing Assistant: *Kyle VanNatter*
Production Supervisor: *Patrick Cash-Peterson*
Manufacturing Buyer: *Debbie Rossi*

Cover Administrator: *Kristina Mose-Libon*
Editorial Production and
  Composition Service: *Preparè*
Interior Design: *NA*
Photo Researcher: *Martha Shethar*
Cover Designer: *[4/c covers only]*

Portions of this text have been adapted from Stephen J. Yanca and Louise C. Johnson, *Generalist Social Work Practice with Families*, published by Allyn and Bacon, Boston, MA, © 2008 by Pearson Education. Adapted by permission of the publisher. Portions have also been adapted from Stephen J. Yanca and Louise C. Johnson, *Generalist Social Work Practice with Groups*, published by Allyn and Bacon, Boston, MA, © 2009 by Pearson Education. Adapted by permission of the publisher.

Library of Congress Cataloging-in-Publication Data

Johnson, Louise C.
    Social work practice: a generalist approach / Louise C. Johnson, Stephen J. Yanca.—
10th ed.
      p. cm.
    Includes bibliographical references and index.
    ISBN–13: 978-0-205–75516–5 (alk. paper)
    ISBN–10: 0-205–75516–X (alk. paper)
    1. Social service.   2. Social case work.   I. Yanca, Stephen J.   II. Title.
    HV40.J64 2010
    361.3'2—dc22   2009020086

10 9 8 7 6 5 4 3 2 1   13 12 11 10 09

ISBN–10: 0–205–75516–X
ISBN–13: 978–0–205–75516–5

www.pearsonhighered.com

Allyn & Bacon
is an imprint of

Contents

Preface   xvii

PART ONE • *Perspectives on Social Work Practice*   1

CHAPTER 1 *Social Work as a Response to Concern/Need*   3

From Concern to Need   4
Need   4
Common Human Needs   6
   Human Development Perspective   6
   Ecological Perspective   7
   Strengths Approach   8
Professions as a Response to Need   9
Development of Social Work Knowledge   10
Social Functioning   13
Summary   14
Questions   15
Suggested Readings   15

CHAPTER 2 *Social Work as a Creative Blending of Knowledge, Values, and Skills*   16

Knowledge   17
Values   21
Skills   25
Creative Blending of Knowledge, Values, and Skills   27
Using Knowledge, Values, and Skills   29
Intervention into Human Transactions   32
The Phases of the Change Process   34
Summary   36
Questions   37
Suggested Readings   38

CHAPTER **3** *Diversity Competent Practice* 39

Becoming Diversity Competent 44

Gender Competence 47

Diversity Competence with People Who Are Gay or Lesbian 49

A Schema for Studying Diverse Ethnic Groups 50

Diversity Competence with People Who Are African American 54

Historical Considerations 55
Cultural Patterns 55
Family 57
Communication Processes 57
Coping Patterns 58
Community Structure 58
Current Issues 59

Diversity Competence with People Who Are Hispanic/Latino 59

Historical Considerations 59
Cultural Patterns 60
Family 61
Communication Processes 61
Coping Patterns 61
Community Structure 62
Current Issues 62

Diversity Competence with People Who Are Native American 63

Historical Considerations 63
Cultural Patterns 64
Family 64
Communication Processes 65
Coping Patterns 65
Community Structure 65
Current Issues 66

Summary 67

Questions 67

Suggested Readings 68

PART TWO • *The Interactional Process and the Ecosystem* 69

CHAPTER 4 *The Worker* 71

Knowledge of Self **72**

The Person as a Feeling, Thinking, Acting System   73
Lifestyle and Philosophy of Life   74
Moral Code and Value System   75
Family and Cultural Roots   77
Life Experiences   78
Personal Needs   78
Personal Functioning   83

The Helping Person **84**

Characteristics of a Helping Person   85
Responsibility and Authority   86
Helping Skills   88

Ethical Decision Making **89**

Accountability **90**

Records   90
Effect of Privacy and Open-Access Laws   94
Use of Computers   94

Summary **96**

Questions **96**

Suggested Readings **97**

CHAPTER 5 *The Client* 98

Becoming a Client **99**

Understanding the Individual Client **103**

Vital Roles   105
Human Diversity   105
Motivation, Capacity, and Opportunity   109
Stress and Crisis Determination   110
Strengths and Uniqueness of Clients   110

Summary **111**

Questions **112**

Suggested Readings **112**

CHAPTER 6 *Environment* 113

Person in Environment as an Ecosystem 114
The Community as a Social System 115
Understanding the Agency 125
Transactions between Person and Ecosystem 133
Working in a Bureaucracy 134
Summary 138
Questions 139
Suggested Readings 139

CHAPTER 7 *Interaction and Engagement* 140

Engagement and Formation of a One-to-One Action System 142
Relationship 148
    The Helping Relationship 149
    Special Influences on the Helping Relationship 151
Communication 155
The Interview: An Interactional Tool 157
    Preparing for an Interview 159
    The Stages of an Interview 159
    Skills Used by the Worker during the Interview 162
Summary 169
Questions 169
Suggested Readings 170

PART THREE • *The Social Work Process* 171

CHAPTER 8 *Assessment* 173

The Assessment Process 175
Selection of the Client System 177
Important Elements of the Assessment Phase 179
    Judgment 183

Stages in the Assessment Phase   **186**

    Identify the Initial Need or Concern   187
    Identify the Nature of the Need or Concern   190
    Identify Potential Strengths and Resources in the Ecosystem   191
    Select and Collect Information   192
    Analyze the Available Information   193

Transactional Assessment   **194**

    The Dual Perspective   199
    Mapping   200
    Social Support Network Analysis   201

Summary   **201**

Questions   **202**

Suggested Readings   **202**

CHAPTER   **9**   *Planning*   203

Empirically Based Practice   **205**

A Model for Good Practices in Generalist Social Work Practice   **206**

Components of a Plan   **208**

    Goals and Objectives   208
    Units of Attention   211
    Strategy   212

Factors Affecting a Plan of Action   **216**

    The Community   216
    The Agency   217
    The Social Issue   217
    The Worker   218
    The Client   219
    Diversity and Populations at Risk   219
    Strengths and Challenges of the Systems Involved   221

The Planning Process   **222**

Agreement between Worker and Client   **223**

Summary   **224**

Questions   **225**

Suggested Readings   **225**

CHAPTER 10   *Direct Practice Actions*   **226**

Action to Enable Clients to Use Available Resources   **230**

The Service Delivery System   230
Referral   233
Broker and Advocate Roles   234

Action to Empower and Enable Clients   **236**

Action in Response to Crisis   **240**

Recognizing Crisis   240
Responding to Crisis   242

Action That Is Supportive   **243**

Use of Activity as an Interventive Strategy   **246**

Actions Utilizing Other Theories and Models   **249**

Brief and Solution-Focused Models   250
Task-Centered Models   251
Person-Centered Theory   252
Narrative Approaches   252
Afrocentric Approach   253
Feminist Practice   254
Practice with People Who Are Gay or Lesbian   258

Summary   **259**

Questions   **260**

Suggested Readings   **260**

CHAPTER 11   *Indirect Practice Actions*   **261**

Action as Mediation   **263**

Influence   **265**

Environmental Change   **268**

Coordination of Services   **272**

Case Management   274

Actions to Change Organizations   **276**

Actions to Change the Community   **277**

Summary   **279**

Questions   **279**

Suggested Readings   **280**

CHAPTER 12   *Evaluation and Termination*   **281**

Kinds of Evaluation   **283**

Single-System Design and Research Techniques in Evaluation   **285**

Evaluation during Phases of the Change Process   **291**

Kinds of Termination   **293**

Planned Termination with Individuals   **297**

Components of Termination   **298**

Disengagement   299
Stabilization of Change   300
Evaluation   301

Summary   **302**

Questions   **302**

Suggested Readings   **302**

PART FOUR • *Multiperson Systems and Good Practices in Generalist Practice*   303

CHAPTER 13   *Generalist Practice with Families*   **306**

The Family as a Multiperson Client System   **308**

Variations in Family Form   **310**

The Change Process with Families   **312**

Assessment with Families   313
The Planning Phase with Families   325
Direct and Indirect Practice Actions with Families   326
Evaluation and Termination with Families   333

Summary   **334**

Questions   **334**

Suggested Readings   **335**

CHAPTER 14   *Generalist Practice with Groups*   **336**

Group Purpose   **337**

Assessment with Small Groups   **338**

Assessing the Small Group as a Social System   339

Planning with Small Groups   **350**

 Planning for a New Group   350
 Planning for Group Sessions   350
 Planning within Group Sessions   351

Direct Practice Actions with Small Groups   **351**

 Actions to Facilitate Group Formation   352
 Actions to Facilitate Discussion Leadership   354
 Actions to Resolve Conflict   355
 Actions to Enhance Group Interaction   356
 Actions to Facilitate Group Development   358
 Actions to Structure Group Activities   359

Evaluation and Termination with Small Groups   **360**

Self-Help Groups   **361**

Summary   **362**

Questions   **362**

Suggested Readings   **363**

CHAPTER **15**   *Generalist Practice with Organizations and Communities*   **364**

Macropractice and Social Justice   **365**

Needs Assessment   **366**

Program Planning and Resource Development   **368**

Changing Organizations from Within   **370**

The Social Worker as a Group Member   **373**

 Issues in Group Participation   374
 Use of the Team   374
 Leadership   376
 Social Work Tasks   377

Involvement of Influentials   **378**

Networking   **379**

Cause Advocacy   **380**

Community Organization   **382**

Summary   **385**

Questions   **385**

Suggested Readings   **386**

CHAPTER 16   *Models and Good Practices in Generalist Social Work Practice*   **387**

Models of Social Work Practice   **388**

Behavior Therapy (Sociobehavioral)   388
Case Management   389
Cognitive (Rational, Reality Theory)   390
Communication (Communicative-Interactive)   390
Crisis Intervention   391
Ecological (Life Model)   392
Feminist Practice (material provided by Mary Bricker-Jenkins)   392
Gestalt Therapy   393
Integrative   393
Locality Development   394
Mediating   395
Problem Solving   395
Social Action   396
Social Planning   396
Strengths Perspective   397
Task   397

Good Practices in Generalist Social Work   **398**

Good Practice in Aging Services   398
Good Practice in Chemical Dependence Services   400
Good Practice in Child Welfare   403
Good Practice in Domestic Violence Services   407
Good Practice in Health Care Settings   410
Good Practice in Mental Health   411
Good Practice in Youth and Delinquency Services   416

Notes   421

Glossary   435

Author Index   443

Subject Index   446

Preface

We are pleased to present the tenth edition of *Social Work Practice: A Generalist Approach*. We are gratified that this text has been in publication for over 27 years. With our companion texts *Generalist Social Work Practice with Families* and *Generalist Social Work Practice with Groups*, we now have a trilogy of texts that cover the entire generalist social work practice curriculum using one model of generalist practice, the Johnson/Yanca model. To our knowledge this has not been done before. Other texts on generalist practice are written with singular texts on generalist social work practice and generalist practice with families and one on generalist practice with organizations and communities. Generalist social work programs that wish to concentrate on studying generalist practice with multiclient systems have to be prepared to teach and have students learn new models of generalist social work practice every time they use a different text. Our three texts will take students from an introductory course on generalist practice to more advanced courses on working with families and with groups and organizations and communities. At the same time, each text can also be used as a stand alone text for a course on any of these areas. This tenth edition of *Social Work Practice: A Generalist Approach* provides a foundation for understanding generalist practice. It continues developing the generalist perspective that past editions have established. It synthesizes historical and current understandings into a logically developed sequence for learning about and teaching the practice of social work. As a textbook on generalist practice, it should be particularly useful for undergraduates in practice or methods courses and as a practice text for first-year graduate students. The material can be used on a one-semester basis or in a two-quarter sequence.

Generalist social work, as developed in this text, begins with the need of an individual or a social system. In generalist practice, the client system can be an individual, a family, a group, an organization, or a community. The social worker explores or assesses the situation in which the need exists with the client system and significant others. Based on the findings of this exploration, a plan for work to alleviate the situation is developed and an agreement between the worker and the client system is reached. The focus of the plan can also be an individual, a small group, a family, an organization, or a community. Once the plan is developed, the worker and client system, and perhaps other persons or systems, work to carry out the plan. At some point, the worker and client system decide whether to terminate the relationship or to continue to work together on further plans.

Students should have certain prerequisites before using the material covered in this book. These include:

1. At least one introductory course covering the history and development of social welfare and an introduction to the profession.
2. A broad liberal arts base providing a wide variety of knowledge pertaining to the

human situation, an appreciation of history, and some understanding about the nature of knowledge.

3. Courses, such as those in psychology, sociology, anthropology, political science, and economics, providing an understanding of human behavior and the social environment. Courses that include understandings of human development and human diversity, including racial and ethnic differences, are particularly important.

A course on human behavior in the social environment taken in a social work program is *not* a prerequisite or a corequisite. This book provides the content needed for integration of social science content into the social work practice frame of reference. Examples of concepts and how they are used in practice situations are given as one means to assist students in applying this knowledge to practice.

Although the book does not attempt to present any one model or approach to social work, it develops an ecosystems strengths approach to the change process and synthesizes material from a number of sources into a coherent whole. It can be used as a framework for any social work model or intervention or approach. At points it may seem that the major focus is on work with individuals; however, this is not the case. It is often easier, however, for students to grasp concepts when their application to work with individuals is presented. These examples can then be used as a base for considering applications to other systems (family, small group, organization, and community). Also, no attempt is made to consider practice with any particular population or social problem area. Rather, the assumption is made that the generalist approach can be used in a wide variety of situations, including urban and rural practice, and with a variety of client populations, such as with people who are older, those who have medical and mental health problems, those who are discriminated against because of diversity, and those who suffer because their social situations do not provide for their basic needs. A chapter is presented that develops the concept of good practices in various settings in which generalist social workers typically practice.

Plan for the Text

In this tenth edition, we have consolidated the material from previous editions in Part One and have reduced this material to the first two chapters. We also added a chapter on diversity competence. Part One develops a framework on which the other three parts are based. It provides a foundation for understanding social work practice and, in particular, generalist practice and diversity competence. It considers practice from the perspective of need and looks at a brief history of social work as a profession. It goes on to examine how knowledge, values, and skills are blended and introduces the change process and the concept of intervention into human transactions. Part Two considers the interactional process and develops the concept of an ecosystem. It presents material on understanding oneself as a social worker, and understanding the client and the environment. Finally, it examines interaction and engagement.

Part Three examines the social work process, which is also called the change process. It is conceptualized as assessment, planning, action, and evaluation and termination. We reorganized Part Three by once again separating chapters on direct and indirect practice actions. To Chapter 10 on direct practice actions we added material on the use of other theories and models, pointing out that the change process in generalist practice can be used as a framework for any social work intervention. To this section we provide material on the use of brief and solution-focused models, person-centered theory, task-centered models, narrative approaches, Afrocentric approach, feminist practice, and practice with people who are gay or lesbian. To Chapter 11 on indirect practice actions we have added material from our text *Generalist Social Work Practice with Groups* on working with organizations and communities. This material includes actions to change organizations and actions to change communities.

Part Four considers multiperson systems (families, groups, and organizations and communities) and the application of the change process to generalist practice with those systems. It also presents models of social work practice and good practices in aging services, chemical dependence services, child welfare, domestic violence services, health care settings, mental health, and youth and delinquency services. These are settings that typically use generalist social workers in serving clients.

The eighth edition was reorganized from earlier editions. Separate chapters were developed on generalist practice with families, groups, and macrosystems (organizations and communities). Those chapters became Part Four along with a new chapter on models and good practices. We made the separation of chapters on multiperson client systems somewhat reluctantly, fearing that the student would lose sight of the freedom to work with any size system, which is a strength of generalist practice. However, our teaching experience indicated that it was difficult for many students to grasp the phases of the change process with various systems when the material was organized solely around those phases. We have continued to emphasize the need to retain the freedom to work with systems of various sizes and hope that the instructor will do likewise in class. In the eighth edition, we introduced our version of diversity competent practice. This was developed further in the ninth edition along with adding social work background material about diverse groups, people who are older, and women that specifically addresses issues of working with these groups. In this tenth edition, we have added to Part One an adapted version of our chapter on diversity competent practice from our text *Generalist Social Work Practice with Families*. Readings that are useful in the development of understanding about practice with diverse groups are suggested.

In order to enhance readability, yet maintain a nonbiased gender content, the pronouns *he* and *she* are used randomly throughout the book, with greater emphasis on the use of *she* because it is expected that the overwhelming majority of readers (and generalist social workers) are likely to be women.

The organization chosen for this text seems most appropriate to the authors, who have based it on years of experience in teaching generalist social work practice. As the concepts are developed, attention is given to building on material presented in earlier sections of the book. Repetition is used to reinforce learning. The authors assume that the present cannot be understood apart from the past; thus historical as well as contemporary aspects of the material covered are noted.

Charts and schemas are provided to help students organize considerable amounts of information into a coherent whole to maximize understanding. The book contains many case examples. Most major sections of each chapter contain vignettes that depict the major concepts in action. In addition, longer case examples are provided and followed up in subsequent chapters. In some chapters, a case may be provided in several parts, illustrating several major concepts. An attempt has also been made to use case examples from practice in a variety of settings. In choosing case material, dimensions of size and kind of community, client age and needs, and agency purpose and source of sanction have been considered. Although much can be learned from a textbook, thorough learning takes place only as the conceptualizations are applied in actual practice experiences. Each chapter contains a summary, a statement of learning expectations for that chapter, study questions, and suggested readings for use by students and teachers. An appendix, with chapter notes, and a glossary of key terms are included at the end of the text.

Acknowledgments

For the tenth edition of this text, we continue to recognize the contributions of several practitioners and students who contributed to the ninth edition. Thanks go out to Karen Pabalis for her feedback on good practice in health care settings and to Jeanne Yonke and her colleagues for their contributions to good practice in domestic violence services. Several students at Saginaw Valley State University provided research materials on working with diverse populations, including Stacie Buszka, Renee Oberski, Roshell Watley-Thomas, Mark Ciacuia, Tunya Hottois, and Eddie Payne.

Thanks are due to the reviewers of this and previous editions of this text, whose suggestions were greatly appreciated and were incorporated into this revision wherever possible: Jean Brooks, Jackson State University; Margaret R. Calista, Marist College; David K. Chenot, California State University, Bakersfield; Shirley M. Clark, Chattanooga State Technical Community College; Jean E. Daniels, California State University, Northridge; Diane Dwyer, State University of New York, Brockport; Ralph J. Gilmore, Westfield State College; Susan Grettenberger, Michigan State University; Kenneth J. Herrmann, Jr., State University of New York, Brockport; Patricia Hunter, California State University, Chico; Lillie C. Kirsch, Marion Technical College; Anna Martin-Jearld, Bridgewater State College; Christine McGill, San Francisco State University; Barbara L. McGregor, Saginaw Valley State University; Judith Norman, Brigham Young University; Jean L. Nuernberger, Central Missouri State University; Art Preciado, California State University, Chico; Emma Quartaro, Seton Hall University; Jeanette Simon, Upper Iowa University; and Louise M. Walton, Norfolk State University. We would also like to thank the reviewers of this edition: Cynthia Bishop, Meredith College; Lori Curtis, University of Missouri—St. Louis; Debra Gohagan, Minnesota State University, Mankato; Anne Kearney Kelso, Syracuse University; Anthony J. Mallon, Virginia Commonwealth University; John D. Matthews, Virginia Commonwealth University; Peggy Pittman-Munke, Murray State University; and Carla Sofka, Siena College.

L. C. J.
S. J. Y.

I

Perspectives on Social Work Practice

Part One provides an overview of the nature of social work practice. When the reader has an understanding of the complexity of the practice situation and has developed a framework in which to place the details, study of practice specifics can follow. The reader likely will wish to return to the concepts presented to develop a greater depth of understanding.

Social work is complex, having a wide variety of applications. Because of this, there are a number of *perspectives* regarding its nature. Five descriptions or perspectives are presented here to provide the overall framework of generalist social work practice. These are most often those referred to in social work literature, which best explains the nature of contemporary generalist social work practice. The approach used in this text is referred to as an *interactive-transactional* approach to generalist social work practice using ecosystems and a strengths approach. Concepts, ideas, and understandings gained from a wide variety of practice literature and experiences are synthesized to describe the realities of generalist social work practice.

A *generalist approach* requires that the social worker assess the situation with the client and decide which systems are the appropriate *units of attention,* or focus of the work, for the change effort. As the units of attention may include an individual, a family, a small group, an agency or organization, a community, or the transactions among these, the generalist approach emphasizes knowledge that can be applied to a variety of systems. Each of the five perspectives discussed in Part One has application to all these units of attention.

Each perspective describes social work practice from contrasting but complementary views. Each may be seen as a different facet of a complex way of thinking, feeling, and doing, and each provides a way of understanding the activity that has come to be known as generalist social work practice. Together, they provide a description of the essential nature of generalist social work practice.

In the first chapter, the first two perspectives address the "why" of social work practice. "Social Work as a Response to Concern/Need," discusses the basic reason for the social work endeavor. It focuses on the desirable outcome of the combined work of worker and client and develops the concepts of need, common human needs, human diversity, social systems needs, social functioning, ecosystems, and a strengths approach. "Professions as a Response to Need," examines practice historically in order to understand why practice exists in its current form. Contemporary practice has many vestiges from the past. Thus, some understanding of the development of practice theory, as contrasted with social welfare history, is important for understanding the major concepts that underlie practice. This section also introduces the concepts of profession, assessment, person in situation, relationship, process, and intervention. These topics were chosen because of their common usage in many conceptualizations of social work practice.

Chapter 2 covers the remaining perspectives—the "how" of social work practice. "Social Work as a Creative Blending of Knowledge, Values, and Skills," discusses how knowledge, values, and skills are used in understanding and taking action in relation to social-functioning needs. The concepts developed are knowledge, values, skills, and creative blending. "The Phases of the Change Process," presents a way of thinking about the process of social work and the steps used in responding to need. It develops the concept of facilitating growth and change based on strengths. This section also discusses the way in which the social worker seeks to bring about growth and change and develops the concept of intervention.

Chapter 3 is our version of what we call "Diversity Competent Practice." It provides a model for becoming diversity competent and presents our version of gender competent practice and diversity competent practice with people who are gay or lesbian. This is followed by "A Schema for Studying Individuals and Families from Diverse Ethnic Groups." The schema is then applied to people who are African American, Hispanic/Latino, and Native American.

The assumption is made throughout the book that the reader is bringing a knowledge base developed through previous social work courses and experiences. Also, it is assumed the reader has some basic understanding of social science concepts, especially those from psychology and sociology. These will be developed in Part Two, which considers the ecosystem, engagement, and the interactional processes present in the social work endeavor. Part Three describes the ongoing process undertaken by worker and client as they seek to respond to need and reach commonly set goals. Part Four focuses on generalist social work practice with families, with groups, and with organizations and communities. Part Four also contains a summary of traditional models of social work practice and of good practice methods in social work settings or with populations that are commonly served by generalist social workers.

1

Social Work as a Response to Concern/Need

Learning Expectations

1. Understanding the concept of need and the ability to identify common human needs.
2. Understanding how concepts about human development are used in identifying need.
3. Some understanding of the following concepts and how they developed: assessment, person in situation, relationship, process, and intervention.
4. Some understanding of how earlier conceptualizations of social work practice affect the nature of contemporary practice.
5. Understanding of social functioning, ecosystems, and strengths as the focus of social work.

The "why" of social work practice is addressed when social work is viewed as a response to a concern or need. This perspective helps identify appropriate goals for service and considers the appropriate target for change given the context of the concern or need. It allows thinking about social work practice to "start where the client is," at the point a concern is felt or a need is identified. Additionally, it begins to provide the means for integrating knowledge about human behavior and the social environment with social work practice to meet human need.

This chapter explores some concepts that clarify this facet of social work practice. These understandings are derived from classical and contemporary themes used by social workers to describe the nature of human need.

From Concern to Need

To begin to understand the complexity of a situation, it is helpful first to identify some of the possible ways concern may be felt in one situation. For example, a parent may be concerned because her child is not doing well in school; a teacher, because a student is disruptive; a merchant, because an adolescent boy is stealing merchandise. A student may be concerned because his family is experiencing financial stress. An agency may be concerned because there are no resources to help families with communication problems. A community group may be concerned that so many young people are in trouble with the law. Each of these concerns may exist around the same situation, and each indicates some difficulty in the relationship between people and social systems.

Human situations, and thus human needs, are complex. The social worker must develop a frame of reference for understanding the reasons behind behaviors. She must also understand environmental factors that influence these behaviors and how the environment is influenced by the behavior. Each situation must be viewed as multifaceted and unique.

Concern is a feeling that something is not right. It is interest in, regard for, and care about the well-being of oneself or others. A feeling of concern is often the result of some behavior that affects the relationship between the individual and other individuals or a social system. All behavior has meaning, and people express and fulfill need through behavior. Need also generates feelings. As a part of understanding what is causing a concern and why the concern is important, feelings relative to the concern should be identified and explored. The social work response to such behavior and related feelings identifies need and discovers alternate ways of need fulfillment so that the needs of each party may be met.

Need

Need is that which is necessary for either a person or a social system to function within reasonable expectations in a given situation. Need is not a want for something that would be nice to have but, rather, is important to the development or functioning of the person or system. For example, if a boy is caught stealing, an unreasonable expectation would be that he keep the stolen items because he felt he needed them. A reasonable expectation would be to identify the reasons behind his desire for the items and to find alternate ways of meeting the related need in a socially acceptable manner.

"They need"—need that is identified by others—has often been a focus of social work. This outside identification of need sometimes leads to people being told what they need. But **felt need**—need identified by the client—is just as relevant. Often the "they need" and the felt need are different or are expressed in different ways. Social workers, using their expert knowledge and professional value system, can sometimes identify need that does not seem relevant or realistic to clients. The felt need of the client and concerned persons must always be considered. This practice is consistent with a basic social work principle: "start where the client is." In using this principle, the social worker starts with the concern or felt need of the client and other concerned persons; identifies various needs (felt needs or "they needs") in the situation; and with the client determines goals based on both kinds of need. In the case example, the debate would be whether services should focus on Jerry and his parents or on conditions that interfere with Jerry's functioning. Questions to be investigated might be: Are the father's working hours too long? What is the school doing to resolve the situation? Are there other needs or concerns in the family?

Case Example

The school referred Jerry Adams, age 13, because of poor school performance. There were also several instances in which negative racial epithets had been exchanged between Jerry and other students. Jerry is the son of Jamilla and Charles Adams. They have four more children. The family is African American, and they recently moved into a neighborhood with a mixture of working- and middle-class households. They are one of only two African American families in the area. The family owns a business. Mrs. A is also concerned because Jerry was caught trying to steal a pair of tennis shoes at a store. Jerry is doing poorly in school this year after being on the honor roll at his former school. Mrs. A believes that most of this is related to racial tension at the new school. Mr. A works long hours at their store and is not home very much. Mrs. A also works there, mainly part time. The store has to compete with the large national chain stores and may not be able to stay open.

The social worker talks with Jerry alone. He confirms that he is not doing well at school and there is stress in his relationships there. He does not feel welcome and wishes he could return to his old school and neighborhood. He admits to arguing with his siblings at times and misses doing things with his father. He is feeling stress from the uncertainty of the family's business. He admits to getting caught trying to take a pair of tennis shoes but blames it on trying to fit in with some peers because they dared him to do it.

The worker speculates about Jerry's needs in this situation. She thinks about the developmental needs of a thirteen-year-old boy. Jerry's need for security and relationships could explain much of what is occurring. She understands that Jerry might be susceptible to peer influences to gain acceptance. Diversity issues have arisen in the school and the community, which is predominantly white. The worker knows that the storekeeper cannot allow his goods to be stolen and that Jerry's parents need to be well thought of by the community and by fellow merchants. The family is an important system. Relationships among the siblings and between them and their parents are especially important with the move to a different community and different schools.

(continued)

Case Example   *(continued)*

In this situation the worker develops an identification of needs for Jerry, his family, and the environment. She identifies which individuals and systems have needs and what those needs are. The components of this situation include the people involved—the child, each parent, the teacher, the merchant, and the child's peers—and the social systems of the family and the school. It also involves the agency, the family's business, and the community. As the needs of each component are identified, the interdependent and reciprocal nature of these needs becomes apparent. This is the beginning of the social work endeavor.

Common Human Needs

Common human needs have been identified as: provision of food, shelter, clothing, health care; opportunity for growth both emotional and intellectual, and meaningful relationships.[1] Abraham Maslow also developed a means for identifying human need. He presented a hierarchy which includes: 1. Physiological needs—food, water, air. 2. Safety needs. 3. Needs related to belonging and being loved. 4. Esteem needs—having status and acceptance in one's group. 5. Needs related to self-actualization. 6. Needs related to cognitive understanding.[2]

Social workers are aware of the need for individuals and groups to feel that they have the power or the control necessary to meet their needs or to change situations that are affecting need fulfillment. The literature has been particularly focused on the need for *empowerment* of discriminated-against groups, such as persons of color and women. The nature of contemporary American society can lead many individuals and groups to feel helpless and hopeless. Thus, consideration of feelings of hope for quality of life and control of resources and situations that affect need fulfillment are important aspects of contemporary social work practice.[3] This theme will be explored throughout this book.

Social workers use several other bases for identifying and understanding human need. These include: knowledge about human development, understandings about human diversity (Chapter 3 will develop these understandings in considerable depth), ecosytems, and a strengths approach. Because of the complexity of the human situation multiple points of view provide the richness needed for an in-depth understanding of human needs. The human development perspective, the ecological perspective, and a strengths approach will be discussed in this chapter. Because of its importance a full chapter (3) will discuss a diversity perspective.

Human Development Perspective

A **human development perspective** indicates that people develop physically, cognitively, socially, emotionally, and spiritually over the life cycle.[4] There are benchmarks that can be used to measure growth in each area. Physically, there are such measures as the age of beginning to walk or the age of onset of puberty. Cognitively, the work of Jean Piaget is often used to examine how a person deals with concepts, or IQ tests are given to measure intelligence.[5] In the social-emotional area, the work of Erik Erikson is often used. His "eight stages of man,"[6] based on the mastery of psychosocial tasks relevant to each age, are useful in determining whether expected psychosocial growth has taken place. Lawrence Kohlberg proposed a theory that identified six stages of moral development.[7] Carol Gilligan offered a theory of moral development for women that has three levels and two transitions.[8] James Fowler proposed a theory of faith development composed of seven stages.[9] Each of these theories is an example of a human development perspective. From a developmental perspective, human need may be identified in two ways. First, at each stage of life individuals should be developing in certain age-specific ways, and for this development to take place, certain conditions must be present. The infant needs love and physical care as well as sensory stimulation. The school-age child still needs physical care, though not to the same degree as the infant. This child needs protection but also the freedom and opportunity to learn skills and develop creativity. The adolescent needs opportunities to resolve the normal conflicts of growing up, to find out who she is, to deal with sexuality, and to make vocational decisions. Adults need opportunities to feel a sense of accomplishment, fulfill their nurturing needs, and participate in group life and society. Older adults need economic security; provision for health needs; and the opportunity to deal with feelings arising from retirement, the aging process, health concerns, and death and dying.

A second way to identify human need is to note development that would be expected at a particular life stage but has not taken place. This includes past needs that have not been met and are contributing to difficulties in present social functioning. It also includes identification of developmental lags or situations in which there is a danger that the expected development will not take place.

In working with Jerry, a social worker would be aware that he is entering the developmental stage of adolescence, a time of confusion for many boys. Jerry is probably trying to discover who he is in relationship to others. He is experiencing new sexual feelings. He is trying out various value systems. The insecurity of his father's business may undermine Jerry's ability to work through these issues.

The response to need from a developmental point of view is to provide the necessary conditions that will allow development to progress and to eliminate those that block development. These conditions are heavily dependent on social interaction between individuals and their environments. In responding to these common human needs, the social worker should have a thorough understanding of human development throughout the life span.

Ecological Perspective

Human need cannot be considered apart from the larger systems in which humans function. These include the family; small groups; the community; and various social institutions, such as the school, the church, and the social agency. All people belong to several larger systems, which often make conflicting demands. These systems are a part of each individual's environment. The demands of these systems are called **environmental demands**. Social systems theory provides a means of understanding these systems and identifying their needs. Social systems theory has been used by social workers to explain and understand these relationships.[10] A more contemporary explanation is found in an **ecological perspective**.

The term *ecology* comes from the biological theory that studies the relationship between organisms and environment. It is closely related to social systems theory, which has been used by social workers to describe human need as it relates to an individual's environment. All people belong to several systems that may be influential in either providing for needs, blocking need fulfillment, or making conflicting demands regarding need fulfillment. Larger systems that are a part of the individual's environment include family, small groups, community, and various social institutions, such as the school, the church, and the social agency to name a few. From an ecological perspective, need is a condition of the relationship between a person or people and the environment. People and their environments have needs and resources. Needs are met when the environment responds to the person in a way that satisfies her need and the person responds to the environment in a way that satisfies needs in the environment. A mutually beneficial interaction between person and environment is desired. When needs are met, then a state of **congruity** exists. There is agreement or harmony—a "fit"—between the person and the environment.

Unmet need reflects an imbalance between the responses of the person and the environment to each other. Sometimes needs are not met because there are insufficient resources available. More often, the interaction between the person and the environment is not balanced in a way that can sustain the needs of either one or both over time. This results in a state of **incongruity**—that is, a lack of agreement or harmony between the person and the environment.

An **ecosystems perspective** involves all the systems in a person-in-environment approach, including the physical environment. It examines the exchange of matter, energy, and information among these systems over time, including past, present, and future. Changes in these exchanges in one part of the ecosystem will affect other parts of the ecosystem.

In planning for change, an ecosystems approach considers the impact of change on all the systems involved. Meeting needs is not simply a matter of meeting the needs of one person at one moment in time. If needs are met at the expense of other people or systems in the environment, and if transactions between systems are not balanced in a way that results in mutual benefit, then over time the client will have difficulty in maintaining any benefits from the social work endeavor. If a balance is not found, there is the likelihood that the situation will either return to its previous state or perhaps worsen. Using this perspective to assist clients in meeting needs means facilitating changes in the person, the environment, and the transactions between person and environment in a way that ensures a balance between needs and resources over time.

Strengths Approach

In a **strengths approach** the worker moves from looking at deficits to looking at abilities and assets. This approach recognizes the importance of empowerment, resilience, healing, and wholeness in working with people. Membership (or belonging) is seen as essential to well-being. The development of this approach has been led by the social work faculty at the University of Kansas, in particular Dennis Saleeby.[11] Two of the basic tenets of this approach are that (1) "every individual, group, family, and community has strengths"[12], and (2) "every environment is full of resources."[13]

In responding to need, social workers should assist the client in identifying strengths and resources in herself and in her environment and use these to create an appropriate response to the need. There are critical reasons for incorporating a strengths approach into the process of meeting needs. Policy changes in human services have resulted in limitations on the length of service and an emphasis on brief, solution-focused intervention. Interventions that focus on deficits and dysfunction and look at the past to understand pathology do not lend themselves to brief intervention. A strengths approach is focused on the future and fits much better with shortened time frames. This approach builds on strengths and capacities that the client and the environment already have rather than relying on the acquisition of new skills and resources. Thus, a more solid foundation for change is ensured. In addition, the worker can identify and build a support system in the existing environment designed to maintain a new balance in the person-in-environment ecosystem.

In this text, an ecosystems approach and a strengths approach are combined with the problem-solving process to form an approach in which the social worker facilitates growth and change as a response to need. The focus will be on the concerns and needs of the client in interaction with her environment. In responding to need, the worker develops an understanding of the person in environment and then assists the client in developing and carrying out a plan for meeting her needs. In accomplishing this, the strengths, abilities, assets, and capacities of the person, family, neighborhood, and community are included.

Professions as a Response to Need

Because not all need can be met by individuals or those in their immediate social structure, there has developed a societal response—**Professions**. There is no clear definition of the term profession. Attempts have been made to develop frameworks for describing the attributes of a profession. Ernest Greenwood stated that "all professions seem to possess (1) systematic theory, (2) authority, (3) community sanction, (4) ethical codes, and (5) a culture."[14] These are the attributes most often referred to in social work literature when discussing social work as a profession.

Leslie Leighninger referred to Greenwood's work as a "trait-attribute" approach. She presented a "process model" focused on movement toward professional status, particularly the development of professional organizations and professional education.[15] Another approach is power/control, which considers the status of a profession. Authority and monopoly of service delivery are indicators of professional status.[16] Elizabeth Howe identified some professions, such as medicine and law, as operating from a "private practice model." She suggested that other professions, such as social work, in which the vast majority of practitioners are employed in agencies, should operate from what she identified as a "public model." The difference between the two models relates to autonomy. Public professions are subject to a greater degree of control by the public. Not only do professionals in the public professions have less autonomy but they are also responsible to clients, the agency, and those to whom the agency is responsible.[17]

When considering social work as a profession, it seems most appropriate to begin by considering Greenwood's attributes. First among these is the possession of a systematic theory. Social work has worked hard to develop this attribute. Because of the complexity of the human situation and other factors, this development is continuing. It is important to consider the process of knowledge development by the social work profession (process model). This allows for considering social work as continuing to develop as a profession and leads to consideration of the influence of the past on the present.

When thinking about the attributes of authority and community sanction, the power/control model becomes useful. The social work profession has not established a monopoly over the delivery of services relative to social functioning. It is only one of several professions (such as education, nursing, and substance abuse treatment) concerned with social functioning. In addition, it has been possible, especially in public social welfare agencies, for employees who carry out certain functions to carry the title of social worker even though they have not had professional social work education. Licensing laws have been most helpful in identifying who is a social worker. That identification is strongly tied to educational qualifications (bachelor of social work [BSW] or master of social work [MSW] degrees). Through licensing and other types of regulations, there now is some authority, community sanction, and recognition of an area of expertise and its services. An ethical code and a culture are provided through the National Association of Social Workers (NASW). The NASW *Code of Ethics,* which was revised in 1996, 1998, and 2008, is discussed in Chapter 2 as a part of the values system a social worker must consider when making practice decisions.

One important area in understanding the nature of social work practice is an appreciation for how its knowledge base has developed over time and how contemporary practice, particularly generalist practice, is part of a continuous development of practices of the past.

Development of Social Work Knowledge

Social work developed not in isolation but in the social climate of the day and the contemporary social welfare scene. It is not possible to present here all the details of either the social history and its effects on the development of social welfare institutions or the history of the profession itself in this book. (It is presumed that the reader will have an introductory understanding of the social welfare system and its history and development.) Five concepts: assessment, person in the environment, relationship, process, and intervention—important in social work practice—will be the focus in discussing the history of social work practice as distinct from social welfare history. The beginning of professional social work was a response to the social milieu of the early twentieth century, a time when new immigrants, with their different cultures and lifestyles, were of concern to the larger society. The major statement of social work practice was Mary Richmond's *Social Diagnosis*[18] in which she developed the original framework for assessment. However, rather than the term **assessment**, she used the term **diagnosis**, borrowing medical terminology from the **medical model**. Richmond saw that it was important to consider the family when developing the diagnosis.

Richmond's work reflects a period when social sciences, particularly sociology, were highly influential on social work practice. Psychology had not yet developed to the point at which personality could be explained. Emphasis was on a broad study because there was still a great deal of uncertainty about which factors were most important for diagnosis. It was assumed that a cause-effect relationship existed; in other words, the social worker was looking for the cause of the problem. The cause of the problem was generally assumed to be either moral inadequacy or lack of appropriate use of social resources. A strong emphasis on diagnosis (assessment) developed and remains an important legacy in contemporary social work practice.

Settlement houses, the originators of group work and community organization methods of social work, responded to the same social conditions differently. They saw the source of problems in the environment and in a lack of understanding about how to cope with one's surroundings. These workers used educational and enriching group activities and worked within the political system to bring about social change.

During the 1920s psychology and psychiatry, with their focus on individuals, began to greatly influence the social casework stream of social work. With this emphasis, the concern for the family as a focus was greatly, though not entirely, dropped from the casework concern. Diagnosis or assessment was better organized with an emphasis on behavior, attitude, and relationships. The individual was seen as the primary source for information. The worker-client **relationship** was primary. Practice was moving from doing *to* or doing *for* to working *with* the client. During this period a group of practitioners from various fields of practice met to identify the commonalities of practice across fields (the Milford Conference)[19]. A major commonality was the use of the social history. They also began to develop the concept of **treatment (intervention)**.

Group work continued to develop as a separate movement. It expanded into youth and recreational organizations using activity and group process as a means to enhance growth, change, and the democratic process. As had been true earlier, there was an emphasis on work with communities and means for better meeting individuals' needs. The developing discipline of sociology provided important understandings to this work, In fact, group work and sociology were often seen as the same.

During the early 1930s (The Great Depression) social workers discovered that older theories about personal deficiencies as the cause of poverty and deviance no longer held up. The public sector (a developing area) was involved in relief and social provision. What came to be called the **private sector** was mostly from a Freudian perspective and came to be known as the **diagnostic approach**. Gordon Hamilton's *The Theory and Practice of Social Casework*[20] provided a clear statement of this approach to practice. Hamilton saw diagnosis as "a working hypothesis for understanding the person with the problem as well as the problem itself."[21] Study, diagnosis, and treatment were the conceptualization of the **process**. Treatment was seen as "furnishing a service" or "behaving toward someone."

Another approach that developed during this period was the **functional approach**, which considered the client neither sick nor deviant, but rather requesting a service. Diagnosis was seen as an attempt for the client and worker to see if there was common ground for working together. Process was seen as beginning, middle, and end. Relationship was professional when the worker was carrying out an agency function using professional knowledge.[22]

During the early 1930s agencies using group approaches began to come together for discussion about commonalities. In the early 1930s the first group-work course in a school of social work was offered at Western Reserve University. In 1936 the American Association for the Study of Groups was founded. In 1946 this organization became The American Association of Group Workers. A method of group work placed emphasis on assisting individuals with normal growth and development, promoting citizen social responsibility. There was importance placed on group process.[23] By 1949 group work had developed to the point that four important texts had been published.[24]

In 1955, seven social work organizations including those related to casework, group work, and community organization together formed the *National Association of Social Workers*. This allowed for a unified profession that included all three divisions—casework, group work, and community organization—to begin to explore commonalities.

In 1957 two important books in the casework area were published. First was Felix Biestek's *The Casework Relationship.* He defined the casework relationship as "the dynamic interaction of attitudes and emotions between the caseworker and the client, with the purpose of helping the client achieve a better adjustment between himself and his environment."[25] The second book was Helen Harris Perlman's *Social Casework: A Problem-Solving Process.*[26] In many ways this text was a blending of the diagnostic and functional approaches, and essentially marked the end of the diagnostic-functional controversy. Perlman saw the casework endeavor as "a person with a problem comes to a place where a professional representative helps him by a given process."[27]

During the 1960s significant changes began to take place in social work practice. First, the domination of psychoanalytical thinking began to lessen. New approaches began to be used—for example, crisis intervention, task-centered, and social behavioral. Work with the family as a system developed. This resulted from the fact that psychiatry had begun to see the importance of work with families and social workers in the clinical realm followed this trend. Another trend at this time was identifying multiple approaches to practice in each of the three methods of practice: casework, group work, and community organization.[28]

Very important was the effort to identify the commonalities of practice theory among casework, group work, and community organization. This became known as **integrative practice**, which is now known as **generalist social work practice**.[29] It should also be noted that the introduction of social systems theory into the social work knowledge base greatly enabled this movement.

In the early 1970s BSW social work programs began to be accredited. Generalist social work came to be the CSWE mandated approach to practice taught by BSW programs. The first edition of this text, *Social Work Practice: A Generalist Approach (1983)* was developed with a problem-solving perspective as a response to a need of students in BSW programs. Over the years the Johnson-Yanca model has evolved into the contemporary ecological/strengths model of change with a strong emphasis on diversity.

In 1986, James K. Whittaker, Steven P. Schinke, and Lewayne D. Gilchrist suggested that the social worker had moved to a new paradigm, or way of thinking, about practice. This way of thinking, the ecological paradigm, is based on "improving social supports through various forms of environmental helping and on improving personal competencies through teaching life skills."[30]

Recently the concept of **best practice** has emerged. This refers to engaging in practice activities that are based on research and is intended to increase successful outcomes. However, most formulations of best practices appear to set the worker up as expert. We prefer to use research in conjunction with practice experience, and in partnership with clients in deciding how to bring about change.

Five concepts have developed over time and form a base for the Johnson-Yanca ecological/strengths approach to generalist social work practice:

Assessment: Understanding the person in the environment as the basis for the action to be taken.

Person in the environment: Uses an ecological approach to identify, develop, and support personal networks.

Relationship: Seen as the cohesive quality of the action system.

Process: Recurrent patterning of a sequence of change over time that is the specification of various stages of the work.

Intervention: Working with clients and others to influence relational patterns between individuals and systems of influence to any situation so that concerns and needs are met.

Thus it can be said that historically, and in the contemporary situation, the response of social workers to concern and need is one that focuses on social functioning of not only individuals but also of social systems important in the individual's environment. These systems include: the family, small groups, and the community (with its agencies and institutions).

Social Functioning

Social workers become involved when individuals are having difficulty living in relationship with other people, growing so as to maximize their potential, or meeting the demands of the environment or when there is a relatively high potential that any developing needs will not be met. It is then that concern and need become apparent. Harriet Bartlett has described this situation as "people coping" and "environmental demands." The bringing together of these two aspects of living in society can be termed **social functioning**.[31] The core of the social work endeavor is the worker and the client interacting to promote healthy social functioning and to alleviate concern over unmet need. The response is one in which the worker and client *together* assess the need in all its complexity, develop a plan for responding to that need, carry out the plan, and evaluate the results of their work together. Both the worker and the client have a responsibility for the work. Because the roles are reciprocal, both must carry out their roles if the process is going to work.

This is, in essence, the meaning of **generalist practice**. In developing a plan, the focal system for change may be any system experiencing or contributing to a lack of need fulfillment. The change strategy is chosen from a repertoire of strategies that the generalist worker possesses. This repertoire contains strategies appropriate for work with a variety of systems (individuals, families, small groups, agencies, and communities).

The **social work process** usually begins with a **feeling** of concern about something. This concern arises because a need is not being met. After **thinking** about the situation in

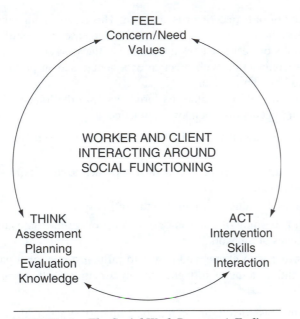

FIGURE 1.1   *The Social Work Process: A Feeling, Thinking, Acting Endeavor*

a particular way—a process called assessment—some **action** is taken. This response—feeling, thinking, acting—is cyclical in nature. As the worker and client think and act together, new feelings of concern arise and new needs become apparent. As they act, they think about what is happening and gain new insights into the situation. The worker's knowledge about human development, human diversity, social systems theory, ecosystems, and a strengths approach is used in thinking about the situation. (See Figure 1.1.)

Summary

One perspective of social work sees social work practice as a response to concern and need. Concern derives from a feeling that all is not right. Social workers respond to concern by identifying any unmet needs in the situation. In doing this, they use knowledge about human development, human diversity, social systems, ecosystems, and strengths. They identify not only the unmet needs and the strengths of a particular client but also the needs and strengths of significant individuals and systems in the environment. The profession of social work has for many years been one of the community entities that responded to concern and need. It is a profession that has developed its ways of working over time in response to what is happening in the world of the day. When people attempt to meet their needs (to cope), and when the environment makes demands on people in response to environmental needs, a process of social functioning exists. Social functioning is a major focus of social work practice. The focus of the social work endeavor is on helping client systems to cope and on the environmental factors impinging on social functioning. The decision on what the focus of service is to be relates to what is causing the difficulty (the barrier to need fulfillment) and on what can be changed—the client, the situation, or both.

Questions

1. What do you consider to be the minimal need level for a person to function in contemporary American society? What would be the ideal need level?
2. How can ecosystems perspective and the strengths approach be integrated into social work practice? What are the differences between the two perspectives?
3. Describe the coping behaviors and the environmental demands in a situation related to your present functioning.
4. How has the development of social work practice enhanced contemporary practice? How has social work been influenced by the social climate of the 20th century?

Suggested Readings

Billups, James W., Ed. *Faithful Angels: Portraits of International Social Work Notables.* Washington, DC: NASW Press, 2002.

Dale, Orren, Smith, Rebecca, Norlin, Julia M., and Chess, Wayne A., *Human Behavior in the Social Environment: Social Systems Theory,* 5th ed. Boston: Allyn and Bacon, 2009 (Chapters 2 and 3).

Edwards, Richard L., Ed. *Encyclopedia of Social Work,* 19th ed. Washington, DC: NASW Press, 1995 ("Generalist and Advanced Generalist Practice"; "Human Development"; "Ecological Perspective"; "Person-in-Environment"; "Social Welfare History"; "Social Work Practice: History and Evolution"; "Social Work Profession Overview"; "Social Work Profession: History").

Erikson, Erik H., Erikson, Joan M., and Kivnick, Helen Q. *The Life Cycle Completed.* New York: W. W. Norton, 1998.

Mizrahi, Terry and Davis, Larry E., Eds. *Encyclopedia of Social Work,* 20th ed. Washington, DC: NASW Press, 2008 ("Distinctive Dates in Social Welfare History," "Ecological Framework," "Generalist and Advanced Generalist Practice," "Human Needs," "Life Span," "Person-In-Environment," "Settlements and Neighborhood Centers," "Social Policy," "Strengths-Based Framework," Strengths Perspective").

Morales, Armando T., Sheafor, Bradford W., and Scott, Malcolm E. *Social Work: A Profession of Many Faces,* 11th ed. Boston: Allyn and Bacon, 2007.

Popple, Phillip R., and Leighninger, Leslie. *Social Work, Social Welfare, and American Society,* 7th ed. Boston: Allyn and Bacon, 2008.

Reisch, Michael, and Gambrill, Eileen, Eds. *Social Work in the 21st Century.* Thousand Oaks, CA: Pine Forge Press, 1997.

Saleeby, Dennis, Ed. *The Strengths Perspective in Social Work Practice.* 5th ed. Boston: Allyn and Bacon, 2009 (Chapters 1, 2, and 5).

Witkin, Stanley L., Ed. "Special Centennial Issue." *Social Work* 43 (November 1998).

Witkin, Stanley L., Ed. "Special Centennial Issue 2." *Social Work* 44 (July 1999).

2

Social Work as a Creative Blending of Knowledge, Values, and Skills

Learning Expectations

1. Understanding of the range of knowledge used by the social worker.
2. Understanding of the nature of values and the value base underlying social work.
3. Understanding of the nature of skills and beginning knowledge of the skills of a generalist social worker.
4. Understanding of the concepts of intervention and the change process.
5. Understanding of the nature of human transactions.

Social work as a creative blending of knowledge, values, and skills is the third major perspective of social work practice. It relates to the "how" of social work practice. Important characteristics of any profession are systematic theory and ethical codes. The development of systematic theory on which to base practice implies that the practice is grounded in a knowledge base and that practitioners are using that knowledge base on their practice decision making. This practice also is based on an ethical code that in part delineates the value base for practice. The value base must consider societal, client, and worker values.

In some ways knowledge, values, and skills are related to the feeling, thinking, and doing construct introduced in Chapter 1. (See Figure 1.1.) Knowledge is a part of the cognitive or thinking component of practice; values are a part of the feeling or emotional component of practice, though in some ways they are also a part of the thinking component. Skills are action, or the doing of social work; they are part of the behavioral component. However, it must be recognized that skills may also be cognitive in nature. Development of the capacity to think about a practice situation—that is, to utilize the broad knowledge base and choose those aspects appropriate to the situation, determine relevant values for consideration, and identify appropriate action—is included in the realm of skill as discussed in this book.

It is important to examine the nature of each of these components of social work practice as well as the content of each component. It is also important to consider how these three components are used together in practice. This gives rise to the notion that the connection among the three results from a *creative blending.*[1] Other issues that must be considered are the use of both science and art in considering the relationship of knowledge, values, and skill and the importance of creativity in combining the three into a coherent practice assessment and plan. The rest of this chapter encompasses the fourth and the fifth approaches to describing generalist practice. The fourth approach is social work as a process of facilitating growth and change. In this section, background information and a brief description of the change process used in this text are presented. The last part of the chapter describes the fifth approach, which is social work as intervention into human transactions. This part will describe the concept of intervention and the need to focus on human transactions in the change process. The fourth and fifth approaches highlight the need to take a transactional approach when using an ecosystems strengths approach in the change process. Facilitating change that focuses on the client and/or the environment is difficult and may be inappropriate. People and systems are not often open to change, especially if the change requires substantial movement or risk. However, changes may be more easily made in how people and systems engage in transactions with each other and what they exchange in their transactions. At the very least, an ecosystems strengths approach to generalist practice calls for considering growth and change in clients, systems in their environments, and transactions among people and systems.

Knowledge

In *The Common Base of Social Work Practice,* Bartlett makes a strong case for the need for social work action to be founded on a strong knowledge base—to be guided by knowledge.[2] **Knowledge** is a term with a broad and varied meaning. Gordon defined knowledge as "the picture man has of the world and his place in it."[3] Max Siporin gives a definition that enhances Gordon's: "Knowledge is cognitive mental content (ideas and beliefs) concerning reality that we take to be true (perceive with certainty, based on adequate evidence), or that we decide is confirmable and has a high probability of truth."[4]

Social work has placed increasing emphasis on knowledge that is scientific as opposed to beliefs in unconfirmed ideas. An attempt has been made to develop a knowledge base that begins to move toward the hardness characteristic of the sciences. Yet the very nature of the social sciences, with their concern for the complex phenomenon of the human being in his social environment, tends to make this difficult and gives a quality of softness to the knowledge base. A manifestation of this is the development of best practices or evidence based practice, which is based on research into the most effective and ethical means of delivering services. In Chapter 9, we develop a version of this that includes practice experience, which we call good practices, and in Chapter 16 we present our suggestions for good practices in various settings in which generalist social workers typically practice.

Social work knowledge, particularly the foundation knowledge used for understanding, has been largely borrowed from the social sciences, particularly psychology and sociology, though anthropology, political science, economics, and history as well as the natural sciences of biology and physiology also contribute. This knowledge base is complex, requiring a breadth of knowledge in various disciplines as well as a depth necessary for more than superficial understanding.

Social work knowledge is what is known about people and their social systems. It is relative to the situation in which it was developed. It is descriptive of the phenomena of persons in environments and explains the functioning of individuals and their social systems. It is used to gain understanding of persons in environments and of larger social systems and to guide the actions of social workers as they seek to enhance individuals' social functioning. It includes knowledge of human development, human diversity, social systems theory, the ecological perspective, and a strengths approach as discussed in Chapter 1. It is knowledge that directs the response to need and includes knowledge about assessment, relationships, the social work process, and intervention.

The knowledge used to guide the action of the social worker with clients has usually been developed by social workers. Much of this knowledge has not been rigorously tested in a scientific manner. However, a small body of practice knowledge can be identified. Task-centered social work is an example of this type of knowledge.[5] However, the use of only scientifically developed knowledge in social work practice fails to account for much that the practitioners know about human beings and how change takes place. Reality is much more than that which has been proven and observed in concrete ways. Ways of knowing other than the narrowly scientific have been referred to as *practice wisdom.* Howard Goldstein has referred to this as "that which we learn from the lives of our clients and from the experiences we share with them."[6] Goldstein also noted that recognition of this knowledge as valid for practice opens up a new range of what are known as generative theories for use in practice.[7]

Practice wisdom must include the ability to appreciate diversity and individuality and to see the strengths in people and their environments. Workers need to value and be open to learning from the lives of clients and from shared experiences. In this way workers grow and strengthen their knowledge base as well as empower their clients. Clients are helped to experience their strengths and capacities rather than focusing on weaknesses or limitations. The focus moves from what is missing to what is possible. A word of caution is offered. In the process of learning from clients, it is important to avoid using those experiences to create stereotypes or generalizations. If anything, practice wisdom conveys that uniqueness and individuality are what really characterize human beings.

Thus, the knowledge base developed for social work is eclectic, interdisciplinary, tentative at best, complex, and often subjective. Social work continues to search for common concepts and common frames of reference and to test hypotheses about the nature of practice to become more scientific. By its very nature, this knowledge base is problematic. Some of these problems include:

1. Problems that come from borrowing knowledge from another discipline. This borrowing often provides yesterday's knowledge rather than the current thinking of the discipline developing the knowledge. Often, such knowledge is given much more certainty by the borrowing discipline than it is given by the developing discipline. Also, borrowing tends to be of a simplified nature.[8] Questionable assumptions may result when borrowed knowledge is improperly used.

2. Problems that arise from separating the knowledge and value elements of practice. Value considerations so influence one's view of reality that observations and facts that conflict with these values are often overlooked. The manner in which knowledge is developed and used contributes to this difficulty.[9]

3. Problems that develop because practice wisdom has often been conceptualized insufficiently to separate fact, perception, ideas, and values. Practice wisdom often has not been tested by applying it to different situations in a controlled manner. Its validity and reliability with respect to different situations has not been examined. Thus, it is difficult to determine if knowledge gained from practice wisdom is appropriate in a given situation.

4. Problems that develop because of the many variables in the human situation and in the worker-client interaction. These make it difficult to generalize knowledge for use in determining intervention possibilities. Of particular concern are cultural factors that change perceptions about behavior and helping situations.

5. Problems that result from a tendency to use terms and concepts without sufficient definition or without agreement as to definition. Without this agreement, the same terms and concepts are sometimes used with different meanings.

6. Problems related to the difficulty in developing relationships among terms and concepts. "Person in environment" and the ecological perspective provide some understanding here.

Although many problems are inherent in the social work knowledge base, it has a major strength. Because social work takes a broad view of person in environment and of social functioning, there is a vast amount of knowledge that can be called on to inform practice. Knowledge that workers have gained from life experiences, observations made about others' life experiences, and understandings developed from a broad liberal arts education are all available.

If a worker is to base practice on a knowledge base, she must have the ability to evaluate the knowledge available, to use judgment in the choice of knowledge to apply to specific situations, and to keep an open mind as to the tentativeness of the knowledge base and the knowledge about client in situation. The worker must be able to think theoretically, systematically, critically, and creatively. Goldstein states that this is far more an art than an applied science. He further states: "Reflectively, creatively, and imaginatively, the mind of the practitioner strives to blend and incorporate fragments of theory, information, intuitions, sensations, and other perceptions into something ambiguously called 'understanding.'"[10]

The sources of knowledge used by the social worker come from a variety of disciplines. The choice of which understandings to use in which situations is problematic, and connecting knowledge bits from a variety of sources is difficult. The human condition is complex. It has been explained in a variety of ways. To have a sufficiently broad knowledge base, a social worker needs the following:

1. *A broad liberal arts base*—This includes a knowledge of the social sciences (sociology, psychology, anthropology, history, political science, and economics) to provide explanations about the nature of human society and the human condition. Study of the natural sciences provides tools for scientific thinking and an understanding of the physical aspects of the human condition. Study of the humanities aids in the development of the creative and critical thought processes; it provides an understanding of the nature of the human condition through the examination of creative endeavors and of the cultures of human society. The latter is especially important for diversity competence. A social worker is a person with a developed and expanded personal capacity gained by exposure to a broad, liberal educational experience.

2. *A sound foundation knowledge about persons, their interactions, and the social situations within which they function*—This includes knowledge about persons from emotional, cognitive, behavioral, and developmental points of view. Such knowledge must consider the age and diversity of the human condition and the effect of age and diversity on functioning and development. Understanding of human interaction in depth is also essential. This knowledge includes one-to-one relationships, family relationships, and small-group relationships and the variety of these relationships found in diverse populations. It also includes understanding of the societal organizations and institutions that are a part of contemporary society and of the social problems that affect human functioning, especially those that are exacerbated by prejudice and discrimination.

3. *Practice theory, with concern for the nature of helping interactions, of the process of helping, and of a variety of intervention strategies appropriate for a variety of situations and systems*—This includes knowledge of professional and societal structures and institutions for delivery of service to individuals in need of help and methods of adapting and developing the service structure for more adequate need fulfillment.[11] It also includes knowledge about effective ways of providing service to members of diverse groups.

4. *Specialized knowledge needed to work with particular groups of clients and in particular situations*—The choice of knowledge each worker includes in this area is dependent on the practice situations and on career aspirations. In diversity competent practice the

worker needs to be knowledgeable about the values and beliefs of the population, its experience with the dominant society, the manner in which help is given and received, and good practices that need to be used with each group.

5. *The capacity to be reflective, imaginative, and creative in the use of knowledge obtained from a variety of sources*—It is especially important to be able to see the strengths in people and in their environment and to be able to use those strengths to build a vision for the future. To become diversity competent, the worker must be able to reflect on her knowledge about herself and knowledge about each diverse group. She must be willing to critically examine her knowledge and be open to considering distortions that might be present as a result of prejudices and stereotypes. She must be able to acquire and use new knowledge about diversity from her client and from professional sources, such as articles, books, professional training, colleagues, and other sources.

6. *The ability to learn new and different ways of acquiring and using knowledge*—In diversity competent practice, the worker needs to become familiar with the different ways of knowing that each diverse group may use in acquiring knowledge.

Values

Knowledge and values are often confused. It is important to distinguish between these two important components of social work practice. Knowledge is at least potentially provable; it is used to explain behavior and to conceptualize practice. **Values** are not provable; they are what is held to be desirable; they are used to identify what is preferred. This includes preferable assumptions about human behavior and preferable ways of helping. Knowledge assumptions and value assumptions are used in different ways in the helping endeavor.

Several definitions of the term *value* are useful for developing an understanding of the term.

Milton Rokeach defined value as "an enduring belief that a specific mode or end state of existence is personally or socially preferable to an opposite or converse mode or end state of existence."[12] He also stated that values, rather than standing alone, exist in systems; that is, individual values are organized in such a manner that they have a relative importance to other values. He construed values as being relatively enduring, as beliefs on which persons act by preference, and as modes of conduct or end states of existence. Value beliefs are conceptions of what is desirable; there is an emotion or feeling aspect to them; and they lead to action.

It is questionable whether, in the contemporary diverse society of the United States, there are, in fact, any generally agreed-on societal values. What does seem to exist are groups of values that various segments of society *believe* should be the societal values and which they tend to want to impose on everyone.

A source from outside the field of social work is useful in the search for understanding the term *value*. The literature of values clarification sees values as (1) guides to behavior, (2) growing out of personal experiences, (3) modified as experiences accumulate, and (4) evolving in nature.[13] This literature provides additional understanding about the nature of values by noting that the conditions in which values operate often have conflicting demands; that is, several values are functioning in the same situation, and each calls for conflicting modes of functioning or end states. For example, working with a frail older woman, the worker is confronted with values of physical safety and self-determination. She wants to remain in her own home, but it is not safe as presently set up. Which value should take precedence? A value judgment is called for.

There are several types of values. *Ultimate values* are the most abstract and tend to be those most easily agreed on by large groups of people. They include such values as liberty, worth, and dignity of people, progress, and justice. *Proximate values* are more specific as to the desired end state. The right to an abortion on demand, freedom to determine how one will do the assignments in a course, and the right to discipline one's child in a specific manner are examples of proximate values. There is apt to be disagreement regarding these values. *Instrumental values* are those values that specify the desired means to the ends; they are modes of conduct. Self-determination and confidentiality are examples of instrumental values. They are means for operationalizing the worth and dignity of individuals.

Values originate, in part, from the society of which a person is a part. If individuals are thought of as evil, it is difficult to believe that individuals have worth and dignity. Factors that influence the values individuals hold include (1) their cultural heritages, (2) values held by individuals and groups with which they are associated or to which they aspire to associate, (3) personal experiences, and (4) the views they hold about human beings and the nature of the human situation.

Social workers have often ignored the importance of religious or spiritual values in the lives of people, but religious beliefs and spiritual frameworks are important sources for the development of beliefs. They strongly influence the value systems of both individuals and cultural groups. To respect a client's values, a worker must recognize the role of religion and spirituality in the development of those values and also how beliefs are important components of human functioning.

Value conflicts develop as individuals are exposed to the differing value systems on which they are expected to act. The *societal value system* contains values generally held by the dominant segment of society. In American society, some of these values that have been articulated are achievement and success, activity and work, moral responsibility, concern for people who are victims of natural disasters and temporary distress, efficiency and practicality, progress, material comfort, equality, freedom, external conformity, science and secular rationality, nationalism and patriotism, democracy, worth of the individual, and superiority of the dominant group.[14] These values have had their origin in a combination of sources, including: (1) the capitalistic-Puritan ethic; (2) the Judeo-Christian heritage; and (3) humanistic, positivist, utopian thinking.[15] Conflicts, tensions, and inconsistencies exist among these various sources as well as among societal values, professional values, and personal values of clients and social workers. Tensions and conflicts become more apparent as one moves from ultimate values to the choice of specific goals and means, that is, as one moves from the abstract to the concrete. Some of these tensions arise because of differences between values about needs of individuals and values about needs of groups of which individuals are a part.

Social work practice is based on a set of values that is often expressed in such principles as the worth and dignity of the individual, the right to self-determination, and the right to confidentiality. Armando Morales and Bradford Sheafor, using Charles Levy's scheme for organizing values,[16] have identified values held by the social work profession:

Preferred Conceptions of People
1. Social workers believe in inherent worth and dignity.
2. Each person has an inherent capacity and drive toward change that can make life more fulfilling.
3. Each person has responsibility for himself and his fellow human beings—including society.
4. People need to belong.
5. There are human needs common to each person, yet each person is unique and different from others.

Preferred Outcomes for People
1. Society must provide opportunities for growth and development that will allow each person to realize his fullest potential.
2. Society must provide resources and services to help people meet their needs and to avoid such problems as hunger, inadequate education, discrimination, illness without care, and inadequate housing.
3. People must have equal opportunity to participate in the molding of society.

Preferred Instrumentalities for Dealing with People
People should be treated with respect and dignity, should have maximum opportunity to determine the direction of their lives, should be urged and helped to interact with other people to build a society responsive to the needs of everyone, and should be recognized as unique individuals rather than put into stereotypes because of some particular characteristic or life experience.[17]

Codes of ethics flow from values; they are values in action, and as such they are preferred instrumentalities for dealing with people. Ethical codes specify what ought to be done in professional practice. At the 1996 Delegate Assembly, NASW adopted a new *Code of Ethics,* replacing a code of ethics adopted in 1960 and amended in 1967 and 1979. Growth and change in the profession of social work as well as shortcomings in the old code made it desirable to develop this new code of ethics. In fact, the 1996 version has been amended in 1998 and 2008. The new code includes issues such as use of electronic media and more specific guidelines for worker behavior in relationships with clients. It also ties ethical principles directly to social work values. A copy of the code in both English and Spanish can be found on the NASW website at *www.socialworkers.org/pubs/code/default.asp*. All social workers should have a copy of the *Code of Ethics* for reference and should be familiar with its contents.

Dealing with values is central to social work practice. The social worker must be concerned with both societal and personal values, with the client's values and with her own. The worker also must function within the framework of social work values and ethics. The worker must be comfortable with discomfort as the search continues for congruence between believing and doing and for resolution of conflict among values. This calls for tolerance and humility. Some of the contemporary issues confronting social work and about which there are conflicting value judgments are abortion, homosexuality, treatment for AIDS victims, extreme health care measures, and treatment of the chronically mentally ill.

When dealing with ethical issues, there is often not a clear course to determining the ethical action in a particular situation. For instance, when does a client have a right to privacy in a situation in which a child may be at risk of abuse? If there is a clear indication of abuse, most legal jurisdictions mandate that the abuse be reported. But what about when there is only an *indication* of risk? Or what about the client who makes threats against another person in the course of service? What about the mentally ill person who makes threats on her own life? All of these situations call for a professional judgment as to the seriousness of the situation. Another contemporary dilemma may arise when working with a person who is HIV positive or one who suffers from AIDS. If that person has not informed a sexual partner of the risk, does the social worker have an obligation to do so? The landmark case of *Tarasoff v. Regents of the University of California* (1976) is often cited regarding the liability of a social worker for failure to warn.[18]

There are no clear-cut answers to any of these situations. The NASW *Code of Ethics* requires the social worker to maintain confidentiality except for compelling professional reasons. It would then follow that the worker must be sure that a real danger to another person exists before breaching the confidentiality ethic. Yet, when a real danger exists, the worker must intervene on behalf of the at-risk other. A first step would be a careful and fully documented assessment of the situation. Next would be an attempt to persuade the client to self-reveal to the at-risk other. If this fails to occur in a timely manner, the worker, usually after informing the client, should take steps to ensure that the other is protected.

Clients should be informed that there are limits to confidentiality. The worker should be aware of laws protecting and limiting confidentiality. The worker also must be aware of liability risks and standard guidelines for informed consent.

Valuing is a common human experience. It allows persons to identify what they hold in high esteem—the objects, instruments, experiences, conditions, qualities, and objectives that are worthy of human effort and interest. It is particularly important for the social worker to engage in the process of valuing. Each worker has developed an individual value system that at least in part is related to the societal and cultural value system of which he is a part. The social work values are also similar to the societal value system in some respects, but there are differences. Social workers must recognize these differences and develop ways of dealing with the tensions and conflicts that result from them. They must be aware of their own values so that unexamined values do not influence their practice.

In valuing, it is important to recognize and value diversity. Too often when people see differences, they fall into the trap of constructing false dichotomies—that is, the tendency to see two things that are different as if one is superior and the other is inferior. As a result, value judgments are made that lead to perceiving differences as good and bad instead of simply different. Perceiving differences in this way provides a rationale for treating people as inferior and leads to prejudice, discrimination, and oppression.

When we value diversity, we open ourselves up to new experiences and to different ways of perceiving and valuing. It allows us to see the richness and the strengths in variety. It is like watching a rainbow through a black-and-white lens and then seeing it for the first time in full color. Valuing diversity is also fundamental to being able to value and respect each individual and to appreciate the uniqueness of each human being.The social work endeavor is based on the dual values of the worth and dignity of individuals and of social responsibility. These values can be expressed in these principles for action:

1. People should be free to make choices.
2. Individuals are important; individual needs and concerns cannot be totally subjected to community needs.
3. Workers should use a nonjudgmental approach to persons and their concerns, needs, and problems.
4. The social work role is helping or enabling, not controlling.
5. Feelings and personal relationships are important.
6. People have responsibility for others, for their needs and concerns.

Skills

Skill is the practice component that brings knowledge and values together and converts them to action as a response to concern and need. A sociological definition of **skill** is also useful in understanding the meaning of the term: a complex organization of behavior (physical or verbal) developed through learning and directed toward a particular goal or centered on a particular activity.[19]

Bartlett uses the term *interventive repertoire* to describe the blending of knowledge and values to respond to problems of social functioning. She describes this interventive repertoire as composed of methods, techniques, and skills. Skill is technical expertise, the ability to use knowledge effectively and readily in performing competently.[20] This formulation seems to encompass two important attributes of this particular component of practice. First, it is necessary to make choices from a variety of possibilities based on knowledge and value considerations. Second, the choices are in regard to action to be taken in relation to a concern or need.

Some of the literature seems to use the term *skill* rather than *interventive repertoire* in discussing the action component of practice. Morales and Sheafor identified the skill of social work as the appropriate selection of techniques for a particular situation and the effective use of those techniques. They discussed how this selection is based on a conscious use of knowledge and stated that social work values filter this knowledge in determining appropriate skills for use in providing service. In their view, skill is needed both for the selection of appropriate techniques and for the ability to use techniques effectively.[21] They defined skill as the social worker's capacity to set in motion—in a relationship with the client (individual, group, community)—guided psychosocial intervention processes of change based on social work values and knowledge in a specific situation relevant to the client. The change that begins to occur as the result of this skilled intervention is based on the strengths and capacities of the client.[22] This would seem to point to a consideration of how to enable the client to use these strengths and capacities not only in the helping situation but in other areas of human functioning.

Social work does not have one skill but a wide variety of skills useful for many different situations. It would seem appropriate to use the term *skills* for the action component of practice and to use the term *skillful* in discussing the competent manner in which skills are used.

Several attempts have been made to identify the core, base, or basic skills needed by all social workers. Betty Baer and Ronald Federico have organized the skills component of practice into four areas: (1) information gathering and assessment; (2) the development and use of the professional self; (3) practice activities with individuals, groups, and communities; and (4) evaluation. They listed the needed skill cluster in each of these areas and translated these skills into ten competencies.[23] Included in these competencies are skills in working with and on behalf of oppressed and disadvantaged populations. This requires an appreciation for and valuing of diversity and an ability to see strengths in those who are different. Given the amount of prejudice in our society, it takes a great deal of skill to overcome the barriers among various groups. This includes skill at recognizing barriers within ourselves as well as those our clients may bring with them. It means being open and creative in building bridges and tolerating complexity rather than seeking simplicity. To do so, social workers need to develop skills in self-awareness, empathy, and relationships, especially as these relate to race, culture, gender, age, sexual orientation, and disabilities. Based in part on this formulation as well as numerous other statements about the nature of social work practice, other formulations have been developed.[24]

The *Educational Policy and Accreditation Standards of the Council on Social Work Education*[25] provides the official statement of the skill level expected of baccalaureate- and master's-level social work graduates. Two types of skills are called for (although it is impossible to completely separate them): cognitive skills and interactive or relationship skills. *Cognitive skills* are those used in thinking about persons in situations, in developing understanding about person and environment, in identifying the knowledge to be used, in planning for intervention, and in performing evaluation. *Interactive skills* are those used in working jointly with individuals, groups, families, organizations, and communities; in communicating and developing understanding; in joint planning; and in carrying out the plans of action. A social worker must be proficient in both types of skills.

Skillfulness develops over time as a result of practice in the use of the various techniques and methodologies. The development of skillfulness involves not only the application of knowledge and the operationalization of values but also the use of the worker's individual attributes and the development of a personal style of work. A useful analogy in understanding the development of skillfulness (and thus competence and personal style) is the musician. Musicians develop their skills and competence only after long hours of practice, practice that starts with learning such simple basics as fingering, note reading, and time concepts, and then progresses to more and more complex techniques and music. The musician's personal style develops in the interpretation of the music. Similarly, it is only as the social worker learns to blend the cognitive and interactive skills that skillfulness develops.

The diversity competent social worker explores ways to serve diverse clients in a manner that is expected within their diverse groups. For instance, a white worker might need to be able to use an Afrocentric approach in working with some of her African American clients or a feminist approach in working with some of her female clients. The professional worker realizes that it is her responsibility to adapt her skills to meet the needs of her client. She meets that responsibility by engaging in lifelong learning activities throughout her career. She reads materials and attends relevant training programs. She seeks to learn from knowledgeable colleagues and members of the community. She realizes the value of learning from her clients about how they would like to be served and incorporates this into her repertoire of skills. She uses diversity-appropriate skills in engagement and relationship building, assessment, planning, action, evaluation, and termination with every client she serves.

Creative Blending of Knowledge, Values, and Skills

The ability to combine appropriately and creatively the elements of knowledge, values, and skills in the helping situation is indeed an important characteristic of the social worker. This characteristic calls not only for choosing and applying appropriate knowledge, values, and skills but also for blending the three elements in such a manner that they fit together and become a helping endeavor that is a consistent whole. This ability involves more than the blending of knowledge, values, and skills; it involves identifying and choosing appropriate, often unrelated, bits of knowledge and using not only social work values but also those of the client and the agency in order to screen the knowledge tentatively chosen for use. It involves skillful application of the knowledge and interactional skill to the situation. Because each person in a situation and each need for help are different, the knowledge, values, and skills to be used are also different. There can be no cookbooks, no standardized procedures that must be adhered to in great detail, though there can be generalized ways of approaching persons in situations. The application of knowledge, values, and skills can be approached only from a creative stance.

The creative stance is often expressed as the *art of social work* as opposed to the *science of social work*. This art is based on hunches and intuition, on previous experience, on very personal attributes of workers that are difficult if not impossible to identify. It is the social worker encountering the knowledge, values, and skills elements and choosing and applying them that makes the helping endeavor indeed a unique work of art. Beulah Compton and Burt Galaway have described this art as having an emphasis on feeling, an empathic quality, and a high degree of subjectivity and of self-consciousness. This art allows for the creation of new vistas and new perspectives.[26] It should be the essence of each worker's individual style.

Much of Lydia Rapoport's description of creativity is useful for understanding the blending of knowledge, values, and skills. She identified qualities that creative people possess. These include a kind of nonconformity in opinion and judgment; high motivation and persistence in task performance; openness and receptivity to new information and ideas; a liking for complexity; a high tolerance for ambiguities; a capacity not to seek premature closure; a tolerance for contradiction, obscurity, and conflict; not too deep a commitment to particular theoretical positions; and thorough familiarity with, and knowledge of, all aspects of the problem.[27]

The blending of knowledge, values, and skills is especially important when working with clients who are from a diversity group. In order to accomplish this, the worker must be able to provide services in a manner that is consistent with the expectations of members of each diversity group. This means acquiring specific knowledge about each group, including its values, norms, and customs; ways of communicating and relating; and other aspects of the group's functioning. The worker must acquire self-knowledge to limit the effects of her own values and culture. She must use social work values and ethics while being cognizant of her own values and those of the diversity group. She must acquire skills that are consistent with the way in which the diversity group seeks and receives help. This is all blended together in a unique way for each diversity group the worker encounters.

The blending of ecosystems and a strengths approach with problem solving to form a change process greatly enhances the social worker's ability to be creative and allows her to organize the complex array of knowledge into a cohesive whole. This approach calls for moving from understanding needs to identifying assets, abilities, and capacities of all of the systems involved in the situation. The worker needs to be open and creative when doing this. She then uses her creativity to assist the client in developing a plan based on his strengths and those of the ecosystem. This perspective avoids the view that the individual is the "carrier of the problem" and must change if the situation is to be resolved. An ecosystems strengths perspective expands the focus to all the systems involved in the person's life and looks for assets, abilities, and capacities in the systems and the individual. Although expanding the focus may initially seem overwhelming, an ecosystems approach is a way of organizing one's understanding of the various systems involved. Enlarging the possible resources available for growth and change brings creativity to the social work endeavor. This perspective also respects the client's ability to control his own life and recognizes that people have the capacity to function well in most areas of their lives even though they may have unmet needs in some areas.

The science and art aspects of social work, rather than being in conflict with one another, are complementary. As science and art are blended creatively in the use of knowledge, values, and skills, the essence of professional social work is expressed.

Case Example

Mrs. Abbott, an eighty-six-year-old woman, is a new resident at the Sunnyside Assisted Living Facility. She is recovering from a broken hip and displays some confusion. Her family and doctor have decided that she can no longer live alone and needs assistance and care the family cannot provide. The social worker is responsible for helping Mrs. Abbott become comfortable in her new situation and for developing the psychosocial aspect of her care plan. To do this, the social worker will draw on knowledge, values, and skills to develop a relationship with Mrs. Abbott and an understanding of her needs.

First, the social worker will look to knowledge of human behavior with particular concern about knowledge of older individuals. The worker knows that potential sources of strength in people who are older include their ways of coping with change; the ways they relate to other people, including family members and friends; and how they are functioning in dealing with the psychosocial tasks of aging. The worker will need to determine Mrs. Abbott's coping patterns, values, and skills; the nature of her interpersonal relationships; and her psychosocial development status.

(continued)

Case Example (continued)

The worker will also look to understandings about crisis and particularly the crisis of leaving a home and familiar surroundings. This yields the knowledge that people who are older may become confused in new situations. When moving to a new living situation, they need support and help in finding their place. Mrs. Abbott is also faced with limited mobility because of the broken hip, which adds to the crisis of change. This knowledge not only gives some understanding about Mrs. Abbott's behavior, but it also informs the worker about the way to work with her. Knowledge about crisis intervention says that the worker needs to be actively involved with the client as quickly as possible after the onset of the crisis and that the client needs to know that someone cares about her.

The worker also knows from experience in working with people who are older adjusting to the same basic situation that certain tasks need to be accomplished. Mrs. Abbott needs to know what the routine of the home will be and what will be expected of her. She needs to know who will be taking care of her and what resources and activities will be available to her. Mrs. Abbott needs to maintain her relationships with family and friends, and the family may also need help in this new situation in order to maintain their relationships. The worker knows how Sunnyside Assisted Living Facility functions and what resources it offers its residents. The worker also knows from experience that it is best not to try to gather too much information for the social history in one interview. Several short interviews are usually preferable to develop the plan.

The worker applies a social work value base in the work with Mrs. Abbott. It is important that Mrs. Abbott feel that she is still able to make choices about her life, that she maintain as much self-determination as possible. Ways in which this can be done include giving Mrs. Abbott the choice of which of her personal belongings will be brought from her home to have in her room and by allowing her a choice of which activities she will take part in from the total program available to Sunnyside residents.

The worker will recognize Mrs. Abbott's worth and dignity in the way in which past experiences and present feelings are discussed with her. These discussions will take place in a quiet, private area so that confidentiality can be preserved. The worker will strive to understand Mrs. Abbott's feelings and behavior rather than make judgments of "good" and "bad" and rather than plan for Mrs. Abbott before sufficient understanding is gained.

The worker will use skill in relating to Mrs. Abbott so that she will feel comfortable in expressing concerns and feelings. As information is gathered, the worker will skillfully develop a social history that will yield the understanding needed for planning. The worker will use skill in involving Mrs. Abbott and her family in the planning process. The worker will present the psychosocial plan to staff in such a way that they can become a part of the integrated care plan.

Using Knowledge, Values, and Skills

In addition to using the creative blend of knowledge, values, and skills in particular practice situations with individuals, families, groups, organizations, and communities, the social worker needs to have an organized framework against which to think about situations and to guide work with them. Originally this text used a problem-solving approach as a response to concern and need. As social work searched for its commonalities in the 1960s, problem solving was one of the concepts found in casework, group work, and community organization. Helen Harris Perlman, in *Social Casework: A Problem-Solving Process,* stated: "The casework process is a problem-solving process in that it employs the orderly, systematic methods which are basic to any effective thinking and feeling toward action."[28]

Murray Ross, in *Community Organization: Theory, Principles, and Practice,* discussed the planning process as a key concept in his formulation of community organization.[29] As one examines Ross's formulation, it is evident that the planning process is indeed an adaptation of the classic problem-solving process. Helen Northen, in *Social Work with Groups,* considered the problem-solving theme in group work.[30] Wide applicability and its use by the diverse parts of the profession seeking unification caused problem solving to become one of the earliest identified commonalities of social work practice. It also became an important concept in developing integrative or generalist practice theory.[31]

Problem solving, of course, is not unique to social work but is an important approach to human need in many helping endeavors. The **problem-solving process** is the scientific process, being a means of addressing the science component of social work practice as contrasted with the creative process, or art, of social work. The scientific process in one of its many formulations is used almost universally by scholars from all disciplines as they seek to develop new understandings of the material they study, to conduct or set up formal research studies, or to answer questions in their discipline.

Even though problems and participation in the problem-solving process are a normal part of life for everyone (as individuals and as members of families, small groups, organizations, and communities), there is increasing concern that a focus on problems highlights deficits while devaluing the strengths of the systems involved. This concern has led to new ways of viewing the problem-solving process. In the field of organizational development, for example, David Cooperrider and Suresh Srivasta have developed the concept of "appreciative inquiry" as an alternative to traditional problem solving in organizational development. This affirmative approach to change begins with valuing those aspects of the organizational system that work well and proceeds to develop collaborative dialogue in exploring possibilities and directions for further development and growth.[32]

In social work, the concern with focusing on the problem is related to the tendency, even on the part of the professional social worker, to blame the victim.[33] This process identifies the ways in which the victim of a social problem differs from those who do not experience the problem and then suggests that these differences help make that person a victim of social problems. In this process there is a tendency to ignore environmental factors responsible for social problems and to also ignore the strengths that have enabled individuals to survive in oppressive environments. Ultimately, there is a concern that a focus on problems may lead to labeling the client as the problem.[34]

Interventions based on most theories from psychology or psychiatry overemphasize the psychological aspects of behavior and have led to interpreting the client's situation in terms of symptoms that represent pathology or disease. This leads to seeking to discover deep-seated causes within the person and then treating him to "cure" the problem. Traditional problem-solving processes used in social work risk considering the client in a similar way by first looking at what is wrong. This makes it difficult to transition from problem to solution. The approach being used in this text defines the **problem** in terms of need. A strengths-based approach considers meeting needs as a normal part of everyone's life. It recognizes that people are able to meet their needs in most areas of their lives. Instead of focusing on causes of unmet need, this approach focuses on marshaling talents and resources to reach goals that will meet needs.

With time we have come to see that two emerging social work approaches—a strengths approach and an ecosystems perspective—add important dimensions to the change process that create a positive, comprehensive approach to meeting needs. In the current formulation of a strengths approach, the problem is given little attention and the focus is on the overall goals and aspirations of the client. An ecosystems perspective offers a way to organize and understand the environment and the transactional nature of person in environment. In this text, a strengths approach and an ecosystems perspective are blended with the traditional problem-solving process to form an ecosystems strengths approach to change. This approach views problem solving as meeting needs in a way that facilitates natural growth and change in the person, the environment, and the transactions between person and environment. It sees the social work endeavor as aimed at identifying and utilizing the assets that are available in the person, the environment, and transactions between person and environment to bring about change that fits with what the client desires and the reality of his situation.

Ecological and strengths approaches have a health-based orientation. Both see growth and change as a natural part of human development over time and consider healthy functioning as a goal and as a reality for most areas of the client's life. It is not necessary to change everything about the person or the situation, only the area in which need is not being met. In general, people are able to meet the majority of their needs in socially accepted ways. Blending these two approaches into assessment, planning, action, and evaluation allows the worker and the client to build on environmental and personal strengths in discovering ways to meet unmet needs.

A strengths-based approach avoids the hazard of "blaming the victim." By searching for abilities, capacities, and assets, a strengths approach shifts attention away from finding deficits and limitations in the person and toward discovering the positive aspects of the person in environment. It attributes the problem to the person in situation rather than attributing the problem to the person alone. Adding an ecosystems perspective gives the worker a means of assessing the entire person in environment rather than limiting the assessment to the "person" side of the equation. This approach also opens up a vast array of possibilities that can contribute to meeting the needs of all involved.

An ecosystems approach sees need as arising out of an imbalance or incongruity in the transactions among systems. Person in environment is viewed as a system of systems in which the client and his natural environment are all a part of one ecosystem. The social worker and the client work together to identify the transactions that are out of balance. Using a strengths approach, they seek to rebalance the transactions based on the abilities, capacities, and resources available within both the client and the environment. The knowledge, values, and skills of social work, along with the strengths and resources within the client and the client's environment, are used in understanding the situation and in identifying possible goals.

Contributions from a strengths approach can become an integral part of the problem-solving process used in social work practice when (1) the focus of the helping process is on the unique individual or client system involved and her environment and on the possibilities for positive growth and change, (2) the strengths and competencies of the client system are respected and valued by the social worker and utilized as a major resource in the helping process, and (3) the client is involved in all phases of the helping process and is given maximum opportunity for self-determination. Social workers who incorporate these principles in their work with client systems will discover that the change process is a useful tool to help the client reach her goals and objectives.

Using knowledge, values, and skills in an ecosystems strengths approach leads to two other concepts for generalist social work practice when addressing concern and needs. The first concept is the focus on change as intervention into human interactions. A second is that the intervention is a process: a change process.

Intervention into Human Transactions

Intervention is the activity of the worker in facilitating change in a systemic sense. It represents a leap in social work thinking from understanding a person in a situation to purposefully bringing about change in the person-situation phenomenon. *Intervention,* as conceived of in this text, is specific action by a worker in relation to human systems or processes in order to facilitate change. The action is guided by knowledge and professional values as well as by the skillfulness of the worker. Intervention is purposeful, goal directed, makes use of the worker's helping repertoire (including creativity, knowledge, values, and skills), and is appropriate for the age and diversity of the client.

As used in social work, intervention does not assume control of either the client or the situation. Not only is absolute control impossible in most human situations but it is also contrary to social work values. What is expected is that the worker will move with the "stream of life," the developmental process of the systems in the relationship. The worker, by means of actions and other input into the situation, will influence that stream of life and will change the course of events. The course of events is also changed by the reactions and interactions of the client and others in the situation. The change can be of a preventive as well as an ameliorative nature. The social work input consists of perceptions and understanding about what is happening, identification of needs in a situation, enhancement of necessary skills, recognition of strengths, and knowledge of specific resources the worker can bring to bear to meet needs. This approach to intervention places considerable stress on enabling clients not only to engage in the helping endeavor but also to become heavily involved in change-producing behaviors of their own. It expands the change process to include any relevant system in the environment and the transactions among systems. Involvement of the client in the change process increases the likelihood of a diversity competent approach provided the worker supports the inclusion of diversity in the process.

Intervention, then, is action guided by the worker's knowledge, values, and skill directed toward the achievement of specific ends. Intervention encompasses the concepts of treatment, planned change, and social intervention as they have been used in social work literature. The diversity competent social worker incorporates diversity into all aspects of the intervention to increase the chances of success and to ensure that her client is served in a manner that is appropriate for his or her diversity.

When using an ecosystems strengths approach to change, social workers consider the transactions between the client system and the environment to be the primary focus of attention. The assessment involves developing an understanding of these transactions, identifying needs in the client system and the environment, and identifying strengths and resources available to meet those needs. Planning develops goals and objectives designed to balance these transactions and meet the needs of the client system and the environment, based on strengths and resources. Intervention into transactions is the practice activity related to the process of facilitating change. The worker intervenes with various parts of the ecosystem to assist the client in carrying out the plan or when barriers to success arise. Intervention calls for the creative blending of knowledge, values, and skills.

This perspective describes a contemporary view of the nature of practice based on a social systems approach and practice wisdom. The interventive approach seems particularly useful when practicing within a generalist framework with a multisystem focus. It is also relevant for diversity competent practice in terms of both content and process. The who, what, where, when, how, and why regarding transactions are heavily influenced by diversity. The way in which transactions occur; the types of transactions; what is exchanged; who is included and who is not; where, when, and how transactions occur and do not occur; and the meaning of this process can vary a great deal depending on age, gender, culture, religion, and other diverse factors. This has profound implications for the work that is done and how it is done.

Social workers recognize that growth and change are natural parts of the life cycle. Needs and meeting needs are constant parts of life, and so are changes in needs and meeting needs. As pointed out earlier, our needs as infants are different from our needs as adults. At each stage of life there are some needs that remain constant, while there are others that change. At the same time, how we get our needs met frequently changes during the course of our life. In addition, the demands and needs that come from our environment also change. Needs tend to be common in global terms but are felt in a very unique and personal way by each individual. The challenge for the social worker is to be able to see the commonality of needs while empathizing with the uniqueness of felt need for each client.

This approach gives the role of expert to the client when it comes to her own life. The worker is recognized as having knowledge and expertise or skills that can be used by the client to create a situation in which unmet needs are being met. The worker uses his knowledge and skill in reaching an understanding of person in environment or the ecosystem, in identifying strengths and resources in the ecosystem (which includes the client), in assisting the client in reaching a decision and developing and implementing a plan, and in evaluating the results.

The term process also needs definition. In a social work context, Sal Hofstein stated: "Process refers to the recurrent patterning of a sequence of change over time and in a particular direction."[35] It is important to note three qualities of this process: (1) occurring in recurrent patterning or stages, (2) taking place over time, and (3) moving in a particular direction. However, this description does not completely explain the nature of process, for there is also a cyclical aspect.

The change process involves making decisions and taking actions to carry out those decisions. In the process of doing this, adjustments are needed in order to successfully implement a decision. New information becomes available about the situation and about the path taken to meet the need. Sometimes new information results in changing the decision or the plan. Sometimes a more serious need is uncovered that requires more immediate attention. The process is rarely linear or step by step, but is cyclical in that the worker and the client return to earlier stages in order to make any adjustments that are needed.

The Phases of the Change Process

It should be recognized that all persons face perplexing situations and reach solutions in a variety of ways. However, the social work process is related to a highly organized and reliable manner of reaching solutions.

People in different disciplines have discussed the change process for various usages and have specified the steps in a variety of ways. The process for meeting needs that is presented in this text is an ecosystems strengths approach to change that includes phases in reaching a decision about change and in developing and carrying out a plan to implement the decision. The basic process is as follows:

1. Assessment phase
2. Planning phase
3. Action phase
4. Evaluation and termination

   1. *Assessment phase*—Assessment is an extremely important phase of the change process because it serves as a basis for the planning and action phases that follow. In most formulations of either problem-solving or change processes, assessment is presented as a single step. However, assessment is a complex process that occurs throughout the change process. The assessment phase used in this text consists of five stages. These stages serve as a guide for students and beginning practitioners in understanding the complex process of assessment. Inexperienced workers may ask such questions as: Where do I start? What is important and what is not? Where do I go from here? How do I know when we are ready to take action? Understanding these stages will help to answer these questions. Eventually, the experienced practitioner learns to use these stages throughout the change process, adding information as it arises and identifying other needs and concerns.

   A quality assessment increases the likelihood of developing a successful plan. The phrase "garbage in, garbage out" used in reference to computers is relevant here. Poor, inadequate, or inaccurate assessment is not likely to produce a good plan. Initially, the student or beginning practitioner needs to understand how to conduct a thorough assessment. Thus, the assessment phase used in this text involves the following stages:

1. Identify concern or need
2. Identify the nature of the concern or need
3. Identify potential strengths and resources in the ecosystem
4. Select and collect information
5. Analyze the available information

Assessment begins with identifying initial needs or concerns. The next stage is identifying the possible nature of the needs or concerns. At the same time the worker identifies potential strengths and resources in the person and the environment. These first three stages determine the fourth stage, which is selecting and collecting information. In this stage, the worker focuses on selecting and collecting information about the nature of the need or concern and about potential strengths and resources. As information becomes available, the worker and the client analyze it with the purpose of understanding person in environment and providing a basis for change that builds on strengths and resources.

In generalist practice, the worker and client may decide to change from the current client system to a different system. Most often this involves moving from individual to family, group, organization, or community. For instance, if the client is concerned about poor communication in her family, the worker and client might decide that the most appropriate client system is the family. Or if the worker has several clients experiencing similar needs, she might decide that a group is the best way to serve them. Generally, changes in the client system will occur during a stage of the assessment phase or in the planning phase. However, whenever it occurs, the worker and the new client system will need to reestablish needs or concerns and proceed through the other stages of the assessment process.

2. *Planning phase*—Information and analysis provide a basis on which the worker can assist the client in reaching a decision about meeting the identified need. However, reaching a decision does not guarantee that it will be carried out. A plan is necessary to ensure that the decision will result in the need being met. Planning is a joint process involving worker and client and is based on the strengths and resources that were identified in the ecosystem during the assessment and that are relevant for the situation at hand. The plan should be feasible and should describe the desired state of affairs in specific, positive terms. The plan includes goals, objectives, and tasks that are designed to bring about the desired change. Goals and objectives are best stated in behavioral terms that describe a desired outcome in as specific a manner as possible. The diversity competent worker develops a plan that incorporates the diversity of her client. She explores goals and objectives that are comfortable for the client given his or her diversity. She realizes that the feasibility of a plan requires that it be consistent with both the client's personal values and those of his or her gender, race, culture, religion, and so on. She includes ways of helping that are consistent with those that are expected within the client's diverse group. She incorporates natural helpers whenever possible.

3. *Action phase*—The action phase involves implementing the plan. Generally, both the client and the worker take action during this phase. These actions relate to the tasks that were identified in the plan. In planning, the client and the worker each agree to carry out certain tasks designed to reach the identified goals and objectives. The worker and the client may need to take other actions when barriers to success arise. For the worker, actions during this phase may involve directly working with the client or clients. These are referred to as direct practice actions. When the worker takes action to change other individuals or systems on behalf of the client, she is engaging in indirect practice actions. In using an ecosystems strengths approach, both direct and indirect actions are generally used in order to mobilize both the client and systems in the environment to bring about change. If the worker has been successful in developing a plan that is diversity competent, then she will be using actions that are consistent with the diversity of her client. Direct and indirect practice actions with individuals, families, groups, organizations, and communities will be covered in the respective chapters in Parts Three and Four.

4. *Evaluation and termination*—Evaluation occurs throughout the change process. The worker needs to constantly evaluate the quality of the assessment and the plan and the process of bringing about change. The diversity competent worker incorporates diversity into her evaluation in terms of both content and process. She is careful to include those factors that are relevant to her client's diversity and evaluates the process in a manner that is consistent with that diversity. This evaluation process will be covered in more detail in Part Three. When the plan is completed, the worker and the client evaluate whether it is successful in meeting the need. Termination of service occurs if the need has been met and there is no further need for service.

The outstanding characteristic of the change process in social work practice is the inclusion of the client as much as possible in the work at each step of the process. The client expresses the need or concern. The client also furnishes much of the information needed in the process, validates information sought from other sources, makes a decision, participates in developing the plan of action and in implementing and evaluating it, and develops problem-solving skills to use in coping with other life situations. Most important, it is the client's unique strengths and competencies that have enabled the client to have her needs met and that can be mobilized to meet both present and future needs.

An ecosystems strengths approach assumes there is a natural drive toward growth and development of one's potential and that unmet needs are challenges to be faced in realizing that potential. Instead of trying to change the client to fit what the worker believes she should be or become, the worker brings out what the client wants to be or become. In this way change becomes part of natural growth and development. By tuning in to the drive toward growth and development as the client is experiencing it, the worker ensures that change becomes a part of the natural life cycle. The worker also is able to be sensitive to the cultural aspects of development experienced by the client instead of imposing his own expectations.

Summary

Knowledge, values, and skills are all used in the social work endeavor. Knowledge is that part of reality that is confirmable. The knowledge base of the social worker is complex, being partly borrowed from other disciplines. It explains the functioning of persons and social situations. It also directs the response to need. Values are what is preferred or can be considered as a guide for behavior. Values that concern social work are those of the client, the social worker, the profession, and the general cultural and societal values of the situation. These values can conflict with one another; in fact, a value system usually has conflicting parts. Social work values contain preferred conceptions of persons, preferred outcomes for persons, and preferred instrumentalities for dealing with persons. The NASW *Code of Ethics* describes expectations for professional practice. Skill brings knowledge and values together and converts them into action. Skills must be developed through use over time. Social workers should have a variety of skills for use in practice. Choices are made as to which knowledge, values, and skills are applied in each practice situation. These choices should be based on appropriate diversity competent practice. The bringing together of these elements calls for creative blending. This creativity is the art of social work.

The change process is a means of responding to concern and need and of applying knowledge, values, and skills to work with clients using the concepts of assessment, person in situation, relationship, process, and intervention. It is a means of proceeding over time through stages in a cyclical manner to meet needs. In social work practice the client is involved in the process to the maximum extent possible. Worker and client together proceed from identification of the initial need through information collection, analysis, planning, action, and evaluation. Throughout this process, the worker focuses on the diversity and unique strengths and competencies of the client system and the environment and the possibilities for growth and change inherent in that ecosystem.

Intervention is purposeful and goal-directed action by a social worker in relation to human systems or processes in order to facilitate change. It implies moving with and influencing the stream of life. Human interaction is transactional in nature; that is, all interactions are affected by other interactions. Social work intervention focuses on these transactions in order to encourage change when social functioning is not meeting the needs of one or more elements in the transactions. Particular attention is given to diversity and to identifying and using clients' strengths.

The interventive-transactive approach calls for the social worker to identify needs; to apply knowledge, professional values, skills, and creativity; and to influence the ongoing transactions relative to the needs so as to bring about a change in the transactions. The change sought is the development of relationships that are need fulfilling for all parties of the relationship. This development may result in new relationships or in a change in existing ones.

This chapter has considered how knowledge, values, and skills are applied to a change process. It shows how the model being presented has moved from a problem-solving approach to an ecosystems strengths approach. It also introduces the notion that intervention is into human transactions and presents a change process that is used in this text.

Questions

1. Identify the knowledge you now have that you believe may be helpful to you as a social worker. How did you obtain that knowledge? Identify knowledge you believe you should gain at this time.
2. What values do you hold about people and their relationships to each other? Do these values seem congruent with social work values and with its code of ethics? How will your values affect the manner in which you work with clients?
3. How are your values congruent or incongruent with societal values as you understand them? How do you deal with situations in which your values and societal values are different?

4. What is the usual manner in which you develop skills in your daily living? How can you use this method in learning social work skills?
5. Discuss the concept of "creativity" as it is used in meeting clients' needs.
6. What is the usual manner in which you meet your needs? What strengths and resources have assisted you? How is your experience in changing and growing similar to or different from the process described in this chapter?
7. What are the advantages of using an ecosystems strengths approach with a client? What are the disadvantages?

Suggested Readings

Abramson, Marcia. "Reflections on Knowing Oneself Ethically: Toward a Working Framework for Social Work Practice." *Families in Society* 77 (April 1996): 195–202.

Congress, Elaine. *Social Work Values and Ethics: Identifying and Resolving Ethical Dilemmas.* Chicago: Nelson Hall, 1999.

Klein, Waldo C., and Bloom, Martin. "Practice Wisdom." *Social Work* 40 (November 1995): 799–807.

Meyer, Carol. "The Ecosystems Perspective: Implications for Social Work Practice." In Carol Meyer and Mark Mattaini, *The Foundations of Social Work Practice.* Washington, DC: NASW Press, 1995 (pp. 16–27).

Miley, Karla Krogsrud, O'Melia, Michael, and DuBois, Brenda L. *Generalist Social Work Practice: An Empowering Approach,* 6th ed. Boston: Allyn and Bacon, 2009.

Mizrahi, Terry and Davis, Larry E., Eds. *Encyclopedia of Social Work,* 20th ed. Washington, DC: NASW Press, 2008 ("Ethical Standards in Social Work: The NASW Code of Ethics," "Social Work Education").

Morales, Armando, and Sheafor, Bradford W. *Social Work: A Profession of Many Faces,* 11th ed. Boston: Allyn and Bacon, 2007 (Chapters 7 and 8).

Reamer, Frederic G. *The Foundations of Social Work Knowledge.* New York: Columbia University Press, 1994.

———. *Ethical Standards in Social Work: A Critical Review of the NASW Code of Ethics.* Washington, DC: NASW Press, 1998.

———. *Social Work Values and Ethics,* 3rd ed. New York: Columbia University Press, 2006.

———. *From the Front Lines: Student Cases in Social Work Ethics,* 2nd ed. Boston: Allyn and Bacon, 2005.

Saleeby, Dennis. *The Strengths Perspective in Social Work Practice,* 5th ed. Boston: Allyn and Bacon, 2009.

Sheafor, Bradford W., and Horejsi, Charles R. *Techniques and Guidelines for Social Work Practice,* 8th ed. Boston: Allyn and Bacon, 2008 (Chapters 1, 2, and 3).

3

Diversity Competent Practice

Learning Expectations

1. Understand diversity competence and the process of becoming diversity competent.
2. Understand gender competent practice.
3. Understand diversity competent practice with people who are gay and lesbian.
4. Understand the development and use of a schema for studying people from diverse ethnic groups.
5. Understand diversity competent practice with people who are African American.
6. Understand diversity competent practice with people who are Hispanic/Latino.
7. Understand diversity competent practice with people who are Native American.

Diversity competence is an important aspect of social work practice. The great majority of clients are members of populations whose diversity places them at risk of experiencing prejudice, discrimination, and oppression. At one time, diversity was seen as a barrier to be overcome. More recently, theories evolved that called for ethnic sensitive practice in which the worker respected and valued the ethnicity and culture of the client. However, being sensitive does not necessarily mean that the worker makes fundamental changes to the manner in which services are delivered. Thus, the next step in this evolution has been to develop **cultural competence** that calls for the worker to be able to practice in ways that are consistent with expectations in the client's culture. In the previous two editions of our text, *Social Work Practice: A Generalist Approach,* we extended this a step further by considering diversity competent practice skills. This extends the concept of cultural competence to all forms of diversity. The Council on Social Work Education identifies diversity as differences related to age, class, gender, gender identity and expression, immigration status, political ideology, color, culture, disability, ethnicity, race, religion, sex, and sexual orientation. The National Association of Social Work (NASW) includes most of these populations in its standards for cultural competence. However, we believe that diversity competent practice is a more descriptive term. The lists of populations for both organizations extend well beyond culture and recognize that people can be different from each other in many ways, and in multiple ways, as well.

The diversity competent social worker explores ways to serve diverse clients in a manner that is expected within their diverse group. For instance, a white worker might need to be able to use an Afrocentric approach in working with some of her African American clients or a feminist approach in working with some of her female clients. The professional worker realizes that it is her responsibility to adapt her skills to meet the needs of her client. She meets that responsibility by engaging in lifelong learning activities throughout her career. She reads materials and attends relevant training programs. She seeks to learn from knowledgeable colleagues and members of the community. She realizes the value of learning from her clients about how they would like to be served and incorporates this into her repertoire of skills. She uses diversity-appropriate skills in engagement and relationship building, assessment, planning, action, and evaluation and termination with every client she serves. She realizes that diversity competence is a lifelong process that is never really achieved, but she seeks to add to her competence with every client she serves.

The importance of diversity competence can be seen in the demographic changes occurring in the United States. During the first half of the twenty-first century, sweeping demographic changes will alter the face of the United States. Population projections indicate that the number of people who are older will increase in the United States and in other industrialized countries. The United States will also experience dramatic changes in its ethnic and racial composition. It appears that sometime in the middle of this century, people of color will surpass whites in population, and we will become a nation of minority groups. Given this demographic, it was inevitable that eventually we would see a person of color elected as president. However, with the election of President Barack Obama this came about somewhat earlier than what would have been expected. The combination of President Obama's ability to mobilize young and old and people of diverse backgrounds coupled with the foreign and domestic crises left by the Bush administration seems to have accelerated this outcome.

By the middle of this century, more than half of our high school graduates will be children of color, as will half of our working-age adults. Martha Ozawa studied these trends and raised concerns about the high rate of poverty among children, especially African American and Hispanic children. She pointed out that federal spending has been eleven times greater for people who are elderly than for children. She concluded that child poverty, especially among children of color, will lead to a decline in our economic and social well-being unless we dramatically increase our investment in children.[1]

In order for the social worker to develop diversity competence, she must take a comprehensive approach to understanding the effects of diversity on herself, her clients, the environment, and the interactions among these. Table 3.1 presents an outline for developing a diversity competent approach to practice. There are two important aspects to this work. The first is the need for the social worker to develop her ability to acquire and use knowledge, values, and skills in a way that makes diversity competent practice possible. This requires developing a view of the world and an attitude toward professional social work

TABLE 3.1   *Outline for Developing Diversity Competence*

   I. Understanding self
- **A.** Understand the social worker's own attitudes and beliefs about diverse groups
- **B.** Understand the influence of attitudes and beliefs of the worker's family on the social worker's own attitudes and beliefs about diverse groups
- **C.** Understand the influence of attitudes and beliefs of the worker's ecosystem on the social worker's own attitudes and beliefs about diverse groups
- **D.** Understand the influence of societal attitudes and beliefs on the social worker's own attitudes and beliefs about diverse groups

  II. Understanding societal influences
- **A.** Understand the history of each diverse group in the United States
- **B.** Understand historical and current stereotypes, prejudice, discrimination, and oppression
- **C.** Understand formal and informal mechanisms in U.S. society that cause or reinforce discrimination or oppression (past and present)
- **D.** Understand privileges and advantages that dominant groups have over the population (male privilege, white privilege, heterosexual privilege, wealth or class privilege, etc.)

 III. Understanding a diverse group
- **A.** Understand the particular culture and circumstances that make each group diverse
- **B.** Understand the values, beliefs, and customs of each diverse group
- **C.** Understand strengths of diverse groups and resources available in their ecosystems
- **D.** Understand the social, psychological, economic, and political effects of historical and current stereotypes, prejudice, discrimination, and oppression on diverse groups

 IV. Developing diversity competent practice skills
- **A.** Develop knowledge regarding relationship building, assessment, planning, action, evaluation and termination that are necessary to provide services in a manner that is expected within each diverse group
- **B.** Develop a personal and professional value system that values diversity
- **C.** Develop skills in providing direct and indirect services in a manner that is expected within each diverse group

practice that is inclusive rather than exclusive, that seeks to include everyone rather than excluding anyone, that genuinely values differences and variation, that taps one's natural curiosity about difference, and that truly values every human being. This means developing a system of thinking, feeling, and acting that opens the door to actively seeking new knowledge, to developing values that are consistent with this approach, and to trying new skills that may be uncomfortable for a while. It means becoming a true professional by giving up the safety of what we know and risking reaching out and learning about what we do not know. This task also involves learning how to acquire knowledge in a variety of ways. It involves learning about values that are different from our own and respecting those values. It involves learning how to use new skills while coping with discomfort that may be associated with doing something different.

The second aspect is to actually acquire and use appropriate knowledge, values, and skills in practice with diverse groups. It means learning how to learn about others. It includes learning where to look, who to ask, what it means, and how to use new knowledge about others. It requires the social worker to learn about his own values and those of others without preconceived notions or judgments that prevent including the client's value system in the work to be done. It means becoming adept at altering one's approach or even abandoning it in favor of one with which the client is comfortable.

To become diversity competent, the worker must be able to reflect on his knowledge about himself and knowledge about each diverse group. He must be willing to critically examine his knowledge and be open to considering distortions that might be present as a result of prejudices and stereotypes. He must be able to acquire and use new knowledge about diversity from his client and from professional sources, such as articles, books, professional training, colleagues, and other sources.

In diversity competent practice, the worker needs to become more familiar with the different ways of knowing that each diverse group may use in acquiring knowledge. In white, male, Eurocentric society, great value is placed on knowledge that is gained by the scientific method. Other groups value knowledge that is more experiential and passed on from earlier generations. Women may value knowledge that is acquired through relationships.

In diversity competent practice, the worker needs to be aware of her own values and the influence these have on her attitudes toward various diverse groups. She needs to be able to change those values that are based on or lead to prejudices and stereotypes so that she is free to accept every client as a valuable human being. This brings her value system in line with the cardinal value of social work, which holds that all human beings have inherent value and worth. She needs to be able to reconcile conflicts between her personal values and those of her profession. The diversity competent worker actively explores her client's values with an open mind. She is aware of how the larger society values or devalues certain groups. For instance, the dominant culture values males over females, heterosexuals over homosexuals, Caucasians over people of color, youth over age, Christianity over other religions, and so on. The diversity competent worker understands how this affects diverse clients and her work with them. She seeks to ameliorate these affects and to reduce the barriers that result. She is constantly aware of the importance of values in her work. She seeks to develop an awareness of her own values in every situation she encounters. She explores her client's values and incorporates appropriate values into the work.

She is aware of value conflicts that may arise between her values, her client's values, the values of the social work profession, and those of the larger society. She actively searches for mutually acceptable ways to resolve these conflicts and engages in lifelong learning to improve her appropriate use of values in diversity competent practice.

The diversity competent social worker tunes in to the attitudes and stereotypes toward diverse groups and the effect that these have on members of each population. He is also aware of the values that each group holds and is alert to value conflicts and their effects on relationships. The worker identifies ways of helping that each group uses and seeks to improve his skills so that he can serve members of each group in a manner with which they are comfortable.

In diversity competent practice, the worker needs to be knowledgeable about the values and beliefs of the population, its experience with the dominant society, the manner in which help is given and received, and good practices that need to be used with each group.

In understanding the environment, it is essential that the worker develop an understanding of responses to diversity from people and systems in the environment. The dual perspective proposed by Dolores Norton is especially relevant. Her discussion of the nurturing environment included family and the immediate community environment. The latter refers to the neighborhood in which the person lives. Norton's sustaining environment consists of the organization of goods and services, political power, economic resources, educational system, and larger societal systems.[2]

In understanding the ecosystem, the worker who is striving to become diversity competent also considers the attitudes toward diversity in his community and agency. He looks at each of the groups identified from his understanding of diversity. He looks for signs that indicate that diversity is valued by the community. He looks at patterns of race and ethnicity in the community. He considers to what extent these patterns represent current or past discrimination toward various groups. He observes how people of color, women, children, and people who are older or disabled are valued and respected. He evaluates community attitudes toward gays and lesbians. Some of these indicators are apparent in the institutions and services available to various groups. Some cannot be seen but can be heard in the stories of people who live in the community. As he becomes more diversity competent, the worker learns to look at the environment from a diversity perspective and to be an active listener.

Of special concern to social workers are diversity factors that exist in the community. The racial and ethnic makeup of the community is important to know. With regard to race and ethnicity, the worker should have knowledge about the degree to which various groups are integrated or segregated. She should note the attitudes of various groups toward each other. Is there respect or valuing of differences? Are there coalitions that have been formed? Are there adversarial relationships? How tolerant or intolerant are these groups toward each other? What groups hold power? Who has little or no power, and how does this reflect the general population? Similar questions should also be asked with respect to gender, age, and sexual orientation.

Becoming diversity competent may seem like an insurmountable challenge, especially for a student or a new social worker. But this work is not done over a semester or over a year. It is done over a lifetime. In fact, it is never really finished. However, the social worker can become more diversity competent if she is open to learning from each and every client she meets and if she accepts the responsibility to engage in the lifelong learning that is expected of a professional. In this chapter and those that follow, we address some of the knowledge, values, and skills that are needed for diversity competent practice, keeping in mind that no single text can do it all. What we seek to do instead is to learn about the process of becoming more diversity competent so that the student or practitioner has the knowledge, values, and skills to begin this endeavor as she experiences diversity in field placement and beginning professional practice. An outline is presented for studying individuals and families from diverse ethnic groups in Table 3.2.

Becoming Diversity Competent

Often students have difficulty in identifying their own diversity. Marty Dewees cited an unpublished paper by W. Nichols that found that "many students from White, dominant, middle-class status, particularly in geographical areas with limited racial diversity, regard themselves as having *no* culture or ethnicity."[3] This observation is consistent with the authors' experiences in teaching BSW students. Some of this lack of cultural identity may be attributed to the mixing of cultures and ethnic groups in U.S. society. However, the inability to identify one's own culture or ethnicity does not mean that one does not have any cultural or ethnic influences. What it means is that one is not aware of these influences. In addition, the authors have consistently observed that many female students have difficulty in recognizing discrimination they have experienced as women. Often, this begins to slowly change when there are discussions about male privilege and who did what around the house when they were growing up or in their current living arrangements. Unfortunately, this type of discrimination is only the tip of the iceberg.

The danger here is that the worker will not recognize or be open to the effects of diversity on the helping relationship and will not be prepared to deal with issues his client experiences that arise out of diversity. To become competent as a social worker, the student must become "diversity competent," or competent in working with diverse clients, especially those who are different from oneself. Competence in working with diversity begins with an awareness of one's own diversity and the affect that diversity has in one's personal life. James W. Leigh suggested that knowing one's own cultural influences is critical to developing cultural competence. He points out that we all carry unconscious cultural influences that either are directly prejudicial toward certain other cultures or lead us in that direction because of cultural differences.[4] Barbara Okum, Jane Fried, and Marcia Okum have discussed the need to develop self-awareness first before being able to develop an awareness of others.[5] Doman Lum cited a number of references that reinforce the need for self-awareness.[6] Jerry V. Diller stated, "It is impossible to appreciate the impact of culture on the lives of others, particularly clients, if one is out of touch with his or her own cultural background."[7] Yuhwa Lu, Doman Lum, and Sheying Chen have developed a conceptual framework for cultural competency that begins with "awareness of cultural and ethnic experiences which are part of the personal and professional socialization of the worker."[8] They included the need to evaluate one's own experiences and reactions to "racism, sexism, homophobia, and other forms of prejudice/discrimination."[9] Two out of the four steps that Marty Dewees proposed for cultural competence with families are related to the need for students to identify their own cultural influences.[10]

Thus, the preponderance of work that is being done on developing models for cultural competence in social work practice points out the need for the student or worker to develop cultural awareness of herself. We propose to extend this requirement beyond culture to all forms of diversity in society. To become diversity competent, the student or worker must begin with an examination of her own diversity, along with an examination of how her experiences have shaped her attitudes toward her own diversity and the diversity of others. Cultural influences play a major role in both of these endeavors. It is not enough to be "color-blind" or "culture blind" or "diversity blind." Assertions of tolerance will not ensure the development of trust in clients who are different from oneself. In fact, it is more likely to lead to mistrust because clients get the message that diversity does not matter when indeed they know that it does. Professing tolerance for diversity can easily come across as insensitivity toward diversity. Diversity competence calls for an active listening approach to diversity that seeks to know more. It uses diversity to create a dialogue with the client that will lead to a better understanding of the client and his environment.

All of the authors in the sources previously cited point to the need for the student or worker to obtain knowledge about the culture to which the client belongs and skills in working within the client's cultural system. Gargi Sodowsky, Richard Taffe, Terry Gutkin, and Steven Wise have added another dimension to the skills related to cultural competence, namely, the multicultural counseling relationship.[11] Again, the requirement to develop knowledge and skills must be extended beyond culture to all forms of diversity in society.

Lu, Lum, and Chen suggested that the worker "engage in inductive learning that promotes investigation and inquiry."[12] Doman Lum also included this in culturally competent practice.[13] The inductive approach is different from **deductive learning** that uses the scientific method. The deductive process involves moving from theory to hypothesis to testing the hypothesis to determine whether the theory is supported. The inductive process involves moving from making observations of phenomena to searching for patterns that may lead to theory development. Applying the **inductive learning** approach to becoming competent in working with diversity means adopting an open-minded inquisitive approach, laying aside preconceived notions, and listening to the experiences of the client. Self-knowledge must come first so that the worker can move away from experiencing the client's story out of her own experience and instead hear the client's story out of his experience.

As a professional, the social worker has a responsibility to engage in a process of lifelong learning. An important area of lifelong learning is learning about diversity. The student begins this process through coursework, research, assignments, reading, class discussions, and examining himself as a person and as a developing professional. He learns to use inductive learning and natural inquiry in his approach to diversity. In field placement, the student is frequently put in a position of working with people who are diverse, often for the first time. Many of these people have experienced considerable prejudice and discrimination related to their diversity. The student learns how to work with diverse clients by applying what he has learned from his academic experiences along with his new field experiences. He learns from his field instructor and from others with expertise who may be available in his agency, community, or university. Most important, he learns to learn from his clients. They are the experts on their own experiences with diversity. As a professional social worker, he learns to continue this learning, and he seeks out additional training through in-service training, conferences, and other continuing education activities.

Becoming "diversity competent" means developing self-knowledge—developing knowledge about one's own diversity. Learning about diversity continues as the student or worker takes an active, inductive approach to learning about diversity in others. This learning lasts for a lifetime as the professional social worker engages in a lifelong process of self-examination, seeks out knowledge about diversity, and develops skills in working with people who are different from her.

The number of individuals and families who are biracial or multiracial has increased substantially during the past several decades and will continue to increase as the United States becomes a more multicultural, multiethnic, and multiracial society. Some of these biracial families are produced by biracial couples. Others are a product of couples who adopt children of another race. In some cases, these are children from foreign adoption. Despite becoming more common, biracial and multiracial individuals and families face the same kinds of prejudice and discrimination as all people of color. In addition, some of these individuals and families find that they are not accepted by either culture or racial group. The children may experience these same attitudes. Biracial parents need to bolster their child's self-image and self-esteem in order to withstand these negative attitudes. Social workers need to support these individuals and families in fighting and coping with the consequences of negative attitudes and actions. Social workers must stand up and fight prejudice, discrimination, and oppression in all its forms.

Families with same-sex partners are a special form of family that has gained greater recognition as gays and lesbians have advocated for legal status as couples. Children in these families may be a product of prior heterosexual relationships, adoption, surrogate mothers, or donor insemination.

In heterosexual families, roles are often assigned by gender and culture. For same-sex couples, there is a need to establish a communication system that can be used to discuss the roles that each partner will take or how these roles will be shared. Egalitarian heterosexual couples have this same need. In many cases, discussing each day who will do what tasks—such as cooking, child care, errands, housework, and the like—is necessary. Same-sex couples and their children often face a great deal of prejudice and discrimination. Children in same-sex families need assistance from their parents in establishing a healthy identity that can withstand these negative social attitudes, along with positive descriptions of their family and family members. For example, in a lesbian family, the child might be encouraged to see himself as having two mothers. It is important that he see this as a strength and that he feel he is just as worthwhile as a child of a heterosexual couple. Families are also headed by single parents who are gay or lesbian. In some respects, these parents become somewhat invisible in terms of their sexual orientation because it is more difficult to tell someone is gay or lesbian if he or she is single. Families may have members who are bisexual or transgendered. People who are bisexual are attracted to both males and females. People who are transgendered feel that they are actually the opposite sex from the one that they are biologically. They frequently describe themselves as being a man trapped in a woman's body or a woman trapped in a man's body. These individuals are people who may seek out a sex change in order to resolve this dilemma. Social workers need to provide support for gay, lesbian, bisexual, and transgendered families to counteract and cope with the consequences of negative attitudes and actions from society. Social workers must be advocates and fight prejudice, discrimination, and oppression in all its forms, regardless of personal values and beliefs.

When considering the ethnic individual or family there are two levels of understanding that are needed by the worker: first is the more general level, which provides overall knowledge; second is the specific level, which provides understanding of a specific individual or family. Table 3.2 presents an outline for studying individuals and families from diverse ethnic groups. We use this outline to examine important factors in working with each ethnic individual or family. However, first we consider the role of gender in families and examine how the generalist social worker develops and implements a gender competent approach to practice.

Gender Competence

Gender is an especially important consideration in working with individuals, families, and groups Expectations for males and females are interwoven into the fabric of nearly every society. These expectations are reinforced by various social institutions. Perhaps the strongest messages about these expectations come from within the family and in the world of work.

During the twentieth century, women in the United States were able to gain the right to vote nationally, have access to higher education, obtain many jobs from which they were formerly excluded, own property, and have other rights that had been denied. However, full equality has still eluded women. Gender-based roles carry the expectation that women will do most of the domestic chores around the home including child care and elder care. Women have not gained access to real power in the economic and political arenas. There are only a very few women who head major corporations or serve on their boards, and there has never been a female president or vice president of the United States. Women are more likely than men to be poor and to be victims of rape and domestic violence.

The plight of women internationally is not much better and in most regards is much worse than in the United States. The exception is western Europe where in most countries women not only enjoy the same or better social and economic well-being but also have achieved real political power that is much greater than that of U.S. women. Globally, women own a very small percentage of the world's wealth. This demonstrates the extent to which women are oppressed.

In developing gender competent practice, it is important to understand feminist practice. A paradigm that is suggested by some social workers as applicable to many populations is the **feminist perspective**. This paradigm is based on five principles: (1) the elimination of false dichotomies and artificial separations, (2) the reconceptualization of power, (3) the valuing of process equally with product, (4) the validity of renaming, and (5) the personal is political. In other words, this approach calls for a holistic view; a wide distribution of power; attention to how goals are implemented; the renaming of action so as to purge discriminatory language; and the recognition that personal problems are often the result of political injustice, requiring that the focus of intervention be on change in large systems.[14] This paradigm seems useful in any situation in which discrimination is of major concern, such as in working with women or minority groups.

Feminist social workers stress the need for teaching clients how to empower themselves as well as how to work with systems that affect them. They also emphasize the importance of working with clients as equals in order to avoid replicating the "one-up" position common in other environmental interactions. Feminist workers attempt to link clients with others who face similar issues in order to build systems that can be used for networking, support, and education. The feminist perspective and method seem particularly relevant in addressing social injustice in that it acknowledges that many of the difficulties faced by populations at risk of discrimination are a result of their interactions with the environment or with the surrounding systems rather than within the clients themselves. The oppression of women around the world presents many challenges for social workers in practicing gender competence with various cultural groups. There are numerous cultures that seek to perpetuate paternalism and have substantial power imbalances between men and women as major cultural constructs for gender roles and expectations. The challenge for gender competent social workers is to engage and work with members of these cultural groups without sacrificing the principles of good gender competence. The risk is that if the worker comes on too strong, the individual, family, or group may be alienated or feel that the worker's values and views are being imposed on them.

The gender competent worker examines his own experiences and background as these relate to gender. He seeks to understand his own attitudes and beliefs about males and females and the influence of his family and his ecosystem, and society's attitudes and beliefs. In understanding societal influences, the worker develops an understanding of the history of societal attitudes toward gender and how these have led to long-standing practices that are discriminatory and oppressive. He understands that there are still mechanisms in U.S. society that perpetuate discrimination and oppression. He understands male privilege and attempts to overcome its effects by creating more equal treatment for women and the elimination of gender stereotyping.

In social work practice the gender competent worker takes an empowerment approach with female clients and supports egalitarian attitudes and behaviors with both males and females. He avoids sexist terminology and models this for his clients. He recognizes that the circumstances for males and females may not be of their own doing, but may be related to the imbalances that have been perpetuated by society, he seeks to raise consciousness regarding these imbalances and their effects, and he models egalitarian values and relationships.

Resources

Affilia: Journal of Women and Social Work.

Bricker-Jenkins, Mary, and Hooyman, Nancy. *Not for Women Only: Social Work Practice for a Feminist Future.* Silver Spring, MD: NASW Press, 1986.

Bricker-Jenkins, Mary, Hooyman, Nancy, and Gottlieb, Naomi. *Feminist Social Work Practice in Clinical Settings.* Newbury Park, CA: Sage, 1991.

Silverstein, Louise B., and Goodrich, Thelma Jean, Eds. *Feminist Family Therapy: Empowerment in Social Context.* Washington, DC: American Psychological Association, 2005.

Valentich, Mary. "Feminism and Social Work Practice" in *Social Work Treatment: Interlocking Theoretical Approaches,* 4th ed., Francis J. Turner, Ed. New York: Free Press, 1996, pp. 282–318.

Van Den Bergh, Nan. *Feminist Practice in the 21st Century.* Washington, DC: NASW Press, 1995.

Van Den Bergh, Nan, and Cooper, Lynn. *Feminist Visions for Social Work.* Silver Spring, MD: NASW Press, 1986.

Diversity Competence with People Who Are Gay or Lesbian

People who are gay or lesbian are probably the object of more hatred than any other groups in the United States, especially by conservative right-wing religious groups and by people who are homophobic. The most common reasons given for negative attitudes are based on religious beliefs.

Recent political battles have been fought over gay and lesbian marriage and gay and lesbian rights. Some states have moved toward recognizing same-sex marriages or civil unions, whereas other states have passed constitutional amendments prohibiting them. This population is the only one that can be legally discriminated against under federal law. In fact, people can be fired for being gay or lesbian without any protection by the federal government. The only protections afforded people who are gay or lesbian are under state and local laws prohibiting discrimination based on sexual orientation. Fortunately, overall prejudice, discrimination, and oppression toward this group have been reduced considerably during recent years. Unfortunately, those who are prejudiced toward people who are gay or lesbian have become more intense in their opposition. Younger generations seem much more tolerant of diversity in sexual orientation, and it would appear that recognition of same-sex marriages and preservation of rights for people who are gay or lesbian is inevitable.

On a professional level, social workers are committed to valuing all human beings and treating everyone with dignity and respect. On a personal level some social workers have religious beliefs that view people who are gay or lesbian negatively. Some may feel conflicted about working with people who are gay or lesbian. However, regardless of the client, social workers should set aside their personal values and act on their professional value system. Generally speaking, when asked, most people say that they would change negative attitudes they have toward people who are gay or lesbian if it were proven that being gay or lesbian was biologically determined. Most studies point in this direction. It is important that social workers use the term *sexual orientation* rather than *sexual preference.* Sexual orientation places sexuality in the biological realm. Sexual preference refers to choice. The term "lifestyle" should also be avoided.

Working with clients who are gay or lesbian involves using similar approaches to those social workers use with other individuals, families, or groups. The main differences lie in areas related to dealing with the social and political ramifications of their sexual orientation. Prejudice, discrimination, and oppression along with homophobia and heterosexism on the part of others result in social and political reactions that affect people who are gay or lesbian and their families. Socially, these negative reactions range from stares and negative comments to hate crimes that include assaults and murders. Politically, most states do not give legal recognition or status to gay and lesbian relationships. This goes beyond the issue of gay and lesbian marriage. It creates difficulties with insurance coverage, inheritance, adoption, medical consents, child custody, and so on. Rights that are taken for granted by heterosexuals are routinely denied to individuals and couples who are gay or lesbian. Thus, advocacy and empowerment are often needed to overcome some of these issues.

Social workers are often unaware of the extent to which heterosexuality is assumed in society at large and even within the practice of social work itself. Estimates of the percentage of people who are gay or lesbian run as high as 10 percent. This means that as many as one out of ten clients is likely to be gay or lesbian. Many of these clients will not reveal their sexual orientation if they do not know that it is safe to do so. Social workers need to become comfortable in working with clients who are gay and lesbian. They should also communicate to their clients that it is safe to reveal this to them. Some subtle ways of doing this are to display materials related to gay and lesbian services or issues. The rainbow is a symbol for gays and lesbians. There are also stickers and other materials that state that the worker or the agency is a safe place for people who are gay or lesbian.

Social workers should not assume that clients are heterosexual. They should incorporate this into their assessment both verbally and in the type of documentation that is used. Most agency materials including assessment documents are biased toward heterosexuality. Social workers should work to change this to an unbiased approach.

Negative reactions by peers toward children in gay and lesbian families can be very difficult challenges. Negative reactions by the general public toward the family as a whole or toward same-sex couples can also be quite challenging. Some same-sex parents will hide their sexual orientation to avoid these challenges. Many find that they have to be very selective about where they live and where their children attend school. They look for neighborhoods or communities where there is either tolerance for their sexual orientation or tolerance for diversity in general. Groups have been formed to assist with these issues and to offer gay and lesbian families opportunities to share time with other gay and lesbian families in order to escape from these challenges and to experience acceptance. These groups offer vacations, trips, cruises, and social events especially for gay and lesbian families.

Resources

Laird, Joan, and Green, Robert-Jay, Eds. *Lesbians and Gays in Couples and Families.* San Fransisco, CA: Jossey-Bass, 1996. A "must have" text for anyone practicing with gay and lesbian couples and families.

Mallon, Gerald P. "Practice with Families Where Sexual Orientation Is an Issue: Lesbian and Gay Individuals and Their Families" in *Multicultural Perspectives in Working with Families,* 2nd ed. Elaine P. Congress and Manny J. Gonzales, Eds. New York: Springer, 2005, pp. 199–227.

Morrow, Deana F., and Messinger, Lori, Eds. *Sexual Orientation and Gender Expression in Social Work Practice: Working with Gay, Lesbian, Bisexual, and Transgender People.* New York: Columbia University Press, 2006.

Silverstein, Louise B., and Goodrich, Thelma Jean, Eds. *Feminist Family Therapy: Empowerment in Social Context,* Washington, DC: American Psychological Association, 2005.

Walters, Karina L., Longres, John F., Han, Chong-suk, and Icard, Larry D. "Cultural Competence with Gay and Lesbian Persons of Color" in *Culturally Competent Practice: A Framework for Understanding Diverse Groups and Justice Issues,* 2nd ed. Doman Lum, Ed. Pacific Grove, CA: Brooks/Cole, 2003.

A Schema for Studying Diverse Ethnic Groups

Table 3.2 displays a schema for studying individuals and families from diverse ethnic groups. It is intended to be broad enough to be used with any individual or family, regardless of ethnicity. It can be adapted for use with clients with mixed ethnic backgrounds by using it multiculturally and covering each cultural background that is relevant. The use of the schema forms the framework for our studies of diversity competent practice with

TABLE 3.2 *Schema for Studying Individuals and Families from Diverse Ethnic Groups*

I. Overall knowledge of diverse ethnic group
  A. History of the particular ethnic group
    1. Significant information about the point of origin
    2. Immigration patterns, when, why
    3. Experience(s) with the dominant society, any legal events, prejudice/ discrimination concerns
    4. Experience in coping or integrating with dominant society
  B. Significant cultural patterns
    1. Spiritual considerations, experiences, beliefs
    2. Relationship beliefs about the physical world
    3. Significant values/value system(s)
    4. Attitudes toward things, time and its use, age, authority, work, display of feeling or emotions
    5. Change and its meaning to group
    6. Past, present, and future orientation
    7. Ceremonies, rituals
    8. Traditional art forms—music—use of in daily or ceremonial life
    9. Taboos
  C. Family patterns and structure
    1. Relationships of importance
      a. Within cultural group
      b. With larger society
    2. Decision-making processes
    3. Generational factors, age, sex considerations
    4. Child-rearing and housekeeping practices
    5. Expectations within the family
  D. Communication patterns
    1. Language usage; concepts, values, philosophies
    2. Nonverbal expression
  E. Traditional coping patterns and mechanisms
    1. Adaptation, compensation, reaction to stress, stigmatization, stereotyping
  F. Community structures
    1. Traditional forms and ways of functioning
    2. Community provision for help
    3. Contemporary society structures relative to this ethnic group
  G. Current issues of the group or regarding the group
    1. Quality of life issues
    2. Economic, educational, spiritual
    3. Group identity
    4. Opportunity provision or restriction
    5. Discrimination, prejudice concerns
  H. Resources for gaining understanding of group
II. Knowledge of the individual or individual family
  A. History
    1. Experience of this particular individual or family

(continued)

TABLE 3.2   *(continued)*

---

    2. Migration, movement within the United States
        a. Social–economic mobility
        b. Identification with ethnic group
    3. Note urban–rural experience
    4. Fit within larger ethnic group
  B. Value concerns
    1. What of traditional ethnic patterns is important to this individual or family? What is not? How do they deal with discrepancies?
    2. Spirituality
    3. Traditions
  C. Family system
    1. How does this family or the family of the client define itself (nuclear, extended, etc.)?
    2. Relationships in this family or the family of the client
    3. How does this family or individual relate to larger ethnic group? To their heritage?
  D. Communication patterns
    1. Within this particular family or the family of the client
    2. With larger society
  E. Coping for this particular individual or family
  F. Community
    1. Relationships to ethnic community, to dominant community
    2. Resources available, usable by this family or individual, experience with
  G. Issues concerning this family or individual

African American, Hispanic/Latino, and Native American clients. It can also be used in learning about clients from various parts of Europe, Asia, and the Pacific Islands as well as those who are immigrants from Central and South America and from Africa. Space prohibits us from covering every type of ethnic group, but three main types that social workers are likely to encounter are covered here.

    When considering the ethnic individual or family there are two levels of understanding that are needed by the worker: first is the more general level, which provides overall knowledge; second is the specific level, which provides understanding of a specific individual or family. At the general level, it is important to consider the history of the ethnic group, including information about the point or country of origin. The worker should gather information about immigration patterns and reasons for the immigration of the ethnic group as a whole. Did this group experience discrimination and oppression in their country of origin? Religious persecution? Economic deprivation? Political persecution? The worker should also seek to uncover experiences the group has had with the dominant group in U.S. society and how they have coped with those experiences or have been integrated into the dominant group.

    Significant cultural patterns provide the next area for examination. Spirituality, values, art forms, taboos, and attitudes and beliefs, including those regarding change and time, should be explored. Ceremonies and rituals are also important aspects of culture.

    Within each culture are family patterns and structure. It is important to know about significant relationships, how decisions are typically made, child-rearing and housekeeping practices, and expectations that families typically have of their members. There are also generational factors and age and sex considerations. These latter factors refer to inter- and intragenerational relationships and statuses, attitudes toward aging and the aged, and sex or gender based role expectations.

The diversity competent social worker needs to pay close attention to communication patterns, especially as these relate to language and to nonverbal communication. Because interaction is the staple of both family life and the social work endeavor, this aspect of culture takes on great significance.

Another area for study is the coping mechanisms that are typically used by members of the ethnic group. How do they respond to stress or to prejudice and stereotyping? What is accepted within the culture and what is not?

Looking beyond the individual or family, the worker needs to be familiar with community structures that are typical for the ethnic group. How does the community typically function within the culture? How is help usually offered and received? What kinds of societal structures are constructed within this ethnic community? Some ethnic groups rely on neighborhood communities or clubs to preserve their identity and their culture. Others rely on religious institutions. Still others have little in the way of formal or informal structures, and, as a result, their ethnic identity may be quickly absorbed into the dominant culture provided they are not identified by skin color or some other recognizable feature that makes them a target for exclusion.

The worker should be familiar with current issues that are important for the ethnic group. For instance, the status of undocumented immigrants is an important consideration within the Mexican American community. Other issues relate to the group's quality of life, economic and educational opportunities or restrictions, identity, and prejudice and discrimination. What are the important issues for this population and why are these important?

Finally, in the area of general or overall knowledge the worker needs to be aware of resources that are available for gaining an understanding of the ethnic group. These range from formal to informal sources of information. Formal sources come from census data, library resources, histories, educational institutions, community resources for the ethnic group, and other community structures. Informal resources tend to be verbal and include colleagues, indigenous workers, experts, and members of the ethnic group, including the individual or the family system with whom the worker is working.

The second area of knowledge is at the specific level, which provides understanding of a specific individual or family. This area recognizes that, although individuals and families may share a common ethnic identity, each individual or family is unique in terms of how they experience and express their identity. The information for this area of study comes mainly from the individual or family. The worker seeks to have clients tell their stories and she listens without any preconceived notions about what she will hear.

The first area for exploration is the unique history of this individual or family. What were their experiences and those of their ancestors? What is their history of migration and their movement within the United States? What is their socioeconomic status and how mobile have they been in terms of increasing their status? What is the individual or family's identification with their ethnic group and how strong is this? Have they lived in rural or urban areas and what affect has this had on the individual or the family system?

Next, the worker should look at values and how the individual or family experiences or adheres to values from their ethnic roots. What has been retained and what has not?

How does the individual or family feel about discrepancies between their values and those of their ethnic heritage? What are the spiritual or religious practices and how do these reflect traditional ethnic practices? What ethnic traditions have been retained and what traditions are no longer practiced?

For the family itself or the client's family, the worker should explore how they see themselves as a family. Who are considered members? How important is the extended family? What characterizes relationships within the family? How does the family relate to the larger ethnic group? How does it relate to their ethnic heritage? What are the communication patterns within the family and between the family and the larger society? What are the typical coping patterns and mechanisms used by this family and how do these relate to those that are typical for its ethnic group? What relationships are there between the family and its ethnic community? How does the family relate to the larger society? What resources are available to this family and how are these accessed and used? What have been the family's experiences with those resources? What are the main issues that concern this family?

The worker uses naturalistic inquiry as he explores these unique areas of family life. He draws out the story and takes the position that he does not know what he does not know. He respects the individual or family as experts on their own lives and their cultural heritage and experience. The diversity competent worker is aware of his own attitudes toward the particular ethnic group and attempts to set those aside so he can be as nonjudgmental as possible. He is also aware of attitudes and stereotypes of the larger society toward the ethnic group and the effects of these on that group. As the worker explores these areas, he builds a meaningful relationship with the individual or family that will carry them through the work to be done.

Diversity Competence with People Who Are African American

Diversity competent practice with people who are African American begins with the understanding that African Americans are diverse while also sharing common experiences. African Americans have diverse roots and histories that create diversity within their culture. At the same time, African Americans share the experience of living in a society that is racist and has continued to marginalize them, even in the face of legal challenges to discrimination and oppression. Despite the election of our first African American president, we still have a long way to go before racism is eliminated. At the same time, the election of President Barack Obama gives hope that we may be closer to that day.

Diversity within the African American culture exists because of variation in their roots. Although most African Americans have their roots in areas of West Africa, some are descendants of former slaves who lived in the Caribbean and West Indies and others are either immigrants from Africa or their descendents. In addition, there was a great deal of variation in their ancestral experiences in the United States during slavery and afterward.

Diversity competent practice with African Americans generally means using an Afrocentric approach. This approach evolved primarily during the twentieth century. Jerome H. Schiele described three basic assumptions regarding Afrocentric social work: "1) that individual identity is conceived as a collective identity; 2) that the spiritual aspects of humans is just as legitimate as the material component; and 3) that the affective approach to knowledge is epistemologically valid."[15] The first two of these assumptions are particularly important in working with African Americans and their families. Whereas individual identity and materialism are highly prized in Eurocentric cultures, individual identity is tied to family, culture, community, and creator for African Americans, and people are seen as being spiritually connected with each other and with the world around them.

Historical Considerations

Most African Americans are descendents of the only non–Native American group that did not immigrate as such; they were brought to the United States against their will to be used as slaves. African American history during slavery and afterward is the predominant issue when it comes to understanding working with African Americans and their families. Although most slaves were brought to the United States from West Africa, there was a great deal of cultural and language diversity among the tribes to which they belonged. In addition, many African Americans are descended from former slaves who lived in the Caribbean and West Indies and had developed a rich and varied culture that was different from African American slaves.

The experiences of African Americans after slavery ended are also important historical considerations. Most former slaves remained in the South and were eventually subjugated again, especially after Reconstruction ended. Few owned any land and the system of sharecropping ensured that they remained poor and in debt. In addition to economic subjugation, African Americans were systematically excluded from voting and holding office. A social and legal system known as "Jim Crow" reinforced their status as second-class citizens. This economic, political, and social oppression was enforced by groups such as the Ku Klux Klan and various vigilante groups who beat, murdered, and lynched African Americans who dared to challenge the system. Some former slaves migrated to the North and the West where they were free but still experienced prejudice, discrimination, and oppression in various forms. With the collapse of the cotton and tobacco economies, especially during the Great Depression, many African Americans migrated to cities in the South, the North, and the West looking for work. They were typically concentrated in poor neighborhoods with overcrowded substandard housing.

More recently, many African Americans have become economically successful and have been able to move to other areas with better housing and more opportunities. Unfortunately, a disproportionate number of African American families have not enjoyed the same success and are still mired in poverty in our inner cities and the rural South. What is remarkable is that the progress that African Americans have made since slavery has been almost entirely at their own hands. Little if any assistance has been given by the dominant culture. In fact much of the progress made by African Americans has actually occurred in spite of barriers that have been and continue to be erected by the dominant culture.

Cultural Patterns

Efforts were made to eliminate African culture as part of the subjugation of slavery. However, African Americans were successful in using their African culture to survive both the ravages of slavery and the further oppression that has followed it. Afrocentricity gives us a view of various aspects of African culture that have survived and contributed to survival.

Schiele's description refers to collective identity and spirituality. These two assumptions are intertwined in that spirituality includes a belief that all human beings are interconnected with each other, with the environment, and with the creator, which is the web that connects everything together. Thus, individual identity does not exist separate from the environment, but as a part of the collective identity of the community, the nation, and the world. This places additional emphasis on the inclusion of family and community in working with people of African and African American descent.[16]

In many traditional African cultures, the community is the most important social entity. This is captured in the African proverb "It takes a village to raise a child." Kinship extended beyond the nuclear family and included both extended family and nonfamily members of the community. Responsibility for child-rearing, preparation for adulthood, and rites of passage were the responsibilities of the entire village. This collective identity resulted in African Americans forming similar communities of related and unrelated kinship networks during slavery and afterward. The community made sure that the elderly, children, and widows were cared for regardless of how poor members were themselves.

The essence of Afrocentricity is best illustrated by the Nguzo Saba of Kwanzaa, which is an Afrocentric value system made up of seven principles. There are numerous renditions of this. The following is from an article by Vanessa D. Johnson regarding its use as a foundation for African American college student development theory:

> *Umoja* (unity): To strive for and maintain unity in the family, community, nation, and race.
>
> *Kujichagulia* (self-determination): To define ourselves, name ourselves, create for ourselves, and speak for ourselves instead of being defined, named, created for, and spoken for by others.
>
> *Ujima* (collective work and responsibility): To build and maintain our community together and make our sisters' and brothers' problems our problems and to solve them together.
>
> *Ujamma* (cooperative economics): To build and maintain our own stores, shops, and other businesses and profit from them together.
>
> *Nia* (purpose): To make our collective vocation the building and developing of our community in order to restore our people to their traditional greatness.
>
> *Kuumba* (creativity): To do always as much as we can, in the way we can, in order to leave our community more beautiful and beneficial than we inherited it.
>
> *Imani* (faith): To believe with all our hearts in God, our people, our parents, our teachers, our leaders, and the righteousness and victory of our struggle.[17]

The values that are expressed in these seven principles reflect values that have been preserved from African heritage. They could easily be used by any group that has experienced oppression.

Given the varied history of African Americans, there are also variations in the extent to which individuals have retained and practice elements of their African heritage. Peter Bell and Jimmy Evans suggested four interpersonal styles they associated with the degree of acculturation. Those who are fully acculturated have assimilated into mainstream white culture and do not typically identify with or express their African American heritage. On the opposite side of the spectrum are those who reject white culture and identify with and express only their African American heritage. In between these are those who are bicultural and who are comfortable with both white and African American culture. A fourth group is traditional. They tend to value their African American heritage and have limited contact outside the African American community. They may show some of the effects of their history under slavery and Jim Crow such as deference to whites.[18]

Family

As indicated under the Nguzo Saba, the family plays a critical role in the life of African Americans.[19] The African American family is an extended family that may also include fictive kin or members who are not related by blood or marriage. This reflects an African cultural heritage in which the community was considered the most important social unit. Unrelated family members may be referred to using the terms *brother, sister, aunt, uncle,* or *cousin*. Grandparents who raise their grandchildren or informal guardians who raise informally adopted children may be called *mother* or *father*.

Probably one of the greatest impacts on African Americans and their families has been the effects of economic deprivation and oppression. Employment opportunities have been extremely limited. One could argue that the only legitimate economic roles readily afforded African Americans by the dominant white society were those associated with slavery, sharecropping, and domestic services. In addition, African American males have generally found it more difficult than females to acquire and maintain employment. Thus, one of the effects of economic oppression on the African American family has been to undermine the role of provider for African American males. From the emasculation of males during slavery and Jim Crow to the collapse of the cotton and tobacco economy, which relied on sharecropping, to the exportation of manufacturing jobs under globalization, many African American males have been robbed of the role of provider. These experiences have contributed to a situation in which the majority of African American families today are headed by females, whereas many of those incarcerated in prison or jail are African American males.

Communication Processes

Although African Americans speak English, a form of English has evolved that is referred to as *Black English* or *African American language*. Valerie Borum differentiates between this and "Standard English" and points out that some African Americans speak only one or the other and some will switch back and forth and are bilingual.[20] She describes African American language as allowing for flexibility and including "highly meaningful nonverbal communication and expression via body language."[21] She sees it as "dramatizing that which Standard English fails to communicate."[22] It "might be regarded as a 'highly exquisite form of pantomime.'"[23]

Accompanying this variation in language are variations in culture and worldviews, which are reflected in the principles of the Nguzo Saba, especially regarding collective identity, unity, and creativity.[24] Relationships are highly prized and are generally valued over the materialism that is seen as characterizing white culture.

Coping Patterns

The coping patterns of African Americans is also reflected in Afrocentricity and the seven principles of the Nguzo Saba.[25] Collective identity, a strong sense of community, and spirituality make for a strong base from which members can deal with adversity. The whole history of African Americans has been fraught with adversity beginning with the diaspora and slavery and continuing through pervasive prejudice, discrimination, and oppression that continues to this day. Through all of this African Americans have persevered and many are quite prosperous in spite of their mistreatment by the dominant white society.

Collective identity gives African Americans a means of overcoming negative messages from the dominant culture, which devalues people of color. By relying on their families, communities, and culture for self-esteem and respect, many African Americans are able to develop healthy self-images despite the actions of white society. Their strong sense of community and the high value placed on mutual aid provided their own safety net during slavery and the following hard times when there were no such structures in the U.S. social welfare system for African Americans. A strong belief in spirituality is the third leg of their coping system. A belief in a creator and a universe where everything is connected has given African Americans the will and determination to persevere.

Community Structure

The word *community* for African Americans means much more than the physical surroundings or place where they live. It is a network of relationships that connect them to each other, to all other human beings, to the world, and to the creator.

Using the Eurocentric concept of community, the physical structure and geography of the African American community varies based on their history. The majority in the North and the West live in urban areas, and traditionally they were restricted by discriminatory practices to the inner city where housing was old and frequently substandard. Most of the rest live in rural areas in the southeastern United States. Some of those living in the North or urban areas of the South have gradually migrated to suburban areas as they have been able to achieve a level of economic prosperity. However, they have generally not been welcomed by their white neighbors who often engage in "white flight" when an African American family moves into the neighborhood. Some of these African American families have experienced various forms of harassment including threats, racist graffiti or publications, or having crosses burned on their lawns.

Most African Americans try to maintain close family ties by either living in close proximity to relatives or by maintaining contact by phone, Internet, and frequent family reunions. Even when close relatives are not nearby, African Americans are able to build their own family networks through the adoption of fictive kin wherever they may live.

The migration of African Americans to urban areas has probably undermined to some extent the strong sense of community that was built in rural areas. Social scientists who study human behavior in crowded communities typically see a breakdown in social structures when people are overwhelmed with a large number of relationships caused by overcrowding. When people are not familiar with their neighbors, they are less likely to establish mutual aid systems.

Current Issues

Current issues for African Americans involve those that typically would be expected. Overcoming prejudice, discrimination, and oppression continues, only in somewhat different forms. On paper it is illegal, but in reality these barriers still exist. Recently, a backlash has developed and there are attacks on such programs as affirmative action, which have opened doors for women and minorities. Poverty remains a reality for a disproportionate percentage of families, especially for a substantial minority of African American children. Substance abuse and incarceration are also overrepresented in the African American community.

Resources

Borum, Valerie. "An Afrocentric Approach in Working with African American Families" in *Multicultural Perspectives in Working with Families,* 2nd ed. Elaine P. Congress and Manny J. Gonzales, Eds. New York: Springer, 2005, Chapter 12.

Boyd-Franklin, Nancy. *Black Families in Therapy: Understanding the African American Experience,* 2nd ed. New York: Guilford Press, 2003.

Fong, Rowena, and Furuto, Charlene, Eds. *Culturally Competent Practice: Skills, Interventions, and Evaluations,* 2nd ed. Boston: Allyn & Bacon, 2001. (See Chapters 3, 8, 9, 16, 17, 24, and 25.)

McRoy, Ruth. "Cultural Competence with African Americans" in *Culturally Competent Practice: A Framework for Understanding Diverse Groups and Justice Issues,* 2nd ed. Doman Lum, Ed. Pacific Grove, CA: Brooks/Cole, 2003, Chapter 9.

Schiele, Jerome H. *Human Services and the Afrocentric Paradigm.* New York: The Haworth Press, 2000.

Willis, Winnie. "Families with African American Roots" in *Developing Cross-Cultural Competence: A Guide to Working with Children and Their Families,* 2nd ed. Eleanor W. Lynch and Marci J. Hanson, Eds. Baltimore, MD: Paul H. Brookes, 1998, Chapter 6.

Diversity Competence with People Who Are Hispanic/Latino

People who are Hispanic/Latino represent a wide variation in race, culture, and roots. We use the term *Hispanic/Latino* to refer to those people whose language is predominantly Spanish and whose culture is at least partially influenced by the cultures that evolved in regions of North and South America that came under Spanish rule during and after the 1500s. This is a vast area with many variations in culture. The most common cultures found in the United States are Mexican, Central and South American, Puerto Rican, and Cuban. There are variations in language among these as well as culture. We have chosen to use the term Hispanic/Latino in an effort to be inclusive, realizing that there are several different terms that are used to describe people from this culture.

Historical Considerations

The Spanish approach to exploration and settlement can probably best be described as one of conquest. Priests often accompanied the conquistadors, and religion, language, and culture were imposed on those who were conquered, often under the penalty of death.

Spanish and indigenous populations intermingled, leaving a wide variation of racial and ethnic groups. Skin color ranged from light-skinned, blond-haired and blue-eyed descendants of Spanish origin to those descended from North and South American First Nations tribes and from African slaves. Portugese language and culture is a major influence in Brazilian culture. Many people in the United States think of those who are Hispanic/Latino as a race, but they are really an ethnic group or culture that includes various combinations of white, First Nations tribes, and African genetic backgrounds.

The Spanish influence in the United States began in the 1500s mainly in the Southeast and the Southwest. The United States acquired Spanish and Mexican territory primarily through force or the threat of it. Florida was ceded to the United States to avoid a confrontation over its acquisition. Texans won their independence from Mexico. Texans included both immigrants from the United States and local residents of Mexican descent. Later, the Mexican-American War was fought so the United States could acquire Texas and California and the lands in between. This represented nearly half of what had formerly been Mexico. After the War, residents of Mexican descent were promised citizenship and property rights, but there were numerous instances in which this was not what ensued. Periodic mass deportations have taken place along with the seizure of land. Cuba was captured from Spain during the Spanish-American War at the end of the 1900s and was later given its independence. Puerto Rico was also captured but has remained a U.S. commonwealth. Puerto Ricans are considered U.S. citizens and they do not need passports or visas to move back and forth between the island and the mainland.

People of Mexican descent are either long-term residents of territory seized from Mexico or they are immigrants from Mexico. People of Central American descent are primarily relatively recent immigrants, mainly either refugees fleeing various civil wars in that region or those seeking improved economic prospects. Most Cubans have settled in the Miami area and are political and economic refugees who left Cuba after the regime of Fidel Castro began in the late 1950s. Most of the immigration policy in the United States during the past century has been aimed at controlling the immigration of Hispanic/Latino populations. Undocumented immigration is a major issue with estimates of as many as 11 million people living in the United States without proper documentation.

Cultural Patterns

Cultural patterns are influenced by the area from which the family comes. However, there are some common patterns of note. *Familismo* is a cultural value that is held by many Hispanic/Latino families. It places a high value on the family and family relationships and sees individual identity as a product of family relationships.[26] Another value that is closely associated with the family is *machismo,* which values traditional gender-based roles and a patriarchal structure within the family.[27] *Personalismo* is a cultural value that emphasizes closeness in interpersonal relationships, which includes valuing people over material objects and emphasizing relationships over individual achievement.[28] Religion plays an important role in the culture, with most families adhering to Roman Catholic beliefs. Pentecostal religions have made strong inroads into this traditional pattern of beliefs in some areas, especially along the Mexican border.

Individuals and families experience a wide range of acculturation, which determines the degree to which cultural heritage and language are retained. Many individuals and families are bicultural and bilingual. However, language skills are frequently lost by younger generations who grow up speaking English at school.

Family

As mentioned previously, *familismo* places a high value on the family. Individual identity depends heavily on family relationships. Many people of Hispanic/Latino heritage would not consider making individual decisions without family input or considering the effects of the decision on the family. Patriarchy and traditional gender-based roles are prominent in most families. The family is generally considered the most important social unit, and cultural values are primarily family centered.

Communication Processes

There are a wide variety of patterns in Hispanic/Latino families with regard to the use of Spanish and English. Some families have a pattern of speaking Spanish within the home and English or Spanish outside of the home depending on the setting. Family members who are older may not speak or understand much, if any, English. This may also be the case for recent immigrants from Spanish-speaking countries. Children may become the first truly bilingual family members as they encounter English when they enter school. This may also be the case for adults who work and acquire English through their work setting. Generally, the latter remain more comfortable with Spanish. Younger Hispanic/Latino family members may have lost their Spanish-speaking abilities and may speak only English although they might understand some Spanish.

Coping Patterns

Religion and spirituality are very important for coping for many Hispanic/Latino families. Celia Jaes Falicov describes how most Latinos attribute adversity to sources that are beyond one's control. She points out that many Latinos will add the phrase "God willing" when discussing the future, which is an indication of the belief that one's life is not under one's control.[29] Falicov describes several coping mechanisms that result from these beliefs. *Controlarse* is "control of the self," which refers to controlling one's mood or emotions as a way of mastering adversity.[30] This concept includes ". . . *aguantarse* (endurance), or the ability to withstand stress in times of adversity; *no pensar* (don't think of the problem), or avoidance of focusing on disturbing thoughts or feelings . . . ; *resignarse* (resignation), or the passive acceptance of one's fate; and *sobreponerse* (to overcome), a more active cognitive coping that allows for working through or overcoming adversity."[31]

The combination of deep religious belief and conviction along with the coping mechanisms mentioned previously give many people who are Hispanic/Latino and their families incredible fortitude when they are faced with adversity. At the same time, these coping mechanisms may not be understood by members of the dominant culture and are easily misinterpreted or stereotyped.

Community Structure

There is variation in the community structure for people who are Hispanic/Latino. Some of this variation is caused by differences among the cultural groups described earlier. For instance, Puerto Ricans are more likely to be found in New York City and several urban areas along the Atlantic Coast. Cubans tend to be clustered in south Florida. People of Mexican descent have large populations in rural and urban areas along the southern boundaries of the border states of Texas, New Mexico, Arizona, and California. They are also found in both urban and rural areas where migrant workers settled.

Wherever they live Hispanic/Latino individuals and families form community networks. The Hispanic/ Latino community typically comes together several times each year to celebrate traditional holidays. Some of these are religious and others are related to events from their native countries, such as Cinco de Mayo, which celebrates Mexican independence. In rural areas, many individuals and families travel to the nearest community with a Hispanic/Latino population. Some will celebrate with only their families or with some close neighbors. In urban areas, people who are Hispanic/Latino often live close together in certain areas. Mexican American communities in larger cities of the Southwest are typically referred to as *barrios*.

Current Issues

Most of the current issues for people who are Hispanic/Latino revolve around immigration, preserving their heritage, and overcoming economic hardship. Most recent changes in immigration law in the United States are aimed at people who are Hispanic/Latino. There is a great deal of disparity regarding experiences between various groups. Puerto Ricans are able to enter the United States legally because they are considered U.S. citizens. Cubans have generally been accepted as political refugees, although some were identified as mentally ill or former prisoners who were criminals in Cuba, and many of these were detained for some time. Immigrants from Mexico and Central American have not been able to immigrate quite as easily. The poverty and lack of opportunity to improve their economic well-being in their own countries lead many to immigrate illegally or without proper documentation. This has become a major political issue with intense debate about what to do to stem the tide of undocumented immigrants along with the question of what to do with undocumented workers and illegal immigrants who are already here.

To some extent, the desire to preserve their language, culture, and heritage is reflected in the community networks that people who are Hispanic/Latino form. At the same time, they have been criticized for not assimilating into the larger culture when they do so. Within the family, including the extended family, it is not unusual to see conflicts over cultural preservation arising between older and younger generations.

Economic hardship is a primary reason for immigration for many people who are Hispanic/Latino and their families. However, economic prosperity is not guaranteed, especially for undocumented workers. They are easily exploited by employers. This exploitation can go beyond financial to include such things as sexual exploitation as well. Many people who are Hispanic/Latino have learned to cope with economic hardship by working hard for long hours and pooling their resources within the family. So, even though several family members may be working at very low wages, the family may be able to experience some prosperity from their combined incomes.

Resources

Falicov, Celia Jaes. *Latino Families in Therapy: A Guide to Multicultural Practice.* New York: Guilford Press, 1998. This book provides a good base for understanding Hispanic/Latino families. Although it uses the term *therapy,* it is written in a way that can be used by generalist social workers working with this population.

Fong, Rowena, and Furuto, Charlene, Eds. *Culturally Competent Practice: Skills, Interventions, and Evaluations,* 2nd ed. Boston: Allyn & Bacon, 2001. (See Chapters 4, 10, 11, 18, 19, 26, and 27.)

Romero, Mary, and Hondagneu-Sotelo, Pierette. *Challenging Fronteras: Structuring Latina and Latino Lives in the U.S.: An Anthology of Readings.* New York: Routledge, 1997. Another look at the lives of Hispanic/Latino families in the United States.

Suarez-Orozco, Marcelo M., and Paez, Mariela. *Latinos: Remaking America.* Berkeley: University of California Press, 2002. A comprehensive look at experiences of Latinos and issues they face.

Zuniga, Maria. "Families with Latino Roots" in *Developing Cross-Cultural Competence: A Guide to Working with Children and Their Families,* 2nd ed. Eleanor W. Lynch and Marci J. Hanson, Eds. Baltimore, MD: Paul H. Brookes, 1998, Chapter 7.

Zuniga, Maria E. "Cultural Competence with Latino Americans" in *Culturally Competent Practice: A Framework for Understanding Diverse Groups and Justice Issues,* 2nd ed. Doman Lum, Ed. Pacific Grove, CA: Brooks/Cole, 2003, Chapter 10.

Diversity Competence with People Who Are Native American

When working with people who are Native American[32] and their families, two understandings are central: First, there are many tribes, each with its own culture, and each considered by most Native Americans as a sovereign nation. Second, each family as it lives in a world dominated by a majority group has its particular ways of dealing with dual perspectives of functioning. This makes it essential that any social worker rely on the Native American client to provide the understandings needed for effective work. An understanding of a person's ties to his culture are of prime concern. The ways in which the family functions are usually closely tied to this cultural base. Rural and urban context is also important. Educational policies and practices are important to understand. The impact of boarding schools, with their emphases, had great implications for Native American individuals and families in the past. This all supports the use of a diversity competent mode of practice that uses the client as the expert in determining what is important and what is to be done in the work together. However, a diversity competent worker strives to understand the client in the culture to the best of her ability. This, of course, suggests that a worker should concentrate on learning about the tribes to which her clients belong. That understanding is far too diverse for this text to provide.[33] However, there are more general understandings that can be provided.

Historical Considerations

First of importance is an understanding of the historical relationship of Native Americans to the U.S. government. Zimmerman and Molyneaux describe this as "dispossession." To quote them, "There were three types of European invasion: physical (the occupation of territory by immigrants), spiritual (the imposition of Christianity), and material (the introduction of goods such as guns and alcohol). Native people were driven out, swindled by unobserved treaties, subjugated, shattered, plied with alcohol, and confined to reservations."[34] Vine Deloria, Jr., describes this as "Promises Made, Promises Broken."[35] Continually changing federal policy regarding removal, resettlement, assimilation, land allotment, and termination has left native peoples with feelings of distrust of the majority society and great uncertainties when relating to a majority person. These practices and policies have also had two major effects on native peoples: the breakdown or even destruction of traditional ways of functioning and the extreme poverty that many Native Americans experience. Land is sacred to Native Americans, thus experiences that interfere or destroy the traditional relationship to the land are particularly destructive to society, the individual, and the family.

Cultural Patterns

Native American cultural patterns, although specific to a tribe or clan, also have some general characteristics. The Native American way of thinking, rather than being linear, tends to be circular or systemic, everything is related to everything else. Past, present, and future are very much intertwined. One means for depicting the native life concept is the circle, which encompasses nature or everything that comes from Mother Earth. Mind, spirit, and body are all seen as major parts yet a part of the whole. All life is sacred and all aspects of nature, as well as all things, all events, and people, are related.

Family is very important and it is the extended family that is the focal point. Children are valued and belong to the tribe and the extended family. Grandparents are of great importance in the raising of children; in fact, they often are of greater importance than parents. Elders are greatly respected. Sharing and giving are important. There is a sense that time is to be used in showing respect and caring for others, not the importance of "being on time."

There is usually a belief in a higher being. Creation stories are important but vary from tribe to tribe. All life is sacred. Spirituality is encompassed in all of daily living. It tends to be more of an individual expression rather than a group expression. Specifics relate to particular tribes' beliefs and experiences. Assimilation of Christianity is related to the historical policy of assigning particular denominations to specific areas. Where Christian beliefs and practices have been accepted, they have a denominational element blended with the native traditions and beliefs. Communal land is sacred. It is tied to the health of the tribe. It is a place to which the tribe can periodically return.

Each tribe has its own rituals and ceremonies. Each usually has traditional art forms, crafts, dances, and so on. Workers would do well to gain appreciation for the meaning of these art forms to the group. Each has various taboos. Many of these relate to relationships among people. Workers must have knowledge of these so as not to offend those for whom they are providing service. In many tribes, eye contact is to be avoided. It is seen as a sign of disrespect.

Family

As has been indicated, the traditional Native American family is an extended one. All members are responsible for one another. All share in child care. They are expected to share what they have with this extended group. This sometimes becomes problematic when some members of the extended family gain opportunities to better themselves through education or other options and are then expected to share with members of the extended family who may be poverty stricken, addicted to alcohol and other drugs, or otherwise not providing for their basic needs. It is expected that decision making will also be shared among family members. Elders are looked to for advice and guidance.

It should be noted that the more isolated the tribe, the less change there will be in family life from traditional ways. Native families in urban areas have been most affected by majority ways of functioning. However, many keep close ties with the "homeland/reservation" or live within an urban enclave of Native Americans. These families tend to relate to two worlds with the tensions inherent in such situations.[36]

Communication Processes

Although most Native Americans speak English, there is a tendency to have a somewhat limited vocabulary and to word sentences somewhat differently from that which majority workers are used to. It is most important to listen carefully and use feedback techniques to be sure that there is mutual understanding. Native culture is strongly an oral culture. Truths and culture are passed along by means of storytelling. It is important to gain an appreciation for this means of communication and develop skill in interpreting the meaning of the stories.

Relationships take time to develop. Time needs to be spent in small talk, in letting a Native American person get to know who you are as a person. Often the provision of some small concrete service will further the development of a relationship.[37]

Coping Patterns

There is a strong emphasis on bringing situations into balance. Ceremonies are used to create or restore harmony with nature that reflects Native American beliefs in a holistic world in which all things are interconnected and interrelated. There is strong reliance on beliefs and sacred wisdom. Because of historical experiences with the majority culture, there are themes of conflict, resistance, and survival.

Native persons are very skilled at hiding emotions. Attitudes toward authority are important because the worker is considered an authority person. Particularly older Native Americans respect authority and often express this respect by agreeing with the worker, although they have no intent to carry out what seems to have been agreed on. Younger Native Americans may display hostility toward workers or other authority figures.

Socialization is of great importance to these people. Each person is valued. When sanctions become necessary, shame and disapproval are the primary methods used.

Community Structure

Tribal structures have been compromised by the imposition of the majority culture's way of governing. Sometimes, the official governmental structure, the tribal government, may be corrupt, and care needs to be taken in assessing its usefulness to the Native American. The strengths of the natural community with its elders, medicine folk, and other natural helpers are often overlooked. In urban areas, this type of strength is often found in the Native American community that has formed.

There are special Native American resources administered by the federal government under the Bureau of Indian Affairs (BIA) and Indian Public Health Services. There are also resources, particularly educational resources in community colleges, which have developed on many reservations. Religious groups still provide resources particularly educational resources. State and federal social welfare systems also provide Supplemental Security Income (SSI), child welfare, and other resources. The Indian Child Welfare Act of 1978 gives tribes jurisdiction over all native children in civil placement. Tribal courts usually carry out this responsibility. Education is today primarily in the public school system, but, as noted, tribal schools and religious schools provide for some students. Today some Native Americans are reaching out to the majority world through the gambling industry and through other recreation opportunities. Social workers can participate in cultural activities but they should avoid tribal politics.

Current Issues

A primary concern is the maintenance of the native culture in contemporary society. Extreme poverty, especially on some reservations, is widespread. Alcoholism and the use of other addictive substances are prevalent, especially where there is significant unemployment. There are many health problems. Rates of tuberculosis, diabetes, and high blood pressure are quite high. The plight of urban Native Americans is concerning as they attempt to live in two cultures. Economic opportunity for those who choose to remain on reservations deserves attention. Educational opportunities in modes that are congruent with native cultures deserve attention at elementary, secondary, and higher education levels. The delivery of health and social services in diversity competent modes is another issue.

Resources

As has been indicated, a primary source must remain the Native American community and individual. If not the client, then other Native Americans become the source.

Brown Miller, Nancy, "Social Work Services to Urban Indians" in *Cultural Awareness in the Human Services*. James W. Green, Ed. Englewood Cliffs, NJ: Prentice Hall, 1993.

Fong, Rowena, and Furuto, Charlene, Eds. *Culturally Competent Practice: Skills, Interventions, and Evaluations,* 2nd ed. Boston: Allyn & Bacon, 2001. (See Chapters 5, 12, 13, 20, 21, 28, and 29.)

Joe, Jennie R., and Malach, Randi Suzanne, "Families with Native American Roots" in *Developing Cross-Cultural Competence: A Guide to Working with Children and Their Families,* 2nd ed. Eleanor W. Lynch and Marci J. Hanson, Eds. Baltimore, MD: Paul H. Brookes, 1998, Chapter 5.

McMaster, Gerald, and Trafzer, Clifford E., Eds. *Native Universe: Voices of Indian America.* Washington DC: National Museum of the American Indian, Smithsonian Institution. This magnificent book, done in cooperation with the National Geographic Society, contains multiple essays by native writers with scholarly recognition. These essays provide contemporary understandings about Native American people.

Riley, Patricia. *Growing Up Native American.* New York: HarperCollins, 1993. This is a compilation of stories by Native American writers about their experiences growing up. It encompasses a number of tribal backgrounds and historical and contemporary experiences.

Weaver, Hilary N., "Cultural Competence with First Nations Peoples" in *Culturally Competent Practice: A Framework for Understanding Diverse Groups and Justice Issues,* 2nd ed. Doman Lum, Ed. Pacific Grove, CA: Brooks/Cole, 2003, Chapter 8.

Zimmerman, Larry, and Molyneaus, Brian Leigh. *Native North America.* Norman: University of Oklahoma Press, 1996. This small, readily available book written by anthropologists who have had considerable experience with the Native American world provides an excellent overview of the variety of tribes and cultural aspects of this world.

In addition there should be a search for tribal-specific literature. Also there are very usable bibliographies on the Internet.

Summary

It is essential for social workers to become as diversity competent as possible so that we can serve individuals, families, and groups in a manner with which they are comfortable. All social workers are called on to serve people who are different from themselves in some way. Differences include race, ethnicity, age, gender, physical or mental ability, physical appearance, religious affiliation, sexual orientation, and socioeconomic standing.

The diversity competent professional social worker seeks to gain knowledge and skills in working with diverse individuals, families, and groups. She begins with a thorough examination of her own diversity and an awareness of her knowledge about and attitudes toward various diverse people. She seeks to add to her knowledge and skills by conducting research, discussing diversity with colleagues who have expertise in this area, and learning from her clients as she uses naturalistic inquiry.

The chapter discusses gender competent practice, especially while working with people from patriarchal cultures and their families. Practice with people who are gay or lesbian and their families is presented along with a schema for studying ethnic individuals and families. This schema is applied to people who are African American, Hispanic/Latino, and Native American.

Diversity competence is never fully achieved and is a lifelong process. Diversity competent social workers continuously work to learn more about serving diverse clients.

Questions

1. List as many diverse groups as you can that have experienced prejudice, discrimination, or oppression at some time during U.S. history. Briefly describe their experiences.
2. Discuss attitudes and beliefs of your family, your peers, or other sources about each diverse group from item 1 to which you have been exposed.
3. Discuss your experiences with any of the groups from item 1.
4. Applying Table 3.2 to a cultural group different from your own and with which you have not had considerable contact, identify factors that you need to find out about to have sufficient knowledge to work as a social worker with people from that culture group.
5. Discuss your current level of diversity competence using Table 3.1. Where would you like to be? How might you get there?
6. What knowledge and skills do you possess that make you diversity competent in working with various individuals, families, or groups? With what kind of clients would you feel comfortable working? With what kind of clients would you feel uncomfortable working? How could you become more comfortable?

Suggested Readings

In addition to the resources identified in this chapter, the following readings are suggested:

Fong, Rowena. *The Contemporary Asian American Experience: Beyond the Model Minority.* Boston: Allyn and Bacon, 2008.

Fong, Rowena, and Furuto, Sharlene, Eds. *Culturally Competent Practice: Skills, Interventions, and Evaluations.* Boston: Allyn & Bacon, 2001.

Lum, Doman. *Culturally Competent Practice: A Framework for Understanding Diverse Groups and Justice Issues,* 3rd ed. Pacific Grove, CA: Brooks/Cole, 2007.

Mizrahi, Terry and Davis, Larry E., Eds. *Encyclopedia of Social Work*, 20th ed. Washington, DC: NASW Press, 2008 ("Cultural Competence," "Feminist Social Work Practice," "Gay Families and Parenting," "Gay Men," "Latinos and Latinas," "Lesbians," "Methods of Practice Interventions," "Native Americans," "Task Centered Practice," "Women," "NASW Standards for Cultural Competence in Social Work Practice).

Saleeby, Dennis, Ed. *The Strengths Perspective in Social Work Practice,* 5th ed. Boston: Allyn & Bacon, 2009.

part

II

The Interactional Process and the Ecosystem

Based on the overview of generalist practice presented in Part One, specific processes integral to the social work endeavor will be considered. In Part Two, the interactional process is explored.

In the simplest sense, the generalist social worker is a provider of services that vary in nature. These include provision of concrete services (such as income maintenance), facilitation of growth and change, developmental services (such as group work in a settlement house), intervention into crisis situations (such as illness or loss of loved ones), and certain therapeutic services. It is not the service but the focus of the service and how that service is given that defines generalist social work. The service focuses on social functioning—the interaction of persons and social systems in meeting human needs.

In order to provide services that focus on social functioning, the worker must interact with individuals and social systems. How the service is provided has two dimensions: (1) the interactions of the worker and other people and social systems as service is provided and (2) the process of service provision. The interactions and service provision are simultaneous, intertwined processes. In this text they are artificially separated to enable students to develop in-depth understanding of each process. Part Two focuses on interactions. It also considers development of understanding of the worker as a helping professional, the individual client, the environment as an ecosystem, and the interactional process. In-depth understanding of these systems and their functioning usually has been obtained from courses in sociology, psychology, economics, political science, anthropology, and human biology as well as from courses titled Human Behavior in the Social Environment or something similar. Discussion in Part Two focuses on the use of this knowledge, including means of organizing it in service of the interactional process. In other words, understanding of the system both from a global and a particular frame of reference is deemed essential for professional relationships. Part Three will treat the process of service provision.

A basic interactional approach is used regardless of the service being offered, although there are modifications and adaptations of that interactional approach depending on the service. In its simplest form, the components of the interactional process are the worker and client interacting in an environment. This is the primary focus of Part Two. However, the generalist social worker often is part of a multiperson worker system (e.g., a team) and often works with a multiperson client system (e.g., a small group or family). Thus, Part Two lays the foundation for exploring these kinds of interactions. Part Three will develop these topics further. Part Four will explore working with multiperson client systems.

Chapter 4 discusses the worker component and considers four concepts: knowledge of self, the helping person, ethical decision making, and accountability. This chapter further develops the concept of common human needs and diversity.

Chapter 5 explores the client component and develops two concepts: becoming a client and understanding the individual client in generalist practice. The concept of human diversity is expanded.

Chapter 6 considers the environment and the interaction and transactions that take place between the client and systems in the environment. This environment includes the community from which the client comes and the community where the service takes place, as well as the agency offering the service. Also discussed is the worker as an agency employee.

Chapter 7 discusses the interaction between worker and client by considering engagement and formation of a one-to-one action system, relationship, communication, and the interview as interactional tools.

4

The Worker

Learning Expectations

1. Development of a framework for a continuous process of developing knowledge of self.
2. Identification of personal needs that arise from human development, human diversity, and membership in social systems.
3. Knowledge about the characteristics of a helping person.
4. Understanding ethical decision making.
5. Understanding of accountability and of various forms of recording.

In the interaction of generalist social worker and client, the social worker is first a person with life experiences, human needs, and a personal lifestyle and value system. The worker is also a helping person with skills for interacting with individuals and groups and for developing relationships. The worker brings to the helping situation a knowledge base that provides understanding about persons in environment, knowledge of helping methods and of means for implementing those methods, and knowledge gained from other helping situations. The worker also brings a value system based on professional values, agency and community values, and her own personal values. The worker must also become competent in working with a wide range of diverse clients.

As a professional the worker is accountable to the client, to the agency, and to her profession. Accountability is a complex issue that often creates ethical dilemmas. A major aspect of accountability for the worker is maintaining client records. In order to do this professionally, the worker must have knowledge and skills in writing and in the use of various forms of records. She must also reflect social work values by maintaining the confidentiality of client records.

In a complex society with complex social problems and multiple human needs, it is sometimes advantageous for the worker to become part of a **multiperson helping system**. A multiperson helping system consists of several workers who are involved in providing the needed service in a collaborative manner. The multiperson helping system is discussed in Chapter 15. Each worker has a special knowledge or skill that is necessary for goal attainment. To explore the meaning of the concept of worker, four topics will be considered: (1) the worker as a person, or knowledge of self; (2) the helping person; (3) ethical decision making; and (4) accountability and recording.

Knowledge of Self

It has been said that the most important tool a social worker possesses is herself. To use that tool skillfully and knowledgeably, a worker must have considerable self-knowledge. It is important that the worker know herself so that she can better understand the differences between herself and her client. For instance, it is essential that she be able to differentiate between her own personal needs or concerns and those of her client. This calls for a kind of introspective stance that seeks to bring personal concerns, attitudes, and values into the area of conscious thought. It calls for a continuous search for self-understanding and for a reasonable degree of comfort with the discovered self.

Social workers develop this self-knowledge in a variety of ways. The process of supervision and the discussion of practice situations and problems with peers have always been two important means of developing self-knowledge. Others can often see how our unrecognized concerns, attitudes, and values affect our interaction with others and our helping capacity. Social workers need to be open to help from others as a means of developing self-understanding.

Another way social workers develop self-understanding is through the study of human behavior. Psychological, sociological, anthropological, and biological knowledge that explains human functioning can be the source of considerable self-understanding. It is important to recognize that one has imperfections, but it is equally important to keep such awareness within reasonable limits. Medical students tend to believe that they have the disease they are studying. The study of psychology and sociology includes examining human behavior that is labeled as pathological, dysfunctional, or deviant. Social work students sometimes believe that they see pathology, dysfunction, or deviance in themselves. If this identification is realistic, it can be helpful to self-understanding. Care must be taken, however, not to become overly introspective and see dysfunction in oneself that is not really there. A balance needs to be reached in which introspection is sufficient to gain needed self-knowledge but not so much as to become overwhelming. Self-knowledge cannot be developed all at once; it needs to grow over a period of time. It is also important to learn to deal with the recognition of one's imperfection in a manner that supports self-worth and dignity.

Another useful way for a beginning social worker to develop self-knowledge is to conduct an organized self-study. This entails thinking about one's lifestyle and philosophy of life, moral code and value system, roots, life experiences, personal needs, and personal functioning.

The Person as a Feeling, Thinking, Acting System

One way to understand oneself as a person is to use an adaptation of Figure 1.1, which represents a human system (the worker-client interaction) as an interplay of feeling, thinking, and acting. Figure 4.1 is an adaptation of Figure 1.1 and depicts the person as feeling,

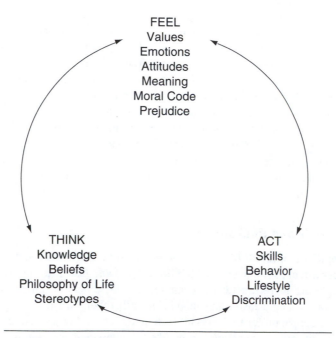

FIGURE 4.1 *The Person as a Feeling, Thinking, Acting System*

thinking, and acting. An understanding of oneself, the client, the environment, diversity, and any human system is not complete without an understanding of each of these dimensions and the ways in which they influence each other. Feelings, thoughts, and behavior are related to each other, not in a linear way but in a cyclical, reciprocal way. The arrows indicate that each of these aspects influences the other two and in turn is influenced by them. These aspects are also influenced by interactions with the environment.

This is a dynamic system in which feelings, thoughts, and actions change as human systems grow and develop, and as they come into contact with each other and interact. At the same time, changes in one of these dimensions will influence the other dimensions. For example, in a friendship our feelings, thoughts, and actions toward each other will change as we experience interactions with each other. We generally have positive feelings and thoughts toward our friends, and we act in positive ways with them. When we get angry at a friend, our feelings have changed, at least for the moment. This change in feelings tends to make us think differently about the person. We may think of the person as no longer being our friend. Our actions will change, and we might avoid contact with this person. If the situation is resolved, our feelings, thoughts, and actions may return to what they were before the incident. Or they may change in a positive or a negative direction. The relationship may become closer as a result of having weathered a storm, or it may drift farther apart as a result of lingering doubts about each other.

Understanding the interaction of feelings, thinking, and actions in people and human systems is important for self-knowledge, for understanding clients, for understanding the environment, for understanding human transactions, for understanding diversity, and for facilitating change.

In understanding diversity, it is important to understand how feelings, thinking, and actions relate to the way in which human systems react to diversity in a negative way. In Figure 4.1, "Prejudice" is listed under "Feel." This represents the way in which prejudice functions as an attitude toward people who are different from oneself. A stereotype is a preconceived idea or belief about members of a diverse group that is consistent with the prejudicial attitude. Discrimination represents an action that is based on prejudice and stereotyping. Oppression occurs when discrimination is institutionalized into systems in society.

In Figure 4.1, one's lifestyle represents action, one's philosophy of life represents thinking, and one's moral code and value system represent feelings. Our family and cultural roots, life experiences, personal needs, and personal functioning represent influences from and interactions with our environment. These in turn affect our feelings, thoughts, and actions.

Lifestyle and Philosophy of Life

People are different because of heredity, life experiences, and environment. Such differences affect the manner in which life is lived and how life's problems are dealt with. Some people are more practical and matter of fact; others are more sympathetic and friendly; others are enthusiastic and insightful; still others are more logical and well organized. Some people prefer to deal with technical facts and objects; others prefer to give practical help and services to people; some like to understand and communicate with people; others like to deal with technical and theoretical developments.[1] Some people are physically strong with no visible disabilities; others may have limited sight or physical stamina or other disabilities. People differ according to gender, socioeconomic class, cultural group, and religious beliefs. People differ in the ways they learn and in their capacity for learning. They have different energy levels. All these factors affect lifestyle. **Lifestyle** is the manner in which we function in meeting our human needs; in interaction with others; and in our patterns of work, play, and rest. It is important not only to describe lifestyle but also to be aware of why a particular lifestyle is preferred.

A philosophy of life—which is related to lifestyle in that lifestyle is affected by philosophy of life—is even more basic to self-understanding. One's **philosophy of life** includes beliefs about people and society and about human life, its purpose, and how it should be lived. In identifying one's philosophy of life, some questions to be asked are: What are my beliefs about the nature of humanity? Is humanity innately good or evil? What should be the relationship between men and women? What is the place of work, family, and recreation in a person's life? When is dependence on another person acceptable? What responsibility does each person have for the well-being of his or her fellow human beings? What is the relationship of persons to a higher being, to God? What is the relationship of persons to the natural world? One's philosophy of life affects all we are, feel, think, and do. A philosophy of life is often strongly dependent on religious teachings or beliefs to which a person has been exposed. It also depends on culture and on family influences. The influence of these early beliefs can result in their rejection or in adherence or commitment to them. It is important that a philosophy of life be well thought out and reflect the person each of us is. One's philosophy of life changes with growth and new experiences.

Moral Code and Value System

A moral code and value system are closely related to one's philosophy of life. A **moral code** is a specification of that which is considered to be right or wrong in terms of behavior. One's *value system* includes what is considered desirable or preferred. The actions and things we consider valuable are also prioritized so that a system of values exists. A person's moral code and value system are affected by cultural heritage, family influences, group affiliations (including religious affiliation), and personal and educational experiences. For some people, the moral code is prescribed and fixed regardless of the situation. For others, the moral code is determined by a set of principles that guide moral and value decisions but that allow for some degree of flexibility; for still others, these decisions are dependent on the situation.[2]

Florence Kluckholm and Fred Strodtbeck have discussed value orientations and identified several dimensions along which people develop a value system:

1. *Human nature*—Is it evil, neutral, a mixture of good and evil, or good?
2. *Relationship of individual to nature*—Should it be in subjugation to nature, in harmony with nature, or have a mastery over nature?
3. *Time orientation*—Is the emphasis placed on past, present, or future?
4. *Activity*—Should activity focus on being, being in becoming, or doing?
5. *Relationality*—Should its nature be one of lineality, collaborability, or individuality?[3]

Identifying one's position on each of these five dimensions can give some indication of basic values—one's way of responding to needs and situations. For example, if a person sees people as basically evil, her response to behavior she does not like may be to punish in order to exact "good" behavior. Such a presupposition carries a belief that people's inclination is to be bad and punishment is needed to curb undesirable behavior. On the other hand, seeing people as good carries a belief that people will try to do what is right, consider others and their needs, and work for what is right. The stance that human nature is good seems more in keeping with social work values than the stance that human nature is bad.

Value conflicts that exist between the dominant society and an ethnic group can often be identified through examining the value orientation of the ethnic group. Some Hispanic people believe that a person's relationship to nature is one of subjugation to nature. Natural disasters, such as floods or hurricanes, are seen as indications that God or the forces of nature are punishing them for some misdoing. Most Native Americans have a value system based on harmony with nature. For many of them, natural disasters may be an indication that in some way they are out of harmony with the forces of nature. For example, floods may be the result of misuse of the land. The response of the dominant American culture tends to reflect a belief in mastery over nature. The response to a flood is to attempt to control future floods with dams and other flood-control mechanisms. These differences often explain why individuals view the same situation differently.

Because many social workers are members of the dominant society, they may experience substantial value conflicts when working with clients who are members of diverse, disadvantaged, or oppressed populations. Some value conflicts occur between the worker's personal values and those of the client. Some conflicts can occur between the values of the social work profession and the values and beliefs of the client. In addition, the worker can experience conflicts between her personal values and beliefs and the values of the social work profession. Self-awareness and a commitment to social work values are critical factors when there are substantial differences between the worker and the client. It takes courage to look at oneself and realize one's inability to accept everyone. Supervision from peers and supervisors is also important. In general, if workers do not discuss and resolve these conflicts, it will affect their ability to form helping relationships. What is not or cannot be discussed frequently becomes a barrier.

Time orientation also is responsible for value conflicts. Some people are heavily influenced by how things have been done in the past and tend to make decisions based on "how it has always been done." Others are focused on the future. These people place considerable emphasis on planning ahead, "saving for a rainy day," and the needs of their children and grandchildren. Still others focus on the here and now. They tend to live a day at a time, to not save money, and to expect children to make their own way. Often those who must use all their energy providing for their basic needs—the poverty-stricken—will have this orientation because they are so overwhelmed by their circumstances that it is difficult for them to think about the future. Again, differences in decisions about similar situations often can be explained by the value difference of time orientation.

Many Americans emphasize activity that results in observable accomplishment. However, some people see value in *being,* that is, in activity that is not outcome oriented. This stance places more emphasis on the person than on the outcome or the production. *Being in becoming* also places emphasis on the person but stresses activity as a vehicle for the growth of individuals. A social worker's belief about the purpose and value of activity will have an important influence on how she practices social work and on her goals with clients. It is important to employ methods and to identify beliefs so that approaches can be chosen that are congruent with the worker's value system.

Another way in which people view the world is how they see relationships among various events or parts of the situation. This relates to the Kluckholm and Strodtbeck dimension of relationality. Relationships are sometimes explained in a cause-effect, or linear, manner. This explanation is not congruent with contemporary generalist social work thinking, which calls for a transactional approach. The transactional approach emphasizes collaboration, that is, seeing the interaction of factors as influencing behavior in a situation. Others see each situation as unique and do not see a relationship with other situations, past or present. This can be considered the individuality approach to reaching conclusions about the nature of situations. These varying views of relationships among events can be caused by different value orientations.

Often people operate from moral codes and value systems of which they are only partly aware. They may have accepted these without fully exploring the meaning or implications of a particular code or system. Sometimes one's beliefs are in contradiction with one another and one is not aware of the value priorities. Social worker self-knowledge calls for specification and understanding of one's moral code and value system. This understanding includes identification of the source of one's moral code and values as well as recognition of and the degree of flexibility regarding priorities.

Family and Cultural Roots

As a person thinks about lifestyle, philosophy of life, moral code, and value system, the importance of roots—cultural and family background—should become clear. Individuals have different reactions to their roots. Some feel comfortable continuing the traditions and lifestyle of past generations; others reject all or a part of that way of life. Many become confused and are uncertain about what should be continued and what should be rejected; others find a balance between using the part of their roots they find useful and making adaptations and changes necessary to function in their present life situation.

One method of gaining understanding about one's cultural heritage is to spend time studying that heritage. This can be done through formal courses; by reading books about people who belong to that culture or about cultural heritage; and by talking with family members about family customs, lifestyle, and beliefs. An attempt should also be made to understand cultural heritage as a response to historical events and situations. Many people find that a journey into their cultural heritage is rewarding and yields considerable self-understanding.

The **genogram**, a family tree that specifies significant information about each individual for at least three generations, is a useful tool for gaining understanding of one's family (see case example in Chapter 13). From studying a genogram one can identify the effect of such things as death, size of family, birth position in family, naming patterns, and major family behavior patterns, to name a few. This method of studying the family as a system can yield much previously unrecognized information and help a person see not only the place she has filled in a family but also how she has been influenced by the family.[4]

There are other ways of considering family influence that aid in the quest for self-knowledge. The study of the family from a sociological and psychological point of view provides insight into the family. Discussions with family members about important events in the life of the family are useful as a method for gaining deeper understanding about the family and its ways of functioning.

The search for one's roots can be a lifelong journey, yielding many fascinating facts. It can also open old wounds and thus be painful. Yet recognizing and dealing with the pain can often result in a person becoming more sensitive to others' pain and a more effective helper. Most of all, it can lead to greater understanding of self, to knowledge of who one is and why one is unique.

Life Experiences

In addition to experiences within the family, other experiences are important, including educational experience—the experience of learning, the knowledge learned, and attitudes toward learning. Other meaningful experiences include those with one's peers and those in one's community and neighborhood and involve all kinds of people—those who are different because of age, race, ethnic background, and mental or physical disabilities. Experiences in organized group situations and in religious activities and experiences related to illness, disability, poverty, or abundance of economic resources are also important.

Identification of life experiences that have significant personal impact is yet another way of developing self-knowledge. It is helpful to evaluate how each of these significant life experiences relates to other life experiences and how each affects ways of thinking, feeling, and acting. Also to be considered is how an experience results from a particular set of previous life experiences.

Personal Needs

Another area of self-knowledge is understanding one's needs and how they are dealt with. This includes personal needs as related to common human needs, needs that result from human diversity, and needs that arise from relationships with social systems (see Chapter 1).

In thinking about common human needs, the focus is on the need for food, clothing, shelter, care, safety, belongingness, and opportunity for growth and learning. An understanding of personal need includes how needs are met and the adequacy of the need provision. It is also useful to consider personal developmental patterns in the area of physical development. An understanding of human development provides information about expected development at a specific age; it is important to consider the development expected in relation to preceding development. Also involved are biological needs, which encompass such issues as health and wellness, disease and disability, physical strengths and limitations, changes in the body and its functioning as a result of aging, and the need for physical closeness.[5] Identification of the current developmental stage is necessary before consideration can be given to the needs of individuals. For example, during the period of rapid physical growth and development in early adolescence, a person has a need for additional food to support the growing body.

Erik Erikson and others have identified psychosocial needs at various stages of human development. Identification of these needs gives rise to developmental tasks that must be accomplished if psychosocial needs during each stage are to be fulfilled. For example, as the young child develops cognitively, there is a need for activities that allow for the exploration necessary for learning. Some have questioned the validity for women of Erikson's formulation of human development.[6] New formulations about differences in male and female development continue to emerge, and these theoretical developments should be taken into account. There have also been questions raised about the validity of Erikson's theory for people of color because it is based primarily on males of European descent. However, there do not seem to be any substantial alternative theories that have gained widespread acceptance. Nonetheless, the application of Erikson's formulation should be done with flexibility and openness to other possibilities. In considering psychosocial need, it is useful not only to determine need at the present stage of development but also unmet needs in earlier stages. Present functioning is in part affected by the way needs have been met in the past. Thus, identification of unmet needs is one means of gaining self-understanding. It is also useful to reflect on how one's cultural group meets the psychosocial needs of its members. Doing so can yield some understanding as to whether personal experience has been typical or atypical for one's cultural group.

Another dimension of human functioning from which common human needs arise is the spiritual dimension. This area is often ignored by social workers because there is little agreement about its nature and content and because there has been little research in this area. Spiritual development has often been considered a part of religious development; although this is frequently the case, there are broader implications. Carlton Cornett defined spirituality as "the individual's understanding of and response to meaning in life; time and morality; expectations regarding what, if anything, follows death; and belief or non-belief in a 'higher power.'"[7] It follows, then, that spiritual development is the process a person goes through in developing as a spiritual being. Although social work has paid little attention to this area, it is one that is extremely important in understanding the formation of a value system and philosophy of life. It is of particular importance to the self-knowledge a social worker needs to develop a professional value base. Some of the most helpful materials are those concerning moral development by Lawrence Kohlberg and Carol Gilligan[8] and faith development by James W. Fowler and Sharon Parks.[9]

A second area of personal need arises because of human diversity. This relates to the effects of identification or affiliation with a particular group. Diversity refers to differences related to age, class, gender, color, culture, disability, ethnicity, marital status, family structure, race, national origin, religion, sex, and sexual orientation.[10] Institutional racism, ageism, sexism, prejudice, and discrimination all have a serious impact on human functioning. Because of this impact, individuals who are a part of certain groups (racial minorities, persons with disabilities, etc.) have distinctive needs. Differences in age, language, physical appearance, and mental ability tend to separate people from some resources and opportunities for meeting needs. Responses to societal expectations and responsibilities are different, as are coping mechanisms. Any understanding of personal need should take into account needs that arise because of different lifestyles and the stresses that accompany such differences.

A third area of personal need arises because of each person's interrelatedness with other persons—his or her membership in social systems. Systems, such as the family, peer groups, institutions of work and education, organizations, the neighborhood and community, and cultural groups, all place expectations and responsibilities on their members. People have a need to respond to these expectations and responsibilities. Individuals can accept expectations and responsibilities and can negotiate with the system to modify expectations and responsibilities.

Making an inventory of personal needs is another way of developing self-knowledge (see Table 4.1). As one comes to understand personal needs, an understanding of behavior, feelings, and responses to a variety of life experiences also develops. This is a necessary aspect of true self-knowledge that has not only psychosocial dimensions but biological and spiritual dimensions as well.

TABLE 4.1   *A Guide for Thinking about Personal Need*

My Common Human Needs

1. What are my needs for food, shelter, and clothing? How do I meet these needs?
2. What are my needs for safety so as to avoid pain and physical damage to self?
   How do I meet these needs?
3. What are my health care needs? How do I meet these needs?
4. What are my needs for love and belongingness? How do I meet these needs?
5. What are my needs for acceptance and status? How do I meet these needs?
6. What are my needs for developing my capacity and potentiality? How do I meet these needs?
7. What are my needs for understanding myself and the world in which I live?
   How do I meet these needs?
8. What other biological needs do I have?
9. How do I describe my spiritual development? What are major sources for this development?
   What are my present needs in this area?

My Developmental Needs

1. What are my needs because of my experience in developing physically? How do I meet
   these needs?
2. What are my needs in relation to my cognitive development? How do I meet these needs?
3. What is my present stage of psychosocial development?
4. What are my needs because of the development tasks of my current stage of development?
5. How well have I accomplished the tasks of earlier developmental stages?
6. What present needs do I have because of challenges related to not accomplishing these tasks?

My Needs Arising from Human Diversity

1. What in my lifestyle is "diverse" from the dominant lifestyle of my community?
2. What is the basis of the diversity—race, cultural group, gender, religion, disabling
   conditions, other?
3. What is the meaning of this diversity to me? How do I feel about myself in relation to
   this diversity?
4. What is the meaning of this diversity to my immediate environment? How does the
   environment deal with me as a diverse person?
5. How do I deal with the stresses and strains that exist because of diversity?
6. What strengths or special needs do I have because of my diversity?

My Needs Arising from Social Systems of Which I Am a Part

1. What expectations do the various social systems of which I am a part have of me?
   (These include family, peer group, school or work, organizations of which I am a member,
   neighborhood or cultural group, etc.).
2. What do I see as my responsibility toward the social systems of which I am a part?
3. What needs do I have in relation to these social systems, including the expectations and
   responsibilities related to them?

Case Example

I am Janie Bryan, a social work student. I grew up in a small town of 10,000. I am the middle of five children in a family that has lived in the same community all of my life. My oldest brother is five years older than I am, married, and a news announcer in a nearby city. My sister, who is two years older than me, married her high school boyfriend, lives in our hometown, and has a three-year-old daughter and a one-year-old son. My sister Mary, who is four years younger than I am, is moderately mentally retarded and is still at home, as is our younger brother, who is nine years younger than me.

I see myself as enthusiastic and insightful. I really get excited about a lot of things and seem to have the ability to sense what is happening in many situations. I seem to understand my friends and their needs and problems. I think I am also logical and ingenious. I like to have time to think about things and to decide what is the logical way to do something, step by step. I guess I like to see where I am going when I start something, but I also like to brainstorm about what can be done and come up with new ideas about how to reach my goals.

It's very easy for me to talk to people. People seem to like me. I have to be careful, however, that I don't try to second-guess where others are coming from based on my experiences. I'm learning to find out from them why they think and feel as they do. In fact, right now I'm trying to learn as much as I can about a lot of different kinds of people. They have really interesting stories and seem to enjoy telling them to me. Also, I'm fascinated with the different kinds of experiences some of my fellow students have had. I am finding I really need to know something about other people to understand why they think the way they do.

I don't consider myself to have any disabilities, though some of my friends think being a woman is a handicap. I am very optimistic that my generation will not have to put up with all the old hang-ups, so I just plan that I can do anything I want to do. My family has always been middle class, never a lot of money but always comfortable. We have had what we needed. Dad has owned a small business for as long as I can remember. He is respected by everyone, and I have always been respected as his daughter. We are Methodists, and the church and its activities are important to our family.

I have always done well in school. I was usually on the honor roll in high school as well as being active in cheerleading, drama, and music. When I got to college, my first semester was not too good. I was not used to the kinds of assignments and tests given here at college. But then I seemed to kind of get the hang of it. I did some structuring of my time and organizing myself, and now I'm getting A's and B's with a C once in a while. I learn best when I am exploring new ideas and when I'm challenged to think and express my own thinking. This year I'm living in an apartment with three other girls. This is great after living in the dorm, but we did have some trouble at first keeping the place livable and getting the cooking done.

I am a positive thinker, optimistic. People are good. I think if you really work at it you can get along with almost anyone. I do like some people better than others, though. I hate to spend too much time discussing all the bad things that are happening and hearing about people's worries over things such as tests next week, and so on. I want to be independent, and it bothers me that I'm still financially dependent on my family. Yet I wonder if I'm not also dependent on my friends, too. I do hope it's in a way that they can count on me when they need it. I really care about other people and want to help them feel good about themselves. So many students seem to not have a lot of self-confidence or feel good about what's happening to them. I wish I could help them.

(continued)

I guess I see the relationship of humans and nature as one of harmony. I am a doer and seem to focus on the present rather than the past or future, though I am concerned about what I will do when I get out of school. I want to see some of the world, maybe work in a big city, though that is scary, too. I would rather work alone but know some things must be done with others. Guess I should develop more skills for working with others.

I've never thought much about my family. Dad's side came from Germany about four generations ago, and Mother's people just moved out from the East about the same time. We seem to have sort of taken each other for granted. My mother's brother is really angry at my mother for letting my grandmother live in a nursing home, but Mom just can't handle her and my sister Mary. Dad is so busy at the store that he can't be much help. He really was the one to insist that Mom can't care for Grandma now. The folks really worry about what is going to happen to Mary. I've learned some things in my social work classes that might help. Last time I was home we talked about this, and I felt real good that the folks said it sure helped. I don't know much about Dad's family. That's something I want to find out more about.

My genogram would help me see that as a middle child I seem to have been more of a helper than the other children. I think this may be because Mary does need special attention and my little brother is so much younger. Mom has had her hands full with them. My older brother and sister sort of left home and got out of the helping. I think maybe I'm more mature because of this experience in my family. These family experiences and the real good experience I had in high school seem to have really prepared me for dealing with college life. I had to learn to use time well if I wanted to do all I did in high school.

As I look at my "common human needs," they all seem to have been met by my family. Mom and Dad still provide part of the money I need to go to school, and I've gotten loans and worked in the summer. Now I have to plan for myself how to deal with the day-to-day needs like eating right; sometimes I don't do so well here. Also, I never thought about health care. Mom has always sent me to the dentist and doctor. I think it's time I took some responsibility for this. I'm going to school to develop my ability to earn money and take care of myself but also to help others. I'm meeting that need by using the opportunities here at school.

I think I've developed normally, but with my sister's problems I understand that this can be a problem for her. I've just never thought about having needs in this area. I'm moving into Stage VI. I'm not yet ready to make any long-term commitments with a man. I want to live a bit and see some of the world first. But I do feel real close to my roommates and sometimes have wondered if they were taking the place of my family. I'm not sure where I am in this area. Maybe this is a sign I am struggling with a developmental task. I guess I need to test myself out as an independent adult person. I'm not sure I really have completed all the tasks of Stage V. I never thought of it, but I've known some role confusion. At home I play mother to my little brother, and I'm not sure what my relationship with Mary should be. I need to think about this and perhaps talk with Mom about it. Otherwise I seem to have gone through the other psychological stages pretty well. I trust people (usually); I feel good about myself; I like to do things and am fairly responsible; I have lots of friends.

I've never thought about diversity. I seem so average. Yet maybe that is my "diversity." Almost everyone I know is different in some way. They have had bad growing-up experiences and now have problems. I've really been lucky. Also, I don't know many people of different races. I need to think about what it means to be different in this way.

(continued)

Because I'm so fortunate I have a lot of responsibility. Maybe that's part of my reason for wanting to be a social worker. Social systems do expect things of me. My parents want me to come home more often than I really want to. I need to talk with them about this rather than just let the problem go on. My instructors place lots of expectations for reading and papers on me. My friends want me to spend time with them. Sometimes it's hard to handle all this and still have the time I need to be alone. I need to work for a good balance. Maybe I need to set up some kind of a schedule for myself.

Overall I see myself as doing pretty well, but there are some things I need to do:

1. I need to continue to find out where others are coming from and to realize everyone has not had the opportunities and experiences I have had. I need to listen.
2. I need to plan for some alone time so I can get to know myself better. This means I need to structure my time better so I can meet all my obligations.
3. I need to get to know more about my extended family. I don't seem to know them very well.
4. I need to talk to my parents about my feelings of growing up and being independent. I'm not at all sure of my role in the family. We need to discuss this.
5. I need to increase my capacity for working cooperatively with others.

Personal Functioning

Self-knowledge includes identification and understanding of one's lifestyle, philosophy of life, moral code, value system, roots, and personal needs. It also includes an understanding of how these factors affect day-to-day functioning. This involves identifying how one learns, how one shares self with others, how one responds to a variety of situations, and how one's biases and prejudices play a role. Also important is how one feels about oneself and how this affects day-to-day functioning. Self-knowledge includes understanding how one meets personal needs; how one deals with freedom and restrictions; how one accepts change, both in oneself and in one's environment; how one views one's responsibility toward the social system of which one is a part; and what one's roles are in those systems.

Fundamental to self-knowledge is a healthy self-image or a sense of positive self-worth or self-esteem. When the worker is able to achieve positive self-esteem, self-knowledge in the areas mentioned previously becomes more accessible. Negative self-worth leads to defensiveness and a greater likelihood that both self-image and one's view of others will be distorted. Positive self-worth is linked to the cardinal social work belief in the innate value and worth of all human beings. This belief is predicated on the realization that human beings are not perfect and that we all have flaws and make mistakes. However, by making mistakes, we prove that we are human. Accepting oneself as worthwhile in spite of one's flaws and mistakes allows one to view oneself and others more genuinely.

If the worker feels inadequate as a person, this will have a negative effect on the way in which help is delivered. The worker may feel good about being needed by the client, and she may yield to the temptation to foster dependency. This may meet her need to be needed, but it undermines the client's need to gain more control over his life and makes it difficult for him to become more independent. However, if the worker has a healthy self-image, she will be able to be more genuine in her care and concern for the client. This care and concern will be based on the client as a human being, not on the worker's own needs. She will be able to work with her client without expecting something in return and can feel good about facilitating his growth and development. She can find gratification in providing a high quality of service rather than taking credit for what the client has achieved. The worker is better able to seek out strengths in the client and in herself because she begins with the basic assumption that both she and her client have value and worth as human beings.

Awareness of one's interactions with the social systems around oneself is important to developing an appreciation for an ecological approach to helping. The more the worker becomes aware of the impact of her environment on herself and her impact on her environment, the more confidence she will have in broadening her work with her client to include the environment. Experiencing a supportive environment is fundamental to growth and change for human beings. Seeking out the strengths in the client's environment provides support for growth and change that is beyond the limited time and scope of the helping relationship.

The kind of self-knowledge discussed here is not easy to develop. It takes time for introspection, for observation of self in a variety of circumstances, and for seeking out others' observations about self. It also requires risk taking. There may be a cost for self-knowledge: dissatisfaction with the self that is found, pain about past experiences, or anger about one's place and role in society. It is a lifelong journey toward self-knowledge and self-acceptance. It is also a necessary journey if the helping person is to be able to use a major tool—the self—skillfully, fully, and with maximal results.

The Helping Person

The generalist social worker is a helper who can effectively use self with other persons to enable them to meet needs or solve problems more adequately. This helping focuses on needs and interactions between the person and the systems that make up the environment. Thus, the generalist social worker must develop the interactional skills necessary for productive interaction with individuals and groups of individuals.

As the social worker approaches the helping situation, she brings first and foremost self. This self brings concern for others; a knowledge base, both substantive and experiential; values, those of the profession and those of self; a view of the nature of change; and skills, both cognitive and interactive. The self is the major tool for working with others.

Many of these skills are characteristic of the helping person. There is a distinction between a helping person and a helping professional. The social work professional is a helping person, but the helping is done in the context of using the knowledge, values, and skills of the social work profession. One major difference between helping and professional helping is that the help given is based firmly in and with conscious use of an identifiable knowledge and value base. Another characteristic of professional helping is that the help is nonreciprocal. That is, help is given with no expectation that the helped will in turn provide help for the helper.

Characteristics of a Helping Person

There have been many descriptions of the helping person. Arthur Combs, Donald Avila, and William Purkey, in a research study, found that the belief system of the worker was an important characteristic of helping. The effective helper believes that people are:

1. More able than unable
2. Friendly rather than unfriendly
3. Worthy rather than unworthy
4. Internally motivated rather than externally motivated
5. Dependable rather than undependable
6. Helpful rather than hindering

They found that the worker's beliefs about self were also important. The effective worker sees self as (1) identified with people, (2) adequate, (3) trustworthy, (4) wanted, and (5) worthy. Some additional traits of the helping person, according to these researchers, are (1) freeing rather than controlling, (2) being concerned about larger issues rather than smaller ones, (3) self-revealing rather than self-concealing, (4) being involved rather than alienated, (5) being process oriented rather than goal oriented, and (6) being altruistic rather than narcissistic. Effective workers approach a task in terms of people rather than things and from a perceptual rather than an objective viewpoint.[11]

Beulah Compton and Burt Galaway saw maturity as another characteristic of helping persons. In their view, maturity consists of the capacities to be creative and to observe self in interaction with others, of a desire to help, and of having the qualities of courage and sensibility.[12] This mature person would seem to be one who is free enough of his own life problems to experiment, to risk, and to give of self in service of another. The quality of sensibility can be expressed as good judgment. Used in this sense, good judgment means the ability to make good decisions that serve the client and her needs rather than the worker's.

David Johnson described the helping person as having another set of attributes. First is the ability to self-disclose while being self-aware and showing concern for what the other person feels about what the worker says or does. This attribute has a quality of honesty, genuineness, and authenticity. Second is the capacity to trust, which entails warmth, acceptance, support, and the capacity to check for meaning. Third is skill in communication. This includes the ability to send messages so that the other can understand, to listen, to respond appropriately, and to clarify what is misunderstood. Fourth is the ability to express feeling; fifth is the ability to accept self and others; sixth is the ability to confront others constructively; and seventh is the capacity to reinforce and model appropriate behavior.[13]

The helping person can be described as one who:

1. Has a generally positive view of individuals and their behaviors
2. Is concerned about others and their well-being for the sake of the other, not for self-centered purposes
3. Is open, trusting, warm, friendly, and honest

4. Works with persons being helped, not for them
5. Responds to people rather than supports the use of a particular technique
6. Is mature, has good judgment, and is willing to take risks in the service of others
7. Is realistic about human situations, the amount of change possible, and the time it takes to change

Anthony Maluccio has reported research that examined the factors influencing outcomes of treatment from both the client's and the worker's perspectives. He found agreement between the workers' and clients' perspectives that the following are desirable worker characteristics: acceptance, interest, warmth, and supportiveness. In addition, the clients saw these characteristics as helpful: being human and understanding; being caring, trusting, and friendly; encouraging work together; looking for solutions; giving advice and suggestions; and releasing anxiety.[14]

In discussing worker styles, Edward Mullen described the helping person as one who exerts personal influence rather than as one who applies techniques.[15] This indicates that the worker's use of self is the major factor in helping. Thus, a primary task in becoming a helping person is a fine-tuning of characteristics that are a part of everyday human interaction. Techniques can be useful tools, but only when used by a person who knows how to use personal influence (self).

The worker is not a cold, objective student of humanity who knows about rather than feels with; nor is he one who has a strong personal need to control, to satisfy his own conscience, to feel superior to other persons, or to be liked. The worker is not an overly confirmed optimist or a person who has solved his own problems but forgotten the personal cost, or a person whose own solutions to life problems are so precarious that the solutions take on a moralistic character. The worker is not afraid of feelings, his own or others. The worker uses knowledge and experience for understanding. This understanding is more than intellectual; it has emotional, or feeling, aspects as well. It is an understanding that leads to sensitive and realistic responses to human need. The helping worker is one who can defer his own needs and both recognizes and is not afraid of those needs; is not impulsive and is aware of his own feelings so they do not cause impulsiveness; is responsible for self and his own tasks in the helping endeavor; is growth facilitating and empathic; and is able to communicate clearly and effectively—concretely and specifically. This worker can clarify roles, status, values, and intentions with the client.

Responsibility and Authority

Two characteristics of a helping person—responsibility and authority—are particularly troublesome to the social worker. These two characteristics are related because each is a part of the personal influence aspect of the helping situation. They are also related in that they often become confused with value judgments related to the right of self-determination. Each worker must learn to manage these two characteristics in relationships with clients.

It is very easy for the social worker to take on responsibilities that do not belong to her. The worker may feel inadequate when she cannot "get the client to see what is best for him." Societal pressures also place a worker in a position of feeling responsible for the client's behaviors. Friends, public officials, and the person on the street ask why the social worker does not "make clients" do something. The worker again begins to accept inappropriate responsibility. Often the worker can see the consequences of a client's behavior and has a great desire to "save the client from self." The right of self-determination includes not only the right to make one's own choices but also the right to suffer the consequences of those choices.

If the worker is not responsible for the client's choices in the helping situation, what, then, is the nature of the worker's responsibility? The worker is responsible for self in the helping situation, which includes:

1. Understanding person in environment as far as possible, given the circumstances of the helping situation
2. Using self in the way that will be most helpful to this client in this situation
3. Creating a climate that makes it possible for the client to use the help
4. Providing a perspective to the client's need, based on the worker's knowledge and experience
5. Providing a structure for thinking about the need, including focusing on, and skillful use of, the process of facilitating growth and change
6. Providing assistance in identifying strengths and information about needed resources along with assistance in obtaining those resources

The worker and client share responsibility for the outcome of the work together. The worker provides resources and opportunities for work on the problem of meeting needs. The client must make use of the opportunities and resources. If the worker carries out the responsibility for providing the opportunity and resources and the client chooses not to use those opportunities and resources, this is not the worker's responsibility.

Regardless of the nature of the worker's responsibility, the client views the worker as a person with authority. Robert Foren and Royston Bailey, in discussing the authority clients ascribe to workers, identified the following as aspects of that authority:

1. Power to enforce standards of child care
2. Personal attributes, social class, education
3. Association with parental figures
4. Knowledge and skill
5. Fantasy-magical power[16]

It is important for social workers to recognize that such authority has been ascribed to them. In accepting the value of the right of self-determination, many workers will deny this authority or be very uncomfortable with it. They see the right to self-determination and the exercise of authority as contradictory, but an in-depth examination of the nature of social work authority reveals that this is not necessarily true. Denial of authority is not useful; the helping person must recognize and become comfortable with the ascribed authority. For example, a worker can examine with a client the exact nature of the worker's authority so that a client knows that the worker will not impose inappropriate standards.

It is also important to help the client become aware of unrealistic authority expectations and free him to be self-determining. Some functions performed by social workers carry a kind of legal authority, which is the means by which certain of society's social control functions are carried out. These areas include protective service for children, the mentally impaired, and the aged and probation and parole work. The needs of social systems must be recognized; people cannot be allowed to act destructively toward others, particularly those who cannot protect themselves. The worker needs to learn to be comfortable with the ascribed authority. There are limits to self-determination.

It is important to help clients understand not only their right of self-determination but also their social responsibility (another social work value). Self-determination, or choice, is limited by social responsibility. If people decide not to be socially responsible, then they choose to take the consequences of their behavior. Social workers must use their authority in helping clients understand the consequences of behavior so that their choices regarding social responsibility are truly self-determining. Workers also must accept responsibility for those who cannot protect themselves, such as children, the frail aged, the abused, and the victims of crime.

To be helping persons, social workers must accept responsibility for those areas of the situation for which they are responsible but not for responsibilities that belong to the client. Social workers also must accept the realistic authority that goes with their role. In exercising this ascribed authority, they must constantly be guided by the values of both self-determination and social responsibility.

Helping Skills

The effective social worker develops helping skills. These skills are not mystical or esoteric; they are the skills of well-functioning human beings. The worker uses these skills with people who have difficulties in social functioning and cannot fulfill the usual responsibilities in human interaction and with people whose sociocultural context for interaction may be different from that of the worker. These factors place greater responsibility for the interaction on the worker than is usual for interaction with people of similar backgrounds. Thus, the skills for human interaction must be fine-tuned and be brought into the conscious awareness of the worker. The skills that need to be developed include the following:

1. *Skills needed for understanding, including understanding of person in situation and helping other people understand themselves in the situation*—Skills in this area are listening, leading the person to express self, reflecting on what has been said, summarizing what has been said, confronting the person with the realities of situations, interpreting the facts as presented, and informing the person of facts.

2. *Skills needed for developing a climate that encourages helpful interaction*—Skills used in making people comfortable in strange or new situations include skills in supporting people, in crisis intervention, in focusing the area of concern to ease a sense of being overwhelmed, and in constructing a comfortable physical and emotional climate.

3. *Skills needed in acting on the needs of the client*—These include skills in problem solving, decision making, planning, referring, modeling, teaching, enabling, identifying strengths and resources, and using activity as well as the skills necessary to any practice strategy the worker may be using.

4. *Skills used in communicating and relating to others*—These include skills in listening and attending to the communication of others; in paraphrasing, clarifying, and checking perceptions; in getting started, encouraging, elaborating, focusing, and questioning; in responding to feelings and to others' experiences; in summarizing and pulling thoughts together; and in interpreting and informing.[17]

5. *Skills in working with diversity*—These include skills in understanding diverse people, the use of naturalistic inquiry, and using assessment, planning, actions, and evaluation and termination in a manner that is comfortable and expected within various diverse groups.

This summary of skills is not meant to be all-inclusive but rather gives some idea of the breadth of skills the social worker needs. Skill development is a continuous task for all social workers if they are to grow as helping persons.

Ethical Decision Making

As professionals, social workers have an obligation to act in an ethical manner and to avoid engaging in unethical conduct. This obligation is both moral and legal. In exchange for the sanction to practice as a professional social worker, society expects that social workers will conduct themselves in a manner that helps rather than harms or exploits clients. Most state licensing boards have adopted the NASW *Code of Ethics* as the ethical code for social work practice. The most recent version of the code was adopted in 1996 and revised in 1999 and 2008.

There are several proposed models for how social workers might apply the *Code of Ethics*. The issue is what is ethical when more than one ethical principle is relevant in a given situation. This is called an *ethical dilemma*. Often social workers find themselves in situations where acting in a way that adheres to one ethical principle would actually violate another. For example, if a client threatens to harm himself or others, the worker would be violating confidentiality if she informed the police about the threat. And yet, protecting the well-being of the client and others is her first obligation. So, in cases of life or death, preserving life clearly takes precedence over confidentiality. However, there are many situations where the decision about what is ethical is not clear-cut.

Philosophically, there are two primary concepts that have been proposed to guide ethical decision making. One involves applying the principle of the "greatest good for the greatest number." In this approach, the worker considers both harms and benefits and makes the decision based on maximizing benefit while minimizing harm. The other approach is based on the idea that certain actions are inherently right or wrong and these can be codified into ethical principles. The NASW *Code of Ethics* describes the purpose of the code as providing a guide to ethical decisions. It recognizes that dilemmas will occur but does not prescribe a specific approach in reaching a decision. The approach that is proposed in this text is based on a blend of these two approaches in adhering to the *Code of Ethics*.

In applying the *Code of Ethics* to working with clients, it seems clear that the worker's first obligation is to her client. We surmise this by examining the code itself. Not only does the ethical responsibility to clients come first in the Ethical Standards but also it is by far the longest of the standards, and the very first standard states: "Social worker's primary responsibility is to promote the well-being of clients."[18] There are some limits to this, such as instances of child abuse, when the worker is obligated to report the abuse, but it is consistent with the idea that society expects professionals to act in the best interests of those they serve provided that other people are not harmed. If we assume that the first obligation is to the client, then identifying who the client is takes on greater significance. For the generalist, the client may be any size client system. Determining the appropriate client system will be discussed in greater depth in Chapter 8.

Another assumption that we will make is that ethical dilemmas are best resolved through open discussion. It seems that what cannot be discussed is most often that which is unethical. So, bringing the dilemma out in the open at the very least tends to protect clients from exploitation. It is very important that this be done in a manner that preserves the client's right to confidentiality. So, the worker does not need to identify the client system except on a need-to-know basis. Revealing the identity of the client to one's supervisor is appropriate because he or she has an obligation to be familiar with the work of those who are supervised. Revealing the identity to one's colleagues may not be necessary, except in formal situations, such as case conferencing or when colleagues are called on to cover for each other. In many instances, it might also be appropriate to involve the client in the discussion when it involves the rights of the client. It is proposed that in applying the NASW *Code of Ethics,* the worker should take the following steps:

1. Analyze the situation and identify the client system
2. Identify the relevant values, ethics, and legal issues
3. Identify potential positive and negative outcomes
4. Discuss with supervisor and/or colleagues and with client when appropriate
5. Decide on the most ethical process and outcome based on ethical principles using a mutual decision making process
6. In implementing this, the worker should thoroughly document each step

Accountability

In recent years, more emphasis has been placed on accountability in the social welfare field. In its simplest form, **accountability** is responsibility. The social worker is responsible to the client for upholding his part of any agreements or contracts and for providing the service agreed on. The social worker is also responsible to the profession for upholding social work values and the NASW *Code of Ethics* in delivering services. The social worker is responsible to the agency that employs the worker for delivering the service within guidelines, programs, and policies developed by the agency.

Records

One important area of accountability regards maintaining records and the use of information about the client. Social work has always placed considerable emphasis on recording. This recording has taken many forms. A commonly used kind of recording is the

problem-oriented record. This method is used not only by social workers but also by all health care professionals. This system has advantages when working in an interdisciplinary setting. It is easily translated to computer databases and is succinct and focused. Problem-oriented records contain four parts. First is a database that contains information pertinent to the client and work with the client. This includes such things as age, sex, marital status, functioning limitations, persons involved (family and other professionals), financial situation, or any test results. Second is a problem list that includes a statement of initial complaints and assessment of the concerned staff. Third are plans and goals related to each identified problem. Fourth are follow-up notes about what was done and the outcome of that activity.

Problem-oriented records take several forms. Usually, they consist, at least in part, of checklists that can be converted into data on a computer. One form is called *soap* (subjective, objective, assessment, plan). In this form, for each identified problem, subjective (the client's report), objective (the facts as determined by clinical activity), assessment (a statement about the nature of the problem), and a plan for dealing with the problem are stated.

The use of the term *problem-oriented record* is inconsistent with an ecosystems strengths approach. However, a similar format is generally used and might be referred to as a *change-oriented record* or *needs-based record* in that it is driven by the identification and meeting of needs. This record should consist of the identification of needs or concerns and an assessment of the person in environment or ecosystem. A plan is developed that is built on the strengths and resources of the ecosystem and designed to meet the needs of the client and the ecosystem. Progress notes are kept that describe the progress toward goals and objectives. Periodic (generally quarterly) reports summarize the progress made and document the need for further service. A termination summary identifies the reasons for ending the service and the outcomes.

Research carried out by Jill Doner Kagle indicated that workers have some difficulty in using what she termed "new records." The *new record* is narrowly focused on defining the need for service, service goals and plans, service activities, and the impact of service on the client situation. She found that many workers felt this kind of recording did not supply all the information needed in providing service. Her work suggests that workers believe they need information on the dynamics of the situation and perhaps on the context of the client. Another difficulty workers encountered with new records was that they did not provide for the "overdocumentation" called for in a world in which all professions are more often threatened with legal actions. The answer to these issues may lie in determining which cases need to have in-depth recording and which can use a new record approach.[19]

Another type of recording often used by social workers is the *summary record*. Though this type of record takes various forms depending on agency policy, it essentially includes entry data, often the social history, a plan of action, periodic summaries of significant information and actions taken by the worker, and a statement of what was accomplished as the case was closed. The periodic summaries may be made at specified periods of time (e.g., every week), or they may be made when it is necessary to document some fact or action. The summary record is shorter and easier to use when considering the total service process. It is focused more on what happens with the client than on the worker's input and sifts out the important elements, discarding the superfluous.

Case Example

Change-Oriented Case Record

Name: Jerry Adams and family   Date: October 30, 2009

Worked on Goal A from the service plan. Met with Jerry and his mother individually and then together. Jerry indicated that school was much better this week. He was able to follow the rules at school this week nearly 100% of the time. There was only one instance when he got into an argument with another boy during recess. The boy called Jerry a name and they pushed each other a few times, but some other boys stepped in and broke it up. We discussed possible ways of handling this type of situation in the future. Mrs. A indicated that she was pleased with the progress that was being made. She felt that Jerry was making an effort to get along and the school seemed to be working hard to decrease the racial taunting. When we met jointly, Mrs. A was able to give Jerry positive feedback, which obviously pleased him. We agreed to continue working on anger management and will meet next Friday to review the progress.

Mary Smith, Social Worker
October 30, 2009

Summary records are used in situations in which long-term, ongoing contact with a client and a series of workers may be involved, such as with residential or day activity programs. These records provide a picture of what has happened with a particular client. Agency policy often specifies the form and content of such records. This policy reflects the agency's need for information for accountability purposes. As summary records may be subject to review by a number of people, questions of how to deal with confidentiality are important. It is usually good practice to include in summary recording only that which is required to be in the record and only verifiable information, not impressions, feelings, or information that can be misinterpreted.

Process recording—a narrative report of all that happened during a client contact, including the worker's feelings and thinking about what has happened—is a form that at one time received great emphasis and was frequently used in the educational and supervisory processes. In recent years it has not been used as often, in part probably because it is extremely time consuming. Also, the intensive individual supervision of workers, which was once considered essential to social work and which made extensive use of recording important, is no longer considered desirable in many settings. Process recording, however, is still a technique that has value for students as they and their field supervisors evaluate their work. It is especially useful to the social worker striving to develop new skills or further develop understanding and skill in difficult situations.

The usefulness of process recording depends on the ability of the worker to recall exactly what happened and in what order and to look at the facts in an objective manner in order to get at underlying feelings and meanings. The worker must be willing to honestly record the actions and communications of both worker and client. When this technique is used in a supervisory process, the worker must have a trusting relationship with the supervisor. Because of its time-consuming nature, process recording should not be used with every case or situation but only with carefully selected cases particularly applicable to the worker's development and learning. Process recording is most often used when working with individuals but can also be used when working with larger systems.

When process recording is used, confidentiality must be preserved. The written record must be kept in a secure place and only seen by those directly involved in the situation or supervising the worker. If a record is to be used for other purposes, such as teaching or as a case example, it must be completely disguised so that neither the person nor the situation can be identified. The purpose of process recording is to aid the worker in understanding the situation and to serve as a tool for learning. After it is used, the process recording should be destroyed. It should not be made part of the permanent record.

A technique used for purposes similar to process recording is taping, either in audio or video format, of interviews, group sessions, or other interactional encounters. This technique can allow the worker to see himself in action with the client. Sometimes it is also useful for the client to view what has happened as a means of evaluating behaviors and interactions. Unless the time is taken to evaluate the underlying elements of the situation (the feeling elements and the reasons behind behaviors), some of the learning potential of this technique is lost. When using the taping technique of recording, workers must obtain written permission from the client to tape sessions. Sometimes taping may inhibit the client and have a negative effect on the work of the session. Again, confidentiality is an important consideration. Tapes should be destroyed or erased after they have served their purpose.

Record keeping is an important part of the social worker's responsibility. It has changed over time as a result of new practice demands and new technologies. Records have many different purposes that range from improving the worker's competence to obtaining data for accountability and research. It is important that social workers develop the capacity to accurately and efficiently maintain records required by any agency in which they are employed.

Clients need to understand not only the confidential nature of their work with a social worker but also the limits of that confidentiality—that is, that information will be discussed with a supervisor or a professional team. Clients should be told what will be recorded, who will have access to their records, and how long these records will be kept. They need to know that records used in agency and program evaluation are depersonalized so that the identity of clients is protected. They need to know what information is shared with whom and why it is shared.

Workers also need to be sure that clients have given informed consent for the use of information in their records. A client should not be asked to give consent when he is desperate for service; at such a time making an informed decision is difficult. It is wise for the worker to discuss the use of information at several points during the work together. If the client decides not to share information and knows the consequences of not sharing it, then the worker should respect the client's right to withhold information to protect her privacy.

Written consent should be specific; that is, it should state the purpose for the sharing of the information, an expiration date, and the persons with whom the information will be shared. Clients should be helped to understand their rights in signing or not signing such consents for release of information. Usually, it is wise to have someone witness the client's signature. Because the release of information could become a part of a legal action, the advice of a legal expert should be obtained in developing a form for the release of information.

Workers should monitor the use of client records to see that information contained in records is not used improperly. When they detect improper or questionable use of records, it is their responsibility to alert supervisors or other responsible persons to the situation. They can suggest ways in which the client's rights can be protected, such as depersonalizing information. If the improper use continues, workers need to advocate preventing unethical use.

Effect of Privacy and Open-Access Laws

Federal and state legislation regulates the use of various kinds of records, including those used for evaluative purposes. This legislation has generated a growing body of interpretation and judicial decisions regarding the application of these laws, which has further complicated issues of record keeping.

The Federal Privacy Act of 1974 (PL 93–579) in essence gives the client the right to see any record containing information about that client. It requires that no disclosure of information in any record be made without written consent from the client and that a record be kept indicating any disclosures of information to other persons. More recently, the Health Insurance Portability and Accountability Act of 1996 (HIPAA) included privacy rules that regulate confidentiality of health records (see *www.hhs.gov/ocr/privacy/index.html*).

Other laws have been enacted that call for open access to public records. In some cases these laws have been interpreted to mean that the records of public agencies and, in some cases, of situations in which governmental funds have been involved are a matter of public record and can be disclosed in a variety of situations, including court proceedings. There seems to be a conflict between privacy and open-access laws that has not been fully resolved.

Another implication of these two sets of laws is that some of them seem to discourage confidentiality. It is essential for social workers and social work agencies to determine exactly what records must be kept and how to best manage those records so that the client's, agency's, and the general public's best interests are met. Social workers should involve themselves in serious discussions to resolve these issues.

Issues of confidentiality and access to records need to be addressed by training, ongoing dialogue, creative thinking, and an ever-present sense of the ethics of the profession of social work. These are not the only issues that have or will arise regarding client records. Every social worker should be alert to identify other issues and to engage in discussions to resolve them.

Use of Computers

The computer is often an important tool in the evaluative process. It can record and analyze large amounts of information and can facilitate the storing and retrieval of data to document accountability.

Social workers need to be aware of what computers can do and what their limitations are. They should know how to process information so it can be computerized, how to enter information, how to access existing data, and how to evaluate the usefulness of both hardware and software for social work purposes. They should know enough about how computers operate in order to communicate with the computer expert or programmer about problems with a piece of equipment or a program. They need to be able to communicate about the tasks they want the computer to perform so that programs can be suggested, written, or modified.

It is also important to understand who can be expected to have access to the information and the purposes for which the information will be used. This helps the worker evaluate whether the most pertinent information is being requested and whether client identification and confidentiality are being protected. If social workers have reason to question whether the information being sought will provide the answers or whether client identification or confidentiality are at risk, they have an ethical responsibility to inform those responsible for the operation of the programs and to ensure that needed modifications are made.

In addition to their use in program evaluation, computers are being used by some agencies to maintain case records. The entire case record is available within the organization's internal network or in some cases it is available online. The advantages of online availability include the ability to access information from distant locations, such as health records being available to an emergency room when the client is traveling out of town. Another advantage is avoiding the need to transfer records by fax or mail risking the possibility of records being lost or confidentiality being broken. It can also save considerable time and expense involved in copying records when these need to be sent to other organizations. However, there are additional concerns over the potential for breaches of confidentiality from unauthorized access.

Interactive programs are available that allow the client (with assistance, if necessary) or the worker to respond to questions about the situation and the needs or concerns. The program then produces a narrative assessment. Some programs are designed to suggest a plan, complete with goals and objectives. Whatever is selected can be modified or new goals added. The computer will then elicit feedback regarding goals when progress notes are entered and will produce quarterly, annual, and termination summaries. With the development of voice recognition programs that receive dictation and of powerful laptop computers, it is likely that in the future nearly all social workers will be using some form of computerized record keeping. Technology has the potential for considerably increasing worker efficiency in meeting "paperwork" demands, which could leave more time available to work with clients.

One of the concerns with computerized records is maintaining confidentiality. Systems can be configured so as to limit access to records, but this can become complicated in large systems having many different workers and clients. One of the advantages of a computerized system is that records can be secured in one place and can also be backed up. Another advantage is that the computer can keep track of who has opened the file, and a breach of security can be identified more easily. This is something that cannot be done with a paper record. One disadvantage is that in a good security system, access is limited, and someone with the ability to access the record may not be available in an emergency. However, having emergency access to a computerized record means that files can be located quickly and are unlikely to be lost. A computerized system must be secure while allowing access to records on a need-to-know basis.

Whenever computers are used to maintain records, a secure, reliable backup system must be used to ensure that records are not lost or destroyed. Mainframe systems should be backed up on a tape system at the end of every day at minimum. Personal computers should use a flash drive, CD-ROM, or zip drive to back up information on the hard drive. The backup system should be kept in a secure area separated from the main information system in case of a fire, flood, or similar disaster. Having two systems in separate places presents some additional challenges to maintaining confidentiality.

Summary

The interactions of worker and client are at the center of the social work endeavor. The worker must develop a high level of self-understanding and healthy self-esteem if she is to maximize helping interactions. The development of self-understanding, which is never complete, is an ongoing endeavor that involves assessing one's values, lifestyle, roots, personal needs, and culture.

The worker's use of self is a major tool in the helping endeavor. Some of the characteristics of the helping person are concern for others, acceptance of others, warmth, supportiveness, and maturity. The helping professional person is one who is grounded in a knowledge base and who uses a professional code of ethics as a guide to the helping endeavor. Good judgment also is a very important factor. The helping person needs to develop skills for understanding clients and their situations, for creating a climate that encourages interaction, for acting on the client's needs, and for communicating with and relating to others. The social worker also needs to develop a degree of comfort with the authority and responsibility inherent in the professional helping role. The professional social worker is aware of ethics and is able to make ethical decisions. Accountability is an important aspect of professional practice. Writing well and maintaining records are major responsibilities of the professional social worker. Confidentiality of client records is also a concern.

Questions

1. What areas of self-knowledge should you examine in order to develop greater helping capacity?
2. What do you see as your strengths as a helping person? Your limitations? What can you do to mitigate your limitations?
3. How well do you believe you have dealt with issues of authority in your life experience? With issues of responsibility? With healthy self-esteem?
4. Describe an ethical dilemma you might experience in practice and how you would use the procedure in the chapter to resolve it.
5. When should the various forms of recording be used? What are the strengths and limitations of each?

Suggested Readings

Abramson, Marcia. "Reflections on Knowing Oneself Ethically: Toward a Working Framework for Social Work Practice." *Families in Society* 77 (April 1996): 195–202.

Dolgoff, Ralph, Loewenberg, Frank M. and Harrington, Donna. *Ethical Decisions for Social Work Practice*, 8th ed. Belmont, CA: Brooks/Cole, 2009.

Erikson, Erik H., Erikson, Joan M., and Kivnick, Helen Q. *The Life Cycle Completed.* New York: W. W. Norton, 1998.

Kagle, Jill Doner. *Social Work Records,* 2nd ed. Prospect Heights, IL: Waveland Press, 1996.

Lum, Doman. *Culturally Competent Practice: A Framework for Understanding Diverse Groups and Justice Issues,* 3rd ed. Pacific Grove, CA: Brooks/Cole, 2007.

Mizrahi, Terry and Davis, Larry E., Eds. *Encyclopedia of Social Work*, 20th ed. Washington, DC: NASW Press, 2008 ("Recording," "Technology").

Prince, Katie. *Boring Records? Communication, Speech, and Writing in Social Work.* Bristol, PA: Jessica Kingsley Publishers, 1996.

Rothman, Juliet C. *From the Front Lines: Student Cases in Social Work Ethics*, 2nd ed. Boston: Allyn and Bacon, 2005

Sheafor, Bradford W., and Horejsi, Charles R. *Techniques and Guidelines for Social Work Practice,* 8th ed. Boston: Allyn and Bacon, 2008 (Chapters 2, 3, 5, and 9).

5 | *The Client*

Learning Expectations

1. Understanding of the term *client* and the meaning of seeking help from a social agency in U.S. society.

2. Understanding of the process a person must go through in becoming a client.

3. Understanding of and the beginning ability to develop a social history of an individual.

4. Understanding of the influence of diversity on the needs of individuals.

5. Development of knowledge of what factors about any culture a social worker must understand in providing service to a client of that culture.

6. Understanding the need to be knowledgeable about client diversity in becoming a diversity competent social worker.

The term **client** in social work usually refers to a person, family, or group that is the focus of the social worker's helping activity. In the generalist approach, this term may be somewhat inaccurate because, as the social worker assesses the situation and develops plans, the focus may not be on an individual or system that has requested help. The focus for change may be on a system that is blocking the need fulfillment of an individual(s) or family(s); the focus for change may be on groups, communities, or institutions/agencies. Nevertheless, the generalist social worker's knowledge base contains understandings about all of the systems on which change might be focused. This chapter focuses on the individual as client, on the person seeking help. Later in the book, material is developed on engaging larger systems as clients and as participants in the helping process. These larger systems are made up of individuals and are social systems as well. Thus, as the generalist social worker works with various sizes of client systems, she uses her knowledge about people as unique individuals and her knowledge of social systems. Understanding the individual client provides a foundation for understanding larger systems that are made up of individual members. The social worker uses relevant aspects of her knowledge of individuals and social systems as she seeks to understand and work with larger systems.

The person seeking help brings to the helping situation concerns, needs, and strengths. He comes to the helping situation sometimes seeking help, sometimes being required to use help, and sometimes not realizing the nature of the help offered or the reason it is being offered. He has concerns and unmet needs. He comes from a societal and cultural milieu, a set of life experiences, and a set of transactions with other persons that make him unique, yet he shares the commonalities of humankind.

Regardless of the reason for coming for help, the client brings much more than concern or need to the helping situation. He also brings the total self as a biological, psychosocial, cultural, and spiritual being. This includes the resources of self and the personal environment and also environmental constraints. Also included are perceptions of self and the situation and patterns of coping with stress and patterns of interpersonal relationships. The present need is affected in part by the way developmental needs have been met and by needs arising from the diverse aspects of the client's lifestyle and from the expectations of the client's environment.

One of the major tasks of the worker-client interaction is to understand the client as a unique person in a unique situation. There can never be total knowledge about a client. The worker seeks knowledge about the client that is needed for giving the service to be delivered. The client is the major source of the facts used to develop the understanding of person in environment.

The social worker must also understand the meaning of seeking and using help, which is a first step to understanding the person seeking help. Understanding of the client also must include consideration of the multiperson client system. In this chapter, client systems in generalist social work practice are discussed. Each type of multiperson system will be considered in later chapters.

Becoming a Client

In the view of Emanual Tropp, the client is one who seeks professional help, one who employs the help of another, or one who is served by a social agency or institution. In discussing each of these definitions, Tropp pointed out that there are inconsistencies. These inconsistencies also permeate the way workers, agencies, and community persons view clients. Several questions arise from these definitions: Is the client a customer or a dependent person? Is the client seen by others as a charge or ward, a person not worthy of respect? Is the client seen as a generally self-reliant person, able to make decisions? Must a client seek help, or may the person who is involuntarily referred be considered a client until she voluntarily seeks the help provided?[1]

Scott Briar and Henry Miller discussed the client in terms of his social role. A social role has normative expectations for the behavior of the person filling the role. These expectations are held by social agencies, reference groups, and the general public.[2]

Allen Pincus and Anne Minahan used the term *client* in a somewhat limited sense. The client system is the system that asks for help; the system that needs to change is known as the *target system*. The system asking for help may not be the system needing to change. A target system may become a client system by realizing a need for change and asking for help.[3]

The client is a person with both needs and strengths. The need may be related to a person the client has a responsibility for; for example, a parent becomes a client when seeking help for needs a child may have. The need may be related to interpersonal relationships, in negotiating with systems in the environment, or in role performance. The need may represent a lack of material means or personal capacity (temporary or permanent) or of the knowledge or preparation needed to carry out social roles. It may be caused by a disturbance or disorder resulting in intrapsychic turmoil, constriction, or distortion; it may be a result of discrepancies between expectations of a person and the demands of various segments of that person's environment or between environmental expectations and demands and personal needs.[4]

For example, a client may be having difficulty because of inadequate income as a result of a layoff at her place of employment; she is a victim of the problem of the workplace. Or she may be a single parent who needs assistance with parenting a young child but is still managing to cope with the help of a good child-care provider. When that provider suddenly becomes seriously ill and is no longer able to help, the parent's unmet need is aggravated by outside conditions over which she has no control. Or the client may not be able to hold a steady job because of excessive use of alcohol and thus be the cause of the need not being met.

The need may rest in interpersonal relationships; for example, a parent may be unable to understand an adolescent child's needs and thus be so strict that there is open rebellion and an inability to discuss the situation between parent and child. The need may rest in an inability to negotiate with systems in the environment; for example, a patient in a hospital may be unable to ask the doctor the questions that bother him or to make his concerns known to the doctor. Or the need may rest in improving role performance; for example, the parent does not meet the nutritional needs of the child or maintain a suitable home for the child.

The need may be one of deficiency; that is, an individual does not have either the material means or the personal capacity (temporary or permanent) to carry out the tasks needed for coping with a situation. Or an older person with a limited income and limited physical capacity may not be able to maintain a home or fix nutritious meals. The need may also be related to not having the preparation needed to carry out a social role. The mother who did not have adequate mothering as a child and has received no instruction in child care may not be able to properly care for her child because she does not know how to care for small children.

Some needs are caused by a disturbance or disorder resulting in intrapsychic turmoil, constriction, or distortion. In these situations, the person may be mentally ill or have some perceptual difficulty that results in using inappropriate or ineffective means for coping with life situations. There may be discrepancies between expectations of a person and the demands of various segments of that person's environment. For example, an individual may expect that food, clothing, and shelter will be provided by a community social agency without work on his part, but the agency can only provide partially for those needs and then only if work is performed for the community. Other needs may be a result of discrepancies between environmental demands and personal needs. For example, a teenage girl whose mother is ill may be expected to care for younger siblings, but she needs time for completing her education and for socialization with her peers.

Diverse clients can experience different needs and also can experience similar needs differently. The need may be directly or indirectly related to the client's diversity. She may be experiencing discrimination as a result of her diversity. Responding to the discrimination may be the need. For instance, a female client may be dealing with sexual harassment at her job. Although this behavior is illegal, informal practices in American society have made such harassment difficult to eliminate. This discrimination may also create a block to fulfilling a need. In working with an African American or Hispanic client in need of employment or housing, the worker might find that the client's efforts are blocked by discriminatory practices. Again, such practices are illegal but still occur.

In practice, a number of terms are used for the client role. The term used depends in part on the setting for practice and carries with it additional meanings. Social agencies generally use the term *client,* but in medical and mental health settings the term **patient** is often used. When using the term *patient,* a social worker might see the client in a more traditional patient role, that is, as sick and dependent rather than as an interdependent person. In a school setting and certain institutions for youth, the client is called a *student.* This can lead the worker into an instructor-learner or a superordinate-subordinate relationship. Psychosocial settings use the term *consumer.* Social workers in advocate roles sometimes see clients as victims. The relationship may then be based on compensating for the wrongs of others and on doing for the client. Whatever term is used, the client should be seen not in a subordinate position but in a collaborative role, as having specific tasks and responsibilities that result in more effective social functioning when carried out in cooperation with the worker.

The worker, the client, and the environment all have expectations about how the client will fill the client role. The worker and the agency supplying the service have expectations about appointments, use of the time during helping sessions, time and place of these sessions, and the client's sharing of information and involvement in the helping process. The community's expectations of clients often center around the client's being grateful for the help provided. The community also has expectations concerning drinking, sexual behavior, child-care practices, and money management concerns. Clients often do not understand what is expected of them in the helping situation. They may expect to be told what to do or to receive certain kinds of advice and help or to be treated as second-rate persons because they need help. Clients usually come for help at times of powerlessness and a lowered sense of self-worth and with anxiety about the unknown helper and the helping situation. Seeking help and taking on the client role can add to the stress of an already-stressful situation.

Before a person seeks help from a social agency, he has usually attempted to meet the need in a way that has worked with previous needs. But if this is not successful, a person may then turn to his natural helping network, such as friends, family, relatives or a minister, teacher, or doctor. Going to a social agency is generally a last resort. Thus, individuals often come to the agency after a period of unsuccessful attempts to meet their needs. Going to an agency or being unable to **cope** can result in anxiety and in feelings of low self-worth or of anger.

When clients have a diversity factor that is different from those providing service, another stress is added. For example, when an African American person must seek help from an agency staffed by white people, the African American person may bring feelings of resentment and anger toward whites because of discriminatory practices he has experienced in other situations. He may be unsure that a white social worker can understand him or his situation because the white worker does not have sufficient knowledge about African American culture.

People come to agencies in varying ways. Frank M. Lowenberg has identified the pathways to help as (1) an informal referral by a neighbor or acquaintance, (2) knowledge of the work of the agency in one's social circle, (3) self-referral, (4) a formal request or referral from another professional or agency, (5) outreach the agency has done to identify persons with needs and encourage these persons to accept service, and (6) mandated participation by a court or some other authority. Lowenberg goes on to note that becoming a client requires a person to admit that he has a problem and to express willingness to give up a behavior if necessary and to cooperate with a relatively unknown person in an often-misunderstood process in an unknown place.[5]

People may resist the acceptance of help from a social agency because of discomfort with strange people and strange or new situations. They may resist because of cultural norms regarding the use of help. Cultural groups prescribe helping mechanisms, attitudes toward the use of help, and the kinds of situations for which one may receive help. People also may resist asking for help because they feel that no help is possible. David Landy has outlined the process a person goes through in seeking help or in becoming a client:

1. The help seeker must decide something is wrong.
2. The help seeker must face the probability that family, friends, and neighbors will know of his disability.
3. The help seeker must decide to admit to a helper he is in distress, failed, or is not capable of handling his own problem.
4. The help seeker must decide to surrender enough sovereignty and autonomy to place himself in a dependent role.
5. The help seeker must decide to direct his search for help among persons and resources unknown to him.
6. The help seeker must decide whether to take time off from a job or from other responsibilities to receive help.
7. The help seeker may realize that in receiving help other of his relationships may be threatened.[6]

In a study of farm families and the use of social services, Emilia Martinez-Brawley and Joan Blundall explored attitudes and preferences in help seeking. They noted that help seeking and help acceptance are very complex processes. The study found that some of the major barriers to seeking or receiving help are concern about community reputation, lack of knowledge about services, feelings about the use of help that originate in the community culture, distrust of workers, and pride.[7] Although the study was limited in the size of the population studied, it provided information about the importance of culture and context in understanding help-seeking feelings and behaviors. It also led to a conclusion that it is important for workers to consider not only the present context or situation of a client but also the client's historical context. For example, many farm families have had to migrate to metropolitan areas because of problems in agricultural communities. In the new setting, stresses and strains often affect the social functioning of individuals and families. Although there may be a need for social services, attitudes and ways of functioning brought from the rural setting are apt to be present, which affect the capacity to seek help.

The role of client is not an easy one to take on. Social and cultural groups have norms that mitigate against easy assumption of the role. Personal feelings of adequacy and self-worth are often threatened in assuming the role. There usually exist considerable discomfort, anxiety, and stress; there may even be a state of crisis when a person enters a social agency. The acceptance of this role also calls for energy when the personal system may have already depleted its energy supply in attempting to meet the need. The worker must understand the phenomena of asking for help and be ready to support the person through the process of becoming a client.

Understanding the Individual Client

Before a worker can adequately respond to an individual's need, develop a working relationship, or engage in decision making and planning with a client, it is necessary to understand that client and his situation. Although there are commonalities among people, there are also differences. These differences include ones that are related to the developmental stage and to present and past adequacy in meeting the individual's common human needs and developmental needs. Differences are the result of diversity, hereditary, and environmental factors.

The human condition is very complex. Each person is a unique bio-psycho-social-spiritual being. When person in environment is examined from a systemic point of view, the various aspects—of both the person and the person's environment—are seen to interact with each other. The outcome of these transactions is a unique person who perceives the world in a unique manner, who reacts to common human needs and developmental needs in an individualized way. The understanding of person in environment is crucial to all of social work practice.

Just as the worker must develop knowledge of self, the worker must also develop knowledge of the client. Some of the same tools used for self-knowledge are useful in gaining understanding of the client. Figure 4.1 depicts the person as a feeling, thinking, and acting system. In developing an understanding of person in environment, the worker seeks to understand the feelings, thoughts, and actions of the client; the human systems in the client's environment; and the transactions between the client and her environment, along with understanding the effects of diversity. The identification of a client's lifestyle, philosophy of life, moral code, and value system is possible only insofar as the client is willing to share of self with the worker and as the worker is able to make assumptions based on his knowledge of the client's background, cultural identification, and life experiences and share these assumptions with the client for confirmation. The extent to which the worker needs to understand these factors about a client depends to a degree on the client's needs and the service to be offered.

Understanding the client's roots, that is, her cultural background, is often crucial in providing service. The worker can use some of the same tools available for understanding his own culture to understand the client. It is most important that the client not be stereotyped because of membership in a particular racial or ethnic group; there are many variations within each of these groups. To gain the needed understanding of any member of a racial or ethnic group, it is necessary to individualize that person.

An understanding of the client's family structure and functioning and of the client's place in the family is very important. Family factors are some of the strongest influences in a person's life. Sometimes the person reacts to these influences by accepting and conforming to the family's lifestyle; other times the person rejects what the family expects. In both situations, understanding of a client's family is necessary to understand the client's needs, desires, and strengths. The genogram is a useful tool to use with clients when developing an understanding of family influences for both worker and client.

It is important to develop an understanding of client needs and ways of functioning to the extent necessary for providing the needed service. Thus, the worker should be selective about the information to be sought and should individualize the nature and depth of the understanding, depending on client need and the service being provided. It is especially important to set the stage for helping by identifying the strengths of the client and of the ecosystem. This provides an essential foundation for the work to be done. Planning that is based on strengths has a much greater chance of success. An ecosystem strengths approach has the potential for meeting the need more quickly than do approaches that emphasize altering the client's skills or lifestyle. An ecosystems strengths approach brings hope by providing a positive approach to difficult situations.

The method used for attaining an understanding of client needs and strengths is often referred to as a **social history**. In Chapter 8, (Table 8.2) we present a schema for the development of a social history of an individual along with a case example. Not all of the material called for will be important or available for all clients. In some agencies, for some situations, and with some clients, other information will be relevant. For example, in a nursing home it is important for the social worker to have information about the resident's avocational interests and friendship ties to enable the resident to remain active and involved with other people. Often, religious ties and experiences will be important. In working with an adolescent who was adopted at age seven, it is helpful to know something about the adoption and the client's attitude and feelings about the adoption. The schema in Table 8.2 is meant not as a fixed outline of what must be included in all social histories but as a guide to be modified and adapted depending on agency practice, client need, and the service being sought. The schema has three major parts: (1) a description of the person in environment, (2) an identification of the concern and needs, and (3) a description of the strengths and challenges of person in environment. The social history should be descriptive rather than evaluative. For example, family relationships should be described in terms of who relates to whom and in what manner rather than by merely stating that the family relationships are "good." Strengths and challenges should be stated as facts rather than as value judgments.

Social histories (both individual and family) are tools that are unique to the profession of social work. Social work developed the social history as a unique tool, and no other profession includes all of the knowledge and skills needed to produce individual and family social histories. In nearly every human service setting (schools, medical settings, human service agencies), social workers are seen as the profession that has responsibility for making this type of contribution to the service delivery team. In the social work change process, the social history serves as the assessment document for individuals and families who are clients. It is the product of the assessment phase and is recorded in the client's case record. In Parts Three and Four, we will be covering the assessment phase of the change process with various client systems. Chapter 8 will cover assessment with individuals. Chapter 13 will look at the change process with families, and Chapter 14 will deal with groups. As we cover assessment in each of these chapters, we will be referring to Table 8.2 and to this chapter as a guide for producing the assessment document.

Vital Roles

Any social history should pay particular attention to vital roles—the roles of work, marriage, and parenting.[8] With children and youth, attention should be paid to how they are being parented and how they are preparing for their work role (education). With older persons past retirement age or after the loss of the mate, attention should be given to how past functioning affects present functioning. Difficulty in one or more of these vital roles underlies most social-functioning difficulties that come to the attention of social agencies and social workers.

Human Diversity

Human diversity is an important factor that merits special attention in developing an understanding of individuals and families. Before a worker can understand the influence of diversity on any specific client, he must understand that person's diversity group generally. It is also important to understand the individuality of each person in the context of her diversity. The worker must also understand how the dominant society has affected individuals of a particular group. A person's needs arise from the expectations of the cultural group and from the attitudes of, and relationships with, the dominant society. In addition, restrictions on the diverse group that arise from the dominant society must be understood. It is also important to consider the range of differences that exist in any cultural group. Cultural understanding recognizes that persons in situations operate uniquely within the diverse group just as they operate uniquely in the larger social setting.

The influence of social class is another factor that must be taken into account in understanding the individual within a culture. In considering an ethnic culture, it is important to separate culture from social class. In other words: How much of the diversity is the result of membership in a cultural group, and how much is the result of the fact that the person lives in poverty? John Longres has stated that minority status is not simply a matter of cultural difference but also is related to relative power, privilege, advantage, and prestige of a group within society (social class is an important consideration here). He pointed out that these factors lead to the individual's perception of her place in society and her identity. This leads to help-seeking and help-using behaviors and influences the ways people of minority status perceive problems.[9] Kenneth L. Chau noted that unless "impediments to individual progress are taken into consideration in needs assessment, the meaning and significance of the client's attempt to solve problems may not be properly understood."[10]

Human diversity is not only ethnic or racial; we are diverse because of age, gender, physical or mental ability, physical appearance, religious affiliation, sexual orientation, geographical area, and socioeconomic standing. When diverse persons form an identifiable group with a common culture, factors of cultural diversity exist, and worker understanding of that culture is important.

Race, color, national origin, religion, geographical area, and ethnicity are aspects of or factors related to culture. Although the United States professes to be a nation that welcomes people with diverse roots or backgrounds, the actual experience of most of these groups has been quite different. Historically, the group that has been dominant politically, economically, and socially in the United States has been males of white Anglo-Saxon Protestant heritage. The signers of the Declaration of Independence were nearly all in this category, along with most of our presidents and our early state and federal leaders. In addition to sharing this heritage, most of our founding fathers were also among the wealthier members of society. People who have not shared this heritage have experienced a long history of discrimination and oppression. The election of President Barack Obama as our first African American president broke the apparent barrier to our highest office, but too many other people of color still have difficulty in gaining political, economic, or social justice and influence. These individuals continue to struggle against prejudice and discrimination, despite laws requiring that people be treated equally.

Native Americans have also had a difficult experience with the dominant U.S. culture. Some would categorize past American policy toward various Native American tribes as genocidal. At the very least, history shows a pattern of broken treaties and promises. Today, many Native American tribes live on reservations where poverty, unemployment, alcoholism, and hopelessness are epidemic. Hispanics have seen half of their native country, Mexico, taken from them as a result of the Mexican-American War. Many of those who remained after the war were deprived of their property and not given the full rights of citizenship that were promised. Today, changes in immigration policy are often aimed at restricting Hispanic immigration. The attacks on bilingual programs launched by certain groups in the United States are aimed at Hispanics, as are the "English only" movements.

Asians have also had a long history of unfair and discriminatory practices with regard to immigration laws. World War II, the Korean War, and the war in Vietnam have been fought against Asian countries, and as a result a considerable amount of prejudice and stereotyping toward Asian Americans lingers. A more extreme example of discrimination against Asians was seen during World War II, when many Japanese Americans living on the West Coast were incarcerated in detention camps. German and Italian Americans did not experience this fate.

In terms of religion, while the practice of most religions has been tolerated for the most part, opportunity for economic, political, and social equality has been limited. Catholics are the largest denomination in the United States, but they have had to fight for a share of political power. The only president of the United States who was Catholic was John F. Kennedy. With the terrorist attacks on September 11, 2001, people of the Islamic faith have been targeted for prejudice, discrimination, and various forms of hate crimes, including murder. It is regrettable that some people have responded to the events of 9/11, which represented one of the most terrible hate crimes in our history, by perpetrating more hate and hate crimes.

This history of prejudice, discrimination, and oppression of groups that are not made up of white Protestant males creates a suspicion and distrust of people who are white in most members of these groups. These attitudes present significant barriers to developing the knowledge and skills needed for diversity competent practice. In addition, most students in the United States are taught a Eurocentric view of American history that primarily concentrates on the exploits of white American males of European descent and is nearly devoid of any of the negative aspects of our history. Thus, the average student knows very little of the struggles that people of color, members of non-European ethnic groups, and members of non-Christian faiths have had to face in fighting for their rights. Instead, many students have been indoctrinated with the conservative view that equal opportunity has been available to all and that those who are not doing well have only themselves to blame.

Elaine P. Congress developed the culturagram as a tool in understanding culturally diverse families. This tool can also be used to understand the culturally diverse individual. Aspects of the culturagram include various circumstances around immigration, along with "language spoken at home and in the community, contact with cultural institutions, health beliefs, holidays and special events, impact of crisis events, and values about family, education, and work."[11] The worker can use the construction of the culturagram to understand the culturally diverse client.

Some types of diversity do not exist as a cultural group. For example, a person with a physical disability may not identify with other persons with physical disabilities; nevertheless, that person may be subject to discrimination, stereotyping, expectations, exploitation, opportunity restriction, and the like. The societal attitudes and behaviors toward the person with diversity are important in identifying need because of diversity; also important is the person's attitude toward self as a person with diversity. It is important to consider the impact labels can have on people with diversity. It is preferable to say the word *person* or *people* first so that the emphasis is on the fact that this is a person rather than on the "differentness" or diversity. Thus, it is better to say "person with a disability" as opposed to saying "disabled person" or "handicapped person."

Age is also classified as a diversity factor. People who are at the extremes of age are often marginalized in American society. Children and people who are old find it difficult for their voices to be heard. They do not typically find themselves valued. Children have limited rights. The predominant view is that parents have the right to raise their children as they see fit. Child poverty and child abuse and neglect are major social problems that seem to make the news only when a child dies. On the other end of the spectrum, older workers may find themselves without jobs when companies downsize. Middle managers and employees with higher salaries are the most likely targets, as opposed to younger workers with lower salaries. Older adults, particularly women, too often find themselves living on limited incomes and with inadequate health care coverage. People who are elderly do not typically enjoy the high regard that these individuals have in many other countries. Issues related to age generally are attributed to overvaluing young adulthood and to the U.S. economic system, which places a high value on wealth and productivity. Children and people who are retired are not participating in the production side of the economy and are even seen by some as economic liabilities. Similar attitudes occur regarding people with physical or mental disabilities. In the not-so-distant past, people with disabilities were isolated in institutions. Before that, many were hidden away by their families in cellars, attics, or sheds. Although attitudes toward people with physical disabilities have improved somewhat, attitudes toward people who are mentally ill continue to be predominantly negative.

Women are not a cultural group, though there is a sense of culture in subgroups of women, such as feminist groups. It is important to see women as having a particular kind of diversity and as having been affected by social factors that can undermine their capabilities, opportunities, and self-perceptions.[12] As we pointed out earler, women have experienced a long history of prejudice, discrimination, and oppression. During times of social change it is particularly important to determine an individual's orientation toward that change by identifying attitudes and self-image in relation to change issues. Major social change has been taking place with respect to the role and function of women. Thus, social workers should be aware of a particular female client's orientation toward this change, of how she perceives society affecting her as an individual, and of her view of her role and function as a woman. It is especially important that female social workers not assume that all women have or should have the same attitudes toward the women's movement that the worker may hold.

Two other groups that have experienced considerable discrimination and oppression are people who are gay and lesbian. There is generally a moralistic or religious basis used to rationalize this discrimination. The assumption is that people who are gay or lesbian have chosen to be attracted to the same sex. Given the overwhelmingly negative attitude of the dominant society toward homosexuality, one might wonder about using the word *choice* or *preference*. Increasingly, research is indicating that human sexuality is much more complex and cannot really be dichotomized into heterosexual and homosexual. Biological and genetic factors seem to play important roles, along with the environment. Even if it were legitimate to use the term *choice* in regard to sexuality, there is no room in social work or in a truly democratic society for discrimination against or oppression of people who are gay or lesbian or against any individual or group.

If the worker is to become diversity competent, he must be able to understand his clients from the client's perspective. Applying Dolores Norton's dual perspective to working with all forms of diversity, the worker needs to understand the effects of both the nurturing and the sustaining systems on the individual.[13] The response of the family and the immediate community environment to the individual's diversity is important to the individual's self-worth and sense of personal well-being. People can face a considerable amount of negative messages from the sustaining systems (organizations and larger societal systems) if there are messages of support, acceptance, and love from the nurturing systems. A good example of this is the "black is beautiful" message. African Americans who receive this message from within their family system can develop a healthy self-esteem even in the face of continuing prejudice and discrimination from the larger society. However, negative messages from the nurturing systems can be devastating, even if the larger society is accepting of the diversity. Of course if the larger society is also negative, the destructive messages can be overwhelming. A good example of this would be the reaction to the coming-out process for people who are gay or lesbian. Although there may be increased tolerance for and even some acceptance of people who are gay and lesbian in the larger society, there can be negative consequences from the nurturing system. If the family is rejecting, the person may feel totally cut off from his nurturing system. If he is fortunate enough to have a substitute nurturing system, such as friends or a gay community, he may be able to receive enough support and acceptance to weather these negative reactions.

Social workers must be attuned to current and past experiences of members of groups that have suffered prejudice, discrimination, and oppression. Some workers may be reluctant to consider historical facts regarding prejudice, discrimination, and oppression toward diverse groups. However, current attitudes are based on and reflect these past practices. The vestiges of these past practices can be found in attitudes held by diverse groups toward people from the dominant group and those held by the dominant group toward the diverse group.

Motivation, Capacity, and Opportunity

In determining a client's strengths and challenges, a useful framework is one that assesses a client's motivation, capacity, and opportunity.[14] Motivation is influenced by what a person wants and how much the person wants it. It is assumed that for a person to meet a need or to use an offered service that person must want to work on the situation or use the service. Factors that can be important for motivation include the push of discomfort, the pull of hope that something can be done to meet the need or accomplish a task, and internal pressures and drives toward reaching a goal.

Capacity can be broken down into three categories: relationship, capacity for growth and change, and physical capacity. In considering relationship capacity, the factor to be determined is the ability of the client to form relationships with a worker or other persons who might be used as resources for helping. Capacity for growth and change is related in part to the cognitive development of the client. The ability of the client to engage in growth and change either independently or with the assistance of a worker should be determined. A person's physical capacity is affected by certain conditions and age.

Opportunity refers to two factors. First is whether the client's environment will allow the client to use the service or to change. A part of this opportunity would be whether the client has sufficient energy for the change activity after the energy expenditure required to satisfy environmental and personal responsibilities. For example, a woman who is a single parent and the breadwinner in a family may not have sufficient energy to engage in an after-work educational activity that would prepare her for work that would yield a higher income. Second, opportunity refers to the availability of resources and services needed to support the change. Attention needs to be paid to whether the particular client can use available resources and services. Cultural or other factors may preclude the usability of resources and services by clients. This results in a lack of opportunity even though the resources or services exist. This conceptualization can also relate to workers' motivation (to work with this client), capacity (in terms of knowledge, skill, and energy), and opportunity (size of caseload, agency sanction, etc.). Opportunity may also be negatively affected by prejudice and discrimination.

Nora Gold has pointed out the importance of motivation when developing an understanding of clients. She noted that two factors seem to be of prime importance. One is **locus of control**. This concern is whether motivation comes from within (an internal process) or from influences in a person's environment (an external process). Also of importance and related to locus of control is the capacity of the individual for self-determination. Here the concern is whether the individual desires or is given the opportunity to make decisions based on internal factors (personal preferences) or external factors (situational imperatives and controls). According to Gold, motivational considerations affect the manner in which people select and define goals, which in turn are influenced by value issues.[15] An emerging goal for change is empowerment (see the section entitled "Action to Empower and Enable Clients" in Chapter 10). If the worker is concerned with empowering the individual, then understanding that individual's motivations can be very important. It is equally important that the worker be committed to assisting the client to maximize her ability to exercise self-determination and be guided by her wishes to do so.

Stress and Crisis Determination

In considering a client's strengths and challenges, another factor to take into account is the degree and nature of the stress the client is experiencing. Stress exists when any internal or external event or condition affects a person or social system so as to upset its usual steady state or way of functioning. Usually, coping and problem-solving mechanisms are used, and the steady state is reestablished. If these mechanisms do not result in some modifications that enable reestablishment of the steady state, or if the severity of the problem or the number of events to be coped with becomes too great, a state of crisis may result.

The crisis state is marked by disequilibrium and disorganization.[16] A true crisis exists when a person who has usually functioned and coped relatively well is rather suddenly in a state of disequilibrium and disorganization. It is important to differentiate between a state of crisis and chronic disorganization. Another factor to examine is how previous crises have been resolved. Sometimes a crisis is resolved in a manner that presents challenges for later social functioning. Inappropriate resolution of a crisis may stifle growth or cause negative relationships or feelings to develop.

Strengths and Uniqueness of Clients

Before leaving the discussion of the person as a client, there are two more considerations. All people have strengths that must be identified and called into play in the helping endeavor, some of which have already been discussed with regard to motivation, capacity, and opportunity. Other strengths become apparent when past problem-solving or coping mechanisms are examined. Strengths also exist in the individual's surrounding network. Elizabeth M. Tracy and James Whittaker have developed an assessment instrument relative to the social supports of individuals and families.[17] It is used to determine the components of a network, its capabilities, and its nonsupportive aspects, among other factors.

Focusing on strengths is an approach that is often difficult for the worker and the client to achieve or maintain. Because the goal of the helping process is to help clients address unmet needs, this tends to focus the process on what is deficient or missing. Earlier social work interventions used problem-focused approaches in working with clients. In using a strengths approach, the worker needs to resist the temptation to look for deficits or signs of dysfunction. Instead, she should seek out the strengths within the client and the various systems that make up his ecosystem. A strengths approach takes a positive "can do" approach that builds a solid foundation for growth and change. The first step is to develop a social history that provides an understanding of the assets, resources, and capacities of the client and the various systems within his ecosystem. There are two fundamental purposes for developing an individual social history. The first should be to gain a better understanding of and appreciation for the client as a unique human being, along with an understanding of the environment and the interaction between client and environment. The second is to develop potential ways in which the client can meet needs that have not been met.

When using a schema such as the one presented in Chapter 8, it is easy to miss the unique qualities of a particular individual or family. According to Jackie E. Pray, it is important to assume "at the outset that the client will differ from all others." She called for the use of the practitioner's practice wisdom and tacit knowledge in considering client uniqueness.[18] Also of importance is the development of mutual understanding between worker and client about the situation and the client, particularly the meaning of the experience to the client based on the client's personal beliefs and life experiences. Thus, the worker must be sensitive to information and understandings not called for in the schema and allow for the inclusion of this material when developing understanding about clients.

Social workers often become involved with clients after they have made considerable effort to cope with a situation, solve a problem, or meet a need. The client may be experiencing a high level of stress, be in danger of a crisis, or even be in crisis. Using a strengths approach gives the client hope and can help him to cope with this stress.

Summary

The client is an individual or social system requesting help or receiving service from a social worker. The client's capacity to request or use help is affected by her culture's attitudes toward receiving help, her past experiences in using help, and pressures and constraints of the context in which the help is given. It is important for a social worker to understand how attitudes about seeking and receiving help affect a client's capacity to function in the helping situation.

Understanding a client's past and present functioning and the various factors that affect functioning is a key skill of a social worker. This understanding is often expressed through the development of a social history. Factors that are particularly important to consider are how the client fills the vital roles of work, marriage, and parenting; how human diversity affects the social functioning of the individual; the motivation that the client brings to the helping endeavor; and the extent of the crisis and stress the client is experiencing.

Questions

1. What images do the terms *patient, client,* and *consumer* bring to mind? How do you think terminology may affect the way help is given?
2. What experiences do you believe help people seek assistance from social workers? What experiences make it difficult to seek help?
3. In what ways are people socialized to use or avoid using help by their culture?
4. Using a cultural group different from your own and with which you have not had considerable contact, identify factors that you need to find out about to have sufficient knowledge to work as a social worker with people from that culture group.
5. Using the human diversity schema, identify your strengths, needs, and challenges related to your diversity.

Suggested Readings

Appleby, George A., Colon, Edward, and Hamilton, Julia. *Diversity, Oppression, and Social Functioning: Person-in-Environment Assessment and Intervention,* 2nd ed. Boston: Allyn and Bacon, 2007.

Fong, Rawena, and Manoa, Sharlene, Eds. *Culturally Competent Practice: Skills, Interventions, and Evaluations,* Boston: Allyn and Bacon, 2001.

Ivanhoff, Andre Marie. *Involuntary Clients in Social Work Practice: A Research-Based Approach.* New York: Aldine de Gruyter, 1994.

Lum, Doman. *Culturally Competent Practice: A Framework for Understanding Diverse Groups and Justice Issues,* 3rd ed. Pacific Grove, CA: Brooks/Cole, 2007.

O'Hare, Thomas. "Court-Ordered Versus Voluntary Clients: Problem Difference and Readiness for Change." *Social Work* 41 (July 1996): 417–422.

Rooney, Ronald. *Strategies for Work with Involuntary Clients.* New York: Columbia University Press, 1992.

Saleeby, Dennis. *The Strengths Perspective in Social Work Practice,* 5th ed. Boston: Allyn and Bacon, 2009.

Sheafor, Bradford W., and Horejsi, Charles R. *Techniques and Guidelines for Social Work Practice,* 8th ed. Boston: Allyn and Bacon, 2008 (Chapter 10).

Voss, Richard W., Douville, Victor, Little Soldier, Alex, and Twiss, Gayla. "Tribal and Shamanic-Based Social Work Practice: A Lakota Perspective." *Social Work* 44 (May 1999).

Weaver, Hilary N. "Indigenous People and the Social Work Profession: Defining Culturally Competent Services." *Social Work* 44 (May 1999).

6 | *Environment*

Learning Expectations

1. Understanding of the importance of the environment as a part of the client's ecosystem and its influence on the worker-client interaction.
2. Understanding of the community as a social system and beginning skill in studying a community.
3. Understanding of the social service agency as a social system and beginning skill in studying a social agency.
4. Understanding of the skill needed for working in a bureaucracy.

The environment of the helping interaction—that is, of the social work endeavor—is the community and the social agency. The client comes from a community or neighborhood that has expectations and resources to be considered in the helping. The worker is usually an agency employee, and there are expectations and resources from that agency. The agency is also a part of a community. The community has expectations about the services being delivered by the agency and also provides resources. The community of the client and agency may or may not be the same. To understand the influence of both community and agency on the helping endeavor, the worker can use a social systems approach as an organizing framework. The helping endeavor takes place not in a vacuum but in an environment. Because of the transactional nature of human interaction, understanding that environment and its effect is essential for effective service.

Sometimes the transactions between community or agency and client are not congruent with the needs of the client, and, therefore, the community or agency or the transactions with them can be targets for change. As generalist social workers develop understandings and assess agencies and communities, they must be alert to when the agency or community is the appropriate unit of attention and when the transactions between the community or agency and the client or clients is the appropriate unit of attention. The first part of this chapter will focus on the content of a community study and an agency study. The last part will look at the transactions between community and client and between agency and client. Strategies for working toward change in these systems are discussed in Chapter 15.

In earlier chapters, the concept of becoming diversity competent was introduced. In understanding the environment, it is essential that the worker develop an understanding of responses to diversity from people and systems in the environment. Here again, the dual perspective proposed by Dolores Norton is especially relevant. Her discussion of the nurturing environment included family and the immediate community environment.[1] The latter refers to the neighborhood in which the person lives. Norton's sustaining environment consists of the organization of goods and services, political power, economic resources, educational system, and larger societal systems. These are the systems we will consider in this chapter as we look at the community as a part of the helping environment. However, the material in this chapter can also be used to study a section of the community, such as a neighborhood. In Chapter 13, we will focus on the family. Chapter 15 will consider using the change process with organizations and communities.

Person in Environment as an Ecosystem

In ecological terms, person in environment represents an ecosystem. An **ecosystem** includes the person(s), all of the systems with which the person(s) interacts, and the larger environment, along with the transactions among the person(s) and systems.[2] Thus, people and their environment are seen as a unified whole in which the various parts are interdependent. People are influenced by their environment and in turn also influence the environment by their actions. Figure 4.1 can be used to depict an ecosystem as a feeling, thinking, and acting system. In developing an understanding of the environment as an ecosystem, the worker seeks to understand the feelings, thoughts, and actions of people; the human systems in the environment; and of the transactions of people and systems in the environment, along with understanding the effects of diversity on the ecosystem.

In using an ecosystems approach that encompasses person in environment, the *in* can serve as the focal point for social work services. The *in* can represent the *in*terface between the person as a system (or a multiperson client system) and the environment. **Interface** is the point of contact between two systems. At the *in*terface there are *in*teractions that occur. To the extent that both the person and the environment exchange resources, energy, or *in*formation via these *in*teractions, **transactions** take place. When these *in*teractions or transactions are balanced, both the person and the environment benefit. *In*terrelationships are formed, and a certain level of *in*terdependence exists. Change in one part of the ecosystem will *in*fluence other parts of the ecosystem. When the *in*teractions or transactions are out of balance, an *in*congruity exists between the needs of the person or the environment and resources available to meet those needs. This imbalance or *in*congruity gains the attention of the social worker and is the reason for and focal point of social work *in*tervention.

A combination of ecosystems and strengths approaches gives the worker a powerful means to assist clients to meet their needs beyond the immediate situation. This approach also brings the environment into play in a positive way and dramatically expands potential resources for change well beyond the worker or the client. Instead of limiting the possibilities to whatever the worker or client brings to the helping situation, the worker and client can seek other possibilities by tapping into resources in the environment. In addition, as the client is able to experience this expanded range of resources with the worker, she is empowered to use this approach in working to meet other needs, now and in the future.

In understanding the ecosystem, the worker who is striving to become diversity competent also considers the attitudes toward diversity in her community and agency. She looks at each of the groups identified from her understanding of diversity. She looks for signs that indicate that diversity is valued by the community. She looks at patterns of race and ethnicity in the community. She considers to what extent these patterns represent current or past discrimination toward various groups. She observes how people of color, women, children, and people who are elderly or disabled are valued and respected. She evaluates community attitudes toward people who are gay and lesbian. Some of these indicators are apparent in the institutions and services available to various groups. Some cannot be seen but can be heard in the stories of people who live in the community. As she becomes more diversity competent, the worker learns to look at the environment from a diversity perspective and to be an active listener.

The Community as a Social System

The **community** is the environment of the worker, the client, and the agency. Different units of that community will have different impacts and influences on each. The interaction of worker and client is influenced by the transactions of the community. Service delivery is a part of the community system. Understanding these impacts and influences is an important aspect of generalist social work knowledge. To gain this understanding, it is first necessary for the worker to see the community as a social system. This knowledge is important not only because the environment influences the worker-client interaction but also because the community may be the client or it may be the target for intervention. In either of these cases, the worker usually works with individuals and small groups to bring about change in the community structure and functioning. For the generalist social worker, effort is usually focused on changing or developing a community resource that will in turn enhance the functioning of individuals and families. Whether the community or some element of it is the client or is the target of change, it is important to understand the community as a social system so that its strengths and resources can be included in promoting growth and change. Particular attention needs to be paid to these elements as the worker studies the community.

At a minimum, such knowledge calls for awareness of the boundaries of the community, its component parts (individuals, families, associations, neighborhoods, organizations, institutions, etc.), and its environment. The worker also needs to be aware of the way the community functions and of its historical development.

The identification of a community's boundaries poses a substantial problem in a society of large cities and multiple institutional catchment areas. Is an agency's community a geographic place, the catchment area from which the clients come? Is a group of persons who support and sanction the agency its community? Is it the immediate geographic neighborhood in which it is located? Should the entire metropolitan area be considered a community? Or are community and neighborhood the same? Each of these questions may be answered affirmatively under certain circumstances.

There is also a time element in the concept of community. The *community system* functions in relation to issues and to provide services (e.g., education). The *community units* may interact only when dealing with those issues and in providing services. Community units are groups (both formal and informal), organizations, institutions, and other social systems that function within the boundaries of the community. Thus, the community system also has a time element; it exists only under certain circumstances.

The community may be seen as a geographic place. *Community* is a term also used to describe "nonplace" associations such as the professional community or the religious community. When considering the kinship group, the extended family, or certain cultural groups, community is a related concept. The community system can have a wide variety of forms that can influence the transactions among individuals, families, and small groups.

Sociology furnishes us with several ways of considering a community. Ferdinand Tönnies saw a change in the relationships among people with the industrialization of society. He described this change as one from **Gemeinschaft** (rural "we-ness") to **Gesellschaft** (individuals related through structures in the community).[3] These differences among communities still exist. Rural or small communities function rather informally; urban or large communities tend to function more through formal structures. In searching for understanding of a community, a worker will find it useful to determine the kinds of relationships that exist in the community. Usually there are different kinds of relationships, depending on the community functions involved.

Understanding the use of land adds a dimension to the study of a community. One method of doing this is to draw maps of a community showing retail stores; wholesale businesses; industry (light and heavy); schools, churches, and other institutions; various types of residential dwellings; and the locations of various ethnic and socioeconomic groups.

Floyd Hunter's studies of community power are also useful.[4] The location of the community power structure is particularly important when trying to develop new services or to change existing services. This power structure may be formal or informal, elected or assigned. The impact of the power is varied depending on how the power holder and others perceive the power. It is exercised through initiating activity, legitimizing activity, giving approval to ideas and plans, implementing decisions, or blocking discussion of issues and of decisions. Usually, the impact of a particular power holder depends on the issue at hand. Some in power tend to have greater influence over economic issues than over social welfare issues. In large communities, where power is more dispersed, there is a greater chance that power is related to specific segments of community life. In small communities, power tends to reside with one small group of people. Identification of not only the individuals in the power structure but also of how they exercise that power and over what issues they have significant influence is another important ingredient of any community assessment.

Eugene Litwak's work on the significance of the neighborhood points out the neighborhood's importance for the individual in meeting need. He identified several types of neighborhoods and their effectiveness in meeting need. The *mobile neighborhood* manages to retain its cohesion despite a rapid turnover of residents. The *traditional neighborhood* is one in which residents are long term and that maintains stability. The *mass neighborhood* is one in which there is no mechanism of integration.[5] Understanding the kind of neighborhood a client lives in helps a worker understand a client and the resources that may be available for that client.

Roland Warren's work, which considers the community as a social system, is especially useful. He identified the locally relevant functions of a community as (1) production-distribution-consumption, (2) socialization, (3) social control, (4) social participation, and (5) mutual support. Each community has community units that carry out these functions. The business community has a major responsibility for production, distribution, and consumption. The schools are involved in socialization. Government is concerned with social control. Various clubs and organizations fulfill social participation needs. Social welfare organizations are involved in mutual support. Warren also noted that many community units have ties with structures and systems outside the community. These links are known as *vertical patterns;* relationships within the community are known as *horizontal patterns.* An example of this conceptualization as it relates to a church (a community unit) would be that the horizontal link would be a local council of churches or ministerial group; the vertical link would be to a denominational body. Warren saw the exploration of these patterns as a primary means for studying a community.[6]

There are differences among communities, just as there are among any category of social system. It is almost impossible to develop a scheme for classifying communities because of the many variables involved. Dennis Poplin identified three areas that seem important when considering differences among communities: size, the nature of a community's hinterland, and social-cultural features.[7]

Differences in size usually have been discussed on a rural-urban continuum. The U.S. Census Bureau uses a population of 2,500 as the division point between rural and urban. This leaves many different types of communities in the urban category. Another division point frequently used is 50,000, the population necessary for a Standard Metropolitan Statistical Area. In looking at nonmetropolitan community service delivery systems,

Louise Johnson identified four types of communities: the small city (15,000 to 20,000), the small town (8,000 to 20,000), the rural community (under 10,000), and the reservation community.[8] In subsequent work, Johnson identified two additional types of small communities: the bedroom community and the institutional community. The bedroom community is found near a larger community that furnishes jobs and often a variety of services for residents of the bedroom community. The institutional community contains a large institution, such as a state mental hospital, an educational institution, or a government site (state capital), which is the major employer in that community. She found that community characteristics are heavily influenced by the distance between communities that contain services (e.g., medical, social, and retail). Small communities that are at considerable distances from services in another community have a richer service system than do communities of the same size that are near communities from which they can obtain services.[9]

Metropolitan areas contain communities that differ: There are the central city, the suburban community, and the satellite city. In addition, some communities are inhabited by the upper class. Some may have a reputation for being inhabited by bohemian, intellectual, or artistic persons; others are middle-class communities. There also are the ghetto and the barrio communities that have always been a particular concern of social workers. Ethnic communities have particular characteristics that come in part from the culture of the groups occupying them. A social worker should possess an understanding of the characteristics of the particular kind of community with which she is working.

A community, then, can be considered as a social system that has a population, shared institutions and values, and significant social interactions between the individuals and the institutions. The institutions perform major social functions. A community usually but not always occupies space or a geographic area and has many forms. In modern society several communities may overlap. They differ in the amount of autonomy they have and the extent to which people identify with their community. When considering the community as a social system, understanding from many sources can be used to provide a theoretical base or to point to characteristics that should be considered in specific communities. In other words, different communities, because of differing characteristics, often call for different choices as to what is important to include in a community study.

In trying to attain understanding about a community and its impact on people, agencies, and institutions, a social worker faces two major problems. First is the identification of the system itself, which varies depending on the situation. Often a political unit is the defined system; this is a fairly easy way to define boundaries, but it is artificial and does not really consider parts of the community system that may lie outside the political boundaries. When looking at the neighborhood system, it is difficult to define boundaries.

Understanding a community calls for identifying the boundaries of the unit to be considered. Too large an area makes the study unwieldy; too small an area makes it too limited. In nonmetropolitan areas the choice may be a small city or town. In metropolitan areas the choice may better be a neighborhood or some other manageable unit. Creativity is necessary in deciding how to define the community.

Social workers function in many different kinds of communities: large metropolitan areas, neighborhood settings, small cities, rural communities, large institutions, Native

American reservations, and so on. Each kind of community has different characteristics. The study of any community as a social system provides understandings that can lead to greater degrees of client-congruent culture, to better use of available resources, to identification of when the community should be the focus of change, and to better identification of which work strategy is best suited to a particular situation.

Of special concern to social workers are diversity factors that exist in the community. The racial and ethnic makeup of the community is important to know. With regard to race and ethnicity, the worker should have knowledge about the degree to which various groups are integrated or segregated. She should note the attitudes of various groups toward each other. Is there respect or valuing of differences? Are there coalitions that have been formed? Are there adversarial relationships? How tolerant or intolerant are these groups toward each other? What groups hold power? Who has little or no power, and how does this reflect the general population? Similar questions should also be asked with respect to gender, age, and sexual orientation.

Some information about diversity can be obtained from census data or community surveys. However, much of this information is obtained more informally, through observation and discussion with key informants who know the history and have personal knowledge about various populations. For instance, knowledge about the gay or lesbian community may only be available from someone who is a member of the gay or lesbian community or from someone who works with these individuals.

The diversity competent social worker tunes in to the attitudes and stereotypes toward diverse groups and the effect that these have on members of each population. She is also aware of the values that each group holds and is alert to value conflicts and their effect on relationships. The worker identifies ways of helping that each group uses and seeks to improve her skills so that she can serve members of each group in a manner with which they are comfortable.

Second, the information that can be collected about any community is vast. It is never possible to obtain complete information. Some decisions must be made as to when there is sufficient information for understanding. Care needs to be taken to ensure that the information is representative of all units in a community. Some information can be found in a library in local history books, census reports, directories, and the like. Other helpful written material can be obtained from chambers of commerce, local government units, and volunteer organizations. Some information is not as easy to obtain; it may be known within the community but not shared with outsiders. This includes information about relationships among people and institutions and the community's decision-making and power structure. Information about norms and values may be obtainable only after observing and being a part of the community for some period of time.

In order to understand community interaction, gathering information from many individuals and small groups is essential. The generalist social worker uses both formal and informal interviews and observes and participates in small groups. The worker carefully observes a wide range of community interactions in order to develop understanding about the community and its impact on the functioning of individuals, groups, and families.

Because of the amount of material, in terms of both volume and variety, it is helpful if an organized plan is developed for gathering such material. Social workers can begin to gather some material before entering a new community. They also need to add to this material as long as they work in the community. As with all social systems, the community system continues to change. In Table 6.1 one means of organizing a community study considers major subsystems related to Warren's locally relevant functions. The table provides a means of identifying possible impacts, influences, and resources in the community system and looks for both horizontal and vertical relationships. Table 6.1 provides a social worker with a guide for developing a working understanding of a community. This table will be used again in Chapter 15, when we look at generalist practice with macrosystems. Just as with the individual social history, the community study represents the assessment document for community practice.

Once a social worker has the necessary information, it is possible to identify and understand current concerns in the community, the decision-making process, and the manner in which that community usually solves its problems. Issues relative to community autonomy become clearer, as do differing service areas for different community agencies and institutions. For instance, the school district, the political boundaries, and the shopping service area are often different. Also, at this point it is possible to identify strengths and limitations of the community system. Because of the size and diversity of the units (subsystems) within the community system, different parts of the system will show different strengths and different limitations. One way of focusing the consideration of strengths and limitations is to consider the overall quality of life as perceived by community residents.

A community study should include at least some consideration of the strengths and limitations of the community system, the manner in which that community solves its problems, and the capacity and motivation for change. Communities that seem most able to fulfill their functions and meet people's needs have the following characteristics:

1. At least some primary relationships exist.
2. They are comparatively autonomous (not overly impacted by outside influences).
3. They have the capacity to face problems and engage in efforts to solve those problems.
4. There is a broad distribution of power.
5. Citizens have a commitment to the community.
6. Citizen participation is possible and encouraged.
7. There are more homogeneous than heterogeneous relationships.
8. They have developed ways of dealing with conflict.
9. There is tolerance for and valuing of diversity.

It is difficult for a community to meet citizen need when (1) the problems lie beyond the capacity of the community to solve, (2) the organizations and institutions of the community lack sufficient autonomy, and (3) the citizens lack identification with the community. These community characteristics should be considered when identifying strengths and limitations of any community system.

TABLE 6.1 *Schema for the Study of a Geographic Community*

I. Setting, history, demography

    A. Physical setting

        1. Location, ecology, size

        2. Relationship to other geographic entities

            a. Ecological, political, economic, social

            b. Transportation, mass media from outside the community

    B. Historical development

        1. Settlement, significant events, change over time, cultural factors

    C. Demography

        1. Population

            a. Age and sex distribution

            b. Cultural, ethnic, racial groups

            c. Socioeconomic distribution

        2. Physical structure

            a. Who lives where?

            b. Location of businesses, industry, institutions

        3. Other

            a. Mobility

            b. Housing conditions

    C. Cultural setting

        1. Community norms, values, and expectations

        2. Community traditions and events

II. Economic system

    A. Employment

        1. Industry: nature, who employed, number of employees, influence from outside community, relationship to community and employees

        2. Distribution-consumption: retail and wholesale business, kind, location, ownership, employees, trade territory

        3. Institutions that employ large numbers of persons: nature, number of employees, types of employees, relationship to community, influence from outside community

    B. Other economic factors

        1. Stability of economy

        2. Leading business persons

        3. Organizations of business or organizations that influence the economic system

III. Political system

    A. Government units (structure and functioning)

        1. Span of control

        2. Personnel, elected and appointed

        3. Financial information

        4. Way of functioning—meetings, etc.

    B. Law enforcement, including court system

    C. Party politics: dominant party and history of recent elections

    D. Influence on social service system

    E. Services provided

(continued)

TABLE 6.1 *(continued)*

IV. Educational system
  A. Structure and administration (all levels)
  B. Financing, buildings
  C. Students
    1. Numbers at each level or other divisions
    2. Attendance and dropout rates
  D. Instructional factors
    1. Teacher-student ratio
    2. Subjects available, curriculum philosophy
    3. Provisions for special-needs students
  E. Extracurricular activity
  F. Community relations

V. Social-cultural system
  A. Recreational-cultural activities, events
    1. Parks, public recreation programs
    2. Cultural resources: libraries, museums, theaters, concerts
    3. Commercial recreation
  B. Religious institutions and activities
    1. Churches: kind, location, membership, activities, leadership
    2. Attitudes: values, concern for social welfare issues, concern for own members
    3. Influence on community
  C. Associations and organizations
    1. Kind, membership, purpose, and goals
    2. Activities, ways of functioning, leadership
    3. Intergroup organizations and linkage within and without the community
    4. Resources available
  D. Mass media in community
    1. Radio, TV, newspapers
  E. Ethnic, racial, and other diverse groups
    1. Way of life, customs, child-rearing patterns, etc.
    2. Relationship to larger community
    3. Structure and functioning of group
  F. Community persons
    1. Power persons; how power is manifest
    2. Leadership and respected persons

VI. Human service system
  A. Health care services and institutions
    1. Doctors, dentists, and other professionals
    2. Hospitals, clinics, nursing homes
    3. Public health services
    4. Responsiveness of health care system to needs of people
  B. Formal social welfare system
    1. Agencies in community: function, persons eligible for service, how supported and how sanctioned, staff, location
    2. Agencies from outside that serve community: location, services available, conditions of service, control of agency
    3. Conflicts among, overlaps, complementary factors of social welfare agencies

(continued)

TABLE 6.1   *(continued)*

      C. Informal helping system
        1. Individuals and organization
        2. How help is given, to whom
        3. Relationship to formal system
      D. Planning bodies
        1. Fundraising, regulatory, consultative

VII. General considerations
      A. Current concerns of community. Who is concerned? Why? What has been done about the concern?
      B. Customary ways of solving community problems. Who needs to be involved?
      C. Community decision-making process
      D. How autonomous is the community? Do various service areas coincide or are they different? How strong is the psychological identification with the community?
      E. Strengths of community in terms of "quality of life"
      F. Limitations of community in terms of "quality of life"

The community can be a nebulous entity that is often understood only intuitively. It can also be a defined system understood through organized study. In fact, through organized study a social worker is most apt to grasp the impacts and influences the community has on the social work endeavor.

Skill in understanding a community includes:

1. A framework to organize information

2. The ability to locate information and resources

3. The ability to identify the information needed in specific situations

4. The ability to analyze the information obtained and to identify linkages and relationships among information and among subsystems in the community system

5. The ability to interact with individuals and small groups for purposes of developing relationships and gathering information about a community

6. The ability for careful observation of community functioning

It is also through organized study that the social worker gains knowledge about the resources a community provides for all members of that community. Knowledge of impacts, influences, and resources leads to effective practice with individuals, families, and small groups. It also leads to a practice that considers interventions into the system of the community and/or its subsystems when these larger systems affect individuals, families, and small groups. Negative impacts, then, may become legitimate targets for change.

One community-centered model of practice, described by Padi Gulati and Geoffrey Guest, is based on experience in Quebec, Canada. It grew out of a conviction that poverty could not be addressed apart from social justice and social rights and that alternatives to

Case Example

Helen, a new graduate, faced her first job with both anticipation and anxiety. She had been hired by the Family and Children's Division of a Department of Social Services in a state adjacent to the one where she had lived all her life and gone to school. Having had field experience in a similar setting in her home state, she had some idea about how such an agency functioned. However, she was also aware of differences. In her home state the Department of Human Services was organized on a district basis. Her new job was in a state that had county administration.

She had spent about a week in the community where she would be working, getting settled in her new apartment. She was glad she could have this time to get settled and to begin to learn something about the community. It would be the community in which she would be living as well as working. She had discovered where the grocery stores were and how to get her utilities turned on. A neighbor who was also an employee of the department had told her about some groups she might want to join.

She had taken time to stop by the library. The librarian had been very helpful in providing her with the resources from which she could begin to develop her understanding of the community. She was glad that her social work class had done a community study and that she knew what to look for and about what to ask. Census directories, community reports, and books about the community were all available. The librarian had recommended one good history, which she had brought home.

She had stopped by the Chamber of Commerce office and had gotten a lot of information, and the local tourist office also gave her some material. She had started to get the local paper. Now that she was settled in, she wanted to get going on her new job.

Helen knew she had made a good start in developing her understanding of the community. She also knew there was a great deal more she would have to learn about it. She knew it would take time, but she already had an outline of the information she needed, and by seeking out that information and asking questions of those she worked with or met at community activities, she would enhance her now-sketchy understanding.

existing service delivery structures should be explored. It contains a strong preventative element and addresses the delivery of both community health and social services. Major features in the model include the use of multidisciplinary teams, universality of service provision, use of community networks, user participation in policy and service delivery, and egalitarianism in the workplace. Although this model developed using a community organization approach to improve services to individuals in a particular political and social environment, it also holds considerable potential for other settings. Generalist social workers with an understanding of community functioning might well consider the community delivery system to be an appropriate focus for change.[10]

The community is a social system. Like any social system, it has a structure, a way of functioning, and a history. It has energy and organization. The functioning of the helping system cannot be fully understood apart from the environment in which it functions, the community.

Understanding the Agency

Social work is an agency-based profession. The **agency** is the immediate environment of the worker-client interaction. This interaction often takes place in an office or building identified as "the agency." The influence of the agency is strong even when the interaction takes place elsewhere in the community. As an employee, the worker is a part of the agency system, and because of this, the worker is accountable to the agency. The form and content of the service offered must be within the agency's purview and guidelines. The manner in which the agency is structured and functions greatly influences the nature of the worker-client interaction. The agency also provides resources for both the worker and the client. To work in and use the agency in service of the client, the social worker must first understand the agency and its way of functioning.

Social workers not only need to understand the agency in which they are employed but they also need to be able to understand other social agencies. This is important if the worker is to help clients use the resources and services of other agencies. In addition, where needed resources are not available or usable, an understanding of the agency is a prerequisite to bringing about needed change.

From an ecosystems strengths perspective, the agency is a part of the worker's ecosystem and also becomes a temporary part of the client's ecosystem as the helping process develops. In addition, the agency has an ecosystem that is made up of the community. An important component of the agency's ecosystem is the human service delivery system within the community of which the agency is a part. Understanding the agency as a system and as a part of the larger ecosystem is essential to maximizing access to important resources for growth and change.

Agencies in which social workers are employed vary as to type and organization. Some are exclusively social work agencies. They provide social services delivered by professional social workers (MSW or BSW). A family service agency might be an example of this. The family service agency may, however, have a homemaker service or use nonprofessional workers in other ways. A family service agency is a voluntary agency; that is, it has a governing board of citizens and raises money for its support in the community (either separately or with other agencies). Once voluntary agencies did not use governmental funds, but since public funds have been used to purchase service from private agencies, this is no longer true.

Other social workers are employed by a variety of governmental agencies. They are in what is known as the *public sector.* These agencies are often state or federally funded. The worker is regulated by law and by governmental policies and regulations. Other social workers are employed in what is known as *host* or *secondary* settings. In this kind of setting, the primary function of the setting is not social service; social services are used to enhance the primary service. The social worker in a hospital is an example of this kind of setting. In other settings the social worker is part of an interdisciplinary team. The prime focus may be social service, or it may be some other service. Work in a community mental health center is an example of this kind of setting.

Barbara Oberhofer Dane and Barbara L. Simon pointed out that social workers in host settings have predictable issues that they must address. These include value discrepancies between social workers and the primary discipline in an agency, an often marginal status assigned to social work in such settings, devaluing social work as woman's work, and role ambiguity and role strain.[11] Thus, agencies vary with respect to several dimensions: size, means of support and governance, nature of the primary service offered, and range of people who are employed.

Another differential aspect of social service agencies is the **field of practice**, or the area on which the service focuses. Some fields are clearly identified, such as medical social work, school social work, and social work in corrections. Others are more difficult to differentiate. For example, where does child welfare end and children and family services begin? The important differentiation in terms of understanding the agency is within what field of practice the agency sees itself. Related to this is how the community sees the problems with which the field of practice is concerned. Does it perceive people who experience these problems as sick, deviant, or inadequate or as persons who deserve some help over rough spots? Community attitudes affect the agency and its capacity to deliver service.

These attitudes lead to another differential that can be described as people-processing, people-sustaining, or people-changing agencies.[12] At the people-processing end of the continuum would be the provision of an information-and-referral service with little follow-up. The goal is to give information. At the people-changing end of the continuum is the highly skilled social work clinician in a mental health agency. Many social service agencies are involved in varying amounts of both people processing and people changing. The people-changing focus of an agency may be seen as socialization or growth oriented, or it may be seen as rehabilitation or treatment oriented. One common problem of service delivery is when worker, agency, and community have different views of the mix of people-processing and people-serving. This leads to incongruent expectations for the outcome of the service.

The community provides financial and other support and sanction for the agency. It also has expectations of the nature and outcome of services. These resources and expectations vary depending on the nature of the agency structure and on the service the agency offers. These impacts also vary from community to community because the agency is one unit in the community system. As changes take place in the larger system, change will be inevitable in the agency system. Social workers who understand this relationship of agency and community are better able to understand and use the agency system in service of the client.

The social service agency is an organization. In its larger forms it is a complex organization or a bureaucracy. This complex organization is made up of subunits, small groups, and individuals. The agency is a social system with distinctive qualities that affect the way it functions:

1. The goals are external to the system. They are not primarily self-satisfying for those who are employed by the agency.
2. They are people serving, not product producing. This service function differentiates social agencies from business organizations, the goal of which is the production and marketing of a product.
3. The goals are change in knowledge, beliefs, attitudes, and skills. The means to achieve these goals are complex, and the measurement of the outcome is also complex.

4. A major component of the agency is professional people. The professional functions with a degree of autonomy and a commitment to the client that often conflicts with the classic and efficient functioning of organizations.

Because of these distinctive characteristics of social service organizations, social workers find themselves functioning with two different kinds of expectations: the professional and the bureaucratic. The larger the organization, the greater the differences. Bureaucratic expectations call for loyalty to the organization; acceptance of authority; working within rules and regulations; formal relationships; and an emphasis on achievement of goals, specialization, and efficiency. Professional expectations call for commitment to professional values and to the service of clients, ability to have a broad span of decision-making power, collegial relationships, and an emphasis on meeting client need and allowing for client self-determination and individualization. These two kinds of expectations lead to tensions in service delivery and are manifest in such issues as (1) How is the competence of the worker to be determined? From a bureaucratic perspective or from a professional perspective? (2) Should workers specialize or be generalists? (3) Should the focus be client need or societal need? (4) What range of professional judgment is to be allowed workers? (5) Are certain services and tasks performed best by professional workers or by technicians? (6) Should service be a clearly identifiable activity, or is there a "mystical something" that happens?

Before a worker can effectively deliver service as a professional in a bureaucratic organization, the worker must first understand the organization. A social systems approach, again, is a means for developing that understanding.

The first task in understanding an agency is to define its boundaries. The entity that operates with a great enough degree of autonomy so that a unique structure and ways of functioning have developed—in which the influences within the structure are stronger than those without—might be identified as the agency. In a Veterans Administration hospital, the social services department might be the choice as the primary system for focus if interaction among departments is limited largely to department heads. If the interaction is greater within a team of doctor, nurse, and social worker, then the unit team might be considered the agency. Because both kinds of interaction are important, however, the total institution might be the better choice. None of these answers is completely adequate. Whatever set of boundaries is used, it should be one that defines the entity with the greatest influence on the worker-client interaction.

The second task is to determine environmental factors that influence the structure and functioning of the agency. These influences involve other social systems and broad socioeconomic factors, including those that have an impact on the agency either by providing resources or by placing expectations. Some of the social systems that may need to be considered include:

1. Any organization or system of which the agency is a part (e.g., a national membership organization, a statewide organization, or an institution of which the social services department is a part)

2. The community (or communities) from which clients come or that provides support for the agency

3. Professional organizations to which the workers belong

4. Foundations or other sources of support
5. Community planning and funding bodies
6. Governmental bodies that regulate or supply support for the services
7. Colleges and universities that educate for the professions employed
8. Other social agencies
9. Individuals and families who are clients or potential clients
10. Organizations, such as churches and service clubs, that may be resources to the agency or its clients

Socioeconomic forces that should be considered include:

1. Economic trends
2. Societal trends
3. Community expectations
4. Community need
5. Political forces
6. Governmental policies or regulations
7. Cultural and diversity needs within the community

The third task is to understand the structure and functioning of the agency system. The factors involved include:

1. *The purposes, objectives, and values of the system*—These are spelled out in articles of incorporation, enabling legislation, agency handbooks, and other official documents. Also important is how these formal expressions are interpreted and implemented in actual service delivery. The agency's value priorities influence this interpretation and implementation. The history of the agency is important in determining how the purposes, objectives, and values developed.

2. *Agency resources, including financial resources*—Resources include the funds provided by the community, through either gifts or tax money; the building or other physical structures the agency leases or owns; and the people resources, both paid and volunteer, including professional and support staff.

3. *The traditional ways of working*—Each agency tends to use particular approaches in its service (such as long-term counseling, crisis intervention, provision of specific resources, group work activity). This can also include specific theoretical approaches, such as task centered, psychoanalytic, and so on. Agencies tend to work with particular systems, individuals, families, groups, or communities. They tend to hire workers with particular educational backgrounds for specific tasks (e.g., MSW, BSW, persons indigenous to the community). They have particular patterns of work (e.g., teams, cotherapy).

4. *Boards or other governing bodies*—An important consideration is the method of sanctioning the agency (public or private). If public, the laws, policies, and other regulations that govern the agency and the organizational structure of the larger organization of which the agency is a part should be identified. If private, the structure and functioning of the board of directors is the focus. Members of the board and their motivations and needs are also important, as is the relationship of the governing body to the agency and its staff.

Another element is the committee structure and functioning. This structure can be one of the board, the staff, or a combination of the two. It is often in committees that new ideas are formulated, that the work of the organization is carried out.

5. *The organizational structure*—This includes both the formal and informal structure, the administrative style, the accepted norms and values, the decision-making and communication processes, and the power and control patterns.

6. *The staff*—Important considerations include who they are as both persons and professionals; the relationships among staff (formal and informal); and the relationship of staff, clients, administration, and governing body. The professional identification and qualifications of staff should also be considered.

7. *The clients*—Often clients are overlooked as a part of the agency system. Without them the agency would have no reason for existence. In an age of consumer advocacy, this aspect of agency functioning takes on new importance. Consideration should be given to client needs, expectations, and ways of relating to the agency. The status, designation (patient or student, etc.), and values relating to clients should also be considered.

8. *Diversity*—Diversity within the agency and other agencies is an important consideration. Some questions to consider are: What are the hiring practices of the agency that ensure a diverse staff? Are there inappropriate attitudes and stereotypes? How do policies and procedures affect service to diverse groups? Do some groups feel excluded because of expectations for receiving help?

Each of these aspects of the structure and functioning of the agency system may overlap with other aspects. In developing understanding of an agency, workers should be aware of these overlaps and of the relationships and linkages between the various aspects. Workers need to be aware of any special aspects of their agency that affect its structure and functioning. In order to gather the information needed for understanding an agency, an organized framework is often useful, such as Table 6.2. This table will be referred to in Chapter 15 as the assessment document when using the change process with an agency or organization.

It should now be apparent that there are several subsystems that function within the agency. First, there are *persons*. Each person in the system brings personal and sometimes professional attributes. As these persons interact in carrying on the work of the agency, their attributes influence interactions. Second, those persons fill *roles*. Some of the roles are defined in job descriptions. Roles imply relationships to other roles. This relationship structure also influences other interactions. Third, there are *small groups*. These small groups may be formal work groups or informal social groups. The functioning of these small groups is another influence on interactions within the agency. Fourth, there is the *formal structure,* which includes the formal lines of authority outlined by the organizational chart. The chart defines the hierarchical relationships: who is responsible to whom and how the various parts of the organization are related. Fifth, there is the *power system*—the system of decision making.[13] It is important to know who makes decisions and how those decisions are influenced in understanding an agency. Each of these systems is important in the functioning of the agency. An understanding of all is necessary for understanding the agency as a social system. It is also necessary if the worker is to work effectively for

TABLE 6.2   *A Schema for the Study of a Social Agency*

I. Organizational Structure
  A. Identify the boundaries of the organization
  B. Discuss the structure of the organization
    1. Mission goals and objectives
      a. The purposes, goals, objectives, and value priorities of the organization
      b. The purposes, goals, and objectives of each program
    2. Describe the organizational structure (Include an organizational chart and narrative description)
    3. The organization resources
      a. Financial (sources and amount)
      b. Physical property
      c. Staff (paid and volunteer)
  C. Identify the organizational structure of any larger organization of which the agency is a part.

II. Organizational Functioning
  A. The sanctioning of the organization (public or private)
    1. If public, identify the laws, policy, and regulations that impact on the organization functioning.
    2. If private, describe the structure and functioning of the board of directors
      a. Describe the board (Describe members as persons and their positions)
      b. Describe the roles and responsibilities of the board (both internal to the board and with the rest of the organization)
      c. Describe the committee structure and functioning
    3. Describe the means of citizen involvement and input
  B. Describe formal and informal functioning of the organization
    1. Describe the accepted norms and values of the organization
    2. Describe communication processes of the organization
    3. Describe decision-making processes of the organization
    4. Describe power and control aspects of the organization
  C. The staff
    1. Describe the staff as persons and as professionals, their relationships, diversity, roles, and ways of working with each other and with clients, administration, and governing boards.
    2. Identify formal and informal staff groups and describe their functioning.
  D. The clients
    1. Describe the clients, their diversity, needs, characteristics, expectations, role, and status
    2. Describe the traditional ways of working with clients
    3. Describe the intake and referral system and how the organization obtains clients
    4. Describe the referral network and the organizations that clients are referred to

III. Development
  A. Describe the history of the organization

IV. Strengths and challenges
  A. Identify the strengths of the organization in terms of serving clients
  B. Identify the challenges the organization experiences in serving clients

needed changes in the agency's structure or way of working. (Specific strategies for working with agencies in a change effort will be discussed in Chapters 11 and 15.)

Recently, health care and mental health agencies have begun to be affected by limitations on funding and on service provision. Various funding sources, including the government, have begun capping funds and services. In these settings, especially, managed care is rapidly becoming the norm. Under managed care, the choice of making referrals to specialists or of continuing service is not left up to the client or the service provider. Instead, a third party is involved as "the manager of care." This may be the physician or an independent agency that contracts with funding sources to regulate services or an insurance company. Sometimes this management of care includes conducting an initial assessment and making a referral to a participating organization. It almost always includes a limitation on the amount of service and a requirement that approval be obtained to provide service beyond those limits.

Although it may seem that other areas of human services are not affected by managed care, various forms of limiting and controlling service delivery are major aspects of the "reforms" that are sweeping through social welfare. Accompanying this reform is a movement toward increasing competition among providers of service and contracting out what traditionally were government services to private corporations, including for-profit organizations. Eventually, all human service providers will likely be affected by these changes. For instance, in the latest version of "welfare reform," the limitation of five years of assistance is basically a capitation of service. When work requirements are added, welfare reform begins to take on some of the aspects of a managed care system, especially because client choice is limited. Several states are looking at contracting out their state social service systems to private for-profit corporations, including major defense contractors.

These changes will have a major impact on how agencies function and how social workers function within agencies. Agencies will have to do more with fewer resources. The competition among agencies for funds will likely intensify because some agencies will be fighting for survival. At the same time that competition increases, there will be a greater need for cooperation in order to coordinate services. To be successful, agencies will need to be able to adapt while walking a tightrope between competition and cooperation.

The emphasis for workers will be on efficiency and on working within limited time frames with clients. There will be a greater need for brief and solution-focused approaches as well as group work services. Although workers will be asked to do more with less, opportunities for creativity and innovation will also be available. Prevention programs and early intervention will become more important, as will more informal support services, such as self-help groups.

Another area that is in desperate need of reform is the amount of paperwork most social workers must do. Computerized records and computers that take dictation are gradually being introduced into the human services. However, what is really needed is fundamental change in the amount and type of information gathered. Much of the information gathered by human service agencies is never used or has little to do with resolving the client's situation. Social workers should take advantage of every opportunity to influence record keeping in their agencies. This is not only the responsibility of a supervisor or administrator; workers should question the record keeping systems under which they operate. Freeing more time from paperwork means having more time to devote to clients. Briefer forms of service should involve briefer records. If workers are expected to deliver services within shorter time frames, they will need to be much more efficient in collecting and recording information.

Case Example

The first morning on the job Helen dressed very carefully, for she knew that first impressions are very important. When she got to the office, one of the secretaries showed her her desk and got her some office supplies—pencils, pens, paper, and so on. One of the workers stopped by her desk and introduced himself. About that time her supervisor came in and said she had an emergency and wouldn't be able to see her until about 10:30; she gave Helen the manual and five case folders for her to read and dashed off.

Helen looked at the manual first. She looked at the table of organization and began to find out how the department was organized. While she was reading, she also observed what was going on in the office and tried to identify who the various people were. As she read the manual she jotted down questions that she had. She was glad she had had a social welfare policy course because she at least knew what the programs were and the federal laws that related to them.

At 10:30 her supervisor came in. Helen got her pad with her list of questions and the case records. The supervisor told her that she could begin to work with these five cases immediately.

They proceeded to discuss each case. Helen asked questions about the manual and the material she had read. She asked about supervision, what was expected of her, and how often she would see her supervisor. The supervisor said that for the first month or so she would try to see her twice a week but that sometimes it might not be at a set time. Then they would decide what to do about supervision. The supervisor said there would be more case assignments later that week. She wanted Helen to go with other workers two or three times on child abuse investigations before she went on one of her own. She should be prepared to do these as they came up. Then Helen was given a lot of employment forms that she was to fill out and give to the supervisor tomorrow.

Helen asked the supervisor if she had any suggestions for getting to know the community and the agency. The supervisor said, "Oh, that just happens, but maybe you would like to go to the interagency luncheon meeting with me on Wednesday." Helen asked if there were some kind of directory of the other agencies in the community. The supervisor told her that the one they had was really out of date but that one of the administrative assistants had a good list of the agencies and it might be a good idea to look at it. The supervisor told her she'd need a map too.

Just as Helen was returning to her office, Bob, another one of the unit workers, told her he had to investigate a child abuse report and asked if she would like to come along. As they drove out to the home, Bob told her that this was a family the agency had worked with in the past. While they were driving to see this family, Bob pointed out a number of things to Helen and talked about the west side of town where many of the agency's clients lived. Helen asked questions about the kinds of problems these clients experience and noted that many of them stemmed from lack of resources.

(continued)

Case Example   *(continued)*

> By the time they got back to the office it was almost 4:00. Helen spent the rest of the day reading records and thinking about how to approach each client. When she got home, she took stock of what had happened that first day and what she needed to do:
>
> 1. She was beginning to get a feel of the community. No one seemed to have all the information she wanted. She would just keep her eyes and ears open and jot down what she learned each night.
> 2. The information about the agency was a little easier to get. She would continue to ask questions and sit back and watch until she got the hang of things.
> 3. She liked the way her supervisor was letting her get started. She intended to try to see all five of her cases this week. Then she would make plans about what to do with each one. She thought that this way she could preserve her power of discretion. She was glad she had some clients to work with right away and could go ahead on her own.

Transactions between Person and Ecosystem

In addition to understanding the community and the agency as social systems in the ecosystem, it is essential to understand the transactions that take place between the client, the worker, and these systems. Sometimes fundamental change in the structure and functioning of the community or agency is necessary in order to improve opportunities for meeting clients' needs. However, most often it is not necessary to undertake such radical change. It may only be necessary to change the transactions so that the needs of clients and these systems can be met. Sometimes change is only needed in the transactions with the particular client system being served. Other times the community or agency's transactions with larger groups may need to be altered. The worker begins by gaining a thorough understanding of the relevant aspects of the community or agency through the schema presented. The worker then proceeds to evaluate the transactions taking place.

People have needs and strengths, as do other systems in their environment. The transactions that take place within an ecosystem include exchanges of matter, energy, and information.[14] Matter is any tangible object. In the social work endeavor this generally represents the physiological or basic needs included at the first level of both Towle's and Maslow's hierarchies of need. These basic needs include air, water, food, clothing, shelter, and health. Food, water, and air are converted by the body into energy. The rest of Towle's and Maslow's needs are intangible and represent transactions that energize a person. These include social, emotional, intellectual, and spiritual growth.[15] When the person's ecosystem supports meeting these "higher needs," he has more energy to meet other needs, both within himself and within other parts of his ecosystem. However, when basic needs are not being met, or the effort to meet those needs drains the person, then he has little energy to spend on meeting higher needs for himself or on responding to needs and demands from the environment.

Transactions that involve exchanging information are of particular interest to social workers. As people in an ecosystem exchange information, they are changed, as are their transactions. Human beings and their social environments are information-processing systems. We seek out information and use it to interpret our environment and to improve our opportunities to meet our needs. In fact, higher needs are met primarily by exchanging information. For instance, social needs are met by interacting with other people. As a society becomes more technological and complex, we become more interdependent. The exchange of information becomes the primary means by which even basic needs for food, clothing, and shelter are met.

The social work endeavor may involve direct exchanges of matter and energy, but most often it involves exchanging information. The worker seeks information from the client, as does the client from the worker. In an ecosystems approach, the worker and client form a partnership in which they also seek information about other parts of the client's ecosystem. This information is used to develop a plan that will meet the needs of the client and her environment. Chapter 7 will take a closer look at transactions involving the exchange of information.

It is clear that people are influenced by their environment while also having an influence on their environment. An ecological approach seeks to provide a theoretical and conceptual base for incorporating both of these factors into the helping process, including the interactions between people and their environment. The addition of a strengths approach means that the focus is on assets, resources, abilities, and capacities that will meet the needs of the client as well as others in the environment. In the long run, it is not in the best interests of the client to have her needs met at the expense of other people or systems in her environment. This would leave the ecosystem out of balance, which means that various parts of the system would experience tension that would eventually be released. When it is released, the ecosystem will seek to rebalance itself. In the process, the client may end up in the same situation she was in to start with or she could even be worse off.

The generalist social worker recognizes the need to examine the exchange of matter, energy, and information between the client and her ecosystem. He observes areas of strength where there is a mutually beneficial relationship that meets the needs of all involved. He also notes areas that need to be strengthened or changed because the transaction is out of balance. When clients experience a balance between the needs and expectations of their environments and having their own needs and expectations met, they are content with their lives and feel good about themselves and about their relationships with others. In addition, they feel competent and in control of their lives. This represents a state in which the client truly experiences as a reality the social work values of dignity and worth of the individual, self-determination, and having socially accepted needs met in socially accepted ways.

Working in a Bureaucracy

With the growth of a service society, many social workers find employment in bureaucratic settings. They are confronted with the conflict between professional and bureaucratic expectations—with human need, human pain, and societal injustices and with agency policy, rules, and regulations. They are confronted with the slowness of change, the seeming unresponsiveness of the system, and demands for accountability by the bureaucratic agency. They are also confronted with the need to find ways to use the agency and its resources to meet the needs of clients. This calls for a set of skills for functioning in a bureaucracy. Ralph Morgan identified five role conceptions that social workers have adopted in bureaucratic organizations:

1. *Functional bureaucrats*—These workers just happen to be working in a bureaucratic organization. Their major orientation and loyalty is toward the profession and its values. They look for interaction with, and recognition from, professional peers. There is resistance to interaction in and with the bureaucracy. These workers are usually very competent practitioners whose services are valued by the agency, so the agency overlooks their lack of bureaucratic loyalty.

2. *Service bureaucrats*—These workers are oriented toward the client but also see themselves as part of the bureaucratic structure. They maintain relationships with both professional peers and agency staff. They are ambivalent about their identification with the agency but believe the agency is the means to help clients reach their goals and to obtain needed resources.

3. *Specialist bureaucrats*—These workers attempt to reconcile "bureaucracy to humans and humans to the bureaucracy." They use the rules and regulations but are also guided by professional judgment. They understand that the human condition is so complex that it can never be encompassed by rules and regulations. They seek means of using professional discretion so as to make the system work in service of the client. They realize that, like all human endeavors, the agency is imperfect. They have a strong professional identification.

4. *Executive bureaucrats*—These workers' major orientation is toward the exercise of power. They are innovators, infighters, and risk takers who tend to enforce bureaucratic norms. They like to manage people, money, and materials.

5. *Job bureaucrats*—These workers have a considerable investment in a bureaucratic career. They seek job security. Their primary orientation is to the agency. They adhere to rules and regulations. They also live by the agency norms.[16]

When working in a bureaucratic setting, a combination of characteristics of the functional bureaucrat, the service bureaucrat, the specialist bureaucrat, and the executive bureaucrat seems most effective. This combination of characteristics would include a professional loyalty, a client orientation, a mediation stance, a sense of realism, a search for areas of discretionary freedom, a respect for rules and regulations, and an innovative approach to services. This is a tall order for a young, inexperienced worker but one that can be sought after. It would seem, then, that the issue is not professional versus bureaucratic but rather a search for means to combine the best of the professional with the best of the bureaucratic.

Robert Pruger has pointed out the necessity for learning bureaucratic skills at a time when it is increasingly impossible to deliver professional service without being a bureaucrat. He indicated that one can be a "good bureaucrat." A first step to developing these skills is the realization and acceptance of the reality that a career in social work will involve work in and with bureaucracies. He sees the key to being effective in a bureaucracy as maintaining the greatest amount of discretion possible. To maintain this discretionary power, a worker must be self-directive. The worker who expects to be told every move to make soon loses this power. The good bureaucrat also knows how to negotiate stresses, opportunities, and constraints. According to Pruger, the worker does this by:

1. Staying with it, not giving up on the first try
2. Maintaining vitality and independence of thought
3. Being responsible by understanding legitimate authority
4. Conserving energy, working only on some issues, and choosing issues that are worth the effort[17]

The bureaucracy, like all human institutions, is meant to serve society's needs. The social worker who can help the social service bureaucracy meet the needs of people can become a valuable employee. This can give the worker leverage to obtain the needed discretion. Another means of gaining this leverage is to gain the competence the agency sees as important. For example, if the agency is developing the case management approach to working with some clients, then the worker should seek information, go to workshops, and collect material about this way of working with clients. In order to maintain discretionary power, it is important for a social worker to demonstrate good judgment. Part of this good judgment is the ability to make decisions that are in compliance with agency rules and regulations, that do not cause negative community reactions, and that lead to effective service to clients. Another part of good judgment is doing the right thing at the right time. The attributes of self-directedness and good judgment are possible when social workers have a realistic sense of their professional self, when they use a knowledge base in making decisions, and when they develop a repertoire of skills. Some ways in which workers can enhance their effectiveness are:

1. Don't seek blame; rather, spend the energy available on seeking solutions.
2. Learn to do a lot with a little. Be realistic about the resources available and make them stretch as far as possible.
3. Be comfortable with uncertainty, ambiguity, and inconsistency. When these are present discretion is necessary.
4. Be self-confident, creative, and responsible.

The use of supervision can be an effective means of becoming a good bureaucrat. The supervisor can provide a great deal of information about the agency, what is happening, and what is allowable. The worker can negotiate with the supervisor for a degree of discretion. The supervisor can be a sounding board for new ideas. To use the supervisory process effectively, the worker must take responsibility for bringing questions and problems to the supervisor. The supervisor needs to have some knowledge of the problems that exist for the worker in order to defend him when questions arise from other parts of the system.

Social workers get into difficulty in a bureaucracy when they make unfounded decisions or do not determine the feasibility of plans they make. Problems also develop if their concerns are not focused but take the form of vague complaints. The expectation that change will take place overnight also can cause difficulty. An understanding of what the agency is trying to do and what is expected of the worker is a base on which to develop effective service. A thorough understanding of the agency as a social system is a prerequisite for being a good bureaucrat.

The development of managed care means adding another layer of bureaucracy to the service delivery system. Under these systems, decisions regarding the amount of service are no longer left to the worker and the client but are reviewed by another agency or entity. Managed care also has had an impact on how workers provide services and on how they document their work. Assessments may need to be reviewed prior to approving services, and justification is required if service continues beyond the allotted number of sessions. This means that documentation and service delivery are more closely tied together. The amount of service is usually prescribed by the diagnosis. Social workers in mental health typically have been reluctant to diagnose because mental health care is based on a disease-based, medical model of service. This reluctance leads many workers to give the most benign diagnosis for the symptoms presented. Under managed care, this generally means briefer service. Thus, it is important to obtain accurate assessment and diagnosis to ensure appropriate services are available.

Social workers are in a good position to adapt to changes brought about by managed care and various forms of limiting services. Their skills in negotiating systems, problem solving, and advocacy are needed by agencies and clients operating within this new environment. Social workers will need to promote the development of prevention approaches and adequate aftercare services in order to ensure that support for change endures beyond the formal intervention period.

Increasingly, managed care companies have employed social workers as service reviewers. Workers employed by companies that are committed to quality service as well as efficiency may find a comfortable niche in facilitating the maximum effective use of limited resources. However, those employed by a company that overemphasizes profits or limiting services will find that ethical dilemmas make it nearly impossible to survive with a commitment to social work values and ethics intact.

The development of managed care and the competition for scarcer resources have added to stress. Workers must account for their decisions and have external and sometimes arbitrary limits placed on the time for providing service. In addition, competition or limits on funding may threaten the survival of the agency. Workers feel stress about job security or how their jobs might change.

One phenomenon that has received considerable attention is *worker burnout*. Christina Maslach described this as "helping professionals losing positive feelings, sympathy, and respect for their clients or patients."[18] **Burnout** may be a symptom of stress in the agency system. It interferes with a worker's capacity to interact with clients and others in a professional capacity. Martha Bramhall and Susan Ezell described some of the symptoms of burnout as feeling unappreciated, loss of the ability to laugh, being literally sick and tired (suffering from headaches, backaches, stomachaches), feeling exhausted, dreading going to work, or having trouble sleeping.[19] Some people seem particularly susceptible to burnout. They tend to be people who take on too much for long periods of time, in a very intense manner. They are often young and enthusiastic about their work. Another group susceptible to burnout are those who use relationships in the work situation to compensate for a lack of meaningful relationships in their private lives. Workers who feel they cannot achieve their objectives or believe they lack control over their activities also seem particularly vulnerable to burnout.

Social workers need to be sensitive to their functioning and to symptoms of burnout. If they are developing, they should engage in a plan to overcome the burnout. Although stress within the agency system can be a source of burnout, the worker can develop lifestyle changes that allow the worker to function within the system. Identification of the condition is the first step. Once burnout is identified as the source of the difficulty, the worker needs to pay attention to personal needs that have been slighted. A regimen that includes sufficient rest, exercise, good diet, and other self-care tasks needs to be undertaken. The worker should develop a network of personal resources that can help in meeting personal need. Having a person who can serve as a sounding board and help in analyzing the situation is particularly useful.[20]

Prevention of burnout should be a goal for all social workers. Preventive measures include providing time and energy for personal needs—the pacing of oneself so as to provide a time to work and a time for self is important. Developing the skills of a good bureaucrat is also important. This includes taking responsibility for maintaining and enhancing one's sphere of discretion.

Using the strengths perspective can help in reducing worker stress and the potential for burnout. It is a positive approach to helping clients and assumes that necessary resources to meet client needs can be found or developed within the client and the environment. Instead of focusing on deficits, it looks at assets, abilities, and capacities. Even though the worker may still feel stress, she is relieved from the burden of being an expert who is responsible for having answers to client problems. Instead, the client is recognized as an expert in his own life, and the worker uses her expertise as a resource for assisting the client in meeting his needs.

Summary

This chapter considers the environment of the helping endeavor, the community and the agency. Both can be understood from a social systems perspective. The transactional nature of human functioning makes it essential that social workers understand the strengths and resources of the community and the agency and the influence of these two systems on the functioning of both worker and client.

If the worker is to be a generalist, this understanding is essential in making decisions as to the target for change and the mode of intervention. If the target is to be the community or agency system, the worker needs in-depth understanding of that target. Communities and agencies are complex systems that must be understood in considerable depth before they become a target for change.

Most social workers are employed in bureaucratic settings. Conflicts between professional and bureaucratic demands are often confronted by the social worker in these settings. It is important that social workers develop skills for dealing with these conflicts and become "good bureaucrats." Social workers are also prone to burnout and need to develop means of protecting themselves against this occupational hazard.

Questions

1. How does conceptualizing the community as a social system enhance a social worker's understanding of any community? How might the community be conceptualized as an ecosystem?
2. Using a community with which you are familiar and the material presented in this chapter, identify information you should obtain if you are to develop greater understanding of the community. Pay special attention to strengths and resources. Where would you go to obtain that information?
3. What factors do you consider the most important influences on the manner in which an agency functions? What might be some potential strengths and resources?
4. What are the differences in agencies where social work is the primary profession and those in which some other profession is primary?
5. How would you go about gathering the information needed to understand any agency in which you might be employed?
6. Using Morgan's classification (see the section "Working in a Bureaucracy"), identify the preferred way for a social worker to function in a bureaucracy. Why did you make the choice?
7. What do you think are some of the ways a social worker can avoid burnout?

Suggested Readings

Homan, Mark S. *Promoting Community Change: Making It Happen in the Real World,* 3rd ed. Pacific Grove, CA: Brooks/Cole, 2004.

Kettner, Peter M. *Achieving Excellence in the Management of Human Service Organizations.* Boston: Allyn and Bacon, 2002 (Chapter 3).

Mizrahi, Terry and Davis, Larry E., Eds. *Encyclopedia of Social Work,* 20th ed. Washington, DC: NASW Press, 2008 ("Environment," "Community," "Organizations and Governance").

Netting, F. Ellen, Kettner, Peter M., and McMurtry, Steven L. *Social Work Macro Practice,* 4th ed. Boston: Allyn and Bacon, 2008.

Netting, F. Ellen, and O'Connor, Mary K. *Organization Practice: A Social Worker's Guide to Understanding Human Services.* Boston: Allyn and Bacon, 2003.

Rivera, Felix G., and Erlich, John L. *Community Organizing in a Diverse Society,* 3rd ed. Boston: Allyn and Bacon, 1998.

Rubin, Herbert J., and Rubin, Irene S. *Community Organizing and Development,* 4th ed. Boston: Allyn and Bacon, 2008.

Sheaford, Bradford W., and Horejsi, Charles R. *Techniques and Guidelines for Social Work Practice,* 8th ed. Boston: Allyn and Bacon, 2008 (Chapters 9 and 16).

Tropman, John E., Erlich, John L., and Rothman, Jack. *Tactics and Techniques of Community Intervention,* 7th ed. Itasca, IL: F. E. Peacock, 2001.

7

Interaction and Engagement

Learning Expectations

1. Understanding of the one-to-one action system as one context for delivering social work services.
2. Understanding of the concepts of engagement and relationship and of their importance in the one-to-one action system.
3. Understanding of the specific characteristics of a professional helping relationship.
4. Appreciation of the complexity of cross-cultural relationships.
5. Knowledge about the use of the interview as a tool in social work practice.

The social work endeavor takes place in an interpersonal interactional process. This interaction is more than an exchange between a worker and a client; the worker also interacts with colleagues, community persons, professionals, and people who are significant to the helping situation (**significant others**). The interaction can be one-to-one, between the worker and another person, or it can take place in multiperson situations such as a family, a team, or a small group. Although there are similarities between the process of interaction of one individual to another and the interaction with multiperson systems, there are also differences. This chapter considers the interaction of the social worker with one other person. Relevant chapters in Part Four will consider the interaction in multiperson situations.

In an ecosystems strengths approach, the work that is done by the worker and the client involves other relevant parts of the client's ecosystem. In most cases, the client mobilizes the strengths and resources available in her ecosystem. This approach empowers the client to take control of her life and get her needs met while meeting the needs of others in her environment. In some cases, the worker may need to assist the client in developing skills. When the client is unable to mobilize resources or there is a major obstacle to doing so, the client and the worker may decide that the worker should intervene more directly either with or on behalf of the client. Many of the skills covered in this chapter and in Parts Three and Four are important for such interventions. Because the worker-client interaction is the core of the social work endeavor, it will receive primary focus; however, one-to-one interactions with members of the client's ecosystem also will be discussed. Much of the knowledge base relative to the worker-client interaction also applies to the interactions a worker has with other persons.

As discussed in Chapter 6, in an ecosystems approach there is an emphasis on the interactions and transactions that take place among systems. Figure 4.1 can be used to depict the transactional nature of an ecosystem. Transactions between people and within an ecosystem can influence the feelings, thoughts, and actions of people and systems and can also be influenced by the feelings, thoughts, and actions of other people and systems. In developing an understanding of the environment as an ecosystem, the worker seeks to understand the feelings, thoughts, and actions of people; the human systems in the ecosystem; and the transactions within the ecosystem as well as to understand the effects of diversity on the ecosystem. The client is considered a part of the ecosystem, and matter, energy, and information are exchanged among various systems that make up the ecosystem. When there is congruity or balance in these exchanges, all of the systems function in a manner that results in needs being met for the client and for other systems in his ecosystem. However, when there is an unmet need, there is imbalance or incongruity in the ecosystem. The work of the social worker and client focuses on restoring balance or developing a new balance. This does not necessarily mean that fundamental changes will be needed in the client or in systems in the environment. Instead, the emphasis is on bringing about a change in the interactions and transactions among systems (including the client). This approach is more realistic than approaches that hope to restructure or change a client's personality or change the basic structure and functioning of a family, an organization, or a community.

The social worker may temporarily provide needed matter or energy either directly or by linking the client with other human services. However, much of the work represents exchanges of information. This includes information that flows from client to worker, from worker to client, from client to other systems in his ecosystem, from worker to other systems in the client's ecosystem, and from worker to other work-related systems in her ecosystem. The purpose of exchanging information is to influence growth and change in various parts of the ecosystem, with the purpose of meeting needs and restoring balance. Much of this process involves changing one-to-one interactions.

Because the exchange of information is the focus of most of the social work endeavor, issues that are important in understanding the one-to-one interaction are (1) engagement and formation of a one-to-one system, (2) the nature of relationship, and (3) communication. Techniques to enhance relationships and communications are also important because they can improve the quality of interactions. As discussed earlier, the worker striving to become diversity competent uses naturalistic inquiry and intuitive learning regarding culture and diversity as she builds a relationship with her client and proceeds through the phases of the change process.

Engagement and Formation of a One-to-One Action System

An **action system** is formed because of the work to be done and because the tasks to be carried out require more than one person. In order for an action system to be formed, the worker must engage the client or client system (family, group, organization, or community). **Engagement** occurs when a helping relationship is established between the worker and the client system. An ecosystem strengths approach is based on the theory that needs are met through interaction. In addition to interacting with the client, the worker may collaborate with a colleague because each may have special areas of expertise relative to the work at hand or because the worker may profit from another view of the situation. The worker may interact with a client's significant other because that other person has some information needed for helping a client or can serve as a support or resource for the client's efforts in meeting needs.

In the worker-client interaction, the efforts of both are also necessary in the helping endeavor. The worker brings to the interaction a professional knowledge base and a professional set of values and skills for helping. The worker also brings the total self, finely tuned, to be used with the client as is appropriate to the needs of the helping situation and the worker's capacity. The worker brings skill in understanding situations, identifying needs, focusing on strengths, and facilitating growth and change. The client brings needs, a perception of the situation, life experiences that influence this perception, and the capacity for growth and change. The client also brings motivational forces for work in meeting needs or for change of self or the situation. In the work to be done, the roles of the worker and of the client emerge from what each brings to the interaction. Felix Biestek identified seven needs of clients in the helping situation:

1. To be dealt with as an individual rather than a type or category
2. To express feelings both positive and negative
3. To receive sympathetic understanding of and response to feelings expressed
4. To be accepted as a person of worth, a person with innate dignity
5. To be neither judged nor condemned for one's situation
6. To make one's own choices and decisions concerning one's own life
7. To help keep confidential information about self as secret as possible[1]

The first encounter is crucial in forming the action system because it determines much that will happen in subsequent sessions. The nature of the interaction, its kind and quality, begins to form at this point. The client will be making decisions as to whether the worker can provide the needed help, can be trusted, and has the capacity to understand the client and his situation.

The initial contact takes place when the person comes to the agency for help, either with regard to a need of his own or with a concern about someone else; or it occurs when the worker reaches out to someone to help with a need. Social workers disagree about whether new workers should read records of a previous worker before meeting the client. Records may present stereotypes or invalid assumptions that can distort the thinking of the new worker. They may focus on problems or deficits rather than strengths and resources. But if records can be read with an open mind and an eye for facts, they can be good preparation for meeting with a client for the first time. The worker needs to be careful not to develop unsupported preconceptions about the client and the situation. Unsupported preconceptions can endanger the formation of the action system.

In preparation for the first contact, the worker may decide to collect and review any available information to determine what is known about the prospective client. Consideration of possible needs this client might bring as well as potential strengths in himself and his ecosystem is also useful. The worker can also get in touch with feelings she might have about the particular client in situation and about possible feelings of the client.

Based on the preliminary understanding of client in situation, the worker can structure the first encounter to make the client feel comfortable. This structuring will also involve environmental factors related to the time and place of the encounter—for example, the nature of the worker's greeting as the client enters the agency and meets the worker, the placement of desks so as not to be barriers between worker and client, and comfort in terms of temperature and privacy for the encounter. Choice of a time for the client is also important.

At the point of contact the worker will attempt to make the client as comfortable as possible. Cultural factors need to be taken into consideration. If the client comes from a culture in which small talk is used before getting on with the task at hand, the worker should engage in a bit of small talk. If, however, the client is anxious about the purpose of the interaction and comes from a culture that wastes few words, the worker will quickly explain what is to be done together. In other words, it is important to structure the initial contact from the interactional framework of the client, not from the worker's framework. The worker should demonstrate to the client what will happen in the work together as soon as possible and to the extent possible. The worker does this by:

1. Being attentive to what the client is saying and being receptive to his feelings
2. Demonstrating a real desire to help the client and giving the client some indication that the worker knows how to help
3. Actively asking the client to share his perceptions of the situation (asking the client about the significance of the need, about the onset and attempts at meeting the need, and about the solutions desired are other ways to involve the client and demonstrate the way of working together)
4. Attempting to answer any unspoken questions the client may have (e.g., he may not be sure if the information being shared will be available to anyone else)

5. Explaining something about the way the agency delivers service, the kind of help it gives, and the procedures for using that help
6. Focusing on strengths and potential resources within the client and within his ecosystem (this reduces feelings of blame and of helplessness or hopelessness and communicates a positive "can do" approach to meeting needs)
7. Trying to reach for the feelings the client is having about what is happening

In other words, the worker does as much as possible to enable the client to become engaged in helping himself in the need-meeting, problem-solving activity. In addition, attention should be given to supporting and developing self-esteem in the client. Partly, this can happen through the realization by the client that he is capable of participating in the search for solutions. Under no circumstances should the worker give unrealistic assurances about the outcome of the service.

As the worker is demonstrating to the client the way in which both can work together, she is also gathering information, understanding client functioning and the need as seen by the client, and enabling the client to think about the situation and perhaps see it in a new perspective. The social history is begun. The worker encourages a climate of trust to develop. Until the client can trust the worker, the relationship is tenuous and the interaction is influenced by the client's concerns about the trustworthiness of the worker. As the client experiences the concern, understanding, and expertise of the worker, there is usually a reduction of these concerns and a strengthening of the relationship. This is further facilitated when the worker uses an ecosystems strengths approach because the focus is on resolving the situation in a positive way rather than an examination of what is wrong.

During this exploratory phase of the initial contact, the worker's task is to test out ideas about the nature of the need and the potential strengths; to gather information about client in situation, with an emphasis on the strengths of the client and his ecosystem; and to define expectations for the client about the nature of service, relationships, and behaviors. The worker is nonauthoritarian, genuine, accepting, and empathic. The client is gathering information about the agency, its services, and the helping process and is also providing information needed to give the worker understanding. The goal is to develop what Nick F. Coady identified as a "therapeutic alliance." He defined this as "an observable ability of the worker and client to work together in a realistic collaborative relationship based on mutual liking, trust, respect, and commitment to the work of counseling."[2]

Sometimes the client presents an angry, hostile, and resistive front. Carl Hartman and Diane Reynolds noted that this front is used when the client is frightened and hurting and lacks trust in the worker and in the process of help. They suggested using an approach that they identify as confrontation, interpretation, and alliance. After searching for the source of the feelings and associated behaviors, the worker first confronts the client about the behavior with questions or other means that communicate that the worker recognizes the feelings and the resistance to help. This is not a hostile, personal confrontation, but one that lets the client know that the worker is willing to accept his anger and hear him out. Immediately thereafter the worker provides the client with an interpretation of the meaning or source of the feelings and associated behaviors. Then the worker provides the client with support and encouragement.[3] This approach often allows the client to feel accepted, which leads to a trusting and working relationship.

When the worker decides that sufficient understanding has developed, she refocuses the discussion to service delivery. During this next stage, the worker and the client discuss whether the need as the client sees it is one that the worker, agency, and client can work on meeting. They discuss whether the client is willing to work on meeting the need in the way expected by the agency, if this seems appropriate. The worker and client discuss other possibilities for need fulfillment. The worker attempts to break down the situation into parts for the client and identify potential strengths so that it does not seem overwhelming. The worker outlines the realities of what the client can expect from the service.

During this phase the worker and client decide whether (1) they can work together on the concern or need brought by the client, (2) some other need should be worked on, (3) the service needed by the client is better delivered by another resource, and (4) the client desires not to use further services. There are times when all a client needs is to discuss a situation and gain a new perspective or knowledge of unthought-of resources. The client can then cope without further service.

In deciding whether to continue to work together (to form an action system), the worker and client need to make explicit the expectations of each person, the possible goals and expected outcomes of the service, the role of each person, and the ways of working together. The worker looks for feelings the client may have and brings negative feelings and disagreements out into the open so they can be examined and discussed. It is very important to discuss the limits of confidentiality connected with the service. Also, the worker should be sure that all terms being used are understood by the client.

If the decision is made to work together, an agreement or preliminary contract may be developed that states the next steps of the work as well as the responsibility of both worker and client and time frames for accomplishing the needed task. The contract or agreement should also indicate hoped-for outcomes of the service. (The concept of contract will be developed in Chapter 9.)

During the negotiation and contract stage, the worker openly faces and deals with resistance. Edith Ankersmit, in discussing contracting in probation settings, has suggested that in dealing with resistance it is useful to help the client discuss two questions: Why am I here? How do I feel about being here? This discussion will allow the client to ventilate hostile feelings. The worker must not deny the existence of such feelings; rather, the worker should actively listen and point out the reality of such feelings. According to Ankersmit, it is important to point out the power the worker has in the situation and particularly note its limits and the power the client maintains. This discussion can communicate to clients that they do have responsibility for their own behavior.[4]

Charles Horejsi called for a motivation, capacity, and opportunity approach in working with clients on probation. He pointed out that it is particularly important to try to identify the problem from the client's point of view and then decide with the client if the problem can be worked on together. He stated that the client must believe that there is hope for a solution and recognize a feeling of discomfort about the problem. The balance between hope for relief and recognition of discomfort is very important; both must be present, yet neither should overwhelm the other. He pointed out that there is discomfort in change. This must be considered when determining the client's capacity for change. Workers should attempt to lessen the discomfort concerning change as one means of lowering resistance.[5] One source of resistance may be environmental factors. For example, if a person's peers are supporting delinquent behavior, it can be difficult for him to give it up. The discomfort of losing the companionship of one's peers may be so great that the change carries too great a price for the client.

During this stage, the worker attempts to provide a climate that allows for productive discussion and a focus for the work together and to identify behavioral, cognitive, and emotional responses of the client to the work at hand and possible future work together. The worker also needs to keep in touch with her own feelings and to share these, as appropriate, with the client.

When agreement about the work together is reached, engagement is established. The worker should summarize what has happened in the previous stages of exploration and negotiation. It is also important to be sure that the next steps, the next session together, and any tasks to be accomplished before the next session are clearly understood.

Engagement and the formation of the action system may be accomplished in one session or several sessions. During this formation the worker attempts to bridge gaps in understanding; set the tone for the work; develop client involvement in the work to be done; maintain a focus on the work; tune in to the client's feelings, way of functioning, and concerns; and identify potential strengths and resources in the client and his ecosystem. In carrying out the worker role, the worker is sensitive to the readiness of the client to move from one stage of work to another.

Several blocks can prevent the formation of a functional worker-client system. The worker should be aware of these and attempt to prevent them from interfering with the system's functioning. First, there is the complexity of human functioning. Relationships between persons with different life experiences and cultural backgrounds are particularly difficult. Misunderstandings happen easily. Bias and prejudice are often present. These lead to differences in perception of what is happening in the work together.

A second block can be the client's fears. He may fear depersonalization, powerlessness, being judged, or having irrelevant goals placed on him. These fears can lead to feelings of anger. The client may keep distance between himself and the worker or avoid appropriate involvement in the work together. The fears may result from prejudices and unrealistic expectations on the part of the client.

A third block can be the worker as an employee of a bureaucratic organization. The complexity of rules and regulations and the inability of an organization to individualize clients often get in the way of providing the needed service. The worker may have feelings of powerlessness and may not feel appreciated by the agency, leading to frustrations that hamper responding to the client appropriately.

A fourth block can be inadequate communication, which can also be related to the differing cultures of worker and client. Because of poor communication, the client may not understand what is expected in the work together. The client also may not be able to sense the worker's interest and readiness to help or may see the worker as incompetent.

A fifth block relates to the worker's sense of purpose. If she has unrealistic expectations for self and clients, the client may sense this and avoid engagement in the tasks at hand. Workers sometimes aspire to heal all, know all, and love all; this leads to unrealistic expectations. Other workers have strong nurturing drives and tend to place clients in overly dependent relationships. Still other workers may avoid conflict, anger, and aggressive behavior. This stifles the expression of feelings that need to be considered in the development of the action system.

A final block is the underlying assumptions or theory base chosen by the worker for explaining the situation. For example, if the assumptions label the client as sick, the worker may be hesitant to demand work from the client, and this may lead to more dependency in the relationship than is merited. If the assumptions assign blame, as might occur with a family of a child who is acting out at school, this will influence the worker's relationship with that family.

When working with the nonvoluntary client, it is particularly important to pay attention to these blocks. Unwilling clients often do not see the need for service, do not believe help is possible, or have difficulty in developing a relationship with the worker. In this situation, workers can sometimes overcome resistance by pointing out the reason for the concern or the consequences of a lack of change. A caring, nonjudgmental approach that focuses on the client's concerns and desires can often provide the nonvoluntary client with a unique helping experience and reduce resistance to help. The nonvoluntary client can be very sensitive to any hint of blame. Thus, using an ecosystems strengths approach can be very helpful in working with a nonvoluntary client because the focus is on changing interactions and transactions in a positive way as opposed to looking for causes.

The worker has a responsibility to attempt to engage a resistant client when services have been mandated by a societal institution or when the client or a person for whom the client is responsible is in danger of significant harm. In doing this, the worker should try to relate as much as possible to the client's frame of reference. She should attempt to use the client's communication patterns and should not catch the client unaware. She should say why there is a concern and what the consequences of not resolving the situation might be. She should openly deal with either hostility or quiet inertia and should support the client's strengths. In working with a resistive client, the worker must be reasonably comfortable with the authority she carries and be reasonable and supportive in its use. Often the resistant client misunderstands the nature of the service, has unmet needs that mitigate against dealing with the situation, has inadequate cognitive capacity to deal with the situation, or is influenced by the environment in a way that prevents need fulfillment. In working with a resistant client, the worker should determine the source of the resistance and attempt to overcome it if possible; otherwise, a functioning action system may not form.

Often a bargaining strategy can be used. The worker can make individuals who are resisting services aware of benefits from working with the social worker. For example, a neglecting mother can come to understand that cooperation with the worker may prevent removal of her children from her care. A juvenile delinquent can come to see that cooperation with the worker can prevent placement in an institution. An institutionalized youth can see that by adhering to certain rules and carrying out prescribed tasks he can gain desired privileges.

In using these strategies, it is important that the worker acknowledge the client's anger and resentment and develop with him a plan that incorporates the object of his concern. For instance, if a client has been ordered by a court to receive services, he is likely to be angry, hostile, and resistant. The worker might begin by asking the client how he feels about working with her. This will likely bring his anger to the surface. At some point, he will express a desire to not be there. Instead of trying to talk the client out of his anger and into liking the situation, the worker should accept these feelings and seek to form an alliance by finding ways in which he will not have to come for service. Of course, this generally means reaching a point at which the client is functioning at a level that will satisfy the court that the situation is resolved. The worker may help the client to see that because he has to be there it is better to work on his concerns rather than waste his time.

The development of the action system may be limited by the time available to the worker and client, by the skill of the worker, by ethical considerations, by the agency function, and by the client's desires. The worker and client must decide together on the desirability and the ways of working together.

Another type of two-person action system that social workers are often involved in is one made up of a social worker and a person who is not a client. This is a common arrangement when using an ecosystems strengths approach because mobilizing potential resources and changing interactions and transactions are the focus of the work. The nonclient is generally a member of the client's ecosystem and can be a significant other in a client's life, a resource provider, or an individual who is or could be involved in a helping endeavor. In utilizing an ecosystems approach, the worker uses resources in the community and within her work-related ecosystem. In this case, the individual might be another service provider, an influential community member, a person who is or could be involved in action plans focused on community or organizational change, or a person whom the worker is seeking to educate about some aspect of service delivery or the social welfare system.

Although worker-nonclient relationships are somewhat different, the worker still must pay attention to the formation of the action system. The same principles apply to these systems as apply to worker-client systems. If a worker uses the process of precontact, exploration, negotiation, and agreement, both parties are more aware of the reason for working together and of the responsibility of each party for that work. Nonclient individuals may also display resistance. Exploration of the resistance is a first step in overcoming it and in deciding if it is possible to form a functional action system. A positive, strengths-based approach tends to result in less resistance than an approach that focuses on deficits or problems.

Relationship

Relationship is the cohesive quality of the action system. It is the product of interaction between two persons. *Relationship* is a term of considerable historical significance in social work practice. It has often been expressed as "good rapport," or engagement, with the client. The development of a good relationship has been seen as a necessary ingredient of the helping endeavor. Helen Harris Perlman has provided a description of relationship and its importance: "Relationship is a catalyst, an enabling dynamism in the support, nurture and freeing of people's energies and motivation toward problem solving and the use of help."[6] In her view, relationship is an emotional bond and is the means for humanizing help. Further, she stated, "'Good' relationship is held to be so in that it provides stimulus and nurture.... [It] respects and nourishes the self-hood of the other.... [It] provides a sense of security and at-oneness."[7]

The social work relationship is both a professional and a helping relationship. A **professional relationship** is one in which there is an agreed-on purpose; one that has a specific time frame; one in which the worker devotes self to the interests of the client; and one that carries the authority of specialized knowledge, a professional code of ethics, and specialized skill. In addition, a professional relationship is controlled in that the worker attempts to maintain objectivity toward the work at hand and to be aware and in charge of her own feelings, reactions, and impulses.[8]

The Helping Relationship

A great deal has been written about the nature of *helping relationships.*[9] The characteristics that appear most often in these discussions include the following:

1. *Concern for others*—An attitude that reflects warmth, sincere liking, friendliness, support, and an interest in the client. It communicates a real desire to understand person in situation.

2. *Commitment and obligation*—A sense of responsibility for the helping situation. Dependability and consistency are also involved. The worker must have a willingness to enter into the world of others, with its hurts and joys, its frustrations and commitments.

3. *Acceptance*—A nonjudgmental, noncritical attitude on the part of the worker, as well as a realistic trust of the client and respect for the client's feelings. Belief that the client can handle her own problems and can take charge of her own life.

4. *Empathy*—An ability to communicate to the client that the worker cares, has concern for the client, is hearing what the client is perceiving, wants to understand, and is hearing and understanding.

5. *Clear communication*—The capacity to communicate to the client in ways that enable the client to fully understand the message being sent.

6. *Genuineness*—The worker's honesty about self and his own feelings. An ability to separate the experiences and the feelings of the worker from those of the client. Genuineness on the part of the worker allows the client to become what the client wants to be. It is present when the worker's communication is understood and comfortable for the client. The worker's personal style of helping should not be an inflexible use of technique.

7. *Authority and power*—The expectation that the client will work to fulfill needs and responsibilities and will want to resolve the situation. This involves encouraging the client to go beyond the present level of functioning and providing guidance and resources so that goals can be reached. It involves insistence that the client do what she can for herself. The worker's knowledge and skills are a base for authority and power. The client must know that the worker's power and authority are not to be used to dominate or control her but to assist her in having her needs, and those of others around her, met in a positive, mutually beneficial manner.

8. *Purpose*—The helping relationship has a purpose known to, and accepted by, both worker and client. According to Beulah Compton and Burt Galaway, this is the most important characteristic of all.[10]

There is some disagreement about the place of advice giving in helping. Traditionally, social workers have thought it unhelpful to give advice; advice was seen as the worker's solution for the client and not the product of mutual problem solving and thus was not useful for the client. Clients, however, often indicate that they expect and are looking for advice.[11] Advice is tangible evidence of help. If advice is given, it should be done selectively and as a result of mutual problem solving by worker and client. It should be presented in a nondemanding manner as something that might be tried, leaving the final decision for its use to the client. When given in this manner, advice may well be a useful tool for helping. However, it is essential that the advice be given by the worker and received by the client in a way that ensures that the client sees it as one of several options. Generally, it is best to use advice as a last resort, when the client is truly stuck or if she seems headed for a situation that is harmful to herself or others or if she is overwhelmed by a crisis.

Another characteristic of the helping situation is that help can be given by the client to the worker. The client helps the worker understand the situation or culture or diversity. This is help and should be recognized as such. When the client evaluates the usefulness of the means of helping and the appropriateness of goals, this is help. Such a view of help enables the client to see the roles as interdependent rather than as superordinal to subordinal. An interdependent relationship encourages growth rather than dependency and is more helpful to the client.

Biestek's classic seven principles of a casework relationship and the worker's role in using each principle are one way of defining the responsibility of the social worker in a worker-client interaction or action system.

- *Principle I: Individualization*—This principle is "the recognition and understanding of each client's unique qualities and the differential use of principles and methods." The worker uses this principle when functioning from a nonbiased, nonprejudicial stance; when applying knowledge of human diversity; when listening and observing to better understand the client; when moving at the client's pace; and when empathizing with the client.

- *Principle II: Purposeful expression of feelings*—This principle is concerned with "the client's need to express his or her feelings freely, especially negative feelings." The worker uses this principle when creating an environment in which the client is comfortable, when expressing the desire to be of help, when encouraging the client to express feeling and then listening to the expression of the feeling, and when avoiding providing advice and solutions before the client's situation is understood.

- *Principle III: Controlled emotional response*—This principle calls for "sensitivity to the client's feelings; an understanding of their meaning; and a purposeful, appropriate response to the client's feelings." The worker uses this principle when responding to the client on a feeling level in a purposefully selective manner, using her self-knowledge to direct her response to the needs of the client.

- *Principle IV: Acceptance*—This principle calls for perceiving and dealing with the client as he really is. It entails recognizing and using the client's strengths and limitations, congenial and uncongenial qualities, positive and negative feelings, and constructive and destructive attitudes and behaviors.

- *Principle V: Nonjudgmental attitude*—This principle "is based on a conviction that the [social work] function excludes assigning guilt, innocence, or degree of client responsibility for causation of the problems or needs" of the situation.

- *Principle VI: Client self-determination*—This principle recognizes the "right and need of clients to freedom in making their own choices and decisions in the [social work] process." The worker carries out this principle by helping the client see problems and needs clearly and with perspective, by acquainting the client with appropriate community resources, and by creating an environment in which worker and client can work together.

- *Principle VII: Confidentiality*—This principle asserts the right of the client to preservation of secret information concerning self that is disclosed in the professional relationship. It is the worker's role to explain the limits of confidentiality and rights of the worker and client within the framework of professional and legal obligations.[12]

These principles are used to guide the professional helping relationship. They help promote a climate in which the client-worker action system can work toward fulfilling client needs. The principles can also be applied selectively to other two-person action systems.

Special Influences on the Helping Relationship

Any difference in diversity between the client and the worker has an influence on the action system's functioning. These include situations in which the worker and the client come from different ethnic or racial backgrounds and those in which the gender of the worker affects the interaction with the client and the environment in which the action takes place. Several obstacles seem to be prevalent in cross-diversity helping relationships:

1. *Mutual unknowingness*—Because of a lack of knowledge about the other's culture or diversity on the part of both the worker and the client, there is a tendency toward stereotyping. Fear of the other is also a result of lack of knowledge and understanding. Inappropriate "good" or "bad" judgments may be made. Social distance that does not allow for the sharing and the trust necessary in the helping endeavor is often present. Of particular importance is lack of knowledge about a client's traditional communication patterns.

2. *Attitudes toward the other culture or diversity*—Negative attitudes may have developed from limited knowledge about a different culture or diverse group. These attitudes may also have developed from negative experiences with persons who belong to the same cultural or ethnic or diversity group as the person being interacted with.

3. *Availability of different opportunities*—Members of different cultural or diversity groups have different opportunities. When the social worker does not understand this difference of opportunity, she can have unrealistic expectations about how clients should use the help offered. This fact can also relate to the use of appropriate resources. Some resources are not usable for a particular diversity group. For example, a culture that does not allow expression of feeling or that uses limited verbal expression and is action oriented will have considerable difficulty with traditional talk therapy. Some resources are available to, and traditionally useful for, particular ethnic groups. For example, Native Americans traditionally use the tribe's medicine man or elders as a resource. They also have the support and financial aid resources of the Bureau of Indian Affairs.

4. *Conflicts between societal and cultural expectations*—These often are difficult to resolve around the helping situation. Clients may have difficulty in identifying these conflicts, and the worker may not be aware of them.

In addition, clients who are members of various diversity groups may have a low sense of self-worth as a result of chronic and acute oppression and discrimination. This can result in low expectations for resolution of situations, in special relationship needs, and in lack of appreciation of their own diversity. There may be a different world view, different expectations for the use of time, and different expectations of male and female behavior. These can get in the way of developing working relationships. The client may have a low trust level toward persons of other cultures or diversity; this may be the result of past relationships that produced pain and anger. A client with a low level of trust may use concealment mechanisms that hinder the helping endeavor. Different mechanisms for showing respect can result in misunderstandings. Different mechanisms for expressing ideas and feelings and different communication patterns can be particularly troublesome. Ann Brownlee has identified some of the areas in which communication differences may exist in cross-cultural relationships, including situations appropriate for the communication of specific information; tempo of communication; taboos; norms for confidentiality; ways of expressing emotions, feelings, and appreciation; meaning of silence; form and content of nonverbal communication; and style of persuasion or explanation.[13] In order to work effectively in cross-cultural situations, the worker should develop an understanding of diverse needs, of the complexities of cross-cultural communication, and of her own biases and prejudices and must also develop considerable skill in accurate perception and tolerance for difference.

In using an ecosystems strengths perspective, it is essential that the worker be diligent, flexible, and creative in uncovering strengths and resources within the client and his ecosystem. Contrary to its professed belief in freedom and tolerance, the United States has a history of oppression and discrimination toward minorities, especially people of color. The basis of prejudice and discrimination is viewing other cultures as weak, inferior, and undesirable. Thus, members of the dominant culture, as well as nondominant cultures, are not accustomed to finding strengths in other cultures. In spite of the social worker's efforts to be nonjudgmental, it will be impossible to avoid all prejudice and stereotyping because these are pervasive and imbedded in the dominant culture. Even if the worker has a predisposition toward seeing strengths, it is unlikely that she will thoroughly know these strengths unless she has had considerable exposure to or conducted research about other cultures. Nonetheless, if the worker and client make a real effort to see strengths and positive opportunities, they can overcome the negative effects of cultural bias.

Gender is another factor that affects relationships. Social work literature contains little discussion of the influence of the worker's gender on the helping endeavor. There seems to be an assumption that a skilled worker should be able to work with both male and female clients. Although this is probably true, social workers should become more aware of gender factors in professional relationships. One study has found that when male and female workers make assessments about female clients, male workers see these clients as less mature and less intelligent than do female workers. Female workers see women as having greater need for emotional expression and less need of home and family involvement than do male workers.[14] Differences in perceptions between male and female social workers, then, seem to exist. These different perceptions are probably a result of sex-role socialization and can affect professional relationships.

Joanne Mermelstein and Paul Sundet have found differences in client expectations in rural areas based on gender factors. In the female worker–female client situation, the client expects nurturing, mothering, and friendship. In the female worker–male client situation, the client sees taking help from a woman as going counter to his definition of manhood. The interaction is also affected by taboos about what is to be discussed with women. In the situation of male worker and female client, the male worker is seen as performing a traditional female nurturing role. The female client expects the male worker to support her, to give her moral guidance and clear direction. In the male client–male worker situation, the male client expects the male worker to prove his masculinity.[15]

Louise Johnson, Dale Crawford, and Lorraine Rousseau found that in traditional Sioux Native American culture it is a mistake for a male worker to go alone to a female client's home. The male worker should go through a male relative because in traditional culture a female speaks through a male relative.[16]

Social workers should examine the expectations for male and female behaviors from the client's perspective and take these into consideration in developing action systems and in understanding and using relationships within these systems. Attention also must be given to the influence of gender of both worker and client on practice, that is, on the functioning of the action system. Workers also need to develop an understanding of how their own gender expectations influence their professional relationships.

Other differences that may exist between worker and client are young workers with older clients; unmarried workers with experienced parents; well-educated, middle-class workers with illiterate, poor clients; heterosexual workers with homosexual clients, or vice versa; and upright, well-behaved workers with norm violators. These and other differences all influence the functioning of the action system—the helping relationship.

Little attention has been given to how the context of the social work endeavor affects practice, particularly the relationship factors of practice. A growing body of literature relative to the practice of social work in rural areas has pointed out the need to pay attention to the context of practice. Again, the work of Sundet and Mermelstein provides an indication of the influence of context on practice. They found that social work roles that call for little risk on the part of the client are most effective when an outside worker enters a new rural community.[17] It may be that this experience provides a useful principle for situations in which cultural distance exists between the worker and the client. Confidentiality is an aspect of relationship that takes on new features when examined in a rural setting. People are more visible in rural settings. In some situations, it is in the client's best interest that certain aspects of the service be known so that misinterpretations about the service do not develop.[18]

Social workers have given little attention to the understanding of the two-person relationship in an action system that does not involve a client—for example, relationships with other professionals, such as a teacher or a pastor, or relationships with community leaders. Yet workers often use this type of action system in serving clients, especially when using an ecosystems strengths approach. In discussing this type of system from an interactional viewpoint, Yvonne Fraley has suggested that mutual problem solving is more effective if this type of relationship is assessed using these six variables: (1) the position of the worker ("actor one")—that is, the location of actor one in an agency or community system; (2) the goal of actor one in the relationship; (3) the position of the other ("actor two"); (4) the goal of the other; (5) the form of communication being used (verbal, written, nonverbal media, etc.); and (6) the method of influence being used by each actor (problem solving, teacher-learner, helper-helpee, etc.).[19] This kind of analysis points out that in the nonclient action system there needs to be some reason for the two actors to work together. If the goals of each are compatible, if one actor does not feel threatened by the position of the other, and if the form of communication and the method of influence are carefully chosen, there is a better chance for gaining the desired outcome.

Regardless of the nature of the action system, the characteristics of the actors (worker-client or other), and the situation in which the interaction is taking place, the relationship of the two persons is a crucial factor in whether the work together produces the desired outcomes. Each person brings much to the system that can aid in, or detract from, the relationship and the work to be done. The social worker must be aware of these factors and use them to further the work by developing functional working relationships with other people. (See Figure 7.1.)

Relationship is not the end-state goal of the helping endeavor or the action system; it is the glue that holds the action system together and as such is a necessary ingredient of a well-functioning action system. It is not a relationship in which there is no conflict and all is happiness and goodwill, nor is it an overly dependent relationship. It is a relationship in which conflict is open and examined and in which there is respect for the position of the other. It is a working relationship, and the purpose of the relationship is the accomplishment of tasks needed to fulfill client need and promote growth and change.

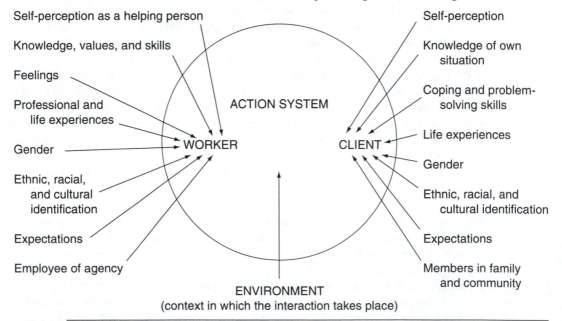

FIGURE 7.1 *Relationship*

Communication

Because effective communication is such an important ingredient of the functioning action system, it is important for all social workers to develop good communication skills. Communication is the sending and receiving of messages between two or more persons. Effective communication occurs when the persons involved in a situation accurately perceive the messages of the other person and in which the messages are sent in a way that allows the receiver to take action or respond to the sender in ways that facilitate the purposes of the communication. The purposes of communication in the social work interaction include:

1. Gathering information needed for the helping endeavor, including strengths and resources
2. Exploring ideas, feelings, and possible ways to meet need based on the strengths and resources within the client and the ecosystem
3. Expressing feelings or thoughts
4. Structuring the work of the action system
5. Providing support, informing, advising, encouraging, and giving necessary directions

Communication is a process. The *sender* conceptualizes the message and through a *transmitter* (the voice or visual production) sends the message to a *receiver* who interprets the message cognitively and affectively. This results in a *response,* another message and/or an action. The response may result in *feedback,* a means for the sender to evaluate the effectiveness of the message. One other factor of the process is *interference* or noise. Interference consists of those influences from outside the process that affect the message while it is transmitted and cause *distortion* of the message as it reaches the receiver. Each part of the process has a particular function and special problems that can interfere with the effectiveness of the communication. The sender must conceptualize the message in a way that is understandable to the receiver. This requires understanding how the receiver deals with and interprets ideas and information. The transmission of the message takes place not only through verbalization but also through nonverbal means. Nonverbal communication takes place through vocal tone and behaviors, such as gestures, facial expressions, and body position. The motivation, needs, feelings, and attitudes of the sender influence the manner in which the message is transmitted. The message has content—the specific words used—and it has meaning—how that content is treated. The choice of words, the order of ideas and words, and the use of humor and silence all contribute to the quality of the message.

Special attention needs to be paid to cultural and personal differences in the meaning of words. Different cultures can have different attitudes, values, and beliefs that influence how words are interpreted and the meaning of nonverbal communication. Beyond the cultural aspect, each of us has unique and individual life experiences. For example, take the word *mother.* For someone who has had a warm, loving relationship with his mother, the word will evoke positive feelings. However, if a person had experienced the death of his mother at an early age, the word *mother* will probably be associated with grief and loss. Even siblings can have different ideas of their mother based on their individual perceptions.

As the message is transmitted, the possibility of distortion is great. Previous experiences, cultural and societal demands, and attitudes and feelings of the receiver can distort the message. Distractions, such as additional stimuli, concerns, and responsibilities, can distort the message.

The manner in which the message is received also influences the effectiveness of the message. The receiver may perceive or interpret the message in a manner different from the intention of the sender. The receiver may not comprehend the meaning of the message as intended or may receive only a part of the message. These influences can occur between any individuals but are especially important when communication occurs between two people who are different in terms of diversity. Feedback is the means of ascertaining whether the message was received and if the message intended by the sender was sufficiently similar to make the communication effective. Feedback is sending a message about a received message to the sender of that message. The feedback is also subject to the problems of the original message.

Effective communication is communication in which the outcome is the accomplishment of the purpose intended by the sender. Messages that have the best chance of being effective are those in which:

1. The verbal and nonverbal messages are congruent
2. The message is simple, specific, and intelligible to the receiver
3. The receiver can understand what is meant by the sender
4. There is sufficient repetition for the receiver to sense the importance of this message from among other messages being received simultaneously
5. There has been sufficient reduction of both psychological and actual noise
6. Feedback has been solicited from the receiver and sufficient time taken to ensure that the original message was received

Effectiveness in communication is affected by the credibility and honesty of the sender of the message. The receiver who has reason to trust the competence and reliability of the sender will tend to be receptive to the message and its expectations. Effective communicators tune into and are sensitive to the feelings and situations of those with whom they are communicating. They are assertive without being overly aggressive or confrontational.

Often the one-to-one communication is not with the client but with other professionals, with significant others in the client's environment, or with people who may in some way be involved in situations that are blocking client need fulfillment. These relationships are particularly important when the focus is on organizational or community change. The principles of communication discussed in this section (regarding clients) apply to interactions with nonclients even though communication may be of a bargaining or adversarial nature. When social workers find themselves in situations where the viewpoint of the other may be different from their own, clear communication is imperative. Sometimes the differences can be resolved through clarification of messages. Other times a clear understanding of the differences allows work to progress.

Brett Seabury has identified several problems that confront social workers in their communications with clients and significant others:

1. *Double messages*—Two contradictory messages are received simultaneously or in close succession.
2. *Ambiguous messages*—These messages have little meaning or several possible messages for the receiver.
3. *Referent confusion*—The words have different meanings to each person, or they may be professional jargon not understood by the other person involved in the communication.
4. *Selective attention and interpretation*—This causes distortion of the message or confusion as to meaning.
5. *Overload*—This is the receiving of more messages than a receiver can interpret and respond to at any one time.
6. *Ritual or order incongruence*—This is the failure of the message sequence to follow expected or habitual behavioral patterns.
7. *Regulator incompatibility*—The use of eye contact and patterns of speaking and listening that regulate the communication of one party in the interchange are not known to, used by, or are unacceptable to another party in the interchange.[20]

Other barriers to effective communication are inattentiveness, assuming the understanding of meanings, and using the communication for purposes different from those of others in the interchange (having hidden agendas). Cross-cultural communication is particularly problematic because the structure of messages differs from culture to culture. Even if the same language is used, words are used differently or have different meanings. Each culture has its own idioms and expressions, and the syntax (form) of the language may be different. The differences make it difficult to listen to the messages and make the likelihood of misunderstanding great. The social worker must overcome the barriers to effective communication if the action system is to function to reach its goals. In social work, communication is dialogue. The worker and client openly talk together and seek mutual understanding. Floyd Matson and Ashley Montagu, in the introduction to *The Human Dialogue,* described communication as:

> not to "command" but to "commune" and that knowledge of the highest order (whether of the world, of oneself, or of other) is to be sought and found not through detachment but through connection, not by objectivity but by intersubjectivity, not in a state of estranged aloofness but in something resembling the act of love.[21]

This is the essence of communication in its most effective form. This kind of communication adds vitality to, nourishes, and sustains the process of working together, the interaction.

The Interview: An Interactional Tool

The **interview** is a primary tool of the social worker. It is the structure for operationalizing the interaction between a worker and a client. Each social worker develops her own interviewing style. Interviewing is an art and a skill, and learning how to interview is accomplished by doing it. Some guides to interviewing can be helpful to the person learning to interview. These guides include preparing for an interview, knowing the stages of an interview, and developing interviewing skills.

Each interview should have a specific purpose or goal. Generally, this purpose may be to obtain the information needed for carrying out some task or function or to work together to meet a client's need or solve a client's problem. The purpose of a specific interview will depend on the stage of working together, the agency function and the method of service, and the client's needs or the nature of the situation at hand. In addition to purpose, there are several types of variables that affect the nature of the interview:

1. *How the interview is initiated*—Is it a voluntary activity on the part of the client? Is it a formal, planned, regular interview or a walk-in request of the client? Or is it a life-space contact (one that takes place in the process of the client's daily activities)?

2. *Where the interview takes place*—Does the interview take place in an office, a home, a hospital room, or some other setting?

3. *The experience of the worker and client with each other*—Have this worker and this client had previous contact with each other? Is this encounter a part of a time-limited or long-term plan?

Each interview will be different. The worker needs to be flexible in structuring and guiding the interview, depending on the interview's purpose and the needs of the client. It should be carried out in a manner that encourages interaction and relationship.

Limited or shrinking resources and the advent of managed care have brought about a greater emphasis on brief and solution-focused intervention. The results are limitations on the amount of time available to work with a client. Some settings still provide unlimited or open-ended services. However, the wave of the future is clearly toward some form of time-limited service throughout the human service delivery system.

Time limits mean that the social worker must place a high premium on the efficient use of time in accomplishing maximum effectiveness. This applies to each interview that is undertaken with a client. It means that the worker must be focused on developing and accomplishing goals and objectives that will bring about necessary change. This might seem to be contrary to the idea of encouraging interaction and relationship. However, if the worker is able to empathize with the client, she would come to realize that the client's needs are met best by moving toward resolution of the concerns that brought the client to the worker. In the process, the client is also well served by learning to bring about change without assistance. This is in line with the social work value of maximizing self-determination for the client. Thus, clients can benefit from a solution-focused approach that builds on their strengths and that results in improved problem-solving skills. It is not so much the amount of time that is spent in building a relationship but the manner in which the worker interacts with the client. When the worker makes it clear to clients that they are valued and respected as human beings and that they are capable of making their own decisions, the foundation for a sound helping relationship has been established. This is not separate from the change process but rather a fundamental part of it.

Preparing for an Interview

In preparing for any interview the worker has three tasks: (1) planning the environment for the interview, (2) planning the content of the interview, and (3) "tuning in." Each of these tasks is carried out before contact with the client.

The worker thinks about the physical conditions of the interview. If the interview takes place in an office, the worker arranges the office so as to encourage working together. This can be done by giving some thought to the placement of desk and chairs (sitting behind a desk may place a barrier between worker and client). An office that is comfortable and does not have too many distracting features is ideal. The worker tries to prevent interruptions such as phone calls and knocks on the door. If the worker plans to take notes or use a tape recorder, arrangements are made so this can be done with full knowledge of the client but in a manner that does not distract from the work at hand. The worker also tries to provide a place for the interview where the conversation will not be overheard by others. Attention is given to the time of the interview so that neither the worker nor the client will be hurried, but the interview will also not be overly long. The worker will think about the impact of his dress on the client. If the interview is held outside the office, the worker will choose a time that is convenient for the client and when the fewest interruptions are likely to take place. For instance, an interview with a mother in the home might best take place when the children are in school.

In planning for the content of the interview, the worker will recall the goal and the purpose of the service and will identify the goal for this particular interview. The tasks to be accomplished will be considered. Any additional knowledge or information needed will be obtained. The worker might review notes about the previous interview if there has been one. The structure of the interview and questions to be asked will be considered. This planning is done to give form and focus to the interview, but the worker is prepared to be flexible and make changes if the client has unanticipated needs.

In tuning in, the worker first tries to anticipate the client's needs and feelings in the interview and to think about his own response to those feelings and needs.[22] The worker tries to become aware of his own feelings and attitudes that might interfere with effective communication. Such awareness should minimize the impact of these feelings and attitudes on the interview. The worker also needs to prepare to help by dealing with personal needs and any work-related attitudes that might interfere with the work of the interview.

Preparation for the interview is one way to promote worker readiness, which communicates to the client that she is important and that the work to be done together is important. Worker readiness prepares the way for effective interviewing.

The Stages of an Interview

All interviews have three stages: (1) the opening or beginning stage, (2) the middle or—working-together stage, and (3) the ending stage. Each stage has a different focus and different tasks. In each interview some time is spent in each stage, but the amount of time spent in each stage may differ depending on the work at hand and the relationship of the worker and client. The stages represent steps in what might be called a "mini" change process. In Part Three of this text, we examine the social work process as a change-oriented approach. The phases are assessment, planning, action, and evaluation and termination. However, these phases are not limited to the overall process but are included during each contact the social worker has with the client.

The opening, or beginning, stage of interviewing corresponds to the relationship-building and assessment phases. The middle, or working-together, stage involves evaluation, planning, and action. It includes evaluating success and barriers to success in carrying out the plan, deciding whether to continue with the plan or to modify it, and taking action to continue success or to remove barriers to success. The ending stage involves termination of the interview.

During the first few interviews with a new client, more emphasis might be needed on the first phases of relationship building and assessment, with planning and action limited to meeting needs that require immediate attention. Likewise, the last few interviews might focus more on termination. However, elements of each phase of the change process should be built into each interview. Besides helping to maintain a focus on the work to be done, this has the added benefit of reinforcing the steps necessary for successful change.

The beginning stage starts when the worker greets the client by name and does whatever seems in order to make the client comfortable. In working with adults, it is important that the worker address the client formally, using *Mr., Mrs., Miss,* or *Ms.,* unless the client asks to be addressed by his or her first name. This is especially important for people of color, such as African Americans, who have experienced situations where the use of their first name is a sign of inferiority or control. Generally, in Hispanic culture, the use of first names with adults is reserved for those who have been accepted into the family system. The worker tries to reduce any tensions and discuss any hostilities that may exist and reaches out to the client to help him become an active participant in the interview. This can be done by asking the client to share any significant events since the last session. This keeps the worker in tune and current with the client and his concerns.

During the beginning stage, the worker defines the purpose of the interview or recalls plans made in a previous session. The client is given an opportunity to discuss this purpose and any special needs he might have at this time. The worker elicits the client's feelings about the work to be done and accepts the client's sense of purpose and need by modifying the purpose and plan of the interview if necessary. Thus, an assessment of the current situation is made while the worker also establishes or reestablishes a relationship by demonstrating care and concern and empathy.

If this is an initial interview, much of the time may need to be devoted to building a relationship and making an initial assessment of the situation. Diversity issues may be especially prominent during these first few interviews. The worker should communicate a respect for diversity and a valuing of difference while also seeking to learn about diversity from the client. However, some of the time should be spent in getting started with the work to be done. At the least, the worker should ask the client what they might do during the next week that might make a difference in meeting his need. A plan for carrying this out should be included.

When the worker senses that the client is ready to proceed with the work to be done, the worker changes the focus of the interview. According to Lawrence Shulman, the worker may have to "demand this work."[23] This is not done in a harsh or demeaning manner, but in a firm manner that helps the client accept the need to begin working on the situation at hand. The middle phase has then begun. The content of this phase depends on the task at hand but should include evaluation of the success of the plan, decisions regarding continuation or modifications of the plan, and actions needed to carry out the plan or to remove barriers. The worker needs to maintain a sense of timing attuned to the client's pace of work as well as time limits that may be relevant, to refocus if the content strays from the task, or to renegotiate the purpose if this is indicated. The worker also should monitor communication for its effectiveness.

Before the agreed-on time for ending an interview is reached or when the purpose of the interview has been fulfilled, the worker again shifts the focus. In bringing the interview to an end, the worker summarizes what has happened during the interview and how it fits into the service being offered. The worker and the client together plan the next steps, which include work to be done by each before the next interview and the purpose, goal, time, and place of the next interview. If this is a single interview or a final interview, the client is helped to say good-bye and given permission to come again if other needs develop.

If the worker has been successful in incorporating termination at the end of each interview, the client may be well prepared for the termination of service when it comes. However, even if the worker is able to do this, some clients may have difficulty with termination. This will be covered in greater detail in Part Three.

Case Example

The case example of Mrs. Abbott in Chapter 2 is a good example of the social worker preparing for an interview. Mrs. Abbott is eighty-six years old and is a new resident at Sunnyside Assisted Living Facility. The interview might proceed as follows.

Beginning Stage

Sue knocked on Mrs. Abbott's door before entering. Mrs. A invited her in. Sue introduced herself and said she was the social worker who would be working on a plan with Mrs. A to make her stay as comfortable as possible. Mrs. A said she would be a lot more comfortable if she were back home. Sue asked Mrs. A about her home. Mrs. A had lived there for more than forty years and had raised four children with her husband who had died four years ago. Tears began to well up in her eyes as she described her family. Sue empathized by recognizing her feelings of loss and coping with having to move. She asked about the fall that caused Mrs. A to break her hip and discussed the need to care for her so she might be able to walk again. Mrs. A perked up somewhat at this and said she was determined to make that happen. Mrs. A asked if it would be possible to return home if she could walk. Sue indicated she did not know but they would cross that bridge when they came to it. As Sue talked with Mrs. A about her concerns, she sensed an alliance was forming. Mrs. A appeared to see Sue as someone who might help her to achieve her goals and meet her needs.

Middle Stage

As Sue sensed her relationship building with Mrs. A, she shifted the focus to her first day at Sunnyside. Mrs. A said it was a nice enough place and the staff seemed very friendly, but it just was not home. Sue asked if there were some things from home that would make Sunnyside feel more like home. Mrs. A indicated she would like some of her furniture and personal items. She had given her daughter a list of pictures and other items, but did not realize she could bring her furniture. Sue and Mrs. A discussed this and worked out what would fit and

(continued)

where it might go in her room. Mrs. A pointed out there was one more thing she missed and that was her friends and neighborhood. Sue said Mrs. A should be sure to make a list of people who were allowed to visit. She pointed out that Sunnyside was close to her neighborhood and had easy access to public transportation. Sue also said as her condition improved she could go with her family or friends whenever she wished. She also invited Mrs. A to call people whenever she felt like she wanted to talk with them. Mrs. A seemed somewhat relieved to hear some of this although she was obviously still hoping to return home. Sue took some time to review some of the activities and programs that were available. She highlighted ones that could accommodate Mrs. A's condition.

Ending Stage

As the interview was coming to an end, Sue summarized what they had covered. She confirmed what Mrs. A wanted from her home and who she wanted on her approved visitor list. She asked Mrs. A if there was anything else she could do to make her stay comfortable. Mrs. A asked about calling long distance to her son and some relatives who lived out of state. Sue said she would arrange this for her. Mrs. A thanked Sue for taking the time to talk with her. Sue said she would be back later in the week to follow up with her.

Skills Used by the Worker during the Interview

As a means of guiding and supporting the work together and of promoting relationship and effective communication, the worker uses six groups of skills during an interview: inductive learning and naturalistic inquiry skills; climate-setting skills; observation skills; listening skills, especially reflective listening; questioning skills; and focusing, guiding, and interpreting skills. The skill of interviewing is, in part, skill in selecting and using the appropriate response at the appropriate time. Like all skills, these must be developed through use over a period of time. The student or worker can improve her communication skills by using them in her everyday life. In addition, many exercises have been developed that are useful in beginning to acquire these skills, but it is only in actual client situations that skill development reaches the professional level. Each of these skills should be utilized in a way that is sensitive to cultural and individual differences.

Inductive Learning and Naturalistic Inquiry. These approaches were identified in Chapters 3 and 4 as important to becoming culturally competent and were expanded to include all forms of diversity. Inductive learning refers to three important concepts. According to Doman Lum, the worker must first take a lifelong learning approach to becoming culturally and diversity competent. This means that learning does not stop but is built into professional development throughout one's career. Second, the worker should use inductive learning as he comes to know each client. This requires an openness to new knowledge as the worker discovers similarities and differences in how each client experiences her diversity. Similarities serve to confirm earlier observations of members of her diversity group. Observing differences allows new learning to take place. Thus, the worker never closes the door to the possibility of advancing his knowledge about diversity. The third concept involves having the client assume the role of teacher while the worker assumes the role of learner each time the worker encounters diversity. This recognizes that each client is an expert in her own diversity and that she experiences that diversity in an individual way.[24] Lum suggested the use of the "Essential Question," which is: "What does X mean to you?" where "the symbol X can refer to a family or social experience, to feelings, beliefs or cultural meanings."[25] For example, in the case in this chapter with Mrs. Abbott, the worker might have asked her what it meant to her to be at home. In the case example of Jerry Adams from Chapter 1 and other chapters, the worker might have asked what his former school or neighborhood meant to him. Open-ended questions and facilitative communication skills are used to deepen the client's narrative.[26]

Naturalistic inquiry comes out of ethnography. It involves the use of the inductive process to learn about a culture. James W. Leigh described this as beginning with the position that one does not know what one does not know. This is different from traditional social work, which uses a deductive process in which the worker uses prescribed guidelines for gathering knowledge, formulates a hypothesis about the current situation, and then designs a plan based on this hypothesis. The emphasis in traditional social work is on knowing what one does not know and then using this knowledge to guide the process of acquiring knowledge. To not know what one does not know means leaving oneself open to whatever unfolds in the interaction with the client. Knowledge acquisition is not prescribed ahead of time but unfolds from the interaction with the client.[27] In the case example of Mrs. Abbott, the worker went with Mrs. Abbott's concerns and inquired about her home and her family. She also sought to discover what would make Mrs. Abbott more comfortable before she assessed her care needs and introduced the activities and programs. Leigh described global questions designed to uncover the client's experiences.[28] The role of the client is as "culture guide," and the role of the worker as "stranger."[29] From this open interaction, the plan and actions emerge.[30]

These approaches fit very well with an ecosystems strengths approach. In fact, Lum pointed out the need to use a strengths approach in becoming culturally competent.[31] In addition, the need to observe the client in the context of her culture brings an ecosystem approach into play. In the case example presented in this chapter, the worker sought to maintain a connection between Mrs. Abbott and her friends, family, and neighborhood instead of trying to break these bonds so that Mrs. Abbott would give up her hope to return home. These are obvious strengths and resources Mrs. Abbott and her ecosystem have. In the case example of Jerry Adams, the worker would look at Jerry's success in his former school and his ability to develop and maintain friendships in his former neighborhood as strengths.

Climate-Setting Skills.   Three attributes have been identified as characteristics of interpersonal situations that seem to produce understanding, openness, and honesty, which are enabling factors in the work of the action system. These three characteristics are empathy, genuineness, and nonpossessive warmth.[32]

Empathy is the capacity to communicate to the client that the worker accepts and cares for the client. Empathy communicates that at this point in time the client's welfare is to be considered before the worker's. Empathy is expressed by openly receiving and recognizing the feelings of the client, by accurately perceiving the client's messages, and by providing the client with concrete feedback about messages.

Genuineness is the capacity of the worker to communicate to the client that the worker is trustworthy. It is expressed by being willing to let the client know the worker as a person in ways that meet the client's need for such information. It also reflects congruence between the worker's verbal and nonverbal messages. In addition, genuineness involves informing the client when the worker disagrees with the client and when the client's behavior and communication are inconsistent. This skill calls for honesty but honesty communicated in a manner that is sensitive to the client's feelings and concerns.

Nonpossessive warmth is the capacity to communicate to the client both a concern and a desire for intimacy; this allows the client to make decisions, to have negative and positive feelings, and to feel worthwhile. It has qualities of nonblame, closeness, and nondefensiveness. A warmth that is nonpossessive is displayed through positive regard and respect for the client and through thoughtfulness and kindness as well as appreciation for, and pleasure at, the client's growth and well-being.

These three attributes are tied to social work values. One of the cardinal values of social work is the belief in the value and worth of every human being. This leads the worker to respect the client as an individual. This does not mean that the worker approves of all of the client's behavior. Some clients will have done things that are wrong, either morally or legally. The worker accepts the client as a human being even with her faults and mistakes. When the worker is able to do this, then he can listen to the client's story without judging her as a person. This helps the worker put himself in his client's shoes and leads to empathy. A genuine belief in the value and worth of every human being allows the worker to be more genuine in treating the client with dignity and respect. It allows the worker to care about the client as a human being even though he may find things about the client that he does not like.

The climate of all interpersonal endeavors greatly affects the nature of the relationship and the quality of the communication. Skills in developing and maintaining an accepting, growth-producing climate are an important part of the worker's repertoire.

Interviewing is only one form of communication. The skills used in the interview can also be used in less formal social work interactions. They are the same skills that encourage relationships to form and to be used and maintained. In the social work endeavor, in the one-to-one action system, it is the responsibility of the social worker to move toward the client so that relationships may form and a common ground for communication may be established. To do this, the social worker must understand the client and be willing to work with her in meeting her needs and in resolving the situation. Improved communication and relationships are central to success in the ecosystems strengths approach. The focus of growth and change is on the interactions and transactions among systems. Success is often determined by the client's ability to change her interactions with others and their interactions with her. Thus, the worker frequently will be in a position to assist the client to acquire these skills in order to bring about growth and change.

In the case example, Sue showed empathy when Mrs. Abbott talked about missing her home and experiencing the death of her husband. She demonstrated honesty when she told Mrs. Abbott that she did not know if Mrs. Abbott could return home if she were able to walk. She showed care and concern by listening to Mrs. Abbott's concerns first before shifting to the purposes of her visit. Sue maintained a positive climate for her work with Mrs. Abbott, which resulted in a positive response. Sue was successful in beginning the process of developing a plan for Mrs. Abbott's care.

Observation Skills. Clients give information and express feeling in nonverbal, behavioral ways. They also provide information and express feeling in the way in which other information is given and discussed. Sensitivity to this nonverbal material is useful for tuning in to where the client really is in relation to the material being discussed, for checking the validity of the client's verbal expression, and for feedback purposes. Workers should observe the following:

1. *Body language*—What is the client communicating by the way she sits, by behaviors such as thumping on the desk with the fingers, and by facial expression?

2. *The content of opening and closing sentences*—These sentences tend to contain particularly significant material. They also may give cues about the client's attitudes toward self and the environment.

3. *Shifts in conversation*—These shifts, particularly when always related to similar topics, can indicate that a particular topic is painful, taboo, or something the client does not want to discuss.

4. *Association of ideas*—Observing which ideas the client seems to associate with which other ideas can often give the worker an indication of unspoken feelings.

5. *Recurrent references*—When the client continues to bring up a subject, this indicates that it is a subject of importance to the client or one with which the client would like help.

6. *Inconsistencies or gaps*—When these are present, it is an indication either that the material being discussed is threatening to the client or that the client is unwilling to openly share in this area.

7. *Points of stress or conflict*—In cross-cultural action systems, stress and conflict may indicate areas of inadequate knowledge about cultural aspects of the client's functioning. This may also indicate misunderstanding on the part of the client or areas of client bias or prejudice.

In the case example, Sue could see that Mrs. Abbott became emotional as she described her home and family. She tuned in to Mrs. Abbott's story and was able to uncover important information that helped Sue to understand Mrs. Abbott and her ecosystem.

Listening Skills. Listening is of vital importance in any interview situation. The worker listens to what the client has to say and how the client responds to questions and responses. Beginning workers often place primary emphasis on what they have to say and on the questions to be asked. Good questioning enables clients to provide necessary information, consider alternatives, and work on the situation at hand. If the worker's listening skills are deficient, the full value of the interview will not be realized. Active listening—being with the client in her struggle to deal with difficulties and problems—is the appropriate response at many points in the interview.

Developing listening skills is also important because social workers often communicate with persons whose language expression is somewhat different from their own. In listening, it is important to try to understand what the client is attempting to communicate. To do this, the worker seeks to understand what the words mean to the client. The worker maintains focus on what the client is saying even though there is a tendency to shut out the communication because it seems strange and is difficult to listen to. It is important to note feeling words and how they are expressed. Listening should reflect an attitude of openness and acceptance. Effective listening involves a sense of timing that allows the worker to focus on the client and what is being said and does not shut off communication by premature evaluation or advice.

Listening skills were a key ingredient for Sue with Mrs. Abbott. Sue's ability to be patient and listen to Mrs. Abbott first helped her to understand Mrs. Abbott's concerns and helped to build a relationship. She listened carefully and observed both verbal and nonverbal behavior. Sue used reflective listening in communicating to Mrs. Abbott an understanding of her losses and the importance of her home. It is much easier to obtain cooperation from others if they know that we are paying attention to what they are saying and experiencing. This demonstrates care and concern for others in a way that has real meaning for them. It is not simply lip service, but demonstrates interest in a genuine way.

Questioning Skills. The essence of this group of skills is knowing the various types of questions to ask and the usefulness of each type of question. A first category of questions includes open- and closed-ended questions. A closed-ended question calls for a specific answer. An example would be "What is your age?" These questions are used to gain factual information. An open-ended question is one that enables the client to define, discuss, or answer the question in any way he chooses. An example would be "How do you feel about being here?" The open-ended question allows expression of feeling and gives the worker the client's perception of the subject at hand. In developing a social history, it is usually advisable to mix open- and closed-ended questions; this allows for discussion between the worker and the client about the facts as well as about the client's life experiences.

There are also leading and responding questions. A leading question is used when it is desirable for a client to continue to explore the subject at hand. An example would be "You have tried to cope with this situation, haven't you?" A responding question follows the lead of the client's response. An example would be when a client has been discussing her family and the worker responds, "Could you tell me more about your son and his family?"

In an answer-and-agree question, the client is expected to answer in such a way as to agree with the worker. An example would be "You are feeling much better today, aren't you?" This usually is not a good form of questioning to use because it blocks discussion and imposes the worker's ideas on the client.

With most clients, it is better to ask questions so that they contain single, rather than several, ideas. A question with a number of ideas might be used when the worker is attempting to help the client recognize connections between the ideas. Whether to ask very broad questions or very specific ones depends on the work at hand and on the worker's style. Some workers like to gain a broad picture first and then explore details. Other workers believe it is more helpful for clients to consider small parts of the situation and then look at the broader picture later. Questioning is one of the means used by a social worker to enhance relationships and communication.

In general, it is better for the worker to avoid asking too many questions; otherwise the client may feel bombarded or put on the spot. Questions also tend to set an agenda that is worker centered rather than client centered. In many respects, questions can be used to control the interview in that the client can end up talking about what the worker wants to discuss, as opposed to discussing his concerns. In addition, questions tend to be one-sided and offer little opportunity for feedback, interaction, or give and take in the interchange. There are other ways to provide guidance or focus that do not use questions but do incorporate client concerns.

In the case example, Sue used mainly open-ended questions with Mrs. Abbott, which led to her opening comments about the importance of her home and about her family circumstances. Sue did not assume that she knew how Mrs. Abbott felt but let her tell her own story. Sue used some closed questions to get information that was needed for her records, but only after she let Mrs. Abbott talk about her concerns. Generally, if the worker shows an interest in hearing the client's story and her concerns, then the client is more willing to give information that may be needed to fill in other parts of the record. In fact, once a relationship has begun and the worker has attended to some of her client's needs and concerns, she can ask the client to do her a favor and help her with her paperwork. This way bureaucratic demands can be used to actually strengthen the relationship rather than weakening it by taking attention away from the client's concerns. Putting the paperwork first can give a message that the paperwork is the most important thing. Putting the client first gives the message that she is most important.

In working with Mrs. Abbott, Sue would use closed questions to find out specific information about her circumstances or her concerns. This could include the names and ages of her sons and daughters and grandchildren. Closed questions can also be used to find out specifics about her care.

Focusing, Guiding, and Interpreting Skills. This group of skills is used by the worker to enable the action system to accomplish the tasks necessary to reach the agreed-on objectives. It includes the capacity to use encouragers; to paraphrase and summarize what has been said; and to reflect feelings, meaning, and ideas. These are skills that incorporate what the client says or does into the worker's response. Thus, they are client centered, but they can be used to guide or focus the interview on what is important to the client and what the worker needs to know about the client, her diversity, her environment, and her needs.

The capacity to confront and to elaborate is important in terms of moving the work toward difficult areas and reaching an understanding of the situation or the work to be done. The effective use of these skills includes a sense of timing as to when to listen, when to focus, when to interpret, and when to direct.

Paraphrasing and summarizing often clarify what has been said. Clarification and elaboration enhance understanding. With understanding of issues and facts, the work can progress as a truly joint effort.

In order to limit questions as much as possible with Mrs. Abbott, Sue employed encouragers, paraphrases, reflections, and summaries to guide the interview when necessary. When she sensed that Mrs. Abbott was talking about something important to her, Sue would nod and indicate that she was listening and understanding her. When she finished talking, Sue would use a paraphrase to reflect her message. For instance, Sue's response, after hearing Mrs. Abbott speak about her children, might have been to say, "So, your family means a lot to you, but you don't want to become a burden to them. Is that right?" In an example of reflection of feelings, Sue could have responded to a story about her husband by saying, "I sense that you loved your husband and really miss him a lot." In hearing what her home meant to her, Sue could reflect the importance of this by stating, "It sounds like your home represents a very important part of your life with your husband and moving is very difficult." These skills would provide focus on and clarification of important material in the interview. They also would serve to let Mrs. Abbott know that Sue was listening and was interested in her and her story. The skills act as a guide because they give messages about areas that Sue was able to understand. Sue would also use a summary at the end of the interview to wrap up her work with Mrs. Abbott by briefly going over what she had said about her home, her husband, and her children and what she wanted to bring with her. This summary would serve as an ending to the interview and let Mrs. Abbott know that she had been heard.

Confrontation and silence are often difficult for the worker. Confrontation is the bringing out into the open of feelings, issues, and disagreements. It involves looking at these elements and attempting to find ways to deal with them. If feelings, issues, and disagreements remain hidden, they may interfere with the work at hand. Silence may indicate resistance, frustration, or anger, but it also can provide a time for worker and client to be reflective. Instead of being uncomfortable with silence, the worker can attempt to understand the nature of the silence and use it appropriately. Times of reflection are useful in the work together. Silence related to resistance can be used to develop sufficient discomfort on the part of the client so that she will have to do something. This can help in focusing on the work together. The worker who senses frustration and anger can bring it out into the open, confront the client, and thus deal with it so that the work can proceed.

Sue did not use confrontation with Mrs. Abbott, but she might need to at some later date. For example, if Mrs. Abbott were to refuse to go to her physical therapy appointments, Sue might construct a confrontation by saying something like: "On the one hand you say that you are determined to walk again, but on the other hand you are refusing to go to physical therapy. How do you explain this?"

It is the worker's responsibility to guide the interview but not to control it. The worker takes whatever material and expression of feeling are given by the client and, by listening, questioning, focusing, guiding, and directing, enables the process of the work together to proceed toward the desired outcome.

Summary

The emphasis in this chapter is on engagement and on one-to-one (worker-client) interaction that takes place in an action system and with members of the client's ecosystem. The formation of the action system requires understanding of the client and skill on the part of the worker. Special consideration must be given in developing action systems with resistant clients.

Relationship is the cohesive quality of the action system and is for the purpose of helping clients. It is influenced by the life experiences of both the client and the worker. Cross-diversity relationships have special characteristics that the worker must understand.

Communication is an important ingredient of the action system. The process of communication can become blocked in a variety of ways. Social workers need to be aware of these blocks and of the means for dealing with them.

The interview is an important interactional tool for use in the one-to-one action system. It is important to prepare for interviews and to make them goal directed. Each interview has three stages: a beginning, a middle, and an ending. Workers use a variety of skills in the interview. These include inductive learning and naturalistic inquiry; climate setting; observation; listening; questioning; and focusing, guiding, and interpreting.

The same principles and skills used in one-to-one interaction with clients are also used when working with significant persons in the situation, with those who may be able to provide resources for the client, or with a variety of community persons. The capacity for forming and using one-to-one relationships is a core social work skill.

Questions

1. What are some of the ways to facilitate the development of a helping relationship?
2. Why is the development of a relationship so essential to the helping situation?
3. What are some ways to encourage nonvoluntary clients to engage in the helping process?
4. How should resistance be viewed in any helping situation?
5. Why is it difficult to communicate across cultural boundaries? How can social workers facilitate such communication?
6. Discuss the needed balance between questioning and listening in a social work interview.

Suggested Readings

Ivey, Allen E., and Ivey, Mary Bradford. *Intentional Interviewing: Facilitating Client Development in a Multicultural Society,* 7th ed. Belmont, CA: Brooks/Cole, 2010.

Lum, Doman. *Culturally Competent Practice: A Framework for Understanding Diverse Groups and Justice Issues,* 3rd ed. Pacific Grove, CA: Brooks/Cole, 2006.

Mizrahi, Terry and Davis, Larry E., Eds. *Encyclopedia of Social Work*, 20th ed. Washington, DC: NASW Press, 2008 ("Interviewing").

O'Hare, Thomas. *Court-Ordered Versus Voluntary Clients: Problem Difference and Readiness for Change.* Social Work 41 (July 1996): 417–422.

Perlman, Helen Harris. *Relationship: The Heart of Helping People.* Chicago: University of Chicago Press, 1979.

Poorman, Paula B. *Microskills and Theoretical Foundations for Professional Helpers.* Boston: Allyn and Bacon, 2003.

Ragg, D. Mark. *Building Effective Helping Skills: The Foundation of Generalist Practice.* Boston: Allyn and Bacon, 2001.

Rooney, Ronald. *Strategies for Work with Involuntary Clients*. New York: Columbia University Press, 1992.

Rothman, Juliet C. *Cultural Competence in Process and Practice: Building Bridges.* Boston: Allyn and Bacon, 2008.

Sheafor, Bradford W., and Horejsi, Charles R. *Techniques and Guidelines for Social Work Practice,* 8th ed. Boston: Allyn and Bacon, 2008 (Chapter 8).

Shulman, Lawrence. *The Skills of Helping: Individuals and Groups,* 6h ed. Belmont CA: Brooks/Cole, 2009.

III

The Social Work Process

The content of the service process—the process of the work of the client and worker in meeting need—is the focus of Part Three. This process of the work can be separated from the interactional process only for purposes of study. Interaction and service are two ways of looking at the professional response to need. The generalist social work process, as developed in this book, is a change process based on knowledge, values, and skill. It is intervention into the transactions of human systems. Part Three will build on material presented in Parts One and Two, offering more depth regarding already-introduced concepts. It will present another facet of the social work endeavor.

The process can be conceptualized as having four major components: assessment, planning, action, and evaluation and termination. Although assessment precedes planning, planning precedes action, and action precedes termination, the process is cyclical in nature. Planning often leads to the need for a new or different understanding of person in environment (assessment). Action often produces new information for use in understanding or demonstrates the need for additional planning. Evaluation, the assessment of what has happened as a result of action, is ongoing in the process and leads to new understanding and sometimes to new plans and action. Thus, all four phases are always present, but at various points in the work one or more may be the focus and receive the most attention.

All four phases as well as the interactional process constitute intervention. All can influence change in the transactions between clients and the systems in their environments. All can influence the social functioning of individuals and social systems. Figure 1 depicts the social work process.

The generalist social worker is prepared to work with individuals, families, groups, organizations, and communities at any point during the change process either as client systems or as the focus of the change process. However, deciding on the appropriate system can be complicated. Students may find it confusing to deal with all of the various size client systems while covering each phase of the change process. In order to help the student gain a better understanding of the use of the change process with various size client systems, Part Three will cover each phase of the change process with a primary focus on working with individual clients. The first three chapters of Part Four will focus on the use

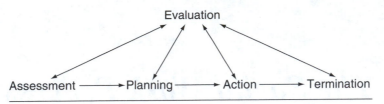

FIGURE 1   *The Social Work Process*

of the change process with families, groups, and macrosystems (organizations and communities). It is important for the student to understand that, in generalist practice, thinking about and working with these various systems is integrated. The generalist social worker keeps an open mind about working with various size systems. She is free to initiate change that is needed at whatever level is most efficient and effective. The text is making an artificial separation of working with various size systems for learning purposes only, to help the student in understanding the use of the change process with these various systems. This should not be construed as encouraging separate methodologies for practicing social work as a generalist practitioner.

Chapter 8 considers the content of the assessment phase with an emphasis on individual clients. Attention is given to the stages in assessment, to the nature of transactional assessment, and to strengths and resources available in the ecosystem.

Chapter 9 discusses planning with an emphasis on individual clients, including the means for developing a plan of action that includes goals and objectives based primarily on strengths and resources in the ecosystem. Units of attention, strategy, roles, tasks, and techniques are also discussed. Factors that affect the plan of action are explored, including diversity and at-risk populations. In addition, there is a discussion of the agreement between worker and client about the plan.

Chapters 10 and 11 identify and discuss important actions used in direct and indirect practice with individual clients by the generalist social worker. The specific direct practice actions identified and discussed are use of resources, including a discussion of the nature of the service delivery system, referral, and broker and advocate roles; empowering and enabling clients; crisis intervention; supportive social work; and use of activity. Chapter 10 also considers the use of our model as a framework for various contemporary theories and models including brief and solution focused models, person centered theory, task centered models, narrative approaches, the Afrocentric approach, feminist practice, and practice with people who are gay or lesbian. Chapter 11 considers indirect practice actions with individuals including the use of mediation, influence, case advocacy, coordination of services, including the strategy of case management, actions to change organizations, and actions to change the community.

Chapter 12 discusses evaluation and termination with an emphasis on individual clients. The chapter includes a look at the kinds of evaluation, the use of research techniques in evaluation (including single-system design), and evaluation during the phases of the change process. It ends with an examination of the kinds of termination, planned termination with individual clients, and components of termination.

Assessment

Learning Expectations

1. Understanding of assessment as a complex process and beginning skill in assessing individuals in generalist practice.
2. Ability to decide on the most appropriate client system to be served.
3. Ability to choose and apply appropriate knowledge to the assessment process.
4. Skill in judgment or decision making.
5. Skill in identifying needs and blocks to their fulfillment.
6. Skill in identifying strengths and resources in the ecosystem and skill in transactional assessment.

The first phase in the generalist social work process is *assessment,* historically referred to as *diagnosis.* Interviews (discussed in Chapter 7) are a very important source of information in assessing the situation. The classic description of the social work process includes "study, diagnosis, and treatment." In the change process, assessment involves "study" and "diagnosis." This is followed by planning and action which corresponds to "treatment." Assessment is the phase being discussed when the term *analysis* is used. The development of understanding about individuals, families, small groups, agencies, and communities is an important aspect of assessment. The understanding about a system required for professional interaction with that system is the core of the assessment stage of the interventive or service process.

Figure 4.1 is used during assessment to understand person in environment as a feeling, thinking, and acting ecosystem. In developing an understanding of person in environment during assessment, the worker seeks to understand the feelings, thoughts, and actions of the client and members of the human systems in the client's environment. The worker also seeks to understand how transactions influence these aspects of the ecosystem and are influenced by them. As with all of the other elements of the social work process, an understanding of diversity is also considered.

Assessment includes identifying strengths and resources that exist within the client, within the systems that make up the client's environment, and in the transactions within this ecosystem. A social study is an assessment. The individual social history is presented in this chapter. In discussing assessment in this chapter, the primary focus will be on assessment with individual clients. However, in generalist practice other systems are also of concern. In fact, the generalist social worker keeps an open mind about what systems she needs to work with in the change process. Although Chapters 13 through 15 focus on the change process with families, groups, and macrosystems (organizations and communities), some reference to these systems will also be made here. In addition, because systems are made up of individuals, elements of individual assessment will be relevant when assessing and working with these other systems, either as client systems or as units of attention for the change effort. Questionnaires and other research tools as well as psychological tests can be used to gather information. Assessment is an essential ingredient for the individualization of people and social systems.

Assessment is made up of both content and process. The content of the assessment for an individual client is exemplified by the schema in Table 8.2. For families the schema is presented in Table 13.1 and for groups, Table 14.1. The schemas for communities and for organizations were presented in Chapter 6 as part of understanding the environment.

Max Siporin defined *assessment* as "a process and a product of understanding on which action is based."[1] It is the collection and analysis of information, the fitting together of available facts so that they yield meaning. Within the perspective of this book, assessment does not include planning, which is seen as a separate step.

Mark A. Mattaini and Stuart A. Kirk reviewed various assessment approaches used by social workers, including the psychosocial, classification systems, and behavioral approaches often used in clinical social work as well as computerized assessment instruments, the ecosystems perspective, and expert systems. The approach that most nearly approximates the one presented for use in generalist social work is an ecosystems approach. Mattaini and Kirk characterized this approach as a way of organizing complex assessment data and suggested that it significantly expands the breadth of assessment without a loss of depth.[2]

Five concepts will be discussed in understanding assessment from a generalist perspective, using an ecosystems strengths approach to change: (1) the assessment process, (2) selection of the client system, (3) the important elements of the assessment phase, (4) the stages in the assessment phase, and (5) transactional assessment.

The Assessment Process

The assessment begins even before the worker meets the client. Generally, a request for service has been made by the client or a referral has been received from another source. Most agencies require some basic information, often called an *intake form*. At minimum, the form will usually have the client's name, address, age or date of birth, marital status, and phone number along with the reason for the request or referral. When the worker receives the form, he has already begun to think about his new client. He sees the initial need or concern expressed in the reason for the request for service. He can usually surmise some basic things, such as gender and perhaps ethnicity by the client's name. He will be able to see by the address in what area of the community or county the client lives. If he is familiar with the demographics of that area, he may know something about its socioeconomic, racial, and ethnic patterns. However, the worker should be careful to avoid making judgments or reaching conclusions about the client ahead of time. He should at least make sure that he checks out the accuracy of the information with the client.

In establishing a relationship with a client who is a member of a population at risk of discrimination or oppression, the worker uses a diversity competent approach as presented earlier in the text. He examines his own experiences and attitudes toward the diversity group. He uses naturalistic inquiry to elicit and hear the client's story. In doing so, he takes the role of learner and allows the client to assume the role of teacher or guide. This creates a situation in which barriers that might exist as a result of diversity are instead used to establish a relationship. Table 3.2 presents a schema that can be used as a guide to understanding diversity.

Nearly every agency will have documentation that is required for the case file. Records were discussed in Chapter 4. Most case records require some form of assessment document. Table 8.2 is a schema for an individual social history that serves as a basic guide for what most assessment documents should cover. The information needed for various parts of the schema was discussed in Chapter 5. The schema contains demographic or background information about person in environment; an understanding of the need or concern; and an assessment of strengths, resources, and limitations. The actual documents used by various agencies will be different in some way. For instance, the specific information needed for the assessment document and the title of the document and its contents will vary. Although much of the basic information is similar, the focus will reflect the types of services offered by the organization. For example, an assessment in a medical setting will emphasize the person's health and medical history. In schools, there will be an emphasis on educational achievement or difficulties.

A student or a new worker is likely to be tempted to use the assessment document as a focus for the initial interview. This is especially so if she is nervous about the interview.

However, it would be a major mistake to use it in that way. Focusing on paperwork sends the wrong message to the client. It says that the paperwork is more important than the client and his concerns. Not showing up for the first interview is a major problem in many cases. The second interview is the next most likely time for the client not to show up. This is mainly because of the worker's failure to connect with the client and form at least the beginning of a helping relationship. It is the worker's responsibility to know what is on the assessment form so she does not have to use it prematurely. In most settings, there is an assessment period of two or three sessions during which the worker can collect information before the documentation is due. Even if the form is due after the first session, there are ways to use the form that will actually assist in forming a relationship, as follows.

The worker studies the case files in her agency to gain an understanding of the documentation system. She attempts to master the basic content areas of the assessment form, knowing that it will take time for her to become completely familiar with it. Before the first interview with each client, she reviews the form. She begins the interview with some small talk (such as comments on the weather or the client's ability to find the agency), and at the appropriate time she asks the client about his request for service, for example, "What brings you to the agency?" If this is a home visit or a session outside of the agency, the worker can say, "We received a request for service. What can you tell me about that request?" This allows the client to start wherever he feels comfortable and does not couch the initial discussion in terms of a problem. As the client tells his story, the worker makes mental notes about information she will need in filling out the assessment document. She asks follow-up questions that focus on areas covered on the form. Good questions relate to who, what, where, when, and how. If the worker understands the answers to these questions, she will have a fairly comprehensive understanding of person in situation. These inquiries will also tell her about the client in environment and can answer many of the questions on the assessment document.

If the worker is patient and focuses first on the client, allowing him to tell his story and express his concerns, she will be building a relationship with him while still gathering information. This is actually similar to the approach described in becoming diversity competent. By focusing on the client, she sends him the message that he is important and that she cares about his needs and concerns. This builds trust and is critical to establishing a helping relationship. Actually, the worker has little choice but to take this approach. If the client fails to return or refuses further service, she will have wasted time gathering information for the assessment. If the client does not trust her, the value or accuracy of the information may not be very great. Once the client feels he has been heard, the worker can ask for his assistance in completing the assessment. This generally comes at the point where the documentation is due. If the worker has another session or two, she can compile the information she has after each session and review what she needs before the next session. If she must complete the assessment after the first interview, she can enlist the client's help with the information during the last few minutes of the session by asking something like the following: "I have some paperwork I need to complete. Would you help me with it by answering a few questions?" By requesting assistance from the client in completing the assessment document, the worker turns a potential liability in relationship building into an asset. She can actually strengthen her relationship by establishing more of a two-way relationship in which the client helps her to help him.

Selection of the Client System

One of the most important decisions to be made is the appropriate client system to be served. As mentioned throughout the text, the generalist approach calls for the worker to be prepared to work with individuals, families, groups, organizations, and communities. Generalist social workers may work with individuals or systems as clients, or they may be the focus of the change efforts on behalf of any size client system. The selection of the client system generally occurs during the assessment phase, although it can also occur during planning. The selection of the focus of the change efforts or the unit of attention is part of the planning process. The selection of the client system determines the focus of the assessment process and the type of assessment to be used (individual, family, group, organization, or community).

The term *client* was discussed in Chapter 5, where it was stated that the client is the person or system that either seeks the help of a social worker or is served by an agency employing a social worker. For students in field placement and for most social workers, an individual is the most frequent type of client system encountered. The next most frequent is the family or subsystems of the family. Groups can be fairly frequent in some settings, such as residential care, day programs, and prevention and growth and development services for children and youth. The least frequent client system for the typical social worker would be an organization or community. The type of client served is determined primarily by the nature of the service delivered by the agency in which the student is placed or the worker employed. It is also determined by the role and the status the worker has in the agency. For example, MSW social workers are more likely to be employed in agencies that provide family work or group work to families or individuals with complicated problems that require therapy. BSW social workers provide counseling and support services to families or in groups, but they are not trained to do therapy. In most agencies, administrators and supervisors are more likely to be MSWs. Part of their responsibility is to plan and implement changes in the agency. Professional community organizers are also more likely to be MSWs. However, BSW social workers will have opportunities to participate in change at the organizational or community level and at times may actually initiate those changes. Thus, the worker must be prepared to work with all of these systems.

Even when the worker has an opportunity to work with systems larger than the individual client, the initial request for service frequently involves an individual or individuals. As the assessment of the need or concern proceeds, the worker may find that the most appropriate client system is the family or a subsystem of the family (marital, parent, parent-child, or sibling subsystems). The worker might believe that the person would be served better in a group, especially one that is made up of members who have similar needs or concerns. He might observe that service delivery or meeting client needs could be improved by changing how an agency functions. He may find that a segment of the community is affected by a situation and that collective action is needed. Table 8.1 outlines several common indications and counterindications for selecting various size client systems and units of attention. Units of attention refers to systems that are the focus of the change efforts, which will be covered in Chapter 9.

As the worker begins to discuss the initial need or concern, he maintains an open mind about the appropriate level for service delivery. This will determine the client system

TABLE 8.1 *Indications and Counterindications with Client Systems and Units of Attention*

	Indications	Counterindications
Individuals	Information giving Information gathering Concrete service Referral service Need relates primarily to an individual without significant family No other involvement feasible Intrapsychic difficulties Individual who with help can involve significant systems in the change process Individual choice	Cannot function in a one-to-one helping relationship Action-oriented service needed Focus on interactional aspects of family or peer group needed Need fulfillment best reached by change in larger system
Family	Major difficulties seem to exist in family interaction One family member undercuts change efforts of other members Family needs to respond to individual need Need for understanding family interaction to understand individual functioning Family needs to examine role functioning or communication Chaotic families where there is a need to restore order Family choice	Irreversible trend toward family breakup Significant impairment of individual family member prevents participation Need for individual help precludes work with family No common concern or goal Worker cannot deal with destructive interactions
Small group	Individuals face similar situations and can benefit from interchange Group influence on the individual is great Development of socialization skills is indicated Use of activity is desirable Focus on environmental change Usable natural groups	Individual overwhelmed by the group Individual destructive to group A common purpose or goal does not exist Sufficient cohesive factors do not exist Environment will not allow the group to function Environment will not allow the group to reach its goal to at least some extent
Organization	Difficulty related to organizational functioning Number of individuals are affected and needs not being met because of organizational factors Workers are overconstrained from providing service to clients	Dangers of further negative results to clients are great Client service will be neglected or negated
Community	Lack of needed resources and services Lack of coordination of services Community influence on organization or family prevents meeting of need Community functioning affects a large number of individuals and families negatively	Same as organization

with whom he will be working. He focuses first on person in environment. He is knowledgeable about the nature of the service delivery system within his agency and for other organizations in the community. He is also aware of issues that concern various segments of the community. The decision about the appropriate client system to be served is a joint decision involving the worker and the client. It is made within the context of person in environment, the service delivery system, and the community.

Important Elements of the Assessment Phase

Assessment is a complex process at the core of the change process. The need for development of an understanding of clients, whether they are individuals, families, or small groups, and of the systems in the client's environment was discussed in relation to the interactional process in Part Two and will be covered in more depth for particular systems in later chapters. These schemas are tools for gathering information, but care must be taken that relevant information that falls outside the schema is not overlooked. Assessment, although a creative process, is also scientific in that it is a manifestation of the scientific method. Some of its most important characteristics are as follows:

1. *Assessment is both product and process*—The stages of the assessment make up the process that the worker goes through in conducting an assessment. The social history is the product that is the outcome of the assessment. Table 8.2 is a schema for development of an individual social history. A case example is included later in this chapter.

2. *Assessment is ongoing*—Assessment takes place throughout the life of the helping endeavor. During the early stages, it is a primary focus. However, during later stages, when the work of doing something about need and of intervening into transactions among systems takes place, assessment is also a concern. As the client system and worker engage in their work together, new information becomes available and new understandings emerge. These then become a part of the ongoing assessment.

3. *Assessment is twofold, focusing both on understanding client in environment and on providing a base for planning and action*—Information must be gathered about the people and systems involved, about their interrelationships and their environment. Information should be collected about the need, blocks to need fulfillment, the situation, and the people and systems significant to the need. It is also important to determine strengths, challenges, motivation for change, and resistance to change that are applicable to the persons and systems involved. When assessing the environment and large systems, it is important to gather information about the demography of the system and the situation being considered.

Information is gathered in many different ways. Of prime importance are the client's perceptions and feelings about the need or concern and the situation. Carefully attending to the client's story conveys respect and acknowledges that the client is the "expert" regarding his life. The manner in which he tells the story, including nonverbal communication, provides important information.

Other sources of information may be previous case records and reports from other interested persons. If a worker uses information sources other than the client, the client

TABLE 8.2   *Schema for Development of a Social History: Individual*

I. The person
    A. Identifying information (as needed by agency): name, address, date and place of birth, marital status, religion, race, ethnicity, gender, referred by whom and why
    B. Family
        1. Parents: names, dates of birth, dates of death, place or places of residence, relationships with each other and family members
        2. Siblings: names, dates of birth, places of residence, relationships
        3. Spouse: names, ages, dates of marriages and divorces, relationships
        4. Children: names, ages, dates of birth, places of residence, relationships
        5. Resources in the family for client—expectations for client
    C. Education and work experience
        1. Last grade of school completed, degrees if any, special knowledge or training; attitudes toward educational experiences; resources and expectations of educational system for client
        2. Work history—jobs held, dates, reasons for leaving; attitudes toward work experiences; resources and expectations of work system for client
    D. Diversity
        1. Disabling factors—physical, mental health history, current functioning
        2. Cultural and ethnic identification, importance to client
        3. Other diversity factors (include religious affiliation or spiritual factors, if any)
        4. Resources and expectations related to diversity characteristics of client
    E. Environmental factors
        1. Significant relationships outside family; resources and expectations for client
        2. Significant neighborhood and community factors; resources and expectations for client

II. The concern or need
    A. Reason for request for service
    B. History of concern or need; onset of concern or need; nature and results of coping attempts; factors that seem to be contributing to concern or need
    C. Capacity to carry out "vital roles" (spouse, employee, student, etc.)
    D. Needs of client (general)
        1. Needs based on common human need/development
            a. Stage of physical, cognitive, and psychosocial development
            b. Adequacy of need fulfillment in previous stages
            c. Present needs (needs for developmental stage and compensation for previous stage deficiency)
        2. Needs based on diversity factors
            a. What dominant societal factors and attitudes affect the way people of this diversity meet common human/developmental needs?
            b. What cultural group factors affect the way people of this diversity meet common human/developmental needs?
            c. Individualize client within the diverse group. What are this client's attitudes toward diversity, means of coping with diversity, adaptation or lifestyle within diverse group, and coping or adaptation relative to dominant societal expectations?
            d. What incongruities exist between this client's way of functioning and societal expectations as a result of diversity?

(continued)

TABLE 8.2 *(continued)*

      e. What needs does this person have because of dominant societal attitudes and expectations, because of cultural factors related to common human need/human development, because of individual factors of attitudes toward the diversity and dominant societal expectations and impingements, or
      because of incongruities between the client's way of functioning and societal expectations based on diversity?

   3. Needs based on environmental expectations
      a. Client responsibilities toward family, peer group, work, organizations, and community
      b. Other environmental expectations of client; client's attitudes toward these expectations
      c. Are responsibilities and expectations of the client realistic?
      d. Client needs because of the responsibilities and expectations

   4. Needs of client in relation to the request for service
      a. What general needs of the client have bearing on the request for service?
      b. What is the specific need of the client in relation to the request?
      c. What factors seem to be blocking the fulfillment of that need?

III. Strengths and challenges for helping
   A. What does the client expect to happen during and as a result of the service to be provided?
   B. What are the client's ideas, interests, and plans that are relevant to the service?
   C. What is the client's motivation for using the service and for change?
   D. What is the client's capacity for coping and for change? What might impinge? What are the individual's internal resources for change?
   E. What are the client's strengths?
   F. What are the environmental resources and the environmental responsibilities and impingements that could support or mitigate against coping or change?
   G. Are there any other factors that affect the client's motivation, capacity, or opportunity for change?
   H. What is the nature of the stress factor?
   I. How realistic are client's expectations?
   J. Summary of strengths and the challenges of client in situation as they relate to meeting need

should be aware of the use of the resources and give suggestions about sources for such information and permission for the worker to obtain the information from other people. The information being collected should always be clearly connected to the concern or need being worked on.

4. *Assessment is a mutual process involving both client and worker*—The client is involved in all aspects of assessment to the maximum of his capacity. The primary content to be assessed arises from the worker-client interaction in the interview. One source of content is the information provided as the worker observes the client in the interview. Content also derives from observations of the client in life situations. The worker discusses observations and other information with the client to establish the meaning of the facts or to gain an understanding of person in environment. The use of a mutual process in assessment is one means of empowering clients because it provides them with a sense of self-worth and demonstrates that what they think and believe is important. They come to realize that they are not passive recipients of help but important partners in the work to be done.

5. *There is movement within the assessment process*—Movement usually occurs from observation of the situation to identification of information needed for understanding. This is followed by collection of information and an explanation of its meaning. The facts and their meanings about various parts are put together in order to understand the total situation.

6. *Both horizontal and vertical exploration are important*—In the early stages of assessment it is usually helpful to look at the situation horizontally; that is, the situation is examined in breadth to identify all possible parts, interactions, and relationships. The purpose of this horizontal exploration is to determine the block to need fulfillment and the strengths and resources in the ecosystem that can be used to meet the need. Later, those parts identified as most important to the situation or to meeting needs are examined vertically, or in depth. The information-gathering process can move from horizontal to vertical and back to horizontal several times as the worker and client explore the need and the situation. Social workers should develop skill in determining when a horizontal approach is most appropriate and when a vertical approach is the one to use.

7. *The knowledge base is used in developing understanding*—The worker uses her knowledge base as one means for developing understanding of client in environment. An understanding of an individual takes into consideration factors of human development and diversity. An understanding of a family is related to what is known about family structure and process. An understanding of an agency considers knowledge of bureaucratic structures. An understanding of community calls for knowledge of economics and political science. An understanding of the ecosystem requires knowledge of systems theory and the exchange of matter, energy, and information among systems.

8. *Assessment identifies needs in life situations and explains their meaning and patterns*—Assessment makes use of the process of growth and change throughout the life cycle in specifying the need and what is blocking need fulfillment. (This idea is discussed more fully later in this chapter.)

9. *Assessment identifies client and ecosystem strengths with an eye toward building on those strengths during intervention*—Individuals grow from their strengths, not their limitations. A thorough assessment of physical, mental, emotional, and behavioral assets must occur in order to work with the client system to set goals, objectives, and tasks that have a high likelihood of success. Identification of client strengths requires identifying resources present in the client system and the environment or situation that can be used to meet needs.[3]

10. *Assessment is individualized*—Human situations are complex; no two are exactly the same. Each assessment is different and is related to the differential situation of the client. Assessment takes into consideration the different parts of the situation and relates these to the unique whole that emerges. This is particularly true when working with populations that differ from the worker's ethnic or sociocultural orientation. It is critical to understand the situation and its meaning to the client system from the client's, not the worker's, perspective.

11. *Judgment is important*—Many decisions must be made regarding each assessment. Decisions include what parts to consider, which parts of the knowledge base to apply, how to involve the client, and how to define the concern or need. The kinds of decisions that are made greatly affect the content and the interpretation of that content. The client system's view of the significance of events must be evaluated carefully; again, what the worker may consider unimportant from his frame of reference may be of great importance to the client system, or vice versa.

12. *There are limits to the understanding that can be developed*—No assessment is ever complete. It is impossible to gain complete understanding of any situation. It is also undesirable. Understanding takes time. Clients in need are seeking help that often must be given quickly. The worker must decide what understanding is necessary to give that help and then be aware of new understandings that develop in giving the help. The worker must be comfortable with the uncertainty of limited understanding and learn to trust in the ongoing process of assessment.

The tasks of assessment, then, are (1) identification of the need or concern and of client and ecosystem strengths and resources, (2) identification of the information needed to further understand the need or concern and to determine appropriate means for meeting the need, and (3) collection and analysis of information. Decision making includes interpreting meanings, ordering information, and discovering relationships among parts of the situation. Decision making considers persons, needs, situations, client and ecosystem strengths, and relationships.

Judgment

Judgment is an important component of assessment. Judgment is, in effect, decision making. According to Harriet Bartlett, "Professional judgment provides the bridge between knowledge and value, on one hand, and interventive action on the other. Assessment is its first application in practice."[4]

Although the discussion of characteristics of assessment may seem to focus on small systems (individuals, families, and small groups), the same characteristics apply to larger systems (organizations and the community). Because individuals, families, and small groups are subsystems of large systems, any assessment of a large system involves assessing the subsystems. The schema provided in Table 6.1 provides a framework for large-system assessments. This schema should, of course, be adapted and individualized depending on the particular system and the understanding needed for the specific service at hand. It is also used to assess the community portion of the ecosystem when working with individuals, families, groups, organizations, or neighborhoods. The generalist social worker must have knowledge and skill in assessing both large and small systems.

Values are very influential in the decision-making process. Our perceptions and thinking are affected by our values, which influence how much of a situation and what parts of a situation we perceive. We tend to screen out that which is not congruent with our values or our thinking. Because of our biases about how things should be, we may miss the unfamiliar or the different. In particular, the perception of what constitutes strength may be very different in various cultures. When working with people from different backgrounds, it is particularly important for the worker to be aware of how her values influence her decisions. Interpretations of meaning from the worker's value perspective may be invalid from the client's perspective.

For example, a worker who adopts a personality theory emphasizing the individual may have difficulty working with a client who is Native American and whose orientation is toward the extended family and the tribe. The worker might determine that the client is not being given appropriate opportunities for self-determination, whereas the client might feel the worker is overlooking the client's responsibilities to family and tribe. The worker would be viewing the situation through her value perspective, which considers individual rights to be of prime importance. The client would be viewing self-determination as irrelevant and be more concerned with how he could better the lot of the collective group. Some resolution of such value-driven difference must take place before a worker and client can work productively together.

Harriet A. Feiner and Harriet Katz have pointed out how deeply held beliefs relating to women and family structure influence the judgments that are made in practice situations.[5] They noted that commonly held myths, such as that women should not compete with men and women should assume the nurturing role, can be detrimental when working with female clients who are struggling to become independent individuals.

Decision making is an important ingredient in professional judgment. Judgments are decisions based on reason and evidence, with the goal of identifying what is a fact, what is an assumption, and what is an inference. The influence that values have on assumptions and inferences is then considered and perceptions are analyzed. In addition, value conflicts and ethical dilemmas are assessed and included in the decisions that are made.

In applying a knowledge base to explanations, it is important that the appropriate knowledge has been chosen. Florence Hollis identified the following three criteria for choosing knowledge for social work education.[6] These can be used in considering knowledge for application to specific practice situations.

1. *The choice should be related to the phenomena being assessed and the situation being considered*—For example, hallucinations have different meanings in different cultures. In white American culture this is considered to be a sign of mental illness requiring treatment. In other cultures this is seen as a gift in which the person has been given access to the spirit world.

2. *The choice should be related to whether the knowledge is useful in a social work context*—Social work takes the view of the human situation that people are self-determining. Thus, knowledge that is deterministic in nature is not appropriate for social work because it provides little hope for change. Determinism negates the idea that people have choices and that by making different choices they can more adequately deal with situations and problems. Without hope for change or the possibility of choice, the social work process is unworkable.

3. *Consideration should be given to the nature of the power the knowledge possesses*—Knowledge developed from working with a small sample in situation does not have the power that knowledge developed by testing a hypothesis under different circumstances with a large sample does. In other words, what has worked with one client may not work with another client because the worker may fail to take into consideration the power of the knowledge being used.

Decisions need to be made jointly with the client and with the client's needs, preferences, and strengths as primary considerations. Principles that can be used when making judgments in assessment include:

1. *Individualization*—Each person and system in a situation is different. In order to assess effectively, the unique aspects of the system need to be identified and understood. This understanding should be derived primarily from the client system.

2. *Participation*—Client participation in decisions and in the assessment process is an important means of developing an assessment that recognizes the client's needs and preferences. Further, it is extremely difficult to assess client strengths without client participation in some manner.

3. *Human development*—Assessment recognizes the developmental process of an individual and a social system as a means to further the understanding of that person or system. One also needs to be aware of the impact of cultural and ethnic influences on developmental stages.

4. *Human diversity*—Recognition of the diverse aspects of individuals, systems, and cultural groups is another important component of assessment. This should take into account strengths that are unique to various populations.

5. *Purposeful behavior*—Recognition that all behavior is purposeful leads to a search for understanding of the underlying meanings of behavior.

6. *Systemic transactions*—The assessment process identifies stressful and energizing life transactions, adaptive and maladapative interpersonal processes, and environmental responsiveness and unresponsiveness when seeking understanding of person in environment.

7. *Strengths and resources*—Identification and acknowledgment of the strengths and positive attributes of clients and their environments are critical.

Through using the principles of individualization, participation, human development, human diversity, purposeful behavior, systemic transactions, and strengths and resources, the worker identifies with the client, the client's needs, and the client's preferences about what needs to be done. This, combined with an awareness of value influences and an appropriate choice of the knowledge to apply, leads to an assessment that yields a valid understanding of client in environment that is useful for planning intervention. Mary K. Rodwell, in presenting a model for assessment based on the naturalistic paradigm of research, described a model similar to the one discussed in this chapter when she stated, "The naturalistic framework frees social work to reach a deeper understanding of person-situation through a holistic assessment style and promotes a sophisticated inquiry into human relationships with social and physical environments."[7]

Stages in the Assessment Phase

Assessment is the first phase of the change process. It lays the foundation for the phases that follow. Each phase is a part of the change process as follows:

Assessment Phase

Identify the initial need or concern

Identify the nature of the need or concern

Identify potential strengths and resources in the ecosystem

Select and collect information

Analyze the available information

Planning Phase

Develop a plan based on analysis of available information

Action Phase

Take action to implement the plan

Evaluation and Termination

Evaluate results during each phase and after the plan is completed

Consolidate change at termination of service

The first five stages comprise the assessment phase. The planning phase will be covered in Chapter 9. The action phase is discussed in Chapters 10 and 11. Evaluation and termination are covered in Chapter 12.

A difficult task in the change process is the specification of the need or concern. The client brings an initial need or concern to the helping situation. Based on material discussed in the first few contacts with the client, the worker may realize that the presenting need is not the actual need. As the worker clarifies the reasons for the initial need or concern, she makes assumptions about the nature of the need or concern. Identification of theoretical knowledge used in thinking about client in environment is another way in which assumptions are created. As assumptions are identified, it is possible to determine the information needed to verify the preliminary formulation of the need or concern and to restate it if necessary. The need to be addressed is formulated after an understanding of client in environment is developed and after the available information has been analyzed.

Formulation of the need or concern is the basis for the next four stages of the assessment. Planning and action can be enhanced by thorough and appropriate formulation of the need or concern. Three steps of formulating the need or concern are (1) identification of need, (2) identification of blocks to need fulfillment, and (3) formulation of the need in terms of removing the blocks to need fulfillment. Once the need or concern is identified, the worker and the client can proceed in considering the nature of that need or concern and potential strengths and resources in the ecosystem that would meet that need. This is followed by selection and collection of information and an analysis of the information available. It should also be remembered that the needs that concern the social worker are those that relate to social functioning and that planned change needs to build on existing strengths and actual or potential resources in the client and her ecosystem.

Identify the Initial Need or Concern

1. *Identify initial need*—The first source of material for identifying need is how the client tells his story. The worker not only listens to the verbal content but also looks for nonverbal communication. The pronouns and words used, the tense of verbs, the tone and inflection all give clues to the meaning of the need. The worker also can note what is not said, what is omitted.

Needs must be considered within the context of the client's diversity. Although all human beings have some common human needs, different needs are associated with culture, gender, age, religion, sexual orientation, and so on. For instance, the dominant American culture places great emphasis on the individual, but in African American, Asian, and Hispanic cultures, the family unit takes on a great deal of significance. As a result, individual needs must be seen in relation to the family. Talking about what is best for the individual without considering the family would be inappropriate. In Native American culture, ancestors, the spirit world, and the tribe are important considerations that supercede the individual. Social workers should consult others beforehand and take time to weigh a decision before making the decision. Women tend to place more importance on relationships, so needs may be expressed in terms of significant relationships and the affect that decisions might have on them. Religious beliefs may require clients to pray or have a sense of peace with their spiritual self. People who are gay or lesbian may consider the need to have their sexual orientation either hidden or revealed and respected as part of the process. For those who are in partnerships, the effects of revealing their sexual orientations may have negative impacts on their partner's circumstances.

The skillful worker often has hunches about what is needed. These hunches are part of the art of social work, the creative nature of the work. Hunches are very useful, but they should be checked out with the client or the system before they are given the power of fact. Hunches are generally based on the worker's experiences rather than the client's; it is, therefore, important to evaluate these ideas in light of the client's reality before sharing them verbally with the client.

As the worker begins to identify the client's need by using the material provided by the client, hunches or ideas that derive from the knowledge base, and information available to the worker from other sources, other systems significant to the situation can be identified. The needs of these systems in relation to the situation being considered should also be identified. Systems that are significant to the situation are those that are affected by the lack of need fulfillment, those that affect the situation, and those that may have resources for meeting the need.

One of the areas that warrants attention is the agency and the service delivery system. If the function of the agency does not include services that can enable the client to fulfill the identified need or needs, the client should be made aware of this. The nature of the service delivery system is sometimes an important factor in the lack of need fulfillment.

2. *Identify blocks to need fulfillment*—Once the need is identified, it is then possible to consider why that need is not being fulfilled. The social worker's past experience, values, and theoretical framework lead to assumptions about the reasons for the blockage. These preliminary assumptions must be checked. Additional information about the client and the situation may be needed. The client and the significant systems should be given an opportunity to provide their points of view. Written materials, such as case records or descriptions of social systems involved, may be useful.

From a diversity perspective, blocks to need fulfillment are often associated with the effects of prejudice, discrimination, and oppression. This is seen in the case example at the end of this chapter. Whenever the worker is engaged in helping a member of a population at risk of these blocks, the worker should consciously incorporate this factor into examining potential blocks. There may be some reluctance to do so, particularly if the worker is a member of a more dominant group, such as males working with females or white workers working with people of color. Collective guilt can come into play or a sense of guilt arising from being a member of a particular culture, race, gender, and so on, that has engaged in prejudice, discrimination, and oppression. Guilt also can be associated with privileges that members of the dominant group enjoy that members of other groups do not. The worker might also be resistant because recognizing such blockages means that change needs to occur in how clients are treated by society and this would be a daunting task to say the least. Obviously, one worker is not going to change societal attitudes and actions. However, the actions of those in the immediate environment of the client may very well be changed. The diversity competent worker considers prejudice, discrimination, and oppression as blocks to need fulfillment in examining the needs of her client.

From an ecosystems strengths perspective, the location of the blockage is sought in the relationships among the significant systems. In this way, the needs of all systems are recognized and the problem is not considered the responsibility of only one system but is seen as interactive in nature.

Carel Germain and Alex Gitterman have identified three situations that seem likely to lead to problems in social functioning: (1) stressful life transitions, (2) communication and relationship difficulties, and (3) environmental unresponsiveness.[8] Assessment of client in environment to see if one of these conditions exists is one means of determining the nature of the blockage of need fulfillment.

Stressful life transitions can result from difficulties in carrying out the tasks of the developmental stages of individuals and other social systems. Thus, the assessment must be concerned with identifying the developmental stage as well as the tasks that are not being carried out. Difficulties may result from lack of opportunity, including opportunity to fulfill tasks in ways congruent with one's cultural or diversity group.

Another potentially stressful life transition is status change. This includes such events as becoming a widow or widower, becoming unemployed, graduation from or dropping out of school, and becoming part of the workforce. Change of status creates new role demands on people. Sometimes there has been no preparation for these demands. The widow with young children who returns to the work force confronts not only the demands of being a single parent and helping the family adapt to the loss of a father but also the demands of a job. Demands of the single-parent role and the work role may conflict or be overwhelming.

Closely related to stressful situations are crisis situations. When change is so great that persons and systems cannot cope and maintain a steady state, a crisis can result. The need is not only for a resolution of the situation but also for the system to regain its steady state so that it can meet the expectations of its environment.

Other social functioning difficulties develop because a person or social system is not effectively communicating with or relating to other people and social systems. Some people from diverse cultures have considerable difficulty relating to the institutions of society. For example, a school's lack of awareness of the needs of children from diverse cultures can undermine the ability of the parents to relate to the school and can result in unmet educational needs of the children. The individual or family may not be able to use existing resources or they may not even know about them. The school may not be able to identify the strengths of the individual or family because of lack of understanding of cultural factors. The underlying issue is lack of accurate communication, which can result in relationship difficulties.

The needs of children from diverse cultures can result from the school's unresponsiveness to their needs. Environmental unresponsiveness is a third cause of stress and coping failure. Environmental unresponsiveness can take two forms: failure to provide the needed service or failure to provide the needed service in a manner in which it can be used by the diverse client. Examples of the latter failure include unrealistic expectations of the client on the part of the social worker, providing the service in a way that requires the client to violate cultural values and norms, and expecting clients to function with ease in a culturally foreign milieu.

3. *Formulate the need or concern*—Once the blockage to the need is identified, it is possible to formulate the concern. Formulation of the need or concern considers the need that is not being fulfilled, the block or blocks to the fulfillment of that need, and factors contributing to the block. It is important to be as specific as possible while still recognizing the transactional nature of social functioning.

The specification of need may be made in several ways. It may be that a concrete resource or service is lacking, such as sufficient income to meet the needs of a nutritious diet or health care. Need can also be specified in terms of psychosocial development needs. An example would be a physically challenged ten-year-old child who does not have the opportunity to develop daily living skills. This might occur because of lack of understanding of the child's need to feel competent or because the mother compensates for her guilt over the child's condition by "overcaring." Need can also be specified in terms of inadequate role fulfillment in the realms of parenting, marriage, or work or in terms of difficulty in life transitions. Another way of specifying need is in terms of relationships among people and social systems.

In formulating the need or concern, the worker includes those that are associated with the diversity of the client. She does this in a way that captures the need from the perspective of the client. The best way to do this is to actively seek out the client's version of what the need or concern is. Paraphrasing and summarizing with a solid checkout is important. In the case example of Jerry Adams, the worker might express this as follows: "So it seems that your former school valued diversity much more than what you have experienced in your new school. Is that what I am hearing you say?" This might be followed up by saying: "So one of the needs that you have is to be respected as an African American. Am I on the right track with this?"

The next step in formulating the concern or need is a statement about what seems to be blocking the need fulfillment, including the recognition of relationships with potential resources. This statement needs to be clearly worded and must recognize the transactional aspects of the blockage.

The case example at the end of this chapter can be used to illustrate the concern or need. Jerry Adams, a thirteen-year-old African American male, is having difficulty at school since moving from the city to a small, predominantly white community. The need is for Jerry to be successful at school. The block to fulfilling this need is prejudice and discrimination, and Jerry's need to learn some coping skills that will improve his academic performance and reduce the likelihood of getting into physical confrontations. This latter need is not intended to place blame on Jerry in these situations but rather to empower him with effective alternative responses when others impose their prejudices on him. Some of Jerry's needs can be formulated in terms of removal of the blockages as follows:

Jerry needs to feel positive about himself and his new school and community.

Jerry needs to be respected as an African American.

Jerry needs to be accepted by his peers and by adults at school and in the community.

Jerry needs to become more successful academically again.

Jerry needs some new skills that would help him to respond effectively to situations of prejudice and to avoid physical confrontations.

The source of a blockage may be in attitudes and values, knowledge and understanding, behavior, coping skills, role overload, environmental expectations, ignorance of available resources, or lack of usable resources. Usually, the source of blockage is not only one but a combination of circumstances. Formulation of the concern or need should recognize this complexity in stating need and specifying blockage to need fulfillment, as in the preceding examples.

Identify the Nature of the Need or Concern

As the worker and the client proceed through the assessment phase, there are assumptions about the person in environment that play important roles in focusing the assessment. At the outset of assessment, the worker determines (1) what information is necessary to understand the situation and (2) what resources are available to meet the needs of the client and his ecosystem. In order to accomplish the first, the worker must make some assumptions about the nature of the concern or need. She uses her knowledge of human behavior in the social environment, of human development and diversity, and of Maslow's and

Towle's systems of identifying needs to determine the underlying nature of the needs. For example, using Maslow's hierarchy, are the needs related to basic needs, such as food, clothing, shelter, or health care? Is the need related to safety and security, socialization, self-esteem, self-actualization, or cognitive understanding?[9] Using Towle's elements of need, does the need represent a need for emotional and intellectual growth, relationships, or spiritual well-being?[10]

As a next step, the worker combines knowledge and creativity in speculating about what might be creating the need in the specific situation. In the case example, the worker might assume that Jerry is overwhelmed by all the changes in his life that have occurred since his family moved from the city to a small community. She could assume that the coping skills that he had used at his former school are not working for him as he faces prejudice and discrimination in his new school. She might assume that the loss of time spent with his father makes Jerry feel like he has to face this alone and that if they spent more time together it would strengthen Jerry's ability to deal with some of these new challenges. She could also assume that if Jerry felt more accepted and the racial comments stopped, he would be as successful at school as he has been in the past. She may assume that the situation in which Jerry was caught trying to steal a pair of tennis shoes was an isolated incident that only occurred because of his desire to be accepted by his peers in the neighborhood. Formulating these assumptions gives focus to the selection and collection of information which follows later.

Identify Potential Strengths and Resources in the Ecosystem

Moving to the third step in the process, the worker might speculate about what would bring about the changes necessary to meet the needs. She begins by identifying potential strengths, abilities, assets, capacities, and resources within the client system and his ecosystem. How does the person, family, group, organization, or community meet its needs? What is going well? What works now or has worked in the past? How does the present circumstance represent a deviation from the client system's typical pattern of meeting needs? The worker then formulates some assumptions about what is needed to develop, maintain, or restore the ecosystem to a steady state in which needs are met on a mutually satisfying basis. In the case of Jerry Adams, these assumptions might be formulated as follows:

1. Jerry is capable of performing well in school because he has been successful before the move.
2. Jerry is a hard worker because he has worked at jobs that were appropriate for his age level.
3. Jerry is able to develop and maintain positive peer relationships because he had this at his former school.
4. Jerry has a strong family system that is capable of supporting him in this new situation.
5. The school is academically sound and could be a resource if Jerry's negative experiences could be turned around.

6. The community could be a resource because it has many opportunities for work, cultural enrichment, recreation, and human services available either within the community or nearby.
7. The school and community are capable of reducing the prejudice and discrimination that has arisen because the Adams family and another African American family moved into the community.

As with the nature of the need, the assumptions regarding potential strengths and resources in the ecosystem provide a focus for the selection and collection of information that follows.

In this part of the change process, the worker tries to be realistic while still allowing herself to speculate about what might be possible. One question that is invaluable in working with any size client system is: What would it take to meet this need? This leads the worker to look at possibilities rather than looking at limitations and deficits.

Select and Collect Information

The assumptions that are made about the nature of the needs and the strengths and resources available are important to setting the stage for collecting information. Information is needed to determine whether the assumptions are true or if some other assumptions need to be made and checked out. The worker should not collect information without a purpose. The two main reasons for having information should be to assist the client in meeting his needs and to meet the bureaucratic demands of the agency or regulatory bodies. In the latter case, certain information may be collected to identify clients, to bill insurance or other third-party payment systems, to meet eligibility criteria, to meet basic standards of accepted professional practice, and so on. Care should be taken that information is gathered in a way that respects the client's right to confidentiality. This was discussed in Chapter 4.

In order to achieve a thorough understanding of the situation, it is useful if the worker asks herself what she knows about who, what, where, when, and how. These five areas of questioning are typically used by reporters when they are covering a story. They are also useful to the social worker to ensure that she has covered all of the aspects of the situation. A sixth area relates to the question "Why," but this will be covered in the analysis portion of the process.

Based on the assumptions made, the worker is able to select the information needed to understand the situation and to lay the groundwork for developing a plan to meet the needs of the client and his ecosystem. Using the various schema presented in this chapter and in Chapters 6, 13, and 14, the worker selects relevant parts of each schema, depending on the size of the client system and the parts of the ecosystem being considered. For example, in working with individuals, the Schema for Development of a Social History: Individual (see Table 8.2) is used as an overall guideline. Relevant parts of the family history schema (see Table 13.1) are used as they relate to understanding the person's interactions with his family, if this is important to understanding the situation and meeting the client's need. Relevant parts of the community schema (see Table 6.1) are used to assess the systems in the community that are impinging on the situation or that might be accessed in meeting the need.

In selecting and collecting information, the social worker considers diversity factors that are present in the situation. She seeks to find out how the client views his or her own diversity. This should include the influence of diversity on thoughts, feelings, and actions. It should also include the response to diversity by both the nurturing and sustaining environment and how these affect the client's thoughts, feelings, and actions. The manner in which information is collected is also important. For the most part, naturalistic inquiry is the best approach to use. By taking the position that she does not know what she does not know, the worker allows clients to take the position of experts in their own lives, including their lives as diverse persons. It allows clients to tell their own stories using their own words in a manner of their choosing. When the worker incorporates diversity in her selection and collection of information, she is better able to see the whole picture in full color, so to speak.

Analyze the Available Information

There are four general areas the worker must analyze as the work proceeds: (1) what the worker understands about person in environment and strengths and resources, given what is known; (2) what changes are needed, given what is known; (3) what further information is needed to better understand the situation; and (4) what further information is needed to bring about successful change.

As the worker analyzes these four areas, she uses critical thinking along with her knowledge base to gain insight into the client and the ecosystem. Throughout the process, she checks out her analysis with the client and with relevant parts of the ecosystem. Paraphrasing and summarizing are particularly valuable in this process. The worker asks the client (or significant person, if it is not the client) if her perceptions about the situation are accurate and if there are other aspects that the client is aware of that might be important. In the case example, the worker might say: "So, Jerry, it sounds like your experience with racial slurs is new for you because you did not hear that at your former school. Is that right?" She might follow up asking: "Could you tell me how you feel when that happens?" This would shift the focus from actions that have occurred to feelings. The worker could change the focus to the thinking aspect by asking: "What were you thinking when that happened?"

The worker asks the client for input into what changes are needed or desired. A good question to ask is: "What would you like to see happen that would meet your needs in this situation?" Or: "If this situation was resolved and your needs were being met, what would it look like?"

Analysis of information should lead the worker to an understanding of person in environment and potential strengths and resources that are sufficient to proceed with planning. It should answer the question "Why?" to the extent that the worker understands the situation from the client's perspective and is able to see what is blocking the need from being met. The worker and the client should be somewhat confident that the strengths and resources necessary to meet the need are present, either in the client and her ecosystem or in the worker's ecosystem (the service delivery system). If greater understanding is needed or if more strengths and resources must be found, then the analysis should indicate this, and the worker and the client should return to an earlier stage of the assessment process for more information.

Quite often, the analysis or other stages of the assessment will uncover new or previously unknown needs or concerns that take precedence over the initial need. This can occur for many reasons, including reluctance by the client to reveal uncomfortable information before trust is established or lack of awareness by the client of the need or that the worker can assist in helping meet the need. In this case, the worker and the client return to stage 1 to formulate the need and then proceed through the remaining stages. There is no need to start over. Rather, it is only necessary to gather information regarding this new need or concern.

In analyzing the available information, the worker uses her knowledge and skills, especially her knowledge of social systems theory and ecosystems, to bring about an understanding of person in environment. She uses a diversity competent approach with naturalistic inquiry to understand the client's diversity from the client's perspective. She uses her practice wisdom and experience to help her to understand the situation at hand and what might be done to meet the need. She uses her critical thinking skills to analyze the gaps between need and need fulfillment. She uses her creativity to uncover strengths and resources in the client, the client's ecosystem, and the service delivery system and to brainstorm with the client about what might work in meeting the client's needs. Thus, analysis is truly the heart of the thinking part of the social work process. (See Figure 1.1.)

Transactional Assessment

The transactional nature of human interaction is complex, and this complexity can cause difficulties in assessment. Transactional assessment depends to a great extent on the worker's creativity and ability to look at a complex situation and bring order and meaning to that complexity. Transactional assessment is particularly useful when considering possible plans of action and the effect those plans might have on the various systems involved in the situation of concern.

The worker needs to understand the strengths and resources within the client and the ecosystem. This includes understanding the transactions that are taking place. As discussed earlier, the types of exchanges that occur among systems involve matter, energy, and information. In analyzing a situation, the worker needs to know what matter is necessary and from where it comes. For instance, how does the client obtain food or clothing? Who is involved? What is obtained? Where, when, and how is it obtained? In terms of energy, the worker might consider which relationships the client finds energizing and which drain energy. In terms of information, using the case example, the worker might need to know what information Mr. and Mrs. Adams have about resources in the community. Who or what is the source of that information? Where and when did they receive it? How does the information influence the way in which the family seeks help? What other information might they need? From whom might they get it? Where, when, and how might they get it?

Case Example

Social Study: Individual

I. The Person

    A. Identifying Information

        1. Personal Information

Name: Jerry Adams   Address: 204 Main, Anytown

Sex: Male   Age: 13 years old

Ethnic Identification: African American

Marital Status: Minor, unmarried   Religion: Baptist, practicing

        2. Referral Information: The school referred Jerry because of poor school performance. There were also several altercations between Jerry and other boys at school.

    B. Family

        1. Parents: Jamilla Adams is 34 years of age and Charles Adams is 37. Mr. and Mrs. A met in college and were married after dating for about one year. Mr. A has a bachelor's degree in business and operates the family business, an appliance store. Mrs. A has three years of college and works part time at their store as the book-keeper. Now that her youngest child is attending kindergarten, she is considering working full time at their business or finding other employment to provide more financial security for the family. Mrs. A reports a very happy marriage but some recent stress since they moved into a small, predominantly Caucasian community. The neighbors have not been very friendly, Jerry has had problems at school, and the store has to compete with the large national chain stores and may not be able to stay open. Mrs. A would like to work part time while the children are at school, but she feels that she might need to find full-time employment with the concerns about the family's business.

        2. Siblings: Jerry's sister, Vanessa, is eleven years of age and in the sixth grade. She and Jerry are close in some ways, but they also have some disagreements. Even though they fight at times, they will always back each other up when one of them has a fight with someone outside of the family. Cory is nine years old and in the fourth grade. Cory seems to get along well with everyone, although he is very quiet and tends to keep to himself. Kendra is seven years old and in second grade. She also gets along well with others and is very outgoing and happy. Jermaine is five years of age and recently started kindergarten. He too seems cheerful and outgoing. As the "baby" of the family, Jermaine has enjoyed a lot of attention from his parents and older siblings and gets along well with everyone in the family. Jerry does not spend very much time with his two youngest siblings, although he will watch them at times when Mrs. A is working or running errands and Mr. A is at the store.

        3. Children: Jerry is a thirteen-year-old, unmarried minor who does not have any children.

        4. Resources and Expectations of the Family: Jerry's family has very strong ties as a family unit, and there is an extensive extended family network. However, the extended family is not as available as they once were since the family moved outside of the city about an hour away. Mrs. A has four siblings; two are married with children and two are single, and both of her parents. Mr. A has a sister who is married with one

(continued)

child and a brother who is single, and his mother. Mr. A's father died three years ago from a heart attack. Mrs. A's mother was very involved in assisting Mrs. A with the children until the family moved. Jerry's parents expect him to attend school and get good grades. They want him to get along with others and stay out of trouble. As mentioned previously, the family owns an appliance store where Mr. A spends many hours working. They bought the store about three years ago. Before that time, Mr. A worked for a major retailer, but he left because he was unhappy with what he called "the rat race" of the corporate world. At first the store did very well, but recently a major competitor built a large outlet nearby that has hurt the business.

C. **Education and Work Experiences**

1. **Education:** Jerry is in the ninth grade and attends the local high school. He is experiencing some difficulties with peer relations and his grades are C's and D's. In his previous school, Jerry had always done well, receiving A's and B's. He enjoyed school until this year. In middle school, Jerry played football, basketball, and ran track. However, he decided not to try out for sports when the family moved because he did not know anyone on any of the teams.

2. **Work Experience:** Jerry has had mainly an informal work history. When he was younger, he mowed lawns, shoveled snow, and ran errands to the store for some of the elderly residents in his neighborhood. Last year, Jerry had a paper route, but he had to give it up when the family moved.

D. **Diversity:** Jerry is an African American adolescent whose family recently moved to a small, predominantly Caucasian community about an hour outside of the city. Jerry has been accustomed to attending a predominantly African American school and his new school has only two other African American students. He and his family have always lived in a mixed racial area of the city until this move. It appears that diversity issues are a primary concern for Jerry and his family.

E. **Environmental Factors:** Although there is a very positive environment within the family, both Jerry and his family are experiencing several environmental stressors associated with being only the second African American family to move to the small town where they live. The neighbors have not been very friendly, and Jerry is experiencing racial tensions at school. Other factors for Jerry include the transition from middle school to high school as well as differences in expectations of the teachers and in the social relationships with peers. Major stressors include the family's business and the time that it consumes as well as the possibility that they may not be able to keep it open. The family moved to the area because their neighborhood was beginning to experience a rapid increase in crime and they wanted to live in a safer community where their children would not have negative influences. It was also closer to the store that they own and operate.

II. **Concern or Need**

A. **Reason for Request for Service**: As mentioned previously, the school referred Jerry because of poor school performance. There were also several altercations and instances in which negative racial epithets had been exchanged between Jerry and other students. Mrs. A is also concerned about a situation in which Jerry was caught trying to steal a pair of tennis shoes at a store.

(continued)

Case Example   (continued)

B. **History of Concern or Need:**   Mrs. A reports that Jerry had always been a good student until they moved. She has gone to the school seeking help for his poor performance and has also been called in for several fights. She has tried tutoring Jerry at home with some success, but he is still receiving poor grades. She believes that racial tensions are the main reason for Jerry's problems at school. She also thinks that he was "set up" by some kids in the neighborhood in terms of getting into trouble for trying to steal the tennis shoes. She admits that her son is not perfect but wonders why he has experienced these problems since the move. Jerry confirms that he is not doing well at school and that there is stress in his relationships there. He feels that he is not welcome and wishes he could return to his old school and neighborhood. When asked about the situation at home, he admits to arguing with his siblings at times and says that he misses doing things with his father. He also talks about feeling stress from the uncertainty of his father's business. He admits to getting caught trying to take a pair of tennis shoes but blames it on trying to fit in with some peers because they dared him to do it.

C. **Capacity to Carry Out Vital Roles:**   Jerry is able to carry out his role as oldest sibling, although he is beginning to resent watching them when his mother is gone, especially when he feels that he has "something better to do." His role as son has been impaired by the fact that his father is gone most of the time, working at the store. His role as student has been seriously impaired by difficulties with race relations at school. The rest of the family members have experienced stressors in their roles that affect Jerry. Besides Mr. A not being as available as a father to Jerry, he is also not as available as a father to the other children and as a husband. His role as primary provider has overwhelmed his ability to carry out these other roles. Mrs. A is also beginning to feel overwhelmed with juggling her role as a parent with the need to either work in the family business or seek full-time employment to provide more financial security for the family. This is more pronounced because she no longer has the support system she had from the extended family.

D. **Needs of Client**

1. **Needs Based on Common Human Need/Development:** Jerry has his basic needs met along with most of his needs for safety, love, and belonging, mainly within his family system. There are some substantial needs for esteem and self-actualization along with developmental needs. Although his developmental needs were met until recently, he now finds himself in a difficult situation. At thirteen, Jerry is in stage V of Erikson's stages, which is entitled "identity vs. role confusion." At this stage, he is beginning to consolidate earlier growth into an identity and developing a sense of self in relationship to others. The changes in his life, coupled with the lack of significant contact with his father, could either delay or skew successful resolution of these issues. Jerry needs to develop a positive sense of himself as a developing male. He needs to see himself as successful in developing and maintaining positive peer relationships. He needs to see himself as having a future in which he can become a productive member of society.

2. **Needs Based on Diversity Factors:** Jerry is experiencing a crisis based on his needs for acceptance of his status as an African American adolescent male. The dominant white culture does not value members of his racial group. Prejudice and discrimination present substantial barriers to social acceptance and economic success. Within his

(continued)

Case Example   *(continued)*

---

cultural group, parents and adults must provide additional acceptance for race and skin color in order to erect barriers to undermining a sense of well-being that almost certainly comes with contact with members of white society. While Jerry was living in the city, he had many experiences that sent him messages about being valued as a person. This has changed radically as he has become the object of prejudice and discrimination. Jerry needs to feel that he belongs and is valued in his new school and neighborhood. He needs to know that the color of his skin will not be a barrier to being socially accepted within his peer group and by adults. He needs support from his father to find and validate positive ways to present himself as an African American male. He needs to become more confident in his academic, social, and athletic abilities so that he can be as successful in his new school as he was in his former school.

3. **Needs Based on Environmental Expectations:** Within his family system, Jerry is expected to be responsible and set a good example for his siblings. He is expected to do his best in school and to stay out of trouble. At school, Jerry is expected to attend regularly, do his schoolwork, and follow the rules. In the community, he is expected to be a responsible citizen who respects the rights of others and develops into a productive member of society. Jerry demonstrated an ability to meet these expectations in the past while he was living in the city. However, at his current school and in the community, racial prejudice is skewing these expectations by virtue of attitudes and stereotypes of others toward African American males. Jerry will need assistance in dealing with these environmental factors if he is to be successful in his new school and community.

4. **Needs of Client in Relation to the Request for Service:** Jerry needs to feel positive about himself and his new school and community. He needs to feel accepted by his peers and by adults at school and in the community. Jerry needs to overcome barriers to success academically, and he needs to feel comfortable competing in athletics, something he very much enjoyed at his former school. One of the main obstacles to success is the prejudice and discrimination that is present at school and in the community.

III. **Strengths and Challenges for Helping:** Jerry and his family hope that with assistance he will be able to enjoy school as he did before the move. Jerry thinks that he could do better if he was able to concentrate instead of worrying about getting into fights at school. He agreed that he might do better with this if he could develop alternative ways of responding that would not lead to physical confrontations. He also thinks that the other students should learn to value diversity instead of overvaluing sameness. He pointed out that he had white and Hispanic friends and teammates at his former school and they got along well with each other. Jerry and his family are highly motivated for change. Jerry has the potential to cope better, especially regarding the negative impact on his grades and his ability to resist negative peer influences in terms of staying out of trouble. Jerry has many strengths. He has been successful academically and in athletics. He has worked at jobs that were appropriate for his age level. He has had positive peer relationships and, until recently, had never been in trouble. Jerry has a strong family system, although the family has experienced some stressors recently. The school is academically sound and could be a resource if Jerry's negative experiences could be turned around. The same is true for the community, which has many opportunities for work, cultural enrichment, recreation, and human services avail-

(continued)

Case Example   *(continued)*

able either within the community itself or nearby. The main impingement would be prejudice and discrimination that has arisen since the Adams family and another African American family moved into the community. If some of these concerns can be overcome and Jerry can experience some success at school, then it would seem that Jerry and his family are quite capable of having a positive experience in their new home.

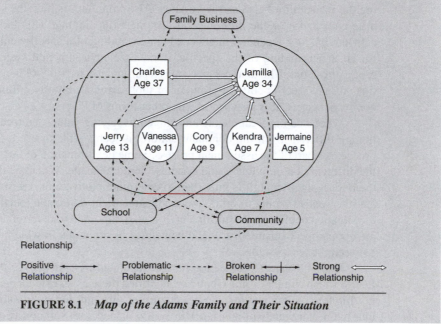

FIGURE 8.1   *Map of the Adams Family and Their Situation*

Some frameworks for transactional assessment have begun to appear. An example is an ecosystems framework developed by Paula Allen-Meares and Bruce A. Lane. They identified variables to be considered and placed them in a three-dimensional framework that consists of kinds of data, data source, and the system to which the data are related. Examination of the framework leads to the conclusion that in order to obtain the breadth of understanding needed for assessment, it is important to collect and place a wide variety of data in a framework that shows some relationship among the data.[11]

In considering the nature of transactional assessment, the generalist social worker needs tools for assessing the functioning, needs, and concerns of individuals, families, small groups, organizations, and communities. Three tools can be useful in transactional assessment: (1) the dual perspective, (2) mapping, and (3) social support network analysis. The use of genograms, as discussed in Chapters 5 and 13, is another transactional assessment technique.

The Dual Perspective

As discussed earlier, Dolores Norton's concept of **dual perspective** depicts the plight of many minority people. The dual perspective is "a conscious and systematic process of perceiving, understanding, and comparing simultaneously the values, attitudes, and behavior of the larger social system with those of the client's immediate family and community system."[12] When the two systems are not congruent in terms of norms, values, expectations, and ways of functioning, conflicting expectations can lead to misunderstanding among individuals, families, and cultural groups.

In making an assessment from the dual perspective, the worker looks for points of difference, especially for conflicting expectations between the two systems. The degree of difference and the number of characteristics that are different are important factors in judging the incongruity between the systems. Also important is how the systems perceive the difference and how the difference affects their functioning. This kind of an assessment calls not only for a general intellectual understanding of a specific cultural group but also for an understanding of the specific, immediate environmental system of the person or group of persons. The dual perspective is a particularly useful tool in assessing the transactions of any specific cultural group or of those from a minority culture within the larger, dominant society. It is also useful with other forms of diversity, as discussed in Part Two.

When dealing with clients and situations having values, culture, and ways of functioning different from the dominant culture, it seems wise to use a dual perspective approach as a part of the assessment process. Some determination of the extent and impact of the difference on individuals and systems should be made. When the difference is great or the impact significant, it is important to determine motivations, resistances, and appropriate interventive points to bring about adjustments in dominant social systems that affect the situation or affect need fulfillment. It is also important to determine with clients if there are coping mechanisms that would be helpful in situations in which incongruencies exist between the two systems.

Use of the dual perspective can be illustrated by considering the characteristics of Puerto Rican culture. Sonia Ghali has identified these as an extended family structure with kinship through godparents; the importance of virginity for an unmarried woman; an emphasis on individualism and inner integrity; a fatalistic, submissive-passive approach to life situations; use of family, friends, and neighbors as the first sources of help; high respect for the advice of pastors and teachers of their own group; use of spiritualism; expectation that helping persons will use authority; belief in mysticism; use of the Spanish language; and an expectation that the wealthy will be paternalistic and benevolent toward the poor.[13] It is, of course, important to determine whether these characteristics hold true for a particular Puerto Rican client. When these characteristics are compared with the characteristics of the majority society, a number of incongruities become apparent, including different language, different expectations about respect, different usage of expression, and so on. An assessment of the incongruities gives an understanding of the transactional influences on a Puerto Rican client.

Mapping

Mapping is a tool for pictorially representing the relationships of the significant parts of any situation. (See Figure 8.1 in the preceding case example.) **Mapping** is a variation of the sociogram discussed in Chapter 14. First, the client or focal point of a situation is depicted with a circle. If this focal point is a multiperson system, the relationships of the person in that system are shown in the circle just as they are in the sociogram.

The other significant systems in the situation are placed around the circle representing the focal system. Various kinds of relationships are drawn, noting which individual in the focal system carries the relationship to these systems.[14]

Mapping can also be useful in assessing the role structure of a situation. The map can be examined for incongruities in role expectations, either within the focal system or with systems in the environment of that focal system. The map can be examined for role overloads and for missing roles.

Use of mapping makes apparent the transactional nature of the situation. It can also be useful in identifying strengths and resources available to the helping situation. Mapping is particularly helpful in understanding the relationships among the parts of an organizational or community system. It also can be used to depict the relationships among key persons in these larger systems.

Social Support Network Analysis

Closely related to the technique of mapping is the analysis of the social support network of an individual or family. Mapping aids the identification of significant social support resources. A **social support network analysis** helps in specifying the nature of the supports and complements the map in the assessment process.

Elizabeth M. Tracy and James K. Whittaker have developed a Social Network Grid for use in a research project. This grid can also be useful in assessing the social support network of an individual or family. Areas to be considered in such an assessment include the area of life in which the support is given (e.g., work, school, etc.), the kind of support (e.g., concrete, emotional, informational, etc.), how often the support is given, whether the support is critical of or problematic to the support receiver, whether the support is in a reciprocal relationship with the support receiver, the closeness of the support to the support receiver, how often there is contact between the provider and receiver, and how long the receiver has known the support provider.[15]

With the goal of identifying and using resources or social supports that are either available or potentially available to individuals, families, and groups, generalist social workers must develop assessment tools for analysis of social support networks.[16] This is particularly crucial when working with disadvantaged or oppressed populations because locating, developing, and using support networks are avenues to empowerment. It is increasingly important in a time of managed care and resource constraints to develop practice knowledge in this area.

Summary

A social work assessment is a picture (however incomplete) made up of all available facts and fit together within a particular frame of reference for a particular purpose. It contains the following elements:

1. Identification of all the entities involved in the situation
2. Development of the needed understanding about each of these entities

3. Arrangement or ordering of these entities in such a manner that the role and relation-ship structure—the transactional nature in the situation—is seen
4. Identification of the need in the situation and of the blockage to need fulfillment
5. Identification of strengths and resources of individuals and systems present in situations, including previously successful efforts to meet needs
6. Identification of conflicting expectations of cultures in which the systems operate
7. Formulation of the concern or need from a transactional point of view
8. Identification of additional information needed, of the knowledge base to be used to enhance understanding, and of the values operating in the situation
9. Evaluation of the information available
10. Identification of relevant social policy, constraints in the situation, expectations of all involved, and actual and potential resources in the situation
11. Identification of possible impacts of potential change in the situation on all systems involved

Assessment is a core skill for any social worker. Like any other skill, it must be practiced if it is to be developed. Professional interaction and professional helping both are heavily dependent on skill in assessment.

Questions

1. Review the material on interviewing in Chapter 7. How do you see the interviewing process used to assess the need or concern and situation with the client?
2. Consider the concept of professional judgment. What are the strengths you now have for operationalizing this concept? What are your current concerns about operationalizing this concept?
3. What is the place of "hunches" or "gut feelings" in the change process?
4. Using the schema in Table 8.2, develop a social history for someone you know.
5. Discuss the advantages of using a strengths perspective rather than only identifying needs and problems in the assessment process.

Suggested Readings

Miley, Karla Krogsrud, O'Melia, Michael, and DuBois, Brenda L. *Social Work Practice: An Empowering Approach,* 6th ed. Boston: Allyn and Bacon, 2009.

Mizrahi, Terry and Davis, Larry E., Eds. *Encyclopedia of Social Work*, 20th ed. Washington, DC: NASW Press, 2008 ("Assessment").

Pardeck, John T. *Social Work Practice: An Ecological Approach.* Westport, CT: Auburn House, 1996.

Saleeby, Dennis, Ed. *The Strengths Perspective in Social Work Practice,* 5th ed. Boston: Allyn and Bacon, 2009.

Sheafor, Bradford W., and Horejsi, Charles R. *Techniques and Guidelines for Social Work Practice,* 8th ed. Boston: Allyn and Bacon, 2008 (Chapter 11).

Planning

Learning Expectations

1. Understanding of the planning process and incorporating good practices into the plan.
2. Skill in developing goals and objectives.
3. Skill in choosing units of attention.
4. Skill in identifying strategies to use in specific practice situations, including choice of roles and tasks.
5. Understanding of the factors that affect a plan of action and skill in identifying the effects on specific practice situations.
6. Skill in identifying resources for use in planning.
7. Understanding of the importance of diversity in planning and the need for empowerment when planning with populations at risk of discrimination or oppression.

Planning is the bridge between assessment and actions focused on change. Often it is seen as a part of the assessment process. Planning and assessment are both such important aspects of the total process that each deserves separate consideration. Planning is based on assessment and is the outcome of assessment. It is based on deliberate rational choices and involves judgments about a range of possibilities.

The assessment process develops understanding of person in environment and identifies potential resources. The planning process translates the assessment content into a goal statement that describes the desired results. Planning also is concerned with identifying the means to reaching goals, which includes identifying the focal system or unit of attention and the strategies, roles, and tasks to be used. It sequences tasks, specifies a time frame, and considers the costs involved.

Planning, when related to social functioning, involves activity designed to enhance people's growth potential and adaptive capacity. It also is designed to increase the capacities of environments to respond to people's needs.

Strategic thinking is the cognitive source of the plan. It is a process of developing a plan with parts that fit together, not by chance, but by choice. This process considers alternatives, evaluates their usefulness, and predicts outcomes of each. The plan considers both process and outcomes by specifying intermediate objectives as well as end goals.

Planning is a skill. The work of the process calls for a complex set of decisions. These decisions are informed by a broad body of knowledge about the nature of human systems and their functioning and of possible interventive strategies. In addition, social work, client, and community values must be considered. The worker's experiences in similar situations also inform the decisions. Planning links purpose to action. Intervention into the transactions between people and social systems is the context of planning. The end goal is planned change. The plan is composed of specified, interrelated parts that have a logical relationship. The reason for each action is specified.

Because of the nature of the human condition and the complexity of the social situation, it is virtually impossible to predict with certainty the outcome of a plan. However, a well-developed plan—one developed with flexibility for change as the process develops—has a better chance of achieving the desired outcome than action not based on such a process.

In developing a plan, it is important to maintain a client-centered perspective and process. During the planning phase, it is easy to leave clients out of the process. Until now, the worker has relied heavily on the client for information. The development of a plan implies that enough information has become available to begin acting toward change. Thus, workers may be tempted to take over and write the plan themselves. This happens all too often in practice. It may occur because workers feel pressured to complete paperwork or workers may be eager to start the change process, which tends to be their primary focus because they see themselves as change agents. When clients do not fully participate in the planning process, the chances of failure increase because they are deprived of an opportunity to become more empowered and to improve their problem-solving skills and their right to self-determination is undermined.

Plans should either be written with clients present or reviewed with them before being finalized. A plan should not be made without the agreement of the client. A plan that does not have the client's consent results in the need to manipulate the client into meeting the expectations of the worker. This would be against social work values and ethics. One way to tell if goals are being written by the worker instead of formulated with the client is to check for repetition. Over a period of time, workers who write goals for clients will use the same or similar goals over and over and have difficulty individualizing plans.

The plan should be sensitive to the background and circumstances of the client. Individual and cultural values and diversity need to be incorporated into the process. The best way to ensure that this happens is to have full participation by the client. The plan should build on the strengths of the client system and environment while seeking to overcome or strengthen areas in which there are barriers or limitations. Populations at risk of discrimination or oppression are especially in need of planning that empowers them and recognizes the need to change the attitudes and stereotypes of others. Assertiveness in interactions with others on the part of both the client and the worker is likely to be needed. This should be built into the plan by identifying targets for change in the environment. Helping members of these groups to adapt to discrimination or oppression is not acceptable. Confronting discrimination and oppression through empowerment and advocacy is generally what is needed for true change to take place.

Empirically Based Practice

As the worker and the client begin the process of developing a plan to meet the client's needs, the worker should consider what approaches are likely to result in a successful outcome. As a professional, the social worker has been trained and educated in the acquisition and use of knowledge and skills to serve her clients. This includes accessing research on a wide range of practice models and techniques and their use in producing outcomes for various client populations. It also includes her own practice wisdom in which she has gained knowledge and skills through direct and indirect experiences as well as attending in-service training, workshops, conferences, and similar lifelong learning activities.

Over the recent past social work, along with other professions, has begun to develop approaches to practice that incorporate empirical data into the decision-making process about interventions. These are generally referred to as "best practices," "empirically based practices," or "evidence-based practices." These approaches advocate the use of research-based outcomes to determine the interventions that are used with clients. The impetus for this comes from a desire to become more scientific and to inform clients about likely outcomes using various approaches to meet their needs. It also seems to come from managed care systems that use similar approaches in medical settings. Although the intent of this is to increase the effectiveness of interventions, we are concerned about how this might be used by social workers. Some workers and other professions may use these as "expert systems" in which someone other than the client is viewed as the expert regarding the client's life and circumstance. This is especially so when one uses the term "best practices" which implies that the worker should only consider using those practices that are identified as such. This is diametrically opposed to what we have tried to present in this text, especially as it relates to the use of naturalistic inquiry. Respecting the client includes respecting the fact that the client is the expert on his or her life. We support the use of research, but we are not in favor of its use in promoting social workers as experts. Instead, we prefer to emphasize the worker's expertise in assisting the client in meeting her needs. The worker should use his expertise in service to his clients as opposed to acting as the expert on what is "best" for them.

If evidence-based-practice approaches are not properly used, they could deprive or undermine the client's right to make her own decisions. This would be the case if the social worker uses research findings to decide what is best for the client without including the client in the decision-making process. This type of approach would basically be the medical model, which is essentially diagnosis and prescription. The expert diagnoses the disease and prescribes treatment to remedy it. This approach does not include the important role that the client plays in determining her own life.

Another consideration is that if evidence-based practices are not properly used they may become too reductionist; that is, they might be used to try to reduce the complexity of human beings and their environments to a more simplistic understanding and intervention. For instance, the term *best practices* implies that there is only one way or one set of ways to provide services to clients who experience certain needs. Although it may be possible to identify protocols for fighting certain diseases and medical conditions, it does not appear this lends itself well to the variety that is found in the human condition. There is a real danger that, in the process of seeking to simplify their interventions or seeking reimbursement from insurances, social workers may preclude the use of more effective approaches because they will not be considered accepted protocols. We do not think that it is wise to limit potential interventions. Instead, we think that it is best to expand possible solutions before deciding on what course of action to take. Chapter 2 described social work as the creative blending of knowledge, values, and skills. Expert-based approaches would seem to miss the inclusion of the creativity of the worker and the client in developing effective change strategies. At the same time, the worker has an obligation to inform the client about the results of any research that is relevant to her situation as well as the experiences that the worker may have had with clients in similar circumstances. If the worker is not familiar with the research in a particular area that is relevant to the client's need, then he should access professional journals and consult with colleagues and his supervisor for guidance. If the client's needs are beyond his skills and abilities, then a referral may be necessary. The referral process will be covered later, in Chapter 10.

Finally, workers should consider that there may not be sufficient research to begin to cover the wide array of challenges that people face in meeting their needs. Research that has not been replicated or confirmed may not be reliable. The subjects may be too different from the client to ensure success. The environments may be quite different also. In addition, research is often driven by a variety of agendas. Clients with unusual or unpopular characteristics and circumstances may not have been studied enough to accurately portray their circumstances.

These precautions do not preclude the use of research in social work practice. We heartily endorse the need for social workers to use research findings in their practice. The question is how that information is used. We are opposed to its use in a way that puts the worker in the position of expert. Research should be used to inform both the worker and the client regarding likely outcomes, and then a mutual decision is made that includes the informed choice and consent of the client.

A Model for Good Practices in Generalist Social Work Practice

It is important to incorporate knowledge gained from research and from practice into working with clients. The approach presented here recognizes both of these needs. We call it *good practices* in generalist practice. It is our version of evidence based practice. **Good practice** is broadly defined as accepted practice in the field or setting or with a population, which is based on empirically based practice, practice experience, and the empowerment of clients. So, in addition to acquiring knowledge and skills through empirical means, the social worker uses her practice wisdom. Good practices also incorporate social work values into each intervention, in terms of both process and content. Good practices use the knowledge, values, and skills of the worker in service to the client. The term *good practices* implies that there are many ways to meet the needs of clients. Our model for good practices is as follows:

1. Through research, practice experience, and lifelong learning, the worker continuously develops the knowledge, values, and skills needed to serve her clients.
2. The worker uses naturalistic inquiry to explore person in environment and shares her knowledge and skills from research and practice experience throughout the change process.
3. The worker and the client mutually decide on a plan that is consistent with the client's diversity and is most likely to be effective in bringing about the desired change.
4. The worker and the client evaluate the outcome to determine whether the desired change has occurred.

These steps are applied throughout the change process as the worker and the client develop an assessment and a plan, then take actions to carry out the plan.

The knowledge and skills necessary for professional generalist social work practice have been identified throughout the text. These include knowledge and skills necessary to build relationships and engage clients in the change process and for completing the assessment, such as knowledge about human need, human development, diversity, person in environment, and ecosystems. Social workers use their knowledge and skills to explore the nature of the need and potential strengths and resources in the ecosystem. In the process they listen to clients' stories about their lives and their situations. Workers use their knowledge and skills to develop an understanding of person in environment or the ecosystem. They share this with their clients, who validate or correct this understanding. In the process of doing this, clients also gain a better understanding of their own lives and the situations with which they are faced. An important aspect of knowledge and skills for practice is understanding the models of practice that are used by social workers. Some of these are presented later, in Chapter 16. The models serve to help the worker formulate ideas or theories about how people develop and function. In turn, this provides workers with a framework for understanding the stories their clients tell. Descriptions of good practices in various settings that follow the models in Chapter 16 help identify areas of knowledge and expertise workers need to serve various populations in various settings.

Social workers develop knowledge and skills necessary for planning. They use their knowledge and skills to assist clients in developing goals, objectives, strategies, and tasks to bring about the changes necessary to meet clients' needs. They incorporate evidence-based practices into their work with clients in a manner that includes clients in making informed decisions. Plans are developed that are consistent with the development and diversity of clients and with good practices. While developing plans, workers teach their clients how to plan. Workers use their knowledge of models of practice and their research in professional journals, which helps them formulate ideas or theories about how people change and which approaches are likely to be successful. This lays the foundation for working with clients to identify change strategies that are likely to be effective in meeting their needs. Good practices give guidance to workers regarding procedures and practices that are necessary to fulfill the expectations of their clients, their agencies, their community, and their profession in a given area of practice.

Social workers acquire knowledge and skills in facilitating the change process through direct and indirect practice actions or interventions. These are used to assist clients in carrying out plans or removing barriers to success. This is the essence or substance of the practice actions presented in Chapters 10 and 11 and the models and good practices presented in Chapter 16. The models provide workers with accepted actions or practice within the profession. When the worker is able to identify the theory or model or method on which her actions are based, she receives some sanction for those actions. In many respects, the models and good practices, along with the professional roles needed to carry them out, exemplify what it means to say: "This is what social workers do." This also gives the client some reassurance that the worker is not merely guessing or experimenting with what might work but that she actually has a theoretical basis or practice background that supports why it should work.

Social work values and ethics are used throughout this process. Social workers use their values to guide both the content and the process of change. Values guide the work and provide a purpose for it. As a result of working with a social worker, clients should feel valuable and worthwhile as human beings. This is achieved by treating clients with dignity and respect and by valuing them as human beings and respecting their positions as experts on their own lives. Self-determination goes hand in hand with this. Respecting clients means respecting their rights to make their own decisions. Social workers should inform clients about what is likely to work or not work, given the workers' knowledge and practice wisdom and information that is available in the professional literature, but clients need to be included in the decisions regarding what is done to meet their needs. A third cardinal value is that clients have a right to have socially accepted needs met in socially accepted ways. Workers should support choices clients make that are congruent with this value.

Throughout the change process, the worker and the client evaluate the process and the outcome. Clients need to be able to give feedback about what feels right and what does not and about what is working and what is not. How change occurs is as important as what change occurs. We are confident that when clients are included in determining the process and the outcome of the change process, the probability of success is increased along with the likelihood that the change will endure over time.

Components of a Plan

Because a **plan of action** relates to a complex human situation to be dealt with over time, identification of the components of a plan helps in managing the complexity of the plan. One formulation of a plan considers three components: goals and objectives, units of attention, and strategies that include the roles of worker and client and the tasks to be performed.

Goals and Objectives

The **goal** is the overall, long-range expected outcome of the endeavor. A goal is usually reached only after intermediate goals or **objectives** have been attained. Objectives may relate to several different persons or social systems involved in the situation. Goals and objectives develop out of assessment related to the needs of the various systems involved and the identification of the blocks to need fulfillment. They are generally related to the removal of a block or to developing new means of need fulfillment.

Students and new workers often find it challenging to write appropriate goals and objectives using an acceptable format. Social workers are prone to qualify or hedge their statements to allow for flexibility or individuality. Much of this comes from a desire to respect client self-determination and to allow for unforeseen difficulties. However, planning calls for direct and definitive statements so that expectations and outcomes are clear and progress can be accurately measured. Otherwise, confusion will occur about who is responsible for what, and measuring progress and outcomes will be impossible. Although goal statements must be definitive, there is room for flexibility in that plans can be changed. When it is obvious that something is not working, the plan needs to be changed. However, the need for flexibility in planning should not obscure the need for clearly defined goals, objectives, and tasks.

Many social workers will see a variety of things that might be improved or changed as they assess the person in environment and will want to fix everything. Clients can easily become overwhelmed by what may be received as a negative message about their well-being. It is best to keep things less complicated and focus on the main areas the client wishes to change and where change will likely make the biggest difference. A general guideline in working with individuals is to limit the number of goals to no more than three at any given time during the process. For individuals facing multiple barriers or difficulties, more goals may be necessary. However, the likelihood that a client will remember to work on more than two or three goals at a given time is very low. Families and groups may need more than three goals, depending on the size of the membership. However, no single member should be asked to keep track of more than two or three goals. For children and those who are under stress or have limitations, one or two goals may be the most they are able to handle at one time.

Goals should also be based on the strengths of the client system as well as the strengths and resources of the environment. A strengths-based approach ensures that the plan is built on the existing capacities of the client system and environment. Without this, the plan might be based on skills the client has not mastered or cannot master or on resources that may not be readily available. The result would be a plan with a great deal of uncertainty, one that depends on too many "if's." The more uncertainty, the greater the chances of failure. Although building on strengths does not guarantee success, it increases the odds and provides the client with opportunities to act immediately rather than waiting to acquire skills and resources.

There is a danger in setting goals that are too broad and general. Broad goals do not lead to the precision that is possible when the outcomes are more specific. It is helpful to specify a general goal that is a statement of the desired end and then to develop specific short-term objectives. These short-term objectives can be placed in a time order to facilitate a plan. In that case, the first objective must be reached before working on the second objective and so on. Objectives should describe a specific desired change in individuals or social systems involved in the total situation. In effect, a miniplan, or a plan within a plan, is developed. This approach allows for evaluation of the progress toward the general goal and for adjusting the plan in progress when there is a change in the situation or because of previously unrecognized influences and consequences.

Care must be taken to express the objectives in terms of the behavioral outcomes desired rather than of how the goal will be reached. In other words, receiving a service is not a goal but rather a task designed to meet a need or achieve the goal or objective. Also, each goal and objective should have a specified date for its accomplishment. Objectives should be specific, concrete, and measurable. Goal statements are usually broader and more general than objectives. If objectives have specific statements about frequency, duration, and time frame, then the goal statement can be more broad. For example, the statement "The interaction between Jerry and his school system will result in successful academic progress" is broad in that it does not specify how much positive behavior or the time frame for completion. In developing more specific, measurable statements for objectives, it is helpful to think in terms of a sequence of questions—namely, who, what, how, where, and when. The "who" refers to the person or persons taking action and the targets of change. The person(s) taking action should appear first in both the goal statement and the objectives. The next word should be *will,* which conveys a positive, unequivocal statement about the desired state of affairs. Next come descriptions of "what" and "how" the situation will appear if the goal or objective were accomplished or the need were to be met. Identifying "who" is the target of change may come next, if appropriate. "When" describes the time, frequency, or duration in which the action is to take place and the time frame for completion. An example of an objective written using these guidelines follows:

> Objective: Jerry will follow the rules at school 100 percent of the time for one week by November 15.

"Jerry" is the "who." "Follow the rules" represents the "what." "At school" refers to both "where" and "when." The expected frequency is "100 percent of the time." "For one week" is the duration, and "by November 15" is the time frame. It is clear from this statement who will do what and where and when he will do it. There should be no confusion about expectations; both progress and outcomes are readily measurable.

Goals should be reasonably feasible; that is, there should be a good chance of reaching them. In thinking about feasibility, consideration is given to time and energy factors. Some questions that should be asked are: Do the worker and the client have the time available to work toward the specified goals? Is sufficient energy available? Are the needed resources available?

It is wise to state goals and objectives in terms of a positive outcome rather than in negative terms. That is, goals should be stated as "Jerry will" rather than "Jerry will not." When goals and objectives are positive, they help to focus on the desired outcome instead of being problem focused. This reinforces behavior that is needed to bring about change. In addition, a positive focus gives the client more hope that the situation can be resolved. Finally, it creates a "self-fulfilling prophecy" that is more likely to result in success than failure. People tend to engage in behavior that is based on a prediction or "prophecy" of what they expect to have happen, not necessarily what they want to have happen. "Self-fulfilling prophecy" means that one's own behavior contributes a great deal to the outcome. When clients are focused on behavior that is likely to bring about the desired change, they are more likely to succeed and are also more likely to receive positive reinforcement from their environments.

Clients can often be most helpful in evaluating the feasibility of a goal; thus, they should be involved in setting goals. This can motivate a client about the work needed to reach that goal. As clients reach objectives, they gain hope for reaching the overall goals.

As with all decisions in the social work process, decisions regarding goals are influenced by value judgments. The choice of goals or end states is based on what is desirable. What is desirable is a value judgment. Social work values also influence the means to the end, or the process and objectives involved in the process. Because people are seen as having the right to make decisions about themselves, workers should not use means in reaching goals that go against the client's desires and values. Workers should respect lifestyle, diversity, and cultural factors in the development of goals and objectives. The worker should constantly evaluate whether the chosen goals are appropriate. There must be flexibility in adjusting goals to changing situations as the plan is implemented.

Different situations call for different kinds of change and different kinds of goals. The kinds of change that should be considered are:

1. *A sustaining relationship*—Used when it appears that there is no chance to change the person in environment and when the person lacks a significant other who can give needed support
2. *Specific behavioral change*—Used when a client is troubled by a specific symptom or behavior pattern and is generally otherwise satisfied with her situation
3. *Relationship change*—Used when the issue is a troublesome relationship
4. *Environmental change*—Used when it is recognized that a part of the need is a change in some segment of the environment or in the transactions between person and environment
5. *Directional change*—Used when values are conflicting or unclear, when a client system is unclear about goals or direction of effort, or when aspirations are blocked in a manner that makes unblocking very difficult or impossible

When setting goals, it is important to consider expectations of the client, significant others in the client's environment, and the worker. These three sets of expectations may be different because each may see the situation differently or have identified the need differently. Consistency and inconsistency among these goals must be identified and reconciled. The client's goals are to be considered of prime importance, and the worker should point out to the client the environmental expectations and the consequences of not meeting these expectations. The worker's goals can be discussed and incorporated or discarded as jointly determined by the worker and the client.

In summary, goals and objectives should relate to meeting a need. They should be stated in terms of an outcome, be specific, and be measurable. They should be feasible and positive in direction and developed with the client to reflect the client's desires.

Units of Attention

The **unit of attention**, or focal system, is the system being focused on for the change effort. This is generally in relation to the overall goals, but there may be different units of attention in relation to specific objectives. This might be either a person, a social system, or the transactions between them. It may be the client or a person or system that has a significant influence on the situation. Units of attention are systems that are the focus of the change activity.

The unit of attention can be an individual client; it can be several clients (a small group) working on meeting a common need or on similar individual needs; it can be an individual who in some way affects the client and his situation; or it can be a group of persons in a community concerned about services to meet the needs of a category of clients.[1] The interactions and transactions among various parts of the ecosystem can be a unit of attention. In the case example of Jerry Adams there is an incongruity in the relationship between Jerry and the school system. Although the unit of attention for specific change may be Jerry or the school, ultimately it is the interaction between them that needs to be changed.

As the change process is divided into activity related to more specific objectives, several objectives and miniplans are often worked on at the same time. It is important to specify the unit of attention related to each miniplan. For example, the overall goal may be a more desirable living situation for a client. It may be necessary to have an objective that relates to understanding the client's situation. To develop this understanding, the focal system may be the client or his landlord as a source of needed information. Another objective may be that a potential landlord be prepared to meet the special needs of the client. The potential landlord then becomes a focal system.

Incorporating diversity into planning means identifying units of attention in the environment, because the blocks to fulfilling a need are often found in prejudice, discrimination, and oppression directed at members of populations who are at risk of experiencing these. The plan should include direct and indirect methods for empowering members of these populations. Often this involves assisting clients to change the interactions between themselves and the environment. The unit of attention in these types of goals is the relationship between client and environment. Some of this may be accomplished by helping clients to change how they respond to prejudice, discrimination, and oppression. For this part of the goal, the client is the unit of attention. Some of it may be accomplished by intervening to change the attitudes and actions of the environmental system. For this part, the unit of attention is the environment.

Units of attention may be individuals, families, small groups, organizations, or communities. Table 8.1 gives some indications and counterindications for the choice of each kind of system. It is important to specify appropriate units of attention for every goal and objective. Units of attention may be clients or other persons and social systems involved in the situation.

Strategy

Strategy is an overall approach to change in the situation. It involves roles for worker and client, tasks to be done by each, and methods and techniques to use. It has been defined as "an orchestrated attempt to influence persons or systems in relation to some goals."[2] The term originated in a military context and relates to a battle plan. It also is used in a game context. Action in the game depends on the action of others. Strategy implies multiple causes. Action is dependent on the action of others; that is, there is anticipation and assessment of the actions and reactions of others rather than reliance on independent action. There is a recognition of the transactional nature of human social functioning.

The worker begins thinking about strategy by considering the feelings, thoughts, and actions of the client and his ecosystem. Figure 4.1 depicts how these factors influence each other. Human systems are made up of individuals. Thus, feelings, thoughts, and actions are woven into the fabric of every human system. In developing a strategy, the worker considers feelings, thoughts, and actions of the client and of the members of human systems in the client's environment as aspects of the units of attention. The unit of attention is the system (individual, family, group, organization, or community) that is the focus of the change strategy. The intended change occurs by changing the feelings, thoughts, or actions of people in that system. The worker assesses the need to influence change in these elements and with the client selects the best option. For example, if the unit of attention is the client, the worker discusses with the client ways in which various combinations of working with his feelings, thoughts, or actions would be preferred in meeting his need or addressing his concern. In the case example later in this chapter, the worker could try to help Jerry change his behavior at school by helping him change how he feels about his new school. The worker also considers how changing transactions will influence these aspects of the ecosystem and will be influenced by them. In the case example, the worker could use knowledge (thinking) as a strategy for changing the approaches (actions) of the parents and of the school to the situation. This is intended to help Jerry feel more positive (feelings) about school and improve the interaction (actions) between Jerry and the school. As with other elements of the social work process, an understanding of the effects of diversity is included in developing and choosing the change strategy. In the case example, the worker tries to get the school to demonstrate (action) valuing diversity (feeling) by adding a study (thinking) of the contributions of African Americans to the curriculum.

One final note, when the unit of attention is an individual or system other than the client system, the ultimate goal of the change strategy is to change the actions of that system or the client's interaction with that system so that the client system's need is met. The interaction is an aspect of action. The worker and the client may accomplish this by changing feelings or thinking, but changes in action are what count. However, assisting the client to change his feelings, thinking, or actions can be the goal of the change strategy if the client is the unit of attention.

When a general strategy is used in many situations, it becomes a category of strategy. Some categories that have been identified are *consensus strategy, conflict strategy, demonstration strategy,* and *bargaining strategy.* Social work has developed a variety of approaches to practice. These may be called theories of practice or models of practice (e.g., crisis intervention, conjoint family therapy, locality development); they provide an overall approach to practice and thus may be considered as strategies.

In choosing strategies the worker must decide if he possesses the knowledge and skills needed for using the strategy. The worker must also determine if the values, explicit and implicit, in the strategy are congruent with those of the client and her situation.

Strategies should not only apply to the client's need but also should be in keeping with the client's lifestyle. For example, in discussing services for African Americans and Puerto Ricans, Emelicia Mizio and Anita Delaney noted that it is important to use strategies that recognize how racism and discrimination affect the lives of these people. They recommended the use of advocacy as a core strategy and the use of counseling strategies based on ecological and systems knowledge.[3] The authors' Native American students indicated that Siporin's situational approach and the functional approach are appropriate for their culture.

Different strategies and different kinds of service call for the social worker to fill different roles. The term *role* is used here in a somewhat different manner than in the strict pattern-of-behaviors sense. Rather, the definition used is that of Robert Teare and Harold McPheeters: "A cluster of altruistic activities that are performed toward a common objective [goal]."[4] The **role** is the way the worker uses self in the specific helping situation. Role is further dependent on the function of the worker and the particular agency offering the service and its function. For example, in short-term, crisis-focused service, the caregiver role will be minimally used, whereas in a nursing home this may be an often-used role.

Teare and McPheeters have identified twelve roles that may be part of the generalist repertoire that social workers fill:

1. *Outreach worker*—Identifying need by reaching out to clients in the community; usually involves referral to services
2. *Broker*—Enabling persons to use appropriate services by providing information, after assessing need of individual and nature of resources; includes contact and follow-up
3. *Advocate*—Helping clients obtain services in situations in which they may be rejected; helping expand services to persons having a particular need
4. *Evaluation*—Gathering information and assessing client or community needs; considering alternatives and planning for action
5. *Teacher*—Teaching facts and skills
6. *Behavior changer*—Activities aimed at specific behavior change
7. *Mobilizer*—Helping to mobilize resources to develop new services or programs
8. *Consultant*—Working with other professionals to increase their skills and understanding
9. *Community planner*—Helping communities to plan for ways to meet human need
10. *Caregiver*—Providing support and care to persons when problems cannot be resolved
11. *Data manager*—Collecting and analyzing data used in decision making
12. *Administrator*—Planning and implementing services and programs[5]

There seems to be one additional role: that of coordinator. The coordinator enables several social workers, other professionals, or other service providers to function so that services are provided in a synchronized manner. The coordinator sees that all involved are aware of and take into consideration the work of all others as they provide service. This role may also be identified as the case manager role. (This will be discussed in Chapter 11.) Another role is the enabler role. (See Chapter 10 for a discussion of enabling as a strategy.)

Ronald Simons and Stephen Aiger discussed role choice in terms of client characteristics and needs. The four client characteristics they noted as important to consider when choosing the worker role are (1) the needs and desires of the client, (2) the resources of the client, (3) the expectations of the client and of the worker regarding the client, and (4) the client's perceived expectations of the worker. Although they defined *role* somewhat differently than did Teare and McPheeters, they identified particular situations and clients' difficulties in which particular roles are important. A lack of resources calls for the broker role; a lack of opportunity, the advocate role; role inadequacy, the teacher role; unrealistic role expectations or behavior, the confronter role; conflicting role expectations, the mediator role; role transition stress, the empathic listener role; role indecision, the clarifier role.[6]

Usually, role and task are discussed in relation to the worker and the worker's functioning. However, role implies action and interaction by and with the client—a reciprocal relationship. Thus, in carrying out the plan attention needs to be paid to the client's functioning and tasks. The plan should specify the role or roles of the worker and consider the reciprocal role of the client. The tasks to be completed by the client and the worker should be specified. A task is a specific action or activity; it is the specification of what needs to be done.

The strategy is developed after tentative goals and units of attention relative to the goals have been identified. After the strategy has been identified, it is possible to develop the operational goal or goals and objectives and to become more specific about roles and tasks. Tasks and objectives are related.

Tasks are steps that are necessary to achieve the objectives and ultimately the goal. Tasks may be used to describe events that occur only once or are ongoing. They should cover the "who, what, how, where, and when" for the actions that are planned. This is generally the first place the worker appears in the plan. The exception would be cases in which the worker might be part of an objective by monitoring, prompting, or rewarding a client to assist him in accomplishing objectives.

The tasks should be sequenced and a time for the completion of each established. This results in an overall time frame or time line for the service. It is important to specify the resources needed to carry out the plan and to indicate how those resources are to be obtained. This would include the time investment of the worker and client. Any monetary investment, such as client fees or agency funds, should be specified. Other needed resources could be the use of an agency or community facility or service or the inclusion of other persons in the action system.

Case Example

In the case example of Jerry Adams, the following plan might be developed.

I. Plan of Action
  A. **Goal A:** The interaction between Jerry and his school system will result in successful academic progress.
    1. **Objective 1:** Jerry will follow rules while at school 100 percent of the time for one week by November 15.
       a. **Client task:** Jerry will be able to recite three basic rules for classroom behavior by October 25.
       b. **Worker task:** The worker will assist Jerry in developing alternative ways of responding to racial slurs.
       c. **Parent task:** Mr. and Mrs. Adams will keep track of the written feedback and reward Jerry for positive behavior at the end of the week according to the number of positive reports they receive.
  B. **Goal B:** The school will reinforce a more positive attitude toward African Americans by incorporating diversity into the curriculum by the beginning of the next semester in January.
    1. **Objective 1:** Teachers will develop and implement an assignment focused on the contributions of African Americans to each part of the curriculum.
       a. **Worker task:** By November 3, the worker will meet with the faculty to discuss the development of assignments for students that involve contributions by African Americans to art, literature, science, history, and mathematics.
       b. **Teacher task:** By December 15, teachers will develop assignments that incorporate contributions by African Americans to art, literature, science, history, and mathematics.

The plan is always based on the information collected and the assessment of that information. It is always developed with the fullest possible participation of the client (or a guardian). The plan is an agreement with the client outlining what the worker will do and what the client's responsibility in the endeavor is.

All plans of action should contain some mechanism for evaluating how well the goals of the plan are met. Evaluation, which is ongoing in the entire interventive process, is discussed in Chapter 12.

Plans should also contain some mechanism for specifying when various objectives are to be met or when specific tasks are to be completed. This can be as simple as specifying a date for the completion of each objective. When working on complex goals, it is often useful to use a task-flow mechanism. The plan must be flexible. As the implementation of the plan progresses, new information is added that may result in a change of plan. The development of the plan calls for specificity. Specific plans are more likely to lead to service that is directed toward client needs and desires and that enhances accountability. Such plans allow for a breadth of possible decisions about the components of the plan, a mark of generalist social work as presented in this text.

When developing plans of action, it is usually advisable to consider several different plans and make choices based on an analysis of each plan and its suitability for the specific situation. This involves considering strengths and limitations of each plan. The chosen plan may be a synthesis of parts of several of the considered plans.

Factors Affecting a Plan of Action

Plans of action reflect the differential nature of social work. Each plan is specific to a situation and to the persons involved. Each plan of action, with its component parts, should be different from every other plan of action. It is important to specify not only the components of a plan but also the various factors that affect the development of that plan. Seven factors that have considerable influence on the plan are: (1) the community in which it is being carried out; (2) the agency sanctioning the plan; (3) the social need that the plan is a response to; (4) the worker involved in the plan; (5) the client involved in the plan; (6) diversity issues among members of all of these systems, along with issues related to disadvantaged or oppressed populations; and (7) the strengths and challenges of all of the above.

The Community

The community is an important influence on the plan of action. The client is a part of a community. The community has expectations for the client. Any plan of action needs to consider the environment in which the plan takes place. What is feasible in one community may not be feasible in another.

The culture of a community is important to consider in planning. Attitudes about receiving help are particularly important, as are accepted coping mechanisms. In communities in which self-help and neighborliness are highly valued, the chosen plan of action may be one that strengthens and enables the natural helping system to function well rather than an extended casework service.

The community's service delivery system is another factor to be considered. An assumption is often made that the ideal service delivery system should be that of a large urban community with many specialized services. However, these assumptions are sometimes inappropriate for small nonmetropolitan settings in which the service delivery system is different.[7]

The Agency

The worker is influenced by constraints and resources within the agency. Constraints may include the kinds of service that can be offered, financial considerations, time priority factors, and the manner in which the agency is organized. Resources to be considered include people (staff expertise), structures, money, and expendable supplies that can be used by the worker and client to enhance the social work process or goal achievement. Skillful use of the agency system in service of the client is an important attribute of planning.

The agency is a component of the community, and is an integral subunit of the community system. It is sanctioned by the community and must, at least in part, express its will. The agency depends on the community for resources. Financial support may be in the form of contributions or taxation. Planning must take into consideration the influence of community needs, values, and intentions for the service being delivered by the agency. It is important that the planning process recognize the influence of agency structure and functioning on service to clients. This recognition gives both the worker and client a sense of the realities involved in the provision of service.

An additional factor to consider is the impact of managed care on how some agencies and workers function. The NASW *Code of Ethics* requires that social workers regard clients' concerns as primary regardless of the interests of themselves or their employers. Managed care plans may limit services available to clients or encourage less care by discouraging more expensive services. Social workers must advocate for policies that allow workers to act in the best interests of clients regardless of the circumstances. Facing the challenges of these situations requires courage and persistence.

The Social Issue

Societal attitudes and expectations about social issues vary. Some social issues are seen as a sign of illness or deviance, and some, as the result of environmental influences.

Elliot Studt has expressed this idea in her conceptualization of the field of practice. She pointed out "three organizing dimensions for describing a field of practice: social problem, social task, and social service system."[8] In thinking about the social issue it is helpful to consider why the issue concerns the community and other social systems. Important are such questions as: How does the issue affect the general welfare of the community? Why does a community see a need for action? What is the condition of central concern? Also important is how the issue affects the social functioning of individuals and families. As these questions are answered and as social policy and programs are developed, the social tasks related to the specific social issues develop. The social task is what the community sees as needing to be done in order to resolve the social issue. Social tasks also include work needed to help the individual affected by the social issue. These tasks develop in part from the expectations of the various segments of the community—taxpayers, professionals, legislators, agents of social control, commercial interests, and so on. Thus, the social task is often unclear and subject to conflicting expectations. This is one of the reasons that accountability is difficult and that goal expectations are unclear.

For example, quite different attitudes are held about someone with a difficulty in social functioning that leads to breaking the law and someone whose difficulty in social functioning is the result of sudden illness. The former enters the corrections field of practice; the latter, the health care field. Social control concerns are greater in the corrections field because the strategy used must protect the community from further threat of lawbreaking. Thus, punishment is often the strategy used. Treatment of illness is the prime concern in the medical setting, and concern with social functioning is in relationship to the illness. Society has considerable compassion for the person whose social-functioning difficulties arise from illness. The strategy chosen must allow for the treatment of the illness and provide means for coping with the resulting difficulties in social functioning. Social policy is often a reflection of societal concerns and attitudes about social issues. Relevant social policy must be considered in developing plans of action. Societal and individual attitudes as they relate to the issue being worked on by the worker and client are important influences on the planning process.

The Worker

Each worker is first a unique person. The worker's primary tool is the self. The worker brings herself as a person, as a professional, as an agency employee, and as a member of the community to the social work endeavor.

Because of workers' individuality, because there is no one theory about the human situation, and because there is no one way to achieve social work goals, workers have preferences about explaining the human situation and practicing social work. One worker may find ego psychology a helpful theory and use psychosocial casework extensively. Another may use a more eclectic theory base and find problem-solving social work and remedial group work useful. A third worker might find that an ecosystems strengths approach provides the most positive and comprehensive approach. Plans of action, though developed by worker and client together, reflect the worker's preferences, priorities, and skills.

As an agency employee, the worker is both constrained and supported. She is responsible and accountable to the agency for her work. She must function within the agency structure and is interdependent with others employed by the agency. As a member of the community, the worker is subject to pressures from that community. The worker's preferences and influences from both the agency and the community also affect the planning process.

When working with a managed care plan, the worker must know how to maximize client benefits to fit the needs of the client and to ensure that the client receives needed services. The worker needs to be knowledgeable about the coverage the client has and be ready to advocate for needed services. The worker should be creative about linking the client to other community services. The worker must be efficient in planning and delivering services within the agency's mandate. Frequently, this means developing time-limited plans that are designed to maximize the impact of the intervention. The worker should be task oriented and outcome focused so that tasks are completed within the limited time frames imposed by the covered services.

Managed care situations necessitate very careful planning to ensure effective outcomes within the limited time frames generally imposed. This requires accurate assessment and development of a plan that is task and solution focused. The restricted time frame can severely undermine the ability of the worker to develop and maintain a helping relationship that will carry the process through to a successful completion. It is imperative that clients be made aware of the limitations of their coverage and the need for immediate action. Otherwise, the client may misinterpret the worker's urgency as a lack of caring. A limited time frame is no excuse for ignoring the need to include the client in planning and decision making. Client self-determination must be central to any approach used by a professional social worker. Helping clients make choices within the context of their situations, advocating for maximum use of their benefits, and using all of the resources at their disposal are the keys to successful planning in managed care situations. An ecosystems strengths approach can be an effective and efficient means of delivering services by using the client's own natural helping and support systems and developing existing strengths and resources. A potential drawback in using this approach is that some managed care systems may not recognize certain worker activities as reimbursable. Again, advocacy and connecting tasks to an approved plan may be necessary to achieve reimbursement.

The Client

The client in his uniqueness brings much to the worker-client interaction. The client comes from a community, a neighborhood, a particular diverse group, and a particular family. The client brings the biological, psychosocial, spiritual being. The client has a self-image, roles in family and community, values, hopes, and expectations. The client has rights—the right to service, the right to participate, the right to fail. The client carries a reference group's expectations as well as the results of interactions with meaningful persons in meaningful situations. The client has strengths, modes of adaptation, and ways of coping. The client brings a particular set of motivations, capacities, and opportunities. This uniqueness will support some interventive strategies and eliminate others. Even more important, the client will have unique expectations and goals for the service. The client may have preferences about the way of working on the need with the worker. The client's need is unique, and the plan must be unique in its response to that need.

The client's role in the plan depends on several factors. Among these are the client's roles in his life situation (parent, child, employee, etc.), the client's role in the agency or organization (patient, inmate, student, etc.), and the role the worker has chosen (the client's role must be reciprocal to it). The client is a vital part of the factors influencing the plan of action.

Diversity and Populations at Risk

Important considerations in developing a plan are the similarities and differences among members of the various systems involved. (The discussion of diversity in Chapter 3 should be reviewed for a better understanding of its implications for planning.) Diversity is an important factor in planning because it permeates the process and affects the worker, client, and agency. For instance, the client might find it difficult to accept help from an agency that has a negative reputation among members of his ethnic or racial group. Alternatively, overcoming this barrier might represent an even stronger commitment on the part of both the client and the agency. Both may realize a benefit in forging a relationship with each other. The agency may see the experience as an opportunity to build a bridge to a part of the community that has felt alienated from its services. The client may see it as a new resource that until now was not accessible.

Clients who are members of populations at risk of prejudice, discrimination, and oppression need to have a plan that reflects empowerment and a means of addressing these issues. Various diversity competent approaches need to be incorporated into the plan. When working with African Americans, Asians and Hispanics, family and cultural traditions are important considerations. Women may desire to change relationships or may want to consider the impact of change on significant relationships. People who are older may be concerned about losing their independence or they may have transportation or health care needs that have to be addressed. These approaches should not be applied as stereotypes but are intended to be used as potential areas for exploration with the client.

The use of naturalistic inquiry should continue during the planning phase. Its use in planning means that the worker looks to the client for guidance in developing a plan that is appropriate with respect to the client's diversity. As the worker gains competence in working with a specific diverse group, she might make suggestions that are consistent with the needs of that group. However, even then she should be sure to get feedback from the client about the appropriateness of the plan. She could ask questions that are specific to the client's diversity, such as: Could you describe what this situation would look like if it were resolved and you were feeling good about the results? What would it mean to you to have this need met? How would this fit with who you are as a (woman, African American, Hispanic, Native American, gay person, lesbian, etc.)? What types of considerations need to be made for you to feel comfortable with this plan? How would your family or community view this? What are some of the approaches to meeting this need that are used within your culture (or group)? Who else needs to be involved in developing a plan?

The answers to these types of questions should open up a discussion about diversity that needs to be incorporated into the plan. Both the types of goals and means of achieving them should be part of this discussion. We do not think that it is wise to prescribe specific approaches to be used with members of each diverse group. The situation is much more complicated than using a step-by-step process. Besides, this would be inconsistent with using naturalistic inquiry. Using a prescribed approach implies that the worker knows what she does not know as opposed to taking the position that she does not know what she does not know. Instead of a prescribed approach, a dialogue about diversity needs to take place, which leads to a diversity competent plan that is specific to the client. Another reason for taking this approach is that quite often clients may be members of more than one diverse group. In addition, each client has unique experiences as a member of his or her diverse group or groups.

Diversity factors in the community at large play an important role in planning. The more homogeneity there is in the culture of a community, the more expectations tend to be standardized. The positive side is that homogeneity creates cohesion and community pride in common heritage and traditions. The negative side is that there often is less tolerance for those who are "different." However, valuing "sameness" does not mean that "differentness" is bad. People can come to realize that there is strength in variety and diversity, but overcoming fear and prejudice is not easy. When the community is relatively homogeneous, there will likely be options for planning that are influenced by community expectations. These expectations may require certain expected behaviors but not tolerate others that deviate from the norm. Similarly, certain behaviors may not be tolerated because they are outside of the bounds of what the community will accept. This situation is probably more common in rural communities and in neighborhoods that have a strong ethnic identity.

Communities that are more heterogeneous may be more tolerant of a wider range of behaviors, but only to the extent that their citizens have been able to overcome their prejudices. Unfortunately, the gap between many ethnic and racial groups and the dominant Caucasian culture in America more often has resulted in devaluing diversity, even to the extent of open prejudice and oppression. When there is a gap between the expectations of the dominant culture and those of the person's ethnic or familial system, the client can feel she is in a double bind: No matter what she does, she will be judged in a negative way by someone. In planning, the worker needs to discuss the implications of diversity and of prejudice and oppression so that the client is not set up for failure.

Strengths and Challenges of the Systems Involved

Each of the systems previously described brings both strengths and challenges to the work to be done. A primary consideration in good planning is building on strengths while addressing challenges. Sometimes, challenges constitute barriers that need to be circumvented or overcome. However, the place to begin is with a strengths-based approach. The worker needs to identify the capacities and potential of the agency, the community, the situation involving the social issue, the worker, the client and his immediate environment, and the diversity factors that might come into play.

To be successful in using a strengths-based approach, the worker must be highly self-aware and sensitive to her own perceptions as well as those of the other systems involved in the situation at hand. When utilizing a problem-focused approach, there is a tendency to perceive the situation in terms of what is going wrong. This can easily lead to blaming, especially blaming the client for having the problem. The implication is that, because the situation is caused by the client, all that is needed is for the client to change. Besides, changing a system seems a more daunting task than individual change.

The person in environment and a strengths approach dictate that all aspects of the situation need to be considered during assessment. Similarly, all aspects of the situation need to be incorporated in planning for change. A strengths-based approach involves basing a plan on the abilities and capacities of clients and systems. Instead of requiring clients and systems to develop new skills and abilities as a prerequisite for change, the plan is based on what the client and systems are already able to do. Finally, a strengths approach clearly fits best with two of the cardinal values of social work, namely, the belief in the value and worth of every individual and the belief in client self-determination. In addition to valuing people inherently as human beings, a strengths approach orients the worker and the client toward abilities, thus valuing the contribution clients can make toward bringing about change. A strengths approach gives clients the tools they need to exercise self-determination and recognizes that clients are major forces in their own lives. Because people are able to make decisions for themselves, they also need to see themselves as acting to make those decisions a reality. Highlighting their strengths helps them realize how they can make self-determination a reality rather than merely an abstract concept.

The Planning Process

Planning is a joint process with the client. Students and new workers often find it difficult to decide where to start and how to determine priorities, time frames, tasks, and other aspects of the plan. In setting a goal, the worker has several approaches she can take. One approach is to take the preliminary statement of need or concern and turn it into a goal. In the case example, if the need statement is "Jerry needs a positive relationship with his school so he can achieve and make satisfactory progress," then a goal can be formulated by changing the "needs" to "will have." Thus, the goal becomes "Jerry will have a positive relationship with his school so he can achieve and make satisfactory progress."

Sometimes the worker or the client may have difficulty in clearly articulating a need in a way that lends itself to converting it into a goal statement. A second way to formulate a goal is to ask the client, "What would your life be like if this need were met (or this concern resolved)?" If he is able to answer, then he has given the worker a goal with which she can work. She should follow this up with questions such as: What would you be doing? What would other people be doing? If the worker and the client can find feasible answers to these and related questions, then a goal can be formulated. The goal might be "Jerry will feel positive about school and be passing all of his subjects."

The next set of questions should relate to setting objectives. If the worker and the client have a clear understanding of the current situation and they have formulated a goal, then they know where the client is and where he wants to go. They have a direction they can take for the work to be done. The objectives should serve as intermediate steps toward the goal and should measure the progress toward the goal. A good way to determine these steps is to ask the client questions such as: What could you do this week (in two weeks, etc.) that would make a difference? or What could you do this month (in two months, etc.) that would make a difference? In Jerry's case, he might say something about ignoring peers when they use racial slurs or not fighting at school. The worker could develop this into the objective that was identified in the case example. The next questions might be: What would it take for that to happen? What do you need to do? What do other people need to do? What do I (the worker) need to do to help? What would you be willing to do if you received a positive response? What would you consider a positive response? What would make it worthwhile for you to change? What resources do you need? Where might we find those resources? The answers to these questions can be developed into tasks similar to those in the case example.

This approach fits well with becoming diversity competent. It relies on the client to articulate goals, objectives, and tasks that are appropriate for his culture or diversity group. If these components of the plan came from the worker, they would reflect the worker's values and perspective. To ensure that the plan is consistent with the diversity of the client, the worker should ask about important factors that are related to the client's diversity. For example, the worker might ask Jerry what value is placed on education in his family or in his culture.

The worker develops a plan in consultation with her client. She uses an approach that is client centered. She respects the client as the expert in his own life and communicates an expectation that he is capable of resolving the situation and getting his needs met. She shows confidence in the client's ability to exercise self-determination. She puts herself in the role of facilitator. She demonstrates how the client can use the change process for himself so he can learn to use it in other areas of his life. As the worker uses this approach with her client, she builds a positive helping relationship and empowers him to act in his own behalf to bring about change that he desires in his life situation.

Agreement between Worker and Client

When the worker and client have worked together in assessment and in developing the plan of action, an agreement develops between them as to what needs to be done and who should do it. This agreement may take the form of a **contract**. The contract may merely be an understanding between worker and client, or it may be a formal, written, signed agreement. The form the agreement takes will be dependent in part on what is best for a particular client and in part on agency practice and policy.

Contracting is an accepted part of the worker-client interaction in many agencies. However, the use of contracts has been challenged in two ways. Pamela Miller asserted that contracts fail to recognize that the service provider is a professional using empathy as an important ingredient of the service. She called for a covenant approach, which implies that the worker has a gift of service for the client.[9] Tom Croxton pointed out that the use of the term *contract* is inaccurate because it lacks an important ingredient—legal implications. This inaccurate use can lead to misunderstandings, vagueness, and even conflict.[10]

Thus, instead of *contract,* the term *agreement* may better describe the worker-client decision. However, *contract,* as used in social work, has never been assumed to have a legal connotation. The concept of contract, as developed in social work literature, seems best to describe an agreement about the plan in the generalist social work sense. A contract or agreement can be thought of as an understanding between the worker and the client as to the work to be done.

Agreements are easiest to develop with motivated, trusting clients. They are very useful with disorganized or forgetful clients who need reminding about the work to be done or about their responsibility for carrying out tasks. Agreements can be more effective if written, but sometimes this is not necessary or even desirable. For the resistant or distrustful client, a signed paper may be a barrier, whereas a verbal commitment might be helpful. For clients in crisis it may be best to quickly get to the work of helping and delay or eliminate the step of a formal agreement. A quick verbal agreement may be all that is necessary. The agreement should be flexible and appropriate to the specific client and situation. It should be a tool to enhance the work together, not a mechanistic procedure to fulfill some outside, imposed requirement. However, regardless of whether the agreement with the worker is written, the plan that is entered into the case file should still be reviewed with the client.

Planning and contracting are means for making clear the who, what, where, when, and how of the social work endeavor. They are means for individualizing the social work process to the person in situation and also provide tools for accountability and evaluation. Planning and contracting tie knowledge about the person in environment to the work of doing something to change the situation for the client. Planning expands opportunity for accomplishing the desired change.

Summary

The following principles for developing a plan of action can give guidance to the planning process:

1. Each plan of action is a part of an overall social work process. This implies:
   - It is based on personal-social need.
   - It is developed through a change process that is based on a strengths approach.
   - It recognizes the impact of diversity on all aspects of the planning process and incorporates into the plan the strengths of the individuals and systems involved.
   - It is dynamic, changing as new knowledge leads to reassessment of situations; reformulation of need; and development of new goals, strategies, and tasks.
2. Each plan of action clearly indicates:
   - The goal toward which it is aimed. This goal should be directly related to personal-social need and should be stated in terms of a positive outcome. Objectives should be clearly stated in positive terms and be observable and measurable.
   - The unit(s) of attention that is (are) included in the plan.
   - The strategy to be used and the role of worker, client, and others and the tasks to be performed by all concerned.
3. The plan of action takes into consideration the community in which the action system functions. This includes the awareness of community expectations, norms, values, service delivery system, and resources.
4. The plan of action reflects the agency's or organization's "way of doing business." Community influences and agency organization structure, functioning, and development all contribute to this "way of doing business."
5. The nature of the social issue is recognized as an important variable in the development of the plan of action.
6. The worker's contribution to the plan of action is based on professional knowledge, values, and skill. It involves the ability to assess and determine the usefulness of various resources as well as the capacity for professional judgment and the ability to make appropriate choices from among various possibilities.
7. The client brings uniqueness to the situation. This includes a perception of the need, a set of values, unique motivation, capacity, opportunity, and goals.
8. The plan of action is the outgrowth of the worker-client interaction. Each contributes from his or her perspective regarding the person in environment. Planning typically results in a contract or agreement between worker and client.

9. The plan of action considers the availability of the resources needed to carry out the plan and the feasibility of reaching the goals.
10. The plan of action includes a time line.
11. The plan contains a means for evaluation.

Questions

1. Set a goal for yourself that you can reach in a week. Write it in outcome terms and identify two objectives that relate to the goal. Identify a task for each objective.
2. Using three of the roles identified by Teare and McPheeters, discuss the complementary client role and possible tasks for client and worker.
3. How might diversity affect the plan and the planning process if you are working with someone who is a person of color? A woman? A person who is gay or lesbian? A person who is physically or mentally disabled?
4. What are at least three strengths that could be considered in planning with someone who is a person of color? A woman? A person who is gay or lesbian? A person with a physical or mental disability?

Suggested Readings

Miley, Karla Krogsrud, O'Melia, Michael, and DuBois, Brenda L. *Social Work Practice: An Empowering Approach,* 6th ed. Boston: Allyn and Bacon, 2009 (Chapter 11).

Mizrahi, Terry and Davis, Larry E., Eds. *Encyclopedia of Social Work*, 20th ed. Washington, DC: NASW Press, 2008 ("Best Practices," "Evidence Based Practice").

Rothman, Juliet. *Contracting in Social Work.* Chicago: Nelson-Hall, 1996.

Saleeby, Dennis. *The Strengths Perspective in Social Work Practice,* 5th ed. Boston: Allyn and Bacon, 2009.

Sheafor, Bradford W., and Horejsi, Charles R. *Techniques and Guidelines for Social Work Practice,* 8th ed. Boston: Allyn and Bacon, 2008 (Chapter 12).

10 | *Direct Practice Actions*

Learning Expectations

1. Understanding of how to enable clients to use available resources.
2. Understanding of strategies for empowering and enabling clients.
3. Understanding of the nature of crisis and of the crisis intervention process.
4. Understanding of the nature and use of support.
5. Understanding of the place and use of activity in helping clients.
6. Understanding the use of various theories and models with generalist social work practice as a framework, including cognitive, behavioral, and cognitive-behavioral approaches, brief and solution-focused models, task-centered models, person-centered theory, narrative approaches, an Afrocentric approach, feminist practice, and practice with people who are gay or lesbian.

Following planning, the next step in the generalist social work process is action. Different clients with different needs in different situations require different kinds of action on the part of the worker. For some situations the actions of the assessment and planning phase provide the help needed so the client can take action for change. Sometimes help comes through the development of the worker-client relationship. This relationship then frees the client to engage in problem-solving activity with the worker. In other situations, action on the part of the worker is required. This action can be helpful in the development of relationships and in assessment. Actions by the worker may be needed to implement the plan or when barriers arise. The social worker may use various kinds of activities with people and with systems other than client systems as a part of the helping process. She may also use any model or theory that is accepted for use by professional social workers.

In understanding direct practice actions, we return to Figures 1.1 and 4.1 and use another adaptation (Figure 10.1) to illustrate how various direct practice actions are aimed at assisting the client in changing feelings, thoughts, or actions. This is not intended to be an exhaustive list of all interventions used by social workers. However, it depicts some of the primary direct practice actions used by generalist social workers in helping clients.

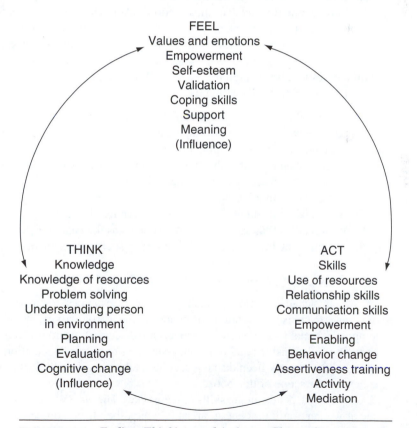

FIGURE 10.1 *Feeling, Thinking, and Action as Change Strategies and Related Direct Practice Actions*

Social workers need to be able to use a variety of theories to guide their helping efforts. An in-depth study of the original sources of these theories is beyond the scope of this book. However, the change process that we present in this text can be used as a framework for applying any of the theories or models that are used in social work practice. We have included a short summary of contemporary theories and models that are most likely to be used by generalist social work practitioners along with their use in the change process. Chapter 16 gives a short summary of the better-known theories, approaches, and models used by social workers along with identifying good practices in settings that typically employ generalist social workers.

One of the marks of a generalist practitioner is the capacity to choose from a wide variety of possibilities the action most appropriate for the specific situation. Social work action falls into two primary classifications: **direct practice** (action with clients) and **indirect practice** (action with people and systems other than clients). Direct practice usually involves action with individuals, families, and small groups. Direct practice is focused on change in either the transactions within the family or small-group system or in the manner in which individuals, families, and small groups function in relation to persons and societal institutions in their environments.

Indirect practice involves those actions taken with persons other than clients in order to help clients. These actions may be taken with individuals, a family, small groups, organizations, or communities as the unit of attention. Some of this type of help will be discussed in Chapter 11. Indirect practice actions with families, groups, organizations, and communities will be covered in Chapters 13 through 15.

Direct practice falls within the following categories:

1. Action taken to enable development of relationships
2. Action taken to enable development of understanding of person in environment
3. Action taken in the planning process
4. Action taken to enable the client to know and use available resources
5. Action taken to empower or enable clients
6. Action taken in crisis situations
7. Action taken to support the social functioning of clients
8. Action taken that uses activity with clients as the base of help
9. Actions that utilize other contemporary social work theories or models of direct practice
10. Action taken in using a clinical model of social work

In this chapter, actions related to the use of resources, to empowerment and enabling of people, to crisis intervention, to support, to the use of activity, and to utilizing other contemporary social work theories or models are discussed. Actions taken to enable the development of relationships and of an understanding of person in situation and in the planning process have already been discussed. Action taken in using clinical models of social work is beyond the scope of this book.

Action depends on the skills of the worker. The NASW *Code of Ethics* mandates that social workers only practice in areas in which they have competence. Depending on the service goals and the usual ways the agency delivers service, workers more often use certain actions rather than others. Skill in using the various types of action develops through use over time. In order to help diverse clients with various needs, social workers can be most effective when they are skilled in using a variety of actions and choose the action best suited to the client and the situation. The generalist practitioner's repertoire includes actions for working with individuals, groups, families, organizations, and communities. Often, several types of action are needed to reach identified goals. There is overlap among possible actions or strategies, and often the worker creatively combines strategies or makes alterations to better respond to specific situations. The art of social work comes into play when action becomes the focus of service. In deciding which kinds of action to take in a particular situation, several principles can be used, including:

1. *Economy*—The action chosen should require the least expenditure of time and energy by both client and worker. Generally, a worker helps the client do for himself whatever is possible to do with help and does for a client only what the client cannot do for himself.

2. *Self-determination of clients*—The action that is most desirable to the client should be used whenever possible. The action of the worker is planned with the client during the planning phase of the helping process.

3. *Individualization*—Any action taken should be differentially adapted to the strengths, needs, and characteristics of the particular client system. The worker should creatively adapt the action to the client's characteristics and situation.

4. *Development*—The action of the worker depends, in part, on the developmental stage of the client system. Different kinds of help are appropriate at different stages of development of the individual, family, and small group.

5. *Diversity*—The action is consistent with the culture and diversity of the client. Diversity competent practice involves delivering services in a manner that is acceptable within the norms and expectations of the culture or diverse group with whom the client identifies.

6. *Interdependence*—The action of the worker depends in part on the action of the client. The activity of the client and the client's capacity to change should always be considered. The actions of the worker and client should be complementary.

7. *Focus on service goals*—The action should be related to the goals for the service as developed by the worker and client together during the planning stage.

Following through with the spirit of naturalistic inquiry, the worker continues to employ the basic aspects of this approach throughout the action phase. If the worker has been successful in employing naturalistic inquiry, she should have an assessment that incorporates diversity as it applies to her client. She should also have a plan that reflects the client's perspective on his or her diversity, including goals, objectives, and tasks that are appropriate for the diversity of the client. Using naturalistic inquiry during the action phase means that the worker consistently dialogues with her client about the actions that are taken. Before she or her client takes action, she discusses who, what, where, when, how, and why. Who is going to take what action? Where and when will it take place? How will it be carried out? Why are we doing this? In addition, the worker confirms that the action is something that the client approves so that it is consistent with his or her diversity or other factors.

When the action takes place over time, the worker carries on a dialogue about the action with the client. She checks to ensure that the client is in agreement and that it fits for him or her and the situation at hand. When the action is completed, she discusses the client's level of comfort with the results and with the means by which the results were achieved.

Most of the actions that follow can be used with members of diverse groups. The actions identified here are those that are used by a generalist practice social worker. The actions are broad enough so that specific approaches may be subsumed under one or more of them. Thus, specific approaches that may be used with members of diverse groups can generally be categorized under one or more of these actions or may require a specific focus as the action is taken. For instance, an Afrocentric approach is mainly one that focuses on the unique contributions of African Americans and takes a world view that values and incorporates African traditions. As the worker works with her African American clients, she seeks out information about how help is given and received within the African American community.

Action to Enable Clients to Use Available Resources

For some clients the major block to meeting need is a lack of resources. Sometimes these resources are available, but the client is not aware of or does not know how to use them. Sometimes the resource is not responsive to some clients. In a complex and diverse society all resources are not amenable to all clients. One part of the generalist social worker's understanding of a community is knowing which resources can meet the needs of which clients. An important part of the social worker's interventive repertoire is the ability to match client and resource and to enable the client to use the available resources.

Enabling clients to know and use resources is especially important when working with diverse groups. Experiences with prejudice and discrimination often result in becoming marginalized and isolated. Members of diverse groups may not be aware of resources or may not feel welcome in using them. The way in which resources are made available or services delivered may not fit with the culture or diversity of the client. In practice with diverse clients, the social worker uses naturalistic inquiry to find out what the client knows about resources that are available. She explores experiences that the client has had or has heard about from others regarding the use of those resources. She incorporates this into the actions she takes in enabling the client to use resources.

To help clients use the available resources, workers should have knowledge and skill in four areas: (1) knowledge of the service delivery systems of the community in which they practice and the community in which the client lives and functions, (2) knowledge of and skill in the use of the referral process, (3) knowledge of the appropriate use of the broker and advocate roles and skill in filling these roles, and (4) knowledge of how to empower clients to take charge of their life situation. The social worker takes action to enable clients to use available resources, with the purpose of enabling clients to meet their needs and thus enhance their social functioning and coping capacity.

The Service Delivery System

When identifying components of the service delivery system, workers usually begin by identifying social service agencies and services provided by other professionals. A broader view needs to be considered. Within many neighborhoods, communities, and ethnic groups, a helping network outside the formal system exists. This **natural helping system** becomes known to social workers as they come into contact with diverse clients and groups in the community. There is, however, much to be learned about how to work cooperatively with this system.

The natural helping system is made up of a client's family, friends, and coworkers. These are the people to whom a person in need goes for help first. When clients come to a social worker, they have probably first tried to get help from these natural helpers. The use of the natural helping system has particular importance in working with diverse cultural groups. Past experiences with discrimination and oppression have led many people of color to rely on systems in their immediate environments for assistance. Often, the relationship between the client and this system may need to be strengthened or restored or the systems themselves may need to be strengthened and supported in providing help. The extended family has always been an important part of the helping system for many ethnic groups and in small towns and rural areas. For example, among Native Americans the extended family is so important that if a social worker fails to involve this system in the planning process, the client may not be able to use any help offered. Ross Speck and Carolyn Attneave have developed a method of working with extended families called *network therapy*, which involves and supports the extended family in helping a family member in need.[1] A **network** is an association of systems that operates through mutual resource sharing.

The work of Eugene Litwak and Ivan Szelenyi supports the use of family, neighbors, and kin as a helping resource.[2] They consider neighborhood ties to be useful because of the speed of response to need. With such ties, the person seeking help has personal, immediately available contact. The person in need is continually observed, and help is provided quickly when situations change. Family or kin are particularly helpful because of the long-term relationships that exist. For example, they are a resource for the care of children when a parent dies or when individuals face long-term medical care or institutionalization. Friendship networks are useful because of the strong emotional element and aspect of free choice.

Also part of the natural helping network are natural helpers in the community, community benefits, and self-help groups. **Natural helpers**, sometimes called *indigenous helpers* or *healers*, are those persons who possess helping skills and exercise them in the context of mutual relationships. These are usually individuals who make helping a part of their everyday life. They are hardworking people who are optimistic about being able to change; mature, friendly people who often have had the same needs as those they are helping; trustworthy people who keep confidences; and people who are available and share a sense of mutuality with others. They usually have had similar life experiences and have similar values as the person they are helping. Members of neighborhoods, small communities, or ethnic groups usually know who these people are. For example, in the Hispanic community the *curandero* is considered the indigenous healer to be consulted when someone needs mental or medical treatment. However, it is often difficult for professional people to identify these healers without help from those who are a part of the community system.

Alice Collins and Diane Pancoast discussed effective methods for working with natural helpers.[3] They believe that social workers should not try to train natural helpers or make them paraprofessionals. Rather, workers should recognize natural helpers as valuable resources and support them in their unique ways of helping. This requires recognition of natural helpers' capacity and competence to help and calls for a consultative relationship.

Community benefits, fund-raising events organized for someone who has had a catastrophe, such as a fire, illness, or death of a family member, are another example of the natural helping system at work. Many cultural groups are more comfortable with this form of support than with support from a formal organization. The challenge to the worker is to use organizational skills in working with the client's native community while at the same time ensuring that leadership and responsibility for the benefit reside in the culture. Some of the guidelines suggested later in the chapter concerning working with natural helping systems can be useful in this regard.

Self-help groups may be considered a part of the natural helping system. Mutual aid is related to the responsibility people feel for one another. One means of carrying out this responsibility is the voluntary small group, often of spontaneous origin, that develops for people who have similar problems. Groups are important in developing connectedness to others at a time when isolation may be experienced. They are useful in encouraging growth and redefinition of self. Some work for change regarding social issues that affect group members. In these groups those who have lived through problems help those who currently experience the problem. Help is given by modeling, positive reinforcement, and emphasis on the here and now. Examples of such groups are Alcoholics Anonymous, cancer support groups, and life-transition groups, such as widow-to-widow groups.[4]

The relationship between self-help groups and formal human service organizations may be problematic because each has different ways of functioning. Such variables as the client group on which service is focused, the need for resources outside the system, and the relationship of helper and those receiving help might differ significantly. Also, relationships among self-help groups and human service organizations vary. Yeheskel Hasenfeld and Benjamin Gidron have identified five relational patterns: competition, referral, coordination, coalition, and co-optation. The ideal relationship would be one of coordination and coalition.[5] Regardless of relational patterns, to maximize the use of self-help groups, social workers must be aware of the relational pattern that exists and, when appropriate, work to facilitate a different pattern.

In working with natural helping systems, social workers must be aware that these systems are primary groups that use an informal, personal means of interaction. Attempting to work with natural helping systems using the methods of formal bureaucratic systems often blocks any meaningful interaction or coordination. Two results can occur: (1) The natural helping system may stop helping and allow the formal system to do the helping; in this situation the natural helping system is destroyed. (2) The natural helping system may withdraw from the formal system and go underground; in this situation the social worker is unable to coordinate and cooperate, and the two systems may offer help that does not allow the client to use both systems effectively. The consultative, enabling stance seems to be the most appropriate approach to functioning with natural helping systems. Social workers must be creative in linking formal and informal networks if the assistance of the natural helping system is to be maximized. It is most important to maintain communication without interfering with the functioning of either the formal or informal systems.

The formal service delivery system includes not only social service agencies but also organizations that either have an interest in specific projects or have resources for their members. The American Legion may be able to provide certain resources for a veteran or his family, particularly if that veteran is a member of the organization. The Lions Club has always concerned itself with visual problems and might help in obtaining glasses for a client. Other organizations may have resources, such as used-clothing stores, that can provide necessary items for clients. The social worker should be aware of these organizational resources.

To help clients use the resources of various community institutions and professionals, the social worker needs a good understanding of the available services and resources and how to access these. Acquaintance with other professionals, such as teachers, ministers, and doctors, can help the worker learn of resources. Skill in coordination, consultation, and team functioning, as discussed in Chapters 11 and 15, is important in helping clients use resources.

Service delivery by social service agencies takes different forms. Agencies use many kinds of workers to deliver different services. MSWs deliver clinical services; BSWs are used in many ways to support clients, to help with meeting needs, and to provide concrete services; paraprofessionals may be used to provide some services. Indigenous workers, who are skilled in working with their particular cultural groups, are another resource. Although they often have no formal education relative to social work, indigenous workers have knowledge of the sociocultural group being helped. Homemaker or chore services may be provided by paraprofessionals or indigenous workers. Volunteers provide some services.

Service may be provided in an agency office only or by outreach to people in need. Agencies may provide only counseling or clinical social work, or they may provide concrete services or resources, such as food or money. Some agencies station workers in small communities or in neighborhoods not easily accessible to the main office. Others use a "circuit-riding" approach to servicing clients in remote areas. In this approach, the worker visits an area on a scheduled frequency to meet with clients. With limited populations or for some highly specialized services, the client leaves the community to obtain service. Social workers must have knowledge of how agencies deliver services and what resources they have if they are to help clients find needed resources. Some agencies may not deliver services in a manner that is usable by some clients. Workers need to be aware of agency limitations so that they do not add to clients' frustration by referring them to services that are unattainable or institutions that are unresponsive.

The first step in enabling clients to use resources is a thorough knowledge of the resources available. The second step is choosing the appropriate resource for the client. This choice is based on matching client need and lifestyle with a resource that can meet the need in a manner congruent with the client's lifestyle. Client involvement in the choice is essential for matching and linking the client to the resource. In addition, workers may use indirect practice strategies to work for change in the relational patterns characterizing segments of the service delivery system so that client need can be better met. (See Chapters 11 and 15.)

Referral

Referral is the process by which a social worker enables a client to know and use another resource. In addition, the referral process involves supplying the referral agency with information that may be helpful in providing service to the client and then following up on the usefulness of the service to the client. The worker must obtain written permission from the client or the client's guardian, usually called a release of information, before sharing any identifying information about the client system with an outside service.

Referral is used when the client's needs cannot be met by services provided by the agency that employs the worker or when a more appropriate service is provided by another agency. The worker uses knowledge of the potential resources and knowledge of the way service is delivered to match potential clients and potential services so that the service is acceptable to and usable by clients. The referral service may be used in conjunction with the service a worker is providing or as the primary service.

Referrals are made only with permission of the client. The worker and client discuss the potential service, and the worker helps the client make the initial contact with the new agency, if necessary. This can be done by giving a phone number or directions for reaching the agency or by making suggestions about how to approach the agency. Sometimes it is helpful for a worker to call the agency for the client or go to the agency with the client for the first contact. The worker must make sure the client has the resources needed to access and utilize the service, including transportation, access to a telephone, financial resources, and day care. The worker and client also discuss the information that would be helpful to the agency. After receiving the client's permission and obtaining a written release of information, a worker provides this information to the worker at the new agency. It is often helpful if the two workers know each other and can discuss the client's needs.

An often-overlooked final step in referral is follow-up. In determining whether the client is receiving the services sought, the worker gains information about the appropriateness of the service for the client and others who may have similar needs. This enables the worker to make appropriate referrals in the future. If the client has not been able to use the service, the worker must advocate for the client or assist her in receiving the needed service elsewhere or determine why she was unable to use the service. Skill in referral is a necessary tool for all social workers.[6]

Broker and Advocate Roles

In enabling clients to use available resources, two primary roles are used: the broker role and the advocate role. It is important for the social worker to understand the difference between these two roles and to choose the one most appropriate to the situation. The **broker** helps a person or family get needed services. This includes assessing the situation, knowing the alternative resources, preparing and counseling the person, contacting the appropriate service, and ensuring that the client gets to the resource and uses it.[7] The goal is to expedite the linkage of client to the needed resource. This involves giving information and support, teaching clients how to use resources, and also negotiating with the agency.

The role of **advocate** consists of "pleading and fighting for services for clients whom the service system would otherwise reject."[8] For example, a lesbian couple may be denied housing because of their relationship, or a person with HIV or AIDS may be denied medical treatment. The worker as advocate seeks different interpretations or exceptions to rules and regulations, points out clients' rights to services, and removes blocks to receiving or using an agency's services.

In the advocacy role, the worker speaks on behalf of the client. Before engaging in advocacy a worker must first be sure that the client desires the worker to intervene in this manner. Then the worker must carefully assess the risks involved for the client if advocacy is used. This includes consideration that any action taken might cause problems for the client or block access to the resources. The client should clearly understand the risks involved and be motivated to use the service if it is obtained. Case advocacy, advocacy for a single client, is most effective when used to obtain concrete resources for which the client is eligible. It is also useful when people and systems impinge on a client's functioning. To be a **case advocate**, social workers must be comfortable with conflict situations and knowledgeable about the means for conflict management. They must be willing to negotiate and be aware of the value of withdrawing application for service if the best interests of the client are not being served. Clients must have considerable trust in the worker before they will be willing for the worker to take an advocate role.

The worker uses the advocate role only when the broker role is not effective. Whenever possible, it is better for the client to act on her own behalf in order to strengthen her belief in self as well as gain a sense of empowerment. There are times, however, when an advocate stance must be taken in order to enable clients to obtain needed services. *Cause advocacy,* which serves groups with similar difficulties, will be addressed in Chapter 15. Mediation as an alternative to advocacy is discussed in Chapter 11.

Case Example

Mrs. Abbott's daughter asked to speak with the social worker at Sunnyside Assisted Living Facility. Sue met with Judy to discuss her concerns. Judy said that she was worried that she would not be able to keep her mother in the facility once her Medicare coverage ran out and private payment began. She was also feeling very guilty about having her mother stay rather than bringing her mother to live with her. She explained that she had three young children and that both she and her husband needed to work. In addition, their house was not very big and could not really accommodate a wheelchair if that is what her mother needed. Sue reassured her that it was okay to have her mother stay. She said that a lot of the families felt the same way. In fact, there was a family support group that she could attend. The group meetings were held at the local Commission on Aging, and families from residential facilities in the area were welcome to attend. Judy took down the information and seemed somewhat relieved. Sue then discussed Medicaid eligibility and the need to spend down assets to become eligible. She referred Judy to the local Department of Human Services (DHS) to find out more information and to meet with a worker.

Judy called the next day very upset. She said that she had gone to DHS and, after a long wait, was told that it was best to wait until after the Medicare ran out before her mother applied. She said that she felt that waiting that long would be too anxiety provoking for her. She wanted to be sure that her mother could stay at Sunnyside. Sue asked if Judy wanted her to contact the worker on her behalf to see what could be done and Judy agreed. Sue had Judy come to her office and sign a release of information form. Sue also explained the situation to Mrs. Abbott and obtained a release of information from her.

Sue contacted the DHS office and spoke with the worker who explained that with recent cuts in state spending along with early retirements, their office was very short of staff. They discussed various options and Sue offered to help in any way she could. The worker suggested if Sue helped Mrs. Abbott and her daughter with the forms and supporting documentation, it would speed up the process. Sue agreed. She met with Mrs. Abbott and Judy several times, and then went with Judy to meet with the worker at DHS. They found that there were several items

(continued)

that were still needed. Judy said that she could get them in a few days. Later in the week, Sue contacted Judy to make sure that everything was settled. Judy indicated that they had done what they could for now and thanked Sue for her assistance. She also said that she had attended her first meeting for families and it was a positive experience. She felt relieved and it was nice to talk with others who were going through the same thing.

Action to Empower and Enable Clients

Most clients can benefit from being able to take an active role in changing the situations impinging on their functioning. Empowerment is "a process of increasing personal, interpersonal, or political power so that individuals can take action to improve their life situation."[9] **Empowerment** has been suggested as a strategy of choice when working with members of minority groups, populations at risk, and women.[10] Empowerment is particularly useful in the contemporary world in which power is an all-pervasive issue and in which the gap between haves and have-nots is growing dramatically. Empowerment means providing clients with the supports, skills, and understanding needed to allow them to take charge of their own lives and use their power in situations in which they have felt powerless.

Those caught in feelings or situations of powerlessness often lack knowledge of how to negotiate systems, feel hopeless that any change is possible, and may lack the self-esteem necessary for engaging in change activity. Empowerment involves assisting clients in negotiating systems. It involves motivating, teaching, and raising self-esteem so clients believe they are competent individuals with the skills needed for negotiating community systems and they deserve the resources necessary for healthy social functioning. Empowerment enables clients to receive the benefits of society and increases their capacity to work toward resolving the conditions preventing them from providing for their needs.

According to Ruth J. Parsons, a literature search confirms that the important ingredients of an empowerment strategy are support, mutual aid, and validation of the client's perceptions and experiences. When these ingredients are present, there is a heightened degree of client self-esteem, more self-confidence, and a greater capacity to make changes or take action. An empowerment strategy calls for building collectives; working with others in similar situations; educating for critical thinking through support, mutual aid, and collective action; and competency assessment, or identification of strengths and coping skills.[11]

Thus, the use of groups, particularly mutual-aid groups, enhances this action strategy. Silvia Staub-Bernasconi pointed this out and called for a focus on consciousness development, social and coping skills training, networking, and mediation. Also, empowerment calls for work with power sources and power structures.[12] This strategy is congruent with the generalist social work model presented in this text. The strong emphasis on maximal client involvement in assessment, planning, and action to meet goals is an important ingredient of empowerment. Teaching clients about meeting needs and about the nature of the systems in their environments is a part of empowerment.

A technique useful in an empowerment strategy is consciousness raising, which involves giving the client information about the nature of the situation, particularly the various environmental forces affecting client functioning. This work can heighten client understanding of self in relationship to others. Workers must feel comfortable with the anger that can result from using this technique and be able to help clients use anger in ways that further the work at hand. When the time is appropriate, it is also important for the worker to help the client move beyond anger into other responses. It is hoped that the client can gain a more realistic view of the situation and then take advantage of change possibilities.

Groups are a powerful adjunct to consciousness raising. It is helpful to the client to see others struggle with new understandings. The group can be involved in collective action and thus enhance a sense of individual power. The group can also be a support system for mutual aid. Participation in a group can lead to enhanced self-esteem and can help clients learn new skills. Groups will be covered in Chapter 14.

The nature of the relationship between worker and client is an important consideration when using this strategy. Using an empowerment approach requires establishing mutual respect, building on client strengths, sharing information and knowledge of resources in a sense of partnership, and considering the client as the "expert" on her own situation. Because the worker may be viewed as yet another person with power over the client, she needs to act as a colleague rather than as a detached professional. This requires the worker to shift her frame of reference from that of an expert to that of a collaborator.[13] As the worker demonstrates belief in the client and points out competencies, the client will gain a sense of self-worth and a belief that she has the ability to bring about change.

Another valuable technique that can be an adjunct to an empowerment strategy is work focused on reducing self-blame. The client needs to see that the difficulties he is facing often have their source in the functioning of systems in the environment. The worker can help the client take responsibility for changing the environment by teaching specific skills for environmental change. Although the worker may also work for environmental change through advocacy and mobilization of resources, it is important that the client participate; otherwise, the feeling of personal inadequacy may be further reinforced.[14]

Empowerment is not a strategy that is used in isolation from other strategies. Instead it aims to reduce helplessness so that clients can take charge of their lives.

Enabling or helping clients reach their goals may seem similar to empowerment, but there are subtle differences. **Enabling**, the broader term, refers to helping an individual or system carry out an activity otherwise not possible. This term recently has taken on negative connotations when used with regard to alcohol and other addictions. For example, a spouse whose actions support the addictive behaviors of the partner is often called an enabler. As used in this text, enabling has a positive connotation in that the action being supported is desirable.

Sometimes in the process of empowering or enabling the client, the worker may need to work directly with the client to enhance positive thinking and actions. Often, the client has had experiences that reinforce a negative view of herself or her situation. She may be frustrated or may have learned that it is safer to predict failure than to hope for success. The client may blame herself or others for the situation. She may engage in self-defeating thoughts or actions. When the worker senses that this is happening, he can assist the client in changing her thoughts or actions so that she can successfully meet her goals and carry out her plan. The thinking part of this strategy is called a *cognitive approach* or *intervention* and is outlined in Chapter 16. The action part refers to behavior, and this is also outlined in Chapter 16. Theorists have combined these two approaches into what is called a *cognitive-behavioral approach*.[15]

The basic idea behind this approach is that thoughts lead to feelings and behavior. Negative thoughts lead to negative feelings and negative reactions, and positive thoughts lead to positive feelings and positive behavior. It is important to be able to work with the client to develop positive thinking and actions as she carries out her plan. The plan contains behaviors that the client has agreed to do. These behaviors are stated in the objectives and tasks. If the client does not think she can accomplish something, she is unlikely to do so. The worker asks the client what she is thinking about the situation and about the proposed goals, objectives, and tasks. The worker listens for thoughts that might be barriers to success and helps the client to see how her thinking can have either a positive or a negative influence on carrying out the plan. A good set of questions to ask are: (1) What do you think will happen if you do this? or What were you thinking when that happened? (2) What do you want to have happen? (3) What could you do to make that happen today? This week? This month? (or Next time?) (4) What could you tell yourself that would make you feel more confident in doing that? (5) What kind of payoff or reward could you identify that would help you to remember to do that?

An important technique in empowering or enabling clients that uses a cognitive-behavioral approach is assertiveness training. In this technique, the worker assists the client to become more assertive about meeting her needs. The worker will generally engage in practicing and role-playing assertive behaviors in situations in which the client needs to advocate for herself. It is important that the worker help the client differentiate between assertiveness and aggressiveness. Assertiveness is the positive expression of oneself and is marked by the use of statements that begin with "I." Aggressiveness is imposing one's thoughts or feelings on others and is generally marked by statements that begin with "You."

Sometimes clients need to be able to use a behavioral approach in their relationships with others. This is especially valuable for parents who need to influence their children's behavior. Social workers are uncomfortable with using negative reinforcement or punishment to modify behavior because doing so usually violates social work values and ethics. In addition, clients may have experienced a great deal of punishment and negative reinforcement in their lives. The use of extinction and positive reinforcement tends not to be a violation of social work values and ethics. Basically, **extinction** involves ignoring undesirable behavior to eliminate it. The parent should be warned that the initial response of the child will be to increase the behavior in order to receive the customary attention. However, persistently using this technique generally results in the desired goal.

Positive reinforcement is giving a reward for or recognizing the desired behavior. Parents can give positive reinforcement whenever they observe the desired behavior, or they can make an agreement beforehand with the child to reward certain behavior. The strongest reinforcements are those that are identified by the person receiving them. If a reinforcement is given too frequently, it is more likely to change the behavior more quickly, but the strength of the reinforcement tends not to last very long. However, if the reinforcement is infrequent or seen as unattainable, it will have little impact on changing behavior. Sometimes a smaller reward or a symbol can be used on a more frequent basis and a larger reward given less often. An example of this would be a star chart where the child receives a star that he can put on a chart for each day of the week. When he earns enough stars, he is rewarded with a toy. In this way the stars serve as positive reinforcement on a day-to-day basis, and the toy serves as a longer-term reward.

Positive feedback is a form of positive reinforcement that is extremely important in developing and maintaining positive relationships. Many clients may not have received much positive support in their lives. Thus, they may not be able to give much positive support. Whenever the worker sees dissatisfaction with a relationship, she should look for the absence of positive feedback. The worker can suggest ways to give positive feedback and ways to receive it. Generally, giving positive feedback results in getting positive feedback in return, although this may take some time if the other person has become accustomed to negative feedback or no feedback at all. Feedback is an important part of parenting. Parents need to give consistent messages about the behavior they expect from their children and then follow up with positive or negative feedback. Positive feedback tends to be the strongest form of reinforcement a parent can give a child.

Actions that assist clients to engage in positive thinking and positive behavior are important to empowering and enabling them. The ability to be assertive may be needed for the client to advocate or speak up for himself. Positive reinforcement and feedback are essential to good parenting and to developing and maintaining successful relationships. The worker incorporates these tools into her work in empowering and enabling clients to carry out their plans.

Case Example

In the case example of the Adams family from earlier chapters, the worker uncovered several concerns that might be resolved using an enabling approach. Jerry mentions that he is upset about being blamed for everything and that it seems like he never does anything right, especially in the eyes of his father. The worker explores this with Jerry and his father and identifies some positive behaviors of Jerry's that generally go unnoticed, such as making his bed in the morning, mowing the lawn, cleaning his bedroom, attending school each day without any unexcused absences, informing his parents of his whereabouts, and abiding by his curfew. Mr. A comments that he does not see why any one should get recognition for "doing what you are supposed to do." The worker asks him if he would go to work if he did not get paid, and Mr. A said that he would not, especially because he needs to support his family. The worker points out that getting positive feedback from one's parent is like "pay day" for children. Mr. A nods his head and says, "I never thought of it that way." The worker turns to Jerry and asks him what he would like to hear when he did something positive. Jerry states that a "Thank you" would be enough or "Nice job on the lawn" would be great. The worker asks Mr. A if he would be willing to give Jerry positive recognition for positive behaviors he sees. Mr. A agrees to try.

In working with Jerry regarding his difficulties at school, the worker discovers that Jerry feels that the teachers do not like him and so his effort is minimal at times. The worker asks for some specific examples of things Jerry sees that indicate that a teacher does not like him. Jerry describes getting a D on a paper and the teacher writing a note that she felt Jerry could do much better than this. The worker asks what Jerry thought the message was from the teacher. He responds that it made it sound like he was lazy or stupid. The worker challenges this and asks Jerry if those were the teacher's words or if they were words that he is telling himself. Jerry admits that they were his own words. The worker then asks how Jerry felt when he interpreted the teacher's comments this way. He says that the whole thing makes him upset; he feels like there is nothing he can do to please the teacher so why try anyway. With some further discussion of the situation, Jerry is able to see how his own negative thoughts are getting in the way of his

(continued)

desire to do well in school. The worker is also able to help Jerry to see that the teacher may
have been expressing her disappointment, but also may be attempting to get him to try harder
by letting him know that such work is not an indication of his potential. The worker asks Jerry
what he could tell himself that would create a more positive attitude toward his work in that
class. Jerry initially cannot think of anything, but with some assistance he decides that telling
himself that he can do it would make him try harder. He agrees to do this before he does his
next assignment. He also agrees to ask the teacher for some assistance.

Action in Response to Crisis

Clients use many coping mechanisms as well as the resources of the natural helping systems and community institutions before coming to a social worker. They often are under
considerable stress and may be in a state of crisis. If the client is in a state of crisis, it is important that the social worker be able to recognize this situation and respond appropriately.
Crisis intervention is a model of social work practice that provides a knowledge base and
guidelines for crisis response. All generalist social workers should develop knowledge of
and skill in working with people in crisis. The major goal of action in response to crisis
(*crisis intervention*) is resolution of the crisis and restored social functioning. If, after this
goal is reached, the worker and the client then decide there is some other goal they want to
work on together, another kind of action is taken.

Recognizing Crisis

A **crisis** exists when a stressful situation or a precipitating event causes a system, such as
an individual or family, to develop a state of disequilibrium, or to lose its steady state. Coping mechanisms that have worked in past situations no longer work, despite a considerable
struggle to cope. A person or family continually in a state of disorganization is not in
crisis; working with such a situation requires a different kind of action.

Crisis is usually a part of the life experience of all people. Workers seeing clients in
crisis should assume that these people were functioning adequately before the crisis event
and should view the helping role as restorative rather than remedial. It is important not to
base an assessment of clients' normal ability to function on the behaviors and coping
mechanisms displayed during the crisis.

A crisis situation can develop because of situational and developmental factors. Situational factors include illness of the individual or close family members, death of a close
family member, separation or divorce, change of living situation or lifestyle, and loss of a
job. These situational factors call either for assuming new roles and responsibilities or for
changing the established way of functioning with others. Sometimes these factors cause
considerable stress only temporarily; after a period of instability and trying new coping
methods, the result is a new and comfortable way of functioning. At other times, an additional stressful situation precipitates the crisis situation.

Developmental stress arises from the unsettled or stressful feelings that may occur as
individuals move from one developmental stage to another. This movement requires new

ways of functioning. Adolescence is a time of stress, a time of new concerns and when needs may not be fulfilled. As young persons learn to deal with their sexual drives, make career decisions, and develop new relationships with parents, they may become overwhelmed, and crises can develop. Families also experience a crisis as they move from one stage to another. The birth of the first child calls for new patterns of social functioning, thus creating additional stress and sometimes crisis.

Figure 10.2 provides an overall view of the crisis process. The hazardous state, the vulnerable state, and increase in upset are precrisis states that are often resolved by the usual means of coping and help from personal support systems. When these means do not bring about resolution, individuals move into a crisis state, and crisis intervention becomes an appropriate strategy for action.

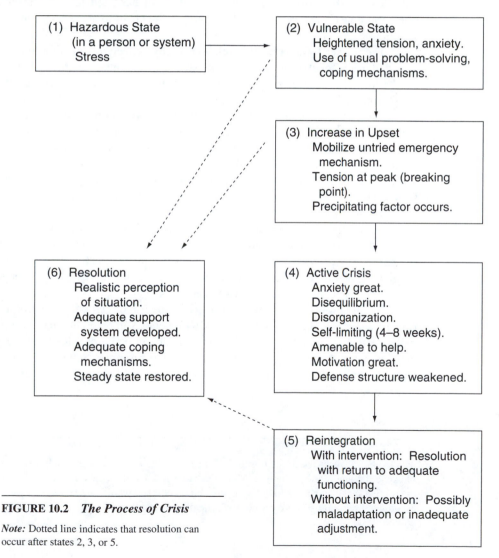

FIGURE 10.2 *The Process of Crisis*

Note: Dotted line indicates that resolution can occur after states 2, 3, or 5.

Responding to Crisis

When working with individuals in crisis, the worker needs to be aware of the time element of crisis. The true crisis situation generally lasts from four to eight weeks. After that time individuals find new ways of coping. Without appropriate help during the crisis stage, the result may be a reduced capacity for effective social functioning. Thus, help for individuals in crisis must be immediate and sometimes fairly intensive.

The worker has two crucial tasks: (1) to develop an understanding about the person in crisis and what precipitated the crisis and (2) to develop the helping relationship. In developing an understanding, the worker searches for the precipitating event—the event that pushed the person into crisis—as well as the nature of the underlying stressful situation.

The worker also determines what the client has tried to do to resolve the stress (the coping mechanisms used) and encourages the client to share how she feels about the situation.

The worker forms a helping relationship by actively responding to the client's concern and need. Together they explore the situation and determine the reality of the client's perceptions. The worker supports the client's strengths by acknowledging the coping attempts and makes specific suggestions for other means of coping. The worker shares with the client his understanding of the situation. The worker communicates realistic hope that the crisis can be resolved and that he will help the client through this difficult time. The client is encouraged to express feelings about the situation. The worker is sensitive to the client's anxiety and to the possibility of depression. If excessive anxiety or depression develops, the worker helps the client seek the services of a competent mental health professional. The worker also links the client to other needed resources.

Through the work together in the four- to eight-week period of crisis, the client usually discovers new coping mechanisms, and the crisis is resolved. In the latter part of this period, the worker can often enhance the client's problem-solving skills and thus prevent future crises. Working with clients in an intensive, fairly directive manner during the crisis helps prevent future social-functioning difficulties and restores the client to a state in which she can manage in an effective manner.

When family systems experience crisis, the use of crisis intervention is also appropriate. Sometimes it is possible to work with persons in crisis in small groups. When the worker has several clients in crisis situations, it can be helpful for these people to share perceptions and experiences as a part of the crisis response. Some crisis groups are open ended, with people in the later stages of crisis gaining help by helping those in the early stages of crisis.[16]

Case Example

Mrs. Abbott was rushed to the hospital after she complained of severe pain in her hip during her physical therapy session. Sue met Mrs. A's daughter Judy at the hospital and they met with the doctor. He said that Mrs. A had developed a blood clot and would need emergency surgery. Judy asked what her mother's prognosis was. The doctor said that, as long as they could remove the

(continued)

Case Example   *(continued)*

clot, her chances were good. However, if it moved or if they found clots in other places, then it might be less positive. After the doctor left, Judy collapsed in a chair, buried her face in her hands, and started sobbing. Sue moved next to her to comfort her. Judy said that she was not sure if she could take much more. She is worried about her mother but also about her job and her family. Her boss was giving her a hard time about taking off so much time from work. She was worried about losing her job. She also said that she and her husband had been having more arguments and that all of this stress was becoming overwhelming. Sue said that Judy needed to take one thing at a time instead of trying to deal with everything at once. They talked about her mother's condition, and Sue pointed out that Mrs. A had been making excellent progress and was starting to walk with some assistance. She had also been noticeably more cheerful and outgoing before this latest setback. Sue believed that the combination of her improved health and mental outlook would help Mrs. A survive this health crisis. Judy said that she hoped Sue was right. Sue said that at the very least, Judy needed to stop worrying about what might happen and just take this situation one hour at a time until they see the outcome. She pointed out that worrying resulted in living one's life as if the worst things are happening even when they do not happen. Judy said she never thought of it that way. She stopped crying and said she was still concerned about her job and her marriage. Sue asked her if there was a human resources department or a union where she worked. Judy said both were available at her job. Sue talked with Judy about contacting both groups to determine what benefits she was entitled to in terms of time off for family health issues. Then she could ask human resources or her union representative to meet with her boss about the situation. Sue then discussed the relationship with Judy's husband. Judy believes that her feelings of being overwhelmed were probably causing most of the stress in their relationship. She feels that her husband does not know what to say when she gets upset. Sue asked if he had attended any of the family support group sessions. Judy said he had not because he was staying at home to watch the children while she went. Sue indicated that it might be worthwhile to get a sitter and have them both go. This would give them more of a feeling of facing this together. Judy said that she had a neighbor with whom she trades childcare time, and she thought it might work to have her watch the children so Judy and her husband could both go. Perhaps they could stop and eat beforehand or afterward. Judy was greatly relieved and thanked Sue for her help. Judy's sister arrived as they finished. She lives about two hours away. They talked briefly and then Sue excused herself to return to her office at Sunnyside. She explained that she had a group to meet with in about an hour. She asked Judy and her sister to keep her abreast of their mother's condition and told them that she would be available to help them with anything that was needed. She asked if they would like to talk with the hospital chaplain or the social worker. They said that either one might be helpful, especially the chaplain. On the way out, Sue stopped by both offices and asked if they could look in on the family.

Action That Is Supportive

Support has been a universal part of helping. As Lois Selby accurately put it, "It is as old as man's humanity to man."[17] Support is part of every generalist social worker's repertoire, yet it is a concept that has received little attention in social work literature. Beulah Roberts Compton pointed out that social work attitudes toward support historically have limited its use to chronic clients or to those for whom no other treatment is possible.[18] There seems to be a notion that support is hardly worth the social worker's time.

Florence Hollis identified sustainment as one of the procedures of social work practice.[19] Her usage of the term *sustainment* seems very close to the notion of support and is primarily expressed by nonverbal means. Hollis identified some of the components or techniques of sustainment as expression of the client's abilities and competencies, expression of interest, desire to help, understanding of a client's situation and feelings about that situation, and use of encouragement and reassurance. Reassurance should be realistic. Emphasis should be on the feeling component and support for the acceptability of having feelings about the situation of concern.

Contemporary social work sees support as an acceptable function. Social work literature recognizes the use of support as a means of helping people to cope with difficult situations and thus to grow. However, little has been written that identifies the nature of support; there seems to be an assumption that social workers know what support is. The use of support seems to be an idea in the domain of practice wisdom of social work knowledge.

Judith Nelson defined supportive procedures as "those intended to help clients feel better, stronger, or more comfortable in some immediate way."[20] She has identified four kinds of support: (1) *protection,* which includes giving directions and advice, setting limits, and giving structure to complex or overwhelming situations; (2) *acceptance,* which includes making clients aware that the worker is with them in their struggles, confirming the worth of the person, and communicating understanding of clients' feelings and situations; (3) *validation,* which includes showing clients ways they are effective and competent persons, giving feedback, providing hope, communicating praise and approval, and encouraging clients in their coping efforts and role performance; and (4) *education,* which includes teaching clients how to cope and function effectively, providing needed information, socializing clients to new roles, and helping clients develop self-knowledge. One of the ways of teaching is modeling effective methods of coping.

Not only is Nelson's classification useful for identifying what support will best meet a client's needs but it also is important in identifying which aspects of a client's functioning the worker desires to support. Two other useful ways to identify the specific area of social functioning that needs support might be in terms of coping tasks or life roles. Using the coping-task approach, the worker identifies the task or tasks a client confronts when coping with a life situation (e.g., acceptance of the limitations of chronic illness). Using the life-role approach, the worker identifies the client's limitations, difficulties, and strengths in carrying out a life role. For example, if the client has difficulty following through with disciplinary procedures as a parent, the worker might first note areas in which the client does follow through, such as meal preparation. The worker then helps the client determine what skills she uses to complete that task and teaches her how to use the same motivations and skills when disciplining her child. This approach builds on the client's strengths rather than weaknesses and reinforces the idea that the client has problem-solving skills useful in various situations.

When using support as an interventive strategy, the worker identifies the client's need (as in all social work practice). This assessment emphasizes the client's perception of the situation and the client's realistic experiences in attempting to fulfill the need. Feelings of threat or deprivation are particularly important to note. The assessment should also consider the client's capacity for hope, the client's strengths, and the support the environment can provide.

The worker then decides what behaviors and attitudes can be supported to enable the client to get the need met. A decision is made about the specific kind of support to provide. Sometimes it is useful to provide the client with concrete resources or tangible services as a means of demonstrating the worker's care and concern. Using a supportive approach, the worker tries to develop a climate for helping that is accepting, understanding, comfortable, and validating and in which the client feels free to discuss concerns and feelings openly. The worker expresses interest and concern, encourages and praises the client for appropriate efforts, expresses realistic confidence in the client's ability to cope and to carry out life tasks, guides the client, and provides needed structure for the client's work.

Problems can arise from the inappropriate use of support. For one thing, there is always a danger that the client will become overly dependent on the worker. Thus, the worker must guard against unrealistic expectations on the part of the client and avoid helping when the client can help himself or when the environment can provide the support. Workers need to be aware of their tendencies to be overly protective or to make up for the wrongs clients have suffered. The worker also needs to be aware that an evaluative tone can create resistance in the client and thus be counterproductive.

Although worker support is an important component of the social work endeavor, the worker also should focus on helping the client build an adequate support system within the client's natural environment. Support from relatives, friends, family, ministers, churches, and so on is essential to healthy functioning. If these systems have not been adequate or have broken down, the worker should assist the client in rebuilding or strengthening these relationships as a means of resolving the current situation as well as meeting future needs. Building a support system is especially important for diverse clients at risk of prejudice, discrimination, and oppression.

In the past, many social workers have become accustomed to spending extra time in a supportive role with clients. However, managed care and limitations on services have reduced the time available for such extra support services. Social workers need to be certain from the beginning that adequate support systems are in place for the client, especially in a situation in which time limits are placed on the service. If support is needed from more formal support systems, then developing a relationship with those systems must be a priority.

Small groups have been found to be effective for providing support. These support groups are of particular value for use with caregivers,[21] those who have family members suffering from chronic or life-threatening conditions,[22] and those who have had common debilitating experiences.[23] The worker should be aware of support groups and self-help groups that are available in the client's area. If a group is needed, the worker may initiate setting up a group through her own agency if appropriate or may approach another agency whose services might potentially include such a group. In the era of managed care and limited services, agencies need to sponsor these groups as a means of providing support beyond the time limits of service. If agencies collaborate and share this task, then the burden of committing staff and resources will not be overwhelming. For instance, a health care agency might agree to sponsor a group for cancer patients, the local senior agency may sponsor a support group for caregivers, and the local substance abuse program may sponsor AA and Al-Anon groups.

Properly used, support can produce growth and not simply maintain the status quo. It provides positive reinforcement and can give clients strength to live and to grow in difficult situations. Support should be a part of the generalist social worker's interventive repertoire.

Case Example

> Mrs. Gold is a sixty-year-old widow. She recently found out that the cancer she suffers from is terminal and that she probably has about eight months left to live; she has been referred to a hospice team. The social worker on the team has determined three foci for work with Mrs. Gold and her family: (1) to see that the resources she needs are provided in such a way that the highest quality of life can be maintained, (2) to help Mrs. Gold problem solve and decide how she wants to live the life left to her and what she wants to happen after she dies (funeral arrangements and disposal of her material possessions), and (3) to provide the support that she so badly needs. In fact, supportive action is the primary focus of the work to be done.
>
> The worker develops a relationship with Mrs. Gold and is careful to let her know what they can do together to make her life more comfortable. She explains the purpose of hospice and how volunteers will be assigned to visit with her and help her with both the activities of daily living and her task of bringing her life to a satisfying close. The worker gives support to the volunteers as they provide services to Mrs. Gold.

Use of Activity as an Interventive Strategy

Activity is doing something or performing tasks as opposed to talking about what to do or about feelings and ideas. Activity can take the form of helping clients carry out normal life tasks. It also take the form of activity constructed by the worker to enhance the helping process, such as role-playing a difficult situation or, in a small group, using an activity that requires cooperation.

Activity can be a means for influencing change in the ways systems and individuals function. Through action individuals learn many of the skills needed for adequate social functioning. Socialization of individuals to the ways of their society and culture (that is, life experience) relies heavily on the use of action. Activity is a means for developing social-functioning skills and also for enhancing self-awareness. Activity leads to accomplishment, which in turn enhances self-esteem and a positive sense of self. Activity also has usefulness in developing an assessment. As the worker observes the client in action, the client's interactional and communication patterns become evident. The worker can also assess the client's competence in functioning and the quality of the functioning by observing the person in action.

Traditionally, activity has been used in certain segments of social work, notably in the use of games and crafts in social group work. The use of play therapy with children has been another use of activity. Milieu therapy (use of the setting) in institutions also uses activity. Some family therapists help families plan family activities. Workers dealing with chaotic families have found activity to be very useful.[24] Literature on the ways people learn emphasizes experiential learning involving activity. Activity has been a major technique in working with children and is considered valuable in working with "action-oriented" persons.

Activity is also useful in a variety of other helping situations and can be used as a technique for meeting many needs of clients. It enhances physical development and neuromuscular control and stimulates intellectual growth. Activity can be an acceptable release for feelings and emotions, teach patterns of behavior and provide self-discipline, enable acceptance by peers, and increase status. It can provide opportunity for making and carrying out decisions, for forming relationships, and for resolving conflict. Activity can also encourage the development of new interests, skills, and competencies. It can enhance social functioning by enabling movement along the normal growth processes and can be useful with persons who may be at risk of not developing. This risk is often related to lack of opportunity, and activity can provide needed developmental opportunities. In this sense, it can be a preventive approach.

Activity can be broadly defined as anything that involves action by the client. This includes structured activities that are a part of individual, group, or family meetings. It includes activities that the worker may participate in as a leader or facilitator. It also includes actions that the client needs to take in order to accomplish various tasks associated with the plan. Some practitioners refer to these latter activities as "homework" in that the client agrees to carry out certain tasks between sessions. There may be practice or role-plays that take place within the session to prepare the client for the work to be done outside the session. For example, in assertiveness training the client identifies a situation that requires him to be more assertive. Alternative ways of speaking up for himself are developed with the assistance of the worker (or the group, if it is group training). The situation is acted out during the session with the expectation that the client will practice between sessions. The client then reports back at the next meeting. It is essential to build activity into the work with the client so that the client can "own" the work to be done. The more active a client is in accomplishing the goals in his plan, the more competent he will feel. Activity is especially helpful to clients who are depressed. Movement toward a goal brings hope and a sense of accomplishment.

Care should be taken in how activity is incorporated into work with clients who have been oppressed or experienced discrimination or excessive control from others. If activities are imposed on these clients, it adds to their feeling of being controlled. The type of activity should enhance opportunities for choice, decision making, and empowerment. The way in which the activity is presented and carried out should also include these elements. Of course, clients should be allowed to decline to participate at any time with any activity without fear of negative consequences.

Social workers must plan activity carefully. This calls for an expanded knowledge of the nature of action and skill in its use. Robert Vinter has identified three aspects of activity: (1) the physical space and social objects involved in the activity, (2) the behaviors essential to carry out the activity, and (3) the expected respondent behavior because of the activity.[25] Before deciding to use any activity, a worker should first assess these three aspects as they relate to the specific activity. A second set of dimensions discussed by Vinter that influence the action include (1) its prescriptiveness as to what the actors are expected to do, (2) the kinds of rules and other controls that govern the activity, (3) the provision the activity makes for physical activity, (4) the competence required for persons to engage in the activity, (5) the nature of participation and interaction required, and (6) the nature of rewards that are inherent in the activity.

A third area that is also important to assess is clients' capacity and use of activity. Areas particularly important to consider include:

1. *The client's particular need and interests*—Need should be identified before deciding to use activity. Interest can be identified by considering the client's stated desires, skills, and interests.

2. *The capacity of the particular client to perform the tasks required in the activity*—An understanding of age-group characteristics is important, as is understanding of the usual activities of a client's cultural or other diversity subgroup.

3. *The client's motivation and readiness to use the particular activity*—Some clients cannot use certain activities because of cultural taboos. Others, who are work oriented, may not be able to use activity that appears to be play. Clients need to have an opportunity to make choices among possible alternatives. Activity that is relevant to the client's lifestyle is usually the activity most useful to the client.

4. *The ability of the client's support system and community to accept and support the activity being used*—Consideration should also be given to these factors.

A fourth kind of assessment that workers using activity should carry out is related to its use in a specific situation and includes:

1. The materials, equipment, and resources needed to carry out the activity
2. The time and capacity required of the worker to help the client carry out the activity
3. The climate and environment in which the activity will be carried out (the environment's ability to allow the activity and its support for carrying out the activity)
4. Directions for carrying out the activity
5. Precautions and safety measures that need to be taken in carrying out the activity
6. Adaptations of the activity that may be needed

Based on these four kinds of assessments, a decision is made to use a particular activity. In preparing to implement the activity, the following tasks may need to be carried out:

1. *An activity may need to be tested or carried out to determine if all aspects are understood*—It is usually best not to use an activity with clients that the worker has not pretested. Adaptations should be made as necessary.

2. *All supplies and equipment must be obtained*—Rooms or other areas must be obtained. Responsibility is allocated for specific tasks to either the worker, other staff, or clients.

As the activity takes place, the worker should be supportive and positive, show rather than tell, and set appropriate limits. It is also important to discuss the process and outcome of the activity with the client after its conclusion.

In using activity as an interventive strategy, the criteria for "good activity" should be kept in mind:

1. Good activity grows out of the needs and interests of the client(s).
2. Good activity takes into consideration age, cultural background, and other diversity factors of the clients.
3. Good activity provides experiences that enable or enhance the physical and psychosocial development of clients.
4. Good activity is flexible and offers a maximum opportunity for client participation.

Because the possibilities for the use of activity are vast and varied, it is beyond the scope of this book to provide information about the use of specific activity. Social workers can make use of literature from the field of recreation, structured group experiences, and social group work to gain knowledge about the use of specific activity.[26]

In using activity the worker employs a creative approach and adapts the activity to the particular client's need. The creative use of activity can be a powerful influence for helping clients. Its use calls for skill and understanding on the part of social workers.

Case Example

A ten-year-old girl is having difficulty expressing feelings. The worker gives her paper and crayons to draw a picture about her feelings. The picture is of a boat that she then destroys with black crayon marks. The worker is then able to help the girl verbalize some of her feelings of fear and insecurity, which the picture represents.

A group of mothers of young children meets in a battered women's shelter. The goal is for the mothers to interact with their children in expressing various feelings. The worker chooses the making of picture books containing illustrations of people expressing various feelings as the main activity. The mothers will use the books with their children. As the books are worked on, the conversation revolves around appropriateness of pictures and how the books will be used.

A family is having difficulty understanding how family members see themselves in the family group. The social worker uses "family sculpting" to draw out the needed information. Family members place other family members in the physical pattern that most nearly depicts the sense of the family as they see it. This active method gives new understanding and enables the family to discuss desired changes.

Actions Utilizing Other Theories and Models

The change process that is presented in this text is highly adaptable. It can be used as a framework for any theory or model that is used by professional social workers. For some theories and models it may be necessary to adapt our version of assessment and planning. Typically what is needed is either special attention to certain aspects of the assessment and plan or some supplementary material that will lay the foundation for using specific theories or models. For most instances, the worker merely uses another theory or model as the action or one of several actions during this phase. In some instances, the worker incorporates another theory or model earlier in the change process. In either case, the phases of the change process would still be used as described in the text—assessment, planning, action, and evaluation and termination.

Several theories and models are presented in Chapter 16, including some that are not used as much as others. In this section we will highlight those that are most likely to be used by generalist social workers in contemporary practice. We have already discussed cognitive, behavioral, and cognitive-behavioral approaches and so these will not be included here. We will consider the use of brief and solution-focused models, task-centered models, person-centered theory, narrative approaches, an Afrocentric approach, feminist practice, and practice with people who are gay or lesbian.

Brief and Solution-Focused Models

In many respects the model for change that we have presented in this text is similar to elements of solution-focused work. For instance, these approaches view the client as the expert on his situation and so he is more likely to know what will or will not work in meeting his needs. There is also an assumption that clients have strengths and resources that can be used to meet their needs and that can be mobilized in doing so. However, in using this model, the emphasis is on bringing about rapid change. Thus there is less emphasis on building a relationship between the worker and the client. There is a belief that understanding the cause of a problem is not necessary for solving it. In addition, the worker spends little if any time focused on reaching a comprehensive understanding of person in environment. Instead, the effort is aimed at bringing about a solution to the problem as defined by the client.

In using these models within our framework, the worker could still use our assessment (Table 8.2), but the emphasis would be on Part II dealing with the concern or need and Part III identifying strengths and challenges for helping. The worker would begin by engaging the client and briefly building a relationship by identifying needs and strengths. In identifying needs, if it appears that a brief or solution-focused approach might be appropriate and the client agrees, then the worker would gather information about what the client has done to try to meet the need. She also seeks to find what the client is currently doing that is working for him in meeting this and other needs even if it is only slightly successful. This is then used to build on for further efforts to resolve the situation.

Planning is likely to look very similar to what we have presented. The main difference would be in the time frames that appear in goals, objectives, and tasks. These would be as brief as possible, supporting the idea that rapid change is possible.

Actions that are used in implementing these models are also aimed at bringing about a successful completion of the plan in as short a period of time as possible. Little or no attention is paid to other needs or concerns. One of the assumptions in these approaches is that small positive changes will have a positive influence on the situation at hand as well as the overall well-being of the client. Thus, each session is spent on identifying what is working or not working in bringing about the solution that has been identified. The worker might use other intervention strategies in conjunction with this effort such as support, behavioral, cognitive, or cognitive-behavioral methods, and the like, provided these are used to strengthen the efforts of the client in implementing the identified solution.

Evaluation in these models is also focused on progress toward resolving the situation and completing the work as soon as possible. Because the work is intended to be brief, termination is planned from the beginning and typically occurs when the need is met. Since there is less emphasis on building a significant relationship, termination is less likely to involve deep feelings of loss or abandonment and will also likely be brief.

Task-Centered Models

Task-centered models are similar to solution-focused models, but the emphasis is on the client carrying out specific steps called tasks to bring about a resolution to the situation at hand. Task-centered models may be used in brief or longer term interventions. Large tasks are broken down into smaller steps and priorities are established. This approach is highly structured with the worker assisting the client in identifying goals and tasks and then monitoring progress toward completing those tasks. Less attention is paid to thoughts and feelings and more emphasis on actions. Taking actions that are successful is seen as leading to increased motivation and momentum. Less attention is also paid to relationship building. This approach places greater emphasis on empirical evidence of task completion. Various techniques from other theories and models can be incorporated into helping clients complete their tasks.

There are elements of this approach in our change process, but we do not limit our focus to carrying out tasks. We believe that the establishment of a helping relationship is important, especially if the work takes more time than a brief intervention or if the client system is faced with multiple or complex needs. In addition, we advocate incorporating exploration of thoughts and feelings as a comprehensive approach to change.

Some clients may prefer this type of approach in implementing the change process. For those who are motivated, taking action may be preferable to taking time to discuss their situation. Involuntary clients may be reluctant to establish a significant relationship or to engage in much revelation regarding their thoughts and feelings. These clients may prefer a more action-oriented approach. For clients who seem immobilized by their situation, it may be necessary to involve them in a highly structured, task-centered activity to help them to overcome this. The approach is more likely to be successful in obtaining services and concrete resources as opposed to resolving issues related to relationships, emotional stresses, or environmental interactions.

In using this model within our approach, the worker would focus on helping the client to identify needs in very concrete terms that are readily observable and measurable. Little if any time would be spent in relationship building or understanding person in environment. Instead the emphasis is on problem solving with the client identifying the problem followed by an exploration of tasks that will resolve it. Thus assessment is focused on the problem or need. The plan is highly structured around specific tasks along with monitoring and measuring results. The emphasis is on client actions with the worker providing mainly secondary actions that facilitate the client completing the identified tasks.

When using this model as an action in our change process we believe it is important to establish a helping relationship if possible and conduct a comprehensive assessment. Once a relationship is established and the assessment and plan are in place, then elements of task-centered models can be used in working with clients on tasks that are necessary to achieving their goals and objectives. Certainly monitoring is important along with measuring observable results.

Person-Centered Theory

The person-centered approach is generally attributed to Carl Rogers. Traditionally, it was very nondirective with an emphasis on building a trusting relationship based on empathy and genuineness. Much of the time was spent with the worker lending an empathic ear and utilizing reflective listening techniques. The theory was that the client would engage in self-exploration and by receiving attention and empathy, her sense of value and worth would be validated and her self-esteem would increase. This approach relied on clients being voluntary with fairly high levels of motivation and overall functioning and a capacity for insight. More recently, person-centered approaches have found their way into the mental health system where person-centered planning is now required within the publicly funded portion.

In our approach we recognize the need to develop and express care and concern for the client based on valuing every human being, along with demonstrating genuineness and empathy in building a helping relationship. We also recommend using reflective listening as the fundamental approach to understanding person in environment and the needs, strengths, and resources in the ecosystem. However, we believe that the worker should be much more active than the traditional nondirective approach when it comes to bringing about change. Thus, we would see the need for the worker to explore areas that will help him to understand person in environment while also identifying strengths and resources for change. Planning is a more mutual process with the worker taking an active role in developing goals, objectives, and tasks, but with a commitment to ensuring that these are consistent with the client's needs and desires and are truly client-centered.

In using person-centered theory within our approach, the worker uses reflective listening along with demonstrating care and concern and genuineness and openness to establish a helping relationship and identify needs. An understanding of person in environment is reached and the assessment is completed. Planning is person-centered with the client determining goals and objectives. These are typically associated with needs for increasing self-esteem or achieving self-actualization. If used to meet lower level, more basic needs, then there is an emphasis on how these are met with special attention being paid to increasing or preserving self-esteem and self-respect.

In using a contemporary person-centered or client-centered approach, the worker offers himself as a tool for the client to use in meeting her needs. He is there to help in identifying needs and in assisting the client in meeting those needs. He encourages, coaches, monitors, advocates, coordinates, and takes any actions that are necessary to achieve success, but is careful to do these *with* the client as much as possible as opposed to *for* the client and never *to* the client.

Narrative Approaches

Narrative approaches are related to naturalistic inquiry that we advocate using in diversity competent practice. These approaches come out of social interaction and social construction theories, which hold that people construct their own "reality" out of their experiences and perceptions or interpretations of those experiences. In using this approach, the worker elicits stories from the client system and carefully listens for themes and tries to understand how the client views "reality." When stories are negative or seem distorted, the worker assists the client in constructing new interpretations and stories that are more positive and functional. In some versions, the client is asked to externalize the problem or separate himself from the problem. The problem is then seen as an opponent to be overcome and the target of change.

These models do not typically use the scientific method in bringing about change, so they do not usually include assessment, planning, and evaluation. However, the worker may use these as techniques in arriving at an understanding of person in environment from which an assessment can be developed. Planning should incorporate the client's view of her situation and be aimed at developing a more positive and functional life situation. Actions can incorporate restorying and the development of a support system for change.

In using this approach within our change process, the worker asks the client to share his stories about how he perceives his situation and what he would like it to be. She notes information that helps her to understand person in environment including potential strengths and resources. Listening to the client's stories is also the means by which she builds a relationship with him. She asks the client how he would like the stories to be and assists him in identifying what might be done to change the stories and their outcomes. This is used to construct plans for change. In taking actions to implement the plan, the worker assists the client in retelling his story and in constructing new interpretations of his situation. She solicits and makes suggestions that will make the story more consistent with the client's desired outcome. She helps him to build a support system that will support the new story and to take actions that will bring this about.

Afrocentric Approach

The Afrocentric approach was described in greater detail in Chapter 3 and will not be repeated here. Instead, we will describe the use of this approach within our change process. We should clarify that all of the actions we have described thus far can be used when working with people who are African American. This is particularly the case when working with those who were described as fully acculturated. For those who are bicultural, the worker presents options to the client and allows a choice. Those who are traditional or who reject white culture may prefer an Afrocentric approach.

In using this approach, the worker will typically expand the work beyond the individual level and include consideration of the family and the community or at the very least these will be considered in the assessment, planning, and action phases. In building a relationship, the worker who is not African American uses naturalistic inquiry and allows the client to be the expert on his culture and heritage. She admits that she does not know what it is like to be African American and displays a genuine interest in listening to the client's story. The African American worker does not assume that she knows what the client has experienced, but allows him to tell his own story.

The worker assesses the unique experiences of the African American client with an ear for how the client views his culture and his experiences with prejudice and discrimination. She also is careful to assess his family experience and his connectedness with the community, especially the African American community. The worker includes spirituality in her assessment to the extent that the client expresses valuing spirituality as a significant aspect of his life and his worldview. She recognizes that the affective approach to knowledge may be more important to her client than the scientific method.

A similar approach is used in planning. The worker considers the effects of prejudice and discrimination and incorporates actions to overcome these including empowerment and advocacy. She recognizes the importance of collective identity and includes family, fictive kin, and the community in the actions to be taken either as participants in the action or as targets for change.

Similarly, the worker's actions need to be aimed at enhancing empowerment, overcoming prejudice and discrimination, incorporating spirituality, and including family, fictive kin, and the community. In addition, the worker listens carefully to the affective aspects of the client's experiences and seeks to find ways for him to feel positive about the work to be done and the outcomes. Feminist theory, which follows, can also be used in working with both male and female clients who are African American.

Feminist Practice

Feminist practice was developed by practitioners as an attempt to integrate feminist theory, commitments, and culture with conventional approaches to social work practice. It goes beyond a "nonsexist" or "women's issues" orientation. The underlying assumptions include the following: (1) The inherent purpose and goal of human existence is self-actualization, which is a collective endeavor involving the creation of material and ideological conditions that enable it; (2) systems and ideologies of domination/subordination, exploitation, and oppression are inimical to individual and collective self-actualization; (3) given the structural and ideological barriers to self-actualization, practice is explicitly political in intent; and (4) women have unique and relatively unknown histories, conditions, developmental patterns, and strengths that must be discovered and engaged by practitioners.[27]

Some aspects of practice theory for feminist practitioners have some similarity to the approach we use in our texts, including this one. For instance, assessment focuses on preferred and available patterns of strength in intellectual, emotional, social, cultural, physical, and spiritual domains. Special emphasis is given to basic, concrete needs, safety, and perceptions of personal power. An underlying principle informing practice is that healing, health, and growth are the purpose of the social work endeavor. Feminist practice sees these as functions of validation, consciousness, and transformative action, which are supported and sustained through resources to meet basic human needs. Feminist practitioners seek the creation of validating environments and relationships that preserve and nurture uniqueness and wholeness. They use a range of conventional and nonconventional approaches. Feminists frequently use groups, which are seen as favorable for developing validation and raising consciousness. They encourage and facilitate individual and collective action and work for open, egalitarian, and collegial relationships with clients. Feminist practice can be used in all kinds of settings, with all populations. Particular attention is focused on women.

In diversity competent practice, the worker explores with the individual, family, or group actions that are consistent with their diversity. She does not impose her own or society's view of what they should do but seeks to find what fits with the client system. One of the difficulties in working with individuals or families from certain cultures is the strict boundaries between male and female role expectations. This generally results in the male being in the role of head of the household, called a patriarchal system. This system may be viewed as oppressive toward women. Most of these cultures define a "good husband" or a "good father" as a man who incorporates the needs and best interests of his wife and children into his decision making. He is obligated to see that the needs of his wife and family are met. This places tremendous pressure on him when faced with limited resources. Some men use their dominant position to meet their own needs or suppress the needs of other family members. Within their culture, this is a deviation from the "good husband and father" role. The worker can assist the husband to define this role within his culture and then work with him to obtain the resources that are necessary to carry this out. The worker might also help him to see that sharing his power is not necessarily a sign of weakness but may indeed be a sign of strength.

There are some substantial dilemmas for the gender competent social worker to resolve in her practice with individuals, families and groups, especially those from patriarchal cultures. These are probably best expressed in terms of several questions: How does the worker respect the client's culture when some of the culture's values conflict with her personal and professional value system? How does the worker support power sharing and egalitarian relationships without imposing her views on the client? How does she maintain her personal and professional value system of valuing all human beings equally while working with an individual or family whose culture does not reflect this value? How does she maintain her personal and professional value system of valuing self-determination while working with a client whose culture does not reflect this value?

A feminist-informed approach appears to hold some promise for developing successful gender competent practice. Shelley A. Haddock, Toni Schindler Zimmerman, and David MacPhee from the Human Development and Family Studies Department at Colorado State University have developed the Power Equity Guide to assist in assessing attention to gender in family therapy. They see a feminist-informed approach to working with families as mainly a philosophical and political perspective rather than a model or set of techniques.[28] The Guide can be used by social workers at all levels of development.

Using the basic philosophy behind feminist-informed practice, the gender competent practitioner would focus on both process and content that reflected gender equity. Process refers to the way in which he works with individuals, families, and groups. Content is what is actually said and done in his work. Because many cultures perceive differences in males and females, especially with respect to specific and overall competence, there are going to be differences in how male and female social workers are perceived. This also influences how male and female social workers are able to work with clients. This includes both the content and process of working with clients. Because of gender differences within the client's culture or family system, male and female social workers may use techniques that are different from each other but have the same effect, and they may use the same techniques but have different effects. For example, a female worker who supports gender equity may be perceived differently by a male client than a male worker may be perceived. The male client may interpret the female worker as being culturally insensitive or threatening to his culturally determined status as head of the family or breadwinner or as a male within his culture. He might interpret the same approach by a male worker in the same way as he interpreted the female worker's approach or he might view it as acceptable because it is coming from another male.

Cross-cultural work with clients is much more complicated when the work is also cross-gender. If the worker is female and the client is from a culture or family system that is patriarchal, it can be very difficult for the worker to gain credibility. Naturalistic inquiry can be especially helpful in these cases. Asking questions and giving the role of cultural guide to the client allows the process to unfold. The client will be more comfortable with a discussion of his cultural background if there is a focus on strengths. Actively incorporating cultural customs and values into the plan is vital. This lays the groundwork for action that is culturally appropriate. It is important for the client to take pride in his cultural heritage and to use that heritage as a source of strength.

The worker needs to be constantly aware of gender differences while also seeking ways to rebalance those differences toward greater gender equity. This is the essence of gender competent practice. It begins with working to develop more egalitarian relationships. This includes encouraging equality in communication, problem solving, decision making, and conflict resolution. Under no circumstances, regardless of the cultural background of the client, should the worker show any tolerance for violence or the threat of violence that may arise when gender roles are used to dominate others.

An important point to be made here in working with families is the need for the worker to allow adult female members of the family to decide how to proceed with encouraging gender equity. This is not a decision for the worker to make independently. It is her client's choice. Feminist practitioners may see this as "selling out," but if the worker is to respect her client's right to self-determination, she is compelled to respect her client's right to make a decision with which the worker disagrees. This does not mean that the worker cannot model gender equity in her work with the family. However, in working with families on making decisions about family structure and functioning, the worker needs to respect their right to decide how they wish to do this.

It is also important to consider the involvement of male family members in this decision-making process, especially those in positions of power in the family. Because they are in the position of exerting power over female members and female members are thereby placed in a powerless or less powerful position, the worker should give preference to the choice of the female members. This generally means that the worker uses influence, persuasion, and encouragement to move the family toward greater gender equity if that is what the female members choose.

In promoting gender equity in families, the worker should encourage sharing responsibility for parenting and household tasks. The worker can point out how men are often deprived of the pleasures of child-rearing and forming close relationships with their children. It is also important for parents to prepare their children for life in a free and democratic society that values independence. This means that children of both sexes need to learn how to take care of themselves by learning and doing all forms of household chores. The worker also encourages parents to support children of both sexes in pursuing education and careers that are growth enhancing and take advantages of opportunities that may not have been available in the home country of their culture. Many immigrants come to the United States for greater economic opportunity. Convincing them to allow their female members to take advantage of those opportunities may not be as difficult as one might expect. Certainly, the greater the opportunities for more family members, the more likely the family will become more prosperous more quickly.

Probably, the area that is of greatest concern for ethnic groups, especially for first-generation immigrants, is retention of their cultures. However, it is almost inevitable that some cultural influences will be diluted as they and their children are exposed to the dominant culture. In fact, this is often an area of great turmoil and conflict between earlier and later generations. Parents need to be realistic about this and select those aspects of cultural heritage that have the highest value for them. These are usually customs and traditions such as holidays and religious or spiritual beliefs. In order to preserve these, parents will likely have to yield some latitude in other areas. This is where gender-based roles may be loosened. In essence, the worker helps the family become bicultural and seeks to do so in a rational way that preserves important aspects of both cultures.

Many culturally diverse families have experienced prejudice, discrimination, and oppression both in their countries of origin and here in the United States. Another approach to use in encouraging more egalitarian relationships is to discuss these experiences and point out the parallels to the treatment of females. Raising consciousness and awareness of these experiences allows the family to decide what aspects of their culture will serve them best in this country. This is an empowering approach. In many respects, empowering the family as a system can lead to freeing it from cultural constrictions. It can empower them to make choices about a bicultural style that is in the best interests of the family as a whole as well as each member.

Some techniques the gender competent social worker can use in her work with families include both verbal and nonverbal. Verbally, the worker encourages everyone to tell their own stories and gives equal credibility to them. She addresses the parents jointly regarding parenting and child-rearing and is careful to initiate and maintain eye contact with both. Workers who are not gender conscious will tend to look at the mother first when it comes to these issues. The worker moves cultural influences from the nonverbal to the verbal level, openly discussing cultural issues and concerns and raising the possibility of decision making and choice. As much as possible, she assists the family through mediation and negotiation in settling disagreements in an equitable manner that is free from power and control.

Most important, the worker is careful to model egalitarianism in his actions and relationships with families. He demonstrates the advantages of an egalitarian approach and points out the disadvantages of power imbalances and control. He discusses the larger social context in which the family finds itself and looks for ways to empower the family and its members to overcome negative aspects of that social context. Similar techniques can be used when working with groups that include members of various ethnicities that are patriarchal.

When working with female clients, the worker needs to incorporate empowerment and power sharing into his approach. This may include consciousness-raising and increasing assertiveness. Groups are great avenues for doing this work. They also provide opportunities for collective endeavors that can enhance self-actualization and empowerment. Consciousness-raising involves raising the client's awareness regarding ways in which she has been subject to prejudice, discrimination, and oppression. It also means considering how exploitation and the political aspects of her situation serve to reinforce an inferior position and is often the cause of her difficulties as opposed to being her fault or her responsibility. Assertiveness means being empowered to assert oneself by expressing one's thoughts and feelings and acting on one's own interests and desires in a way that exercises one's own rights while respecting the rights of others. Power sharing means ensuring that one's power as a worker is truly shared with the client. This includes giving equal or greater weight to the client's perspective and preferences. It means ensuring that the relationship is a partnership. Actually, naturalistic inquiry fits very well with this approach. Exploring the client's thoughts, feelings, and actions along with her perceptions of her situation without preconceived notions lends credibility to those thoughts, feelings, actions, and perceptions.

Practice with People Who Are Gay or Lesbian

In some respects, the description of feminist and feminist-informed practice described in the previous section on gender competent practice also applies to working with gay and lesbian individuals and families. This is especially the case regarding the need for empowerment and the principle that the personal is political.

In working with clients who are gay or lesbian, there are three primary areas we examine here. These are concerns related to coming out, especially with families of origin; working with couples who are gay or lesbian; and assisting gay and lesbian parents and their children with social issues related to sexual orientation.

Concerns related to coming out as a gay man or a lesbian woman are quite common when working with clients who are gay or lesbian. The dilemma is a need to be open about being gay or lesbian and to be accepted. The fear is that acceptance will be lost or rejection will occur if others know the person is gay or lesbian. This fear has a great deal of reality to it as many people who are gay or lesbian experience rejection from their families and friends and may even be fired from their jobs if they reveal their sexual orientation. This causes stress for many people who are gay or lesbian. Having to hide an important aspect of one's true identity can cause a great deal of stress and strain. It can also be quite complicated for couples because if one of them comes out the other person's sexual orientation is also revealed. Support, advocacy and mediation are important direct actions.

Working with adolescents who are gay or lesbian is quite challenging because of the extreme reactions by their peers, negative reactions by their families, and the volatility of adolescence itself. Both suicide attempts and completions are reported to be much higher for youth who are gay and lesbian as compared to heterosexual teens. The social worker must be vigilant about depression and suicidal thinking when she works with this population. It is best if these youth can work with a trained therapist in dealing with these issues. However, generalist social workers also work with this population. They need to be sensitive to the possibility that as many as 10 percent of their youthful clients are struggling with their sexual identity and the social stresses related to it.

Working with gay and lesbian couples and their families involve all of the same issues and approaches that are relevant in working with heterosexual couples and their families. However, one thing that is different is the issue of gender-based roles. In heterosexual relationships, various cultures may prescribe certain roles to the male and others to the female. This will not work for same-sex couples. A common myth about same-sex couples is that one of the partners assumes the male role and the other the female role. Some same-sex couples do this, but the majority do not. It appears that many are able to develop egalitarian relationships and may even provide good models for heterosexual couples who are struggling with developing shared-role relationships. The key to developing shared-role relationships is communicating effectively and using an efficient and effective decision-making process. Roles cannot be assumed and need to be discussed every day to determine who is going to do what.

Social workers may become involved with assisting parents who are gay or lesbian and their children with social issues related to sexual orientation. Dealing with the reactions of others can be quite challenging. Fortunately, there are books and materials that are becoming available to help same-sex couples and their children with these issues. Same-sex couples become parents in a variety of ways. Some were formerly in a heterosexual relationship in which children were produced. Some people who are gay or lesbian have been able to adopt children, although only one of them is typically a legal parent to the child. Some same-sex couples use formal and informal fertility options, including artificial insemination and surrogate mothers. Those couples who produced children in previous heterosexual relationships often experience a great deal of difficulty with the legal system regarding custody and visitation if their sexual orientation is revealed. The same can be true for adoption.

Summary

The choice of which kind of action generalist social workers take with a client should be based on the principles of economy, self-determination, individualization, development, interdependence, and focus on service goals. The choice also depends on the skill of the worker and the worker's interventive repertoire. The dimensions of using action follow:

- Action to enable clients to use available resources requires a thorough knowledge of the service delivery system, skill in use of the referral process, and skill in the use of the broker and advocate roles. The service delivery system includes the informal helping network as well as the formal system.

- Action that enables the clients to bring about change in their environments and its institutions allows for empowerment of powerless people.

- Action that enhances positive thinking and positive actions on the part of clients enables them to utilize strengths in themselves to bring about change.

- Action in response to crisis calls for skill in recognizing a crisis situation. Response to a crisis should be immediate and active.

- Action that is primarily supportive is focused on particular positive behaviors and attitudes. It guards against overdependence and can promote growth.

- Action in the form of activity is especially useful when working with action-oriented persons.

- Action as a tool. When using activity, the worker considers the client's lifestyle and characteristics. Also to be considered are the inherent characteristics of the activity and the process for carrying it out.

- Action that utilizes other contemporary social work theories or models of direct practice. The change process presented in this text can be used as a framework for using other theories, models, and approaches.

Questions

1. Empowerment has been considered of particular importance when working with women, people of color, and populations at risk. Why do you think empowerment is important in such situations?

2. Consider a situation that you are facing and describe a negative thought or feeling you have about it. Change the thought to a positive one that predicts a successful resolution and describe the feeling that accompanies it. How would acting on the positive thought change your behavior in that situation?

3. Describe the crisis process in a situation in which you have been involved. What was most helpful in the resolution of the crisis?

4. Name some situations in which you believe support is an appropriate action for a social worker to take.

5. Choose an activity that you think will be helpful in a specific situation. How did you go about choosing this activity? How should it be structured and presented?

6. Describe how you would use one of the contemporary theories to facilitate change with a hypothetical client.

Suggested Readings

Dobson, Keith, Ed. *Handbook of Cognitive-Behavioral Therapies,* 2nd ed. New York: Guilford Press, 2000.

Ellis, Albert. *Better, Deeper, and More Enduring Brief Therapy: The Rational Emotive Behavioral Therapy Approach.* New York: Brunner/Mazel, 1996.

Epstein, Laura, and Brown, Lester. *Brief Treatment and a New Look at the Task-Centered Approach,* 4th ed. Boston: Allyn and Bacon, 2002.

James, Richard, and Gilliland, Burl. *Crisis Intervention Strategies,* 5th ed. Pacific Grove, CA: Brooks/Cole, 2005.

Miley, Karla Krogsrud, O'Melia, Michael, and DuBois, Brenda L. *Social Work Practice: An Empowering Approach,* 6th ed. Boston: Allyn and Bacon, 2009 (Chapters 12–14).

Mizrahi, Terry and Davis, Larry E., Eds. *Encyclopedia of Social Work*, 20th ed. Washington, DC: NASW Press, 2008 ("Advocacy," "Behavioral Theory," "Brief Therapies," "Cognitive Therapy," "Crisis Interventions," "Direct Practice," "Feminist Social Work Practice," "Gay Families and Parenting," "Gay Men," "Latinos and Latinas," "Lesbians," "Methods of Practice Interventions," "Narratives," "Native Americans," "Task Centered Practice," "Women").

Norman, Elaine. *Resiliency Enhancement.* New York: Columbia University Press, 2000.

Reid, William. *The Task Planner: An Intervention Resource for Human Service Professionals.* New York: Columbia University Press, 2000.

Roberts, Albert R. *Crisis Intervention Handbook: Assessment, Treatment, and Research.* New York: Oxford University Press, 2005.

Sheafor, Bradford W., and Horejsi, Charles R. *Techniques and Guidelines for Social Work Practice,* 8th ed. Boston: Allyn and Bacon, 2008 (Chapters 6, 13, and 15).

Worell, Judith, and Remer, Pam. *Feminist Perspective in Therapy: Empowering Diverse Women.* New York: John Wiley and Sons, 2002.

11 | *Indirect Practice Actions*

Learning Expectations

1. Understanding of the use of mediation in helping clients.
2. Understanding of influence and its use.
3. Understanding of environmental manipulation as a strategy.
4. Understanding of action to coordinate services.
5. Understanding of actions to change organizations or communities.

In the generalist approach to social work practice, the worker is not only involved in direct work with clients but is also involved in work with individuals, small groups, agencies, and communities on behalf of individual and family clients. This work has often been characterized as indirect practice. It is very often work with the agency and community systems, which is sometimes described as *macropractice.*

There is a historic debate in social work referred to as the cause-function debate. This debate involves two kinds of need: private troubles and public issues. Work with individuals and families usually falls in the function and private-trouble domain of response to need, whereas work focused on agencies and communities tends to fall in the cause and public-issue domain.

One of the identifying characteristics of the generalist social worker is the worker's ability to respond to both private troubles and public issues. Furthermore, the generalist social worker identifies both the private troubles and the public issues inherent in any practice situation and then decides on the appropriate focus of the action for change. This focus may be on private trouble (individuals and families) or on social issue (agency and community) concerns. Often the focus may call for work with both private parties and the public. Thus, the generalist practitioner must possess knowledge and skills for indirect as well as direct practice and be able to combine the two when appropriate.

This chapter discusses six approaches that may be used in indirect practice, particularly with individual clients:

1. Action as mediation
2. Action that involves the use of influence
3. Action designed to change the environment
4. Action relative to coordination of services
5. Action to change organizations
6. Action to change communities

Before discussing these actions, attention will be given to influence as it relates to action with clients and on behalf of clients. As the social worker works with clients, influence for change is heavily based on the worker-client interaction, particularly on the relationship between worker and client. In indirect practice, the worker often works with individuals and small groups in order to meet needs of clients either as small systems (individuals and families) or as collectives (community segments affected by a dysfunctional delivery system or a social problem). Relationship remains an important aspect of influence, though other factors (such as the knowledge and expertise of the worker and the material resources and services the worker might have available) are also important. The worker's status and reputation are also sources of influence. All these influences are used when the work together is collaborative and cooperative in nature. Sometimes persuasive techniques must be used for the other system or systems involved to become convinced that a collaborative or cooperative approach is of value to all concerned. Sometimes cooperation and collaboration are not possible, and confrontation, bargaining, and even coercion are necessary to reach the desired goals.

Sometimes the social worker initiates and participates in the action on behalf of clients. Sometimes mediation between systems is called for. At other times the social worker stimulates others to carry out the action. Regardless of who takes the action, some means of legitimizing any action taken must be sought. The social worker does not act in isolation but as a representative of an agency. Sometimes the social worker can act with or through an organization to which she belongs. Without the support of legitimization, the worker lacks the influence needed to support the change effort. Without legitimization, ethical issues can come into play.

Action as Mediation

Sometimes as the worker and client explore the client's needs, concerns, and situation, it becomes apparent that the way in which a client and a system in the client's environment interact is not functional. Often the situation is of a conflictual nature. For example, a mother seems unable to communicate with a probation officer so that they can work together in setting limits for her son. The mother is afraid of the authority represented by the probation officer and does not respond to his suggestions. The probation officer is frustrated and believes the mother is indifferent to her son's need for limits. The worker knows this is not the case. In such a situation, a **mediation strategy** can be useful.

Mediation is in many respects a bridge between direct and indirect practice actions. We have chosen to include it with indirect practice actions because it requires the worker to remain neutral and avoid taking sides. In many ways the worker takes the side of the relationship and tries to facilitate change that will lead to a successful relationship.

William Schwartz described this strategy as "to mediate the process through which the individual and his society reach out for each other through a mutual need for self-fulfillment"[1] and as "helping people negotiate difficult environments."[2] The worker's concern—and the focus of the mediation action—is the social functioning of both the client and the system. The transaction between the two is the concern, the target for change.

Mediation is basic to an ecosystems approach to social work practice. This approach views need as arising out of incongruity between the client and systems in his environment. Restoring or developing a balance between the needs of the client and the needs of individuals and systems in his environment is necessary for the situation to be resolved. A mediating role allows the worker to work with the client and individuals or groups in his environment without taking sides. Mediation is also used whenever the social worker is working with multiclient systems including families, family subsystems, and groups. It is essential the worker remain neutral and not take sides when working with more than one client.

In the example of the Adams family in Chapter 10, the worker used a mediation approach in working with Jerry and his father to increase positive feedback to Jerry for positive behaviors. Mr. Adams wanted his son to reduce his negative behavior and increase his positive behavior. Jerry wanted to hear that his positive behavior is appreciated. The worker was able to convince Mr. Adams that giving positive feedback would reinforce positive behavior from Jerry. In working with this situation, the worker also could have inquired if Jerry would be able to accept criticism for negative behaviors if he knew that he would also receive recognition for positive behavior. Jerry might be expected to agree with this because it is an evenhanded approach. The worker did not take sides but was able to help both Jerry and his father come to a middle ground.

William Schwartz and Serapio Zalba and Lawrence Shulman have written extensively about this type of action and strategy.[3] Shulman has identified three blocks in the interactions of individuals with environmental systems:

1. *The complexity of systems*—The development of institutions and the bureaucratizing of their functioning has made it less possible for individuals to understand how to approach these systems or to use the resources they provide. These complex systems seem strange, impersonal, and often overwhelming to many clients.

2. Self-interest—The self-interest of systems often is in conflict with the interests of others or of the larger system of which they are a part. When such self-interest is predominant, it is necessary to make that system aware of the interdependence, and thus of the mutual interest, necessary for the functioning of the larger system.

3. *Communication problems*—Often, the inability of systems to work together is a result of a lack of communication or of inaccurate communication and thus of misconceptions about the other.[4]

In overcoming these blocks, the worker and client both have tasks. The purpose of mediation is not for the worker to be an advocate and challenge one or the other system but to help the two systems reach out to each other so that together they can achieve a common goal. The worker helps or enables each of the two systems to accomplish the tasks necessary but does not do the work leading to the goal. That work belongs to the client and the environmental system. The worker has three major tasks to accomplish: (1) to help the client reach out to the environmental system, (2) to help the environmental system respond to the client, and (3) to encourage both the client and the environmental system to do the work needed to reach the common goal.

In helping the client reach out to the environmental system, the worker first points out to the client the common interests and goals of the client and the environmental system. The worker also identifies the blocks that seem to be preventing the client from reaching these goals. The worker challenges these blocks by pointing out ways they can be overcome and the advantages to the client of overcoming them. The worker tries to give the client a vision of what can happen if the client and the environmental system find a means of working together. In doing this, the worker reveals her own commitment and hopes for a society in which people and institutions work together for the common good. Through this the worker gives hope to the client. The worker helps the client define what needs to be done in the reaching out, and together they decide how the client is to do it. The worker is careful to define the limits of what may be expected so that the client does not develop unrealistic expectations.

When helping the environmental system to respond to the client's reaching out, the worker points out their common interest and concerns and the obstacles that seem to prevent cooperative functioning. The worker tries to help the environmental system mobilize its concern and its resources for helping. Where appropriate, the worker can provide the environmental system with information that will enhance its understanding of the situation. In a sense, both the individual client and the environmental system are clients. In some situations (e.g., divorce) a social worker may be engaged as a mediator on initial contact. Both parties immediately are seen as clients under these circumstances.

In using this strategy, the worker negotiates a contract or agreement with the client and, when possible, with the environmental system as to the work (tasks) each will do in attempting to overcome problems. The worker helps both carry out their tasks by helping them adhere to the contract, clarifying what is expected in the situation, and requiring that they do their tasks. Schwartz and Zalba have identified a four-step process for working with a client when using a mediative strategy:

1. *"Tuning in"*—The worker gets ready to enter the process of transactions in the situation.

2. *Beginning together*—The worker helps the various individuals involved to reach out to one another and identify what needs to be done. Contracts are negotiated.

3. *Work*—This is doing what needs to be done.

4. *Transitions and endings*—This consists of leaving the situation, ending the work together, and the worker separating from the situation.[5]

Ernesto Gomez has adapted the four steps or phases of work for use with Chicano clients. He places particular emphasis on the tuning-in phase. He notes that in this phase it is very important to "tune in" to the culture by focusing on how culture may be affecting client in situation. This includes concern for linguistic and other cultural practices as they relate to the specific client's needs in the situation for which help is sought. As worker and client begin together, a cultural assessment helps to pinpoint how cultural factors contribute to the situation and how the culture can provide resources for dealing with the difficulty.[6] This approach can be useful when working with diversity group members.

When working in a mediation mode, the units of attention are both the original client and the environmental systems involved. Each is helped to acknowledge the common interests and to become aware of the feelings, needs, and demands of all. This requires that the worker be aware of the rules and roles within the situation. The worker provides focus and structure for the work to be done. Based on his knowledge and understanding, the worker also supplies ideas and suggestions as to how the systems might better work together. Clarification and problem solving are important tools of the endeavor.

Although the mediation strategy was developed to use with small groups, it has proven equally effective in working with individuals and is particularly useful with institutionalized individuals.[7] It should be used with families and groups and is often useful in situations in which empowerment is a goal. Thus, it is frequently used in serving clients at risk of experiencing prejudice, discrimination, and oppression.

Influence

"Reality demonstrates influence, not control" best describes the worker's effect on a situation. The social worker does not have complete control and cannot guarantee a specific outcome when working from an interventive-transactional stance. Clients and others involved in the situation maintain the ability to decide what their behavior will be in the situation. This ability makes control by the social worker impossible except in those areas in which he has been given the authority to control certain aspects of the client's behavior, such as in some institutional situations, some work with children, protective service work, and probation and parole work.

Influence has been defined as "the general acts of producing an effect on another person, group, or organization through exercise of a personal or organizational capacity."[8] Influence is powerful. It can produce change, persuade or convince, overcome obstacles, motivate, and bring about attitudinal changes. The social worker's input is to create a climate favorable for the needed work, heighten the motivation of those needing to do the work, "provide a vision"[9] for the work to be done together, and reduce the resistance involved.

An important base for influence is the skill and knowledge of the social worker in developing and using relationships with a variety of persons in a variety of situations. Influence can be exerted by those who know about and can use a planned change process. Influence derives from understandings about human development, human diversity, the variety of social problems, and the availability of services and resources. Social workers use not only their own base of influence but also that of other people with whom they are working. When working for change in situations, in organizations, and in communities, people with influence are very useful. Influential people may be elected or appointed to positions of authority, are respected and admired, have control over resources and information, and are involved in important decision making. They often are people who control from behind the scenes. Values are another important factor to consider in relationship to influence. People are more apt to be influenced for change when the change is within their value system and provides something that is important to them.

Workers need to be aware of the nature of the power and influence they wield in relationships with clients. Influence can be an inherent outgrowth of the power differential in the worker-client relationship. Every effort needs to be made to guard against the potential for abuse of power with clients. In addition to professional expertise, which workers possess by virtue of their skill, values, and knowledge base, certain personal characteristics may also contribute to a worker's influence with a client.

Influence was included in parentheses in Figure 10.1 as a way of recognizing that the worker has influence on the client. However, the use of influence as a planned strategy with clients has many complications for the social worker because it tends to undermine self-determination. Thus, it should only be used as a last resort when clients are in crisis or are headed for disaster or are truly stuck. Influence as a planned strategy is commonly used as a direct practice action with organizations and communities. This will be covered in Chapter 15. Influence is used as an indirect practice action with individuals and environmental systems on behalf of the client, as is environmental change and coordination of services. These are discussed later in this chapter. Generally, indirect practice actions are intended to be used to bring about changes in the environment, especially the actions of systems. Changes in feeling and thinking may be used as tactics in accomplishing this, but changing actions is the basic strategy.

Clients do have some choice of whether they will be influenced. To be influenced, clients must have at least some motivation for change. Some factors that affect willingness to be influenced include discomfort with the situation and a belief that it can be changed, a desire to gain position or resources, and a desire to change the situation for someone else.

According to Nora Gold, "Social workers can be very useful as motivators to their clients by increasing their sense of competence and control and helping them to recognize the power in 'seeing oneself as a potential force in shaping one's ends; and changing one-self with making whatever changes must come about.'"[10] Gold's quote is from none other than Helen Harris Perlman, the originator of the problem-solving approach in social work. This statement is very close to describing a process of enabling.[11]

Resistance is the opposite of motivation and is sometimes a sign that other influences on a person are stronger than the need for change. Barriers to change—to accepting influence—can be cultural in nature. Ideologies, traditions, and values are all part of cultural influences on situations. Barriers also may be social in nature. The influence of a person's family or peer group, the norms of the situation, or the reputation of the change agent can be social barriers to change. Or the barrier may be organizational in nature: a competitive climate or an organizational climate that considers procedure rather than people. Family communication patterns can be a barrier to change. Personal barriers, such as fear, selective perception, or lack of energy and skill, also affect an individual's capacity to accept influence and to change. All of these barriers may be part of the transactive nature of relationships in a helping situation.

The influence process is carried out in a relationship with one or more of the systems involved in the transaction. This relationship is transactional in nature, in that it is affected by other relationships. The relationship between the social worker and the system being influenced is a major source of a social worker's influence. A major task in the social work endeavor is to foster the kind of relationships that allow the worker to bring other sources of influence to bear on the situation. As the worker applies these various sources of influence to the situation, change takes place in the relationships among the subsystems involved. The worker's knowledge and skillfulness as well as social work values guide the decisions about what sources of influence to use and how to use them.

There are also ethical considerations regarding the use of influence. Of particular importance is concern about the difference between influence and manipulation, control, or abuse of power. Clients and others typically do not understand the limits of the social worker's span of control and ascribe more authority to the worker than is legally allowed. Clients may believe that the worker can withhold an income maintenance check if they do not do what they think the worker wants them to do. Such situations can become complex when the client acts according to what she believes the worker wants rather than what the worker has said. Workers can use their ascribed authority to control clients. However, this negates the value of self-determination and also raises concerns about who has the right to do what and on what grounds.[12] In the contemporary situation, social work values, such as the right to self-determination and confidentiality, are often limited by agency mandates, statutory reporting laws, or other constraints of practice. All three of the following questions can be used to determine if influence is being used within social work values:

1. Whose needs are being met by the use of the influence? If it is the client's needs, it is within the social work value system. If it is the worker's needs, it is not.

2. Have the goals been established by the worker and client together as part of a collaborative process?

3. Has freedom of choice for all concerned been considered and maintained to the maximum extent possible?

Case Example

The Hispanic mother of an eight-year-old girl has been urged by the school nurse to seek medical help for her daughter's skin rash. The mother has not followed up on this recommendation, and the school social worker has been asked to see what can be done. The social worker should consider cultural attitudes toward health care; the family's experiences with the school, school nurse, and local health care system; the family's relationships; and the family's decision-making process. The difficulty or inability to follow through on the recommendation may be influenced by factors arising from any of these areas. Difficulties can also arise from a language barrier, a lack of knowledge of health care and financial resources, or other family problems. The relationship of the mother and the school nurse or the social worker should be seen as transactional in nature.

In this case, the worker can influence the situation in several ways. He can discuss the cultural implications with the school nurse to see if the nurse's recommendations can be given in a manner more congruent with the Hispanic culture. In doing this he is changing the situation by working for a change in the relationship between the nurse and the mother, thus changing the transactional nature of the situation. The social worker could influence the mother to follow the nurse's recommendations by either explaining their importance or by enabling the mother in seeking the health care needed, perhaps making a referral to an affordable health clinic or even taking the mother and daughter to the first appointment. If a Hispanic aide is available, the worker could explain to this aide why the care is needed and ask her to work with the mother in obtaining the care, thus influencing a third party, who in turn will influence the mother. If the worker has seen several similar situations, he might work for change in the school system by such means as staff education about the Hispanic culture or by influencing the health care system as to ways to make that system more usable by these clients. The social worker could also influence the educational system to be more responsive to the needs of all Hispanic children and their parents.

Influence is a major consideration for the social worker to take into account in planning and implementing interventions in transactions among people and their systems. Because a power differential often exists between social workers and their clients, attention must be given to prevent misuse of influence. Influence, or use of self, when used within the social work value system serves as an enabling function.

Environmental Change

Environmental manipulation is the strategy that brings about alteration in the environment of a client as a means of enhancing the client's social functioning. Specifically, three factors in the environment are considered as appropriate targets for change: space, time, and relationships. Environmental change has been a strategy of social work since the time of Mary Richmond. The term *environmental treatment* appears in the work of Florence Hollis, who discussed treatment of the environment as bringing about change in the situation of the client.[13] Max Siporin defined situational intervention as "actions that alter structural, cultural and functional patterns."[14] In discussing "change in behavioral setting," Siporin pointed out that "an environment has profound effects on the behavior, feelings, and self-images of the people who inhabit or use that setting."[15] Richard Grinnel and Nancy Kyte reported a study of the use of environmental modification by social workers in a large public agency. The authors stated that this is a much more intricate technique than is widely believed.[16] This may be related in part to the fact that the environment is a complex system that transacts with clients and impinges on their functioning.

Environmental psychology provides some of the knowledge needed to understand the impact of the environment on individuals.[17] This knowledge relates the effects of crowding on individuals, the need for privacy, distance as it relates to different kinds of relationships, territoriality, and other aspects of individual functioning. As this field has developed, social workers have gained more understanding about the use of this strategy.

Carel Germain and Alex Gitterman, in *The Life Model of Social Work Practice,* emphasized the ecological aspects of human functioning. They differentiated between the social and physical environments, pointing out that people in the environment not only can provide resources for clients but also can affect the client's behavior by their responses to that behavior. When considering the physical environment, both the "built world" and the "natural world" are included.[18] Although social workers have long used the strategy of environmental manipulation, the knowledge base has remained in the realm of practice wisdom or common sense. Germain and Gitterman provided a beginning knowledge base to use when manipulating the environment.

In using an ecosystems strengths approach, action takes place to change the transactions between the individual or family and formal and informal systems in the immediate environment. In identifying the immediate environment, both proximity and relationships are important. For an individual, the family is often a primary system in the immediate environment. School or places of employment are important systems for individuals and families, as are the neighborhood, extended family, friends, and other significant individuals or systems. The first choice in working with clients is for the client himself to be able to mobilize these systems to assist him in meeting his needs. However, often the relationship between the client and significant individuals and systems in his environment needs to be developed, enhanced, or restored. This may be the reason needs are not being met and the client requires assistance from the social worker. In working on behalf of the client, the worker may need to have contact with these significant individuals or systems and take actions that will develop, enhance, or restore important relationships.

Mediation is an important action with systems in the environment. Mediation can be used with both formal and informal systems. Other important skills are improving communication, bargaining, negotiation, problem solving, and conflict resolution. The worker may work jointly or separately with the client and systems in the environment. When working separately, the goal is usually to move toward some kind of joint effort to resolve the situation.

The social worker uses her communication skills to facilitate good communication. (See Chapter 7). She models good communication and asks people to change their communication patterns to reflect good communication.

Decision-making and problem-solving skills involve the ability to work together to develop a plan that will resolve the situation. Because the social worker is familiar with various models of problem solving, he can assist clients and members of their ecosystems in doing this. In addition, the worker can assist them to develop an ongoing process of reaching decisions or solving problems.

Bargaining, negotiation, compromise, and conflict resolution are used when unresolved differences persist. These approaches involve identifying the needs and concerns of the parties involved and finding ways to meet those needs. As needs are identified, the worker elicits responses to need from others. She may ask those involved in the situation to give and take in order to have their needs met. She may suggest ways of reciprocally meeting needs between parties. Throughout the process, the worker attempts to reach a mutually beneficial arrangement that can be sustained over time. Some questions that might be used are: (1) What would you like to see happen in this situation? What would meet your needs? What would it take to satisfy you? (2) What would you be willing to do to resolve this? (3) Would you be willing to…? (4) If…, then would you be willing to…? (5) What do you want to do with this? These questions are designed to move people toward having their needs met by meeting the needs of others in their ecosystems. When needs are balanced, then the ecosystem is balanced.

When planning for change in the environment, a worker can use the variables of relationship, space, and time as a framework. Relationships should be influenced to enhance the competence of the client. Consider the situation of a person with physical disabilities. If those in this person's environment provide care so that the client makes few decisions and little use of the physical capacity she possesses, she will feel less competent. If caregivers encourage appropriate self-reliance, however, her competence will be enhanced.[19]

Changes can be made in the spatial aspects of a client's environment. Space should be appropriate for the person who occupies it. According to Irene Gutheil, some of the factors important when considering physical space are the features of a space and whether they are fixed or can be changed through modifying the design of the building and placement of furniture. Also important are issues of territory, personal space, crowding, and privacy.[20] These concerns are particularly important in residential situations but should also be considered in evaluating offices and other areas where services are provided.

For people with physical disabilities, physical barriers can be a block to self-sufficiency. A sense of competence is enhanced when barriers are removed. The physical environment should provide for the privacy a person needs. The effects of color and light in influencing feelings and behavior should be considered.

The activity to take place in the space and the manner in which people interact during the activity are important considerations. There must be provision for appropriate closeness of people; being too close or too far apart can lead to discomfort and cause people to withdraw.

Spatial arrangement that allows for eye contact is important in some situations. A circle arrangement encourages people to talk to one another because each can see everyone else. Room arrangements in which all individuals face a speaker discourage group interaction and encourage attention to the speaker only. Social workers can use their understandings of clients and their needs and of spatial arrangements to determine how space can be changed to enable people to function more adequately.[21]

When a social worker working with a group arranges chairs at the meeting space to bring about interpersonal interaction, she has manipulated space and created environmental change. The way the physical environment of a social agency is arranged can make clients feel comfortable or uncomfortable and can cause undesirable behavior or enable constructive activity. Physical arrangement can sometimes make the difference in whether the client uses the services offered or fails to get needs met.[22]

Placement of a child in a residential treatment facility is a form of environmental change. That facility uses the milieu (the arrangement of the space, program, and staff relationships) to help the child. Milieu therapy involves attitudes and relationships of the persons who occupy the space as a therapeutic tool. Hospitals, nursing homes, and other institutions can make use of milieu therapy.[23] Another example of environmental change is in the case example of Jerry Adams. In Chapter 9, the social worker develops a plan to work with the school to reduce racial tensions by incorporating diversity into the curriculum.

Any environmental change should be preceded by a thorough study and assessment of the situation, with particular emphasis on relationship, space, and time factors that may be impeding the client's social functioning. Attention should be given to how culture and lifestyle prescribe the use of the physical environment and time so that the plan does not conflict with the client's culture and lifestyle.

Time factors can be changed in service of clients by changing the schedule for activity. There is a time for physical or mental activity and a time for quiet in people's lives. By considering client need at various times, the social worker uses the time allotted in ways that are congruent with the client's need. For example, when children have been in school all day, after school they are usually ready for physical activity rather than for sitting quietly. When working with a mother, the worker should realize that times when family demand is high are not times the mother can reflect on her own needs. The timing of appointments should take into consideration the time rhythms of the client's life. Institutions often develop schedules to meet staff desires rather than considering the daily rhythms of those being served. Social workers can be alert to these time elements and work for changes in schedules so that service to clients can be facilitated.[24]

When using the strategy of environmental manipulation, the worker assesses the situation and plans changes in relationships, space, and the use of time. In planning for change it is essential that the worker use her understandings about relationships, space, and time. The social worker also should be creative in structuring environments to support clients' efforts in social functioning.

Case Example

A social worker in a nursing home notes that some patients, who must share rooms with other residents because of funding policies, need an opportunity to be alone for parts of the day. These same residents seem to need a private place to visit with those who come to see them. The social worker brings this need to the weekly staff meeting. At first the staff takes the attitude that this is just the way it is and states that there is no room for a private space. The social worker makes a tour of the facility to identify space that may not be used 100 percent during the day and early evening hours. She finds a craft facility that is only used two hours each morning and afternoon. She also finds a couple of alcoves in hallways that could hold a couple of comfortable chairs. In addition, she notes that there is outdoor space that in nice weather could be used for visiting if comfortable seating were provided. At the next staff meeting she presents her findings. The administrator then asks who is going to provide the needed furniture. The activities director states that she would welcome a comfortable corner in the craft room. She also says that the auxiliary has been looking for a project and wonders if this would not be a good one for them. Within a couple of months the identified space is converted to comfortable private space, and the residents have been involved in developing guidelines for its use.

Coordination of Services

Coordination is the working together of two or more service providers. Coordination of activity can be focused on a client, such as an individual or family (microlevel coordination), or on persons in a particular category, such as persons with AIDS or developmental disabilities (macrolevel coordination).

Collaboration and coordination are often used as if they were synonymous, but, as used in this text, there is a difference. Collaboration is the working together, or teamwork, of two or more helpers using a common plan of action. Coordination does not imply a common plan of action; in fact, there may be two or more plans of action. Collaboration and teamwork are two kinds of coordination. In this section several other methods of coordination are presented.

For coordination to be effective, there must be a spirit of working together toward a desirable end. For example, this end could be a common goal, such as maintaining in the community a person with chronic mental illness. This would require coordination of different services provided by different agencies, such as socialization and vocational rehabilitation services as well as housing services, medical monitoring services, income maintenance services, and the like. Public social services as well as mental health and vocational rehabilitation units and perhaps other agencies would all need to be involved.

In another example, the end may be the common goal of providing a range of services to a particular community to enable it to meet the needs of its aging members. This might involve coordination of the services of the senior citizens' center, the public health nursing agency, public social services, and the variety of other services available in the community. The goal would be to help specific clients who are older while enabling existing services to respond more appropriately to all people who are older. The common end would be a network of needed services usable by a broad range of people who are older.

An important aspect of coordination is the mutual satisfaction of all concerned. The persons or agencies involved need to believe that it is advantageous to coordinate their services with others. This feeling of common benefit leads to open exchange and feelings of satisfaction, which are necessary for productive relationships. Coordination can involve a range of resources broader than those of formal social service agencies. It can involve professionals from a variety of disciplines: service providers of community institutions, such as schools and churches; community self-help group leaders; and the informal resources of friends, family, and work colleagues.

One factor that can hinder coordination relates to the differing perspectives on clients and clients' needs held by those of different professional disciplines. A doctor might see an older person's frail health status as the primary need. A social worker might consider this person's lack of a support system as the main issue. A senior citizens' center director might identify the need for socialization to prevent isolation. Each professional would advocate for a different need for the client. The physician might push for a nursing home placement. The senior citizens' center director might want to involve the client in the activities of the center. The social worker might attempt to develop an individualized support system after ascertaining the client's desires.

Each profession has its own societal task to perform, its own way of functioning, and its own values and knowledge base. When social workers work with other disciplines, it is important to have an understanding of the other professions' perspectives. Issues of concern to other professions and areas of overlapping interest and service should also be identified. The social worker should also be aware of potential tensions among professionals. The expectation that every professional should think in the same ways about a client or a client's needs is a major block to coordination. Understanding differences is a first step to working together in a coordinated manner. This understanding aids in identifying the distinctive capacities of each professional that can be used in developing a coordinative relationship and can lead to respect and acceptance. Respect for and acceptance of another profession's contribution are necessary components of coordinative action.

When coordinating resources and activities from the informal arena, it is important to be aware of the different ways formal and informal resources function. Eugene Litwak and Henry Meyer pointed out the differences in functioning of the primary group (natural system) and the bureaucracy (formal system). *Primary systems* are diffuse, personal, have an affective bond, and call for face-to-face contact. They can best deal with nonuniform, relatively unique events. They are adaptable and flexible and have the capacity to respond quickly. *Formal systems* tend to be impersonal, specific as to what they can do, and operate within rules and regulations. They function with professional and technical expertise and deal with large numbers of people in an impartial manner. Both kinds of service systems are important and should be coordinated. An important contribution of Litwak and Meyer is what they called the *balance theory of coordination*. According to this theory, the important aspect of coordination is communication. If the two types of systems (formal and informal) are too far apart, communication does not take place. If they are too close together, their differences hinder each other's functioning. There is a midpoint of social distance between the two systems at which each system can function best. (The midpoint is the point at which the two systems can communicate with each other but are not so close that the functioning of either system is impaired.)[25]

Social workers who get to know community influentials and natural helpers in relatively informal community groups can develop relationships that will facilitate coordination with the informal system. If individuals who function in the informal system know the social worker, they will be more apt to consult with her or to refer someone to her. Social workers in turn can discuss common concerns in the informal settings in which these helpers are more comfortable.

Another consideration is the difference between the ways in which men and women communicate. Traditionally, women tend to seek cooperation when communicating, whereas men tend to be more competitive. Women tend to be more comfortable in relatively less structured settings, whereas men are drawn to settings with more formal lines of communication. The natural helping system seems to be more often a female system. The formal system, although staffed with both men and women, functions in a formalized manner that is more akin to traditional male communication. Male social workers should be particularly aware of differences in communication styles when working with the informal helping system.

Coordination can be carried out through several mechanisms. One is to locate those who serve similar populations in common settings, often called multiservice centers. This can be done by either locating the agency or the individual service deliverers (e.g., family service worker, community health nurse, income maintenance worker) representing a variety of agencies in a common setting close to those needing service. It is assumed not only that this will make services more accessible to clients but also that close proximity will encourage sharing among the professionals.

Another means of linking services has been an information and referral service; this can serve as a coordinative mechanism, depending on its means of functioning and on the capacity of those who staff it. If the emphasis is on providing information about services, the coordinative function will probably not be carried out. If the emphasis is on referral and enabling clients to access needed services, then a coordinative service is enhanced by follow-up and evaluation of the service delivered. Evaluation can also lead to identification of unmet needs and of needed services that are not available and thus to program development. A coordination approach that merits special consideration is case management.

Case Management

Case management has received considerable attention as a coordinative approach to service delivery. It has been found to be useful in the fields of child welfare, mental health (particularly with the chronically mentally ill), developmental disabilities, and gerontology. Its use is often indicated when a client needs a range of services from several social service or health providers. Provision for such services is supported by federal legislation.[26]

Although the process of case management has been identified in a varying manner from field to field, a common thread has emerged. According to Karen Orloff Kaplan, the process contains five components: (1) case identification; (2) assessment and planning; (3) coordination and referral; (4) implementation of services; and (5) monitoring, evaluation, and reassessment.[27]

Assessment and planning involve consideration not only of client needs but also of the resources available within the client's informal network of relationships and in the immediate community. Assessment is carried out with maximum client input and involves identifying the needed resources and weaving them into a plan that is congruent with the client's desires and lifestyle. This weaving together can be described as developing a *complementary resource pattern*. The case manager provides an integration so resources are not duplicated or at cross-purposes, and the client can sense a holistic concern for need fulfillment. The case manager reaches out to the various resources to obtain their cooperative input and to provide the information needed for coordinating services. She may need to creatively develop a new resource or modify an existing one. Often the case manager provides a part of the needed service. Regular monitoring is another task of the case manager.

Several case management models have been developed, usually addressing service in a particular field of practice (e.g., child welfare, services to older adults). One developed by Jack Rothman seems to depict the process most thoroughly and clearly. This model begins with access to the agency through outreach or referral and proceeds through intake and assessment, which may have both short- and long-term psychological, social, and medical components to goal setting. From this point a variety of options are possible: intervention planning, resource identification and indexing, and linking clients to formal agencies or informally to families and others. Counseling, therapy, advocacy, and interagency coordination, including policy considerations, may also be used but are outside the process loop and are used only when needed. Monitoring, reassessment, and outcome evaluation are also within the loop. Rothman noted that the process is meant to be used flexibly and is cyclical in nature.[28]

Two goals are often discussed in relation to case management: continuity of care and maximum level of functioning. *Continuity of care* is important because many of the clients who benefit from the use of this approach need services for an extended period of time, if not for the rest of their lives. This care may need to be provided in a range of different community and institutional settings. A holistic plan for services is considered desirable, and case managers can often provide the desired continuity. *Maximum level of functioning* is important because many clients with whom this approach is used operate at a less-than-independent level of functioning. Because of the multiple needs involved, they may not be functioning at the highest level of which they are capable. A case management approach provides an overview that can lead to planning, which encourages a maximum level of functioning.

Stephen T. Moore noted that case management should be an enabling and facilitating activity. A major thrust is to ensure that formal service complements family care and other informal helping rather than competing with or substituting for such care. This can add to the complexity of the service. The case manager may not only need to consider the current and potential strengths, limitations, and ways of functioning of the informal care system but also may need to develop a potential for help within these systems. He may need to provide support and other services to the informal system to enable it to perform as the needed resource. It is important to be aware of the stresses on the informal system as well as the needs of the helping system.[29]

Case management calls for the social worker to use both direct and indirect approaches. It is truly generalist social work practice in that it weaves together a variety of strategies so that the range of needs of clients with multiple challenges can be met. Coordination is a major concern of the case manager.

Case Example

Larry is a thirty-five-year-old man with a developmental disability who needs to be placed in a group home because his parents' advancing age makes it impossible for them to care for him.

A case manager for the agency to which Larry has been referred for placement carefully conducts a comprehensive assessment. He talks to Larry and sets as a short-term goal that he adjust to community living with involvement in sheltered work and recreational activities. The worker chooses a group home in a small town with a sheltered workshop. The case manager believes that Larry should not have to adjust to big-city life, which might be confusing at this time. The staff of this facility has been very successful in working with individuals like Larry.

The case manager discusses Larry's interests and experiences with the sheltered workshop staff, who make suggestions about work assignments and ways of working with Larry. The community into which Larry is to be placed is particularly rich in recreational activities because it is a college town and students are available to work with group home residents. The group home director and the case manager make specific plans for using this resource.

During the initial placement stage, the case manager plans to monitor the situation carefully, with weekly contacts with Larry, the group home, and the sheltered workshop. The group home manager will take responsibility for setting up the recreational program. After a period of adjustment, the case manager hopes that monitoring can be less frequent. At such a time, it will be important to set up long-term goals with Larry.

Actions to Change Organizations

Organizational and community change processes will be covered in more detail in Chapter 15. We decided to include some aspects of considering these changes here to highlight their use as indirect practice actions. When an organization or a community is the client system, actions are considered to be direct practice actions. This is covered in Chapter 15. However, it is rare for BSW or inexperienced MSW social workers to be placed in this position. Thus, most of the time the organization or community is the target of change. As such the actions of the worker are considered to be indirect.

Most indirect actions with organizations fall under the umbrella of advocacy. We described case advocacy, which is advocacy on behalf of an identified client, in Chapter 10 under the broker and advocate roles. Cause advocacy is advocacy on behalf of a population. This is discussed in Chapter 15. In case advocacy, there are several levels of assertiveness that are possible. The most extreme are actions that involve the worker fighting for the client and doing whatever is feasible to secure resources or services to which the client is entitled. However, as we pointed out these actions have potential consequences for the client as well as the worker and her agency. These actions can lead to more intense negative actions toward the client, the worker, or the agency.

There are actions that are less extreme that the worker can use that are less likely to result in a negative response. We still consider these as a form of advocacy. The least assertive or aggressive is to assume that a mistake was made in denying resources or services. Asking the other worker to explain the denial gives them an opportunity to save face and change the decision. If this fails, the social worker might involve her supervisor who can intervene and advocate with the supervisor in the other organization, or the social worker might discuss this possibility with the other worker before doing so. This lets the other worker know that the social worker is not taking "no" for an answer and is willing to bump this up to the next level. Typically the supervisor will want to review the case record in which case the other worker will want to make sure that everything is in order. In some cases it may be necessary to elevate the issue to higher levels of both organizations. The social worker needs to be certain of the correctness of her position when this occurs.

Actions between staff at various levels of both organizations typically involve some form of negotiation with the hope that a resolution can be reached. In most organizations workers at lower levels typically do not have the power to make exceptions or to determine that potential clients who do not meet all of the eligibility criteria can still be served. However, at some level there is typically someone who can exercise some discretion in this area. Sometimes, the resolution involves an exchange of "favors." This usually takes the form of making an exception or waiving some eligibility criteria with the expectation that the social worker's organization will reciprocate at a later date.

We refer to this type of advocacy as "reactive advocacy" because it involves reacting to a situation. We see a different form as "proactive advocacy," which is advocating before a problem arises. One way for the social worker to do this is to accompany his client to the other organization or call ahead of time to let the other worker know that he is involved. This lets the worker know that another professional is interested in the decision regarding resources or services. It is a form of influence. We all are susceptible to being influenced by others. When workers know that a fellow professional is involved they are more likely to be careful to ensure that they do not make a mistake in denying resources or services. Of course, everyone who presents themselves for services should receive equal consideration, but the reality is that consciously or unconsciously workers are influenced by the involvement of other professionals. We want to have the respect of our colleagues.

Another form of proactive advocacy occurs when the social worker takes the position of what is in the best interests of clients whenever new services are being considered or a change of services is contemplated or is needed. The worker is more frequently in a position to do this in her own agency as opposed to other organizations, but occasionally the opportunity may present itself. Whenever it does, as a social worker it is incumbent on her to advocate for the removal of existing barriers to service or to anticipate these and make suggestions to make it easier for clients to use needed services or access important resources.

Another form of change actions in organizations are policy changes. The worker should engage in similar proactive advocacy actions in influencing policy changes in his agency as well as other organizations. The worker should become familiar with how policies are formulated and changed within his agency and in other organizations. He can then be in a position to advocate for the best interests of clients when the opportunity presents itself. This type of advocacy with other organizations comes closer to what is called cause advocacy.

Actions to Change the Community

There are parallel actions with communities that are similar to what we just described under actions with organizations. One might argue that changing other organizations is an aspect of community change. As with organizational change, it is rare for BSW and inexperienced MSW social workers to be in positions of serving communities as client systems. More often the actions are indirect on behalf of clients. Even these actions are relatively rare.

Occasionally the social worker will be in a position to influence change in her community. In urban areas this may be limited to a neighborhood or area of the city. In rural areas, it is much more common for the worker to be involved in community change for the community as a whole. Various forms of community change are described in Chapters 15 and 16.

In our companion text *Generalist Social Work Practice with Groups*, we have included engaging in macro practice with organizations and communities and working with various types of task groups with these systems. The reader is referred to that text for a more in-depth description of macro practice.

Rothman and Tropman presented three models of community organization practice that can be used to address social issues and promote change, as follows:

1. *Locality development*—This model is used when the desired change is to facilitate community cooperation and interaction and foster self-help. It is primarily a process model in that it focuses on efforts to involve large numbers of concerned citizens in an area rather than on a specific change per se.

2. *Social planning*—This model is used when the goal is planned change regarding a specific issue. It utilizes "experts" rather than grassroots planners and is commonly used in governmental, educational, and private institutional settings. There may be very little, if any, community involvement in the process.

3. *Social action*—This model utilizes a coalition of a disadvantaged segment of the population to take action regarding a social problem that affects them directly. This is discussed in more detail in Chapters 15 and 16.[30]

Rothman and Tropman's models are classic examples of professional community organizing strategies. They provide an excellent base for understanding community practice as a professional social worker working as a community organizer. However, many generalist social workers need to understand community practice from a generalist perspective and as a worker who needs to work with the community as a part of her work with other client systems. It is also important for her to understand how to work with various task groups in the community. From this perspective it is important to consider the involvement of the worker, the involvement of members of the community, the involvement of community organizations, and the involvement of governmental agencies and bodies. Each of these may vary considerably. In addition, the unit of attention for the change effort may be the community or a segment of the community, organizations in the community, or governmental systems. In an ecosystems approach to change, the unit of attention could also be the interaction among any of these systems. Let us look at the various types of change efforts.

The community or neighborhood or segment of the community may be the initiator of the change effort or the unit of attention. When change is initiated by the community or any group of community members, we generally refer to it as a *grassroots movement*. In working with a grassroots movement, the worker may be a participant as either a representative of his organization or as a private citizen. In either case, the worker may provide valuable knowledge and skills in organizing, campaigning, advertising, media relations, and similar activities that may be vital to the success of the change effort. When the worker initiates the change effort, either alone or with a group, we consider this to be an *activist movement*. Similar activities as those with a grassroots movement typically take place, but an effort to involve the community or affected segments of it is generally the first priority in using this approach. In a grassroots movement, the community is already involved and the worker joins the effort and lends his expertise. In either of these instances, community organizations may or may not be involved as supporters of the change effort. Some community organizations may be the unit of attention. Most often, these two approaches do not involve governmental systems as partners in the change process, at least not initially. However governmental systems are frequently the unit of attention either primarily or secondarily. In the first instance, the change effort is aimed directly at a governmental unit. In the second instance, influencing the governmental unit may be necessary in order for the effort to be successful.

One or more community organizations may initiate a change effort that is directed at the community or a segment of it or at governmental systems or at other organizations. We refer to this as an *organizational task force*. It might also be called an *organization* or *agency collaborative* or *cooperative*. Governmental systems may also set up a task force which we refer to as a *governmental task force*. When members of the community are included in an organizational task force we refer to it as a *community partnership*. When members of the community are included in a governmental task force, we call it a *community task force*. Community task forces may also include representatives of community organizations. Most often task forces are developed to address social or economic issues in either the community at large or a segment or area of it. Task forces might be set up to reduce crime or drug activities or to reverse urban decay or promote economic revival. The worker is usually a representative of her organization and her knowledge and skills are used in a more formal way by the task force to facilitate the change effort.

With each of these types of community groups the worker takes actions that are consistent with her role in the task group. She also uses other skills described throughout this text in assisting the group as whole or individual members of the group.

Summary

The social worker takes actions on behalf of clients as well as directly with them. We refer to these as indirect practice actions, which include:

- Action that uses mediation, which can be useful when the client and environment are not interacting in a functional manner. The worker helps client and environment reach out to each other so they can fulfill common needs. Mediation is also used when working with any multiclient system, including families, family subsystems, and groups.

- Action involving influence is an important component of the interventive repertoire of a social worker engaging with others on behalf of the client. The social worker should be able to use influence and to work with influentials.

- Action to bring about environmental change is a strategy used to alter structural, cultural, and functional patterns in the client's environment. Patterns that are particularly important are those of relationships, space, and time. This strategy calls for creative action by the social worker.

- Action to coordinate services calls for a thorough understanding of the service delivery system. Communication is an important ingredient of coordination. The social worker instigates coordination by helping service deliverers communicate with one another. Case management and networking are strategies for developing coordination.

- Action to change organizations typically involves some form of advocacy or policy change.

- Action to change the community may also involve advocacy. Various models of working with task groups are typically involved when the worker engages in actions to change the community.

Questions

1. In what kinds of situations would the mediating model be appropriate? When would it not be appropriate?
2. When is it appropriate to use influence? When is it not appropriate?
3. Describe a situation in which environmental manipulation would be appropriate. Give an example that involves relationship. An example of time. An example of space.
4. Describe the important tasks involved in providing case management and give an example of each.

5. In a community with which you are familiar, identify a need you believe a community task force can fill. An activist movement can fill. A grassroots movement can fill. Using one of these resources, how would you go about working to provide a needed service or meet a community problem?

Suggested Readings

Yanca, Stephen J. and Johnson, Louise C. *Generalist Social Work Practice with Groups*. Boston: Allyn and Bacon, 2009 (Part III: Generalist Practice with Organizations and Communities, Chapters 10–13).

Alinsky, Saul. *Rules for Radicals*. New York: Random House, 1967.

Brueggemann, William G. *The Practice of Macro Social Work,* 3rd ed. Belmont, CA: Thomson-Brooks/Cole, 2006.

Haynes, Karen S., and Mickelson, James S. *Affecting Change: Social Workers in the Political Arena,* 5th ed. Boston: Allyn and Bacon, 2003.

Long, Dennis D., Tice, Carolyn J., and Morrison, John D. *Macro Social Work Practice: A Strengths Perspective*. Belmont, CA: Thomson-Brooks/Cole, 2006.

Miley, Karla Krogsrud, O'Melia, Michael, and DuBois, Brenda L. *Social Work Practice: An Empowering Approach,* 6th ed. Boston: Allyn and Bacon, 2009 (Chapters 12–14).

Mizrahi, Terry and Davis, Larry E., Eds. *Encyclopedia of Social Work*, 20th ed. Washington, DC: NASW Press, 2008 ("Advocacy," "Case Management," "Community," "Community Organization," "Organizational Development and Change").

Netting, Ellen F., Kettner, Peter M., and McMurtry, Steven L. *Social Work Macro Practice,* 4th ed. Boston: Allyn and Bacon, 2008.

Netting, Ellen F., and O'Connor, Mary K. *Organization Practice: A Social Worker's Guide to Understanding Human Services*. Boston: Allyn and Bacon, 2003.

Norman, Elaine. *Resiliency Enhancement.* New York: Columbia University Press, 2000.

Rae, P. Ann, and Nicholas-Wolosuk, Wanda. *Changing Agency Policy: An Incremental Approach.* Boston: Allyn and Bacon, 2003.

Roberts, A. L. and Greene, G. J. Eds., *Social Worker's Desk Reference.* New York: Oxford University Press, 2002. See: Jack Rothman, "An Overview of Case Management"; Joseph Walsh, "Clinical Case Management"; Jannah H. Mather and Grafton H. Hull, Jr., "Case Management and Child Welfare"; David P. Moxley, "Case Management and Psychosocial Rehabilitation with SMD Clients"; Charles A. Rapp, "A Strengths Approach to Case Management with Clients with Severe Mental Disabilities"; W. Patrick Sullivan, "Case Management with Substance Abusing Clients"; Candyce S. Berger, "Social Work Case Management in Medical Settings"; Carol D. Austin and Robert W. McClelland, "Case Management with Older Adults"; Brian Giddens, Lana S. Ka'opua, and Evelyn P. Tomaszewski, "HIV/AIDS Case Management."

Rothman, Jack. *Guidelines for Case Management: Putting Research to Professional Use.* Itasca, IL: F. E. Peacock, 1992, and *Case Management: Integrating Individual and Community Practice*. Boston: Allyn and Bacon, 1998.

Rothman, Jack, Erlich, John L., and Tropman, John E. *Strategies of Community Organization—Macro Practice*, 6th ed. Belmont, CA: Thomson-Brooks/Cole, 2001.

Rubin, Herbert J., and Rubin, Irene S. *Community Organizing and Development,* 4th ed. Boston: Allyn and Bacon, 2008.

Sheafor, Bradford W., and Horejsi, Charles R. *Techniques and Guidelines for Social Work Practice,* 8th ed. Boston: Allyn and Bacon, 2009 (Chapters 6, 13, and 15).

Shulman, Lawrence. *The Skills of Helping: Individuals, Families, Groups, and Communities,* 6th ed. Thomson-Brooks/Cole, 2009.

Tropman, John E., Rothman, Jack, and Erlich, John L. *Tactics and Techniques of Community Intervention,* 4th ed. Belmont, CA: Thomson-Brooks/Cole, 2006.

12 | *Evaluation and Termination*

Learning Expectations

1. Understanding the importance of and skill in the use of evaluation in the social work process.
2. Understanding of the use of research techniques in the evaluation process.
3. Understanding of the place of the termination process in the social work process.
4. Understanding of the components of the termination process.
5. Understanding of both the transfer and the referral processes.

Evaluation and termination are covered together in this chapter. Although each is distinctive in many ways, they are also linked to each other. In the successful completion of a change process, evaluation provides a basis for termination by determining that the goals have been achieved and the need has been met. Evaluation occurs throughout the change process. At the same time, unplanned termination can occur at any point during the process and for a variety of reasons. The worker must be prepared to respond to the needs of the client, even when unplanned termination occurs. Thorough, ongoing evaluation provides the worker with important knowledge in determining a response to planned and unplanned termination.

As an ongoing part of the social work process, **evaluation** is the means for determining if the goals and objectives of the social work endeavor are being reached. (See Figure 1) It also involves looking at the means being used to reach goals and objectives. Evaluation identifies unexpected outcomes, both negative and positive, from the helping activity. Evaluation should be continuous, but it becomes particularly important as each step is completed. It should occur after assessment to see that the information collected is valid and reliable and that appropriate conclusions about the meaning of the information and about client in situation have been drawn. After planning, there should be evaluation to determine if the plan is complete and feasible. After action has been carried out, evaluation should be used to determine if the desired goals have been reached. Evaluation is also an important part of the termination process.

Evaluation, then, is finding out if what is expected to happen is really happening. It looks at completed work and determines which methods and strategies worked and why. It is an opportunity to check with clients and significant others to see how it is going from their viewpoint. Evaluation of one's work is a professional obligation for every social worker and should be a continuous process. Programs and agencies are obligated to carry out an ongoing evaluation of their mission, purpose, and goals. Evaluation is necessary if social workers and the agencies are to be accountable to clients, support sources, and the general public. Social workers participate in evaluation in some way, regardless of their place in the agency hierarchy. Agency and program evaluation will be discussed here and in Chapter 15. In terms of evaluation, this chapter will consider various kinds of evaluation, research techniques in evaluation, and evaluation during each phase of the change process.

The final stage of the social work process is **termination**, or the ending stage. Although ending the process is often slighted, it is nevertheless an important aspect of the social work endeavor. Termination is planned from the beginning of the work together. A social work relationship that focuses on meeting the needs of the client terminates when those needs are met. The time line that is a part of the plan of action specifies the anticipated time for termination.

In termination, it is important to consider the background of the client system and the reasons for termination. Life is full of beginnings and endings. The end of one experience usually signals the beginning of another. Termination work can enhance the client's social functioning. Any ending can arouse strong feelings. These feelings can be used as a means for growth, or they can be denied or suppressed, perhaps to arise and interfere with later social functioning.

In considering termination, three areas will be discussed: (1) kinds of termination and reasons for clients' and workers' terminating, (2) planned termination with individuals, and (3) components of the termination process—dealing with feelings, stabilizing change, and evaluating with clients.

Kinds of Evaluation

Planning for evaluation, when developing a plan of action, is one way of ensuring that the plan of action is carried out in a way that yields maximum information to the worker, the client, and the agency. If the information to be used in evaluation is identified before the social work process begins, there is a better chance that such information will be available for use in evaluation.

In order to plan effectively and efficiently for evaluation, an understanding of the various kinds of evaluation and some of the means for carrying out the evaluative process is useful. Evaluation serves many purposes and takes a variety of forms. In its most simplified form, it is a worker thinking about what has happened and why it happened. During the termination phase of the social work process, the worker and client together determine if the goals set out in the contract have been reached and then discuss what enabled the goal attainment. Evaluation involves discussing what has been helpful to the client and what could have been done differently. Program evaluation is more complex, generally involving statistical data or other research methodology. Evaluation may be summative or formative. **Summative evaluation** is concerned with outcomes and effectiveness. **Formative evaluation** is concerned with looking at the process of the work, at how the work during the various steps in the service influenced the final outcome. This evaluation would look at such things as the nature of the relationship, the content of sessions, or the setting in which the work took place. Both types are important in social work practice and should be included in the evaluation process.[1] The kind of evaluation employed is in part dependent on the stage of the social work process or on the program or agency need for data related to accountability.

One way to develop an understanding of evaluation is to consider various classification schemes used relative to evaluation. The first classification to be considered is whether the evaluation is of a particular case, of a program within an agency, or of the agency itself. When considering a specific case, evaluation focuses on whether the goals set by the worker and client together were attained. Evaluation of the process of the work should focus on how the various components of the plan of action contributed to reaching the goal. Evaluation of the process of work is a joint endeavor of the worker and the client because the client is usually the best source of information about goal attainment and about the process of the work together. Workers often do some additional thinking about the client in situation and how the client and his situation relate to other clients they have had. This is done so that the worker can develop an understanding of how to approach future clients who may be in similar situations.

Program and agency evaluations determine the effectiveness of agency functioning. These kinds of evaluation are often concerned with efficiency of service provision and usually are not as personalized as a case evaluation is. Different kinds of evaluation require different methods and techniques.

Program evaluations serve four purposes. First, they are necessary to meet the requirements of outside funding and accreditation bodies. Second, they can provide indications of client satisfaction. Third, they can provide information that can be used in developing new practice knowledge and worker competence. Fourth, program evaluations can document the need for new services or service effectiveness to other service providers, funding sources, and the general public.

A second classification is qualitative versus quantitative evaluation. With quantitative data, an effort is made to measure satisfaction by using numbers and averaging the responses of those surveyed. The advantage of this procedure is that statistical computations can be used to determine whether the outcome is a result of random error or is likely to be associated with the service. The disadvantage is that the data may not be very meaningful because they lack the richness of individual experiences. Qualitative data tend to derive from asking people to relate their experiences. This has the advantage of providing a comprehensive picture of service from the client's perspective. However, gathering qualitative data is more time consuming and thus more costly than quantitative data collection. In addition, samples of the client population tend to be smaller, and the data are more difficult to analyze. The contemporary service delivery system has been highly influenced by organizational management trends and the use of a quantitative base for evaluation. Clinical practice has also been influenced by behavioral psychology and its emphasis on measuring behaviors. The trend toward computerization of information and records also supports the demand for quantitative data. However, most social workers maintain that not all information can be dealt with in a quantitative manner because of the qualitative factor in human functioning. Although behaviors can be measured, feelings and emotions are difficult to quantify, and qualitative measures are a better mechanism for evaluating these factors. Most client surveys should include both quantitative and qualitative data in order to tap the advantages of each.

A third classification is that of clinical versus management evaluation. Although this classification might be closely related to the quantitative-qualitative classification (management generally uses quantitative data; clinical generally uses qualitative data), the application of these two types of evaluation is quite different. Management evaluation is used to make internal staffing and program decisions and to substantiate need for services and resources to support services. Clinical evaluation is limited to use by professional persons (worker and supervisor) and the client involved in the situation being evaluated. Because of the different usage, different information is sought for use in different types of evaluation, and different kinds of outcomes are expected. Sometimes data are used for both types of evaluation, which is more efficient in that it avoids collecting two sets of data. It can be difficult to use the same information for two different purposes. Management evaluation is apt to call for statistical data that can be broken down into categories of problems. Clinical evaluation is usually concerned with the type of need dealt with and specific information as to how the need and its resolution affected the client and her situation. This information loses some of its meaning when converted to categories or statistics.

A classification developed by Michael Key, Peter Hudson, and John Armstrong,[2] identified a hard line–soft line continuum. Hard-line focuses on aims and objectives are set before the implementation of programs. Some scientific objectivity is involved in this type of evaluation. Soft-line is based on impressions and opinions. Each approach yields different kinds of information. The worker needs to determine if hard-line information will adequately provide for the evaluation needs and tell the necessary story. If not, then soft-line information should be used either to tell the story or to supplement the hard-line information.

Each type of classification points out a different dimension of evaluation. Each evaluation can be classified along a continuum related to each of the four classifications. It is important to consider the requirements of the situation being evaluated, keeping all four possible classifications in mind (case or program/agency, quantitative or qualitative, clinical or management, hard or soft), and choosing methods that match the requirements of the situation.

Single-System Design and Research Techniques in Evaluation

Research techniques are very useful in carrying out evaluations because evaluation and research share common considerations and concerns. The main reasons social workers need to be familiar with research and evaluation techniques in practice are (1) to evaluate the success or failure of their services, (2) to evaluate themselves and their strengths and limitations as practitioners, (3) to evaluate the potential use of various approaches and techniques found in professional literature or obtained through training programs, and (4) to evaluate programs in order to make them more effective while maximizing the efficient use of resources and to report these results as a part of accountability. This last area will be covered in the next section.

The purpose of this discussion is to point out the relationship between practice and research when evaluating social work practice and to discuss research methods and techniques that are particularly suited for evaluation of practice single-system design and goal-attainment scaling. **Single-system design** is a research method that fits very well with problem solving, the change process, or any solution-oriented approach. It is a natural follow-up to the measurable goals and objectives that were identified in Chapter 9. It is important that the worker and the client develop a plan which measures progress toward meeting needs and overcoming barriers. Otherwise, the work can seem aimless rather than focused on suitable outcomes. An essential ingredient for change is hope. When the client sees progress, she feels more hope that the situation will change for the better. If the plan is based on strengths of the client, then progress will come sooner and the overall plan will have greater chance of success. The client will feel empowered because she is acting on abilities and capacities she already has. As the client sees progress, she will experience positive reinforcement for change. Even the completion of tasks can be very uplifting for the client.

Single-system design can be used with any size client system. It is a variation of time-series design. A series of measurements of the same system are made over time. The system can be an individual, a family, a group, a program, an organization, or a community.

The simplest traditional experimental design uses control experimental groups. Participants are randomly assigned to each group to avoid biasing the outcome. The experimental group receives services, and the control group does not. Differences between the two groups at the end of the experiment are assumed to be caused by the service. Statistical methods are typically used to estimate the probability that the results were a result of error rather than the service. The problem with this approach is that it is unethical for a social worker to withhold services to clients, especially if the client would benefit from the service.

Occasionally, social work evaluators can develop a research project using a traditional experimental design in which the control group consists of clients on a waiting list for service. The control group might also be offered service at a later time. However, it is nearly impossible to randomly assign clients to a waiting list, and so these designs are considered quasi-experimental.

In single-system design, no one is refused service for experimental purposes. There is no need to apply statistical methods or to use random assignment to ensure that the control and experimental groups are equivalent. Instead, the client system serves as its own control by measuring a target behavior, condition, or event before the intervention or service begins and then measuring the same thing during or after the intervention or service.

In single-system design, clients can be informed and can consent to the evaluation by participating in the process itself. Throughout the change process, the client participates as a partner in change efforts. Including clients in measuring and evaluating change is essential to sound ethical practice. Researchers who are "purists" would be highly critical of this approach. Their concern would be that one would have difficulty in determining whether the intervention or some other influence brought about the change. They would be especially concerned that clients would "contaminate" the process by doing something out of the ordinary that would either enhance or sabotage the results. However, practitioners are interested in assisting clients in changing their circumstances rather than in maintaining purity in research design. If the purpose is to measure client goals, then the concerns of the "purists" are irrelevant.

If the worker needs to generalize the results to determine the effectiveness of an intervention method, a service, a program, or the like, then care needs to be taken to control for bias. For most purposes it is sufficient to limit claims of success or failure to the situation at hand. Another option is to be scrupulous in describing how the evaluation was designed and carried out, allowing others to decide for themselves the validity or reliability of the results.

For an individual client **single-subject design** may be used. During the assessment phase a baseline of behavior is established. Intervention methods, goals, and measurable objectives related to a desired change in the behavior are identified. At specific points during the intervention, the target behavior is measured to determine the progress toward reaching the goal. After completion of the intervention, a final measurement is made to determine the extent to which the goal was reached. Proponents of this method claim that measurable results or outcomes of the intervention can be obtained. They feel that single-subject design provides a reliable means of validating practice. It is also critical in developing what is called "practice wisdom," which consists of benefits gained through experience. The more the social worker adds empirical evidence to her experience, the greater her confidence in practice decisions.

Critics of single-subject design believe that the range of applicability is limited because the technique is only useful within a behavioral framework for practice. They also believe that there are qualitative questions that are not addressed by this methodology. Questions also are raised as to the lasting quality of the change when measurements are made during and directly after intervention. Is the planned intervention the cause of the desired change, or have other factors, either in the treatment situation or in the environment, contributed to the change?[3] The major contribution of single-subject design is its focus on goals and outcomes and the provision of a methodology for measuring outcomes, which moves evaluation toward the hard end of the soft–hard continuum.

The simplest single-system design involves a pretest before intervention and a posttest afterward. Another variation involves several measurements during the baseline period, with continued measurement during the intervention. This is called AB design, where A represents time when the intervention is not taking place and B represents time when it is.

Careful attention is paid to measurement in single-system designs. To ensure validity and internal reliability, measurement must be as consistent as possible. A good way to monitor this is to pay attention to the who, what, where, when, and how of measurement. To be consistent, the same person or group (who) needs to measure the same thing (what) with the same client system (who) at the same place (where) and time (when) using the same instruments or observation techniques (how). Any variation in any of these raises doubts about the validity and reliability of the data or information; that is, whatever is being observed or measured may change because the person sees or interprets it differently or because the time and place are different. If what gets measured or how it gets measured changes, then the worker is actually comparing two different things that may be not be related at all. The worker will have to prove that the relationship exists before the results can be used with any confidence.

It should be noted that measuring lack of progress is as important as measuring progress. Evaluation is not only a matter of measuring success but also of measuring failure. Finding out that something is not working allows the client and the worker to change the plan. If the worker finds that certain techniques or approaches do not work in certain situations or with certain groups, she has added important information to her practice wisdom. In addition, with managed care it is essential that the worker be as effective and efficient as possible. There may be little if any room for error before the client's benefits or reimbursement are cut off or exhausted. To prevent financial hardship for the client or the agency, the worker must be focused on resolving the situation and will need to establish time frames and track progress quickly and with a minimum of effort.

Single-system design can be used with any size client system. As long as what is being examined can be observed and measured, change can also be measured. Indications of the effectiveness of an intervention, service, or program can be determined, with some caution regarding generalizing the results. Extra caution should be used to protect the consistency of measurement when larger client systems are being evaluated and when ongoing or long-term evaluation is planned.

A technique often used with the single-subject design is **goal-attainment scaling**. Goals are set so that the outcomes can be measured on a five-point scale. The five points on the scale are (1) most unfavorable outcome thought likely, (2) less-than-expected outcome, (3) expected outcome, (4) more-than-expected outcome, and (5) most favorable outcome thought likely. Allowance for recording several goals is made by the development of a grid, with goals on one axis and levels of predicted attainment on the other axis.[4]

The major strength of goal-attainment scaling is that it allows for several measurements of success and failure to reach an outcome. By specifying a continuum of outcomes, the technique includes a growth factor. It also offers an evaluative mechanism (the five points on the scale) that can be converted to symbolic codes needed for computerization of data. The grid provides a quickly read summary of the outcomes of a specific episode of service.

Case Example

In the case example of Jerry Adams and his family, the worker might construct a single-system evaluation design to evaluate the outcomes of a plan. The following is an example of a report that a student might submit for a field assignment on evaluating the effectiveness of her interventions.

I. **Identifying Information**
   A. Name: Jerry Adams (The names would be disguised for purposes of confidentiality.)
   B. Age: Jerry is thirteen.
   C. Jerry is a first-year student in high school.
   D. Presenting need: The school referred Jerry because of poor school performance. There were also several altercations between Jerry and other boys at school. The family is African American and recently moved from a mixed neighborhood to a predominantly white community. Jerry reports missing a positive relationship with his father because Mr. Adams works long hours.
   E. Significant others in the client system: Jerry's parents. Mr. and Mrs. Adams own their own business. Mrs. Adams works part time in the family business. The school system and community do not have much experience with diversity.
   F. Targeted behavior to be altered: Jerry needs to follow the rules at school so he avoids disciplinary actions, such as suspension. He needs some new coping skills as alternatives to responding to racial comments. He also needs more positive attention from his father. (Note: This case example only focuses on Jerry and his family and does not include changes in the school's response to diversity.)

II. **Intervention Chosen and Rationale**
   The interventions chosen are positive feedback and anger management. Positive feedback is a form of behavior modification. The intervention will call for Jerry to receive positive feedback from his parents and from the worker regarding his adherence to rules at school. The rationale for this is to give Jerry support for handling the situation in a positive manner and to change some of the negative interactions between Jerry and his parents. Jerry will also receive positive feedback from his father for doing things around the house. The rationale for this is to reestablish a more positive relationship between Jerry and his father. The worker will work with Jerry on anger management. This will give him some alternative ways to handle racial situations that provoke his anger. This is a cognitive-behavioral technique. The rationale for this is to empower Jerry and give him more control over these situations. Role-plays with the worker will be used to practice and reinforce methods of managing anger.

III. **Outcome Desired for the Intervention**
   Goals and Objectives
   Goal A: Jerry will have a positive interaction with his school.
      Objective 1: Jerry will follow rules at school 100 percent of the time for one week by November 15.
      Client task: Jerry will be able to recite three basic rules for classroom behavior by October 25.
      Worker task: By October 25, the worker will arrange for the school to give written feedback on his behavior each week. The worker will also work with Jerry on anger management techniques during each session and will role-play these with him.

(continued)

Case Example   *(continued)*

Parent task: Mr. and Mrs. Adams will keep track of the written feedback and reward Jerry for positive behavior at the end of the week based on the number of days of positive reports.

Goal B: Jerry and his father will have a more positive relationship.

Objective 1: Jerry will receive positive feedback from his father at least five times in one week by November 15 for doing his chores.

Client task: Jerry will do his chores without being asked and will report to his father when his chores are completed.

Worker task: The worker will meet with Mr. Adams to discuss feedback techniques as needed.

Parent task: Mr. Adams will give Jerry feedback on his chores. He will make a positive statement when they are completed in a satisfactory manner and will give corrective feedback if they are not. Each week that Jerry receives at least five positive feedback statements, he and his father will spend at least an hour together in an activity that they mutually select.

IV. Measurement Method Used to Monitor Client Outcomes

Mrs. Adams will track the feedback from the school on a calendar in a folder. She will give Jerry feedback on it every Friday afternoon after school and will bring it to sessions with the worker. Jerry and Mr. Adams will keep track of feedback and activities on a calendar in another folder. They will meet every Saturday morning before Mr. Adams leaves for the store to determine the number of positive statements given during the past week and to plan activities according to the results.

V. Baseline Data Report

This was a retrospective baseline, in part because there was no other reason to delay the intervention. During the assessment, Mrs. Adams was asked to have the school report any violations of school rules and Jerry was asked to track the number of times he received positive feedback from his father. Both of these activities occurred during a two-week period of time. As a way to validate the data, Mrs. Adams was asked to check with the school to see how typical these two weeks were compared to the previous two weeks. Mrs. Adams and Jerry were also asked how typical the feedback was from Jerry's father. During the first week Jerry had five violations of school rules; three were altercations that included racial comments and two were for being tardy for class. During the second week there were four violations: two tardies and two altercations. Mrs. Adams confirmed with the school that this was fairly typical. During the first week of tracking feedback from Mr. Adams, Jerry reported one positive comment; he reported none the second week. Mrs. Adams and Jerry reported that this was typical.

VI. Intervention Data Report (A graph of the data would be included in an appendix.)

During the first week of the intervention, Jerry was able to limit his tardies to one, but he had two altercations. The second week he was successful in eliminating all tardies but still had two altercations. The third and fourth weeks were the same as the second. In terms of receiving positive feedback from Mr. Adams, the schedule reveals that Jerry received positive feedback four times the first week and six to seven times each week since then.

(continued)

Case Example   *(continued)*

VII. Assessment of Change in the Targeted Behavior

There have been some changes in the interaction between Jerry and his school but the goal has not yet been achieved. It seems that although Jerry has been successful at developing new ways to respond in these situations, some of the students have chosen to keep escalating their response until they get a negative response from Jerry. However, Jerry feels much better about his ability to deal with these situations and wants to continue the work until the end of the semester. Thus, the target date for completion has been extended until January 31. Jerry reports a great deal of satisfaction with the results of Goal B. He feels very good about his relationship with his father. They have spent time on activities such as going to a basketball game and throwing the football back and forth. Jerry asked if he could help out at the store and he is now working every Saturday afternoon, cleaning and running errands.

VIII. Conclusions Regarding Interventions Based on Data and Subjective Observations

It appears that the use of positive feedback and anger management worked to improve the relationship between Jerry and his school even though these were not completely successful. Although Jerry improved in eliminating his tardiness and in his response to altercations, the intervention was not able to control the behavior of the other students. It is hoped that the implementation of the school's diversity project will have some impact on this. If these incidents can be limited to a few identified students, then more direct interventions with those students can be implemented. Jerry's positive attitude toward the intervention and his desire to extend it for the rest of the semester would indicate that it has been successful in helping him to feel more in control when these situations arise.

A limitation of goal-attainment scaling is the time needed to set up the scales for measurement. Some social workers believe the time spent in setting up the scales would better be used in working with the client. Also, some desired outcomes are very difficult to specify in the manner needed in this technique. Goal-attainment scaling has some of the same limitations as single-subject design, such as questions about the relationship of the change to the intervention, the emphasis on the outcome of goals, and the sustainment of the change over time.

Other forms of evaluating practice outcomes include *task-achievement scaling (TAS)*. Two of the major contributors to this approach are William Reid and Laura Epstein, who have written about task-centered practice.[5] Joel Fischer and Kevin Corcoran have compiled a sourcebook of more than 320 *rapid-assessment instruments (RAIs)* that can be used quickly in assessing numerous client conditions. RAIs generally have the additional advantage of being able to be used over and over with the same client while retaining their validity and reliability.[6] *Individualized rating scales (IRSs)* can be used for developing what are called self-anchoring scales.[7]

One of the most common uses of research for practitioners is for professional development activities. Professional social workers must increase their knowledge and skills and should aspire to contribute to the knowledge base of the profession. This means commitment to continuing education throughout their careers. This includes attending in-service events, workshops, conferences, and training programs along with researching and reading professional literature. To be a competent consumer and user of new techniques, the social worker must be able to evaluate the quality of the material presented and its applicability to various clients, practice settings, and circumstances. A solid foundation and knowledge base in the area of research and evaluation is required in order to accomplish this. In addition, competent and appropriate supervision is needed when trying new approaches or techniques.

Social work has become more professional, and demands for accountability have increased, especially from managed care systems. This has led to an increased expectation for research and practice to become more closely associated with each other. Social workers are expected to become more knowledgeable about the effectiveness of their approaches. However, it is not enough to evaluate the effectiveness of interventions. As research has expanded, social work has begun to develop an approach called **empirically based practice**, also called evidence-based or best practice. This approach calls for identifying research approaches that are most likely to succeed with various clients experiencing certain needs or concerns in various settings. In Chapter 9 we proposed incorporating these along with practice wisdom and an empowerment approach into what we call *good practices*.

Not every social worker will have an opportunity to write or publish an article or a book. However, opportunities to make contributions to the profession occur on a daily basis. These include sharing articles and educational materials with colleagues, conducting in-service training and workshops, sharing practice wisdom through peer or formal supervision, and networking with other social workers and human service professionals. These daily contributions are fundamental to how social workers have functioned from the very beginning of the profession.

Evaluation during Phases of the Change Process

Validity and reliability are two important concepts from research that are also relevant for evaluation. **Validity** refers to the accuracy of the information. **Reliability** is concerned with whether repeated measurement would yield the same results. In using naturalistic inquiry for diversity competent practice, knowledge is considered to be tentative. What we think we know we consider to be fluid and not fixed. In practice, information is exchanged within the context of human interaction. Thus, the information includes interpretation and perception that is subjective. Yvonne Lincoln and Ergon Guba described negotiated outcomes and negotiated meanings and interpretations as important in naturalistic inquiry. In a person in environment approach, the worker is interested in understanding "reality" from the client's perspective. The worker seeks to understand the meanings and interpretations of the client. She also realizes that the client's willingness to disclose her true thoughts and feelings depend on the quality of the helping relationship and the level of trust.[8]

Because we are concerned about the client's interaction with her environment, it is not necessary and probably impossible to know with certainty the objective accuracy of the information. What is important is that the worker has an understanding of the client's interpretation and perception of the information. The question is not whether a client should feel or think what she does. The question is what does she feel or think and how does that influence her actions? Validity is established when there is an understanding between the worker and the client regarding the client's perception of herself, her environment, and the interaction between herself and her environment.

Reliability in practice situations relates to how well the understanding the worker and client have about a given situation will carry over in time or in similar situations. In other words, does the same thing happen over and over again whenever the same situation arises? Does the same thing happen in situations that are similar? If so, then we can be more certain that we understand person in environment. If there is inconsistency, then we need to explore our understanding further with the client. However, in naturalistic inquiry and diversity competent practice, the worker refrains from making judgments or drawing absolute conclusions from his observations. In other words, inconsistency does not represent deception. Rather, it represents a lack of understanding on the part of the worker or a lack of mutual understanding or the trust in the relationship may not be sufficient for the client to openly reveal her thoughts and feelings.

We believe that clients will reveal what they can about themselves. If the client does not trust the worker, she would be foolish to reveal things about herself that might cause her harm. None of us would do this until we could feel that we trusted the other person. Instead of making judgments about the client, the worker takes responsibility for not having established sufficient trust and seeks ways of improving trust in the relationship.

The social worker engages in evaluation throughout the change process, as depicted in Figure 1. As the worker adds new information to his assessment, he evaluates that information to see how it helps in his understanding of the situation. He checks out his perceptions and interpretations with the client. Agreement means he can have more confidence in the information in building a foundation for change. Disparity means negotiating an understanding.

In understanding need, the worker approaches the situation from an ecosystems perspective and seeks an interpretation based on incongruity between person and systems in the environment. What the client needs or wants to have happen is not happening. The worker looks for blocks to fulfilling need. He considers the nature of the need and makes assumptions about why the need is not being met. He makes assumptions about potential strengths and resources in the client, her environment, their interactions, and his own ecosystem. Throughout these stages of the assessment, he constantly evaluates the information he has, the assumptions he has made, and the information he needs to determine whether his assumptions are supported and his understanding is appropriate.

The worker selects and collects information that is used to further his understanding of person in environment and of strengths and resources in the ecosystem. The selection of information is based on his assumptions. The worker evaluates information that he needs to check his assumptions and the degree to which the information he collects supports those assumptions. Verification of assumptions adds to understanding. Assumptions that are not verified are either discarded or remain in question if more information is needed.

Evaluation of the analysis is critical. The worker must determine whether he has sufficient information to proceed or if he needs to gather more information. At some point, the analysis yields enough information to provide a basis for the plan. These are judgments that the worker must make. They involve evaluating the quality of his understanding of person in environment and strengths and resources. A major source of feedback is the client along with other sources of information in the environment. When his understanding is consistent with the client's and is supported by information from the environment, the worker and the client have a high level of confidence in the decisions that are made. Minor discrepancies or differences that can be accounted for as variations in perception mean keeping the door open for more information, but the work can usually proceed. Major discrepancies mean that more work needs to be done.

As the work proceeds into the planning phase, the worker must evaluate the quality of the goals, objectives, and tasks. As described in Chapter 9, the worker determines whether the goals are feasible. He looks at the objectives to see if they are clear, measurable, and aimed at accomplishing the goal. If so, then the objectives can be used to measure progress toward completion of the goal. He looks at both the objectives and tasks to decide if they clearly identify who, what, where, when, and how in terms of the work to be done. Finally, the worker and the client agree on the plan and develop a mechanism for monitoring progress and completion.

As actions take place, the worker evaluates their effectiveness. Is the plan working? If not, why not? What needs to be done to change the plan or remove barriers to success? Does the action need to be modified? Are new actions needed? Should the plan be scrapped and a new or an alternative plan be implemented? Is there a need to return to a stage of the assessment that should be modified? Is there a new need that takes precedence over the initial need? The answers to these questions require the worker and client to constantly monitor and evaluate their work as they proceed with the change process.

On completion of the plan, the worker and the client evaluate the results. The first questions are: Are we done? Did it work? Was the need met? If measurable objectives were set, the first question has been answered. If the client no longer experiences the need then the next two questions have been answered. If the need is still there, then the worker and client should evaluate what went wrong and return to an earlier stage of the process, perhaps even back to the beginning. Evaluation as a part of termination will be discussed later in this chapter.

Kinds of Termination

For clients who are successful at achieving their goals, ending their work with the worker signals a resolution of their difficulties and greater independence. It may also trigger anxiety over the ability to succeed without the worker's assistance. For workers leaving an agency for another job or for students graduating from college, the end of an experience in one setting can be accompanied by excitement and anxiety at the prospect of a new phase in their career paths. This represents the ambivalence frequently related to termination.

Because human beings are mortal, it is the nature of all relationships to end. Dwelling on this fact might lead some clients to avoid relationships for fear of the pain or loss associated with the ending. This fear can obscure the need to be free to enjoy relationships with others and go on to other phases in life. Many clients have experienced pain, loss, abandonment, or rejection in some of their significant relationships. Often patterns of loss have been handed down from one generation to the next. Overcoming the results of these experiences may be the central issue that needs to be resolved in the social work process. Thus, termination issues can be a focus of the change process itself. Termination of the worker's involvement is inevitable. Helping clients to successfully terminate is essential to solidifying any change that has taken place. Thus, handling a termination is an important skill for social workers to develop.

Termination is an aspect of social work that is often given inadequate consideration. Endings can be painful for workers as well as for clients. Workers sometimes make decisions about the desired goals of service that prolong the time of service beyond what the client desires.[9] This has resulted in many unplanned terminations (those in which the client fails to keep appointments). According to William Reid, research has shown that:

1. Recipients of brief, time-limited treatment show at least as much durable improvement as recipients of long-term, open-ended treatment.
2. Most of the improvement associated with long-term treatment occurs relatively soon after treatment has begun.
3. Regardless of their intended length, most courses of treatment turn out to be relatively brief.[10]

There is a growing emphasis on short-term service. This service considers the client's desires and expectations in the planning to a greater extent than in long-term service. Plans are much more specific, with specific goals and time frames for reaching those goals. Goals are measurable, making it easier to know when the purpose of the service has been fulfilled, the goals met, and the contract satisfied. The ending is more apt to be planned by the worker and the client rather than the client deciding that the worker's help is no longer needed.

Termination can take place at any point in the process: when the goals set by the worker and client have been reached and the client feels comfortable in carrying out those goals without help from the worker; when clients feel that sufficient help has been given so they can meet the need or deal with the problem on their own; when it becomes apparent that no progress is being made or that the potential for change is poor; or when a worker or an agency does not have the resources needed by the client or does not have the sanction of the agency to deliver the service needed. This last condition may result in a referral, which was discussed in Chapter 10. Sometimes clients terminate because the systems on which they depend are threatened by the possibility of change.

If a worker is leaving an agency, termination activity may result in transfer to another worker within an agency or referral to another agency for continued service. It may result in a decision by the new worker and the client to work on another goal or use another strategy in reaching an elusive goal and thus continue with a new plan of action. However, termination usually results in separation of the client from both the worker and the agency.

Termination is an expectation discussed with clients from the beginning of the work together; it is planned for by the worker and the client together. When a worker senses that the client is not using the help being offered, or when the client is missing appointments or in other ways indicating that termination may be advisable, it is time to discuss the possibility of termination. This is done to maximize the benefit that can come from a planned termination and to minimize feelings of anger and guilt that might interfere with seeking help in the future. Many times what a client wants is someone to talk to about his need. This discussion can lead to a better understanding of the need, identification of resources, or planning what can be done about the need. The client does not always need or want any other interventive activity from a social worker or a social agency. Figure 12.1 shows the place of termination in the social work process.

When the worker-client relationship is terminated because the worker is ending employment or being transferred to a new position, special consideration should be given to the client's feelings. In some cases this is also a good time for the client to terminate with

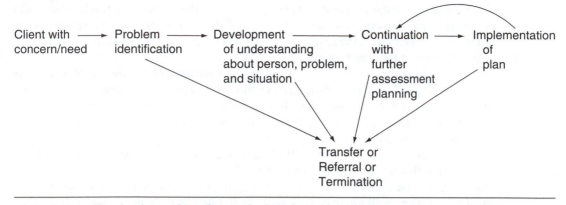

FIGURE 12.1   *Termination and Its Place in the Social Work Process*

the agency as well. At other times, the decision is made to transfer the client to a new worker. The client may be angry because the worker is breaking an agreement. The client may feel deserted or may have a reawakening of old feelings about previous separations. The worker may experience feelings of guilt about leaving the client and breaking the agreement. The worker also may be absorbed in plans for a new job or in the demands of a new situation. When transfer becomes necessary, it is important to recognize and deal with feelings that may impede the continuation of service to the client.

When a worker engages in the termination process with a client because she is leaving her current position, it is important to bring the client's feelings into the open, however painful. Sometimes clients can also deal with previous painful separations in this process. The worker should be prepared to accept the client's anger and resentment and, whenever possible, should help the client accept the new worker. A useful technique is for the worker to introduce the client to the new worker and for all three to discuss the work that has been done and the possibilities for future work. After this session, the worker and the client should have a last session so that they can terminate their relationship.

Whenever a worker takes over a case from a former worker, feelings about termination should be discussed with the individual, family, or group. Clients need time to adjust; if they are rushed, they will not be ready to accept help from the new worker. Beginnings and endings occur together. How the last relationship ended will determine whether unresolved issues will create barriers or negative expectations for the next relationship. Allowing the client to talk through these feelings can be a strong bridge to building a new helping relationship. For this reason, the worker should discuss with a new client any previous experiences the client may have had and his feelings about those experiences.

In order for a social worker to be effective in terminating with clients, she needs to be aware of some blocks to effective termination that arise because of her feelings and attitudes. There may be a tendency for the worker to hang on to clients. This may arise because the worker is reluctant to terminate a relationship that she has enjoyed. Other reasons for hanging on may be that the worker expects more of the client or the situation than is warranted or that she is ambitious and is seeking "the perfect case." Sometimes a worker wants to compensate for what the client may have suffered. Awareness of these feelings and a focus on the client's needs and goals can prevent these blocks to effective termination.

The nature of the worker-client relationship is another factor. Any time a close working relationship develops, both the worker and the client are apt to have strong reactions to termination. When this is the case, more time must be allowed for the termination process so that feelings of loss can be handled.

It should not be assumed that all clients view termination as loss; some, especially those mandated to service, may view termination with relief. Other clients view the work together as a necessary interlude in their lives but are pleased that they have gained understanding and coping skills so they can get on with the business of living without further help from the worker.

Research by Anne E. Fortune, Bill Pearlingi, and Cherie D. Rochell indicates clients can have positive feelings about termination. They can feel pride and a sense of accomplishment in what they have been able to do. This study has limitations because it was carried out with a small group of voluntary practitioners in a small geographic area. Also, case selection may have been limited to those for whom there was success.[11]

Howard Hess and Peg McCartt Hess pointed out differences in termination, depending on context. The nature of the relationship required in the work and the expected ongoing relationships with others who have been a part of the process affect the impact of termination. Hess and Hess discussed the difference between termination of the one-to-one relationship and the formed group, in which the loss is not only of the worker but of other group members.[12] In the family and the friendship group, the only person terminating is the worker. The authors also note the differences in termination when the strategy has been counseling, education, or resource mobilization. The nature of attachment and the impact of termination are different in each of these situations. The content of the termination phase will be different in each situation.

If worker and client have developed the habit of consciously terminating each session together, they have developed a good base on which to conduct the final termination of work together. Summarizing each session—what has been done and what is to be done—gives the client a good sense of the process and how much time there is before the work is completed and termination takes place. Planning termination helps avoid a surprise ending and the feelings of desertion that go with such endings. Evaluating at the end of each session gives the worker an understanding of the client's sense of the work together and allows for corrections so that unplanned or precipitous termination does not take place. What has been done in a small way at the end of each session can then be done in a more complete manner at the end of the work together.

Issues related to diversity need to be included in termination. Individual values and experiences as well as cultural values, attitudes, and beliefs play an important role. The ultimate termination is death, and individual and cultural attitudes and beliefs about death often reflect attitudes and beliefs about termination. The worker should be aware of the stages of termination and be sensitive about individual experiences and about cultural mores.

In many cultures, there are customs, such as gift giving, when termination occurs. Even without this, some clients will want to give the worker a gift as a sign of appreciation. This presents some ethical dilemmas for the worker because the social worker should not benefit from her service to the client except through compensation from her agency or through the financial arrangements that were made ahead of time. Gift giving can also signify "the repayment of a debt" by the client, which would be a misunderstanding of the social work relationship. Expensive gifts should clearly not be accepted. Inexpensive ones might be allowed by an agency's policies. In either case, the worker should discuss the situation with the client and with her supervisor to ensure an ethical outcome.

For individuals at risk, termination can represent a crisis in their quest for power and control over their lives and for acceptance and recognition. Empowerment that was gained during the intervention may be ascribed to the worker, and inner doubts and anxieties about the client's own abilities may arise again. Helping clients solidify their gains and assert and advocate for themselves without the support of the worker are major issues during termination with people who have experienced discrimination or oppression. Clients need to know that the fight against discrimination and oppression is both personal and collective. Efforts to connect clients to groups engaged in this cause should be made during the intervention to ensure continuation of support.

Continued success by clients after termination rests to a great degree on the extent to which the plan was based on clients' strengths and their environments and on building strength in areas in which limitations and barriers exist. Client success also rests on the degree to which the worker helped the client learn new skills while resolving his situation and was able to assist him to experience social work values as a part of the helping relationship and as something integral to his everyday life. This is what represents true social work and differentiates it from other human service professions. If clients feel more valuable as human beings based on inherent worth, if they are able to exercise greater self-determination and control over their lives, and if they can access appropriate resources to meet socially accepted needs, then they have truly been empowered. This means that the social work intervention has been successful not only on a short-term basis but also at a deeper, more significant, and long-term level.

Planned Termination with Individuals

Individual clients may experience termination in a very personal way. They may have derived a great deal of satisfaction from the relationship. They may also be vulnerable to feeling pain, loss, abandonment, or rejection. Helping them to resolve these issues is important in determining how permanent any changes might be. Throughout the intervention, the worker should be aware of the effect of relationships and termination on the client. She should note how clients handle termination in other areas of their lives. Sensitivity to the client's attitude toward termination is fundamental to planning for successful termination.

When the worker has been able to support independence and interdependence instead of dependence, she has already begun to prepare the client for termination and for life without the social worker's involvement. However, clients may want to give credit to the worker for the work that was done. Statements that the client may make can be extremely flattering, such as "You were wonderful. Thank goodness that I found you. I don't know how I could have made it without you." The worker should resist the temptation to accept accolades or credit. To do so will undermine the client's sense of empowerment and the need to recognize who did the work. The social work plan identifies clients as the primary force behind change, and clients deserve credit and recognition when they are successful at achieving their goals and objectives. If they had not done what they needed to do, then no real change would have taken place.

At its worst, crediting the worker with the change is a form of magical thinking in which the client makes the worker "the savior." The worker should quickly dispel the myth that she is the only one who could have helped the client. She should credit the client for his courage in facing his difficulty and for the hard work he did in resolving the situation. If there were things that the worker did that were especially helpful, she should point out that such help is available from other social workers who practice the way she does.

Planned termination with individuals should allow enough time to resolve issues related to feelings of termination. These may be similar to, and as intense as, a grief process. Thus, the worker should plan for at least three or four sessions to work through unresolved issues. In the end, the client should have access to positive feelings and a sense of accomplishment as opposed to feeling abandoned or rejected. Some clients stop meeting rather than face the feelings associated with termination. In these instances, the worker should follow up with the client and offer an opportunity to experience an appropriate termination process. If the client refuses, the worker should at least make a follow-up contact at a later date to ensure that the client is still open to receiving help if needed. Unplanned termination initiated prematurely by clients should be handled similarly, except that clients should be offered a transfer or a referral if it is feasible.

Planned termination can include time-limited services imposed by design, regulations, funding sources, limited resources, or other circumstances. The advent of managed care has resulted in limitations on the amount of services that are reimbursed by insurance companies. Although this is viewed by those companies as a form of efficiency and cost savings, in essence it is rationing services for the benefit of the insurer. Managed care can place social workers in the awkward position of either denying continuation of services when they believe continued service is needed or continuing services without receiving reimbursement. At times, the existence of the agency can be threatened by reduction in revenue. Refusing needed services is a violation of the NASW *Code of Ethics*. Social workers should consider becoming active in organizations that advocate for providing services based on client needs or for decision making on services by those without a financial stake in limiting services. Allowing service decisions to be made by bureaucrats or to be arbitrarily set by diagnosis is not acceptable for clients or social workers.

In the era of managed care, termination is an issue from the onset of service. Social workers need to become proficient in providing brief and time-limited services. Clients are not as likely to invest themselves as significantly in a relationship when termination is an ever-present issue. When there is a significant investment, some form of brief follow-up may be needed to smooth the client's transition. Workers need to develop extensive referral networks for posttermination services. Social workers should be aware of the benefits and rights of clients and ensure that clients are so informed. Workers should be prepared to advocate for needed services and to assist clients in appeals processes and other advocacy actions. Finally, social workers should be open to greater use of natural helpers and nontraditional services, such as self-help and support groups.

Components of Termination

Allen Pincus and Anne Minahan identified three major components of the termination process: disengagement, stabilization of change, and evaluation.[13] As with other aspects of the social work endeavor, these are intermingled in practice and are separated only for purposes of discussion and study.

Disengagement

Endings bring about a cessation of relationships. If relationships have been meaningful, feelings are aroused. An unplanned termination leaves the client to deal with these feelings on her own, which results in a sense of unfinished business. It is assumed that the client is aware that termination will take place when goals have been reached. Nevertheless, when faced with actual termination, the client and the worker should acknowledge the reality of their feelings.

These feelings will vary from situation to situation; however, some common expectations about feelings at termination have been identified. The initial reaction is often one of denial, either of the reality of termination or of the feelings associated with it. Denial is a defense mechanism used to avoid painful feelings. An indication of this mechanism is the phenomenon of flight. This phenomenon is manifested by a client not keeping appointments after termination is discussed. The temptation is for the worker to let the client go and to assume that he wants to deal or not deal with the termination feelings in this manner. However, it is important for the worker to elicit feelings at this point so that client and worker can move through the termination process.

The next stage is usually a period of emotional reaction. Feelings or emotions may arise from fear of loss or the unknown. There may be feelings of sadness or grief over the impending loss as well as anger. There may be a return of feelings associated with old wounds from previous disappointments and separations. There can be regression to old patterns of behavior. Regression may be a client's attempt to say that she is not ready for termination. At this point it is important for the worker to accept the client's feelings and to help her examine these feelings and the fears, anxieties, and past experiences that are the source of the feelings. Acceptance and help in examining feelings enables the client to work through them. In a sense, the client is helped to go through a process of mourning and is enabled to disengage from the relationship in a helpful manner.

Another means of dealing with disengagement is reminiscing about or reviewing what has been done in the work together. Doing this can help clients see the positive aspects of the work together and develop the understanding that growth often has pain associated with it. At this time, workers also should try to minimize any guilt the client may have about the work together.

Clients sometimes introduce new problems as termination nears. The worker and client together need to examine why these new problems have appeared and whether there is a valid reason for continuing the service with a focus on the new problems or the client can work on these problems in other ways.

Clients' feelings about termination vary in intensity and nature. If the intensity of the relationship or the period of time involved has been minimal, the feelings about termination will usually be less than if the relationship has been intense or fairly long. Involuntary clients may be relieved that service is terminating. Clients with feelings of success or satisfaction will have different kinds of feelings about termination than those whose service experience has not been as positive. Clients who have had significant losses or separations in their lives—particularly if they have not had opportunities to deal with feelings about those losses—will have different feelings about separation from clients for whom loss has not been as significant. The client's capacity for independence or need for dependence will also influence feelings. A significant factor in the way a client deals with termination is what is happening in his life at that point in time. If a client is called on to cope with many changes or other demands, termination may either be more difficult or may come as a relief.

The social worker needs to develop skill in disengaging from relationships with clients. This should be done with consideration for, and sensitivity to, a client's feelings and needs. A useful technique for disengagement is to taper off involvement with the client as feelings are dealt with and other work of termination is completed. Appointments may be set further apart or more emphasis placed on what the client is to do for herself.

The worker needs to develop self-awareness about her own reactions to separation and loss. If the worker has difficulty with these tasks, she will be less able to help the client deal with the tasks of separation. The worker may wonder how to react to the intense feelings of the client that may arise in the process of termination. These feelings may be related not only to loss or grief but also to dissatisfaction about what the worker and client have been able to do together. Most people tend to ignore or downplay feelings that are uncomfortable. If, because of their own discomfort, workers do not adequately encourage the client's feelings about termination and about their work together, they will fail to allow the client to learn management of feelings in coping with life tasks.

The work of disengagement is related to the immediate social work situation and to past and future losses of the client and social worker. In helping the client disengage, the worker is helping the client deal with past losses and unresolved feelings about those losses. The client is being provided with coping mechanisms for dealing with future loss, with understandings for dealing with grief and loss that are part of human functioning. To bypass or minimize the disengagement process is to lose an opportunity for client growth.

Stabilization of Change

In helping a client deal with the feelings of termination and disengagement from the relationship, the client and the worker often review what has happened in the work together. This is useful in stabilizing the change that has taken place and helps clients understand how they have grown and what has led to the growth. This gives clients guidelines on how future problems might be approached and dealt with. It enables clients to know they have resources that can help them to make it on their own and what those resources are.

One way to work on stabilization of change is to review what has occurred. The time together should be seen as one step, an important step, of the growth that results in better coping with life tasks. This view implies there are other steps to be taken, not with the worker but through new relationships or in ongoing responses to life situations. Continued growth is one way of stabilizing the change that has taken place. Worker and client discuss the next steps and how the client can go about taking these steps. They then plan ways of obtaining needed supports and resources the client can use in taking these steps.

Together, the worker and the client explore possible ways for dealing with situations similar to the one that brought the client to the agency. They consider how new learning can be transferred to other situations. They may identify other resources in the client's environment that would be useful in coping with life situations. These may be natural helpers or other community systems, such as recreation programs, groups of people with similar concerns, and the like. These resources can be substitute or replacement support systems.

Usually, the worker offers the client the option of returning to the agency if future problems become overwhelming. It is important for the client to know that the agency makes the service possible and that even if the worker is no longer available, the agency will provide someone else to help. The client needs to be aware that workers come and go but that the agency continues to provide the service. This awareness is particularly important for the client who may be terminating service against the advice of the worker.

Stabilization of change can be encouraged by discussing possible goals for further growth and resources that can be used to enable growth. This discussion can examine how change took place as the worker and client worked together. The process that was used can be examined, and the worker can maximize the client's understanding of this process. Through the work of stabilizing the change, the worker supports within the client a sense of accomplishment and competence. The client's fears are recognized and examined, and suggestions are made about how to deal with them.

Stabilization of the change is an important stage in growth and change. Without conscious efforts to carry out the tasks involved in stabilization, the client's capacity to sustain the desired change may be lessened.

Evaluation

The third component of termination is evaluation. Evaluation is an ongoing part of the social work endeavor and a particularly important component of the termination phase. As the worker and client engage in evaluation during termination, the focus is on the goal or goals set in the plan of action and on the client's need or needs, identified in the assessment process. The major question to be answered is: Did we accomplish what we set out to do? If the goal was achieved and the need met, then the purpose of the service has been accomplished. If the goal was met but the need remains troublesome, then the goal may not have been the right goal or other goals must be met as well.

When considering the outcome of service, it is useful to look at the process of reaching the goal and identify what has and has not been useful. Any unexpected consequences of the work together should be noted. This aspect of evaluation is useful for both worker and client in that it helps the client better understand how to meet needs in the future. It helps the worker gain greater understanding of the helping process and of means for working with clients.

The worker's openness to evaluating what has happened involves a certain amount of risk because the worker's mistakes and limitations may come to light. The client may be overly critical or display undue dissatisfaction, which may be one way the client expresses negative feelings related to termination. The worker needs to accept these feelings without becoming defensive and carefully examine with the client the negative feelings and sort out current feelings from past feelings of abandonment or unrealistic dissatisfaction. Perhaps one of the reasons workers have not put sufficient emphasis on the termination process is that it is a time for examining the performance of the worker. This is a threatening experience but one that is essential for good social work practice.

Competence in guiding the termination process is one way of influencing client satisfaction over the work together. The client reviews what has happened, acknowledges improvement or progress, discovers his part in the process and how the experience may be transferred to other life experiences, and assesses how he can continue his growth.

The social work endeavor is terminated through the interwoven activities aimed at disengagement, stabilization of change, and evaluation. Through these activities the client is helped to deal with feelings so that these feelings will not inhibit future social functioning. The client is readied to continue to grow and to cope with activities of living and with the environment and its expectations.

Summary

This chapter has considered evaluation as an ongoing part of the social work process. It has discussed various kinds of evaluation and their usefulness. The use of research tools in the evaluative process was explained. Evaluation during each stage of the change process was discussed. Evaluation is a skill that all social workers must possess and a process that all social workers must engage in if they are to adhere to the ethical principles of the social work profession.

The last stage of the social work process is termination. It is planned from the beginning of the process. Termination may lead to transfer of the client to another worker. There are three components of termination work: disengagement, stabilization of change, and evaluation. Social workers who engage the client in a well-thought-out termination process strengthen the client's capacity for social functioning in the future. They also enhance their own professional capacity through evaluating with the client what led to the desired outcome. Termination is an integral part of the total social work process.

Questions

1. How do the change process and single-system research design fit with each other?
2. What are some ethical concerns that social workers might have with respect to the use of the traditional experimental method and with other research designs?
3. Discuss your feeling about losing a relationship with someone who is important to you.
4. Discuss some of the reasons clients may terminate prematurely.
5. How can a worker appropriately deal with issues during termination?

Suggested Readings

Bloom, Martin, Fischer, Joel, and Orme, John G. *Evaluating Practice: Guidelines for the Accountable Professional,* 6th ed. Boston: Allyn and Bacon, 2009.

Miley, Karla Krogsrud, O'Melia, Michael, and DuBois, Brenda L. *Social Work Practice: An Empowering Approach,* 6th ed. Boston: Allyn and Bacon, 2009 (Chapter 16, "Integrating Gains").

Mizrahi, Terry and Davis, Larry E., Eds. *Encyclopedia of Social Work,* 20th ed. Washington, DC: NASW Press, 2008 ("Best Practices," "Evidence Based Practice," "Program Evaluation," "Qualitative Research," "Quantitative Research," "Research," "Single System Designs," "Termination").

Sheafor, Bradford W., and Horejsi, Charles R. *Techniques and Guidelines for Social Work Practice,* 8th ed. Boston: Allyn and Bacon, 2008 (Chapter 14).

Tripodi, Tony. *A Primer on Single-Subject Design for Clinical Social Workers.* Washington, DC: NASW Press, 1994.

Weinbach, Robert W. *Evaluating Social Work Services and Programs.* Boston: Allyn and Bacon, 2005.

Yegidis, Bonnie L., and Weinrich, Robert W. *Research Methods for Social Workers,* 6th ed. Boston: Allyn and Bacon, 2009.

York, Reginald O. *Evaluating Human Services: A Practical Approach for the Human Service Professional.* Boston: Allyn and Bacon, 2009.

part IV

Multiperson Systems and Good Practices in Generalist Practice

Part Four continues the social work process by examining generalist practice with families, groups, organizations, and communities. Focusing on each of these systems in separate chapters is done for educational purposes only. This work is not separated when practicing within a generalist framework. In the concept of generalist practice using an ecosystems strengths approach presented in this text, the social worker is free to work with individuals, families, groups, organizations, or communities as client systems or as units of attention in the change process whenever it is appropriate to do so. They are separated here to give the student a better understanding of the use of the change process when working with each system. The term *client system* refers to an individual, a family, or a system that has either sought help or is served by the agency. *Unit of attention* refers to the focal system or the system or systems on which the change activity is focused. The unit of attention may be the client system, a system in the environment, or the interaction between the client system and a system in the environment. Part Four ends with an examination of models used in social work practice and good practices in various settings.

The social worker is often called on to interact with more than one person at the same time, particularly when working from a generalist approach. This happens when the client is a family, a small group, an institution, an agency, or a community. When the agency, institution, or community system is the client, the interaction is usually with individuals or groups of people within the system. When the focus is on the development of new resources, task groups are usually involved. In using an ecosystems strengths approach, the worker may interact with more than one person at a time when working with systems within the client's ecosystem, such as members of the client's family. The social worker works with more than one person at the same time when she is functioning on a team or a case conference or as a member of a committee or a planning group. These groups can have a fact-finding, evaluation, policy-making, planning, education, problem-solving, or therapeutic purpose; they can be casual, appointed, ongoing, or self-formed. Multiperson interaction is used when people share a common task or purpose and when the situation does not lend itself to one-to-one interaction. Situations that often call for the use of multiperson interaction include the following:

1. Those in which individuals cannot reach their goal except by working with others (e.g., when a group of persons works for some environmental change)
2. Those in which individuals cannot function on a one-to-one basis with a professional person but can function with peers (e.g., a group of delinquent adolescents)
3. Those in which the group has considerable influence over the individual (e.g., the family influence on individual functioning)
4. Those in which the task or purpose needs the contribution of several persons (e.g., the interdisciplinary team)
5. Those in which persons are faced with similar needs or concerns (e.g., parents of developmentally disabled children)
6. Those in which working with systems in the client's ecosystem is more effective when it takes place with all of the system or with significant parts of the system (e.g., family, parents, etc.)

Much of what was discussed in Chapter 7 about one-to-one interaction also applies to family and group interaction and interaction with individuals in organizations and the community. Relationships between individuals are important for the facilitation of the tasks to be accomplished. Family or group process and task accomplishment are also enhanced by effective communication. Relationships and communications become more complex when additional people are involved; in this case the transactional nature of the interaction must receive greater attention. In effect, the interview becomes family or group discussion. Thus, many of the techniques useful in facilitating the interview are also useful in facilitating family or group discussion.

In using an ecosystems strengths approach, the worker must keep in mind that clients hold memberships in many different groups that are a part of their ecosystems. As a result, the worker may be directly involved in multiperson interaction when she works with systems in the client's ecosystem. In addition, she will need to assist the client in developing necessary skills in multiperson interaction as he comes into contact with various systems in his environment. This does not mean that the client needs to become skilled in leading groups or in working with families. It does mean that the client probably will find himself in groups and in interactions within his family system on a daily basis. When he does, he will need to know how to meet the needs of others while also meeting his own needs. This is often the very crux of the matter that brings the client to the agency for help. Relationships with others in the ecosystem may be out of balance or in conflict. Or relationships important to meeting needs may not be functioning in an effective way. These relationships may be one-to-one or multiperson. The client needs to have mutually beneficial interactions in both cases.

When social workers work with multiperson systems, they come into direct contact with interactions and transactions among people. Chapter 7 covered the worker's interaction with individuals. In working with individuals, the worker is a part of the interactional system. Thus, she is responsible for her part of the interaction. The worker needs to be aware of the direct influence she may have in these instances because she is a major part of the interaction. When working with families, groups, organizations, and the community, the worker is a part of a much larger interactional system. Much of the interaction is not between the worker and individual members but among the members of the multiperson system. In fact, there is a great deal of interaction that goes on among members of multiperson systems outside of the time when the worker is meeting with them. As a result, although the worker may influence the interaction, her influence is much more indirect because she cannot control the actions of others.

Because the worker may not be directly involved with all interactions among members, she usually has less influence on what is happening in working with multiperson systems. For the most part, the appropriate role for her is that of facilitator. The questions pertaining to this role are: What should the worker facilitate? When should she observe and when should she intervene? What should happen when conflict or difficulties arise? The answers to these questions are heavily influenced by values. The worker must always be aware of the experiences she brings with her from her own family and from groups and organizations and the community to which she belongs. These experiences, especially those with her own family, are value laden. Because families are conduits for culture and values, it is important for the worker to respect the values of the members of the multiperson system with whom she is working while also being aware of her own values and those of her profession.

While being aware of the impact of culture and values in relationships, the worker can facilitate the development of relationship skills. Typically, the worker has knowledge and skills in communication, facilitating growth and change, conflict resolution, and behavioral change. Teaching these skills to the family or group is essential to improving individual, family, and group functioning. The use of these skills within a framework of social work values and within the cultural systems to which the family or group members belong can provide a basic foundation for meeting the needs of individuals, families, and groups.

Chapter 13 focuses on generalist social work practice with families. It continues this examination of multiperson interaction and discusses the use of the change process in working with families, including assessment, planning, direct and indirect actions, and evaluation and termination.

Chapter 14 focuses on generalist social work practice with small groups as multiclient systems. It includes discussions of group purpose and assessment, planning, actions, and evaluation and termination with small groups.

Chapter 15 focuses on generalist social work practice with macrosystems. It begins with a discussion of macropractice and social justice. The chapter includes descriptions of the process of conducting a needs assessment, program planning and resource development, changing organizations from within, and the social worker as a group member in working with macrosystems. The chapter concludes with a look at community change actions, including involving influentials, networking, cause advocacy, and community organization practice.

Chapter 16 presents models of practice that are typically used in social work and good practices for working with populations or in settings that are typical for the generalist social worker.

13 | *Generalist Practice with Families*

Learning Expectations

1. Understanding of the importance of working with the family in generalist social work practice.
2. Knowledge of the role and function of the generalist social worker with the family and with the family's ecosystem.
3. Understanding of the nature of the generalist social worker's interaction with the family system in the various forms the family takes in U.S. society.
4. Knowledge of working with families as client systems and as the unit of attention in the change process.
5. Knowledge of assessment, planning, action, and evaluation and termination with families.

Nearly everyone starts out life in a family. Families may look quite different from the nuclear family that has been the image of what a family is for white society in the United States. The absence of a family experience can be devastating unless a suitable replacement is provided. The family is the first and most important multiperson interaction we have.

A basic assumption guiding this consideration of multiperson interaction is that the fundamental issue for all human beings is answering the question: Can I be an individual and still be loved and accepted by others? The tension between acting on one's own needs while preserving relationships with others is basic to human relations. Initially, this tension is played out in the family between the young child and his parents. The child vacillates between the search for autonomy and independence and the desire for meaningful attachment. When parents successfully communicate the message that the child is loved and accepted unconditionally for himself, then attachment is secure and provides a base from which the child can establish individual autonomy. When the message is something else or if it does not get through, then doubts begin to occur and self-confidence is more tenuous.

In simple terms, if the answer to the preceding question is "yes," then the child can internalize this and feel more secure about loving and accepting himself. This is the essence of self-image, self-esteem, self-worth, and self-respect. What does one think or feel about oneself? If the answer to the preceding question was a conditional "yes" (I love you if . . . or I love you when . . .), then the child begins to look outside himself for the approval of others and for his value and worth. If the answer was "no," then the child may conclude that he is not worthwhile or may reject others as the source of influence on his behavior.

This last circumstance is what happens when children are abused or neglected. These children often have very low self-worth. They may learn to treat others as objects just as they were treated as objects. In the first case the person says to himself, "If my parent(s) do not love me, who will? I must be unlovable." In the second case, the person says, "If my parents do not care about me, why should I care about anyone else?" This is the reasoning of most people who go to prison, many of whom were abused or neglected as children. These individuals conclude that acting on self-interest is the only way to survive.

Whatever our experience was as a child, we carry it with us outside of the family and reflect it in our expectations of ourselves and others. This fact is fundamental to multiperson interaction and affects the client, the social worker, and the people in the systems with whom we have contact. Understanding who we are means understanding the impact our family had on us. Before undertaking work with clients, especially with families, the social worker should first have insight into her own background and how it influences her perceptions of herself, her clients, and her world. Self-awareness and a healthy self-esteem are necessities in developing oneself as a competent professional social worker.

When working with individuals, families, and groups, it is important to keep in mind how the client's self-image and relationships with others have been shaped by family experiences. Working with clients in families or groups is an opportunity to help them to find a positive response to the question of acceptance and individuality. In fact, the social work value of belief in the inherent value and worth of every human being represents a positive response to this question. Thus, if the social worker is successful in communicating this value to others and in getting the family or group to experience it, then individuals can reexperience the question of self-worth in a more positive way. A more positive experience can have a profound impact on a client's future experiences.

Understanding the influence of family on self-esteem and on relationships with others is fundamental to assessment and intervention with individuals, families, and groups. The ways families influence individual development and relationships provide a key to what the worker needs to focus on in multiperson interaction. It is important to view the family as a system and understand its structure, functioning, and development or history. It is also important to understand the needs of each member and the system as a whole. Examining strengths and challenges provides a basis on which to build strategies for change.

When the social worker uses social work values to guide her work with families and groups, the answers to the questions raised about the facilitator role in the introduction to Part Four become more clear. The worker should facilitate interactions in families and groups that reflect dignity and respect for each person. She should support this type of interaction when it occurs and intervene when it does not. She should be aware of differences in culture and values and respect those differences. She should help members to work out their conflicts with respect and with the recognition that each person needs to have a voice in the final resolution. Win-lose situations will inevitably produce losers. If one feels like a loser or belongs to a family or group in which others feel like losers, then everyone in the system will eventually feel this impact. Win-win situations support all parties in having their needs met. Being open about the values that social work espouses reduces the chances that the worker will impose values or manipulate. The social worker supports valuing human beings and treating each other with dignity and respect whether she is working with a client or with members of the client's ecosystem.

This chapter will examine the family as a multiperson client system. This is followed by consideration of variations in family form. Finally, the bulk of the chapter will examine how the phases of the change process apply to working with families. Assessment, planning, actions, and evaluation and termination with families will be examined.

The Family as a Multiperson Client System

Some approaches to working with the family as a system are summarized in Chapter 16. It is beyond the scope of this book to consider any of these in depth; rather, what will be presented about working with the family as a system will be understandings and principles of action that enable the worker-family interactional process to develop and facilitate use of the change process. The first step in working with families is the development of a social history of the family unit (see Table 13.1) so the worker gains the necessary understanding of the family. The family is seen as a system using knowledge of social systems, small-group processes, and family structure and functioning. The family group has many of the same characteristics as the small group (see Chapter 14). The family is a special small group—one that is usually intergenerational, exists over an extended period of time, and has very strong bonds because of the amount of time members have spent together and the strength of the influence a family has on its members. The family has its own developmental process that is related to the developmental stages of the family members.

An important principle is that a caring, understanding relationship be developed with the total family unit, not only with certain members. The social worker must recognize that the family is a well-established system. The worker should not become entangled with that system; neither should she take sides with individual family members. The contribution of all family members is sought and valued, and each family member is respected as an individual.

Another principle is that responsibility for the situation is to be owned by the family. It is important to gradually confront families with the realities of the situation—that is, with the responsibility of the whole family for family-related problems. This can be done by conveying an exploratory attitude toward the presented situation. It can help if the worker explains to the family that problems are often an indication of a blockage in the growth of the family or may be a sign that family members are not meeting needs or having their needs met, either within the family or in interactions with the environment. Anxiety can often be relieved by clarifying the situation. Most important, the family needs to understand that the helping situation is a safe place in which to work on meeting its needs. By demonstrating a nonblaming attitude that respects the rights of all family members, the worker provides them with a model of how they might begin to work together on the family's needs. The worker helps the family take responsibility for the situation as a total system. The family is then expected to develop and carry out plans for meeting unmet needs for the family as a system, for individual members of the family, and between the family (or members) and the environment. The worker's role is to enable the family in this process.

A related principle is that blame and guilt are to be avoided because they place responsibility on specific members. In using an ecosystems strengths approach, the worker helps the family realize that unmet needs may be related to interactions within the family system and to its interactions with the environment. The worker helps the family find ways of rebalancing interactions and transactions. The influence of environmental factors and the need to develop skill in meeting family needs are also stressed, when appropriate.

When working with the family, the worker encourages members to speak for themselves. She discusses with the family how the work will be done and how communication is to take place. This should be done in a way that is sensitive to the culture and value system of the family. Each member is given the feeling that this is a safe place to work on concerns. Attention is paid to the physical setting in which the work takes place. If young children are involved, provision is made for them to move around and play quietly. The expectations and concerns of each member are clarified so that each understands those of other members.

The worker seeks to help the family develop consensus about the nature of the needs or concerns within the context of their culture and diversity. He helps the family develop an agreement among the members as well as with the worker about what needs to be done and who should do it. He uses an educational approach when members of the family lack understanding and skill necessary for effective family functioning. These skills include communication, problem solving, conflict resolution, positive reinforcement, cognitive restructuring, and the like. Skill in dealing with resistance to change is most important because families often have entrenched ways of functioning that are not only the source of difficulties but also are very hard for individual members to give up.

Variations in Family Form

When working with the family, social workers often encounter difficulty because they either are not aware of or have not resolved some of their own concerns and feelings about their families of orientation (the families in which they grew up). Workers may also make unfounded assumptions about the functioning of families based on their personal experiences. Thus, an important prerequisite to working with family groups is recognition and resolution of how the worker has been affected by her own family.

Often the assumption is made that a family consists of two parents and two or more children. In contemporary American society this is often not the case. Many couples choose to remain childless; some parents have multiple divorces; some have children outside of marriage; more couples are living longer after their children have left home; and the number of single-parent families, families with grandparents raising grandchildren, and blended families is growing. Social workers need to adapt models for work with families to these varied situations. Couple or marital therapy can provide a basis for working with a family made up of only a husband and wife. When working with older persons, either as couples alone or with their adult children and their families, consideration must be given to the developmental tasks of the later years. Role reversal of parents and adult children is to be avoided. Unresolved or poorly resolved issues from the past may need to be dealt with. Two tasks that often are important for families with older persons are (1) to help the family find and use community resources that will allow older persons to live in the least restrictive environment possible and (2) to help families maintain supportive, helpful relationships that do not overburden any family member.

When working with single-parent or blended families, it is important to consider the influence of the absent parent. Different concerns may be present if the absent parent is dead, a divorce has taken place, or there has never been a marriage. The father or mother may be the custodial parent, or there may be a joint-custody agreement. When working with the single-parent family, it is particularly important to consider role overload and the needs of the single parent. There may be unresolved feelings or issues resulting from death or divorce. Inappropriate expectations of family members may be present. Children may be filling the role of the absent parent in a way that places too much stress or responsibility on the child. This type of family often has a need for supportive community resources.

Blended families present special challenges for the social worker. The **blended family** is one in which the parents have had previous marriages or relationships and have children from these marriages or relationships. There may be children from the current marriage or union, along with children from other relationships. Some of the children may be "half siblings." Everyone in the family has a "step" relationship with at least one other member. Some of the children may leave to visit their other biological parent. Some children may come to visit their noncustodial parent. All of this can be very confusing for the family as well as the worker. One of the fundamental issues that all blended families face is how to adjust to living together as a family, given all of these various types of relationships. Most second marriages fail because family members are not able to adjust. Thus, the work to be done generally revolves around the development of appropriate relationships in the face of what are often difficult circumstances. It is especially important that children be assisted in accepting their parents' decisions regarding divorce and remarriage. The work also should include helping the family to restructure itself around the current reality and to adapt its communication and functioning to meet each member's needs.

Some of the families that social workers work with may be seen as multiproblem or chaotic families. Child abuse, spousal abuse, and substance abuse are often what bring these families to the social agency. These families usually do not come to social workers voluntarily but are ordered by the court or some other authority to seek service. When working in these difficult situations, a first step must be the development of a relationship based on trust of the worker. To do this, the worker must be consistent and flexible and avoid any type of retaliation. The worker must be honest with the family about why they are there and what the consequences of lack of cooperation may be. Concern and empathy expressed in a nonjudgmental manner are very important. In many of these cases, the worker will find a history of difficulties that goes back to previous generations. In addition, the worker will generally find individuals who are unable to get their needs met in socially acceptable ways or who simply do not know how to get their needs met. Often the family's interactions with its ecosystem are limited or fraught with conflict. These families often need help in setting priorities and developing skills of social functioning. Their communication skills may be limited. It is most important that these families develop a sense of competency.

The worker must understand the differences in family functioning and structure within different cultural groups. When working with families from a minority cultural group, workers should not presume an understanding of family function until they have checked out with the family how it operates within its cultural group. Usually, meeting with families in their homes and using short-term, action-oriented modes is a successful approach. The worker helps the family work out its own solution in a manner that is supportive of the extended family and immediate ethnic community system. Often, work with minority group families involves helping them deal with the external dominant society system and its institutions. This is when an ecosystems strengths approach is especially beneficial. Advocacy or mediation with individuals, groups, and institutions within the majority culture may be needed. An important goal when working with all families, but particularly with families who have experienced discrimination, is to enable the family and its members to take control of their own lives and work toward changing their situations by influencing the transactions with their ecosystems. (Enabling as a practice strategy was discussed in Chapter 10.)

The social worker needs to develop understanding of the various forms families take in our society. Workers need to develop skill in assessing a family and its situation and then creatively developing means for working with the family. Skill is necessary in interacting with the family so as to provide the needed information and to enable participation in the planning and work necessary for need fulfillment and enhanced social functioning.

Families that are biracial or multiracial have increased over the past several decades and will continue to increase as the United States becomes a more multicultural, multiethnic, and multiracial society. Some of these families are produced by biracial couples. Others are a product of couples who adopt children of another race. In some cases these are children from foreign adoption. Despite becoming more common, biracial and multiracial families face the same kinds of prejudice and discrimination as families and children of color. Some of these families find that they are not accepted by either culture or racial group. The children may experience these same attitudes. Biracial parents need to bolster their child's self-image and self-esteem in order to withstand these negative attitudes. Social workers need to support these families in fighting and coping with the consequences of negative attitudes and actions. Social workers must stand up and fight prejudice, discrimination, and oppression in all its forms.

Families with same-sex partners are a special form of family that has gained greater recognition as people who are gay and lesbian have advocated for legal status as couples. Children in these families may be a product of prior heterosexual relationships, adoption, surrogate mothers, or artificial insemination. In heterosexual families, roles are often assigned by gender and culture. For same-sex couples, there is a need to establish a communication system that can be used to discuss the roles that each partner will take or how these roles will be shared. Egalitarian heterosexual couples have this same need. In many cases, discussing each day who will do what tasks—such as cooking, child care, errands, housework, and the like—is necessary. Same-sex couples and their children often face a great deal of prejudice and discrimination. Children in same-sex families need assistance from their parents in establishing healthy identities that can withstand these negative social attitudes, along with positive descriptions of their family and family members. For example, in a lesbian family, the child might be encouraged to see himself as having two mothers. It is important that he see this as a strength and that he feel he is just as worthwhile as a child of a heterosexual couple. Again, social workers need to provide support for these families to counteract and cope with the consequences of negative attitudes and actions from society. Social workers must be advocates and fight prejudice, discrimination, and oppression in all its forms, regardless of personal values and beliefs.

Finally, the worker assesses the strengths of the family and of the systems in the family's environment. There is a tendency to see families that are different from the traditional nuclear family as being inferior. In reality, all families have strengths, regardless of their structure, function, development, ethnicity, or culture. Even chaotic families are able to provide for most of the needs of their members. There is also a tendency to focus on what is missing rather than what is already there. If the worker and the family are able to see the strengths of the family system and its ecosystem, then growth and change can be built on these strengths and on the transactions within the ecosystem instead of undertaking a major overhaul of the whole system. If people decide to make a change, they need to do so from a position of strength, not a position of weakness. It is more likely that change will occur and be sustained if it is based on existing strengths the system already possesses. It is up to the worker to identify and point out the strengths when the family is not able to do so.

The Change Process with Families

Most often, the initial request for social work services involves contact with an individual or a family subsystem (marital, parental, parent-child, or sibling). Later, the work may be expanded to include the entire family or certain subsystems in the family. The initial request for family work is often with subsystems, such as a parent-child concern. In this text, family work is work that is focused on any part of the family system. Receiving an initial request to work with an entire family is not as common for most workers, although in some settings (such as child welfare) it may be more frequent.

The worker and the client system may decide that it is best to provide service to the family as a whole or with subsystems. This process was discussed in Chapter 8, along with the indications and counterindications for working with the family (see Table 8.1). The family may agree to become the client system or it may be designated as such by the referral source (such as a court system). In some instances, the family or a subsystem or a specific member may be the unit of attention in the change process while the client system continues to be an individual (or another subsystem). In these instances, the worker works with the client to change her interaction with the family (or certain members). She works with the family on behalf of the client to influence changes that are needed. In working with families, the worker uses the same phases of the change process that were described in Chapters 8 through 12. Assessment is followed by planning and action. Evaluation takes place throughout the process and at the completion of the plan. Termination takes place when services end.

Assessment with Families

Assessment with families is similar to the assessment described in Chapter 8. The worker identifies needs and concerns and makes assumptions about the nature of the need or concern and about potential strengths and resources in the family ecosystem. Information is selected and collected that may or may not support these assumptions. The worker analyzes the available information to understand family in environment and to build a foundation for change based on the strengths of the family and resources in the ecosystem. If the client system is the family, then the primary assessment document is the family social history, which uses relevant portions of the individual social history to understand individual members. If the client system is an individual and the family is the unit of attention, then the individual social history is the primary assessment document, and relevant portions of the family social history are used to understand the family.

When the client is a multiperson system, the worker must understand not only the persons who are members of the system but also the subsystems that exist within the system and the system itself. This includes understanding the relationships among the individuals and subsystems. Social systems theory provides one means for describing multiperson systems. All social systems have structural, functional, and developmental aspects. An analogy from photography helps to differentiate these three aspects. Structure may be seen as a snapshot; it describes the parts and their relationship to one another at a given point in time. Functioning may be seen as the movie; functioning describes the nature of the process of the system. Development may be seen as time-lapse photography; development describes stages of family functioning and is also concerned with roots and history and with significant past events in the life of the system.

The family is the system most apt to influence the functioning of the individual; it is the primary system responsible for providing for needs of individuals. Challenges to individual functioning often arise from family functioning, past or present. Often, without change in the family system, the needs of individuals cannot be provided for and the challenges that the individual faces cannot be met. To bring about this change in the family system, it is necessary to understand the family as a social system. Knowing about an individual's place in his family system is also often necessary for understanding that individual. When the change needed is in transactions among members of the family system, the family may be either the unit of attention or the client system. The social worker determines the family system's strengths, motivation, capacity, and opportunity for change and engages the family system in the helping process. The family goes through the process of becoming a client.

Just as the social history is the assessment document for working with individuals, so the family social history is the assessment document for working with the family system. (See Table 13.1 for a family schema.) The family schema contains four parts: (1) necessary identifying information, (2) a description of the family as a system, (3) the identification of concerns and needs of the family system, and (4) identification of the strengths and challenges of the family system and the environment for meeting needs.

TABLE 13.1 *Schema for Development of a Social History: Family*

 I. Identifying Information (as needed by agency)
   A. Names and birth dates of family members, dates of death
   B. Dates of marriage, dates of previous marriages
   C. Religion, race, cultural background
   D. Language spoken in the home
   E. Date of first contact, referred by whom

 II. The Family as a System (note the strengths, resources, and challenges for each section)
   A. Family structure
      1. Identify all persons within the functioning family system. Include members of extended family and nonrelated persons if they function as part of the system. Describe each person using appropriate parts of "Schema for Development of a Social History: Individual" (Table 8.2).
      2. Subsystems—Describe the relationships and functioning of the marital, parental, sibling, and parent-child subsystems or other subsystems.
      3. Family cohesiveness—Describe the manner in which the family maintains its system, boundary, and relatedness. Include the issue of connectedness and separateness among family members, specification of family rules and norms, and emotional climate.
      4. The family's environment—Describe the family's:
         a. Living situation
         b. Socioeconomic status
         c. Nature of community or neighborhood and the family's relationship with the community or neighborhood. Include community organizations and institutions important for the family and the nature of the relationship with these. Describe community and neighborhood resources and responsibilities and impingements for this family in this community.
         d. Extended family: involvement with; significant persons in the extended family; strength of the influence of this family system; and resources, responsibility, and impingements from it.
   B. Family functioning
      1. Communication patterns
      2. Decision-making patterns

(continued)

TABLE 13.1 *(continued)*

     3. Role performance
        a. Work and housekeeping standards and practices
        b. Parenting and child-care standards and practices
        c. System member support; growth encouragement, care, and concern
     4. Family's customary adaptive and coping mechanisms
     5. Construct an eco-map for the family. (See Figure 8.1 as example)
  C. Family development—history
     1. Roots, influence of cultural group and previous generations on the family system
     2. Significant event in the life of the family
     3. Developmental stage of family life
     4. Construct a genogram (See Figure 13.1)

III. The Concern or Need
  A. Why did this family come to the agency? What service is requested?
  B. Needs of individual family members (See Table 8.2)
  C. Needs of subsystems within the family. (Particular attention should be paid to the marital system and the parental system.) Identify resources and other assistance or change needed for appropriate functioning.
  D. Needs of the family system. Consider how the needs of individuals and subsystems impact on the family system. Also consider environmental responsibilities, expectations, and any diversity factors that impact on the family as a system. Identify blocks to the family system's meeting these needs.

IV. Strengths and Challenges for Meeting Needs
  A. What does this family want to happen as a result of the service provided?
  B. What are the family's ideas, interests, and plans that are relevant to the service?
  C. What is the family's motivation for using the service or for change?
  D. What is the family's capacity for coping and change? What might impinge?
  E. What are the family's resources for change (internal to the system)?
  F. What are the environmental resources, responsibilities, and impingements on this family that could support or mitigate against change?
  G. Are there any other factors that affect the family system's motivation, capacity, or opportunity for change?
  H. Are the system's and the environment's expectations realistic for this family?
  I. What are the strengths and challenges for family in situation as they relate to meeting need?

In studying the structure of the family, it is useful first to understand each family member in considerable depth. Use of appropriate parts of Table 8.2 (a schema for an individual social history) would be a helpful tool for development of such understanding. The family should be considered as a system. System members are those persons who have stronger relationships among themselves than with other persons. The boundary of the family—the separation of the family from the environment—should be drawn so as to include other significant persons and reflect the family's view of itself.

Thus, the family system may include some members of the extended family who may or may not be living in the home, such as a grandparent or an aunt. It may include an unrelated person living in the home or a neighbor. The children who have left the home for whatever reason need to be considered, depending on the nature of their functioning with the family system. Attention should be paid to absent family members—those who have died or left the family through divorce. Their influence on the family system and its functioning should be ascertained. The determination of who is in a family system is particularly difficult in the case of a blended family. Often in blended families, custody and visitation of children from previous marriages creates a changing mix of individuals and relationships, which results in a state of flux. In addition, relationships between stepparents and stepchildren and between stepsiblings may be tenuous or conflicted. These family relationships may be even more complicated by multiple divorces, live-in partners, and children born out of wedlock.

Another part of the structure of the family is its subsystems—the marital, the parental, the sibling, and the parent-child subsystems. The marital subsystem includes the husband and wife or couple as partners. Their relationship should be described in terms of separation from each partner's family of origin and the ability of each partner to support and validate the other partner. The parental subsystem includes the mother and father or couple and their interactions as parents or stepparents. The understanding of the sibling subsystem is concerned with how the children relate to one another. The parent-child subsystem is intergenerational in nature; of particular concern is how limits of authority and responsibility are drawn between the generations.[1] Other subsystems may exist in a family, and these should be identified and the nature of relationships described. Ann Hartman and Joan Laird pointed out that an intergenerational perspective is very helpful in developing understanding of the family system, which can be aided by the use of a genogram.[2]

A third consideration in describing family structure is cohesiveness. This binds the family together. It is the emotional or feeling tone of the family, the we-ness of the family, the connectedness of family members with one another. Healthy family relationships allow for both connectedness and separateness.[3] The mechanisms for both connectedness and separateness are described. Family rules and norms (the way this family does things or behaves) are means of expressing cohesiveness. Description of what is allowed and under what circumstances is another means of discovering the interrelatedness of family members.

The family system is part of a larger environment. That environment has expectations for the family, which involve the functioning of the family as a system internally and responsibility toward other systems in the environment. In a society of cultural diversity, there are often conflicting expectations that should be identified. Impacts of prejudice and discrimination because of family diversity should be identified. It is important to determine the nature and extent of the influence of systems, such as church, school, cultural group, extended family, and the like, that impinge on the family or have expectations of responsibility for the family. It is also useful to identify environmental systems that may be resources to the family. As one way of gathering this information, Hartman and Laird developed the technique of constructing an eco-map.[4]

Important features to consider regarding family functioning are the communication patterns, the manner in which decisions are made, and the way in which roles delegated to family members are carried out. Families having difficulty often have communication patterns that do not serve the needs of their members. Some of these patterns may involve parents communicating through children, lack of freedom to communicate, and conflicting messages.[5] Identification of these patterns is important in understanding the functioning of the system.

In understanding the functioning of any social system it is important to know how decisions are made. This includes identifying which decisions are individual ones, which are made in the subsystem, and which belong to the total system. It includes influences on the decisions and how those decisions are communicated, performed, and enforced. In most families, there are communication patterns that meet the needs of various members; however, these patterns may be limited to certain relationships. For example, a child may have a pattern of positive interactions with one parent but may not have such a relationship with the other parent. A positive pattern of communication is a strength, and the goal is to extend this pattern to other relationships in the family.

The family is a major institution of society. For society to function, families must carry out the roles delegated to them by society. These functions include the primary provision of common human needs for individuals, the care and nurturing of children, and the continuance of the culture. In order to perform these functions, adult members of the family perform work roles, including the homemaking role, the income-providing role, the parenting role, and the childcare role. These are vital roles in meeting common human needs and developmental needs of all family members. Through carrying out work, parenting, and marriage roles, the family provides support, encouragement of growth, and care of and concern for all family members. Knowing how these roles are filled provides an understanding of family functioning. These roles are often an important source of strength in the family, even when one or more of these roles present challenges. In fact, meeting challenges in fulfilling these roles is a sign of resilience and strength.

Change is a part of all human functioning. The family is subject to change in several ways: (1) growth of family members; (2) birth, children leaving the family home, death, and divorce; (3) changed functioning of family members as a result of illness or disability; and (4) changed environmental resources, impacts, or responsibilities. All systems develop mechanisms for coping with changes or for adapting to changing conditions. These adaptive and coping mechanisms are identified and examined for their contribution to appropriate flexibility of the family system in meeting changes both within the social system and in the environment. These are important indications of strength and resilience.

A final area for understanding the family as a social system is the development of the family, which begins in a family's roots. Current structure and functioning are in part a product of its roots. Again, the genogram is a useful tool to use with a family in considering these roots. Also important is an understanding of the family's cultural background (see Table 3.2). Events that have called for significant change, adaptation, and coping within the family system are also important in understanding a family's development. Family culture is part of a family's roots, and pride in one's culture and family heritage can be a foundation for growth and change. Self-knowledge begins with knowing where we came from and how our values, beliefs, and lifestyle reflect our past and that of our family and our culture. Understanding and appreciating family and cultural heritage strengthen the family and its members.

All families go through stages as the composition and needs of family members change. Sonya Rhodes identified seven stages of family life:

1. *Intimacy vs. idealization or disillusionment*—The dyadic relationship of husband and wife is formed. Developmental task involves developing a realistic appreciation of one's partner.

2. *Replenishment vs. turning inward*—The stage between the birth of the first child until the last child enters school. Developmental task involves developing nurturing patterns for family members.

3. *Individualization of family members vs. pseudomutual organization*—The stage where the family has school-age children. Tasks include parents separating their own identities from that of the child and the enabling of the development of support and opportunities for individual family members outside the family system. Another task is the individualization of each family member.

4. *Companionship vs. isolation*—The stage of teenage children in the family. Important themes are separation and sexuality. The tasks are development of parent-child relationships based on the knowledge of the child's growing independence and a marital relationship based on companionship.

5. *Regrouping vs. binding or expulsion*—This is the stage of the children leaving home. The task is a regrouping on generational lines and development of an adult-to-adult relationship between parents and children.

6. *Recovery vs. despair*—The couple renegotiates a relationship that does not involve parenting children in the home. Parent-child relationships are also changed. The task then is renegotiation of relationships.

7. *Mutual aid vs. uselessness*—Parents are now retired. Couples often are grandparents. The task is to develop a mutual-aid system among the generations.[6]

A study of the family as a social system also includes the identification of that system's concerns and needs. Though the needs of individual members and subsystems contribute to the family system needs, the needs of the family system are different from those of the parts. The needs of the family system relate to what will enable the family to maintain itself as a system and still fulfill its responsibility to its members and to its environment.

Of particular importance when working with families in which ethnicity and social class must be considered is use of a multisystem model. Here the focus is on the interacting level of family functioning (within the family, within the extended family, and with the various formal helping agencies involved). This type of approach will lead the worker toward more appropriate interventive strategies, whether they are strategies better suited to a particular ethnic situation or toward a choice that will bring about change in the larger system that negatively affects the family's healthy functioning.[7]

It is important to identify the strengths and challenges of the family in situation as a base for developing a professional relationship and for considering intervention into the transactions among family members and between the family and its environment. Through intervention into these transactions the social worker can enable families to meet the needs of the family as a system, as well as those of the individual members, and can help families improve social functioning. The understanding of the family as a social system is a means of identifying its strengths and challenges and of planning for intervention.

Case Example

Social Study: Family

I. Identifying Information

A. Names and Birth Dates of Family Members

Father:	Jorge Perez	Born: January 21, 1974
Mother:	Maria Perez	Born: April 2, 1975
Children:	Juan	Born: July 14, 1993
	Carmen	Born: June 20, 1994
	Arturo	Born: October 8, 1998
	Juanita	Born: December 7, 2001
	Jose	Born: February 25, 2005
Extended family:	Guadalupe Hernandez (maternal grandmother)	
	Born in Mexico. Date of birth uncertain.	

B. Marriage: August 24, 1993. First marriage for both.

C. Religion: Catholic, attend regularly.

D. Cultural/Racial Background: Both parents are Mexican American.

E. Language Spoken in Home: Spanish and English.

F. Date of First Contact: February 2009 referred by school because Juan has been skipping school.

II. The Family as a System

A. Family Structure (See Figure 13.1 - Family Genogram)

Jorge dropped out of school in tenth grade and is employed as a laborer. He works long hours but barely makes enough money to meet the family's needs. Maria did not return to school when the couple was married just before her senior year of high school. She has always stayed at home to care for the children and has never been employed outside of the home. Her mother, Guadalupe Hernandez, has lived with the family since her husband's death five years ago. She was born in Mexico and grew up in a migrant family. She married Felix Hernandez and they moved to Texas when Maria was twelve years old. Shortly after they arrived in the area, Jorge and Maria met and have been together since that time. Mrs. Hernandez understands and speaks some English but is most comfortable conversing in Spanish. Both Mr. and Mrs. Perez are bilingual.

Juan is fifteen and in tenth grade. He has been an average student until this year when he began skipping school and his grades plummeted. He has never been very active in extracurricular activities and does not especially like school. Juan feels that because his parents did not complete high school, it should be okay for him to drop out. He has had two minor problems with the law in the past six months, a curfew

(continued)

Case Example   (continued)

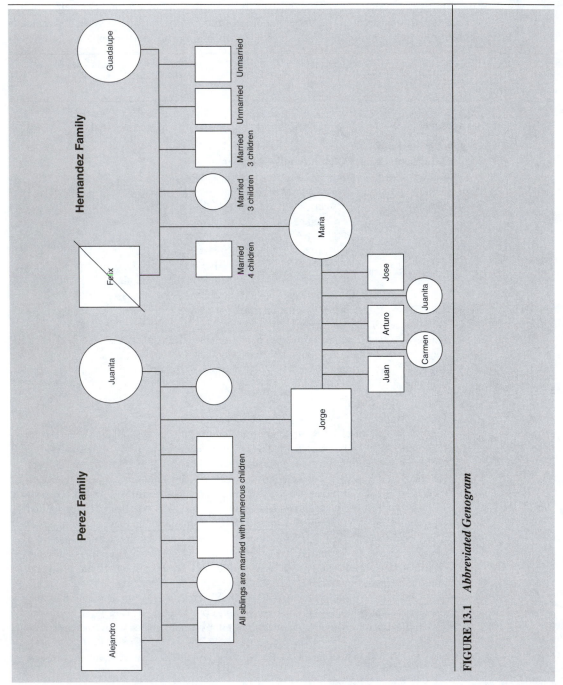

FIGURE 13.1 *Abbreviated Genogram*

(continued)

violation and a shoplifting complaint. Carmen is fourteen and in ninth grade. She has always been a good student and very active in school activities. Carmen has never been in trouble. However, since entering high school, Carmen has had a number of boys who are interested in dating her. Mr. and Mrs. P are opposed to this and expect that Carmen will follow traditional expectations of waiting until she is fifteen to date and then only under chaperoned circumstances. She sees this as being "old-fashioned." Arturo is ten years old and in fifth grade. He is very affable and outgoing. While he has been a good student, he is also somewhat of a class clown, which gets him into trouble periodically. He has not been in any trouble in the community. Juanita is seven years of age and is in second grade. She is a good student but is very quiet and shy. She rarely plays with the other children at school, and, if she does, it is generally with only one friend. She prefers to spend her recess reading and would actually prefer to stay inside where it is quiet. Jose is four years old and is in Head Start. He also seems outgoing and happy. He shows an interest in learning and readily socializes with the other children.

There is generally good communication between Mr. and Mrs. P. Each fulfills traditional gender-based roles in the family with Mrs. H sharing many tasks with her daughter. Mr. P wants a clean house, well-cooked meals, and well-behaved children.

The children have had close bonds with each other until recently when both Juan and Carmen began to rebel against the expectations of their parents and grandmother. The younger children get along well with each other and there are few arguments. The parent-child system is primarily focused on mother-child with Mrs. H serving as a surrogate mother of sorts. Mrs. P has experienced a loosening of the bonds of parental authority with her two oldest children but retains good control over the younger three. She has tried to elicit assistance from Mr. P, but his long hours at work limit the amount of time he has to devote to this. Mr. P, for his part, has tried ordering Juan and Carmen, which works while he is home but has little effect when he is not. Mrs. H has tried to intervene, but Juan and Carmen do not see her as an authority figure per se. They are fond of their grandmother but feel that her way and that of their parents is the old way and they want to do the same things that their friends are doing instead. The adults in this family expect to follow traditional family roles and ways of functioning. However, the two teens want to break away from this and, as a result, there are some serious cultural clashes occurring. Although there is cohesion in protecting each other as family members, the two oldest children seem caught between loyalty to the family and their ethnic identity and the lure of what is seen as a more permissive attitude by the dominant Anglo culture. This has led to tension within the family system as the adults attempt to preserve traditional cultural expectations and their two teens seek to break away from those very traditions.

The family lives in an older, two-story, five-bedroom home in a predominantly Hispanic neighborhood. Mr. and Mrs. P have their own bedroom upstairs along with the children. Juan has his own room and the two girls and other two boys share a room. Mrs. H has a room off the dining area on the first floor that she uses as her bedroom.

(continued)

Mr. P's parents are both alive and live in the area. He also has six mostly older siblings who live nearby. Mr. P's family has always been very close. The extended family gets together regularly for every American and Mexican holiday and for other important family traditions. Juan and Carmen have begun resisting attending these events, especially because their aunts and uncles try to influence them to adhere to the family and cultural traditions. Mrs. P has a sister in the area, but all four of her brothers have moved to other parts of the United States in search of work. Her mother is not able to live with her sister because her home is much too small. Mrs. P's family has also been very close. She misses the family gatherings that they once had. When any of her brothers come to town, they make it a point to celebrate the occasion.

B. Family Functioning

There is good communication between Mr. and Mrs. P on the whole, although this has become strained by the need for Mr. P to work long hours and the couple's frustration at the rebelliousness of their teenage children. The communication between Juan and Carmen is good, but this tends to serve as an alliance against the parents. The two communicate very little with the rest of the family, and they try to be absent from home as much as possible, preferring to be with their friends. The younger children communicate well with each other and with their parents and grandmother except that Juanita tends to keep to herself, preferring to read in her room. Mrs. P relies heavily on her mother for communication in the absence of her husband. This is almost exclusively in Spanish. Juan and Carmen understand and speak some Spanish but have drifted away from any serious effort to retain their Spanish-language skills. The younger children show some interest in speaking Spanish because they have had their grandmother living with them for a significant portion of their formative years. Thus, they have some proficiency.

Mr. P makes all of the major decisions in the family; however, day-to-day decisions have to be made by Mrs. P because he is gone most of the time. Mrs. P usually consults with her mother when she is not able to delay a decision until her husband is available. Housekeeping standards are high and Mrs. P and her mother do well at maintaining the home inside. The house needs some paint and some minor repairs, and Mr. P tries to get to these when he is not working. Parenting is left primarily to Mrs. P, with assistance from her mother. However, recently, Mr. P has become more involved with parenting and discipline with the two oldest children, but, because he is frequently absent from the home, this has had minimal effect on them. This is a source of great frustration for Mr. and Mrs. P and Mrs. H as well. They are at a loss as to how to get their teens to respect their authority. They are worried that they will lose Juan to the streets and that Carmen will become sexually active and become pregnant. Mr. P has resorted to physical threats with Juan, but he wants to avoid crossing into physical confrontation. He is at a loss as to how to deal with his daughter's rebelliousness. The family is not in a position to reward or sanction behavior financially. Even if they were, it does not appear that the nature of the conflict would lend itself to this type of intervention. They have tried grounding, but the teens simply leave when Mr. P is not at home.

There is an obvious bond of affection within the family despite this latest difficulty. This is especially true with the younger children. There has always been some

(continued)

Case Example   *(continued)*

stress in the family as a result of their poor economic situation. However, the strain in the relationships among the adults and the teenagers has increased the stress tremendously. Ordinarily, the adults in the family have found that turning to their faith has been the best way to cope with major difficulties. They also talk with each other and with extended family members. Usually, the family and extended family pull together whenever there is a crisis. However, the current situation has challenged their abilities to cope in the usual ways. The children generally cope either by denying any problems and trying to forget about them, or by going to their parents for help. Under the current circumstances, Juan and Carmen have turned instead to their friends, which in turn has driven them further away from their parents. The younger children do not discuss the situation and seem oblivious to it but are obviously watching and waiting to see what will happen.

C. Family Developmental History

This couple is very tied to their traditional Mexican-American roots. It is these very traditions that are now being challenged by their two teenage children who want to break away from them and become part of the dominant Anglo culture. The family is experiencing a great deal of stress concerning issues of acculturation. This is quite common as members of various ethnic groups assimilate into American society. Earlier generations often seek to preserve their ethnic heritage, whereas younger generations either straddle between ethnic traditions and current trends in the larger society or seek to break from the traditions of their parents.

Until this time, the two most significant events in this family have been the dropping out of school of Mr. and Mrs. P and the death of Mr. H. The fact that neither parent completed high school has frozen them into a life on the brink of poverty. The only thing that has kept them from going over the edge is the fact that Mr. P works as many hours as he can. Now he is stuck between working long hours and being gone from the family or cutting back on his hours so he can deal with the crisis at home. If anything were to happen that would prevent him from working, the family would be economically devastated. The death of Mr. H was a severe blow to everyone in the family. He was loved by all and is still mourned.

The family is in stage 4 (Companionship vs. Isolation) in Rhode's stages of family life. The important themes in this stage are teenagers who are in the midst of separation and sexuality. This describes the family as it struggles with the emerging independence and sexuality of the two oldest children. However, the cultural clashes that are occurring have created a crisis about how to resolve these issues.

III. Concern or Need

The family was referred for assistance in dealing with unexcused absences at school by Juan. They are also concerned about Carmen's desire to date. In addition, customary disciplinary approaches have not been successful in dealing with the situations. Mr. P might be able to improve his circumstances if he was able to complete high school or get a GED. Mrs. P could also benefit from this and might be able to relieve Mr. P of some of the burden of providing for the family. Mrs. H needs to know that her grandchildren will value the heritage that she and her late husband tried to pass on to them. Juan needs to find a way to meet his need to belong with a positive peer group while also satisfying his

(continued)

parents' expectations of him. He needs to see that completing high school and having a skill are important to escaping from the poverty that his family has experienced. Carmen has a positive peer group but needs to avoid becoming overly involved with males, especially older ones, until she is mature enough to manage a relationship. She needs to be able to negotiate some compromise with her parents that will satisfy their need to know that she will abide by some of their traditions until she is old enough to decide for herself what she will retain from her heritage. Arturo needs to continue to do well in school and not let his zest for life and sense of humor interfere with his success academically. Juanita needs some assistance in becoming more social. Her teacher is aware of this and has brought it to the attention of her parents, but they have not had the energy to focus on this because they are trying to deal with the situation at hand. Jose needs to continue to receive nurturing and support from his family and not have his needs overlooked because of the stress of the current situation.

The couple needs support in preserving the strength of their relationship, which is being challenged by Mr. P's long hours at work and the strain of dealing with two rebellious teenagers. They need to maintain some separation between the demands of parenting and the intimacy in their marriage. As parents, they need to present a united front in dealing with the demands of parenting. A major aspect of this is the need for increased communication regarding discipline and a mechanism that will address the challenges at hand. In terms of parent-child relationships, Mr. P needs help in reestablishing his parental influence over his older children and Mrs. P needs support in disciplining Juan and Carmen when he is not home. Juan needs to find a way to meet his individual needs for peer relations while maintaining positive father-son and mother-son relationships. Carmen has similar needs, but these are focused on dating and boy-girl relationships. Mr. and Mrs. P need to be able to continue to maintain strong parent-child relationships with the younger children while dealing with the stresses of the relationships with Juan and Carmen.

The family needs some relief from the stresses of economic hardship and needs to find a way to preserve important aspects of their heritage while also recognizing the influence of the dominant Anglo culture. Mr. and Mrs. P were moderately successful in accomplishing this, although they have not enjoyed much economic success. Their children have all proven to be at least adequate students, and Mr. and Mrs. P will need to encourage success at school if they hope to see a bright future for the children. At the same time, school and work bring the children in more contact with others who do not share their heritage, and this will inevitably increase the tension between their heritage and other cultures.

IV. Strengths and Challenges in Meeting Needs

In addition to dealing with Juan's truancy and getting into trouble, the family wants assistance in dealing with the crisis of the cultural clashes that are occurring between the adults and the teens. They would like to have the stress reduced so that they can deal with the economic issues that they face. The parents want the teens to abide by the parents' wishes and to adhere to the traditions of their heritage. The teens would like to have their parents accept their decisions to reduce their involvement with their ethnic traditions and to become more Anglo in their cultural activities. The parents are highly motivated to resolve the situation. The teens are much less motivated, fearing that the resolution will not be in their favor. There is the potential for change, but there are also major impingements.

(continued)

Case Example   *(continued)*

Both sides will need to be ready for some give and take. Regardless of what the parents do and even if they were to be successful at curbing the recent unrest, it is inevitable that the children will reach a point where they are able to make these decisions for themselves. The question will be how much influence will the parents have and will they be successful at retaining the important aspects of the traditions that they value the most. The teens need to realize that some of their parents' wishes with regard to adhering to traditions are in their best interests, regardless of whether they are associated with their heritage. For example, Juan needs to stay out of trouble and in school if he is to put himself in a position of achieving economic success. Carmen needs to avoid getting overinvolved in a relationship prematurely so that she can mature and make good decisions about her future. Within the family, the parents have a strong marriage, Mrs. H provides emotional support and assistance with household tasks, and the family has retained a strong sense of love and care and concern. The extended family system on Mr. P's side of the family is intact and very supportive. There are resources available in the community, such as adult education, job training, and family service agencies. The school is concerned and has some resources to support academic success. The turmoil in this family has not reached the point where irreparable harm has occurred. The referral has occurred early enough to hold out hope that some resolution will be feasible. This should add to the family's motivation and capacity for change. Many Hispanic families have successfully dealt with these same issues, which makes the family's expectations realistic, even though there are clearly some major differences between parents and teenagers. The main strengths of the family lie in their love for each other and their desire to maintain a positive family system. The challenges that they face are in large part cultural in nature, and, although they are substantial, they are not insurmountable.

The Planning Phase with Families

In developing a plan with a family system, the challenge is to balance the needs and goals of each individual with each other and with those of the system. The first task is to identify individual or personal goals for each member. Although the worker may have discussed these beforehand, it is important for members to state their goals to other members of the family.

The next step is for the worker to assist the family in articulating a common goal that includes everyone in the system. This inclusion process helps to establish and reinforce a sense of belonging and teamwork and increases a sense of cohesion. It is sometimes difficult to develop an all-encompassing goal; thus, the worker should keep the goal simple and straightforward. For example, for a family a common goal might be to get along better with each other. Sensitivity to diversity and to at-risk populations is essential when planning with families, as is building on the strengths of individuals, the family system, and the environment.

Once the family has established a common goal, the task is to assist them in finding ways to help each other achieve individual goals as well as to identify roles in helping the family to achieve its overall goal. The worker will need to use mediation and negotiation in helping the family in this process. Goals should build on the strengths of individuals and the family as a whole, as well as the strengths and resources available in the larger ecosystem.

In addition to personal or individual goals and a common goal for the family, there are two other types of goals that are important: mutual, or shared, goals and reciprocal goals. Mutual goals require two or more members to participate or act in certain ways regardless of the actions of others. An example would be a goal in which everyone agreed to use "I" statements when talking to each other in order to improve communication. If one person forgets, it does not excuse others from using the word *I* as a reminder. The respondent should not say, "You forgot to use 'I'!" Instead, they would need to say something like, "I would like to hear that in an 'I' statement."

Reciprocal goals require different actions on the part of two or more members. An example would be a goal in which a parent agrees to cook the family's favorite meal and the family members agree to make a commitment to sit together as a family for that meal. Reciprocal goals may also be contingent. This is usually stated as "if-then." For example, parents can agree to give each child an allowance based on completion of certain chores. This might be stated as "If Jerry cuts the grass when requested, then Mr. A will pay him $20.00."

In setting goals with the family, the units of attention may be within the family system or in the environment. Units of attention can be individuals, subsystems, or the family as a system. The unit of attention may include the structure, the functioning, or the development of the system or subsystems. Change may be focused on internal or external boundaries, relationships, cohesion, interactions, communication, decision making, roles or role performance, support, coping mechanisms, or various skills. Change may be focused on the growth and development of individuals, subsystems, or the family system as a whole.

The unit of attention may be in the environment. In particular, it is important for the family to be able to access and use needed resources. With families that have experienced discrimination and oppression, this is vital. These families have limited access to necessary resources and little hope of changing the situation. The worker's role is to assist the family in gaining access to resources and to advocate for people's rights when there are barriers.

As presented in Chapter 9, a set of objectives and tasks are used to describe who, what, where, when, and how the worker and the family members will work to carry out the plan. The elements of good goals, objectives, and tasks are the same and will not be repeated here. However, the focus is different in that family work generally occurs with more than one person and is often aimed at the interactions.

Direct and Indirect Practice Actions with Families

The direct and indirect practice actions that were covered in Chapters 10 and 11 are also relevant for working with families. The work can be focused on individual family members, the family, or a subsystem as the client system. The environment can also be the unit of attention in the change process. The worker has a dual focus when the family is the client system. He uses actions in helping the family to achieve its goals while also helping the family to acquire skills in using these actions. Helping clients to use the change process gives them the power to bring about change on their own in the future. This brings true meaning to the social work value of client self-determination.

In diversity competent practice, the worker explores with the family actions that are consistent with the diversity of the family. She does not impose her own or society's view of what the family should do but seeks to find what fits with the family system. One of the difficulties in working with families from certain cultures is the strict boundaries between

male and female role expectations. This generally results in the male being in the role of
head of the household, called a patriarchal system. This system may be viewed as oppressive toward women. Most of these cultures define a "good husband" or a "good father" as
a man who incorporates the needs and best interests of his wife and children into his decision making. He is obligated to see that the needs of his wife and family are met. This
places tremendous pressure on him when faced with limited resources. Some men use
their dominant positions to meet their own needs or suppress the needs of other family
members. Within their culture, this is a deviation from the "good husband and father"
role. The worker can assist the husband to define this role within his culture and then
work with him to obtain the resources that are necessary to carry this out. She might also
help him to see that sharing his power is not necessarily a sign of weakness but may
indeed be a sign of strength.

Cross-cultural work with families is much more complicated when the work is also
cross-gender. If the worker is female and the family system is patriarchal, it can be very
difficult for the worker to gain credibility. Naturalistic inquiry can be especially helpful in
these cases. Asking questions and giving the role of cultural guide to the family allows the
process to unfold. The family will be more comfortable with a discussion of its cultural
background if there is a focus on strengths. Actively incorporating cultural customs and
values into the plan is vital. This lays the groundwork for action that is culturally appropriate. It is important for the family to take pride in its cultural heritage and to use that
heritage as a source of strength.

With diversity factors, such as family structure and same-sex partners, a similar nonjudgmental, inquiry approach is essential. Helping the family to define itself and see its
diversity as a strength is the key to success. Often these families do not have role expectations that are clearly defined. Much of the direct practice work may involve assisting the
family with expectations or in filling roles with flexibility. The family needs to ensure that
necessary tasks are carried out in a positive way that strengthens the family.

The strategies and actions in Figure 10.1 are relevant for working with families. The
worker helps family members to use these actions to change what they think, how they
feel, and how they act with each other and with their environments. The worker focuses on
the family as a system and assists its members in finding ways to meet everyone's needs
within the structure and culture of the family system. In Chapter 10, we covered direct
practice actions. These are also relevant for working with families.

1. *Actions taken to develop relationships*—Relationship is the key element in working
with families. Well-functioning families have healthy, well-functioning relationships.
Often, direct practice actions with families as the client system or the unit of attention
involve developing, repairing, restoring, or strengthening relationships among its members
as either the primary need or concern or the means by which the primary need or concern
will be met.

A good relationship requires the ability to do three things: (a) communicate effectively, (b) make decisions and solve problems, and (c) resolve conflict constructively. Effective
communication begins with the use of "I" statements (statements that begin with the word *I*).
A successful process for decision making and problem solving needs to be one that the
parties agree on and results in everyone's needs being met. The ability to resolve conflict
in a constructive manner is using a win-win approach, as opposed to win-lose.

In constructive conflict resolution, a willingness to negotiate and compromise is a must. The parties should stick to the issue and stay in the present, not the past. Using "I" statements will tend to encourage expression of feelings. "You" statements tend to create defensiveness and can easily lead to name calling and attacking the other person. These situations are related to win-lose. Changing the subject, talking about the past, attacking the other person, using or threatening violence are ways that people use to win at the other person's expense. It is crucial to avoid violence and threats of violence. The problem with win-lose in family systems is that someone has to be a loser, which does not lead to a successful family outcome.

The social worker uses his knowledge and skills in developing relationships to build a relationship with the family and to assist family members in strengthening relationships with each other. He models effective communication and teaches and guides members in communicating effectively with each other. When inappropriate or harmful interactions occur, the worker helps those involved restructure the interaction. For instance, calling someone a derogatory name generally occurs because the person is angry. The worker asks the person what she was thinking and feeling before she called the other person a name. As the reasons for the name calling emerge, the worker asks for a direct statement about the person's real feelings using "I" statements. The person might say, "I feel hurt and angry because…." Behind negative interaction in families is unmet need. Family members need positive relationships to grow and develop and succeed. Good communication skills, an effective decision-making/problem-solving process, and constructive conflict resolution are necessary for maintaining positive relationships.

2. *Actions to enable the family to use the change process*—Helping families learn to use the change process is important for their long-term success in meeting needs. This approach should be included mainly when the family (or subsystem) is the client system. When a family develops a better understanding of itself and its environment, it has learned the first step in the change process—assessment. This understanding allows the family to change the interactions between itself or its members and the environment. In an ecosystems strengths approach, need represents an imbalance in the transactions in the ecosystem. Changing the transactions is necessary to meet the need. Understanding the ecosystem is critical to restoring balance and meeting need. It helps the family identify strengths and resources within the family system and in the environment.

Understanding family in environment is the foundation for successful planning. Families can learn planning skills as they work together on resolving the current situation. Teaching planning skills is an important direct practice action with all client systems. The actions that follow can be learned in order to facilitate implementation of plans the family formulates and to remove barriers.

3. *Actions to enable the family to know and use available resources*—Frequently, the block to fulfilling need is a lack of resources. The family may need to become aware of resources and how to access or use them. Even when the family is not the client system, it may be important to help the family to meet its needs in order for the family to respond to the needs of the client. The worker uses brokering skills to refer family members to resources in the community. When there are barriers to accessing resources, the worker advocates for the family. Ultimately, the goal is to help the family to be able to advocate for itself.

4. *Actions to empower or enable families*—Empowerment and enabling involve validation of feelings, positive reinforcement, feedback, assertiveness, and cognitive and behavioral change. The family can learn to use these actions to build strong members. These actions are primarily used when the family is the client system and the unit of attention is the change process. The most powerful validation, reinforcement, and feedback come from one's parents. The fundamental basis for good self-esteem is love and acceptance from one's parents. Unconditional love for being, not doing, allows the child to internalize unconditional acceptance of himself as a human being that has worth. This is not unconditional acceptance of the child's behavior. It is the parent's responsibility to socialize the child so that he learns what is acceptable and not acceptable behavior. The message is: "I love you as a person no matter what you or I feel, think, or do. However, your behavior is a separate matter. I do not have to love or even like your behavior and neither does anyone else." The worker helps the parent to use validation and reinforcement and feedback to build healthy self-esteem in the child while also shaping appropriate behavior. She also helps the family to appropriately use cognitive and behavioral change strategies in meeting each others' needs.

5. *Actions taken to resolve crises*—Frequently, the family is in a crisis when the service is initiated. Unmet need can create a crisis situation. In systems theory, when one part of the system experiences stress or unmet need, it affects other parts of the system. Situations in which families may experience a crisis include financial woes, health problems, relationship difficulties, trouble with the law, and the like. During a crisis, the family's normal coping mechanisms are overwhelmed. The worker helps the family to restore its coping abilities by developing and working on a plan that will meet needs and resolve the crisis. When faced with a crisis, there are two types of families: those that pull together and those that pull apart. Of course, nearly every family wants to be one that pulls together. The idea of pulling together can be used as a motivation for change. When inappropriate or destructive actions occur, the worker can ask how those fit or contribute to the family pulling together. He can follow this up with a discussion of what actions would do this.

6. *Actions taken to support the social functioning of families*—Support is an important aspect of healthy family functioning. Most of us place a high value on having the support of our families. When we have it, we feel we can face almost anything. When we do not, we may despair or look to others to make up for the loss. Support may be used when the family is the client system or the unit of attention. When working with individual clients, especially those in crisis, establishing support from the family is often a vital action.

For couples, having the support of one's spouse or significant other makes all the difference in the world. Sharing a life together means sharing happiness and unhappiness. When couples are at odds with each other, they are using their power and energy against each other instead of using it to deal with life's challenges. The worker shows them how disagreements can be used to either weaken or strengthen their relationship. Unresolved issues and destructive interactions will weaken it. Constructive conflict resolution can strengthen it. The couple can feel a deeper understanding and appreciation of each other when they successfully face an issue together. Commitment to the relationship is strengthened. In the end, a disagreement can be seen as an opportunity to demonstrate one's love by allowing the other person to have his or her way. This must be done with no strings attached; otherwise, it will be manipulation.

7. *Actions taken that use activity with families*—Activity can be used with families, but it is usually limited to when the family is the client system or when the family or family members need to act on the environment. "Homework assignments" help to carry over the work that is done in family sessions to everyday life. Once family members begin to use the work from the sessions, they can build on their success. The worker asks members to describe in detail what happened and how they felt about it. If they feel good about the change, the worker discusses what it would take to make this happen more frequently.

8. *Actions taken to mediate with family members*—Mediation within the family system is critical to successful family work, whether the family is the client system or the unit of attention. When the worker takes sides, she loses credibility with the other side. Taking sides increases conflict and competition by creating the illusion of winning the worker over to one's side. In any work that involves ongoing relationships, the worker must take and be given the position of mediator. The worker helps the two sides reach common ground and resolve their differences. She engages in a dialogue of negotiation and compromise, asking questions such as: "What would you like to do with this? What do you want to see happen? What would satisfy you? What would you be willing to do? As the issues emerge, the worker asks each party about the give and take that is necessary to reach a compromise: "If he does …, would you be willing to …? What would it take to get you to …? Would you be willing to …?" While mediating and negotiating a compromise, the worker is also modeling how family members can do this among themselves. The worker can also use mediation when there is a block to accessing resources. Mediation is generally the first choice before engaging in advocacy.

9. *Action taken that uses various theories and models with generalist social work practice as a framework, including cognitive, behavioral and cognitive-behavioral approaches, brief and solution-focused models, task-centered models, person-centered theory, narrative approaches, an Afrocentric approach, feminist practice, and practice with people who are gay or lesbian*—The generalist practice approach provides a framework for using any other models or theories used in social work practice with any size client systems including families and family subsystems.

Indirect practice actions are also used with families as client systems; as units of attention; or on behalf of individual members, subsystems, or the family as a system. Indirect actions are aimed at bringing about change in the environment. Indirect actions can be learned by family members so they can act on their own behalf in the future. The indirect practice actions discussed in Chapter 11 were (1) mediation, (2) the use of influence, (3) changing the environment, (4) coordinating services, (5) changing organizations, and (6) changing the community.

1. *Actions that use mediation between families and systems in the environment*—The actions that the worker uses to mediate between families and systems in the environment are similar to those used with individual clients and systems in their environments.

2. *Actions that use influence*—Generally, the worker uses influence on behalf of his client system and refrains from using it with the client system except in a crisis situation or as a last resort, when his client is truly stuck. The use of influence in family work typically takes place when the client system is an individual and the family (or subsystem or members) is the unit of attention. In that case, the family is considered as part of the environment, and influence can be used to bring about change on behalf of the client. For example, if the client has been alienated from her family but needs assistance, the worker might contact the family (with his client's permission) in an effort to restore the relationship or at least agree to work at it. Influence includes bringing about changes in the thoughts, feelings, and, especially, the actions of individuals and systems in the environment.

Quite often, when people or staff in other agencies know that there is a worker involved with a client, this changes the way that they act. People may give more credibility to the client's need because the worker has done so. They may be willing to defer to the worker because of his position of authority. Workers in other agencies may do this as a matter of policy or as a professional courtesy. Workers are more conscious of their work when a fellow professional is also involved. The majority of workers are conscientious and hardworking, regardless of the circumstances. However, the worker will naturally want to make a good impression on fellow professionals, and this fact alone can influence change on behalf of the client. For example, if the worker calls for services on behalf of the client whose situation requires immediate action, it increases the likelihood that the client will receive services more quickly. Similarly, accompanying the client to an agency sends a strong message about the importance of the service.

The use of influence has potential ethical problems. The worker should only use influence with his client when absolutely necessary. This also applies to influencing other systems. The worker should not routinely use his influence as a shortcut or to gain favor for his client over other clients. This undermines client empowerment and self-determination. It can lead the other agency to see the worker in a negative light over time, limiting his ability to obtain services when he has a client who really needs immediate attention. Other agencies will expect reciprocity when they have clients who need immediate or special attention. A worker who abuses his influence may build up expectations with other agencies that cannot be met by him or his agency.

3. *Actions taken to change the environment*—Changes in time, space, and relationships are also relevant in family work. Relationships were discussed earlier, under direct practice actions. With indirect practice actions, the relationships between family members and the environment are the focus. Reviewing these earlier sections and the discussion of interaction in Chapter 7 gives the student a foundation for working on these relationships. In an ecosystems strengths approach, family needs may involve incongruity in the transactions among family members and the environment. If one or more members of the family experience unmet need from the environment or excessive demands, it affects other family members, as others try to cope or meet the need. Changing the transaction to meet the need not only returns balance to the individual and his ecosystem but also restores balance to his family system by reducing the stress in his family.

Changes in time with family work generally mean flexibility in scheduling, which is much more difficult with families than with an individual. Family size, the ages of its members, and environmental demands, such as work or school, affect the time that members have available to meet and to carry out various tasks. Not only must the visits with the worker be coordinated but also scheduling services and activities can be complicated. Working with families generally involves more complicated scheduling and arrangements.

Changes in space can range from accommodating the family for an office visit to assisting in major moves, such as changing place of residence for the family or for one of its members. When the family decides to make a move from its current residence, the worker may need to assist in locating other living options, especially in instances that involve government funding. The family may need access to resources to assist with security deposits and other costs. Families may experience discrimination and need to have their rights protected. The social worker could be involved in accessing day programs or in arranging for residential, institutional, or alternative placement for one of the members of the family. This is common in child welfare, mental health, disability services, health care, aging services, delinquency services, corrections, and similar settings. Social work services can include making referrals and securing placement, providing services to the family while the member is in care, or providing aftercare services. Social workers often provide services within a program including residential settings, day programs, and the like.

4. *Actions taken to coordinate services*—Coordination of services can be used on behalf of the family as a system or for family members. When a family is in crisis or faces severe or multiple needs, it may require assistance in coordinating needed services. This is a common situation with social workers who work in the settings mentioned previously. Case management is usually the model that is used. Child welfare cases involve families who are having difficulty in meeting children's needs or are abusive. In the majority of cases, there are multiple needs experienced by the family and by individual members. The worker may assume initial responsibility for coordinating services, with the expectation that the family will eventually assume responsibility or will experience a reduction in the need for services. Various family preservation models have emerged since the 1970s that are designed to prevent out-of-home placement of children. These are mainly short-term, intensive, in-home services.[8] Given the tremendous rise in costs, various alternative models to residential and institutional care have evolved for the mentally ill, developmentally disabled, or mentally retarded. The juvenile and adult corrections systems have seen similar efforts. Services for aging individuals are becoming more community based and will inevitably require more alternative services as the costs of residential and institutional care mount. All of these services require the social worker to provide coordination or to participate in situations where another worker is the primary coordinator of services.

When the family is the client system and coordination of services is needed, the worker involves the family with the process as much as possible. Over time, some families will be able to do this for themselves. Others will no longer need the array of services. Still others will require some assistance over an extended period of time. When working with an individual, the worker attempts to involve the family in the process, if this is possible and the client is agreeable. The assumption is that the family will be an important and more consistent source of ongoing assistance in securing services. For some clients, this may not be so, but in most cases, the family remains an important resource. Sometimes all that is needed is for the worker to mobilize the family or give information to key members. Other times, the worker may supplement what the family provides, or he may find resources for the family that will ease some of the burden.

5. *Action to change organizations*—The worker uses the same actions in changing organizations on behalf of families as she would on behalf of individual clients.

6. *Action to change the community*—Similarly the worker also uses the same actions in changing communities on behalf of families as would be the case when working with individual clients.

Evaluation and Termination with Families

Most of the discussion of evaluation in Chapter 12 can also be applied to working with families. However, evaluation with families is more complex because families have members of varying ages who have different interactions with systems in the environment. Additionally, the worker must evaluate the family as a system. This involves evaluating family structure, functioning, and development. Also, as with other situations involving clients, the social worker must work within the culture, diversity, and value system of the client system. The best way to ensure diversity competence is to include the family in the evaluation process. The worker relies on naturalistic inquiry. She asks questions about how the family's structure, functioning, and development are viewed within the cultural system. Frequently, families in the United States are multicultural because couples from different cultures have children. Questions will need to be answered with respect to the relevant cultural backgrounds. The worker asks questions about how the family perceives or experiences attitudes held by the larger society toward the family and its circumstances. The worker is interested in how help is viewed, whether her assessment is accurate, and what kinds of goals and actions are acceptable within the cultural or diversity systems. This gives her a sense of whether the help and the services are likely to be effective and appropriate.

Termination with families is likely to be much different from individual termination, although individuals in the family may express feelings similar to those of individual clients. For families, termination generally represents the end of the social work process experience but not the end of their relationships with one another. This is especially true if the worker has been successful at reinforcing and strengthening the positive functioning of the family system by supporting appropriate family roles and relationships and positive interaction with the family's environment. At such times, successful termination brings good feelings as well as a desire to terminate. It is not unusual for family members themselves to conclude that they are ready to try things on their own. They may announce at the beginning or at the end of a meeting that they do not intend to return. If the worker has been tuned in to the family, he may be able to plan for it.

Because the family goes on after termination, less time may be needed to resolve any issues. At the least, members should be given an opportunity to express how they feel about terminating. For children, this might be structured in terms of what they liked best and least about meeting and what they will miss most and least. Sometimes an informal celebration may take place, such as going out to dinner or having a picnic, to mark this significant event in the life of the family. Generally, the worker does not participate in these events.

Evaluation at termination is focused on whether goals have been achieved and needs met. This includes evaluating the family's ability to continue to meet its needs as a system and the needs of its members. The worker asks the family to evaluate the service. He asks what was helpful, what was not helpful, and what would have been helpful. If appropriate, he asks everyone to answer these questions. With younger children, it may be necessary to rephrase these questions. Questions about what it was they liked best or least and what they will miss the most or the least are likely to elicit this feedback.

Summary

Frequently, the social worker must work with multiperson systems, either as client systems or as units of attention in the change process. To be effective, the worker must have knowledge and skills in working with multiperson interactions. The family is a multiperson system that is often involved in social work practice. The worker begins by understanding influences from her own family and societal attitudes toward various families. She understands the various forms that families take in society. She works at becoming diversity competent by remaining nonjudgmental and using naturalistic inquiry in working with diverse families.

The change process is used when working with families to assist in meeting the current need and in helping the family to become more effective in meeting needs in the future. The assessment phase involves understanding the family as a social system, along with understanding individual members. Planning includes developing a common goal and either reciprocal or shared goals. Direct and indirect practice actions are used to facilitate successful completion of the plan, to remove barriers, and to teach the family skills for acting on its own behalf. Evaluation occurs throughout the process and includes looking at the structure, functioning, and development of the family as a system. Successful termination is different with families because the family goes on and only the work ends.

Questions

1. What issues do you think you should consider when working with a family? Identify those issues that may be unresolved or important to you personally in your own family situation and that may get in the way as you work with a family.
2. Discuss the differences when working with the family as a system as contrasted with working with individuals who may be family members. Why is it important to work with the family as a system rather than work with individuals in a family?
3. Do your own family social history. What did you discover about your family's structure, functioning, and development? What do you see as your family's strengths? Its challenges?
4. What knowledge and skills do you possess that would be strengths in working with families? What knowledge and skills do you need to acquire? How might you get these?
5. What knowledge and skills do you possess that would make you diversity competent in working with various diverse families? With what kind of diverse families would you feel comfortable working? With what kind of diverse families would you feel uncomfortable working? How could you become more comfortable?

Suggested Readings

Yanca, Stephen J. and Johnson, Louise C. *Generalist Social Work Practice with Families.* Boston: Allyn and Bacon, 2008.

Anderson, Stephen A., and Sabatelli, Ronald M. *Family Interaction: A Multigenerational Developmental Perspective,* 4th ed. Boston: Allyn and Bacon, 2007.

Becvar, Dorothy Stroh, and Becvar, Raphael J. *Family Therapy: A Systematic Integration,* 7th ed. Boston: Allyn and Bacon, 2009.

Boyd-Franklin, Nancy. *Black Families in Therapy: Understanding the African American Experience,* 2nd ed. New York: Guilford Press, 2003.

Carter, Elizabeth A., and McGoldrick, Monica. *The Expanded Family Life Cycle: Individual, Family, and Social Perspectives,* 3rd ed. Boston: Allyn and Bacon, 2005.

Flores, Maria T., and Carey, Gabrielle. *Family Therapy with Hispanics: Toward Appreciating Diversity.* Boston: Allyn and Bacon, 2000.

Fong, Rowena, and Furuto, Sharlene, Eds. *Culturally Competent Practice: Skills, Interventions, and Evaluations.* Boston: Allyn and Bacon, 2001.

Kilpatrick, Allie, and Holland, Thomas. *Working with Families: An Integrative Model by Level of Functioning,* 5th ed. Boston: Allyn and Bacon, 2009.

McGoldrick, Monica, Giordano, Joe, and Pearce, John K., Eds. *Ethnicity and Family Therapy,* 3rd ed. New York: Guilford Press, 2005.

Mizrahi, Terry, and Davis, Larry E., Eds. *Encyclopedia of Social Work,* 20th ed. Washington, DC: NASW Press, 2008 ("Family," "Family Services," "Family Therapy").

Nichols, Michael, and Schwartz, Richard. *Family Therapy: Concepts and Methods,* 8th ed. Boston: Allyn and Bacon, 2008.

Nichols, Michael P., and Schwartz, Richard C. *Essentials of Family Therapy,* 4th ed. Boston: Allyn and Bacon, 2009.

Shulman, Lawrence. *The Skills of Helping: Individuals, Families, Groups, and Communities,* 6th ed. Belmont, CA: Thomson-Brooks/Cole, 2009.

Van Wormer, Katherine, Wells, Joel, and Boes, Mary. *Social Work with Lesbians, Gays, and Bisexuals: A Strengths Perspective.* Boston: Allyn and Bacon, 2000 (Chapter 11).

Walsh, William M., and McGraw, James A. *Essentials of Family Therapy: A Structured Summary of Nine Approaches.* Denver, CO: Love, 2002.

14 | *Generalist Practice with Groups*

Learning Expectations

1. Understanding of the importance of the small group in generalist social work practice.

2. Understanding various direct service groups offered within generalist practice.

3. Understanding the use of the change process in generalist practice with groups.

4. Understanding of group process so as to be able to recognize its various aspects in the functioning of a small group or a family.

5. Understanding of how the social worker can facilitate the work and process of any small group.

6. Beginning skill in facilitating small-group interaction.

This chapter examines working with groups within a generalist social work practice framework. There are two general categories of groups: those that provide direct services to clients and task groups that are used to facilitate change in organizations and communities. Direct service groups will be the focus of this chapter. The purpose of these groups is to provide a benefit to members. The change process is used in several ways in direct service groups. Assessment and planning occur before the group begins and throughout the life of the group. Assessment includes understanding the small group as a social system. Assessment, planning, and direct practice actions are used to facilitate the group and are often taught to group members. Evaluation occurs throughout the group. Termination can be planned and unplanned and can be experienced by the group as a whole or by individual members as they leave the group. Assessment, planning, actions, and evaluation and termination with direct service groups will be examined. Task groups will be discussed in Chapter 15.

Group Purpose

A group is a system of clients or a multiclient system. To the extent that the worker works with the group as a whole to facilitate achievement of its purpose, the group can be considered as a system. Direct service groups are a means by which services are delivered to several clients who have common needs or interests. In this discussion of direct service groups, the primary purpose of the group is to serve the needs of its members. The nature of the concern or need considered here in this text will be (1) the need for growth and skill development, (2) the need for prevention services, (3) the need for support, and (4) the need for counseling. Therapy groups are for those clients who need to overcome major difficulties in social functioning. We assume that providing therapy is limited to MSWs with advanced training and is beyond the scope of this text.

MSW's and BSW social workers under supervision provide group work services aimed at facilitating growth and skill development and providing prevention services, support, and counseling services. Most growth and skill development groups are offered to the general population, although these services can also be provided to people experiencing greater need. Examples are recreation groups, education groups, parenting groups, social skills training, and various youth groups, such as scouting, church groups, and the like. It is assumed that the benefits gained from this type of group come from participation.

At the other end of the spectrum are counseling or change oriented groups. Counseling groups are defined as serving the needs of individuals who are faced with important decisions or difficult problems. In this view, counseling groups are for clients who are capable of making and carrying out decisions or solving problems with assistance. In contrast, therapy groups are for clients who need assistance in overcoming major barriers to social functioning before they will be able to participate in growth and skill development activities or make and carry out decisions and solve problems. For example, a child who is exhibiting disruptive behavior or is emotionally unstable may need therapy to overcome these difficulties before he is able to participate in a recreation group. Placing him in a group that is not designed to meet his needs usually leads to scapegoating and other harmful experiences.

When offering direct service groups, the worker must be careful to avoid a wide range of social functioning among members. If there is too much disparity in social functioning, members will have difficulty relating to one another.

Support groups are offered for a variety of situations. Typically, members have either already been through a difficult situation and need support, or they need help coping with a situation that is beyond their control. In the first type of support group, members need assistance in continuing changes that they made in individual or group counseling. Because managed care programs increasingly are limiting the length of service, these groups are important resources. Support groups are not typically considered to be reimbursable but it is important that agencies offer this service so that clients receive support after counseling ends. The second type of support group is designed to help clients and family members cope with situations such as cancer, bereavement, incurable conditions, and the like. Coping with these situations can be especially difficult because of feelings of helplessness and hopelessness. Giving and receiving support from others in similar circumstances can be a powerful aid in facing these challenges.

Prevention groups are designed to serve the needs of those who are at risk of experiencing difficulties in social functioning. Prevention groups may follow a specially designed curriculum, or they may use growth and skill development activities or decision-making and problem-solving processes. The difference here is that membership is limited to those who are identified as being at risk. For example, a drug prevention group would be appropriate for youth who have a family member who has abused drugs or alcohol or for youth who live in an area where drugs are prevalent. This type of group could use a curriculum that educates about drugs and offers strategies for avoidance. Recreation or outings could be offered as rewards for attendance and participation. Skill development and decision making can help encourage members to refuse drugs.

The purpose of the group influences decisions about membership. Age, gender, developmental stage, and social functioning are important considerations. The purpose of the group also dictates the role of the worker and the types of services rendered. Group purpose must be understood and incorporated into every facet of the work to facilitate success for the group as a whole and to ensure maximum benefit for members.

Assessment with Small Groups

There are two major types of assessment needed for small groups: product and process. Assessment as product includes collecting and organizing data on each potential group member prior to beginning the group. This involves utilizing the steps described in Chapter 8. Data collected are similar to those described in Chapter 8, although the emphasis is on assessing the individual's "fit" with both the group's purpose and with other potential members. The worker who is forming a small group should conduct an individual assessment from two viewpoints at the same time: (1) What are the issues, needs, concerns, and strengths of the individual being interviewed? (2) How would this individual fit with the other potential group members and the overall purpose of the group?

Although the purpose of the group will influence member selection, it is generally desirable to have members who are somewhat similar in socioeconomic status, age, and level of concern regarding the group's purpose. An ethnic, cultural, and gender balance can also be important, again depending on the overall goals of the group. Because in small groups members learn from and use each other's strengths, diversity in this area can be an asset for group functioning. Diversity in members' experiences can also be helpful if the disparity is not too great because members can learn from one another about how to deal with situations relevant to the purpose of the group. It is also important to determine how potential members might interact with others in a group setting and what role they might be expected to assume. Communication skills, social skills, and developmental level must also be assessed in light of potential group membership.

In some instances, commonalities rather than diversity, and diversity rather than commonalities, are preferred. For example, a group for people who have been sexually abused would probably function better if all members are of the same sex. A group for people who are dealing with the death of a family member, however, may benefit from members who are in various stages of the grieving process. Again, the purpose of the group determines the composition.

Once the group has begun, group assessment skills may include utilization of the tools described in Table 14.1 and the sociogram depicted in Figure 14.1. These provide information about the group at a particular point in time and may contribute to an understanding of group dynamics or indicate when the group leader should intervene. Ongoing periodic assessment of members' progress and interactions, as well as group dynamics, will also help the worker shape or reshape the structure and intent of the group.

Assessing the Small Group as a Social System

The term *group* is often used in an imprecise, broad sense. The designation of *small group* as a social system places some limitation on the term. As a social system, a **small group** is composed of three or more persons who have something in common and who use face-to-face interaction to share that commonality and work to fulfill needs and solve common problems, their own or others. An effective small group allows each person in the group to have an impact on every other person in the group. The group is an entity or system that is identifiable, and it is more than the sum of its parts. For best results, the group should not exceed eight to ten members. A task group may require more members to accomplish its tasks. Support groups may be larger, but membership fluctuates. Groups, like all social systems, have structure (the form of a system at any point in time), a way of functioning or behaving in order to accomplish tasks, and development that takes place in stages over time.[1] (See Table 14.1.) To develop sufficient understanding for effective interaction in and with a small group, a social worker needs to assess all three of these dimensions.

The group has an ecosystem, and each group member has an ecosystem unique to that member, although certain systems may overlap, such as community systems in which group members share membership. The purpose of most groups is generally to assist members in getting their needs met from their ecosystems and meeting the needs of others in those systems. Members are expected to use what they gain in the group to bring about growth and change in their lives outside the group. In a task group, the purpose is changing the ecosystem of the group. Thus, the worker needs to develop skills in facilitating the group in accomplishing its goals and objectives, both within and outside of the group.

TABLE 14.1   *A Schema for the Study of the Small Group as a Social System*

I. Structure

    A. Boundary

        1. What is the purpose, mission, or task of this group?

        2. Identify members of the group. Describe them as persons. (Use appropriate parts of Table 8.2.)

        3. What are the factors that separate these persons from other persons? How were the members chosen? Under what circumstances would a person no longer be a member of this group?

        4. What is the history of this group? How and why was it formed? How long has it been meeting?

        5. What is the position of the worker with this group?

        6. What is the influence of the environment on this group and its functioning? Include environmental expectations, impingements, and resources.

        7. Describe the open/closed character of the boundary. Include communication and energy exchange and openness to new ideas and ways of functioning.

    B. Relationship framework

        1. Describe any rating/ranking of group members.

        2. Draw a sociogram.

        3. Describe the manner in which members fill roles. Are all needed roles filled? Are any roles overfilled? Which members fill several roles?

    C. Bond

        1. What is it that holds members of the group together? Note common interests and friendships.

        2. Describe the climate of the group.

        3. What are the goals of the group? Are they explicit and known to, and accepted by, all group members?

        4. What are the norms or rules for functioning in this group? How did they develop? Are they known to, and accepted by, all group members?

        5. What are the rewards of membership in this group?

        6. What priority do members give to the group?

II. Functioning

    A. Balance/stability

        1. How does this group adapt to changing conditions? Consider change both in the environment and within the group.

        2. How much time is spent on group maintenance and how much on group task? Is this balance appropriate?

    B. Decision making

        1. How does this group make decisions about norms, goals, and plans for work?

        2. Describe group problem-solving mechanisms. Do any members engage in diversionary or blocking tactics that inhibit problem solving?

        3. Describe leadership as it facilitates or inhibits the group's decision making.

        4. How do group members influence group decisions?

        5. How is conflict resolved? Is it recognized and kept in the open?

    C. Communication

        1. Describe communication patterns of the group.

        2. Does the group have adequate feedback mechanisms? Is attention paid to nonverbal communication?

(continued)

TABLE 14.1   *(continued)*

  3. Do all group members have adequate opportunity to communicate? Do any members tend to overcommunicate?
  4. Are there any content areas that seem to be troublesome when communicating?
  5. Is attention paid to communication difficulties that arise from cross-cultural or cross-professional interaction?
  D. Task implementation
  1. Describe the manner in which the group carries out its tasks. Describe the quality of interaction in carrying out tasks.
  2. Do any members engage in diversionary or blocking tactics that inhibit carrying out plans?

III. Development
  A. Identify the stage of development in which the group is operating.
  B. Describe any factors that may be inhibiting continued group development.

IV. Strengths and Challenges
  A. What are the strengths of the group?
  B. What are the challenges for the group?

Structure.   Three major dimensions of structure are boundary, relationship framework, and bond. **Boundary**, in a social system, is the point at which the system of interaction around a function no longer has the intensity that the interaction among the members has. Sometimes membership in a group is clearly defined; at other times, the determination of boundary may be difficult to establish. For example, a drop-in group at a community center will have sporadic attendance.

When considering boundary, it is important to take into account who the group members are. All members have personal histories, current needs, and responsibilities toward other systems. These affect each person's functioning in the group. Each group member receives certain rewards for participating in the group, and these need to be identified. The history of the group, how and why it was formed, and any change in focus, membership, or way of functioning as it influences current structure are important for a group assessment.

The worker's role in the group is another component of relationship. Henry Maier has identified three orientations to member-worker interactions. A Type A relationship has a strict boundary between the work of the group and larger life situations. The worker is considered an expert; as such he functions from a position of separation from the rest of the group yet exercises considerable control over the functioning of the group. In a Type B relationship, the worker is more a part of the group yet has the distinctive role of facilitator of group functioning. In a Type C relationship, the worker is a member of the group, and there is no role differentiation. The Type C relationship would likely include such groups as community groups or interdisciplinary teams, which is covered in Chapter 15.[2]

The environment of the group also affects the group's functioning. The environment places expectations on, and furnishes resources for, the group. The boundary may be relatively open or closed. When a group has an open boundary, it is fairly easy for individuals to join the group, and the group is open to new ideas and other communication from the environment. When the boundary is more closed, membership is restricted, as is communication from outside. However, as mentioned earlier, the purpose of the group is to either act on the environment as a group or for members to act on their environments as individuals in order to bring about balance in meeting needs. The boundary helps to define the group, but members continue to have lives outside the group that influence their functioning in the group and that is influenced by their functioning in the group. The relationships among the members can be examined in several ways, three of which include:

1. *The rating-ranking pattern*—In some groups one (or more) member clearly has higher status than the others. When examining relationships from this perspective, it is important to look not only at the status hierarchy but also at the reason for members' status as well.

2. *The sociogram*—The **sociogram** shows patterns of liking and nonliking.[3] It can also show subgrouping and strength of relationships in a group. Figure 14.1 describes a group of delinquent boys in a group home. Reggie and Isaiah have a very strong relationship, as do Gary and Eddie. There are mixed relations among others.

3. *The role structure*—Kenneth Benne and Paul Sheats have identified three categories of roles that may develop in groups: group task roles, group-building (or group maintenance) roles, and individual roles. **Group task roles** are related to the accomplishment of the function or task of the group. In discussion groups, roles include the initiator or contributor of ideas, the information seeker, the clarifier of ideas, the information giver, the opinion giver, the opinion seeker, and the orienter. **Group-building (group maintenance) roles** are those that focus on the maintenance of the group as a system. Roles that fall into this category include the encourager, the harmonizer, the compromiser, and the gatekeeper. The gatekeeper is the one who controls the flow of communication by allowing, encouraging, and blocking messages from the various group members. The third category is composed of the **individual roles** that satisfy individual need but detract from the work of the group. These roles include the dominator, the special-interest pleader, and the blocker.[4]

Often, leadership is considered to be a role. **Leadership** can be thought of as filling a number of roles, particularly those needed for effective group functioning. The identification of who fills which roles, which roles are not being filled, and which members tend to carry many or crucial roles clarifies group structure.

Bond is the cohesive quality of the group; it is a "we feeling" as opposed to an "I-he-she feeling." It is expressed in common group goals, in norms for group behavior, and in

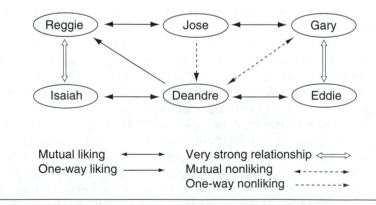

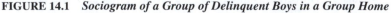

FIGURE 14.1 *Sociogram of a Group of Delinquent Boys in a Group Home*

common values held by group members. In systems terms, steady state is a related concept. *Steady state* is a particular configuration of parts that is self-maintaining and self-repairing. In other words, it is a state of systems that leads to both stability and adaptability. The functional group needs to maintain stability while still being adaptable to changing conditions and situations.

Description of the bond existing in a group identifies what holds the group together: common interests or tasks, friendships, desire for relationships, and the like. Also important is the identification of group goals, norms, and values as well as the ability of the group to adapt to changing conditions and situations.

Group structure is described by identifying the aspects of boundary, relationship structure, and bond. The structure changes as the group interacts and carries out its function over time. The social worker strives to enable the group to develop a structure that enhances the quality of the interaction of its members while also enhancing the group's ability to achieve its purpose. Generally, this involves either balancing the interactions between the group and its ecosystem (as in a task group) or enhancing the ability of members to meet their own needs and the needs of their ecosystem (as in counseling or support groups).

Function. Group interaction is a complex process influenced by the actions of group members and by the interactions among the various members. These actions and interactions in turn are influenced by group members' needs and responsibilities. The process is also influenced by the needs of the group as an entity accomplishing tasks and maintaining itself. The situation or environment in which the group functions also influences the functioning. This functioning, which is quite complex, is transactional in nature.

One way of describing group functioning is in terms of the *use of energy.* Every system has a limited amount of energy, and there is always a state of tension as to the way the energy will be used. Tensions may be expressed in terms of energy allotted to group tasks or to group building. They may be expressed in terms of stability versus change or adaptability issues. Each group develops ways of dealing with these energy issues.

Another way to describe group functioning is in how it uses information. As mentioned earlier, much of the social work endeavor involves the exchange of information. Group members share information within the group and use information from outside the group. They also take information from the group and use it in their interactions with their ecosystems. The bulk of the work in groups involves exchanges of information designed to achieve goals and objectives for the group and its members. Members are expected to use what they learn to either act on the group's ecosystem (task groups) or to act on their own (counseling or support groups). The need for confidentiality can restrict the flow of personal information from the group. (See Chapter 4 for more on confidentiality.)

Another aspect of the group's functioning is its *decision-making* and *communication processes.* Groups make decisions about which roles and tasks belong to which members, about how to communicate and implement group decisions, and about the use of energy. Decisions are made in different ways in different groups. Sometimes a rational or problem-solving process is used; sometimes compromise is a method; sometimes one or more group members impose their will on the rest of the group. Often groups merely function on the basis of past experience.

Closely related to decision making are issues of leadership, power, control, and conflict. **Conflict** is often viewed as a negative ingredient of group interaction. Properly managed it can be a force that enhances group creativity and problem solving. Conflict is expected in a situation in which people of varying backgrounds work together. Conflict is the struggle for something that is scarce. In a group this may be attention, power, status, influence, roles, and so on. Groups make decisions about how conflicts will be resolved. One of the tasks of a social worker in fostering group interaction is to identify conflict areas and help the group work toward healthy resolution of the conflict.

Communication is the heart of the process of group interaction and thus a most important aspect of its functioning. Information, decisions, and directives are distributed through communication among group members. Communication is the means of forming and modifying opinions and attitudes. The *communication process* is described by focusing on who communicates to whom and about what.

Another way of describing the group's functioning is to note the *task implementation process,* that is, how the group accomplishes its task. The task implementation process is concerned with who does what and whether individuals carry out delegated tasks.

Group functioning is simply movement in carrying out the group's function. The structure changes as movement takes place. This change is related to the development of greater organization, which results in specialization and stabilization. As the worker strives to influence the group's interaction, he enables the group to carry out its function and tasks.

Development.   As the group functions and the structure changes, it passes through a series of expected, identifiable stages. At each stage, the group has differing group maintenance needs. The capacity for the group to fulfill its function grows as it progresses through the stages of development. Groups develop at different rates. Factors that encourage group development include:

1. The strength of the members' commitment to the group's function, tasks, and goals
2. The satisfaction of the mutual needs of the members
3. The liking or caring that the members feel for one another
4. Reciprocation rather than competition for roles
5. Respect for diversity among group members
6. The amount of time the group spends together
7. Interaction that encourages individual growth
8. A degree of homogeneity that allows group norms and goals to form
9. A degree of heterogeneity that provides different ideas and points of view among the members

The stages of group development may be conceptualized as follows:

1. *The orientation stage*—Members come together for the first time, seek similarities in interest, and make an initial commitment to the group. There is also an approach-avoidance mechanism at work. Patterns of functioning around tasks begin to develop. Task roles begin to emerge. Emphasis is on activity and orientation to the situation. Individuals make decisions about the desirability of belonging to the group and whether to become dependent on other group members.

2. *The authority stage*—There is challenge to the influence and control of the group by individual members. Conflict develops; members rebel and search for individual autono-

my; power and control are issues; there may be dropouts. Structure and patterns of functioning are revised. Members share ideas and feelings about what the group should do and how the group should function. Norms and values develop through this sharing.

3. *The negotiation stage*—The group confronts, differs, and engages in conflict resolution. Goals, roles, and tasks are designated and accepted. Group traditions are stronger, norms develop, personal involvement intensifies. Group cohesion is stronger, and members are freer in sharing information and opinions.

4. *The functional stage*—A high level of group integration is reached. There is little conflict about structure, and ways of functioning have been established. Roles are differentially assigned to members and accepted by all. Communication channels are open and functional; goals and norms are known and accepted. The group has the capacity to change and adapt. Conflict and tension are managed with minimal energy use; a problem-solving capacity develops. Members are interdependent. Plans are implemented, tasks are completed, and goals are reached. The group can evaluate itself and its work.

5. *The disintegration stage*—At any of the first four stages, a group may begin to disintegrate. Signs of disintegration include the lessening of the bond. There is a reduction in the frequency and strength of group interaction, in common norms or values for group members, and in the group's strength of influence on members. At the same time that this is occurring, members will generally be strengthening and increasing their interaction with their ecosystem outside of the group.

Identifying a group's stage of development allows a worker to respond to that group with greater understanding about the structure and functioning of the group. It also provides an informed response to that group's functioning, which is a means for enhancing the interactional processes of the group.

Understanding the small group as a social system is a prerequisite to effective work as a group member or to working with the multiclient system. This understanding is a guide for the worker's interactions and interventions when working in and with groups.

Case Example

Group of Delinquent Boys in a Group Home
I. Structure
A. Boundary

1. **Purpose:** The boys in the group have been placed in the group home by juvenile courts. Each has a history of property crimes or involvement with drugs. The purpose of the group is to work on the life skills needed to resolve situations that are barriers to success at home, at school, and in the community. The group plans and carries out community service projects.

2. **Group members:** There are six members in the group. Reggie, 16, is African American and has been in the home for 11 months and is nearing discharge. Reggie was living on the street before being sent to the home and had a series of thefts and drug possession charges. He claims that his mother's live-in boyfriend

(continued)

was abusive toward him so he left home. He is uncertain where he will go after discharge, but he is hoping that his grandparents might agree to take him. Isaiah, 15, is African American and has been in the home for 11 months and is also nearing discharge. Isaiah had a long history of delinquency, including burglary and drugs. He and his two older half sisters were raised by his grandmother. Jose, 16, is Mexican American and has been in the home for 8 months. He was sent there for assault and car theft, which he committed with members of a gang. His girlfriend was pregnant when he was placed and has since given birth to a boy. Jose wants to marry her when he leaves and get a job. Gary, 14, is Caucasian and has been in the home for 3 months. He was sent by the court for a series of burglaries, which he committed with a group of friends. His parents are divorced and have married other partners. Eddie, 14, is Caucasian and has been in the home for 3 months. He is the youngest of six children and was sent to the home for a series of car thefts. Deandre, 14, is African American and has been in the home for a month after he was caught working in a drug house as a guard. Deandre had run away from home after being released on probation from the youth home.

3. **Why these boys constitute a group:** This is a nonvoluntary group that is a part of the boys' rehabilitation program. Failure to complete the program will likely mean placement at the state boys' training school or some restricted setting. The boys will not leave the group until they are discharged.

4. **History of the group:** The group is ongoing based on admission and discharge from the program. The group must unanimously recommend members for discharge. Candidates must present a thorough assessment of the difficulties that resulted in their placement, an assessment of their strengths and challenges, and a comprehensive discharge plan that includes a place to live and educational, vocational, and community service plans. The group meets daily Monday through Saturday. The current group membership has been together for a month since Deandre arrived.

5. **Workers and the group:** There are two social workers who facilitate the group either jointly or on a rotating basis to cover Saturdays. The workers have a combination of A and B characteristics (see Maier's typology). They are definitely in a professional role, which would be Type A, but they allow the group to do much of the work. They also spend a great deal of time with the boys outside of the group, especially with community service projects, family work, and individual counseling sessions. This makes them more Type B in the group members' view of them.

6. **Environmental influences:** Group members have what amounts to two ecosystems: the one they left when they were removed from their families and the one they share with each other in the group home. Since most of their time is spent together in the group, they share many of the same experiences with the environment. The situation is somewhat different at school, since they attend either the middle school or the high school, and have different classes. The group home has been operating for ten years, and the local community has become accustomed to it. The community service projects that the group undertakes have had a very positive influence, but the boys are still seen as outsiders and regarded warily by some parts of the community since they are delinquents. The local Boys and Girls Club has welcomed them, and the group members have established a relationship with the YMCA. Some of the boys participate in athletics and clubs at school.

(continued)

Case Example   *(continued)*

7. **Meeting arrangements:** The group meets in the living room daily from Monday through Saturday after dinner for ninety minutes.
8. **Open/closedness:** The group has a closed boundary, since membership is determined by admission and discharge from the program.

B. **Relationship framework**

1. **Ranking:** There is no rating and ranking in this group. All are seen as equal, and ideas from all are accepted. However, boys who are preparing for discharge are expected to take a positive leadership role to demonstrate their readiness for life outside of the home.
2. **Sociogram** (see Figure 14.1): It should be noted that there is a generally positive relationship among all group members but that there is a tendency for the boys to pair up based on race or ethnicity and age.
3. **Roles:** Reggie is the organizer and a natural leader in the group. He is serious and reminds everyone of their responsibilities when they forget and is also most active in organizing community service projects. In the meetings, he is quick to point out unsuccessful behaviors in group members and participates in finding positive alternatives. Isaiah is probably the most popular member. He is very humorous and always seems to have a smile on his face. Sometimes his humor takes the group away from their task, but he is also very adept at pointing out difficulties in a humorous way that seems to put members more at ease in terms of accepting responsibility. Jose is a listener. He makes his contribution by working on his own agenda but sharing his work with the group for their comments. In some ways he models for the rest of the group the work to be done in that he is making an effort to take the responsibility that parenthood has thrust on him. Gary is a follower who seems to be willing to go along with whatever the group wants. Recently, however, he has been distracting the group from their task at times by making funny sounds or changing the subject. Although this is a blocking activity, it seems like it is a sign that his individuality is coming out. It also seems to relate to subjects with which he may be uncomfortable. Eddie is a questioner. He often seems to be stalling group discussion, but what he is really doing is asking the group for some direction, and, at times, this helps the group to look at itself and how it is functioning. Deandre is still being rebellious by challenging positive activities in the group and refusing to accept responsibility for his actions. He has not found a positive role with the group as yet and feels like he is being picked on.

C. **Bond**

1. **What it is:** The commonality of their situations of being adolescent boys living together in a group home is a major component of the bond. The desire to return home is of major importance. They must have approval from all of the members of the group before a release goes to the staff for approval.
2. **Climate:** The climate is most comfortable when planning a project or an outing in which everyone participates. It is less comfortable when the group is working on life skills, especially when an unsuccessful behavior or attitude has been identified in a member.
3. **Goals of the group:** The group goal is for each member to learn to make successful decisions that result in positive life outcomes. This includes learning life skills such as social skills, conflict resolution, decision making, planning, and personal and social responsibility.

(continued)

Case Example   *(continued)*

4. **Norms of the group:** Most group norms are explicit in terms of the program and the expectations for individual and group behavior. The norms of the group are that members must attend all meetings, which last an hour and a half; members must be on time; the material discussed is confidential and must not be discussed elsewhere; and that the group will spend part of the time focusing on individual situations and part of the time planning group projects or outings.

5. **Priority of the group:** Group members give high priority to the group because it is important to their success in the program and their discharge.

II. Functioning

A. Balance/stability

1. **Adaptation:** Recently, the group has not had a stable environment and membership because of turnover. Deandre took the place of a member who was removed by the court when he eloped, broke into a home, and stole a car. Deandre is having difficulty in adjusting to placement. Before that time there were several successful discharges. The group spent a lot of time discussing its most recent failure, and this seems to have helped it to regain some stability. Most of the boys were able to admit they had thought of doing the same thing when things got tough or they were homesick. Thus, they seem able to turn a negative into something positive. Members have been very patient with Deandre and seem determined to help him to become part of the group.

2. **Maintenance vs. task:** During the first meeting with Deandre, the group spent considerable time on maintenance, discussing how the group works together. A contract is developing detailing some of the work to be done with Deandre. This is still in progress. For most meetings, minimal time is spent on group maintenance because the group meets so frequently. At the beginning or end of each meeting, there is some discussion about projects and how well the group is fulfilling its contract with one another. As the group is working well together, the balance is appropriate.

B. Decision making

1. **Method:** Decisions are made by consensus. For example, when discussing projects or outings, members discuss several possibilities and, as a group, decide on the specific plans.

2. **Problem solving:** Problems tend to relate to a particular group member's struggle to make successful decisions. The pattern is for members to throw out ideas as to possible solutions and then together consider each solution. Group solutions are implemented after consensual decision making.

3. **Leadership:** Reggie and Isaiah tend to share the leadership role. Both tend to be facilitative leaders. At times Jose calls for the worker to take this role by asking the worker to be more directive and tell them what to do.

4. **Influence on decision making:** Group members all have influence on the decisions through their contributions to discussion. Reggie and Isaiah seem to have the most influence because of the quality of their contributions.

5. **Conflict:** Conflict is either denied or is taken as a challenge. The worker notes that when members recognize a conflict, they tend to ask for input from him as to a decision or task. They refuse to recognize this as a mechanism of avoiding conflict, even when this is pointed out. However, after this denial, they work as a group in a problem-solving mode to resolve the differences.

(continued)

Case Example   *(continued)*

C. Communication

1. **Patterns:** The group gives each person an opportunity to discuss each issue. There are some blocks, as mentioned previously. Older or more veteran group members are aware of the communication process and of the need for listening as well as talking. Occasionally, newer or younger members will get into a side conversation. Other members will call attention to this, which ends the intrusion into the work of the group.

2. **Feedback:** The veteran group members often ask each other for feedback. Newer members do not solicit feedback but are given it by veterans.

3. **Opportunity:** Each member is encouraged to add his thinking to the group discussion. If one member gets off on a tangent and holds the floor too long, someone steps in and brings the discussion back to the subject.

4. **Troublesome content areas:** Personal responsibility is the biggest trouble area. Veteran members have come to realize the importance of this area, not only for graduating from the program, but also for life afterward. Newer members are very evasive and much more willing to blame others for any difficulties.

5. **Cross-cultural factors:** There is a tendency for the group to pair up by race and ethnicity. Much of this has been reduced by sharing experiences with each other. Members seem to have come to the realization that underneath their skin, they are all human beings. However, there is still some separation that appears in the group.

D. Task implementation

1. **How tasks are carried out:** Projects and outings bring about the most enthusiasm. Discussing personal responsibility is usually met by some denial, with veteran members moving quickly to acceptance. The group tends to get down to business on its own unless there has been a recent conflict. Discussing chores and daily living concerns generates a lot of complaints initially, but the group tends to find ways of resolving issues without too much intervention.

2. **Blocking tactics:** Denial is a primary blocking tactic that all use at some time. Newer members use it frequently. Deandre's rebelliousness and Gary's distractions are blocking tactics but are predictable.

III. Development

A. **Stage:** The group demonstrates elements of various stages depending on the circumstances. With the recent addition of a new member, the group has experienced some orientation and authority stage elements when working with Deandre. Overall, it seems to be primarily in the negotiation and functional stages, with newer members setting goals and veteran members fulfilling goals.

B. **Inhibiting factors:** Denial and projection have been such basic defense mechanisms for so long that it is difficult to give these up. Veterans do so fairly quickly, but these responses still occur as an initial reaction to most difficulties.

IV. Strengths and challenges

A. **Strengths:** The group is self-organized with well-focused tasks, especially with projects. The relationship framework, bond, decision-making process, and use of the problem-solving process are all very functional.

B. **Challenges:** The group itself is functioning well; however, individual members face obstacles to success, especially when they return home. The immaturity of younger members is frustrating for those who are nearing graduation.

Planning with Small Groups

There are four ways that planning is used with small groups. These include: (1) planning for a new group, (2) planning for each group session, (3) planning within group sessions, and (4) facilitating the development and use of planning skills by group members. This last use of planning is similar to that used with individuals and families and will not be repeated here. The worker uses the small-group experience to teach skills in planning and to support the successful completion of goals, objectives, and tasks.

Planning for a New Group

In starting a new group, the worker needs to formulate a plan or proposal that can be used in working with supervisors, administrators, other staff, and other agencies and in recruiting potential members. Generally, administrators and supervisors will be concerned about efficiency and effectiveness, so these issues should be addressed. Other staff and other agencies will be concerned with why they should refer clients to the group and who would be appropriate. Potential group members will wonder what benefit they could expect from participating.

There are several formats that can be used for constructing a proposal if one has not been developed by the agency. Essentially, the worker should answer the questions why, who, what, where, when, and how. The question "why" is answered by a thorough discussion of the purpose of the group and the potential benefits for participants. The proposal should include a description of who the members will be and how they will be recruited. It should have a description of what will take place during sessions and over the course of the group. If a curriculum is to be used, a table of contents and a sample of a session is generally attached as an addendum. The plan should describe where and when the group will take place, length of sessions and when the group will end. There should be a description of resources needed and how these will be obtained. The cost of these resources may be formulated in a budget format. Examples of recruitment fliers or letters, informed consent forms, and other materials should also be attached. In addition, the process for evaluating the group should be described.

Planning for Group Sessions

The worker's role in planning group sessions can vary considerably. Factors include group membership, the structure of sessions, the type of group, and coleadership. Groups with young members or members with developmental delays or a significant impairment (such as mental retardation or mental illness) generally require more planning and direction from the worker. Members with lower social functioning need structure to ensure successful completion of tasks. Usually, sessions are structured around the use of discussion and activity. The most common structure is discussion-activity-discussion, or DAD. The worker leads a discussion of events during the week and of the activity for the session. The group engages in the activity. This is followed by a discussion of the activity itself, including any benefits, and its use in everyday life. Planning for the next session may also be discussed.

Growth and skill development groups generally require considerable planning and preparation. Education groups require the most preparation because the worker is often in the role of teacher or presenter. Skill development groups usually use a curriculum that has structured activities involving more preparation by the worker. In addition to becoming familiar with the activity, the worker is also responsible for securing supplies and facilitating participation. Prevention groups often use a curriculum or structured activities. Support groups for older adolescents and adults are usually less structured. Planning for support groups generally requires providing resources, such as information, speakers, videos, and similar materials. Counseling groups are the least structured and require less planning ahead of time, but planning is used more within the group process.

In coleadership, workers must use planning before and after each session to coordinate their roles and activities so they complement each other. Workers need to be consistent and avoid contradictions and confusion. Maintaining consistency is difficult but important to avoid sending mixed messages to group members.

Planning within Group Sessions

The use of planning within group sessions may involve engaging the group in planning for activities that will take place during group sessions, between sessions, or in the future outside of regular sessions. In addition, planning is used within groups that are intended to assist members in learning to use the change process, decision making, or problem solving. Members use the group to develop goals, objectives, and tasks designed to make changes in their daily lives. Group goals are similar to common or shared goals with families (see Chapter 13). Individual goals are similar to those covered in Chapter 9.

In groups using a DAD structure with higher-functioning members, either discussion phase may include planning for future activities. The ending phase often includes planning for the next session. Groups that live together in group homes, residential programs, and institutions generally use group sessions to plan activities that will take place between sessions or in the future. Because members are living together, they also need to use groups to manage their daily living activities and resolve problems that arise. The change process is used to facilitate decision making and problem solving. Planning is an important phase in these activities. These groups may be used for long-term planning for group activities and projects, such as community service activities, outings, and field trips.

In counseling groups, members use the group to assist in decision making and problem solving. The change process facilitates these activities. Members use the group to help assess the situation and develop a plan. The group provides support for carrying out the plan. In the course of making decisions and solving problems for themselves and with each other, members gain knowledge and skills in use of the change process for the future.

Direct Practice Actions with Small Groups

Working with the small group as a multiperson client system means the worker facilitates the group in terms of structure, functioning, and development while ensuring members obtain maximum benefit from their experiences in the group. Thus, group work involves a constant process of balancing needs of the group in maintaining itself as a group and needs of individual members. Because needs of individual members are important, all of the direct practice actions and strategies that were identified in Chapter 10 can be used in working with small groups. (See Figure 10.1.) In addition, interaction skills that were covered in Chapter 7 are vital to working with groups. Finally, direct practice actions with families discussed in Chapter 13 are also relevant for small groups. These include actions related to relationship building, the change process, resources, empowering and enabling, crisis resolution, support, activity, and mediation. Practice actions are used to facilitate completion of the plan, removal of barriers to the plan, and the functioning of both the system and individual members. These practice actions will not be repeated here, but the student should review this material before proceeding and include them in her work with small groups. This section will focus on actions to facilitate group development and functioning, including actions taken to (1) facilitate group formation, (2) facilitate discussion leadership, (3) resolve conflict, (4) enhance group interaction, (5) facilitate group development, and (6) structure group activities.

Indirect practice actions may be needed on behalf of individuals in the group or on behalf of the group as a whole. In instances when influencing the environment or environmental change is needed, the worker should make every effort to either support the group in acting on its own behalf or include the group in actions the worker takes.

Actions to Facilitate Group Formation

Although social workers sometimes work with already-formed systems or groups, at times it is necessary to form a group. People considered for group membership may not be acquainted with one another. The handling of the formation process is an important factor in whether the group will be able to function to meet its goals. There are four stages to the formation of a group: (1) establishing the group's purpose, (2) selecting members, (3) making the first contacts with prospective members, and (4) holding the first meeting of the group.

The group's purpose may develop from a client request or from an agency staff decision that there is a need that can be met through developing a group. Some of the reasons for forming a group are (1) when several people facing similar situations can benefit from sharing their experiences; (2) when group influence on individuals is great, such as during the teenage years; (3) when the target for change is in the environment, such as the development of a new community service; (4) when a natural group exists; (5) to improve relationships with others; and (6) to aid those experiencing social isolation. The group is an excellent vehicle to use for reality testing because it is a social microcosm of the larger society. Groups should not be used to save workers' time when a common goal or purpose does not exist, when an individual is in danger of being overwhelmed by the group, when there is insufficient commonality for a cohesive climate to develop, or when the environment impinges on the group's functioning or prevents it from reaching its goals. Groups can work together on individual needs, on relationships within or outside of the group, on decision making or task achievement, or on targeting for change in the larger community.

For a group to function, group members must have some commonality (in part, the purpose and function provide the commonality). At this stage of the formation process, the worker and agency identify a common need and translate the need to the purpose for the prospective group. The worker formulates tentative group goals. Based on the purpose and tentative goals, the worker begins selecting members. Consideration is given to how many people should be in the group. When members have good interactional skills, the number can go as high as ten or twelve and still allow for interaction among all members. For clients with little interactional capacity, the size of the group should be limited to five or six persons.

Group commonality is in part based on the attractiveness prospective members have for one another. People are attracted to other people because they admire them, hold common values with them, respect them, or support their functioning in some way. People feel most comfortable with those who are similar to themselves. For a group to be productive, however, it is necessary for the members to have sufficient differences so that unique contributions can be made by each group member. The worker must determine how much commonality is necessary for the group to be attractive to prospective members and how much difference is necessary to carry out the function of the group.

In choosing prospective members the worker must evaluate how well these individuals can be expected to function in the group and what their contributions might be. The choice of prospective members is based on multiple factors that relate to the need for balance and the individual qualities of these members.

In facilitating group formation, the worker considers diversity of its members. In most groups, it is generally best to try to have members with a variety of diverse backgrounds. If only one member has a particular diversity background (such as being the only woman or African American in the group), that person is likely to feel out of place and is at risk of leaving the group. If at least one other member shares the same diversity, the chances that both members will stay improve considerably. In terms of the functioning of the group regarding diversity, the worker should facilitate open discussions of the differences that exist among members and help the group see the strengths in others who are different and realize how diversity strengthens the group itself. She should not assume that everyone shares her view of valuing diversity. It is likely that the prejudices that are present in society will also be present in the group. The worker's role is to facilitate positive exchanges that will help group members to know each other as human beings. Identifying commonalities is generally the first step in this process. If members can appreciate each other as human beings, they can begin to look at what makes each group member unique and individual, including his or her diversity. Given the prejudice in society toward people of color, women, homosexuals, non-Christians, various ethnic groups, and the like, this work is very delicate and must be undertaken with caution and planning. It is best if ahead of time the worker has developed some degree of competence with respect to the diversity in her group. This can be done in part during screening interviews and by conducting a self-assessment and some research. During the screening interview, the worker uses naturalistic inquiry to discover the prospective member's perceptions regarding his or her diversity. In the group, the worker models naturalistic inquiry and respect for diversity. If the group can solidify an appreciation for the diversity of its members, members can learn a great deal from one another, and the group will have access to a wider variety of experiences from which it can draw on as resources.

Other factors in forming a group are the resources and expectations that arise from the prospective group's environment. These factors affect the prospective member's ability to function in the group and also affect the manner in which the group can function.

When the worker has completed the process of choosing prospective members, the next step is an initial contact with each person. During the initial contact, the worker explains the purpose of the group and the reason for considering the person for group membership. Together they explore how the group may function and come to a decision about the prospective member joining the group. In many ways, this session is similar to the worker's initial interview with an individual client. The major purpose of the session is to begin to engage the member in the group and to orient the member to the group.

The first meeting of the group is crucial for group formation. The group function and the way of operating are discussed again. The worker enables members to share their reasons for joining the group and their individual goals with respect to the group. The worker facilitates communication among the members and helps them begin formulating group norms and goals. The group begins to work on the tasks of carrying out the function of the group. Every attempt is made for this first session to be a positive experience for all members.

Adequate group formation is time consuming, but, if properly done, saves time later. It reduces the chances of having a mismatch of group members and prepares members for functioning in the group. In this way, time in the group can be spent on its function and tasks, not on unrelated individual needs.

When the group is ongoing and not time limited, the group must decide how it will add new members. If it is an open group, as are support groups and self-help groups, members can join or leave at any time. For these groups, a certain member or members should be identified who can quickly orient new members to the norms of the group and help introduce them to the group.

In closed groups that are ongoing, new members are usually only added when someone leaves the group. The worker generally takes responsibility for screening prospective members. In groups with voluntary members, the group may be responsible for the decision of whether to accept a prospective member after the worker describes the person and his or her situation, or the worker may have responsibility for making a decision. In nonvoluntary groups, such as the one in the group home from the case study earlier in the chapter, the staff members of the agency decide who to accept through an intake process. The worker should ensure that the group has resolved any termination issues and is ready to accept the new member. Termination will be discussed in more detail later in this chapter. In either case, the worker typically will orient the new member prior to the group meeting and then facilitate having the group complete the orientation process during the first session the new member attends. This orientation should include introductions, a discussion of group rules, and a discussion of what is expected of the new member in terms of participation. Periodic checks should be made with the new member and feedback given for the first few sessions to facilitate having him or her join in the group process.

Actions to Facilitate Discussion Leadership

Discussion is the means of communicating within the group. The worker carries the task of enabling the discussion to develop until such time as leadership emerges in the group. This enabling takes place through:

1. *Climate setting*—The worker pays attention to the physical atmosphere. Chairs are placed so that all members can have eye contact and are neither too close nor too far apart. The atmosphere should be warm, friendly, and relaxed.

2. *Stimulating*—The worker encourages the sharing of ideas. The worker also helps group members disagree without developing hostility.

3. *Encouraging mutual respect and understanding*—The worker helps members understand their commonalities and differences. The right of people to be different is considered. The worker demonstrates respect for all members and their ideas. This modeling often helps members respect one another.

4. *Reducing overdependence*—The worker encourages the group to develop its way of functioning. The worker seeks ideas and facts from the members and helps group members fill the essential roles.

5. *Drawing in nonparticipants*—The worker helps a member who is not active in the discussion to contribute by asking questions or asking for information.

6. *Checking overaggressive participants*—The worker points out to the group the need for each member to have an opportunity to participate.

7. *Helping the group define and verbalize goals and needs*—The worker stimulates group thinking and helps the group in making decisions and developing plans.

8. *Helping the group to problem solve*—The worker helps the group clarify issues, analyze problems, discover solutions, evaluate solutions, and carry out decisions. Also, the worker helps the group focus when it gets off course and summarizes as appropriate.

9. *Helping the group appreciate member diversity*—The worker encourages appropriate exploration of the diversity of its members through the use of naturalistic inquiry. The worker helps the group to value diversity and appreciate the strengths each member possesses from that diversity and the increased strength this brings to the group as a whole.

10. *Helping the group deal with conflict*—The worker points out symptoms of conflict, helps individuals clarify viewpoints and state positions, and seeks commonalities.

In providing discussion leadership to a group, the worker is also teaching members of the group how to take responsibility for their own leadership. The worker needs to help the group avoid placing undue pressure for conformity or dependency on its members, allowing harmful and unsupportive responses to vulnerable members, and tolerating assertive and talkative members receiving all the attention. As soon as group members are able to carry any part of this responsibility, the worker encourages the discussion leadership to begin to rest in the group members and then assumes the enabler role.

Actions to Resolve Conflict

For many people conflict is frightening. There is a feeling that disagreements can lead to fighting, and fear of uncontrolled fighting explains, in part, the fear of conflict. Other people believe that conflict can result in nothing positive and thus attempt to avoid it. Conflict does not need to result in uncontrolled fighting. It can lead to development of new ways of functioning that give rise to new ideas.

Conflict is to be expected when people of different backgrounds and differing experiences interact with one another. Conflict in small groups is not to be avoided; it is to be managed. Differences about what the task and function of the group is, who will fill roles, and what the norms of the group will be should be discussed and negotiated. Mediation is a process in which all parties in a conflict state their points of view and reasons for them. These points of view are examined to discover whether there is any faulty thinking and if there are any aspects the parties are willing to accommodate; attempts are made to reconcile the disagreement. Often, faulty communication is a part of the disagreement. Usually, each point of view has something that can contribute to the work of the group. Conflict is not to be avoided but rather to be brought into the open and dealt with by the group. Following are some aids to the resolution of conflict:

1. Define the conflict not as one person's problem but as the group's concern.
2. Listen to all points of view and seek to identify similarities as well as differences among them.
3. Seek clarification so that each point of view is fully understood.
4. Try to avoid win-or-lose solutions.
5. Do not ignore cues that conflict exists; check them out.
6. Work for a cooperative rather than a competitive climate.

Because social workers have skills in understanding people and their behaviors, the worker can help the group recognize conflict. The recognition of conflict is the first step toward its management and resolution. When conflict is not recognized, it can be most destructive to the group's interaction.

Actions to Enhance Group Interaction

Four factors are particularly helpful in enhancing interaction so as to enable the group to reach its goals and to carry out its tasks or functions: (1) member involvement; (2) decision making about norms, goals, and roles; (3) group discussion skills; and (4) structuring of meetings.

Member involvement is a prerequisite to effective decision making and problem solving. The climate of the group is a major contributor to member involvement. The ideal group climate encourages participation; is friendly and accepting; and is supportive of, and sensitive to, the needs of individual members. The group climate is one in which effectiveness is expected and self-actualization and innovation are encouraged. There is a stress on inclusion and trust. Members seek to collaborate with each other. The ideal group distributes influence and power among the members rather than relying on an authoritarian power figure. Influence and power rest in the knowledge and skills of the members. Conflict is not suppressed but is dealt with in the discussion process. Members engage in periodic evaluation of the work of the group.

A troublesome area is bringing in a new group member. An effective group does this in an organized manner so that the new member understands how the group functions, what its goals are, and what is expected of the new member. The new member needs time to get to know the group and its members, and the group needs time to get to know the new member.

A second contributor to effective functioning is the *decision-making process*. In making decisions about norms, goals, and roles, it is important that all members be involved in the process and that consensus be reached whenever possible. Not all group decisions must be made in this way. After norms and goals are set, some decisions can be made by voting or by individual members with permission from the group.

The process of developing norms is known as **norming**—the process by which implicit norms or expected ways of behaving are made explicit. The norms are examined to discover whether they are appropriate to the task. Periodically, the norms should be evaluated to determine their usefulness. Changes are made in the norms as necessary. Norms that are most useful to group functioning are those that allow recognition in decision making and that support individuals and the cohesiveness of the group. Another important norm is that feelings are valid information.

The *development of goals* is another shared responsibility. Goals should be clear to, and accepted by, all group members. Whenever possible, a match should be sought between individual and group goals. Goals should not be imposed on the group. It is helpful if the goals are prioritized.

Role definition also belongs to the total group. No member should automatically take on a specific role without permission from the group. Messages should be clear to all members about the acceptability of members filling roles. A conflict over roles—the desire of two or more persons to fill the same role—should be openly negotiated and alternatives sought. Compromise is an appropriate mechanism in resolving role conflict. No one person should have a role overload, that is, be filling too many of the needed roles. One means of encouraging participation is to spread the roles among the members. Periodic evaluation to determine how roles are filled is helpful.

A third characteristic of good group functioning is *group discussion skill*. Group discussion is to the small group what interviewing is to the one-to-one action system: a means of structuring communication. One definition of group discussion is: "Two or more people talking with one another in order to achieve mutually satisfactory understanding of each other's images or beliefs or a solution to a problem."[5] Cooperative interaction is influenced by each individual's perception of the topic under discussion and the group process. Two factors are particularly important for good group discussion: good communication and the use of the change process as a guide to group thinking.

Good communication calls for skill in sending messages and receiving messages so that all can know what is happening. No one person monopolizes the conversation. The feedback is:

1. Descriptive rather than evaluative
2. Specific rather than general
3. Such that it considers the needs of all persons involved
4. Directed toward that which the receiver has control over
5. Well timed

Actions to Facilitate Group Development

When a social worker works with a group of unrelated people, the focus is on group inter-action. Because the system may not have formed, in the early stages the worker may be in-volved in interaction that enables the group system to form. Again, the interactions are to enable individuals to become part of the group and to function in the group. The major focus is on group interaction, not on worker–individual member interaction; otherwise, the worker is not working with the group system but with individuals in the presence of other individuals. The worker influences the group process in a number of ways, including:

1. *Acceptance*—The worker accepts individual members with their feelings, attitudes, ideas, and behaviors. Through such acceptance, other members come to see the member's contribution, realize that their feelings can be respected, and appreciate difference. In being accepted by the worker, group members gain strength to carry out their roles in the group.

2. *Relationships*—The worker helps each group member relate to other members and gain interactional skill. The worker also uses relationship to help members find their commonalities.

3. *Enabling and supporting*—The worker helps members accept themselves and others, express themselves, have a feeling of accomplishment, and involve themselves in the activity and decision making of the group. In addition, the worker helps the group and its members gain understanding of their group process and how it may be modified. The worker contributes facts and understanding that enable the group to function.

4. *Limiting behavior*—When behavior of individual members is harmful to themselves or to others or is destructive of property or relationships, the worker helps the group or the individual member to limit such behavior.

5. *Guiding*—The worker helps the group by providing guidance for the discussion process, such as helping the group keep on focus or task, and teaching effective decision-making and planning skills. The worker also guides the activity and the movement of the group in its process.

6. *Alleviation*—The worker relieves tensions, conflicts, fears, anxiety, or guilt that may be interfering with group functioning.

7. *Interpreting*—The worker helps the group understand the function of the agency and of the worker in relation to the group's task. The worker may also interpret the meaning of the feelings or actions of the group or its members.

8. *Observation and evaluation*—The worker constantly tries to understand what is happening in the group and why it is happening.

9. *Planning and preparation*—The worker plans for the group as needed to enable the group to function and carry out its purposes.[6]

Throughout the process, the worker helps the group members to identify strengths in themselves and in their ecosystems. The worker facilitates the ability of members to assist each other in identifying these strengths. Thus, the role of the worker is to help the members reach out to one another in such a way that they can help one another in meeting their needs or in some way influencing their environments so that group and individual needs are met. Helping the group as a system to carry out its task is the focus of the social worker when working with a multiclient system.

The social worker's role is influenced by the stage of group development and by the stage of individual development of group members. During the orientation stage the worker is very active with the group. The worker helps group members to share their needs and concerns; structures group meetings so the members can get a vision of how the group can function; enables group members to maintain distance while making decisions about the group and their role in the group; and attempts to maintain a comfortable, accepting climate.

As the group moves to the authority stage, the worker allows members to challenge ideas and ways of functioning. The worker helps members recognize and deal with conflict. The worker supports the group and its members as they struggle to find ways to work together.

As the group begins to negotiate differences, the worker supports this negotiation and continues to assist the group in dealing with conflict. The group is helped to identify norms and values, establish goals, and negotiate roles. The worker clarifies feelings and ideas.

In the functional stage, the worker allows the group to function as independently as possible. The worker serves as a resource person and as an observer and helps the group evaluate its process. During this stage the worker's contribution to the group's process and work depends on what will be useful as the group engages in its work together.

When a worker senses the onset of disintegration, a decision should be made with the group as to whether the group has served its purpose; then the disintegration should be allowed to progress or an attempt should be made to help the group reverse the disintegration. If the decision is to reverse, the worker's role is to help the group determine the reasons for the disintegration and take the steps needed to restore the group to an appropriate level of functioning. A change process is used with the group. If the group has served its purpose, then the worker helps the group understand what is happening and feel good about the group's accomplishments.

Actions to Structure Group Activities

The group can be enabled to function through the use of activity. Activity can be tasks the group does together, such as games, crafts, or other program materials, or it can be structured exercises. The way in which a worker structures these activities can affect the group's development. Activity can also give the group data on which to make decisions about its functioning. Another part of structuring is the use of the physical facility and the time and place of the meeting.

When working with the multiperson client, the worker has four primary tools: (1) the worker and the way he uses self, (2) the use of group process, (3) discussion as a means of communication, and (4) structure and activity. Using these tools, the worker enables the group to function and carry out the tasks that lead to goal fulfillment.

The generalist social worker's interactive repertoire includes skill in working with small groups as well as in one-to-one interaction. To develop this skill the worker needs knowledge of group process and means for enabling the functioning of the multiperson client group.

Case Example

> ### Session Summary of a Group of Delinquent Boys in a Group Home
> January 18: Today was Deandre's first day in group, replacing an earlier member, Frank. Although Deandre had met everyone earlier, the group spent some time telling him why they were in placement, what they were working on, and where they were at in terms of progressing through the program. When asked about his situation, he bragged about working as a guard in a drug house and about how he and another boy had shot up a guy's car. Reggie challenged him on this and asked Deandre where that had gotten him. Deandre tried to act tough by saying that it didn't bother him to have to do some time. Jose asked him what would have happened if he had killed the guy. Deandre admitted that he could have faced life in prison. When asked by Reggie if that would have been worth the twenty dollars the man owed, Deandre was very quiet. He did not say very much for the rest of the session. The group spent some time discussing their last community service project, which was singing Christmas carols at some nursing homes and at an activity center for developmentally disabled adults. They decided that they wanted to do something at one of the local nursing homes for Easter but would also like to follow up with the developmentally disabled adults, especially when the weather got better.

Evaluation and Termination with Small Groups

As with individuals and families, evaluation takes place throughout the work with the group and on completion of either group or individual plans. The evaluation process is similar to working with families in that the worker must be aware of evaluating the functioning of the system and of individual members. Evaluating the system is somewhat different, because the stages of group development are different from the stages of family development. Individual evaluation takes place throughout the group just as with families. However, in some groups, members leave after completing their work. In these groups, individual evaluation of progress and of completion of plans is necessary. For time-limited groups in which everyone terminates at the same time, the worker asks for feedback about the experience just as she would do in family work.

Successful termination in small groups depends on whether the group is an ongoing group or one that is time limited. If an individual is leaving, as in the case of an ongoing group, the individual may have ambivalent feelings. He may feel good about achieving his goals but sad at the prospect of leaving those who have assisted him. The degree to which the group has been cohesive represents a bond or a sense of belonging that is now being left behind. This may be similar to what young adults feel when they become emancipated. Termination by an individual is a reminder for everyone in the group that some day they will also leave or that the group may come to an end. Each member wonders when termination will happen for him. Some may be spurred on to achieve their goals. Others may shrink from the prospect and even regress out of fear or anxiety.

Termination for individuals leaving an ongoing group may include some kind of graduation ceremony, certificate, or ritual. At the least, a member needs to be able to say his good-byes so that he can go on with his own work. This is also essential in order for the group to become ready for the new members who will follow. Members should be encouraged to allow for two or three sessions before finalizing their termination from the group. If members drop out without notice or suddenly announce their termination, the remaining members may need time to work out their feelings before they can trust one another again or are ready for a new member.

In time-limited groups, termination is an issue from beginning to end, and members choose how much to invest themselves based on this fact. Those who remain with the group will experience termination together. Often, a celebration or graduation should be planned to mark the occasion and to highlight the success of the group and its members. For some groups, certificates of achievement may be appropriate. At the least, members should be given an opportunity to express their feelings about the group experience.

In both types of groups, members may drop out. When this occurs, the worker should contact those members to see if they will return to the group. The worker may be called on to help overcome a barrier or to negotiate a problem between the absent member and the group or one of the other members. If a member cannot be convinced to return or if a return is not appropriate, the worker should arrange for alternate services. Because the group has invested time and energy in the absent member, they need feedback after the follow-up contact.

Self-Help Groups

Self-help groups are another resource social workers can help develop. These voluntary small groups are an important component of mutual aid. In the modern world, it is not always possible on one's own to find a supportive group. Social workers can help those with similar life situations and challenges find each other and provide mutual aid to one another.

Because people facing a new situation or difficulty often feel helpless, it is advisable to include individuals who have worked on the same issue or adjusted to a similar situation. They often are glad to help others because this further facilitates their return to more stable functioning. The widow-to-widow program is a good example. Newly widowed persons can be visited by others who have been widowed for a year or more; the visitor can encourage participation. In the group, the newly widowed person finds others who can help with the many concerns and decisions she faces. Much needed information is shared.

Brian and Gail Auslander have suggested that a *consultation model* is appropriate when working with self-help groups. They identify three roles for the consultant: (1) discussion of client-related needs and possible interventions, (2) discussion of the self-help group's policies and procedures in the hope of obtaining desired change, and (3) linking with resources that the group or individuals in the group may need.[7] The latter role would include providing information about and consulting on the procedures for accessing needed resources. Information about how similar groups function can also be provided.

Self-help groups are not the answer for all clients. Some groups foster inappropriate dependence or encourage simplistic solutions to complex situations. Some develop a strong antiprofessional bias. Some of these negative characteristics can be avoided if, in the process of development, an ongoing consultative role for the social worker can be planned. Social workers can support self-help groups by helping groups find meeting places, encouraging them to find needed financial resources, providing them with information and training, referring appropriate persons to them, helping the group develop credibility with the community and with professionals, and providing social and emotional support.

Summary

Multiperson interaction is an important generalist social work activity. To be effective in multiperson interaction, a social worker should understand the small group as a social system. Understanding the structure, functioning, and development of the group gives the worker direction for effective interaction. The purpose of the group affects the nature of the group, including groups for the purposes of counseling, support, and prevention, among others. There are two types of assessment of groups: product and process.

Social workers work with small groups to carry out tasks and to serve clients. They can enable these groups to function by (1) helping all group members participate in the group, (2) clarifying the decision-making process, (3) stimulating the discussion process, and (4) structuring group meetings.

Generalist social workers work with multiperson clients to enable the system to function. In doing this, the social worker helps groups to form and uses group discussion techniques and activities to facilitate group functioning. The direct practice actions a social worker uses to work with small groups involve self, group process, discussion, and activities.

Planning and evaluation and termination are important processes at the beginning and ending of work with groups.

Questions

1. Using the schema for study of a small group, describe a group in which you have participated. How does this help you understand what was happening in that group?
2. Think about groups of which you are now a part. How do you think you might enable that group to function more effectively?
3. Identify a conflict situation in a group with which you are familiar. What was the cause of the conflict? How did the group handle the conflict? Was there a better way to handle the conflict?
4. How would you justify to an agency administrator the amount of time needed for good group formation?
5. Identify a self help group in your community. Obtain information regarding the group including eligibility, leadership, involvement of professionals, agency or organizational sponsorship, and any other information that you would need to refer a client to the group.

Suggested Readings

Yanca, Stephen J. and Johnson, Louise C. *Generalist Social Work Practice with Groups*. Boston: Allyn and Bacon, 2009.

Gitterman, Alex, and Shulman, Lawrence. *Mutual Aid Groups, Vulnerable and Resilient Populations, and the Life Cycle,* 3rd ed. New York: Columbia University Press, 2005.

Grief, Geoffrey, and Ephross, Paul, Eds. *Group Work with Populations at Risk,* 2nd ed. New York: Oxford University Press, 2004.

Haslett, Diane C. *Group Work Activities in Generalist Practice.* Belmont, CA: Thomson-Brooks/Cole, 2005.

Jacobs, Ed, Masson, Robert, and Harvill, Riley. *Group Counseling Strategies and Skills,* 5th ed. Belmont, CA: Thomson-Brooks/Cole, 2006.

Johnson, David W., and Johnson, Frank P. *Joining Together: Group Theory and Group Skills,* 9th ed. Boston: Allyn and Bacon, 2006.

Mizrahi, Terry and Davis, Larry E., Eds. *Encyclopedia of Social Work*, 20th ed. Washington, DC: NASW Press, 2008 ("Group Dynamics," "Groups," "Group Work," "Self Help Groups").

Northern, Helen, and Kurland, Roselle. *Social Work with Groups,* 3rd ed. New York: Columbia University Press, 2001.

Shulman, Lawrence. *The Skills of Helping: Individuals, Families, Groups, and Communities,* 6th ed. Belmont, CA: Thomson-Brooks/Cole, 2009.

Toseland, Ronald W., and Rivas, Robert F. *An Introduction to Group Work Practice,* 6th ed. Boston: Allyn and Bacon, 2009.

Zastrow, Charles. *Social Work with Groups: A Comprehensive Workbook,* 7th ed. Belmont, CA: Thomson-Brooks/Cole, 2008.

chapter

15

Generalist Practice with Organizations and Communities

Learning Expectations

1. Understanding of the need to work with organizations and communities in generalist practice.
2. Understanding of the role of the social worker as a group member.
3. Understanding of the use of task groups in bringing about change in organizations and communities.
4. Knowledge of the change process in working with organizations and communities.
5. Knowledge of various methods of community organization practice.

This chapter deals with the change process in generalist social work practice with macrosystems. It is rare for the BSW-level worker to be called on to work directly with organizations or communities in bringing about change. However, it is very common for workers to be involved with the change process as a member of the agency staff and as a participant in community task groups. When the social worker engages in these activities, she acts on behalf of clients to ensure that changes that are made at the organizational and community levels benefit clients who are in need of services and resources. The worker brings her knowledge and skill in working with groups and in assessment, planning, direct and indirect practice actions, and evaluation to the change process with organizations and communities.

The first part of the chapter discusses macropractice and social justice. This relates to the importance of empowering populations at risk of discrimination and oppression through macropractice actions. Discussions on conducting a needs assessment, program planning and resource development, changing organizations from within, and the social worker as a group member follow. Community change actions include involving influentials, networking, cause advocacy, and community organization practice.

Macropractice and Social Justice

Generalist practice includes working with organizations and communities to bring about change on behalf of client systems. This is an essential aspect of social work practice with clients at risk of discrimination and oppression. Current and historical attitudes and actions have denied these groups equal access to political, economic, and social power. Although most forms of discrimination are illegal, barriers still exist and prejudice seems firmly embedded in U.S. society. Practice with these groups that only focuses on the person or family and the immediate environment may not bring about real change.

A cardinal value of social work is that people have a right to have socially accepted needs met in socially accepted ways. If people are expected to give up some freedom so that everyone's rights are protected, then they have a right to expect that their rights will be respected as well. A just society is one in which everyone has an equal opportunity to participate in its political, economic, and social benefits. A major ethical principle expressed in the NASW *Code of Ethics* is that "social workers challenge social injustice." Most often this takes the form of advocating for clients when they are denied services or resources. It is also embodied in cause advocacy and social action organizing, which will be discussed later in this chapter.

It takes courage to fight prejudice and discrimination. We as social workers must adopt the attitude that we will not tolerate intolerance. We must stand up for what is right and just. However, it is not enough for social workers to merely react when social injustice occurs. Taking a proactive approach to organization and community practice is also needed. Social workers must constantly be aware of opportunities to bring about change in their organizations; in other organizations; and in the community that will improve opportunities, especially for women, people of color, people who are homosexual, and other groups that have been oppressed. We must have the courage of our convictions in pursuing equitable treatment for all of our citizens. Social workers use their skills on behalf of clients to facilitate needed changes in the agency, the human service network, and the community. They assist in assessing needs, planning programs, and developing resources, and they act to bring about changes that will ensure equal opportunity for everyone. They speak up on behalf of those who are not able to speak for themselves. They practice in a way that empowers and enables those who cannot feel or experience their own power. They use their influence to support these changes. In doing so, they support their professional organizations on a state and national level as well.

Needs Assessment

Assessment of a community and its resources, assessment of a group of people, or assessment of a client in a situation may result in the realization that needed resources are not available. Social workers have a responsibility to work toward the development of needed resources. One of the first steps is carrying out a **needs assessment**. Funding sources usually require some data relative to the nature and extent of need be gathered before they will support new projects or programs. Some governmental funding agencies and accreditation bodies require a needs assessment as part of their ongoing review of programs. A needs assessment may be undertaken by an agency, a group of agencies, or a community group.

The assessment can be carried out in several ways. First, general opinions about the service or the need for service can be obtained from various segments of the community, such as service providers, consumers, and community influentials. This is the most common form of needs assessment. A major problem with this type of information gathering is that it represents opinions, not hard facts. However, this mechanism can provide information that may not be obtainable through other means. It can be a preliminary step in designing an assessment instrument that captures a complete picture of the problem and can be used to involve the community in the assessment.

A second mechanism for needs assessment is to survey current users of service. Often professionals forget that the *I need* perspective is just as important as the *they need* perspective. Involving users in needs assessments may provide important information about the design of services. However, it is not always possible for users to articulate their needs, so the mechanism may not provide a complete picture of the need. For example, older people may have some difficulty admitting to need. They may feel that the admission of limitations would force them into nursing homes or to come to grips with the aging process in ways they prefer to avoid.

Another mechanism of determining need is through the use of statistical data. For example, if a community has a high percentage (compared to similar communities) of people who are older or people below the poverty level, it is likely that there are needs not being met. The worker must be careful in using statistical data because the use of this mechanism may lead to assumptions that later prove unfounded.

Usually, in designing a needs assessment it is desirable to use several means for collecting data. Need can be identified in terms of gaps in services, redundancy of services, availability of services to various groups of people, accessibility of services to those who are in need, and usability of service (e.g., is it provided within a framework that can be used by various diversity groups?).

Before designing a needs assessment instrument for a community, it is important to be thoroughly familiar with the community, the need area, and the population to be targeted. A schema for the study of a community was presented in Chapter 6. (See Table 6.1.) Involving community influentials or community organizations can be very helpful in planning the assessment. These people can help interpret the need for the assessment, give it community sanction, and provide input for its construction; this will make the assessment acceptable to the community and result in a greater chance of an accurate response. Other social systems significant to the study also need to be identified, as well as all possible data sources. The latter category includes demographic statistical profiles, key informants (those in direct contact with those experiencing problems), consumers of service, individuals experiencing difficulty or having potential for doing so, and the general public. A preliminary statement of the concern or need should be developed at this stage and assumptions about the nature of the concern or need and potential resources stated.

When the needed background information has been gathered, the worker is ready to begin the design of the needs assessment. Decisions must be made about the type of data needed, the individuals who can best provide the information, and the most appropriate means for gathering that information. Information can be gathered in person; by phone interviews; through mailed questionnaires; or through existing data, such as agency or census records. Generally, it is wise to develop an instrument that will allow the collection of the same information from each respondent. Information sought may include demographic data, such as race, gender, age, marital status, educational level, and length of residence in the community; perceived problems; where information about services is obtained; factors that hinder the seeking of help; and services needed. The development of the needs assessment design requires creativity to individualize it for the situation.

As the needs assessment design is being developed, two other areas need attention. The first is publicity if groups in the community will be surveyed. Public knowledge of the assessment and its purpose is necessary if people are to provide accurate information. A publicity campaign can include news releases, television and radio spots, posters, and announcements at meetings and community activities. It can make use of the community members who have been involved in the development of the needs assessment. These individuals can give sanction and lend credibility to the effort. When considering a needs assessment, it is important to consider timing of the survey. The worker must be aware of other activities going on in the community and plan the assessment for an appropriate time.

Another consideration relates to the confidentiality of information obtained, or the human rights concern. All publicity should indicate how the information will be used and assure confidentiality. Interviewers must be trained not only in confidentiality issues but also in how to conduct the interview. Often, it is helpful to first test an instrument with a small sample of people representative of those who will be contacted during the assessment. This test case can alert the designer to questions that are problematic and apt to be misinterpreted or not answered. This helps ensure that the outcome of the assessment will be accurate. The evaluation and interpretation of information are part of the assessment design and relate to the particular information. Once this stage has taken place, it is important to share the findings with those who have participated in the assessment. Needs assessment, when properly carried out, is an involved process but an important part of meeting the needs of individuals and families.

Program Planning and Resource Development

Planning on an organizational or community level generally involves some kind of task group. The planning process may take up a considerable amount of the group's time. Just as in small groups, it is important to establish a common goal that is inclusive and relates to the purpose of the group. Initially, the common goal may be stated in very broad terms. However, care should be taken to avoid stating the goal in terms of solutions. Task groups are usually made up of factions or representatives of organizations who may have a considerable investment in the outcome. For example, a community task force on juvenile gangs is likely to be made up of representatives from law enforcement, the juvenile court, the schools, substance abuse agencies, and youth organizations. Each of these brings its own perspective on the problem and is invested in solutions related to that perspective. Usually, the solution is viewed as a need for more resources for that particular organization or a need for a different response from one of the other organizations. Thus, law enforcement is likely to see the problem as related to not having enough police officers or of the courts not being tougher on juveniles. The juvenile court may see the problem in terms of needing more court workers or more money for placement options. The schools may see the goal as the need for a new program in the schools or for the court to be stricter with school truants. The substance abuse agencies and youth organizations are likely to see a need for more programs to treat substance abuse or to keep young people off the street. Generating a common goal that involves a community response is the key to holding these groups together. For example, the group could be encouraged to adopt a community goal of reducing gang membership by half. To accomplish this goal, each organization would have to do its part and make a collaborative effort.

Social workers can sometimes use program planning to mobilize different and creative kinds of resources that are relatively inexpensive financially. Two resources that fall into this category are volunteers and self-help groups.

Program development uses the planning process developed in Chapter 9. As the plan is developed, special attention must be given to means of generating support for the plan. Support must come not only from the agencies involved (both workers and administration) but also from the community. Most programs needing community resources cannot be developed without community support.

Usually, in developing a new program, it is advisable to begin small or to serve at first only a portion of the population that might benefit from the program. It is also advisable to begin with that portion of the population with which the chances of success are the greatest. If done in this way, it is easier to find and correct the deficiencies in the plan. Another point to remember is that it is easier to obtain support for small programs that relate to popular causes.

Jack Rothman, John Erlich, and Joseph Teresa discussed promoting an innovation in an agency.[1] This idea can be related to planning new community programs. They pointed out that the literature on the "diffusion of innovations" supports the advisability of beginning small and of demonstrating the new program before planning for widespread use. Three guidelines are helpful when planning programs to develop or mobilize new resources:

1. Develop and rely on good relationships.
2. Clarify goals and plans for developing the program.
3. Be realistic about the resources that may be available to the program.

Program planning can take place within an existing agency structure or from a community base. If the program is to function within an existing agency structure, the support and involvement of the agency administration and staff are crucial. If the program is to develop from a community base, community members will carry primary responsibility for its functioning. These people need to be involved in the planning as early as possible. Usually, it is important to discuss the proposed plan with several community influentials as a first step. This discussion will provide the social worker with information needed for developing the plan. It also involves these important persons in obtaining support for the project. Often, it is advisable for a community person to initiate and conduct a meeting to discuss the project. The social worker may need to identify and motivate a suitable leader. The worker then prepares the leadership person for the meeting by making the arrangements for a meeting place, attending to the meeting details, and evaluating with the leadership person after the meeting.

If the decision is made to develop a program, some kind of structure should be set up to do the necessary work. This can be a provisional board or a planning committee and should allow for appropriate involvement of community persons in the process. This group may find it useful to conduct a needs assessment. The group should also be involved in the development of the program structure and policies. Other tasks are to obtain support for the proposed program, which may involve grant writing and other fundraising activities, and recruitment and hiring of personnel. The social worker can fill the role of enabler by helping the community group reach the goals it has adopted. Also, the worker can fill the role of technical expert by providing information about how to accomplish certain tasks.[2]

Sometimes an established community group becomes aware of a need and wishes to do something about it. In this situation a social worker can help the group document the need, obtain support (money, people, etc.), and develop the program or resource. For example, a community group was concerned with services for the elderly. The social worker helped the group carry out a needs assessment that indicated that housing for older single women was a prime need in this community. The group was able to interest a local realtor in focusing on this need and worked with the realtor to develop an understanding of the housing needs of older women and plans for making more suitable housing available for them.

At other times, groups of people interested in a particular problem emerge. Social workers can also work with these groups to develop community resources. For example, a women's group was concerned about battered women. The social worker's function was to provide understanding about battered women and their needs. This group talked to women who had worked on the problem in other communities. The group set up a training program and developed a telephone response service, a safe house, and a self-help group.

As these examples show, grassroots groups can be useful when developing community resources for clients. When working with such groups, social workers should not take over the planning; they should respect the group's way of functioning and facilitate the work. Workers must gain and maintain the trust of the group. They should enable individuals to carry out the necessary tasks, suggest ways of proceeding and resources to be tapped, and mediate the group's difficulties with professionals and other community groups. This latter task is sometimes necessary because established services or other professionals may be threatened by a grassroots group or concerned about its ability to provide quality service. In a time of shrinking federal and state resources, maximizing local resources is necessary if human needs are to be met. Program planning and resource development with grassroots groups thus becomes an important task for social workers.

The social worker who attempts to mobilize the community or a group of concerned individuals to address a particular issue may want to form a **task group**. Task groups are also used within agency settings to address a specific concern. Task groups are groups organized to reach a specific goal. They tend to have clear lines of responsibility and specific tasks. Because task groups often include influentials, potential consumers, and service providers (people with various agendas and varying social statuses), it is important to address both interpersonal and task issues throughout the work of the group. Each member must feel he has something valuable to contribute, and this contribution needs to be perceived by other members. It is important to have members who can offer various skills, resources, or services to achieve the goal. For example, if the goal is to establish a hospice service for persons with AIDS, it would be important to have a member who can raise funds, an influential who can work effectively with the community to allay fears or concerns, and someone who can network with people who have AIDS. In task groups, the work is generally divided into subgroups, which then work toward various objectives to reach the goal. This implies that there must be shared leadership, with each leader and subgroup given a specific charge and sufficient autonomy to attain the desired objective. Typically, subgroups meet frequently, with the group as a whole coming together less often to share progress, ensure coordination of efforts, and reevaluate the overall plan.[3]

Changing Organizations from Within

Historically, consideration of the organization as a target for change has received little attention in social work literature. Yet in working with clients, workers (particularly in the public sector) are well aware that the functioning of the agency (policy, procedures, etc.) often is a source of blockage to client need fulfillment. It follows that social workers should develop a means for influencing agency change. Organizational change as a strategy can be defined as "a means of enhancing the effectiveness of human service organizations in their relations with clients.... [It] is a set of interrelated activities... for the purpose of modifying the formal policies, programs, procedures, or management practices.... The intended outcome... [is] to increase the effectiveness of the services provided and/or to remove organizational conditions that are deleterious to the client population served."[4] This strategy focuses on means of change from within the organization and is carried out by those in middle or lower levels of the organization.[5]

The social worker begins with assessment. Some of the understandings a worker must develop when using a *change-from-within strategy* include:

1. The agency as a social system (See Chapter 6 for a discussion of a schema for developing this understanding.)
2. The source of the block to need fulfillment (Is it in policy or procedure? Is it caused by lack of agency resources? Is it caused by methods used to deliver service?)

3. The forces within the agency and the community that influence the agency functioning in relation to the need
4. The usual processes used to bring about change in the agency
5. The source of decision making in the areas needing to be changed
6. Any influences to which the decision-making source is particularly sensitive
7. The decision maker's receptivity and resistance to the change sought

The assessment process should identify what requires changing if client needs are to be fulfilled. It is not sufficient to say that change must take place.

In planning change within an organization, it is important to be inclusive. Often, there is a temptation to bring about change by issuing memos or directives. This can lead to resentment, resistance, and even sabotage by those who are affected by the change. How change occurs is as important as what gets changed. Getting input from those affected ensures greater investment in carrying out the change and helps to avoid barriers. Getting input from clients should be done whenever applicable and feasible. At the least, client needs and concerns should be considered as primary, and "proactive advocacy" should be used by the social worker. "Proactive advocacy" means advocating for clients before barriers are encountered by avoiding policies that are not in the best interests of clients.

In a small agency, it may be possible to include everyone in the planning process. When major change is planned in larger agencies, it is usually wise to establish a *task group* made up of representatives from various levels of the agency. The representatives should solicit input from the groups they represent. The task group is generally given responsibility to recommend changes to the executive. Generating several options, along with an analysis of the advantages and disadvantages of each, will allow the administrator to retain her decision-making role while incorporating input from other levels of the agency.

It is important that both the place where the change should take place and the desirable change at that site be specified. The assessment should specify what change is possible and what limitations may exist. There should be some consideration of timing factors that need to be taken into account in planning for change.[6] For example, if management is under stress because of changes being imposed from a central office, the chances that management will be receptive to discussing other changes with line staff is doubtful. However, if management is concerned with a problem of service delivery, it may be receptive to discussing change that could result in better service and also alleviate the problem. According to Herman Resnick and Rino Patti, the change process is:

1. Practitioner's perception of a problem in agency functioning
2. Discussion of problem among practitioner and like-minded colleagues, including an assessment of change potential
3. Commitment to the change effort by persons involved in the assessment
4. Formulation of the goal to be sought
5. Analysis of resistance to change
6. Development of an action system and mobilization of resources (needed persons added and group development takes place)
7. Formulation of a plan of action
8. Submission of proposal to the decision makers; take other action as needed

At this point the change is either accepted, rejected, or modified. At each step goals may change as new information or input is gained.[7]

An important consideration is who to include in the change effort. At least some participants should have a good understanding of the agency functioning. Some should be respected, valued members of the staff. Some should be those who can influence decision makers; some should have skills in negotiation and mediation and in carrying out the particular change. Agency change can originate from the efforts of one person, but to implement a change-from-within strategy, others who possess the characteristics and skills needed also must be involved.

A number of techniques or methods can be used to bring about change in organizations. Patti and Resnick identified eight collaborative and nine adversarial activities. Collaborative activities are to (1) provide information, (2) present alternative courses of action, (3) request support for experimentation, (4) establish a study committee, (5) create new opportunities for interaction, (6) make appeals to conscience or professional ethics, (7) use logical argument and data, and (8) point out negative consequences. Adversarial activities are to (1) submit petitions, (2) confront in open meetings, (3) bring sanctions against the agency, (4) engage in public criticism through use of communication media, (5) encourage noncompliance, (6) strike, (7) picket, (8) litigate, and (9) bargain.[8]

Collaborative activities should always be tried first. The use of adversarial activities should be restricted to situations in which collaborative activities have not worked. Before using adversarial activities, workers should determine whether such strategies will bring harm to clients and whether they are willing to take the personal risks involved.

Rothman, Erlich, and Teresa identified four means of bringing about change in organizations:

1. *Promoting an innovation*—This is carried out by testing a new or modified service with a small group of clients. If it is successful, it may later be adopted for use on a larger scale. An example would be using a group approach to deliver a service.

2. *Changing an organization's goals*—One way to do this is to change the structure of influence by increasing the power of appropriate groups within the agency. For example, developing a clients' advisory group would increase client input into decision making and provide a new source of information or influence.

3. *Fostering participation*—This is a means of encouraging broader participation in the functioning of an agency. For example, a staff group could be involved in the planning for a new program. One means of fostering participation is through providing some kind of benefit for the participation, such as public recognition.

4. *Increasing the effectiveness of role performance*—This can be carried out by clarifying the role performance expected of those working in an agency. It can also be carried out by encouraging various kinds of staff development.[9]

In-service training for workers can be used to introduce new service delivery ideas. If the social worker is skillful in the use of group interaction, he can sometimes enable a staff group to examine and adopt a new idea. Sometimes social workers are given the opportunity to lead an in-service session; in doing this, the knowledge from adult education and staff development literature can be useful.[10]

Edward Pawlak pointed out that an ideal time for bringing about change in an organization is when leadership changes. He provided suggestions for workers who wish to engage in organizational change, including influencing the selection of new leadership and altering the manner in which rules are interpreted and enforced. Revising of roles, or role interpretation, is another means for change.[11]

It should be apparent that a number of approaches and techniques are available for changing organizations. The choice of approach depends on the change being sought and the situation. Two factors must be considered: risk for the worker seeking the change and resistance of other persons within the organization.

Three kinds of risks may be involved when a social worker engages in changing from within: job loss, restricted upward mobility, and strained working relationships.[12] Not all of these risks may be present, but a careful assessment should indicate the extent of the risk. Each social worker must then make the decision as to whether he is willing to take the risks involved before using this strategy.

Resistance is almost always present to some degree in change activity. Change upsets the system's functioning and causes uncertainty. Thus, the social worker must be prepared to modify the plan to mitigate resistance. When dealing with resistance, an attitude of compromise is often necessary. Workers who are determined that their plan be accepted are most apt to encounter a negative response. Those who engage in joint consideration of a problem likely will find a solution acceptable to all. Understanding the nature of the resistance and dealing with it are essential skills when using a change-from-within strategy.

Because social work is primarily practiced within organizations, particularly bureaucracies, the change-from-within strategy is important to the social worker's repertoire. The social worker's ethical responsibility is to work toward the humane delivery of social services in a manner that meets client needs. To do this, it is often necessary to bring about change in organizations. The social worker can use the change-from-within strategy to bring about change.

The Social Worker as a Group Member

The social worker is frequently called on to participate as a member of various groups. These include task groups, teams, and staff meetings. The worker uses his knowledge and skills in use of the change process in working with groups to facilitate successful achievement of group goals and tasks for groups of which he is a member. The change process with these groups involves assessment, planning, action, and evaluation.

Use of the change process in group discussion is a means of structuring group thinking. All members of the group should understand the change process and be aware of which step in the process the group is using. In this way, group thinking can progress from need identification and formulation, to analysis of the situation, to identification of possible goals, to analysis of the possibilities, and to choice of a plan. Thus, the plan becomes the property of the group rather than the contribution of an individual member. Several areas that often give groups difficulty as they attempt to change are:

1. Lack of clarity in stating the need
2. Lack of necessary information
3. A critical, evaluative climate
4. Pressure for conformity
5. Premature choice of a goal or plan

If a plan for implementation is a result of group thinking, there is a better chance that it will be carried out.

Some attention should be paid to the structure of group meetings to further enhance the group's capacity. There should be preparation for group meetings, just as there is preparation for an interview. Various members should be responsible for bringing needed information to the meeting. Someone should take the responsibility for ensuring that the meeting room is comfortable and arranged so that each member can have eye contact with each other member. Someone should be responsible for seeing that agendas and other needed printed materials are available and for keeping minutes or recording decisions in some way.

The planned agenda should be reviewed and revisions made, if necessary, at the beginning of each meeting. Everyone should know what the meeting is intended to accomplish and what the time limitations are.

The middle part of the meeting is spent on the task of the day. When necessary, the group should deal with any group maintenance issues that seem to be impeding the work at hand. Discussion should focus on tasks or goals or on the process of carrying these out. All members should be urged to participate. Someone should be responsible for keeping the group on task and helping it move through the change process in an orderly manner. Before the allotted time is over, the group should review what has been accomplished at the meeting, and plans should be made for the next meeting.

In helping the group involve members, make decisions, have productive discussions, and structure the discussion, social workers can be valuable resources for the group. Knowledge of group process and of the problem-solving process and skill in group discussion form the base of effective membership in a group.

Issues in Group Participation

Several issues of group participation are of particular concern to social workers when they participate as members of small groups, including (1) the use of the team, particularly the interdisciplinary team, as a means of service; (2) leadership in its delegated form; and (3) conflict management, which was discussed in Chapter 14. Each of these issues confronts the social worker and, if not understood, can block effective group functioning.

Use of the Team

Although the well-functioning team can be very effective in providing service to clients, there are often problems that cause some social workers and agency administrators to question the team approach. These problems need to be understood and some ways for overcoming them considered.

The team has been defined as "joining the essentially dissimilar skills which colleagues in diverse occupations bring to bear upon different aspects of a common problem."[13] This definition is most applicable to the interdisciplinary team, and it is the interdisciplinary team that presents the greatest hazards for working together. Dissimilarity of backgrounds and work expectations are a major cause of these hazards, as is overlap of the expertise of the various helping professions. This can lead to conflict over turf. Some of the most frequent problems encountered by teams are:

1. *The time and energy needed for team building*—The task of the team is to provide service to clients. Often, the immediacy of the need for service and number of clients needing service place expectations on the team that militate against the use of time and energy for team building. These expectations may come from within the team or from the agency within which the team or any of its members operate. Yet effective team functioning requires time and energy from the team members. The allocation of time and energy for team building can be problematic.

2. *Communication*—The use of technical language by any member of the team that is not understood by all other members of the team blocks communication. Persons from different disciplines often use the same terms but with somewhat different meanings. When this happens, there are problems in communication.

3. *Decision-making traditions*—Professions and agencies develop traditions as to how decisions are made. In bureaucratic organizations decisions are made from above, and lower-status persons are expected to implement the decisions. A team in such an organization may have a leader appointed by the administration; the appointed leader may assume an authoritative stance. In health care, the doctor, as the high-status professional, has traditionally used this authoritative stance. This is needed in an operating room, but it is not helpful in a protective service situation. Other decision-making models may call for everyone to have equal decision-making power about all aspects of service. All team members may not have equal knowledge or understanding of certain aspects of the team's service. One of the purposes of a team is to accommodate differing types of expertise to be used in service of the client. The decision-making process needs to allow for this diversity of understanding yet facilitate the process so that it is reasonably expedient.

4. *Use of the change process*—As with all small groups, goals need to be accepted by all. Differences in goals among team members can arise from inadequate need identification. If team members see the situation differently and do not understand or accept the team goals, hidden agendas can develop. If team members are functioning at different stages of the change process, confusion in planning results.

5. *Implementation of plans and carrying out tasks*—Team members usually have other tasks and other influences on how they prioritize their work. This can result in assigned tasks not being carried out, particularly when those tasks are imposed on members.

6. *Functioning within a complex organization*—Sometimes organizations institute or sanction the use of the team approach without full understanding of the implications of teamwork. The organization may not allow sufficient time for team functioning, may impose leadership that does not enable team functioning to develop, or may interfere with the team's ability to function in other ways.

Each team is unique and must discover its own way of functioning. Some will function in a cooperative manner in which an integrated approach to client service is the mode. Others will use a collaborative approach in which the team decides on the services needed; appropriate members then provide those services in an autonomous manner. Other teams will use various combinations of the two approaches. Regardless of approach, teams that function best have members who are dedicated, share a common ideal, and have confidence in one another. Members also have a willingness to work together, to learn from one another, and to share clients. They have a cooperative rather than a competitive climate, flexibility, and good communication and problem-solving processes. They also have the support of the agency of which they are a part. Social workers can contribute to the enhancement of the decision-making process by helping the team to identify the issues confronting the team so that it can work for resolution.

Leadership

Because leadership has differing meanings for different persons, it is often the source of problems in group functioning. Some people perceive a leader as being one who tells everyone else what to do. Others see the leader as one who consults with the other group members but in the end makes the decisions. Still others see the leader as the one who enables the group to function. Some people who carry the title "leader" are appointed, some are elected, and others emerge from the group. Some people resent leadership or leadership by certain people or professions. Others expect the leader to take full responsibility for the group or expect a member of a particular profession to automatically be the leader.

More and more, leadership is being understood as "interpersonal influence"; in this sense the meaning of leadership, as used here, is captured. Such influence can be exerted in a variety of ways, some of which are more helpful in furthering the functioning of the group than others. The idea that only one person, elected or emergent, carries the entire leadership responsibility is fallacious. If group members understand leadership as a shared responsibility, much interpersonal conflict can be avoided. The group can then use the knowledge and skills of all group members, and the leadership can change, depending on the task at hand.

As a group member, the social worker can influence, or enable, the group to carry out its task and function. Some of the tasks involved in this enabling include:

1. *Seeing that decisions are made*—(but not making them for the group).

2. *Being sure the group knows what it is doing*—Are there goals that are known to all the members? Does the group know its purpose? Are group norms explicit?

3. *Making certain the group knows how it is doing*—In what stage of the change process is the group functioning? Are the essential roles in the group being filled? Are all group members' contributions accepted? Is communication open and understood by all?

4. *Being sure that when things are not going well or feeling good, the group stops to evaluate what is wrong.*

Social workers with a knowledge of group process can carry out these tasks for any group, regardless of their position in the group. To do this they must use good judgment about how and when to exercise this kind of influence. In this way they exercise leadership and influence the group's functioning.

Social Work Tasks

Social workers who are group members are qualified to carry out three tasks that can be very useful for the group in its functioning: consultation, facilitation, and coordination. The *consultation task* calls for the worker to ask for and offer information and suggestions; there is no demand that the suggestions be accepted. Consultation provides an expectation that all group members will examine the information and suggestions in light of their particular perspective and provide feedback on the usefulness and validity of the social worker's contributions. This type of consultation is a means of enabling the group to engage in a joint process of thinking about clients and situations to identify strengths and resources and to develop plans for action. Through consultation, the social worker contributes the expertise she brings to the group. This expertise can be in the area of group functioning, or it can be in the form of contributions to the task of the group.

Facilitation is the process of enabling others to function. Facilitation of the group process is one form of the *facilitation task.* Social workers can carry out this task in a number of ways. They can support helpful behaviors of other group members, model useful behaviors, ask appropriate questions, or provide appropriate observations and feelings about the group. They can teach other group members about group process and functioning. Other means of facilitating are helping members stay on the topic, summarizing what has been said or decided, and letting other members know their feelings are accepted. Because of their skills, social workers can help the group state problems so that they can be worked on. Workers can partialize problems, which is done by breaking a problem into parts, prioritizing which part should be worked on, and/or deciding the order for working on the various parts. They can identify strengths and resources.

Some behaviors to avoid are criticizing others or their values, forcing ideas on the group, making decisions that belong to the group, and talking too much. The social worker studies the group and its functioning and decides what will most help the group at any point in time.

A third task, the *coordination task,* calls for monitoring to assess whether all members are carrying out their assigned tasks and whether, in carrying out the tasks, the work of each group member is done in a way that complements that of other members. Coordination ensures that the work of various members does not conflict but rather complements the work of other group members. Social workers are especially able to perform this role because of their broad view of personal and social functioning. They can view the various parts of a plan, ascertain how the parts fit together, and when misfit exists, identify means of modifying misfitting plans.

Much of this coordination is done by building relationships. The social worker attempts to understand the position of every other group member and to gain an appreciation of the needs of each member in relation to the group's task. Through relationships with group members, the social worker can mediate differences and provide observations about group functioning. In this way, the social worker assists the group in its work and helps the group coordinate its work.

Social workers can contribute a great deal to groups of which they are members. Knowledge of group process; understanding of issues that can inhibit group functioning; and skill in carrying out the tasks of consultation, facilitation, and coordination provide the social worker with a firm base for making this contribution.

Task groups usually end when the task has been completed, when the group gives up its efforts to effect a change, or when its authority to operate ends, as might be the case for a time-limited task group. Generally, a celebration of some sort is in order when the task is completed. If the group fails to complete its task, some sort of debriefing may be necessary, and a report may be generated outlining its accomplishments and analyzing the reasons that the effort failed. This may help group members resolve some of their disappointment and can help future groups avoid some of the same difficulties. Such a report may also be needed for accountability to various authorities with an interest in the outcome.

Unlike small groups in which relationships are important, task groups are focused on the task itself, and relationships are secondary to the group's purpose. When individual members drop out, the decision regarding follow-up is generally made based on how critical the person or her organization is to the task at hand and whether she is likely to support or oppose the group's efforts. Follow-up can be done by any member.

Involvement of Influentials

One means of gaining support is through the involvement of influentials—people within a community or an organization who have power or authority. Individuals may have power because they have a reputation that assigns power to them. They may have power because they are in positions to make crucial decisions, such as which projects get funded, who reports to top administrators, or how regulations are written. Other individuals have power because their role or function involves control over ideas, information, fiscal resources, and so on.

Influentials have the ability to use power to affect the actions of others. These people can persuade others to act in specific ways, gain support for their points of view or ways of functioning, and effect compliance with desired ways of functioning. They often have control of needed resources (money, manpower, etc.), can reward or punish others, and can effectively block action they do not favor. They may be influential in all aspects of an organization or community or only in certain segments of the system's functioning. Influentials relate to one another in patterns; this is called the power structure. Social workers can work with influentials in several ways when:

1. Approval for projects or programs must be obtained from influentials in order to facilitate development of the projects or programs.
2. An attempt must be made to have an influential initiate the action in order to gain the support of others.
3. Influentials must be informed about what is being planned and why to prevent them blocking a project.

The first step in working with influentials is to identify these persons. This can be done by asking those who know the system well ("system knowledgeables") which people have the reputation of being influential or who of these must be included in decision making. Influentials are not always the same as those who hold authority positions; often, they are less visible and function behind the scenes in the informal system. An understanding of the community and its power structure is essential when working with influentials.

When social workers work with influentials, they need to be clear about the desired change and why it is needed. They can then present facts in a convincing, logical manner. It is often useful to show the influential how the desired change is in her self-interest. This first step for involving influentials allows them to see that the social worker can be an ally in carrying out community projects. Social workers should remain open and flexible when working with influentials. It is important to incorporate appropriate input from influentials into the plan.

The art of **opportunity seizing** is another important skill useful for working with influentials. This involves a keen sense of timing and a sense of when influentials are ready to become involved and make use of the social worker's help and expertise. Involvement in community activities can provide social workers with opportunities to get to know influentials and for influentials to get to know workers.

Persuasion skills are important when working with influentials and often can be useful in helping an influential understand the desirability of working for change. Social workers need to learn how to work with and utilize the support of influentials to effect change in organizations and communities.

Networking

Networking also is a form of coordination.[14] **Networking** is the development and maintenance of communication and of ways of working together among individuals of diverse interests and orientations. This technique can facilitate macrolevel coordination. Networking holds promise as a means for formal system helpers and natural helpers to work together. The technique of networking calls for developing some means of face-to-face communication among people who have the potential for developing a relationship based on a common interest.

One technique used to develop a network is a "fair." People delivering services in a particular area (such as services for women) are invited to set up displays and provide an informed person to be present to discuss informally the services provided. The fair is usually seen as an opportunity for the community to find out about the services. In informal, open discussion at the fair, professional and other helpers discover commonalities of interest and concern. From this discussion decisions begin to be made about working together. A sensitive facilitator can then encourage further planning for activity that will strengthen the network.

Another technique is a monthly meeting of community agencies that can be expanded to include a wide range of community resources. Agendas for these meetings can consist of various agencies presenting their programs and services. Time should be provided for informal discussion and discussion of current community needs. The long-term goal is for relationships to develop among the participants and for a network to emerge.

Because of the differing patterns of functioning and communicating, formal systems must not expect informal systems to accept their approach. Networking calls for the establishment of innovative patterns that allow both formal and informal systems to function together. Informality must not be stifled but rather respected and encouraged when using this form of coordination.

When coordinating with natural helpers, it is important not to place professional expectations on them. Professionals tend to consider these individuals in a paraprofessional capacity and take a supervisory stance in the relationship. This is not appropriate, for two reasons. First, it may destroy any chance of developing the relationship because the natural helper feels demeaned in such a relationship. Second, it may destroy the natural helper's distinctive way of helping and thus his contribution to the situation.[15] Professionals who use a consultative stance are more likely to develop coordinative relationships with natural helpers.

Blocks to effective coordination include lack of respect for, or confidence in, the other helpers involved; lack of adequate sharing of information among helpers; differing perspectives or values about what is to be done regarding clients; lack of capacity to share and work together; lack of time to develop cooperative relationships; and lack of agency sanction and support for coordination. A productive, satisfying coordination is possible when mutual understanding, shared goals, a feeling that it is advantageous to work cooperatively, a capacity to work together, and the sanction needed to develop cooperative relationships are present.

Three social work skills are useful for social workers in facilitating coordination: (1) skill in sensing commonalities and differences and in communicating them appropriately to those involved in the situation, (2) skill in facilitating communication among the participants, and (3) skill in exciting and motivating helping persons to see the advantages of coordinating services. Underlying these skills is the capacity to develop opportunities creatively for open and relaxed communication.

Much has been said about the need for, and the advantages of, coordination in interorganizational and interprofessional relationships. Less has been identified with respect to skills and techniques in developing and maintaining those relationships. Applying understandings about the nature of other relationships and the means for encouraging and maintaining them can enhance this knowledge base. Coordination is needed for providing complex services in complex situations. Coordination depends on functional relationships among helping people.

Cause Advocacy

Social workers using a systemic approach to assessment should be sensitive to situations in which the block to need fulfillment lies in the functioning of societal institutions. Often these blocks affect not only one person or family but also groups of individuals. In these situations a strategy that focuses on change in societal institutions needs to be considered. A cause advocacy strategy is one option.

Cause advocacy has been a concern of social work since its earliest days. Early-twentieth-century social workers in settlement houses were concerned with social conditions as they affected the people with whom they worked. During the unsettled 1960s, cause advocacy was a major focus of some social workers. The cause-function debates of the profession relate to social work's concern with changing social institutions. This represents the function side that refers to societal aspects of social problems.

The literature on advocacy recognizes both *case advocacy* (advocacy in service of a client) and cause advocacy (advocacy in service of a class of persons who are victims of a social problem). George Brager has identified an advocate as the professional who identifies with the victims of social problems and who pursues modification in social conditions.[16] According to Robert Teare and Harold McPheeters, the advocate role is helping clients obtain services in situations in which they may be rejected or helping expand services to persons in particular need.[17] (See also Chapter 9 for a discussion of the Teare-McPheeters role classification.)

There are a number of means to use in advocating for a class of persons. Robert MacRae identified the following:

1. Preparation of carefully worded statements of policy on lively social welfare issues
2. Careful analysis of pending legislation
3. Individual consultation with key legislators on the implications of pending measures
4. Persuasion of influential organizations outside the welfare field to oppose or support pending legislation
5. Creation of an ad hoc citizens' committee composed of representative citizens of influence and prestige
6. Continuous interpretation of social needs[18]

J. Donald Cameron and Esther Talavera discussed an advocacy program in which the emphasis was on participation in "important community planning and development groups, and other community organizations." The goal of this activity was "to keep the community needs of Spanish-speaking people visible and to effect the flow of resources to meet these needs."[19] Almost all the literature on social work with diverse racial groups calls for advocacy as an important component of any service provided to these groups.

Robert Sunley suggested the following as useful in a family advocacy program: (1) studies and surveys, (2) expert testimony, (3) case conferences with other agencies, (4) interagency committees, (5) educational methods, (6) position taking, (7) administrative redress, (8) demonstration projects, (9) direct contact with officials and legislators, (10) coalition groups, (11) client groups, (12) petitions, (13) persistent demands, and (14) demonstrations and protests.[20]

There are two major approaches to cause advocacy. The first is influencing the political process; the second is organizing the people affected, or **social action**. Before discussing each of these major approaches, some issues pertinent to the use of advocacy will be considered. First is the position of an agency employee, particularly an employee of a public agency, in advocacy activity. Constraints in public employment policy make it difficult, if not impossible, for public employees to engage in cause advocacy. This fact places an additional responsibility on social workers not so constrained to be cause advocates. However, public employees can find some legal means to advocate. These include taking annual leave to testify at legislative hearings, providing factual data on the effects of policy on individuals, and giving clients information about organizations that can help them fight for their rights.

Second, advocacy activity may cause a backlash. Policies and procedures meant to assist one group of clients may cause additional difficulties for another group of clients. Money used to fund a needed program for one group of clients may be taken from an equally valuable program for another group. All workers who engage in advocacy need to carefully assess the possibility of backlash or the effect of the desired change on other parts of the service delivery system. They then must make interventive decisions in light of ethical considerations.

A third issue is related to the ethics of engaging in cause advocacy for persons who have not asked for or do not want such action. Some clients are afraid of recriminations and feel they have more to lose than to gain from advocacy activity on their behalf. Others do not trust professionals.

Before engaging in cause advocacy a social worker should carefully assess and thoroughly understand the situation. The worker should be certain that other means for alleviating the difficulty are not available. The risks involved should be thoroughly explored and seem worth taking for the anticipated outcomes. The expected outcomes should be realistically determined. Resources needed to complete the project should be available. Facts to be used should be verified, appropriate, and to the point. Research techniques should be used when possible because they strengthen the case for change. With all the facts at hand, the social worker can then decide whether to work to influence the political system or to organize the people affected by the problem.

Community Organization

Community organization is a field of study unto itself and is beyond the scope of this book. However, community organizing will be discussed here briefly, so that the student has some awareness of its role in indirect macropractice and how it can be used to bring about change in a community. Rothman and Tropman's three models of community organization practice were presented earlier in Chapter 11 along with our models of community practice. These models can be used to address social issues and promote change.

Much of the service delivery system is heavily influenced by actions that take place in the political arena. Public social policy is an outcome of legislative action. Policy determines which programs will be supported and to what extent by governmental funds. Some social workers have always attempted to influence that political process, with varying degrees of success. The political process is heavily influenced by the climate of the times, so in times of a more liberal political climate, social workers tend to have more influence; in times of conservatism, less influence.

Recently, the political climate in the United States has increasingly tended toward conservatism. Nonetheless, it is critical that social workers continue to advocate, especially because there are fewer avenues available for populations at risk to voice their concerns. All social workers, not only those in indirect service positions, should become politically active. Direct service workers are in the best position to fully understand the impact of social and political change on their clients.

As with all social work strategies, influencing the political process takes understanding and skill. A thorough understanding of local, state, and national political processes is a must, as is a thorough understanding of the issues involved. It is important to view political decision makers as individuals and know how they respond to others. Reliable data about how the issue of concern affects people are very important. These data should include not only how the problem affects the client group but also how it affects other segments of the population. The cost of proposals under consideration is important knowledge to have. Also, an assessment should be made of possible sources and nature of resistance to any proposed change.

Gathering the information needed to develop this understanding of the political process takes time and skill. Social workers should learn how to use governmental publications and documents as well as statistical material. These materials are available through state and federal representatives, libraries, and various Internet sources. Participating in political activities and establishing working relationships with key political figures can be a means of gathering other needed information.

After the social worker has gained information and understanding about the political process and the particular issue involved, a decision should be made about the appropriate tactics to use in influencing that process. This decision will depend in part on where that issue is in the political process. If it is still in the discussion stage, then suggestions for possible legislation might be the option to pursue. Some of the means social workers use to influence the political process include:

1. Researching issues and providing facts to decision makers
2. Testifying at hearings (using facts whenever possible)
3. Lobbying or being present while the legislative process is taking place and influencing legislative votes when possible
4. Forming coalitions with service providers to present information to legislators regarding the local impact of current policies
5. Sharing disguised anecdotal information regarding the impact policies have on clients with state and national groups concerned with the issues
6. Working for the election of candidates who are sympathetic to social issues and to the needs of people
7. Letter-writing/e-mail campaigns to inform decision makers

Influencing the political process is a complex endeavor. Although most social workers are not in a position to be heavily involved, they can and should use the tactics available to them to influence the political process. Workers have an obligation to develop an understanding of the process and of the issues so they can participate in political advocacy in a responsible manner.[21]

Social action organizing has been a part of the social work response to human need from its earliest days. Jane Addams organized for social action when she advocated improved social conditions. The approach was widely used during the period of social unrest in the 1960s. Since that time a theory base has developed that supports the use of this approach to organizing oppressed peoples. The focus is on changing the societal power base and basic institutional change. A theory proposed by Saul Alinsky and Richard Cloward and R. Elman is sometimes referred to as a grassroots approach.[22] It begins with people who see themselves as victims, not with professionals who decide what is needed.

The principal thrust of this approach is the organizing of groups of people so that they can exert pressure on power structures, institutions, and political bodies. Adherents believe that equity in society will come about only when existing power structures recognize the power of oppressed peoples; in other words, when the societal power base is broadened to include new groups of people. Tactics used include: (1) crystallization of issues and action against an enemy target; (2) confrontation, conflict, or contest; (3) negotiation when appropriate; and (4) manipulation of mass organizations and political processes.

The social worker's first task is to organize people and get them involved in the action. In many ways, this is a self-help approach in that it relates directly to client empowerment and may be an outgrowth of a mutual aid group. The worker then enables the individuals to carry out the action.

Social workers need to develop advocacy skills if they are to help social institutions become more responsive to the needs of all people. How the individual social worker uses these skills depends on three variables:

1. *The position of the worker in the social welfare system*—Some agencies place constraints on workers' involvement in cause advocacy. Also, workers who work cooperatively with decision makers will probably not want to use conflict tactics.

2. *The client's desires regarding action*—If clients do not wish to take the risks involved in an advocacy action, these desires should be respected.

3. *The risks involved in the action*—If advocacy actions have the potential for bringing about backlash or negative influences on the client or on the social service system, advocacy should be used cautiously and only when the client or service system fully understands the possible negative ramifications.

The worker serves as an expert, an enabler, a negotiator, or whatever is needed by the people who direct the change activity.[23]

Case Example

About a year after David, a family services social worker, had organized communitywide efforts to develop a homeless shelter, the housing issue in his community became the focus of attention. Many homeless people were employed or had income from various social welfare programs but were unable to find affordable housing. During the year since the shelter opened, David and his original task group had gathered information regarding the lack of low-income housing in the community. Many existing low-income housing units had been lost to other purposes or had been torn down for commercial or other housing developments.

The issue came to a head when the city council was asked for a zoning change that would allow a parking ramp to be built on property now containing an apartment that housed many low-income people. David organized and met with a small group, including a member of the city council who showed concern about the homeless, a former state legislator, the director of the county social services agency, a low-income resident housed in the apartment, and several other concerned citizens from the original task group.

(continued)

Case Example   *(continued)*

This group needed to move quickly because a zoning change proposal was to come before the city council in about two weeks. The group assessed the information David had gathered about affordable housing for low-income people in the city. They asked the newspaper to run a feature article, which aroused some citizen concern. With the help of the city council member, they contacted city council members and city staff who had been involved in planning the zoning proposal and discussed the impact of the loss of housing on low-income people. They planned and carried out public testimony at public hearings regarding the zoning change. They were present with the apartment residents at the council meeting at which the matter was considered.

The outcome was that the city council tabled the zoning change and appointed a committee made up of council members and concerned citizens to study the situation further. David and his committee planned to continue to monitor the work of this committee, to collect and provide them with needed information, and to testify as needed.

Summary

Generalist social work practice with macrosystems involves changing organizations and communities on behalf of client systems. Often, this involves making needed resources available to clients. The assessment process begins with a needs assessment.

Program planning and development involve the use of the planning process to develop new resources. Program planning may take place within an agency or be used by a community group.

Changing organizations from within may be the strategy of choice when agency functioning is the cause of the block to client need fulfillment. To use this strategy, the worker first assesses the social system of the agency. Emphasis is placed on decision making and resistance to change. This strategy is important because of the ethical responsibility of social workers to work for humane delivery of social services.

Cause advocacy is concerned with changing societal institutions. Two main approaches are used: influencing the political process and organizing the victims.

The generalist social worker provides service to individuals, families, small groups, organizations, and communities. The focus is on transactions among systems, that is, on social functioning. This approach to social work calls for a wide variety of strategies, including those that do not focus on the client. These strategies involve action with other systems on behalf of clients and focus on situations in the client's environment that affect social functioning. Ethically, a social worker must not only work with the client but also with systems that impinge on the client.

Questions

1. Identify a need in your community. Discuss how you would go about conducting a needs assessment.
2. How would you go about planning and developing a program to meet the need you identified in question 1?

3. Describe a role you would play as a social worker in a task group organized to meet the need you identified in question 1. Who would you want to have as members of your task group? Why would you select these people?

4. What are the ethical considerations of working in an agency that is not meeting the needs of clients (needs for which it has responsibility)? How much risk would you be willing to take in bringing about needed change in an agency? At what point do you think it would be appropriate for you to use a change-from-within strategy?

5. When engaging in cause advocacy, should the response be to injustice or to client wishes? How can these two perspectives be reconciled?

Suggested Readings

Yanca, Stephen J., and Johnson, Louise C. *Generalist Social Work Practice with Groups.* Boston: Allyn and Bacon, 2009 (Part III: Generalist Practice with Organizations and Communities, Chapters 10-13).

Bobo, Kim, Kendall, Jackie, and Max, Steve. *Organizing for Social Change: A Manual for Activists,* 3rd ed. Carson, CA: Seven Locks Press, 2001.

Brueggemann, William G. *The Practice of Macro Social Work,* 3rd ed. Belmont, CA: Thomson-Brooks/Cole, 2006.

Edwards, Richard L., Ed. *Encyclopedia of Social Work,* 19th ed. Washington, DC: NASW Press, 1995 ("Citizen Participation," "Community," "Community Needs Assessment," "Community Organization," and "Community Practice Models").

Haynes, Karen S., and Mickelson, James S. *Affecting Change: Social Workers in the Political Arena,* 5th ed. Boston: Allyn and Bacon, 2003.

Homan, Mark S. *Promoting Community Change—Making It Happen in the Real World,* 4th ed. Belmont, CA: Thomson-Brooks/Cole, 2008.

Kirst-Ashman, Karen K., and Hull, Grafton H., Jr. *Generalist Practice with Organizations and Communities,* 4th ed. Belmont, CA: Thomson-Brooks/Cole, 2009.

Long, Dennis D., Tice, Carolyn J., and Morrison, John D. *Macro Social Work Practice: A Strengths Perspective.* Belmont, CA: Thomson-Brooks/Cole, 2006.

Mizrahi, Terry and Davis, Larry E., Eds. *Encyclopedia of Social Work*, 20th ed. Washington, DC: NASW Press, 2008 ("Citizen Participation," "Community," "Community Organization," "Macro Social Work Practice," "Media Campaigns," "Organizational Development and Change").

Netting, F. Ellen, Kettner, Peter M., and McMurtry, Steven L. *Social Work Macro Practice,* 4th ed. Boston: Allyn and Bacon, 2008.

Netting, F. Ellen, and O'Connor, Mary K. *Organization Practice: A Social Worker's Guide to Understanding Human Services.* Boston: Allyn and Bacon, 2003.

Rae, P. Ann, and Nicholas-Wolosuk, Wanda. *Changing Agency Policy: An Incremental Approach.* Boston: Allyn and Bacon, 2003.

Rothman, Jack, Erlich, John L., and Tropman, John E. *Strategies of Community Organization—Macro Practice,* 6th ed. Belmont, CA: Thomson-Brooks/Cole, 2001.

Rubin, Herbert J., and Rubin, Irene S. *Community Organizing and Development,* 4th ed. Boston: Allyn and Bacon, 2008.

Tropman, John E., Rothman, Jack, and Erlich, John L. *Tactics and Techniques of Community Intervention,* 4th ed. Belmont, CA: Thomson-Brooks/Cole, 2006.

Weinbach, Robert. *The Social Worker as Manager,* 5th ed. Boston: Allyn and Bacon, 2008.

16

Models and Good Practices in Generalist Social Work Practice

Learning Expectations

1. Understanding models used in social work practice.
2. Understanding good practices in aging services.
3. Understanding good practices in chemical dependence services.
4. Understanding good practices in child welfare.
5. Understanding good practices in domestic violence services.
6. Understanding good practices in health care settings.
7. Understanding good practices in mental health.
8. Understanding good practices in youth and delinquency services.

As social work has grown into a profession, various theories, models, and methods have been developed to guide social work practice. In this chapter most of the major models that are used by generalist social workers are presented. Good practices in settings or with populations typically served by the generalist social worker are also covered. The latter includes suggestions for the use of the models of social work practice and suggested readings that assist the student or worker in developing a deeper understanding of practice.

Models of Social Work Practice

Social work practice theory has been developed in a manner that gives a rich variety of approaches to practice. The various models or practice theories available have been developed in different situations, based on various underlying assumptions, for use in many types of circumstances. Thorough study of each model is needed in order to use it with clients. The summaries presented here can be used to gain a preliminary understanding of the salient points of the various models of practice and to help students decide on those models in which they desire to develop further understanding. Specification of models is primarily based on those appearing in:

Robert W. Roberts and Robert H. Nee, Eds., *Theories of Social Casework* (Chicago: University of Chicago Press, 1970).

Catherine P. Papell and Beulah Roberts Rothman, "Social Group Work Models: Possession and Heritage," *Education for Social Work* 2 (Fall 1966): 66–77.

Joan Stein, *The Family as a Unit of Study and Treatment,* Monograph One (Seattle: Regional Rehabilitation Institute, University of Washington, School of Social Work, 1969).

Jack Rothman, "Three Models of Community Organization," in Fred M. Cox, John L. Erlich, Jack Rothman, and John E. Tropman, Eds., *Strategies of Community Organization* (Itasca, IL: F. E. Peacock, 1970), pp. 20–36.

Francis J. Turner, Ed., *Social Work Treatment: Interlocking Theoretical Approaches,* 3rd and 4th eds. (New York: Free Press, 1986 and 1996).

Robert W. Roberts and Helen Northen, Eds., *Theories of Social Work with Groups* (New York: Columbia University Press, 1976).

Eleanor Reardon Tolson and William J. Reid, Eds., *Models of Family Treatment* (New York: Columbia University Press, 1981).

Jack Rothman with John E. Tropman, "Models of Community Organization and Macro Practice Perspectives: Their Mixing and Matching," in Fred M. Cox, John L. Erlich, Jack Rothman, and John E. Tropman, Eds., *Strategies of Community Organization,* 4th ed. (Itasca, IL: F. E. Peacock, 1987).

Behavior Therapy (Sociobehavioral)

Source: Edwin Thomas, University of Michigan, School of Social Work, based on behavioral psychology. Developed as a reaction to the lack of specificity in traditional methods.

Proponents of this model include Sheldon Rose (groups), John Wodarski (families), Richard Stuart (families), and Ray Thomison (families).

Underlying Theory: All behavior is learned. Behavior is sometimes controlled by consequences; at other times, it is controlled by stimuli (stimulus-response). Behavioral psychology is the underlying theory.

Practice Theory: Assessment specifies behaviors; defines baselines; and specifies stimulus, antecedents, and consequences. Frequency, magnitude, and direction of problem behavior are monitored during and following intervention. Goals are very specific to behavioral change.

Practice Usage: In situations in which behavioral change is the goal.

Sources
Richard F. Farmer and Rosemary O. Nelson-Gray, *Personality-Guided Behavior Therapy* (Washington, DC: American Psychological Association, 2005).
Mizrahi, Terry and Davis, Larry E., Eds., *Encyclopedia of Social Work,* 20th ed. Washington, DC: NASW Press, 2008 ("Behavioral Theory").
Michel Hersen and Johan Rosqvist, *Encyclopedia of Behavior Modification and Cognitive Behavior Therapy* (Thousand Oaks, CA: Sage, 2005).
Joseph Plaud and Georg Eifert, *Behavior Theory to Behavior Therapy* (Boston: Allyn and Bacon, 1998).
Barbara Thomlison and Ray J. Thomlison, "Behavior Theory and Social Work Treatment" in Francis J. Turner, Ed., *Social Work Treatment: Interlocking Theoretical Approaches,* 4th ed. (New York: Free Press, 1996).
Geoffrey Thorpe and Sheryl Olson, *Behavior Therapy: Concepts, Procedures, and Applications,* 2nd ed. (Boston: Allyn and Bacon, 1997).

Case Management

Source: Case management seems to have grown out of the roots of social work practice, in particular what was called *casework*. The traditional form of casework developed from the Charity Organization Societies, which sought to alleviate poverty and other social ills by working with individuals. The settlement house movement offered a different approach, which focused on environmental change through social action and advocacy. Modern case management developed during the 1960s to 1980s when deinstitutionalization of people who were mentally ill and developmentally disabled necessitated the coordination of community services for those who were vulnerable. A major contributor to the formalization of this approach is Jack Rothman.

Underlying Theory: The purpose of case management is to ensure that people receive services that they need. The growing complexity of human services makes it difficult for most client populations to negotiate the system. Vulnerable populations find it impossible without assistance. Vulnerable populations can live and have their quality of life enhanced when they receive the services they need within the community. Without this coordination, these populations are more likely to use more costly services, such as hospitals and residential care.

Practice Theory: Several models have evolved, but all of them include various forms of assessment, planning, and coordination of services. Case finding, intake, and referral are included in most models, as is reassessment. Brokering, mediation, and advocacy are used to access necessary services, with the latter two coming into play when barriers are experienced.

Practice Usage: Case management is used with any client, but reimbursement tends to be limited to more intensive services to vulnerable populations. These include people who are mentally ill, developmentally disabled, mentally retarded, elderly, medically fragile, children, child welfare clients, and the like.

Sources

Mizrahi, Terry and Davis, Larry E., Eds., *Encyclopedia of Social Work,* 20th ed. Washington, DC: NASW Press, 2008 ("Case Management").

Jack Rothman, *Guidelines for Case Management: Putting Research to Professional Use.* (Itasca, IL: F. E. Peacock, 1992) and *Case Management: Integrating Individual and Community Practice* (Boston: Allyn and Bacon, 1998).

A. L. Roberts and G. J. Greene, Eds., *Social Worker's Desk Reference* (New York: Oxford University Press, 2002). See: Jack Rothman, "An Overview of Case Management"; Joseph Walsh, "Clinical Case Management"; Jannah H. Mather and Grafton H. Hull, Jr., "Case Management and Child Welfare"; David P. Moxley, "Case Management and Psychosocial Rehabilitation with SMD Clients"; Charles A. Rapp, "A Strengths Approach to Case Management with Clients with Severe Mental Disabilities"; W. Patrick Sullivan, "Case Management with Substance Abusing Clients"; Candyce S. Berger, "Social Work Case Management in Medical Settings"; Carol D. Austin and Robert W. McClelland, "Case Management with Older Adults"; Brian Giddens, Lana S. Ka'opua, and Evelyn P. Tomaszewski, "HIV/AIDS Case Management."

Cognitive (Rational, Reality Theory)

Source: General category includes Alfred Adler's individual psychology, Albert Ellis's rational-emotive psychotherapy, William Glasser's reality therapy, and Harold Werner's rational casework. An alternative to Freudian psychotherapy, which concerns itself with conscious thinking and behavior.

Underlying Theory: Behavior is mainly determined by a person's thinking and willing. Intensity of acts depends on strength of will. Cognitive theory important. Perceptions, goals, and patterns are principal concerns.

Practice Theory: Assessment focuses on present thinking, feeling, and behavior. The goal is to change the client's consciousness (the sum of thoughts, emotions, and behaviors). The interaction focuses on problem solving and having client examine way he or she thinks and behaves in the living situation. Emphasis on "accurate thinking."

Practice Usage: Can be used with individuals, groups, families, and communities when resolution of problems is a focus. Should not be used to treat phobias, addictions, or psychoses.

Sources

Albert Ellis and Catherine MacLaren, *Rational Emotive Behavior Therapy: A Therapist's Guide* (Atascadero, CA: Impact Publishers, 2005).

L. Sherilyn Cormier and Paula S. Nurius, *Interviewing and Change Strategies for Helpers: Fundamental Skills and Cognitive Behavioral Interventions* (Pacific Grove, CA: Thomson-Brooks/Cole, 2003).

William Glasser, *Reality Therapy in Action* (New York: HarperCollins, 2002).

Michel Hersen and Johan Rosqvist, *Encyclopedia of Behavior Modification and Cognitive Behavior Therapy* (Thousand Oaks, CA: Sage, 2005).

Jim Lantz, "Cognitive Theory and Social Work Treatment," in Francis J. Turner, Ed., *Social Work Treatment,* 4th ed. (New York: Free Press, 1996).

Keith Dobson, Ed., *Handbook of Cognitive-Behavioral Therapies,* 2nd ed. (New York: Guilford Press, 2001).

Communication (Communicative-Interactive)

Source: Work of Don Jackson and Jay Haley in the project on "Family Therapy in Schizophrenia" at the Palo Alto Research Foundation (initiated, 1954). Virginia Satir exemplifies social work of this model. Judith C. Nelson has expanded understanding of the use of communication theory in social work practice with particular emphasis on work with individuals and families.

Underlying Theory: Broad communication and transactional base. "Double-bind" communication, metacommunication, and family homeostasis are important concepts. Emphasis is on improved family functioning, particularly improved communication.

Practice Theory: Analysis of family functioning with emphasis on role functioning, rules, and communication modes. Often uses a "Family Life Chronology." Worker is seen as therapist and modeler of communication. Techniques include showing how a person looks to other family members, building self-esteem, making explicit roles and rules, and pointing out nonverbal communication.

Practice Usage: With family group with verbal orientation and willingness to make a time investment. Particularly useful when communication is problematic.

Sources
Virginia Satir, *Con-Joint Family Therapy* (Palo Alto, CA: Science and Behavior Books, 1967).
Virginia Satir, James Stachowiak, Harvey A. Taschman, et al., *Helping Families to Change* (Northvale, NJ: Aronson, 1994).
Virginia Satir, *The Satir Model: Family Therapy and Beyond* (Palo Alto, CA: Science and Behavior Books, 1991).
Gil Green, "Communication Theory and Social Work Treatment," in Francis J. Turner, Ed., *Social Work Treatment: Interlocking Theoretical Approaches,* 4th ed. (New York: Free Press, 1996).

Crisis Intervention

Source: Study of a natural disaster and work of Erich Linderman and Gerald Caplan. Concepts of brief treatment. Work of Lydia Rapoport and Howard J. Parad, Smith College, School of Social Work (1962). The leading proponent is Naomi Golan.

Underlying Theory: Eclectic theory base with emphasis on ego psychology and stress theory. Concerned with cognitive process. Uses public health model. Goal is the restoration of social functioning and enhancement of coping capacity.

Practice Theory: Assessment of client's personality structure, basic defenses, habitual adaptive patterns, the nature of the upset, potential for adaptive response, and resources available. Makes maximal use of the period of upset, reduces client tension and anxiety, gives hope, gives support, and helps with crisis situation. Teaches new patterns of problem solving and coping and corrects perceptions. Short-term service.

Practice Usage: In situations in which developmental or situational crisis is limiting adequate social functioning. Can be used with individuals, families, or groups of individuals in crisis.

Sources
Eileen Ell, "Crisis Theory and Social Work Practice," in Francis J. Turner, Ed., *Social Work Treatment,* 4th ed. (New York: Free Press, 1996).
Alan A. Cavaiola and Joseph E. Colford, *A Practical Guide to Crisis Intervention* (Boston: Lahaska Press, 2005).
Richard K. James and Burl E. Gilliland, *Crisis Intervention Strategies,* 5th ed. (Belmont, CA: Thomson-Brooks/Cole, 2005).
Kristi Kanel, *A Guide to Crisis Intervention* (Pacific Grove, CA: Brooks/Cole, 2003).
Albert R. Roberts, *Crisis Intervention Handbook: Assessment, Treatment, and Research* (New York: Oxford University Press, 2005).

Ecological (Life Model)

Source: Carel B. Germain, Columbia School of Social Work (1970).

Underlying Theory: Ecological approach. Concepts about transactions between people and their environments, adaptation, reciprocity, mutuality, stress, and coping. Also considers growth and development, identity, competence, autonomy, and relatedness. Uses Erikson. Concerned with environmental quality, organizations, and social networks.

Practice Theory: Assessment carried out by worker and client together seeking to understand meaning; focus on person and problem in order to set objectives and devise appropriate action. Engages positive forces in client and environment. Attempts to remove environmental obstacles and change negative transactions. Uses a process of engagement, exploration, contracting, ongoing, ending. Concerned with client need and vulnerability. Focus on life transitions, unresponsiveness of environments, crisis events, and communication-relationship difficulties. Action designed to increase self-esteem and problem-solving and coping skills. Also works to facilitate group functioning and influence organizational structure, social networks, and physical settings.

Practice Usage: For problems in social functioning.

Sources

Carel B. Germain and Alex Gitterman, *The Life Model of Social Work Practice,* 1st and 2nd eds. (New York: Columbia University Press, 1980 and 1996).

Alex Gitterman, "Advances in the Life Model Approach to Social Work Practice," in Francis J. Turner, Ed., *Social Work Treatment: Interlocking Theoretical Approaches,* 3rd ed. (New York: Free Press, 1996).

Susan P. Kemp, James K. Whittaker, and Elizabeth M. Tracy, *Person-Environment Practice: The Social Ecology of Interpersonal Helping* (New York: Aldine De Gruyter, 1997).

Carol Meyer and Mark Mattaini, "The Ecosystems Perspective: Implications for Social Work Practice," in Mark Mattaini, Christine Lowery, and Carol Meyer, Eds., *The Foundations of Social Work Practice* (Washington, DC: NASW Press, 1998), pp. 3–19.

Carel Germain and Martin Bloom, *Human Behavior in the Social Environment: An Ecological View* (New York: Columbia University Press, 1999).

John T. Pardeck, *Social Work Practice: An Ecological Approach* (Westport, CT: Auburn House, 1996).

Feminist Practice (material provided by Mary Bricker-Jenkins)

Source: Developed by practitioners as an attempt to integrate feminist theory, commitments, and culture with conventional approaches to social work practice. Goes beyond a "nonsexist" and/or "women's issues" orientation.

Underlying Theory: The inherent purpose and goal of human existence is self-actualization, which is a collective endeavor involving the creation of material and ideological conditions that enable it. Systems and ideologies of domination/subordination, exploitation, and oppression are inimical to individual and collective self-actualization. Given the structural and ideological barriers to self-actualization, practice is explicitly political in intent. Women have unique and relatively unknown history, conditions, developmental patterns, and strengths that must be discovered and engaged by practitioners.

Practice Theory: Assessment focuses on preferred and available patterns of strength in intellectual, emotional, social, cultural, physical, and/or spiritual domains; special emphasis given to basic, concrete needs, safety, and perceptions of personal power. Underlying principle informing practice is that healing, health, and growth are functions of validation, consciousness, and transformative action, which are supported and sustained through resources to meet basic human needs, the creation of validating environments and relationships that preserve and nurture uniqueness and wholeness. Uses a range of conventional and nonconventional approaches. Frequent use of groups. Encourages and facilitates individual and collective action. Works for open, egalitarian, and collegial relationships with clients.

Practice Usage: In all kinds of settings, with all populations. Particular attention focused on women.

Sources
Affilia: Journal of Women and Social Work.
Mary Bricker-Jenkins, "Feminist Issues and Practices in Social Work," in Albert Roberts and Gilbert
    Greene, Eds., *Social Worker's Desk Reference* (New York: Oxford University Press, 2002).
Nan Van Den Bergh, *Feminist Practice in the 21st Century* (Washington, DC: NASW Press, 1995).
Mary Valentich, "Feminism and Social Work Practice," in Francis J. Turner, Ed., *Social Work Treatment:
    Interlocking Theoretical Approaches,* 4th ed. (New York: Free Press, 1996).
Christine Saulnier, *Feminist Theories and Social Work* (Binghamton, NY: Haworth, 1996).

Gestalt Therapy

Source: Work of Fritz Perls, adopted by many social workers because of emphasis on "beginning where the client is."

Underlying Theory: Holistic, organismic, emphasis on hunger rather than sexuality, development of self through awareness and responsibility. One must take responsibility for one's own existence. Normal personality characterized by unity, integration, consistency, and coherence. Sovereign drive is self-actualization. Concern for paradoxes.

Practice Theory: Assess what the client is experiencing, what client wants. Process: lay groundwork, establish contact; negotiate consensus between client and therapist; grading, experiment within client's ability; surface client's awareness; locate client's energy; generate self-support; generate theme; choice of experiment; enact experiment; insight and completion.

Practice Usage: In situations in which worker and agency have time and inclination to allow client to develop self-knowledge and to engage in self-exploration. Most effective in oversocialized, restrained, constricted individuals.

Sources
Elaine P. Congress, "Gestalt Theory and Social Work Treatment," in Francis J. Turner, Ed., *Social Work
    Treatment: Interlocking Theoretical Approaches,* 4th ed. (New York: Free Press, 1996).
Michael Blugerman, "Contributions of Gestalt Theory to Social Work Treatment," in Francis J. Turner, Ed.,
    Social Work Treatment: Interlocking Theoretical Approaches, 3rd ed. (New York: Free Press, 1986).

Integrative

Source: Nathan Ackerman was an early source of basic ideas. Family agencies an important source. Work of Otto Pollak, John Spiegel, Frances Beatman, and Sanford Sherman also influential. Frances Scherz an important contributor (1966).

Underlying Theory: Based in a psychoanalytic frame of reference with particular emphasis on ego psychology and role theory. Eclectic in nature. Incorporates systems theory, small-group theory, family development tasks, and communication concepts. Assumes family is the link between the individual and the larger society.

Practice Theory: Assesses family structure, functioning, and history with emphasis on placement of current problems. Goal is to modify or change aspects of the family relationship system that are not functional. Worker enables and supports family members. Emphasis is on the here and now. Task oriented. Uses advice, education, and guidance. Demonstrates techniques. Encourages appropriate role development, communication patterns, decision making, and family responsibility. Deals with resistance to change and fears of feelings and of destruction of the family. Helps family members expose hidden feelings and observe themselves.

Practice Usage: In situations in which there is a parent-child, family, or marital problem.

Sources

Frances H. Scherz, "Theory and Practice of Family Therapy," in Robert W. Roberts and Robert H. Nee, Eds., *Theories of Social Casework* (Chicago: University of Chicago Press, 1970), pp. 219–264.

Laura Sue Dodson, *Family Counseling: A Systems Approach* (Muncie, IN: Accelerated Development, 1977).

Sonya L. Rhodes, "Family Treatment," in Frances J. Turner, Ed., *Social Work Treatment: Interlocking Theoretical Approaches,* 3rd ed. (New York: Free Press, 1986), pp. 432–453.

Sanford N. Sherman, "A Social Work Frame for Family Therapy," in Eleanor Reardon Tolson and William J. Reid, Eds., *Models of Family Treatment* (New York: Columbia University Press, 1981), pp. 7–32.

Locality Development

Source: William W. Biddle, University of Missouri (1965). Contributing influences include work of United Nations in underdeveloped countries, experimental and demonstration projects of the Ford Foundation, Mobilization for Youth, Peace Corps, and work of settlement houses.

Underlying Theory: Eclectic. Draws from sociology, anthropology, and social psychology. Has an existential leaning. Sees community as eclipsed and lacking relationships. Uses problem-solving capacity of community persons.

Practice Theory: Assessment is problem solving with citizens. Process includes exploration, organization of community persons, discussion of problems, action, new projects, continuation. The goal is the development of community capacity and integration. The worker is an enabler, catalyst, coordinator, and teacher. Citizens participate in interactional problem solving. Involves a broad cross-section of people. Uses small task-oriented groups that seek consensus. Problem solving is primary.

Practice Usage: To involve a total community or neighborhood in discovering and solving problems.

Sources

William J. Biddle, *The Community Development Process: The Rediscovery of Local Initiative* (New York: Holt, Rinehart and Winston, 1965).

Fred M. Cox, John L. Erlich, Jack Rothman, and John E. Tropman, Eds., *Strategies of Community Organization,* 4th ed. (Itasca, IL: F. E. Peacock, 1987), pp. 3–26 and Part Three, pp. 351–383.

Jack Rothman, "Approaches to Community Intervention," in Jack Rothman, John Erlich, and John Tropman, Eds., *Strategies of Community Intervention* (Itasca, IL: F. E. Peacock, 2001).

Mediating

Source: William Schwartz, Columbia University, School of Social Work (1962). Lawrence Shulman also a major contributor. Work of Clara Kaiser and Helen Phillips also suggests this focus. Lawrence Shulman has continued to develop and expand usage with individuals, families, groups, and communities.

Underlying Theory: Social systems theory, symbolic interaction. Sociological understanding about organizations, institutions, and communities as systems; game theory and small-group theory.

Practice Theory: Assessment is a systems assessment of the blocks to need fulfillment. Focus is on individual in interaction, group process, and impinging environment. Process includes tuning in (worker readies self to move into process), beginning together, work, and transitions and endings. Goals related to mutual need for self-fulfillment as individuals and society reach out to each other. They are specified. Worker is a mediator and enabler, helps client reach out for what he or she needs, demands work, mobilizes healing powers of human association and mutual aid. Clarifies communication and makes use of problem-solving process.

Practice Usage: Helping people negotiate difficult environments.

Sources
William Schwartz and Serapino R. Zalba, *The Practice of Social Group Work* (New York: Columbia University Press, 1971).

Lawrence Shulman, *A Case Book of Social Work with Groups* (New York: Council on Social Work Education, 1968).

William Schwartz, "Between Client and System: Mediating Function," in Robert W. Roberts and Helen Northen, Eds., *Theories of Social Work with Groups* (New York: Columbia University Press, 1976), pp. 171–197.

Lawrence Shulman, *The Skills of Helping: Individuals, Families, Groups, and Communities,* 6th ed. (Belmont, CA: Thomson-Brooks/Cole, 2009).

Problem Solving

Source: Helen H. Perlman, University of Chicago (1957). Blending of psychosocial and functioning models.

Underlying Theory: All human living is a problem-solving process. Eclectic, using ego psychology, John Dewey's rational problem solving, role theory, and symbolic interaction.

Practice Theory: Assessment identifies and explains the nature of the problem, focuses on aspects of personality involved in the problem. Continuous appraisal of client's motivation, capacity, and opportunity. Goal is to help client cope as effectively as possible in carrying out social tasks and in relationships. Relationship with client of prime concern. Uses time in process. Conceptualized as a *person* with a *problem* comes to a *place* where he or she is offered help through a *process*.

Practice Usage: With individuals motivated to use help in a cognitive and interactive process.

Sources
Helen H. Perlman, "The Problem-Solving Model," in Robert W. Roberts and Robert H. Nee, Eds.,
    Theories of Social Casework (Chicago: University of Chicago Press, 1970), pp. 129–179.
Helen H. Perlman, *Social Casework: A Problem-Solving Process* (Chicago: University of Chicago Press,
    1975).
Helen H. Perlman, "The Problem Solving Model," in Francis J. Turner, Ed., *Social Work Practice: Inter-
    locking Theoretical Approaches,* 3rd ed. (New York: Free Press, 1986), pp. 245–266.

Social Action

Source: Saul Alinsky and Richard Cloward (1960s).

Underlying Theory: Eclectic and selective. Little theory development. Concepts used include disadvantaged population, social injustice, deprivation, inequality. Concerned with power, conflict, confrontation. The community is seen as made up of conflicting interests that are not easily reconcilable and as having scarce resources.

Practice Theory: Goal is the shifting of power relationships and resources as well as basic institutional change that benefits "me and mine." The worker is an advocate, agitator, negotiator, and partisan. Client is seen as victim and employer of worker. Strategy is to crystallize issues and develop organization to take action against enemy target. Also uses conflict, confrontation, and negotiation. Manipulates mass organizations and political processes.

Practice Usage: When individuals are seen as victims of an unjust system.

Sources
Saul Alinsky, *Rules for Radicals* (New York: Random House, 1967).
Fred M. Cox, John L. Erlich, Jack Rothman, and John E. Tropman, Eds., *Strategies of Community Organi-
    zation,* 4th ed. (Itasca, IL: F. E. Peacock, 1987), pp. 3–26 and Part Three, pp. 384–422.
Jack Rothman, "Approaches to Community Intervention," in Jack Rothman, John Erlich, and John
    Tropman, Eds., *Strategies of Community Intervention* (Itasca, IL: F. E. Peacock, 2001).

Social Planning

Source: Conventional community organization in planning and funding organizations and governmental planning agencies.

Underlying Theory: Sees the community as an entity with many interacting systems. Particular emphasis on decision making, power control, and the agency system. Political and economic considerations as important as substantive knowledge about social problems. Emphasis is on rationality, objectivity, and professional purposefulness.

Practice Theory: Assessment identifies social problem, its cause, and its possible resolution. The process includes study and assessment of the problematic situation; determining preferences and influences relevant to the problem; examining alternative goals and strategies and their consequences; selection of goals, strategies, and programs; obtaining commitments to desired change; and designing and implementing a feedback-evaluative system. Worker is a fact gatherer and analyst, program designer, implementer, and facilitator. Consumers tend to be power structure of the community.

Practice Usage: Where rational planning toward the alleviation of social problems is desired.

Sources

Robert Perlman and Arnold Gurin, *Community Organization and Social Change* (New York: John Wiley and Sons, 1972).

Fred M. Cox, John L. Erlich, Jack Rothman, and John E. Tropman, Eds., *Strategies of Community Organization,* 4th ed. (Itasca, IL: F. E. Peacock, 1987), pp. 3–26 and Part Three, pp. 308–350.

Jack Rothman, "Approaches to Community Intervention," in Jack Rothman, John Erlich, and John Tropman, Eds., *Strategies of Community Intervention* (Itasca, IL: F. E. Peacock, 2001).

Strengths Perspective

Source: Originally developed for working with persons with mental illness but has been extended to other population groups and fields beyond direct practice. Major contributors include Dennis Saleeby, Ann Weick, Richard Rapp, W. Patrick Sullivan, Walter Kisthardt, Charles Cowger, and Julian Rappaport, University of Kansas, School of Social Welfare (1992).

Underlying Theory: Respects the unique strengths, abilities, and aspirations of clients and recognizes resources within the client's natural environment. Focuses on people's innate capacity and motivation for growth and change. Views difficulties in life as sources of challenge and opportunity.

Practice Theory: Focuses on regeneration and healing from within and on empowering or discovering the power within people. Respects the resilience of people in overcoming adversity. Builds on the client's knowledge of his or her own situation and aspirations for change. Views the role of the social worker as that of collaborator. Recognizes the role of dialogue, membership, and interrelationships in caring communities in generating resources and contributing to empowerment.

Practice Usage: Applicable to all client systems: individuals, families, small groups, organizations, and communities.

Sources

Karla Krosgrud Miley, Michael O'Melia, and Brenda L. DuBois, *Generalist Social Work Practice: An Empowering Approach,* 6th ed. (Boston: Allyn and Bacon, 2009).

Elaine Norman, *Resiliency Enhancement* (New York: Columbia University Press, 2000).

Dennis Saleeby, *The Strengths Perspective in Social Work Practice,* 5th ed. (Boston: Allyn and Bacon, 2009).

Task

Source: William J. Reid and Laura Epstein, University of Chicago (1972). Influenced by Reid and Shyne's work, *Brief and Extended Casework.* Developed as an approach whose results (outcomes) can be empirically researched.

Underlying Theory: Eclectic. Selective. Use of general systems theory, communication theory, role theory, psychoanalytic theory, and certain parts of learning theory.

Practice Theory: Assessment is specification of target problem and desired outcome. Specifies tasks needed to resolve problems. Helps client carry out task as necessary. Goals are specific and limited and related to what the client wants. Uses communication to explore, structure, enhance awareness, and direct.

Practice Usage: For time-limited treatment of problems of living.

Sources

William J. Reid, "Task-Centered Social Work," in Francis J. Turner, Ed., *Social Work Treatment: Interlocking Theoretical Approaches,* 4th ed. (New York: Free Press, 1996).

William J. Reid, *The Task Planner: An Interventive Resource for Human Service Professionals* (New York: Columbia University Press, 2000).

Laura Epstein and Lester Brown, *Brief Treatment and a New Look at the Task-Centered Approach,* 4th ed. (Boston: Allyn and Bacon, 2002).

Good Practices in Generalist Social Work

This section will describe good practices typically used by generalist social workers practicing in various settings. Much of the discussion derives from our own practice backgrounds along with research into practice methods that have evolved over time and are described in the literature. Each method includes a client-centered approach by describing the areas of service, identifying needs of client systems, describing services that are considered good practice in meeting those needs and identifying models of practice that are typically used, and suggested readings for more in-depth examination of good practices. In using these methods, the social worker employs the four steps that were identified under good practices in Chapter 9 to ensure that the client is included in the decision-making process and the implementation of services.

Good Practice in Aging Services

Description of Practice Areas. The primary practice areas in providing services to people who are aging are related to maximizing their independence and maintaining people in what is called the least restrictive environment. In order to provide for the needs of people at various stages of independence, a continuum of care is needed. At the highest level of independence, people who are older receive support for living in their own homes, condominiums, apartments, or retirement communities. Those who have needs for lower levels of care may either directly receive services to meet those needs or may have caregivers who receive services to support their caregiving. Those who have intermediate needs may live in community living facilities including group homes, adult foster care, or assisted living facilities. Those with more advanced needs will likely need nursing home care. Social workers provide valuable services at all these levels.

Good practices in aging services requires a thorough understanding of the aging process. In addition, the worker must come to terms with her own aging and mortality and be able to provide support when clients experience grief and loss. A commitment to maintaining people's dignity in the face of declining abilities is a must. People who are experiencing increased dependence need reassurance that their status as adults will be respected. The two main areas of decline that lead to greater dependence are physical and mental capacities, or both. Even though these may cause people to become more childlike in their behaviors or more dependent on others, they are not children and should never be treated as such. People who are able to provide high-quality service do so in a way that reflects a version of the Golden Rule. They approach the situation by asking themselves how they would like to be treated if they were in need of care. What would I want for myself or my loved ones? How can I respond to this situation in a way that demonstrates care and concern and respect?

Client Needs. There are common areas of concern in delivering services to people who are older at all levels of care. These are related to Maslow's hierarchy of needs, which were listed in Chapter 1. At each level of care, the worker seeks to ensure that as many of these needs are met as possible within the context of the client's mental and physical status. The degree to which various levels of need are met determines the quality of life for the client. If the ecosystem is not functioning in a way that maximizes the client's quality of life, then the worker either marshals resources to do so or seeks to change to a higher or alternative level of care that will fulfill this need. As we consider Maslow's hierarchy of needs with regard to working in aging services, we can see where meeting basic or physiological needs means ensuring survival. Safety needs may relate to being safe from becoming a victim of crime or abuse, or the need to be safe from injury. It also relates to the need for quality medical care to maintain one's health. These first two levels of need tend to drive much of the work that is done in aging services. The third level is also important: Maintaining a connection with others and meeting social needs regarding belonging and love are necessary for maintaining our mental health and this can also affect physical well-being. The other three levels of Maslow's hierarchy for people who are older are primarily determined by how people are treated by those around them, the extent to which the environment provides opportunities and stimulation, and the extent to which people are able to come to terms with their own aging and mortality. These are also important considerations in providing services to this group of clients.

Service to Clients. Most people who are older and living on their own do not receive services unless they experience a temporary need, such as a medical emergency. They rely on themselves, their families, their friends and neighbors, or staff at retirement communities for assistance if any is needed. This is especially the case for people who are middle and upper class and have financial resources available. To a great extent, the need for services is also driven by financial well-being. People who are wealthy can purchase services while maintaining their independence. There is a direct relationship between wealth and the ability to maintain independence in old age. The greater one's wealth, the more likely it is that one can maintain oneself at a higher level of independence, even in the face of advanced levels of care. Middle-class people can do so as long as they maintain their mental and physical health, but their resources can easily be overwhelmed if they need care outside of their family systems. People who are poor are the most vulnerable in terms of losing their independence, unless their families are able to support their needs for care.

In general, good practice in aging services requires the ability to provide support and assistance with grief and loss. As we age, we lose various physical abilities. With each loss we need to grieve in order to reach acceptance and resolution. Otherwise, the losses can accumulate to the point where it interferes with our quality of life. Workers should be familiar with the stages of the grief process.

Services to people who are older and living independently revolve around maintaining independence and enhancing their abilities to meet higher-level needs for socialization, esteem, self-actualization, and cognitive understanding. Proper nourishment and medical care are two major areas of focus with regard to basic needs. Congregate meal sites are available in all urban and most rural areas. In addition to meals, these sites provide opportunities to socialize and engage in activities. Case managers provide assessment and referral for medical needs and various programs designed to meet needs.

For people who are older and receiving family care, the social worker's role becomes more involved. The change model presented in this text is perfect for this work. Assessment, planning, action, and evaluation revolve around meeting needs and maintaining the caregiving system. Assessment focuses on the person's ability to perform adult daily living skills (ADLSs) and the ability of the ecosystem to provide support for those skills that the client is unable to perform independently. When needs are identified, then a plan is developed to meet those needs. The first choice for most clients is to have their informal helping systems provide for these needs. If this is not available, formal systems are employed. Nearly all of the models identified earlier in this chapter can be used in some aspect of services to people who are aging and their families.

Suggested Resources. The NASW has developed *Standards for Social Work Services in Long-Term Care Facilities, Standards for Social Work Case Management,* and *Standards for Social Work Practice in Palliative and End of Life Care,* which are available at social-workers.org/practice. Recent publications include:

Berkman, B., and D'Ambruoso, S. *Handbook of Social Work in Health and Aging* (New York: Oxford University Press, 2006).
Berkman, B., and Harootyan, L. *Social Work and Health Care in an Aging Society: Education, Policy, Practice, and Research* (New York: Springer, 2003).
Friedan, B. *The Fountain of Age* (New York: Simon and Schuster, 1993).
McInnis-Dittrich, K. *Social Work with Elders: A Biopsychosocial Approach to Assessment and Intervention,* 2nd ed. (Boston: Allyn and Bacon, 2005).
National Institute on Aging, U.S. Administration on Aging. *Resource Directory for Older People* (Bethesda, MD: U.S. Department of Health and Human Services, National Institutes of Health, Administration on Aging, 2001).
Roberts, A. L., and Greene, G. J., Eds. *Social Worker's Desk Reference* (New York: Oxford University Press, 2002). See: Arnold, E. M., "End-of Life Counseling and Care: Assessment, Interventions, and Clinical Issues"; Brownell, P., "Elder Abuse"; and Giddens, B., Ka'Opua, L. S., and Tomaszewski, E. P., "Case Management with Older Adults."

Good Practice in Chemical Dependence Services

Description of Practice Areas. The practice areas in chemical dependence includes prevention, outpatient treatment, and inpatient or residential treatment. In many settings, there also tends to be some separation between services aimed at alcohol dependence and those that are targeted toward dependence on other drugs. However, services tend to be similar under each.

Good practice with chemical dependence is founded on various combinations of professional treatment and the twelve-step system provided by Alcoholics Anonymous and various offshoots of it. Some programs offer only one or the other, but most offer a combination of both. There has been a long debate over the use of recovering staff versus professional staff in providing services. It is our sense that recovering staff tend to be especially valuable in confronting people who are chemically dependent during the initial stages and getting them past their denial. However, without further education and training, recovering staff have only their own experiences on which to rely and may be limited in assisting clients to find their own way through recovery. On the other hand, professionally trained staff who are not recovering may tend to be less rigorous in their initial confrontations of clients' denials but have typically been trained to use a client-centered approach that allows for more individual variation in recovery. Perhaps the ideal staff are a mixture of those who have both types of background along with some who are professionally trained and educated and recovering. Some states and localities combine chemical dependency services with mental health services.

An important aspect of good practice in this area is the acceptance that recovery from chemical dependence is a lifelong process. Relapse is prevalent and can occur at any time, even after many years of abstinence and recovery. This may be difficult for some professionals to accept. The idea of "cure" is so ingrained in American medicine that maintenance is generally not valued as much.

Client Needs. The most obvious need in American society is to curb the use of chemicals that alter the mind. These come in the form of both legal and illegal products that permeate American culture. Alcohol, nicotine, and caffeine are legal drugs that are consumed by the majority of Americans daily. Pharmaceutical companies market various chemical products on television and radio. The use of marijuana, cocaine, and methamphetamine has been categorized as epidemic. Although the use of these illicit drugs clearly is a major social and health problem in the United States, the use of legal drugs is by far the most pervasive problem. Hundreds of thousands of people die each year from conditions caused by the use of tobacco and alcohol. Thousands more die in accidents caused by alcohol. The vast majority of people in jail or prison were either drunk or high when they committed their crimes, or committed their crimes to get drunk or high. Incarceration has become the favored method of "treatment" for chemical dependence in the United States. At the same time, prevention amounts to a minuscule portion of the time and money spent on this problem. When the cost of incarceration along with that of law enforcement and the legal system is compared with expenditures for chemical dependence services, funding for treatment of chemical dependence is also quite small.

The most obvious need for clients who are chemically dependent is to abstain from the use of drugs or alcohol. However, this is easier said than done. Dependence and addiction are complex conditions that have physical, mental, and environmental aspects. Some theories hold that the prolonged use of some chemicals may bring about physical changes in the body that cause overwhelming cravings. Some theories indicate that some people are more prone to dependence or addiction because of their mental makeup. Still other theories point to influences in the environment. It may be that various combinations of these factors are present for nearly all clients in this practice area. Thus, clients have a myriad of needs associated with recovery. Some may need pharmacological treatment to reduce their cravings to a manageable level. Most will need counseling or therapy to change ingrained thoughts, feelings, and behaviors associated with the use of chemicals. Nearly all will need to modify their environments, which tend to be permeated with systems that support continued use and which tend to encourage high resistance to recovery.

Services to Clients. Good practice in chemical dependence generally includes active prevention programs along with the use of a full spectrum of services. Prevention needs to be aimed at children and adolescents as well as adults. It should be in the schools, in the media, and throughout the community and it must be ongoing. The most common forms of prevention tend to be those that provide information about the physical, mental, and environmental consequences of chemical dependence. Some programs offer ways to resist the pressure to use drugs and alcohol. It is difficult to measure the effectiveness of these programs, and, as a result, they are often reduced or eliminated in times of economic difficulties.

Good practice in treating chemical dependence should include the availability of both outpatient and inpatient or residential services. It should include a combination of professional counseling and therapy and variations of the twelve-step program. It should offer both individual and group formats and be available to voluntary and involuntary clients. It should support abstinence while also focusing on overt and covert mechanisms that support continuing use. These include physical, mental, and environmental factors. Good practice recognizes the high risk of relapse, and any limitation on the use of services should be considered as contrary to good practice. Unfortunately, many insurers and employee assistance programs place limits on the frequency or availability of covered services.

Nearly any of the models of practice may be used in some aspect of service delivery in chemical dependence. Behavioral and cognitive-behavioral approaches are quite popular and are offered in both individual and group formats. Twelve-step programs appear to be as effective or more than the use of traditional models. It is our sense that the supportive aspects of twelve-step programs are probably what make them more effective. People can find a group nearly any day of the week, at least in urban and suburban areas. In addition, the use of sponsors who are available 24/7 is probably the most effective service in maintaining sobriety. Professional services cannot provide this kind of response on such a personal level. Another important aspect of this approach is the helper effect in which people feel good about themselves when they are able to help others. This boosts one's self esteem, which in turn strengthens one's ability to maintain one's own sobriety.

Suggested Resources. There are many websites devoted to this subject. Those that seem most relevant for good practice are Alcoholics Anonymous (alcoholics-anonymous.org), Narcotics Anonymous (na.org), Al-Anon and Alateen (al-anon.alateen.org) for family and friends of alcoholics, the Substance Abuse and Mental Health Administration (samhsa.gov and ncadi.samhsa.gov), the U.S. National Library of Medicine and the National Institutes of Health (nlm.nih.gov/medlineplus/substanceabuseproblems), the National Institute on Alcohol Abuse and Alcoholism (niaaa.nih.gov), the National Council on Alcoholism and Drug Dependence (ncadd.org), and The Partnership for a Drug-Free America (drugfree.org). Recent publications include:

Craig, R. J. *Counseling the Alcohol and Drug Dependent Client: A Practical Approach* (Boston: Allyn and Bacon, 2004).

Fisher, G. L., and Harrison, T. C. *Substance Abuse: Information for School Counselors, Social Workers, Therapists, and Counselors,* 3rd ed. (Boston: Allyn and Bacon, 2005).

Johnson, J. *Fundamentals of Substance Abuse Practice* (Pacific Grove, CA: Brooks/Cole, 2004).

Lewis, J. A. *Substance Abuse Counseling,* 3rd ed. (Pacific Grove, CA: Brooks/Cole, 2002).

McNeece, C. A., and DiNitto, D. M. *Chemical Dependency: A Systems Approach,* 3rd ed. (Boston: Allyn and Bacon, 2005).

Good Practice in Child Welfare

Description of Practice Areas. Child welfare includes child protective services (CPS), foster care, and adoption. CPS is the responsibility of the public welfare system. It includes investigation of complaints regarding child maltreatment, including physical, educational, and medical neglect, and physical, sexual, and emotional abuse. Private agencies may provide prevention and family preservation programs. Foster care is used when children cannot remain in their own homes because of an ongoing risk of maltreatment. It is considered to be a temporary arrangement until the risk is removed or parental rights are terminated and a permanent plan is implemented. If family reunification is not possible, then permanency planning generally requires an effort to place children for adoption. Adoption services include domestic, foreign, and specialized adoptions.

Client Needs in CPS. Good practice in CPS begins with a thorough investigation. Protection of the child from harm is coupled with the need to preserve the family unit if possible. The long-term interests of children are to have parents who are able to provide for their needs. Removal from the home should be undertaken as a last resort if necessary to protect the child from further harm. The worker assesses the situation and the risk of future maltreatment. Several inventories have been developed to assist in assessment along with structured interview formats. Generally, the more cooperative the parent or guardian is, the lower the risk. Higher risk is associated with substance abuse, criminality, and poverty. Sexual abuse seems more difficult to assess in terms of risk, and generally, separation from the perpetrator is the primary protection. A protective response by the nonoffending parent or guardian lowers the risk in most of these cases.

Services in CPS. The success of treatment techniques is mixed, with some focusing on the parent and others taking a family systems approach. Treatment may be rendered within the public welfare system but is often provided by private agencies. The alleviation of risk factors is the focus for the most part. A comprehensive treatment program for substance abuse is required whenever it is present. Parenting classes and improving the family's economic well-being can reduce risks. The social work intervention role is case manager to ensure the effective use of resources. Social workers may also provide counseling, substance abuse treatment, and parenting classes. Risks are reduced when the parent admits to the maltreatment and acts to alleviate the risks.

A number of models can be used in good practice with CPS. The family preservation model has been required by the federal government as the first choice in CPS. A strengths approach is a must for any form of family preservation or reunification efforts. Crisis intervention is important with respect to both parents and children, especially when removing children from the home. Behavior therapy may be used to assist younger children in adjusting to foster care. For older children and for parents the cognitive-behavioral, communication, mediation, problem solving, solution-focused, or task models can be employed, depending on the needs and desires of the parents and children. Case management is required for all cases to ensure access to services and resources.

Working in CPS can be risky for the worker. The use of teams and police protection may be necessary, especially when removing children from their homes. Workers should use cell phones, a system of tracking their locations, and regular check-ins with the office. Risks are considerably elevated if there are drugs, alcohol, or criminal activity in the home. Urban settings may include elevated criminal activity in the neighborhood. In rural settings, isolation and distance reduce law enforcement's ability to respond to emergencies.

Client Needs in Foster Care. Foster care is used when it is determined that children have to be protected from further harm as a result of neglect or abuse and their parent or parents are either the source of the risk or are not able to protect the children from further harm. Generally, the first choice is to place children with relatives. In these cases, similar services are provided as would be the case if the children were in nonrelative foster care. If a relative is not available or it is determined that the children would not be safe with a relative, regular foster care is needed. While they are in foster care, children have a full spectrum of needs, including physical, social, emotional, and educational needs. The foster parents need support in assisting children to adjust to living with the foster parents and in arranging for services, such as medical, dental, mental health treatment, and educational planning and placement. There is a special need to balance assisting the child in adjusting to temporary care while preserving the relationship with their parents and siblings so reunification can take place if possible. The biological parents need assistance in overcoming the circumstances that resulted in the loss of custody.

Services in Foster Care. Good practice in foster care involves recruitment and training of foster parents and case management activities associated with maintaining children in care and with reunifying the family. Formal recruitment involves using various forms of publicity to recruit from the general public. Generally, the wider the range of recruitment activities, the wider the range in motivations for becoming a foster parent. Many people have unrealistic expectations of what is involved. Most workers find that their best recruiters are their experienced foster parents. Training should be ongoing. There are several curricula that are available through the public welfare system and private entities. Foster parents need to view fostering as a lifelong learning pursuit, just as professional social workers are expected to continue to improve their practice skills. Monetary support and child care are important. Case management is the primary role of the worker. Children in care have a full spectrum of needs as mentioned previously. The worker provides support for the foster parent in arranging for services, arranges appropriate visitation with the biological family, and provides case management services necessary for successful reunification if appropriate. The latter often includes such services as parenting skills, counseling, homemaker services, referrals for job training, and so on. Referrals to appropriate community services are needed, such as mental health facilities. Social workers, usually practicing in private agencies, community mental health settings, substance abuse services, and the like, are often involved in providing direct services to biological parents and foster children. Models that are typically used in foster care are the same as those described for CPS. In addition, a psychoeducation model involves teaching parenting and social skills.

Client Needs in Adoption. Adoption is intended to provide children with a permanent home. It also meets the needs of adoptive parents who wish to have the opportunity to raise children. For infant adoptions, pregnant mothers need assistance in making decisions about their pregnancies, especially regarding their emotional response to the pregnancy and to the possibility of terminating the pregnancy or the decision of adoption. Older children need to be prepared to bond with new parents who are not their biological parents. Prospective adoptive parents need to be prepared for the challenges of bonding to and raising a child who is not biologically theirs. Some prospective adoptive parents may decide to adopt because they are not able to conceive or bear their own children. Alternative methods of overcoming infertility may not be successful or are not acceptable to them for various reasons. In these instances, the couple needs to be able to adjust to their infertility before they will be ready to adopt. Some prospective adoptive parents may wish to add to their existing families. They will need assistance in helping their families to adjust to an adoptee. Some parents are single and the challenges of being a single parent must be addressed. Some couples may be gay or lesbian. They will need assistance in overcoming the additional prejudice and discrimination that they will face. They also need assistance in helping the child to deal with these issues.

Adoption Services. Good practices in adoption services include recruitment, assessment, training, matching, supervision, and knowledge of the legal process. Adoption of healthy white infants generally involves infertile couples seeking to adopt, and little, if any, recruitment of parents is needed. Most adoption agencies have long waiting lists of couples wishing to adopt healthy white infants. The primary service here is providing problem pregnancy counseling to mothers who are considering adoption and ensuring that she receives appropriate health care. The worker helps the pregnant mother to make a decision to keep the child and raise it, to terminate the pregnancy, or to offer adoption. In the first instance, good practice means assisting the mother to prepare for the child both emotionally and practically. Emotionally, the mother's attitude toward herself and the biological father and the reaction of her family become primary areas for exploration. Practically speaking, the mother needs to make financial preparations and living arrangements, such as accommodations, furniture, supplies, and so on. In cases where the mother is considering terminating the pregnancy, good practice methods require that the worker respect the client's right to make this decision. If the agency's policy allows for counseling and making arrangements for abortion, the worker proceeds with providing these services. If not, or if the worker's personal values conflict with these services, professional ethical practice requires that the social worker refer the client to an agency or worker who provides these services. Imposing one's own values or that of the agency on the client is not acceptable. Social workers should avoid practicing in agencies whose policies conflict with their own personal values or the values and ethics of the profession. For pregnant mothers who decide to offer adoption, the worker counsels the mother about her decision and prepares her for the adoption process.

Adoption of older children, minorities, and those with special needs requires recruitment. This can take many forms, including the use of the media, contact with churches and community groups, advertising, and so on. After recruitment, assessment and screening need to take place. As in the case of foster care, people may have unrealistic expectations that need to be corrected. Motivation for becoming an adoptive parent is an important consideration. For couples, it is also important that both parents share the motivation to adopt. If one of them is considerably more motivated, it will often lead to relationship difficulties when the inevitable challenges of even routine parenting arise. Adopting older children and those with special physical or emotional needs has many additional challenges for which parents need to be prepared. Motivation should also be balanced between the desire to meet the needs of the child and their own needs. Prospective parents should view adoption as meeting needs that they have and not so much an altruistic act for which the child will be grateful. The latter is a prescription for a failed adoption because altruism will not last very long in the face of difficult parenting experiences.

Social workers need to do background and reference checks as part of screening and assessment to ensure that the parents are appropriate for consideration. The worker generally provides a series of training programs where the adoption process and the role of the adoptive parent are discussed. These may be individual or in group formats. One or more home visits are made to determine the suitability of the living arrangements. Social workers gather information and develop a family social history.

Workers are involved in matching prospective parents with children. For infant adoption, some agencies may place an adoptee based on a waiting list where couples with seniority receive the next child. Some may give preference to older parents, giving some consideration for the age gap between parent and child and the likelihood that such marriages may be more stable than those of younger couples. Divorce is not only a higher risk at younger ages but it is also greatly increased for infertile couples. Some agencies may consider gender preferences. Other agencies may attempt to do some matching based on ethnicity. Matching is especially important for older children, minorities, and those with special needs. In fact it is the key ingredient in successful adoption of these children. Usually, these adoption arrangements are made between two agencies. States are required to list children who are available for adoption. Children in these categories have most often become available through the CPS system in which parental rights have been terminated. Foster parents are given first choice of adoption if the child has been placed with them for a sufficient length of time. There are also national listings available. The child's worker lists important characteristics and needs and, in many cases, includes a picture. The worker for the prospective adoptive parents seeks out information from the parents about their desires and looks for potential matches. When a potential match is found, visits are arranged. Generally, a mutual agreement between parents, child, and workers needs to take place before a permanent move is made. In some jurisdictions the worker may prepare and file the necessary legal documents. In others, the worker provides the family history and other information to an attorney for managing the legal aspects. The worker then provides supervision before finalization, generally for one year.

Adopting children from foreign countries generally involves an organization that specializes in this area, with a local social worker providing all of the previously mentioned services except the matching process, which is usually performed by the organization. One of the challenges with this type of adoption is helping Caucasian parents to have realistic expectations for raising children of color. This is also the case for any form of cross-racial adoption. Being able to see themselves as the parent of a child of a different race is a part of this process. In addition, consideration needs to be given to maintaining ethnic and cultural awareness and identity. Parents also need to be prepared for the prejudice and discrimination that they and their child will face in U.S. society.

The model of practice most commonly used in adoption services is psychoeducation. In working with adjustments to foster care, a behavioral approach is often used with younger children and most of the models for CPS and foster care can be used with older children and those with special needs.

Suggested Resources. The NASW has developed NASW *Standards for Child Welfare,* which is available at socialworkers.org/practice. The Child Welfare League of America (cwla.org) has a number of publications in this area, including the *Standards of Excellence for Services to Strengthen and Preserve Families with Children, Standards of Excellence for Family Foster Care*, and *Standards of Excellence for Adoption Services*. Recent publications include:

Berg, I., and Kelly, S. *Building Solutions in Child Protective Services* (New York: W.W. Norton, 2000).
Brittain, C., and Hunt, D. *Helping in Child Protective Services: A Competency-Based Casework Handbook* (New York: Oxford University Press, 2004).
DePanfilis, D., and Salus, M. *Child Protective Services: A Guide for Caseworkers,* 3rd ed. (Washington, DC: U.S. Department of Health and Human Services, http://purl.access.gpo.gov/GPO/LPS33451, 2003).
Ellis, R. A., Dulmus, C. A., and Wodarski, J. S. *Essentials of Child Welfare.* (Hoboken, NJ: John Wiley and Sons, 2003).
Kluger, M., Alexander, G., and Curtis P. *What Works in Child Welfare* (Washington, DC: CWLA Press, 2000).

Good Practice in Domestic Violence Services

Description of Practice Areas. Good practice for generalist social workers in domestic violence services includes prevention, dissemination of information, and services to victims and perpetrators. Prevention can include early intervention with children to prevent family violence; policy changes that promote intervention by law enforcement, prosecution, and courts; and community education on the dynamics of domestic violence. Dissemination of information is essential because victims are often isolated and controlled by their perpetrators. Publicizing facts about domestic violence, raising awareness, and informing victims about accessing services are critical in reaching victims. Services to victims should include nonresidential and residential components along with support for legal matters. Services to perpetrators include treatment to reduce the risk of further violence.

Client Needs. Although victims of domestic violence can be both male and female, the overwhelming majority of victims served by domestic violence programs are women. In addition to being victims of physical abuse, victims are typically emotionally and psychologically abused and may even be killed if they attempt to leave a domestic violence situation. Victims of domestic violence have a range of needs as they progress toward establishing a life that is free of violence. The first need is to be safe. In some instances, the removal of the perpetrator along with a personal protection order may be sufficient to protect the victim from further harm. However, it is often necessary for the victim to be removed from the home or residence, and steps may need to be taken to keep her from being found by the perpetrator. This might mean moving in with friends or relatives or entering a shelter. In more extreme cases of danger, the victim may need to be moved out of town, out the area, or even out of state. Domestic violence programs have developed networks that make these options possible.

A major consideration for women who are mothers is their children. Domestic violence is closely related to family violence and child abuse, causing many mothers to leave the abusive situation with their children. This could complicate the ability to secure temporary shelter with friends and relatives. Domestic violence shelters readily accept families, but space may be limited at times. Other complications associated with children include school and recreation. Children may not be able to attend their regular school because of the ease with which the perpetrator can locate them and ultimately their mother. Adjusting to a new school under these circumstances can be quite difficult. Children also need to be entertained and be able to play. While in a shelter, these activities need to take place under supervision.

Women who leave their partners may literally leave with the clothes on their backs. Although accessing their residences may be possible, it is rare that all of their belongings are recovered or their half of any possessions in the home. So those who leave permanently are usually starting over with practically nothing. Many victims do not have cars or the means of maintaining one, so transportation is a challenge. In addition, many women may not be employed, and those that are may have to leave their employment for fear of being located by their partners. Thus, receiving education or job training and finding employment and child care are often challenges. Securing new housing generally requires substantial assets to pay for security deposits and the first month's rent. Food, furniture, and housewares must also be acquired.

Assistance with legal matters is another need. Both criminal and civil proceedings may be involved. Victims need support and advocacy in order to persevere in securing justice for themselves and their children. They are often faced with financial barriers in covering the cost of legal representation, and it may be difficult to obtain pro bono services from attorneys.

Perpetrators of domestic violence need to eliminate violence or the threat of violence from their behaviors and establish healthy behavior patterns in relationships. Accepting responsibility is usually the first step. Alternatives to violence classes, substance abuse treatment, and mental health treatment are usually necessary in order to reverse long-standing and underlying patterns of domination and violence in domestic partnerships.

Services to Clients. Good practice in domestic violence services requires courage and fortitude. Some perpetrators are not beyond threatening workers who assist their victims. Quite often, victims decide to return to their abusing partners. In fact, victims may return multiple times (according to national statistics, an average of seven times) before they decide to leave. Women are especially vulnerable in the area of financial hardship in part because of the disparity between male and female income levels. It is much more difficult for women to obtain employment that will support themselves and their children. The cost of child care and setting up a new residence is daunting. Securing child support and spousal support may be difficult and could be dangerous if it ends up revealing the victim's whereabouts.

Knowledge of the tactics of power and control and the cycle of violence is necessary for good practice. Lenore Walker developed the concept of the cycle of violence in her book, which is cited in the resources section that follows. The cycle begins as tension builds and an incident of abuse occurs. This is followed by making up and then a period of calm before tension begins to build toward another incident (see domesticviolence.org/cycle.html for an adaptation of this). Good practice includes educating both victims and perpetrators regarding the dynamics of power and control. With victims, it is important for them to focus on their own safety by using supportive services or leaving their partners and establishing personal independence. They also need to be aware of the potential to become involved in future relationships that could be abusive. If they can recognize the warning signs ahead of time, they can avoid these types of relationships. Educating perpetrators of abuse involves helping them change their thoughts, feelings, and/or behaviors and helping them recognize how they have used power and control to manipulate their victims. Teaching alternatives to violence can be particularly useful in this process.

An empowerment approach is essential in providing domestic violence services. Victims need to recover personal power that is lost through the victimization process. Psychological and emotional abuse go hand in hand with physical abuse and often cause victims to feel worthless and powerless. Because the initial contact generally occurs during a crisis, it may be necessary to be more directive to ensure the victim's safety. However, once services begin after the crisis stage, it is better to provide support for decision making and goal setting. Empowerment means helping victims to restructure their thoughts, feelings, and behaviors to increase their power and control over their physical, psychological, emotional, social, and economic well-being. Victims may need to build or rebuild self-esteem destroyed by their experiences. Group work, including support and cognitive restructuring, is typically employed along with personal counseling. This can occur on either a nonresidential or residential basis.

Advocacy and legal representation is vital. A positive relationship with law enforcement, prosecuting attorneys, and the courts needs to be established and maintained. Case management and referrals are also part of the core of services. Access to a full spectrum of services is important. Service gaps tend to lose clients. When clients are lost because a service is not available, it can easily become a life and death situation.

Suggested Resources. The National Coalition against Domestic Violence provides information and resources. Their website is ncadv.org. The National Domestic Violence Hotline also provides information and referral at ndvh.org. The U.S. Department of Justice provides information at usdoj.gov/domesticviolence/htm. Recent publications include:

Kennedy-Dugan, M., and Hock, R. R. *It's My Life Now: Starting over after an Abusive Relationship or Domestic Violence* (New York: Routledge, 2000).

Lissette, M. A., and Kraus, R. *Free Yourself from an Abusive Relationship* (Alameda, CA: Hunter House, 2000).

Paymar, M. *Violent No More: Helping Men End Domestic Violence* (Alameda, CA: Hunter House, 2000).

Potter-Efron, R. T. *Handbook of Anger Management: Individual, Couple, Family, and Group Approaches* (New York: Haworth, 2005).

Stith, S. M. *Prevention of Intimate Partner Violence* (New York: Haworth, 2005).

Walker, L. *The Battered Woman* (New York: Harper and Row, 1979).

Wilson, K. J. *When Violence Begins at Home: A Comprehensive Guide to Understanding and Ending Domestic Abuse* (Alameda, CA: Hunter House, 2005).

Good Practice in Health Care Settings

Description of Practice Areas. The primary practice areas in health care settings include hospital social work, home care and community services, and hospice. It also includes practice in extended care facilities, which was covered under aging services and will not be repeated here. Although the great majority of residents of extended care facilities are people who are older, young people and adults may also become residents. This is typically as a result of the need for rehabilitation and care caused by a medical condition or an injury. Much of what was covered under aging services is also relevant for health care settings because the majority of patients in most settings are people who are older. Thus, it is suggested that social workers who work in health care should follow the good practices previously described under aging services.

Client Needs. In most health care situations, clients need assistance in negotiating the health care system. This system can be confusing and overwhelming. In addition, health insurance coverage and financial concerns are frequently issues. Clients and their families also need assistance in dealing with the emotional and psychological affects of threats or challenges presented by health care needs and the condition or treatment. In the community, clients with medical conditions that limit their independence need assistance to maintain independence and quality of life at home and in the community. Clients may need rehabilitation services to overcome a challenge or limitation or to maximize recovery. They may need to learn to engage in various activities again or learn new ways of accomplishing daily tasks. The general public needs information about potential health-threatening situations and about behaviors that can lead to health problems, such as smoking, alcohol abuse, and the like. Clients who are terminally ill need palliative care to make them comfortable and to assist their families as their life comes to an end.

Services to Clients. Four important aspects of good practice in health care are (1) the ability to use a strengths-based approach, (2) a thorough understanding of community resources, (3) an understanding of medical terminology, and (4) competence in crisis intervention and grief work. A strengths approach has been discussed throughout the text. It is important for the generalist social worker practicing in a health care setting to be able to focus on health and abilities as opposed to disease and disabilities. This approach emphasizes hope and the curative aspects of health care. It balances losses that patients may experience with what they are still able to do.

Case management and discharge planning are central tasks for most social workers in health care settings, so a thorough knowledge of the full range of services available is necessary in order to ensure that the full range of needs are met. Workers cannot limit themselves to only the medical aspects of clients' situations. They must take into account clients' abilities in caring for themselves and their levels of independence. A wide range of home health care and homemaker services are available in urban and suburban areas. Rural areas may be quite limited in terms of available services. Case management often includes assisting clients with maximizing their health care benefits and advocating for services, especially when dealing with various managed care systems. Familiarity with Medicaid and Medicare is a must. Clients often need assistance in applying for benefits.

Good practice in health care means mastering the medical terminology and abbreviations that are used in these settings. In some respects, it is almost like learning a foreign language. While it is not necessary for the worker to take a course in medical terminology (although it is very helpful to do so), she must be able to quickly acquire knowledge in this area as she develops her practice skills. Because health problems can lead to disabilities and to life-threatening conditions and to death itself, good practice means developing competence in crisis intervention and grief and loss. Crisis intervention was covered in Chapter 10. Support groups are important services for those who suffer from debilitating or terminal conditions and for their families, who need support while providing care and assistance. As with aging services, good practice includes the need for the worker to accept her own aging and mortality, which health care conditions can bring to mind. Models of practice used are primarily case management, crisis intervention, ecological, problem solving, and task.

Suggested Resources. The NASW publishes a journal entitled *Health and Social Work.* It also identifies health and various health-related areas as speciality practice sections that offer resources to members. The website is socialworkers.org/sections/default.asp. The Agency for Healthcare Research and Quality is a governmental agency that provides information and resources on a wide variety of health care issues at ahrq.gov. The American Health Care Association has a website at ahca.org. The Mayo Clinic provides information on health care at mayoclinic.com and WebMD has a website providing information at webmd.com. The Centers for Medicare and Medicaid have a website at cms.hhs.gov. Recent publications include:

Cowles, L. A. Fort. *Social Work in the Health Field: A Care Perspective* (Binghamton, NY: Haworth, 2003).
Csikai, E. L., and Chaitin, E. *Ethics and End of Life Decisions in Social Work Practice* (Chicago, IL: Lyceum Books, 2005).
Gehlert, S., and Browne, T. A. *Handbook of Health Social Work* (Hoboken, NJ: John Wiley and Sons, 2005).
Johnson, J. L., and Grant, G. *Casebook: Medical Social Work* (Boston: Pearson/Allyn and Bacon, 2005).
Yuen, F. K. O., and Skibinski, G. J. *Family Health Social Work Practice: A Knowledge and Skills Casebook* (Binghamton, NY: Haworth, 2003).

Good Practice in Mental Health

Description of Practice Areas. The primary practice areas for generalist social workers in mental health are case management, partial hospitalization, inpatient, clubhouses, emergency services, assertive community treatment, day activity programs, sheltered workshops, supported employment, and residential care. Generalist social workers can be found in each of these areas. Typically, outpatient therapy is provided by MSW social workers with clinical expertise along with psychologists and psychiatrists. Thus, therapy will not be covered here, but the other areas of practice will be discussed. Because there is considerable overlap with regard to clients who use these services, the organization for this method will focus on clients with severe or chronic mental health care needs and those who are developmentally disabled or mentally retarded.

The mental health system is comprised of both public and private service delivery systems with some overlap. The private system is made up of nonprofit and for-profit organizations. The public mental health system is mainly supported by a combination of state and federal funding, including Medicaid. It includes community mental health programs, which cover every county in the United States, and the state mental health system, comprised of state hospitals and various residential options. Some reimbursement may also be obtained from fees for services or other insurances, although this tends to be minor because many clients do not have these benefits. Each state has its own public mental health system and its own system of reimbursement from Medicaid called a "Medicaid waiver." Thus, although there may be a great deal of similarity from state to state, there can be differences in services. Services to people who are mentally retarded or developmentally disabled are generally either provided by the public system or through contracts for services with the private system.

The private system is usually supported by fees for services and insurance. The public system may contract for services with private organizations, depending on the service delivery system that is available in various geographical areas. In rural areas, the private system is often limited, distant, or nonexistent, so the public system may be the only service that is available. Even that system might be distant as well. The recipients of services in both of these systems tend to be different in urban areas. The private system tends to serve those who have resources, including those with active family support systems. The public system must serve anyone in need, and in urban areas it tends to primarily serve those who have few, if any, resources and may also have little or no active family support. Sometimes family support is available, but the mental health symptoms have created barriers. Sometimes symptoms have estranged family members. Unfortunately, there are also some families who do not function well in terms of support, even without the challenges presented by mental health needs.

Client Needs.   There are two primary types of clients who use most of the services provided in the areas of practice previously identified. The first are people who have symptoms of major mental illness and the second are people who are developmentally disabled or mentally retarded. The two main types of clients who experience major mental illness include people who experience various psychotic symptoms and those who experience serious symptoms of depression. Most of the first type of clients are diagnosed with some form of schizophrenia. The latter are those whose depression places them at risk of suicide. These are typically people who are diagnosed with major depression or with bipolar disorder. People who experience anxiety are a third major area of service, but they generally receive services through outpatient treatment and medication, so they will not be covered here. Some people who experience severe or chronic depression may also experience psychosis, and most people who experience psychosis also have periods of severe depression. Both groups are at high risk for suicide. The symptoms of psychosis and depression require a number of acute and ongoing types of services. At the same time, the symptoms make it difficult for people to receive those services because both of these types of mental illness interfere with the ability to function cognitively. Generally, people with acute or chronic psychosis or depression need support in meeting the full spectrum of needs identified by Maslow and by Towle when their symptoms are active and interfering with their cognitive functioning. Many people with these conditions will fluctuate in terms of their abilities to function and meet their own needs, and so their needs for various services will also fluctuate. However, some are never able to experience relief from having symptoms and will need ongoing support. Because these conditions are often either chronic or cyclical, maintaining full employment can be difficult. This limits many of the resources that are available, such as income and health insurance. In turn, this affects the quality of life and puts people at high risk of living in poverty. There are no cures for these conditions. Although people can recover from major depression, they are typically at risk of experiencing periodic episodes in the future. Many people are able to function with pharmacological treatment, but some may not experience full or continuous benefit. Thus, in addition to needing support for meeting their full spectrum of needs at various times, people with these conditions need constant monitoring of their medication regimen.

People who are developmentally disabled or mentally retarded need support for a full spectrum of needs depending on the extent to which their mental or physical symptoms affect their independence. Their conditions are almost always chronic, but their levels of functioning and independence may be increased with consistent support. People with these conditions face similar challenges to those who are mentally ill in that their conditions can present barriers to accessing services. In addition, those with fragile health conditions may need substantial medical monitoring and services.

Services to Clients. Good practice in mental health for generalist social workers often includes providing case management to clients who are experiencing acute or chronic symptoms. Some mental health agencies only employ master's-level staff, but the BSW worker is perfect for this type of service. Case management in the mental health system follows the typical model for case management identified in the Chapter 11. Case managers provide assessment, planning, coordination of services, and crisis intervention. For clients with acute or chronic mental illness and those who are mentally retarded or physically disabled, these services are vital in advancing their quality of life and in ensuring that their basic needs are met. Case managers monitor medication and health needs and ensure that clients have access to psychiatrists and doctors. People experiencing psychotic or depressive symptoms must have their medications monitored in order to function on their own and to protect against potential decompensation, which often leads to hospitalization and, in the case of depression, an elevated risk of suicide. Case managers ensure that periodic medication reviews take place and that the medication is effective in maximizing their clients' abilities to function. For clients who are physically or developmentally disabled, case managers ensure that they receive the necessary health care needed to address their condition. They meet with clients in the office and on home visits to determine whether basic needs are being met. They arrange for participation in any of the programs mentioned previously as needed. A primary goal is to assist clients in maintaining themselves in the least restrictive environment. In other words, case managers try to help clients to maintain a maximum level of independence. This can range from complete independence with employment and their own homes or apartments to residential care in a group home or in adult foster care. In between these extremes, clients may be in supported or semi-independent living situations or they might live with their families. Case managers assist in arranging for changes in living circumstances when the client's condition or situation requires such change. This may mean movement toward more or less independence, depending on the client's abilities at a given time.

Generalist social workers are employed in all of the services previously mentioned under practice areas. In inpatient settings, they provide supportive and habilitation services, such as coping skills, training in life skills, activities, and so on. These are generally provided in a group format. The same types of services are provided in partial hospitalization. Typically, the main difference between these two types of settings is that clients go home at night when they are attending a partial hospitalization program. Day activity programs offer socialization and training in social skills as well as personal care and similar areas. Some are designed for people who are mentally ill, but most are for people who are mentally retarded or developmentally disabled. Clubhouses have begun to substitute for partial hospitalization and day activity programs. Clubhouses are operated by the participants with support available from staff who are usually social workers. Generalist social workers also provide supportive services in sheltered workshops where clients who cannot function in a competitive employment situation are able to learn work skills and receive payment for their work, which is often done on a piecework basis. In supported employment, clients receive support services, such as coaching in a competitive employment situation. Emergency services staff provide crisis intervention and assessment for inpatient hospitalization. All community mental health programs must provide this service twenty-four hours a day, seven days a week every day of the year. Social workers are frequently used to staff this service. In urban areas, emergency services and crisis centers may be housed independently or in hospitals with emergency departments and inpatient units. Usually, rural areas cover crises at the office during business hours and rely on hospital emergency departments after hours. Inpatient units are usually located in a more urban area at a distance from residential areas. In rural areas, staff will carry beepers or cell phones for coverage after hours and will talk over the phone or meet with clients in the emergency department. Assertive community treatment teams are designed to meet the needs of people who are chronically mentally ill and who have histories of multiple or long-term psychiatric hospitalizations. The team approach is used to prevent hospitalization or shorten the client's stay when he is hospitalized. It generally consists of a doctor, a nurse, and one or more social workers. Some teams may also have a psychologist. A team provides twenty-four-hour response to a small group of patients as well as intensive case management on a frequent basis, daily if necessary. Residential care involves a range of options from independent or semi-independent living to group or foster care. Independent living generally consists of the client living in some sort of supported living arrangement, but staff are not on site. Generally, a case manager visits and maintains contact with the client to ensure that the client's needs are met. In semi-independent living, clients usually live alone or with a roommate in an apartment, and staff are available on site to assist them. In foster care clients live with a family or in an adult foster home. In a group home, clients live together with staff who work in shifts to provide supervision and basic needs. Social workers provide case management services to most of these groups of clients.

Good practice in mental health settings must include crisis intervention skills, the ability to assess for hospitalization, and suicide assessment and intervention. A model for crisis intervention was presented in Chapter 10 and in this chapter. Because each state has its own mental health code, assessment for hospitalization will vary somewhat from state to state. However, at the very least, all states and good practice dictate that hospitalization occur when the client's condition results in immediate danger to himself or others. Voluntary hospitalization means that the client is able to sign himself into the hospital. It also means he can sign himself out. Involuntary hospitalization requires that a petition for hospitalization be initiated. Petitions are usually permitted to be signed by an adult, a law enforcement officer, or a health care professional who has direct knowledge of the situation. All social workers, but especially those working in mental health settings, should be knowledgeable about their state's requirements with regard to the process of hospitalizing people who are mentally ill, both voluntarily and involuntarily. The time to gain this knowledge is before the social worker needs to use it, not afterward. If a client is admitted to a mental hospital or unit voluntarily, but wishes to sign out against medical advice, then it is up to the hospital staff to file a petition for involuntary admission if the client is deemed to fall under the statutes for that state. Petitions require court involvement in whatever court system is applicable in that state.

Suicide assessment and intervention is an important skill that all social workers should acquire. Because they work with people who are vulnerable to experiencing depression, social workers need to know the signs of suicide risk and how to respond effectively. When clients are depressed, they should be asked if they have been thinking of harming themselves. If so, the next question should be whether they have a plan. If they have a plan, then assessing the risk is based on how effective the plan is likely to be. Higher risk is associated with more specificity, more lethality, more availability of the means, and less likelihood of interference from others. In cases of medium to high risk, the first option is to access the emergency services system at the community mental health agency that is responsible for the county involved. Intervention involves reducing these risk factors by removing the means of carrying out the plan and reducing isolation, which is generally necessary for the plan to succeed. For instance, the client's family would typically be instructed to remove or lock up guns, ammunition, sharp knives, and so on, and the person should not be left alone until the risk subsides. Lower-risk clients may continue to be served by negotiating a safety contract in which they agree not to harm themselves without seeing the worker in person to discuss their feelings. They should also agree to inform the worker of any such thoughts and the worker should monitor this closely.

Chronic and severe mental illness generally requires medication to treat or reduce the symptoms. Antidepressants are used for major (as well as less severe) depression. Some form of lithium-based medication is used for bipolar disorder. Major tranquilizers are used for schizophrenia and other psychotic disorders. However, medication alone is not always sufficient. Various combinations of the services previously identified are often needed. For depression, outpatient therapy should also be arranged.

Good practice by generalist social workers in mental health settings nearly always involves case management to ensure that necessary services are received. A thorough understanding of the *Diagnostic and Statistical Manual of Mental Disorders*, fourth edition, (DSM-IV) is also needed to work effectively in mental health settings. Nearly all of the models identified earlier in this chapter are used in various aspects of providing mental health services.

Suggested Resources. The NASW has developed the NASW *Standards for Social Work Case Management,* which is available at socialworkers.org/practice. The American Association of Suicidology has excellent resources available at suicidology.com. The Crisis Intervention Network has resources listed on its website at crisisinterventionnetwork.com. Recent publications include:

American Psychiatric Association. *Diagnostic and Statistical Manual of Mental Disorders,* 4th ed. (DSM-IV) (Washington, DC: American Psychiatric Association, 1994).

Bentley, K. J. *Social Work Practice in Mental Health: Contemporary Roles, Tasks, and Techniques* (Pacific Grove, CA: Brooks/Cole, 2002).

Holt, B. *The Practice of Generalist Case Management* (Boston: Allyn and Bacon, 2000).

Jacobs, D. G. *Harvard Medical School Guide to Suicide Assessment and Intervention* (San Francisco, CA: Jossey-Bass, 1999).

Roberts, A. R. *Crisis Intervention Handbook: Assessment, Treatment, and Research* (New York: Oxford University Press, 2005).

Stout, C. E., and Hayes, R. A., Eds. *The Evidence-Based Practice: Methods, Models, and Tools for Mental Health Professionals* (Hoboken, NJ: John Wiley and Sons, 2005).

Thyer, B. A., and Wodarski, J. S. *Handbook of Empirical Social Work Practice, Volume 1, Mental Disorders* (Hoboken, NJ: John Wiley and Sons, 2004).

Good Practice in Youth and Delinquency Services

Description of Practice Areas. The primary practice areas for generalist social workers in youth and delinquency services are community-based services and residential care. Community practice involves promoting growth and development, prevention, and juvenile probation. There are further subdivisions within delinquency services between youth who commit crimes and those who are classified as status offenders. Status offenses are only offenses because of the age or status of the offender. Status offenses include home truancy, school truancy, and incorrigibility (failure to obey the reasonable and lawful commands of one's parents). Residential care ranges from foster care and group homes to state training schools.

Client Needs. All youth need their basic needs met along with the need to grow and develop according to the stages of development. A glance at Erikson's stages of development shows that children go through five stages of development before they reach young adulthood. Each stage presents challenges for successful growth and development. All children and youth need opportunities to complete the tasks of each stage. Some will need assistance in overcoming barriers.

An important task in delinquency services is balancing the needs of youthful offenders against the need to protect society from victimization. This task has become increasingly more difficult, especially in many urban areas, as ever more youthful offenders have become involved with drugs, gangs, and guns. Delinquency seems to stem from a combination of family experiences and environment, with a number of theories about its etiology.

Boys from fatherless homes seem to be especially vulnerable as are youth whose families are engaged in various criminal enterprises. Additional risk factors are similar to those identified for families experiencing neglect or abuse as previously identified. In many cases, the difference between children who enter the child welfare system and those who enter the delinquency system is age, with younger children entering the former and older children the latter. So, substance abuse in the family increases the risk along with the presence of neglect or abuse. Growing up in a neighborhood with a high rate of crime and delinquency increases the risk regardless of the presence or absence of a father. Poverty is also a risk factor. There is evidence that untreated attention deficit hyperactivity disorder may also increase risk. So it would appear that the needs of most male delinquents are for a stable family unit with a father, a middle-income level for the family, and an environment free from crime. Although minority youth are much more likely to be officially found to be delinquent by the courts, controlling for social class generally results in little difference between white youth and those of color.

Given the tremendous differences in U.S. society between whites and people of color and between the poor and those who are not poor, it is very difficult to ameliorate the risk factors for delinquency. In fact, the task is often one of convincing the youthful offender to overcome or transcend his circumstances and to become a productive citizen in spite of his situation and society's attitude toward him. Similar challenges are present in terms of successful treatment of family members who abuse alcohol or drugs. For some delinquents, the threat of punishment is sufficient to deter them from further criminal activity. Others need a meaningful relationship with an adult who genuinely cares about them and their future. Some need a positive peer group to whom they can relate along with positive activities that meet their need for attention and for access to resources. Many need positive experiences at school in order to have access to legitimate employment opportunities.

Girls are more often brought to the attention of the court for status offenses than are boys. Girls do engage in criminal activity, but they tend to be less violent and aggressive. For instance, boys more frequently offend in terms of stealing cars or breaking and entering. Girls are more likely to shoplift. One of the factors that influences the greater use of status offenses with girls is the concern over sexual activity and pregnancy. Thus, there tends to be a double standard in delinquency.

Services to Clients. Good practice in youth and delinquency services for generalist social workers ranges from providing growth and development activities to prevention services to juvenile probation to residential care. Examples of growth and development activities are youth recreation, scouting, youth groups, Boys and Girls Clubs, and similar programs. Prevention programs include drug prevention, gang prevention, runaway services, diversion programs, and similar youth initiatives. Juvenile probation involves working within the court system to assess, plan, and intervene with youthful offenders. Residential care involves the rehabilitation of offenders away from their homes and communities. This includes foster care, group homes, open and closed residential facilities, and boys and girls state training school programs. Nearly all of the models identified earlier in this chapter are used in various aspects of providing services to youth and delinquents.

Good practice in growth and development generally involves inclusion and participation. This includes setting up and operating programs that address the needs of young people to be successful at home, in school, in the community, and with their peers. It is assumed that if the program addresses these needs then participation will meet the needs of the children and youth who are served. Generally, services are delivered in group formats with activity as a core of the program. Most groups follow a discussion-activity-discussion structure in which the activity is introduced and structure or directions are provided. This is followed by the activity itself. Afterward, debriefing takes place in which the experience is discussed along with its utility in life outside the group.

Good practice in prevention includes identifying the population at risk and developing and providing programs to reduce the risk factors. For younger children and young adolescents, games and other "fun" activities are usually coupled with messages about avoiding drugs, gangs, and other negative activities. With adolescents, more sophisticated approaches are necessary, such as decision making and refusal methods with peers. Role-plays, assertiveness training, and similar techniques may be employed. Good practice in runaway services include working with the youth and family on issues that led to the home truancy, maintaining the youth in foster or residential care if they are unable to return home immediately, and providing case management and after-care services. An important aspect of these services is connecting the youth and the family with community resources to alleviate factors that increase the risk of further truancy. Diversion programs include diverting youth from the juvenile justice system and diverting youth from out-of-home placement. The latter will be discussed under probation services. Generalist social workers may be employed in programs designed to divert first-time offenders or youth involved in minor delinquent activities from formal court involvement. Some courts use what may be called *informal probation* in which formal court action is held in abeyance for a period of time. Good practice in diversion programs involves identifying likely causes of the delinquent acts and either providing direct services or referring the youth and possibly the family to community agencies. Restorative justice programs have been initiated in which youthful offenders engage in community service or meet with the victim and negotiate appropriate restitution for the offense. In some programs, victims may choose the organization to which the community service is provided.

Good practice in probation services follows the change process presented in the text: assessment, planning, intervention, and evaluation. Generally, the juvenile probation officer provides the court with a social history that identifies functioning at home, at school, and in the community. A recommendation is also made to address the balance between the needs of the youth and those of society. The worker then carries out the decision of the court. Probation includes monitoring, case management, and often some form of counseling with regard to avoiding further delinquent activity.

Diversion from residential care involves intensive services that are generally focused on the youth and the family in an effort to avoid the human and financial costs of care. The human costs are related to the risk of learning more criminal activity when youth are placed with other delinquents. The financial costs of out-of-home placement are also substantial. Intensive counseling and case management along with crisis intervention and close monitoring are usually the services that are provided. Generalist social workers provide counseling and case management to youth who are placed in various forms of residential care, which is intended to temporarily remove the youth from a situation that is promoting further delinquency or which is intended to protect society from the youth.

Suggested Resources. The NASW has developed *Standards for the Practice of Social Work with Adolescents,* which is available at socialworkers.org/practice. Information and resources are also available through the National Criminal Justice Reference Service at ncjrs.org., the Office of Juvenile Justice and Delinquency Prevention at ojjdp.ncjrs.org, and the National Council on Crime and Delinquency at nccd-crc.org. Recent publications include:

Bartollas, C., and Miller, S. J. *Juvenile Justice in America* (Upper Saddle River, NJ: Pearson Prentice Hall, 2005).

Glicken, M. D., and Sechrest, D. *The Role of the Helping Professions in Treating the Victims and Perpetrators of Violence* (Boston: Allyn and Bacon, 2003).

Heilbrun, K., and Goldstein, N. E. Sevin. *Juvenile Delinquency: Prevention, Assessment, and Intervention* (New York: Oxford University Press, 2005).

Jackson, M. S., and Knepper, P. *Delinquency and Justice* (Boston: Allyn and Bacon, 2003).

Rapp-Paglicci, L. A., and Dulmus, C. N. *Handbook of Preventive Interventions for Children and Adolescents* (Hoboken, NJ: John Wiley and Sons, 2004).

Notes

Chapter 1

1. Adapted from Charlotte Towle, *Common Human Needs* (Washington, DC: National Association of Social Workers, 1945), p. 37.

2. Adapted from Abraham H. Maslow, *Motivation and Personality* (New York: Harper and Row, 1954).

3. One of the best discussions of the empowerment perspective is Lorraine M. Gutierrez, "Working with Women of Color: An Empowerment Perspective," *Social Work* 35 (March 1990): 149–153.

4. Anne Minahan, Ed., *Encyclopedia of Social Work,* 18th ed. (Silver Spring, MD: National Association of Social Workers, 1987), "Human Development: Biological Perspective," "Human Development: Psychological Perspective," "Human Development: Sociocultural Perspective," pp. 835–866.

5. Jean Piaget, *The Origins of Intelligence in Children* (New York: International Universities Press, 1952).

6. Erik H. Erikson, *Childhood and Society* (New York: W. W. Norton, 1950), chap. 7.

7. Lawrence Kohlberg, *Stages in the Development of Moral Thought and Action* (New York: Holt, Reinhart, and Winston, 1969); and Lawrence Kohlberg, *The Philosophy of Moral Development* (New York: Harper and Row, 1981).

8. Carol Gilligan, *In a Different Voice: Psychological Theory and Women's Development* (Cambridge, MA: Harvard University Press, 1993).

9. James Fowler, *Stages of Faith: The Psychology of Human Development and the Quest for Meaning* (San Francisco: Harper and Row, 1981); and James Fowler, *Faithful Change: The Personal and Public Challenges of Postmodern Life* (Nashville, TN: Abingdon Press, 1996).

10. See Carel B. Germain, Ed., *Social Work Practice: People and Environments* (New York: Free Press, 1976); Carol H. Meyer, Ed., *Clinical Social Work in the Eco-Systems Perspective* (New York: Columbia University Press, 1983); and Carel B. Germain, *Human Behavior in the Social Environment: An Ecological View* (New York: Columbia Press, 1991).

11. Dennis Saleeby, Ed., *The Strengths Perspective in Social Work Practice,* 2nd ed. (New York: Longman, 1997).

12. Ibid., p. 12.

13. Ibid., p. 15.

14. Ernest Greenwood, "Attributes of a Profession," *Social Work* 2 (July 1957): 45–55.

15. Leslie Leighninger, *Social Work Search for Identity* (New York: Greenwood Press, 1987).

16. Gary R. Lowe, Laura Rose Zimmerman, and P. Nelson Reid, "How We See Ourselves: A Critical Review of Text Versions of Social Work's Professional Evolution" (unpublished paper).

17. Elizabeth Howe, "Public Professions and the Private Model of Professionalism," *Social Work* 25 (May 1980): 179–191.

18. Mary E. Richmond, *Social Diagnosis* (New York: Russell Sage Foundation, 1917; reprint, Free Press, 1971).

19. *Social Casework: Generic and Specific* (New York: American Association of Social Workers, 1929).

20. Gordon Hamilton, *The Theory and Practice of Social Casework* (New York: Columbia University Press, 1940), p. 153.

21. Ibid., p. 167.

22. Jessie Taft, Ed., *A Functional Approach to Family Casework* (Philadelphia: University of Pennsylvania Press, 1944); and Herbert H. Aptekar, *Basic Concepts in Social Casework* (Chapel Hill: University of North Carolina Press, 1941).

23. Gisela, Knopka, *Social Group Work: A Helping Process*, 2nd ed. (Englewood Cliffs, N. J. : Prentice-Hall, inc. 1972, Chap. 2*).*

24.   Gertrude Wilson and Gladys Ryland's *Social Group Work Practice: The Creative Use of the Social Process* (Boston: Houghton-Mifflin, 1949); Harleigh B. Trecker's *Social Group Work: Principles and Practices* (New York: Woman's Press, 1949); Grace Coyle's *Group Work with American Youth: A Guide to the Practice of Leadership* (New York: Harper, 1948) and Gisela Konopka's *Therapeutic Group with Children* (Minneapolis: University of Minnesota Press, 1949).

25.   Felix P. Biestek, *The Casework Relationship* (Chicago: Loyola University Press, 1957).

26.   Helen Harris Perlman, *Social Casework: A Problem-Solving Process* (Chicago: University of Chicago Press, 1957).

27.   Ibid., p. 4.

28.   These include: Catherine P. Papell and Beulah Rothman, Social Group Work Models: Possession and Heritage," *Journal of Education for Social Work* 2 (Fall 1966); Jack Rothman, "Three Models of Community Organizatin Practice," in *National Conference on Social Welfare Social Work Practice* (New York: Columbia University Press, 1968). pp.16–47; and Robert W. Roberts and Robert H. Nee, Eds., *Theories of Social Casework* (Chicago: University of Chicago Press, 1970).

29.   Important in this development were: Carol H. Meyer, *Social Work Practice a Response to Human Need* (New York: Free Press, 1970; Harriett M. Bartlett, *The Common Base of Social Work Practice* (New York: The National Association of Social Workers, 1970; and Allen Pincus and Anne Minahan, *Social Work Practice: Model and Method* (Itasca, IL: F. E. Peacock, 1973). The first edition of this text; Louise c. Johnson (1983) followed in this modality.

30   James K. Whittaker, Steven P. Schinke, and Lewayne D. Gilchrist, "The Ecological Paradigm in Child, Youth, and Family Services: Implications for Policy and Practice," *Social Service Review* 60 (December 1986): 483–503.

31.   Harriet M. Bartlett, *The Common Base of Social Work Practice* (New York: National Association of Social Workers, 1970), chap. 6.

Chapter 2

1.   For another early formulation of this perspective, see Werner W. Boehm, "The Nature of Social Work," *Social Work* 3 (April 1958): 10–18.

2.   Harriett M. Bartlett, *The Common Base of Social Work Practice* (New York: National Association of Social Workers, 1970), chap. 5.

3.   William E. Gordon, "Notes on the Nature of Knowledge," in *Building Social Work Knowledge* (New York: National Association of Social Workers, 1964), p. 70.

4.   Max Siporin, *Introduction to Social Work Practice* (New York: Macmillan, 1975), p. 363.

5.   For examples of this, see William J. Reed, "Task-Centered Approach," in *Encyclopedia of Social Work,* 18th ed., Anne Minahan, Ed. (Silver Spring, MD: National Association of Social Workers, 1987), pp. 757–765; Scott Briar, "Incorporating Research into Education for Clinical Practice in Social Work: Toward a Clinical Science in Social Work," in *Sourcebook on Research Utilization,* Allen Rubin and Aaron Rosenblatt, Eds. (New York: Council on Social Work Education, 1979); and Martin Bloom, *The Paradox of Helping: An Introduction to the Philosophy of Scientific Practice* (New York: John Wiley and Sons, 1975).

6.   Howard Goldstein, "The Knowledge Base of Social Work Practice: Theory, Wisdom, Analogue, or Art?" *Families in Society* 71 (January 1990): 41.

7.   Ibid., pp. 38–41. Included as humanistic alternatives are Narrative Theory, Social Constructionism, Cognitive Theory, Moral Theory, Faith and Spirituality, and Feminist Theory.

8.   Based on material in Alfred Kadushin, "The Knowledge Base of Social Work," in *Issues in American Social Work,* Alfred J. Kahn, Ed. (New York: Columbia University Press, 1959), pp. 67 ff.

9.   Note Berger and Luckmann, *The Social Construction of Reality;* and William E. Gordon, "Knowledge and Value: Their Distinction and Relationship in Clarifying Social Work Practice," *Social Work* 10 (July 1965): 32–35.

10.   Goldstein, "The Knowledge Base," p. 41.

11.   For another formulation of the knowledge base, see Betty L. Baer and Ronald Federico, *Education of the Baccalaureate Social Worker: Report of the Undergraduate Curriculum Project* (Cambridge, MA: Ballinger, 1978), pp. 75–78.

12.   Milton Rokeach, *The Nature of Human Values* (New York: Free Press, 1973), p. 5.

13. Lewis Raths, Merrill Harmin, and Sidney B. Simon, *Values and Teaching* (Columbus, OH: Charles E. Merrill, 1966).

14. From Robin Williams, *American Society: A Sociological Interpretation,* 2nd ed. (New York: Alfred A. Knopf, 1967), as discussed in Charles S. Prigmore and Charles R. Atherton, *Social Welfare Policy: Analysis and Formulation* (Lexington, MA: D. C. Heath, 1979), chap. 2.

15. Alan Keith-Lucas, *Giving and Taking Help* (Chapel Hill: University of North Carolina Press, 1972), chap. 8.

16. Charles S. Levy, "The Value Base of Social Work," *Journal for Education for Social Work* 9 (Winter 1973): 34–42.

17. Armando Morales and Bradford W. Sheafor, *Social Work: A Profession of Many Faces,* 4th ed. (Boston: Allyn and Bacon, 1987), pp. 205–207.

18. For further discussion, see Frederick G. Reamer, "AIDS, Social Work, and the 'Duty to Protect,'" *Social Work* 36 (January 1991): 56–60; Marcia Abramson, "Keeping Secrets: Social Workers and AIDS," *Social Work* 35 (March 1990): 169–173; and Sandra Kopels and Jill Doner Kagle, "Do Social Workers Have a Duty to Warn?" *Social Service Review* 67 (March 1993): 101–126.

19. George Theodorson and Achilles Theodorson, *A Modern Dictionary of Sociology* (New York: Crowell, 1969), p. 382.

20. Bartlett, *The Common Base,* pp. 80–83.

21. Morales and Sheafor, *Social Work,* chap. 9.

22. Ibid., p. 140.

23. Baer and Federico, *Education of the Baccalaureate Social Worker,* chap. 9.

24. One of the more important statements of social work functions and tasks is found in Allen Pincus and Anne Minahan, *Social Work Practice: Model and Method* (Itasca, IL: F. E. Peacock, 1973), chap. 1.

25. Found in *Educational Policy and Accreditation Standards* (Washington, DC: Council on Social Work Education, 2001), pp. 9–12.

26. Beulah Roberts Compton and Burt Galaway, *Social Work Process* (Homewood, IL: Dorsey Press, 1979), p. 28.

27. Lydia Rapoport, "Creativity in Social Work," in *Creativity in Social Work: Selected Writing of Lydia Rapoport,* Sanford N. Katz, Ed. (Philadelphia: Temple University Press, 1975), pp. 3–25.

28. Helen Harris Perlman, *Social Casework: A Problem-Solving Process* (Chicago: University of Chicago Press, 1959), p. 3.

29. Murray Ross, *Community Organization: Theory, Principles, and Practice* (New York: Harper and Row, 1955).

30. Helen Northen, *Social Work with Groups* (New York: Columbia University Press, 1969).

31. See Kurt Spitzer and Betty Welsh, "A Problem Focused Model of Practice," *Social Casework* 50 (July 1969): 323–329. See also Beulah Roberts Compton and Burt Galaway, *Social Work Processes,* 3rd ed. (Homewood, IL: Dorsey Press, 1984), chap. 8.

32. For further information regarding this approach, see David L. Cooperrider and Suresh Srivastva, "Appreciative Inquiry in Organizational Life," *Research in Organizational Change and Development* 1 (1987): 129–169.

33. William Ryan, *Blaming the Victim,* rev. ed. (New York: Vintage Books, 1976).

34. Dennis Saleeby, *The Strengths Perspective in Social Work Practice,* 2nd ed. (New York: Longman, 1997), p. 3. This book provides a thorough analysis of the philosophical basis of the strengths perspective and its application in social work practice and research.

35. Sal Hofstein, "The Nature of Process: Its Implications for Social Work," *Journal of Social Work Process* 14 (1964): 13–53.

Chapter 3

1. Martha Ozawa, "Demographic Changes and Their Implications," in *Social Work in the 21st Century,* Michael Reisch and Eileen Gambrill, Eds. (Thousand Oaks, CA: Pine Forge Press, 1997).

2. Delores Norton, *The Dual Perspective* (New York: Council on Social Work Education, 1978).

3. W. Nichols, "Portfolio," unpublished analytical paper (University of Vermont, Burlington), as cited by Marty Dewees in "Building Cultural Competence for Working with Diverse Families: Strategies from the Privileged Side," *Journal of Ethnic and Cultural Diversity in Social Work* 9, 3 (2001): 41.

4. James V. Leigh, *Communicating for Cultural Competence* (Boston: Allyn and Bacon, 1998), pp. 31–33.

5. Barbara F. Okum, Jane Fried, and Marcia L. Okum, *Understanding Diversity: A Learning-as-Practice Primer* (Pacific Grove, CA: Brooks/Cole, 1999), chaps. 2 and 3.

6. Doman Lum, *Culturally Competent Practice: A Framework for Understanding Diverse Groups and Justice Issues* (Pacific Grove, CA: Brooks/Cole, 1999).

7. Jerry V. Diller, *Cultural Diversity: A Primer for the Human Services* (Belmont, CA: Brooks/Cole and Wadsworth, 1999), p. 14.

8. Yuhwa Eva Lu, Doman Lum, and Sheying Chen, "Cultural Competency and Achieving Styles in Clinical Social Work: A Conceptual and Empirical Exploration," *Journal of Ethnic and Cultural Diversity in Social Work* 9, 3/4 (2001): 6.

9. Ibid, p. 7.

10. Marty Dewees, "Building Cultural Competence for Working with Diverse Families: Strategies from the Privileged Side," *Journal of Ethnic and Cultural Diversity in Social Work* 9, 3 (2001): 33–51.

11. Gargi Roysircar Sodowsky, Richard C. Taffe, Terry B. Gutkin, and Steven L. Wise, "Development and Applications of the Multicultural Counseling Inventory," *Journal of Counseling Psychology* 41 (1994): 137–144.

12. Lu, Lum, and Chen, "Cultural Competency and Achieving Styles in Clinical Social Work," p. 7.

13. Lum, *Culturally Competent Practice,* chap. 6.

14. Nan Van Den Bergh and Lynn B. Cooper, Eds., *Feminist Visions for Social Work* (Silver Springs, MD: National Association of Social Workers, 1986), Introduction, pp. 1–28; and M. Bricker-Jenkins and N. Gottlieb, *Feminist Social Work Practice in Clinical Settings* (Newberry Park, CA: Sage, 1991).

15. Schiele, Jerome H. "The Contour and Meaning of Afrocentric Social Work," *Black Studies*, 27, 6 (July, 1997) p. 805.

16. Ibid.

17. Vanessa D. Johnson, "The Nguzo Saba as a Foundation for African American College Student Development Theory," in *Black Studies*, 31, 4 (March 2001), pp. 416–417.

18. Peter Bell and Jimmy Evans *Counseling the Black Client: Alcohol Use and Abuse in Black America* as cited by Ruth McRoy "Cultural Competence with African Americans" in *Culturally Competent Practice: A Framework for Understanding Diverse Groups and Justice Issues* Doman Lum Ed. (Pacific Grove, CA: Brooks/Cole, 2003).

19. Vanessa D. Johnson, "The Nguzo Saba as a Foundation for African American College Student Development Theory," in *Black Studies*, 31, 4 (March, 2001), pp. 416–417.

20. Valerie Borum, "An Afrocentric Approach in Working with African American Familes" in *Multicultural Perspectives in Working with Families*, 2nd ed. Elaine P. Congress and Manny J. Gonzales, Eds. (New York: Springer Publishing, 2005), p. 252.

21. Ibid, p. 253.

22. Ibid, p. 252.

23. Ibid, p. 252.

24. J. P. Butler (1981) as cited by Valerie Borum, in "An Afrocentric Approach in Working with African American Familes" in *Multicultural Perspectives in Working with Families*, 2nd ed. Elaine P. Congress and Manny J. Gonzales, Eds. (New York: Springer Publishing, 2005), p. 252.

25. Vanessa D. Johnson, "The Nguzo Saba as a Foundation for African American College Student Development Theory," *Black Studies*, 31, 4 (March, 2001), pp. 416–417.

26. M. K. Ho (1987) as cited by Roy A. Bean, Benjamin J. Perry, and Tina M. Bedell in "Developing Culturally Competent Marriage and Family Therapists: Guidelines for Working with Hispanic Families," *Marital and Family Therapy*, 27, 1 (January 2001), pp. 43–54.

27. Ibid.

28. Roy A. Bean, Benjamin J. Perry, and Tina M. Bedell in "Developing Culturally Competent Marriage and Family Therapists: Guidelines for Working with Hispanic Families," *Marital and Family Therapy*, 27, 1 (January 2001), pp. 43–54.

29. Celia Jaes Falicov. *Latino Families in Therapy: A Guide to Multicultural Practice.* (New York: Guilford Press, 1998), p. 149.

30. Ibid, p. 150.

31. Ibid, pp. 150–151.

32.   We have chosen to use the term Native American rather than American Indian the term imposed by European settlers. It should however be noted that various native persons use either term as their preference or other terms such as First Nations People.

33.   Larry J. Zimmerman and Brian Leigh Molyneaux, *Native American North America*, (Norman: University of Oklahoma Press, 1996). This book provides an excellent summary of characteristics of tribes in various regions of North America.

34.   Ibid p. 20.

35.   This excellent essay is found in Gerald McMaster and Clifford E. Tratzer, editors. *Native Universe:Voices of Indian Americans* (Washington D.C. National Museum of the American Indian, Smithsonian Institution in association with National Geographic).

36.   See Longres, JohnF. *Human Behavior in the Social Environment* (Itasca, IL: F.E, Peacock Pub. Inc. 1990, pp. 240–247).

37.   The material on relationship is based on Louise C. Johnson's experiences of working with and dialog with Native American, students and others as Director of the Social Work Program at the University of South Dakota.

Chapter 4

1.   Adapted from the work of Isabel Briggs Myers, *Introduction to Type* (Gainsville, FL: Center for Application of Psychological Type, 1976).

2.   For development of this idea from a Christian viewpoint, see Joseph F. Fletcher, *Situational Ethics: A New Morality* (Philadelphia: Westminster Press, 1966).

3.   Florence Rockwood Kluckholm and Fred L. Strodtbeck, *Variations in Value Orientations* (Evanston, IL: Row Peterson, 1961), pp. 10–20.

4.   Ann Hartman and Joan Laird, *Family-Centered Social Work Practice* (New York: Free Press, 1983), chap. 10.

5.   See Dennis Saleeby, "Biology's Challenge to Social Work: Embodying the Person-in-Environment Perspective," *Social Work* 37 (March 1992): 112–117.

6.   See Carol Gilligan, *In a Different Voice* (Cambridge, MA: Harvard University Press, 1982); Jean Baker Miller, *Toward a New Psychology of Women* (Boston: Beacon Press, 1976); and Alice S. Rossi, "Life-Span Theories and Women's Lives," *Signs* 6 (Autumn 1980): 4–32.

7.   Carlton Cornett, "Toward a More Comprehensive Personology: Integrating a Spiritual Perspective into Social Work Practice," *Social Work* 37 (March 1992): 101–102.

8.   For a discussion of moral development in a social work frame of reference, see Wayne A. Chess and Julia M. Norlin, *Human Development and the Social Environment,* 2nd ed. (Boston: Allyn and Bacon, 1991), pp. 231–237; Charles Zastrow and Karen Kirst-Ashman, *Understanding Human Behavior and the Social Environment* (Chicago: Nelson-Hall, 1997), pp. 283–288; and John F. Longres, *Human Behavior in the Social Environment* (Itasca, IL: F. E. Peacock, 1990), pp. 474–481.

9.   James W. Fowler, *Stages of Faith* (San Francisco: Harper, 1995); and Sharon Parks, *The Critical Years: Young Adults and the Search for Meaning, Faith, and Commitment* (San Francisco: Harper and Row, 1991).

10.   See *Educational Policy and Accreditation Standards* (Washington, DC: Council on Social Work Education, 2001/2002), p. 7.

11.   Arthur W. Combs, Donald Avila, and William W. Purkey, *Helping Relationships: Basic Concepts for the Helping Professions* (Boston: Allyn and Bacon, 1971).

12.   Beulah Roberts Compton and Burt Galaway, *Social Work Processes,* 3rd ed. (Homewood, IL: Dorsey Press, 1984), pp. 245–248.

13.   David W. Johnson, *Reaching Out: Interpersonal Effectiveness and Self-Actualization,* 7th ed. (Boston: Allyn and Bacon, 1999).

14.   Anthony N. Maluccio, *Learning from Clients: Interpersonal Helping as Viewed by Clients and Social Workers* (New York: Free Press, 1979).

15.   Edward Mullen, "Differences in Worker Style in Casework," *Social Casework* 50 (June 1969): 347–353.

16.   Robert Foren and Royston Bailey, *Authority in Social Casework* (Oxford, England: Pergamon Press, 1968), p. 19.

17. Based in part on Lawrence M. Brammer and Ginger MacDonald, *The Helping Relationship: Process and Skills,* 7th ed. (Boston: Allyn and Bacon, 1999).

18. NASW *Code of Ethics.* (Washington, DC: National Association of Social Workers, 1999), Standard 1.01 Commitment to Clients.

19. Jill Doner Kagel, "Record Keeping: Direction for the 1990's," *Social Work* 38 (March 1993): 190–196.

Chapter 5

1. Emanual Tropp, "Three Problematic Concepts: 'Clients,' 'Help,' 'Worker,'" *Social Casework* 55 (January 1974): 19–29.

2. Scott Briar and Henry Miller, *Problems and Issues in Social Casework* (New York: Columbia University Press, 1971), chap. 6.

3. Allen Pincus and Anne Minahan, *Social Work Practice: Model and Method* (Itasca, IL: F. E. Peacock, 1973), chap. 3.

4. Helen Harris Perlman, *Persona* (Chicago: University of Chicago Press, 1968), p. 207.

5. Frank M. Lowenberg, *Fundamentals of Social Intervention: Core Concepts and Skills for Social Work Practice* (New York: Columbia University Press, 1977).

6. David Landy, "Problems of the Person Seeking Help in Our Culture," in *Social Welfare Institutions: A Sociological Reader,* Mayer N. Zald, Ed. (New York: John Wiley, 1965), pp. 559–574.

7. Emilia E. Martinez-Brawley and Joan Blundall, "Farm Families' Preferences toward Personal Social Services," *Social Work* 34 (November 1989): 513–522.

8. Perlman, *Persona,* pp. 207–211.

9. John F. Longres, "Toward a Status Model of Ethnic Sensitive Practice," *Journal of Multicultural Social Work* 1, 1 (1991): 41–56.

10 Kenneth L. Chau, "Social Work with Ethnic Minorities: Practice Issues and Potentials," *Journal of Multicultural Social Work* 1, 1 (1991): 23–39.

11. Elaine P. Congress, "The Use of Culturagrams to Assess and Empower Culturally Diverse Families," *Families in Society* 75, 9 (November 1994): 531–540.

12. Sharon Berlin, "Better Work with Women Clients," *Social Work* 21 (November 1976): 492–497.

13. Dolores Norton, *The Dual Perspective* (New York: Council on Social Work Education, 1978).

14. Lillian Ripple, Ernestina Alexander, and Bernice P. Polemis, *Motivation, Capacity, and Opportunity: Studies in Casework Theory and Practice,* Social Service Monographs, Second Series (Chicago: School of Social Service Administration, University of Chicago, 1964).

15. Nora Gold, "Motivation: The Crucial but Unexplored Component of Social Work Practice," *Social Work* 35 (January 1990): 49–56.

16. Howard J. Parad, "Crisis Intervention," in *Encyclopedia of Social Work,* 17th ed., John B. Turner, Ed. (Washington, DC: National Association of Social Workers, 1977), pp. 228–237.

17. Elizabeth M. Tracy and James K. Whittaker, "The Social Network Map: Assessing Social Support in Clinical Practice," *Families in Society* (October 1990): 461–470.

18. Jackie E. Pray, "Respecting the Uniqueness of the Individual: Social Work Practice within a Reflective Model," *Social Work* 36 (January 1991): 80–85.

Chapter 6

1. Dolores Norton, *The Dual Perspective* (New York: Council on Social Work Education, 1978).

2. See Carol Meyer, "The Ecosystems Perspective: Implications for Social Work Practice," in *The Foundations of Social Work Practice,* Carol Meyer and Mark Mattaini, Eds. (Washington, DC: NASW Press, 1995), pp. 16–27.

3. Ferdinand Tönnies, *Fundamental Concepts of Sociology* (Gemeinschaft und Gesellschaft), trans. Charles P. Loomis (New York: American Books, 1940).

4. Floyd Hunter, *Community Power Structure* (Chapel Hill: University of North Carolina Press, 1953).

5. Eugene Litwak and Ivan Szelenyi, "Primary Group Structures and Their Function: Kin, Neighbors, and Friends," *American Sociological Review* 34 (August 1969): 465–481; Phillip Fellin and Eugene Litwak, "The Neighborhood in Urban American Society," *Social Work* 13 (July 1968): 72–80; and Eugene

Litwak, *Helping the Elderly* (New York: Guilford Press, 1985), chap. 8.

6. Roland L. Warren, *The Community in America* (Chicago: Rand-McNally, 1963).

7. Dennis E. Poplin, *Communities,* 2nd ed. (New York: Macmillan, 1979), chap. 2.

8. Louise C. Johnson, "Human Service Delivery Patterns in Non-Metropolitan Communities," in *Rural Human Services: A Book of Readings,* H. Wayne Johnson, Ed. (Itasca, IL: F. E. Peacock, 1980), pp. 55–64.

9. Louise C. Johnson, "Services to the Aged: Non-Metropolitan Service Delivery" (unpublished paper delivered at NASW Symposium, Chicago, IL, November 1985).

10. Padi Gulati and Geoffrey Guest, "The Community-Centered Model: A Garden Variety Approach or a Radical Transformation of Community Practice?" *Social Work* 35 (January 1990): 63–68.

11. Barbara Oberhofer Dane and Barbara L. Simon, "Resident Guests: Social Workers in Host Settings," *Social Work* 35 (January 1990): 63–68.

12. See Phillip Fellin, *The Community and the Social Worker* (Itasca, IL: F. E. Peacock, 1987), chap. 9.

13. This identification of systems is based on Armand Lauffer, Lynn Nybell, Carla Overbeiger, Beth Reed, and Lawrence Zeff, *Understanding Your Social Agency* (Beverly Hills, CA: Sage, 1977).

14. See J. G. Miller, *Living Systems* (New York: McGraw-Hill, 1978); and Margaret M. Bubolz and M. Suzanne Sontag, "Human Ecology Theory," in *Sourcebook of Family Theories and Methods: A Contextual Approach,* Pauline G. Boss, William J. Doherty, Ralph LaRossa, Walter Schumm, and Suzanne K. Steinmetz, Eds. (New York: Plenum Press, 1993), chap. 17.

15. See Charlotte Towle, *Common Human Needs* (Washington, DC: National Association of Social Workers, 1945), p. 37 and Abraham H. Maslow, *Motivation and Personality* (New York: Harper and Row, 1954).

16. Ralph Morgan, "Role Performance in a Bureaucracy," in *Social Work Practice 1962* (New York: Columbia University Press, 1962), pp. 115–125.

17. See Robert Pruger, "The Good Bureaucrat," *Social Work* 18 (July 1973): 26–32, and "Bureaucratic Functioning as a Social Work Skill," in *Educating for Baccalaureat Social Work: Report of the Undergraduate Social Work Curriculum Development Project,* Betty L. Baer and Ronald Federico, Eds. (Cambridge, MA: Ballinger, 1978), pp. 149–168.

18. Christina Maslach, "Job Burnout: How People Cope," *Public Welfare* 36 (Spring 1978): 56–58.

19. Martha Bramhall and Susan Ezell, "How Burned Out Are You?" *Public Welfare* 39 (Winter 1981): 23–27.

20. These ideas are further developed in Martha Bramhall and Susan Ezell, "Working Your Way Out of Burnout," *Public Welfare* 39 (Spring 1981): 32–39.

Chapter 7

1. Felix P. Biestek, *The Casework Relationship* (Chicago: Loyola University Press, 1957).

2. Nick F. Coady, "The Worker-Client Relationship Revisited," *Families in Society* 74 (May 1993): 293.

3. Carl Hartman and Diane Reynolds, "Resistant Clients: Confrontation, Interpretation, and Alliance," *Social Casework* 68 (April 1987): 205–213.

4. Edith Ankersmit, "Setting the Contract in Probation," *Federal Probation* 40 (June 1976): 28–33.

5. Charles R. Horejsi, "Training for the Direct-Service Volunteer in Probation," *Federal Probation* 37 (September 1973): 38–41.

6. Helen Harris Perlman, *Relationship: The Heart of Helping People* (Chicago: University of Chicago Press, 1979), p. 2.

7. Ibid., p. 24.

8. Ibid., p. 62.

9. See Lawrence M. Brammer, *The Helping Relationship: Process and Skills,* 3rd ed. (Englewood Cliffs, NJ: Prentice-Hall, 1984); and Beulah Roberts Compton and Burt Galaway, *Social Work Processes,* rev. ed. (Homewood, IL: Dorsey Press, 1979), chap. 6.

10. Compton and Galaway, *Social Work Processes,* p. 224.

11. See Anthony N. Maluccio, *Learning from Clients: Interpersonal Helping as Viewed by Clients and Social Workers* (New York: Free Press, 1979).

12. Quoted material in this list from Biestek, *The Casework Relationship,* pp. 25, 35, 50, 72, 90, and 103, respectively.

13.   Ann Templeton Brownlee, *Community, Culture and Care* (St. Louis: C. V. Mosby, 1978), chap. 3.

14.   Joel Fischer, Diane D. Dulaney, Rosemary T. Frazio, Mary T. Hadakand, and Ethyl Zivotosky, "Are Social Workers Sexists?" *Social Work* 21 (November 1976): 428–433.

15.   Joanne Mermelstein and Paul Sundet, "Education for Social Work in the Rural Context," in *Educating for Social Work in Rural Areas: A Report on Rural Child Welfare and Family Service Project of the School of Social Work,* Lynn R. Hulen, project coordinator (Fresno: California State University, June 1978).

16.   Louise C. Johnson, Dale Crawford, and Lorraine Rousseau, "Understandings Needed to Work with Sioux Indian Clients" (unpublished paper).

17.   Joanne Mermelstein and Paul Sundet, "Worker Acceptance and Credibility in the Rural Environment," in *Rural Human Services: A Book of Readings,* H. Wayne Johnson, Ed. (Itasca, IL: F. E. Peacock, 1980), pp. 174–178.

18.   Janet Kirkland and Karen Irey, "Confidentiality: Issues and Dilemmas in Rural Practice," in *Second National Institute on Social Work in Rural Areas Reader,* Edward B. Buxton, Ed. (Madison: University of Wisconsin—Extension Center for Social Studies, 1978), pp. 142–149.

19.   Yvonne L. Fraley, "A Role Model for Practice," *Social Service Review* 43 (June 1969): 145–154.

20.   Adapted from Brett A. Seabury, "Communication Problems in Social Work Practice," *Social Work* 25, 1 (January 1980): 40–44.

21.   Floyd W. Matson and Ashley Montagu, *The Human Dialogue: Perspectives on Communication* (New York: Free Press, 1967), p. 6.

22.   See Lawrence Shulman, *The Skills of Helping: Individuals and Groups,* 2nd ed. (Itasca, IL: F. E. Peacock, 1984), chaps. 2 and 4.

23.   See ibid., pp. 65–72, for discussion of this task.

24.   See Doman Lum, *Culturally Competent Practice: A Framework for Understanding Diverse Groups and Justice Issues* (Pacific Grove, CA: Brooks/Cole, 1999).

25.   Ibid., p. 155.

26.   Ibid.

27.   James W. Leigh, *Communicating for Cultural Competence* (Boston: Allyn and Bacon, 1998), p. 19.

28.   Ibid., chap. 8.

29.   Ibid., chap. 5.

30.   Ibid., p. 19.

31.   Lum, *Culturally Competent Practice,* pp. 152–154.

32.   This triad is based on the work of C. B. Truax and R. R. Carkhuff, *Toward Effective Counseling and Psychotherapy* (Chicago: Aldine, 1967). For an excellent discussion of this material, see Eveline D. Schulman, *Intervention in the Human Services,* 2nd ed. (St. Louis: C. V. Mosby, 1978), chap. 8.

Chapter 8

1.   Max Siporin, *Introduction to Social Work Practice* (New York: Macmillan, 1975), p. 219.

2.   Mark A. Mattaini and Stuart A. Kirk, "Assessing Assessment in Social Work," *Social Work* 36 (May 1991): 260–266.

3.   Ann Weick, Charles Rapp, W. Patrick Sullivan, and Walter Kisthardt, "A Strengths Perspective for Social Work Practice," *Social Work* 34 (July 1989): 350–354; and Florence Wexler Vigilante and Mildred Maileck, "Needs-Resource Evaluation in the Assessment Process," *Social Work* 33 (March–April 1988): 101–104.

4.   Harriet Bartlett, *The Common Base of Social Work Practice* (New York: National Association of Social Workers, 1970), p. 159.

5.   Harriet A. Feiner and Harriet Katz, "Stronger Women—Stronger Families," *Affilia* 1 (Winter 1986): 49–58.

6.   Adapted from Florence Hollis, "And What Shall We Teach? Social Work Education and Knowledge," *Social Service Review* 42 (June 1968): 184–196.

7.   Mary K. Rodwell, "Naturalistic Inquiry: An Alternative Model for Social Work Assessment," *Social Service Review* 61 (June 1987): 231–246.

8.   Carel B. Germain and Alex Gitterman, *The Life Model of Social Work Practice* (New York: Columbia University Press, 1980), chap. 1.

9. Abraham H. Maslow, *Motivation and Personality,* 3rd ed. (New York: Harper-Collins, 1987).

10. Charlotte Towle, *Common Human Needs,* rev. ed. (New York: NASW Press, 1957).

11. Paula Allen-Meares and Bruce A. Lane, "Grounding Social Work Practice in Theory: Ecosystems," *Social Casework* 68 (November 1987): 315–321.

12. Dolores Norton, *The Dual Perspective* (New York: Council on Social Work Education, 1978), p. 3. Also see Dolores G. Norton, "Diversity, Early Socialization, and Temporal Development: The Dual Perspective Revisited," *Social Work* 38 (January 1993): 82–90.

13. Sonia Badillo Ghali, "Culture Sensitivity and the Puerto Rican Client," *Social Casework* 58 (October 1977): 459–468.

14. Ann Hartman and Joan Laird, *Family-Centered Social Work Practice* (New York: Free Press, 1983), chap. 11.

15. Elizabeth M. Tracy and James K. Whittaker, "The Social Network Map: Assessing Social Support in Clinical Practice," *Families in Society* 71 (October 1990): 461–470; and Elizabeth M. Tracy, "Identifying Social Support Resources of At-Risk Families, *Social Work* 35 (May 1990): 252–258.

16. Also see Charles Froland, Diane L. Pancoast, Nancy J. Chapmen, and Priscilla J. Kimboko, *Helping Networks and Human Services* (Beverly Hills, CA: Sage Publications, 1981); and James K. Whittaker and James Garbarino, *Social Support Networks: Informal Helping in the Human Services* (New York: Aldine, 1983).

Chapter 9

1. This formulation is similar but not identical to a format developed by Ruth R. Middleman and Gale Goldberg, *Social Service Delivery: A Structural Approach to Social Work Practice* (New York: Columbia University Press, 1974), chap. 1.

2. Fred M. Cox, John L. Erlich, Jack Rothman, and John E. Tropman, Eds., *Strategies of Community Organization,* 4th ed. (Itasca, IL: F. E. Peacock, 1987), p. 258.

3. Emelicia Mizio and Anita J. Delaney, Eds., *Training for Service Delivery to Minority Clients* (New York: Family Service Association of America, 1981).

4. Robert J. Teare and Harold L. McPheeters, *Manpower Utilization in Social Welfare* (Atlanta, GA: Southern Regional Education Board, 1970), p. 34.

5. Ibid.

6. Ronald L. Simons and Stephen M. Aiger, "Facilitating an Eclectic Use of Practice Theory," *Social Casework* 60 (April 1979): 201–208.

7. For a discussion of nonmetropolitan service delivery, see Louise C. Johnson, "Human Service Delivery Patterns in Non-Metropolitan Communities," in *Rural Human Services: A Book of Readings,* H. Wayne Johnson, Ed. (Itasca, IL: F. E. Peacock, 1980), pp. 55–64.

8. Elliot Studt, *A Conceptual Approach to Teaching Materials* (New York: Council on Social Work Education, 1965), pp. 4–18.

9. Pamela Miller, "Covenant Model for Professional Relationships: An Alternative to the Contract Model," *Social Work* 35 (March 1990): 121–125.

10. Tom A. Croxton, "Caveats on Contract," *Social Work* 34 (March–April 1988): 169–171.

Chapter 10

1. Ross V. Speck and Carolyn L. Attneave, *Family Networks* (New York: Pantheon, 1973).

2. Eugene Litwak and Ivan Szelenyi, "Primary Group Structures and Their Function: Kin, Neighbors, and Friends," *American Sociological Review* 34 (August 1969): 465–481.

3. Alice H. Collins and Diane L. Pancoast, *Natural Helping Networks: A Strategy for Intervention* (Washington, DC: National Association of Social Workers, 1974).

4. Alan Gartner and Frank Riessman, *Self-Help in the Human Services* (San Francisco: Jossey-Bass, 1977).

5. Yeheskel Hasenfeld and Benjamin Gidron, "Self-Help Groups and Human Service Organizations: An Interorganizational Perspective," *Social Service Review* 67 (June 1993): 217–236.

6. For a good discussion of effective referral, see Elizabeth Nicholas, *A Primer of Social Casework* (New York: Columbia University Press, 1960), chap. 9.

7. Robert J. Teare and Harold L. McPheeters, *Manpower Utilization in Social Welfare* (Atlanta, GA: Southern Regional Education Board, 1970), p. 34.

8. Ibid.

9. Lorraine M. Gutierrez, "Working with Women of Color: An Empowerment Perspective," *Social Work* 35 (March 1990): 149–153.

10. Barbara Bryant Solomon, *Black Empowerment: Social Work in Oppressed Communities* (New York: Columbia University Press, 1976); and "Social Work Values and Skills to Empower Women," in *Women, Power, and Change,* Ann Weick and Susan T. Vandiver, Eds. (Washington, DC: National Association of Social Workers, 1980), pp. 206–214.

11. Ruth J. Parsons, "Empowerment: Purpose and Practice Principle in Social Work," *Social Work with Groups* 14, 2 (1991): 7–21. Also contains an excellent case example.

12. Silvia Staub-Bernasconi, "Social Action, Empowerment and Social Work—An Integrative Theoretical Framework for Social Work and Social Work with Groups," *Social Work with Groups* 14, 2 (1991): 35–51.

13. Karla Krogsrud Miley, Michael O'Melia, and Brenda L. DuBois, *Generalist Social Work Practice: An Empowering Approach* (Boston: Allyn and Bacon, 1995), p. 31.

14. Good discussions of techniques are found in Gutierrez, "Working with Women," and in Solomon, "Social Work Values."

15. The approach that follows is a simplified version of cognitive and behavioral approaches. See Cognitive Therapy and Behavioral Therapy in Chapter 16. Also see Albert Ellis, *Better, Deeper, and More Enduring Brief Therapy: The Rational Emotive Behavioral Therapy Approach* (New York: Brunner/Mazel, 1996); Judith Beck, *Cognitive Therapy: Basics and Beyond* (New York: Guilford Press, 1995); Jim Lantz, "Cognitive Theory and Social Work Treatment," in *Social Work Treatment,* 4th ed., Francis J. Turner, Ed. (New York: Free Press, 1996); Mark Mattaini, *Clinical Practice with Individuals* (Washington, DC: NASW Press, 1997); and Bruce Thyer and John Wodarski, *Handbook of Empirical Social Work Practice* (New York: John Wiley and Sons, 1998).

16. See Chapter 16 for an outline of this model.

17. Lois G. Selby, "Supportive Treatment: The Development of a Concept and a Helping Method," *Social Service Review* 30 (December 1956): 400–414.

18. Beulah Roberts Compton, "An Attempt to Examine the Use of Support in Social Work Practice," in *Social Work Processes,* 5th ed., Beulah Roberts Compton and Burt Galaway, Eds. (Pacific Grove, CA: Brooks/Cole, 1994), pp. 472–479.

19. Florence Hollis, *Casework: A Psychosocial Therapy* (New York: Random House, 1972), pp. 89–95.

20. Judith C. Nelson, "Support: A Necessary Condition for Change," *Social Work* 25 (September 1980): 388–392.

21. Patricia Ferris and Catherine A. Marshall, "A Model Project for Families of the Chronically Mentally Ill," *Social Work* 32 (March–April 1987): 110–114.

22. James Kelley and Pamela Sykes, "Helping the Helpers: A Support Group for Family Members of Persons with AIDS," *Social Work* 34 (May 1989): 239–242.

23. Carolyn Knight, "Use of Support Groups with Adult Female Survivors of Child Sexual Abuse," *Social Work* 35 (May 1990): 202–206.

24. See Elizabeth McBroom, "Socialization and Social Casework," in Roberts and Nee, *Theories of Social Casework* (Chicago: University of Chicago Press, 1970), pp. 315–351.

25. Robert Vinter, "Program Activities: An Analysis of Their Effects on Participant Behavior," in *Readings in Group Work Practice,* Robert Vinter, Ed. (Ann Arbor, MI: Campus Publishers, 1967).

26. See Ruth R. Middleman, "The Use of Program: Review and Update," *Social Work with Groups* 3 (Fall 1980): 5–23. The Suggested Readings in this text contain many important sources for this material as well.

27. Mary Bricker-Jenkins in Louise C. Johnson and Stephen J. Yanca, *Social Work Practice: A Generalist Approach,* 9th ed. (Boston, MA: Allyn and Bacon, 2007) p. 408.

28. Shelley A. Haddock, Toni Schindler Zimmerman, and David MacPhee, "The Power Equity Guide: Attending to Gender in Family Therapy," in *Marriage and Family Therapy,* 26, 2 (April, 2000), pp. 153–170.

Chapter 11

1. William Schwartz, "The Worker in the Group," in *Social Welfare Forum 1961* (New York: Columbia University Press, 1961), p. 154.

2. William Schwartz, "On the Use of Groups in Social Work Practice," in *The Practice of Group Work,* William Schwartz and Serapio R. Zalba, Eds. (New York: Columbia University Press, 1971), p. 5.

3. See Schwartz and Zalba, *The Practice of Group Work;* and Lawrence Shulman, *A Casebook of Social Work with Groups: The Mediating Model* (New York: Council on Social Work Education, 1968), and *The Skills of Helping Individuals and Groups,* 2nd ed. (Itasca, IL: F. E. Peacock, 1984).

4. See Shulman, *The Skills of Helping Individuals and Groups,* pp. 9–10.

5. Schwartz and Zalba, *The Practice of Group Work.*

6. Ernesto Gomez, "The San Antonio Model: A Culture-Oriented Approach," in *Our Kingdom Stands on Brittle Glass,* Guadalupe Gibson, Ed. (Silver Spring, MD: National Association of Social Workers, 1983), pp. 96–111.

7. See Shulman, *A Casebook of Social Work with Groups.*

8. Irving Spergel, *Community Problem Solving* (Chicago: University of Chicago Press, 1969), p. 106.

9. William Schwartz, "The Social Worker in the Group," in *The Social Welfare Forum Proceedings* (New York: Columbia University Press, 1961), p. 157.

10. Nora Gold, "Motivation: The Crucial but Unexplored Component of Social Work Practice," *Social Work* 35 (January 1990): 49–56.

11. Helen Harris Perlman, *Social Casework* (Chicago: University of Chicago Press, 1957).

12. See Charles S. Levy, "Values and Planned Change," *Social Casework* 53 (October 1972): 488–493, for another discussion of these factors.

13. Florence Hollis, *Casework: A Psycho-Social Therapy,* 2nd ed. (New York: Random House, 1972), pp. 81–85 and chap. 9.

14. Max Siporin, *Introduction to Social Work Practice* (New York: Macmillan, 1975), p. 302.

15. Ibid., p. 305.

16. Richard M. Grinnel, Jr., and Nancy S. Kyte, "Environmental Modification: A Study," *Social Work* 20 (July 1975): 313–318.

17. See Robert Sommer, *Personal Space* (Englewood Cliffs, NJ: Prentice-Hall, 1969); Edward T. Hall, *The Hidden Dimension* (New York: Doubleday Anchor, 1969); and William H. Itlleson, Harold M. Proshansky, Leanne G. Rivlin, and Gary H. Winkel, *An Introduction to Environmental Psychology* (New York: Holt, Rinehart and Winston, 1974).

18. Carel B. Germain and Alex Gitterman, *The Life Model of Social Work Practice* (New York: Columbia University Press, 1980).

19. For additional discussion, see Anthony N. Maluccio, "Promoting Competence through Life Experience," in *Social Work Practice: People and Environments,* Carel B. Germain, Ed. (New York: Columbia University Press, 1979), pp. 282–302.

20. Irene A. Gutheil, "Considering the Physical Environment: An Essential Component of Good Practice," *Social Work* 37 (September 1992): 391–396.

21. See Carel B. Germain, " 'Space': An Ecological Variable in Social Work Practice," *Social Casework* 59 (November 1978): 515–529.

22. For further consideration of this topic, see Brett A. Seabury, "Arrangement of Physical Space in Social Work Settings," *Social Work* 16 (October 1971): 43–49; and Thomas Walz, Georgina Willenberg, and Lane deMoll, "Environmental Design," *Social Work* 19 (January 1974): 38–46.

23. See Richard E. Boettcher and Roger Vander Schie, "Milieu Therapy with Chronic Mental Patients," *Social Work* 20 (March 1975): 130–139.

24. Carel B. Germain, "Time: An Ecological Variable in Social Work Practice," *Social Casework* 57 (July 1976): 419–426.

25. Eugene Litwak and Henry F. Meyer, "A Balance Theory of Coordination between Bureaucratic Organizations and Community Primary Groups," *Administrative Science Quarterly* 11 (March 1966): 31–58; and *School, Family and Neighborhood: The Theory and Practice of School-Community Relations* (New York: Columbia University Press, 1974).

26. Karen Orloff Kaplan, "Recent Trends in Case Management," in *Encyclopedia of Social Work,* 18th ed. (supplement), Leon Ginsberg, Ed. (Silver Spring, MD: NASW Press, 1990), pp. 60–77.

27. Ibid., p. 62.

28. Jack Rothman, "A Model of Case Management: Toward Empirically Based Practice," *Social Work* 36 (November 1991): 520–528.

29. Stephen T. Moore, "A Social Work Practice Model of Case Management: The Case Management Grid," *Social Work* 35 (September 1990): 444–448.

30. Jack Rothman, with John E. Tropman, "Models of Community Organization and Macro Practice Perspectives: Their Mixing and Phasing," in *Strategies of Community Organization*, 4th. ed., Fred Cox, John L. Erlich, Jack Rothman, and John E. Tropman, Eds. (Itasca, IL: F. E. Peacock, 1987), pp. 3–26.

Chapter 12

1. For further discussion of this balance, see Beulah Roberts Compton and Burt Galaway, *Social Work Processes,* 5th ed. (Homewood, IL: Dorsey Press, 1994), chap. 16.

2. Michael Key, Peter Hudson, and John Armstrong, "Evaluation Theory and Community Work," in *Strategies of Community Organization,* 3rd ed., Fred M. Cox, John L. Erlich, Jack Rothman, and John E. Tropman, Eds. (Itasca, IL: F. E. Peacock, 1979), pp. 159–175.

3. See Roy A. Ruckdeschel and Buford E. Farris, "Assessing Practice: A Critical Look at the Single-Case Design," *Social Casework* 62 (September 1981): 413–419.

4. Thomas J. Kiresuk and Geoffrey Garwick, "Basic Goal Attainment Scaling Procedures," in *Social Work Processes,* 2nd ed., Beulah Roberts Compton and Burt Galaway, Eds. (Homewood, IL: Dorsey Press, 1979), pp. 412–421.

5. See William Reid and Laura Epstein, Eds., *Task Centered Practice* (New York: Columbia University Press, 1977); Sharon Berlin and Jeanne Marsh, *Informing Practice Decisions* (New York: Macmillan, 1993); and Catherine Alder and Wayne Evens, *Evaluating Your Practice: A Guide to Self-Assessment* (New York: Springer, 1990).

6. See Joel Fischer and Kevin Corcoran, *Measures for Clinical Practice,* 2nd ed., two vols. (New York: Free Press, 1995). There are also several reference texts available containing assessments for families, groups, organizations, and the like.

7. See Martin Bloom, Joel Fischer, and John Orme, *Evaluating Practice: Guidelines for the Accountable Professional* (Boston: Allyn and Bacon, 1995); and Joel Fischer and Kevin Corcoran, *Measures for Clinical Practice,* 2nd ed., two vols. (New York: Free Press, 1995).

8. See Yvonne S. Lincoln and Ergon G. Guba, *Naturalistic Inquiry* (Beverly Hills, CA: Sage, 1985), as cited in James W. Leigh, *Communicating for Cultural Competence* (Boston: Allyn and Bacon, 1998), p. 18.

9. See William J. Reid and Anne Shyne, *Brief and Extended Casework* (New York: Columbia University Press, 1969).

10. William J. Reid, *The Task Centered System* (New York: Columbia University Press, 1978), p. 5.

11. Anne E. Fortune, Bill Pearlingi, and Cherie D. Rochell, "Reactions to Termination of Individual Treatment," *Social Work* 37 (March 1992): 171–178.

12. Howard Hess and Peg McCartt Hess, "Termination in Context," in *Social Work Processes,* 5th ed., Beulah Roberts Compton and Burt Galaway, Eds. (Belmont, CA: Wadsworth, 1994), pp. 529–539.

13. See Allen Pincus and Anne Minahan, *Social Work Practice: Model and Method* (Itasca, IL: F. E. Peacock, 1973), chap. 13.

Chapter 13

1. For further discussion, see Curtis Janzen and Oliver Harris, *Family Treatment in Social Work Practice* (Itasca, IL: F. E. Peacock, 1980), pp. 6–12.

2. Ann Hartman and Joan Laird, *Family-Centered Social Work Practice* (New York: Free Press, 1983), chap. 10.

3. Janzen and Harris, *Family Treatment,* pp. 12–16.

4. Hartman and Laird, *Family-Centered Social Work Practice,* chap. 8.

5. Janzen and Harris, *Family Treatment,* pp. 15–20.

6. Based on Sonya L. Rhodes, "A Developmental Approach to the Life Cycle of the Family," *Social Casework* 58 (May 1977): 301–311.

7. See Joseph D. Anderson, "Family-Centered Practice in the 1990's: A Multicultural Perspective," *Journal of Multicultural Social Work* 1, 4 (1992): 17–29; and Rocco A. Cimmarusti, "Family Preservation Practice Based upon a Multisystems Approach," *Child Welfare* 71 (May–June 1992): 241–256.

8. See Jill Kinney, David Haapala, and Charlotte Booth, *Keeping Families Together: The Homebuilders Model* (New York: Aldine de Gruyter, 1991); and Insoo Kim Berg, *Family-Based Services* (New York: W. W. Norton, 1994).

Chapter 14

1. This discussion of the small group as a social system is a synthesis of knowledge about small groups primarily based on three schools of thought: (1) Field theory or group dynamics. The work of Kurt Lewin is the original source. Darwin Cartwright and Alvin Zander, *Group Dynamics: Research and Theory* (Evanston, IL: Row Peterson, 1960), is another source. (2) Interactional process analysis. Paul A. Hare, Edgar F. Borgotta, and Robert E. Bales, *Small Groups: Studies in Social Interaction* (New York: Alfred A. Knopf, 1965), is a source for this school of thought. (3) Homans's systems theory. George Homans, *The Human Group* (New York: Harcourt, Brace and World, 1960), is the third primary source. Another excellent source on group process is Margaret E. Hartford, *Groups in Social Work* (New York: Columbia University Press, 1972).

2. Henry W. Maier, "Models of Intervention in Work with Groups: Which One Is Yours?" *Social Work with Groups* 4 (Fall/Winter 1981): 21–34.

3. For a full description of this technique, see Mary L. Northway, *A Primer of Sociometry,* 2nd ed. (Toronto: University of Toronto Press, 1967).

4. Kenneth D. Benne and Paul Sheats, "Functional Roles of Group Members," *Journal of Social Issues* 4 (1948): 41–49.

5. John K. Brilhart, *Effective Group Discussion* (Dubuque, IA: Wm. C. Brown, 1974), p. 5.

6. Based on a formulation developed by Henriette Etta Soloshin, "Development of an Instrument for the Analysis of Social Group Work Method in Therapeutic Settings" (Ph.D. diss., University of Minnesota, Minneapolis, March 1954). Also see William Schwartz, "The Social Worker in the Group," in *Social Welfare Forum 1961* (New York: Columbia University Press, 1961), pp. 146–171.

7. Brian A. Auslander and Gail K. Auslander, "Self-Help Groups and the Family Service Agency," *Social Casework* 69 (February 1988): 74–80.

Chapter 15

1. Jack Rothman, John L. Erlich, and Joseph G. Teresa, *Promoting Innovation and Change in Organizations and Communities: A Planning Manual* (New York: John Wiley and Sons, 1976), chap. 2.

2. For more information about each of the tasks identified, see Bradford W. Sheafor, Charles R. Horejsi, and Gloria A. Horejsi, *Techniques and Guidelines for Social Work Practice,* 4th ed. (Boston: Allyn and Bacon, 1997), pt. IV, sec. B.

3. Ronald W. Toseland and Robert F. Rivas, "Working with Task Groups: The Middle Phase," in *Strategies of Community Organization,* 4th. ed., Fred Cox, John L. Erlich, Jack Rothman, and John E. Tropman, Eds. (Itasca, IL: F. E. Peacock, 1987), pp. 114–142.

4. Herman Resnick and Rino J. Patti, Eds., *Change from Within: Humanizing Social Welfare Organizations* (Philadelphia, PA: Temple University Press, 1980), pp. 5–6.

5. This strategy is based on the work of Resnick and Patti, *Change from Within,* and the discussion that follows is heavily influenced by their work. For an early version, see Rino J. Patti and Herman Resnick, "Changing the Agency from Within," *Social Work* 17 (July 1972): 48–57.

6. See Rino J. Patti, "Organizational Resistance and Change: The View from Below," *Social Service Review* 48 (September 1974): 367–383.

7. Resnick and Patti, *Change from Within,* pp. 9–11.

8. Patti and Resnick, "Changing the Agency from Within."

9. Rothman, Erlich, and Teresa, *Promoting Innovation and Change in Organizations and Communities,* chap. 2.

10. See James D. Jorgensen and Brian W. Klepinger, "The Social Worker as Staff Trainer," *Public Welfare* 37 (Winter 1979): 41–49.

11. Edward J. Pawlak, "Organization Tinkering," *Social Work* 21 (September 1976): 376–380.

12. Resnick and Patti, *Change from Within,* p. 12.

13. John J. Horwitz, *Team Practice and the Specialist* (Springfield, IL: Charles C. Thomas, 1970), p. 10.

14. For further discussion, see Seymour B. Sarason, Charles Carroll, Kenneth Maton, Saul Cohen, and Elizabeth Lorentz, *Human Services and Resource Networks* (San Francisco: Jossey-Bass, 1977); and Louise C. Johnson, "Networking: A Means of Maximizing Resources in Non-Metropolitan Settings," *Human Services in the Rural Environment* 8, 2: 27–31.

15. See Alice H. Collins and Diane Pancoast, *Natural Helping Networks: A Strategy for Prevention* (Washington, DC: National Association for Social Workers, 1976).

16. George A. Brager, "Advocacy and Political Behavior," *Social Work* 13 (April 1968): 15.

17. Robert J. Teare and Harold L. McPheeters, *Manpower Utilization in Social Welfare* (Atlanta, GA: Southern Regional Education Board, 1970), p. 30.

18. Robert H. MacRae, "Social Work and Social Action," *Social Service Review* 60 (March 1966): 1–7.

19. J. Donald Cameron and Esther Talavera, "Advocacy Program for Spanish-Speaking People," *Social Casework* 57 (July 1976): 427–431.

20. Robert Sunley, "Family Advocacy: From Case to Cause," *Social Casework* 51 (June 1970): 347–357.

21. It is expected that understandings to carry out these activities will come from political science courses and a course in social welfare policy.

22. Saul D. Alinsky, *Reveille for Radicals* (Chicago: University of Chicago Press, 1946); and Richard Cloward and R. Elman, "Advocacy in the Ghetto," in *Strategies of Community Organization: A Book of Readings,* 1st ed., Fred M. Cox, John L. Erlich, Jack Rothman, and John E. Tropman, Eds. (Itasca, IL: F. E. Peacock, 1970), pp. 209–215.

23. Cox, Erlich, Rothman, and Tropman, *Strategies of Community Organization,* 4th ed. (1987); pt. III, sec. IV, "Social Action," is an excellent source for this.

Glossary

accountability   Evaluation of efficiency and effectiveness factors relating to the delivery of social services.

action   The process of carrying out a plan developed through the assessment and action phases of the social work process.

action system   System of people and resources involved in carrying out tasks related to goals and strategy of the helping endeavor.

activity   Doing something or performing tasks as opposed to talking about what to do or talking about feelings or ideas.

agency   The organization that employs the worker and manages resources used to help the client.

assessment   Ongoing process of the social work endeavor that develops an understanding of person in situation to use as the basis for action.

best practices   Engaging in practice activities that are based on research and intended to increase successful outcomes.

blended family   A family in which the parents have had previous marriages or relationships and have children from those marriages or relationships, as well as possibly having children from the present relationship.

bond   Emotional tie that determines the cohesiveness of a group; expressed in "we feelings" and commonly held values.

boundary   Point at which the interaction around a function no longer has the intensity that interaction of system members or units has. For example, when considering who is a member of a family system, the boundary is the point that divides those who are continually interacting around family concerns and issues and those who have little or no input into family functioning.

broker   A social work role in which the worker provides the client with information about available resources and helps link the client with the resource.

burnout   A condition that some social workers develop. It is characterized by feelings of lack of appreciation, illness, tiredness, inability to laugh, dreading to go to work, and sleep disturbances.

case advocate   A social work role in which the worker pleads or lobbies for services for a client whom a service provider would otherwise reject.

case conference   Members of a team or a multiperson helping system in a formal meeting share information and plan for services to individuals and families they are all serving in some manner.

case management   A method for coordinating services in which a worker assesses with a client which services are needed and obtains and monitors the delivery of the services.

cause   Movement directed toward eliminating a social evil or toward meeting human need in a new way.

cause advocacy   Concern about and action on behalf of the victims of social problems that works toward the modification of social conditions.

cause-function debate   Debate about whether to emphasize removal of an evil in community life that impacts the individual's social functioning or to emphasize response to individual malfunctioning.

client   One who has either sought help from a social worker or is served by an agency employing a social worker.

closedness   A quality of social systems that describes the lack of ability of the system to allow information or individuals to permeate the system's boundary.

collaboration   The working together of several service providers with a common client toward a common goal.

community   Immediate environment of worker, client, and agency that is manifest as a social system.

community benefits   Organized efforts by the natural helping system to meet needs of a member of the system. Usually the effort is in response to a catastrophic situation.

concern   A feeling that something is not right. Interest in, regard for, and care about the well-being of self and other persons.

conflict   A struggle for something that is scarce or thought to be scarce.

congruity   A situation in which the interactions or transactions within an ecosystem are balanced, resulting in mutual benefit for the person and the environment.

consultation   A way of two or more people working together in which the consultant provides knowledge and expertise but has no power to require the consulted to accept the help or advice. The consulted examines the input from the consultant as to its usefulness in the situation under consideration.

contract   An agreement, verbal or written, between worker and client about the work to be done together. Goals, objectives, and tasks to be carried out by worker and client are specified.

coordination   The working together of two or more service providers in activity focused on a particular client or focused on persons in a particular category (e.g., the aged). Coordinative mechanisms include colocation of services, networking, linking, case management, collaboration, and a team approach.

cope   A person's efforts to deal with some new and often problematic situation or encounter or to deal in some new way with an old problem.

crisis   A state of disequilibrium or a loss of steady state as a result of stress and a precipitating event in the life of a person who usually has a satisfactory level of functioning.

cultural competence   The ability to provide services to clients from a particular cultural group in a manner that is consistent with the norms and customs of that culture.

deductive learning   Involves moving from theory to hypothesis to testing hypothesis to determine whether the theory is supported.

diagnosis   A term borrowed from the medical field. It relates to developing a statement as to the nature of the client's need and the situation related to that need. A more contemporary term is *assessment.*

diagnostic approach   A historic model of social work practice that places a primary emphasis on diagnosis. The contemporary model is usually referred to as the *psychosocial approach.*

direct practice   Action with individuals, families, and small groups focused on change in either the transactions within the family or small group or in the manner in which individuals, families, and small groups function in relation to individuals and social systems in their environments.

diversity competence   The ability to provide services to clients with a particular diversity factor in a manner that is acceptable within that diversity group.

dual perspective   Process of consciously perceiving, understanding, and comparing simultaneously the values, attitudes, and behaviors of the larger social system and those of the immediate family and community system.

ecological perspective   A way of thinking about practice that involves a focus on the client's surrounding environment.

ecosystem   A system of systems including the person(s) and all of the interacting systems in the environment along with the transactions among the person(s) and systems.

ecosystems perspective   An approach that examines the exchange of matter, energy, or information over time among all the systems in a person-in-environment approach.

ecosystems strengths approach   A blend of the ecological and strength perspectives with the problem-solving approach to form a process for facilitating growth and change.

empirically based practice   Practice that is based on knowledge that has been tested by empirical or scientific methods and found to be effective.

empowerment   A process for increasing personal, interpersonal, or political power so that individuals can take action to improve their life situations.

enabling   Making it possible for an individual or system to carry out some activity they might not be able to engage in without support or help.

engagement   The establishment of a helping relationship between the worker and the client system.

entropy   The quality of systems that describes the loss of energy and the capacity to carry out functions.

environmental demands   Expectations that people or social systems in an individual's or social system's environment place on themselves relative to their social functioning.

environmental manipulation   A strategy to bring about change in a client's environment in order to enhance the client's social functioning.

equifinality   The capacity of two systems to achieve identical goals when starting from different conditions.

equilibrium   A fixed balance in a social system among the various subsystems and their functioning. Tends to represent a quality of stability and closedness.

evaluation   Collection and assessment of data about the outcomes of a plan of action relative to goals set in advance of implementing that plan.

extinction   The technique of ignoring undesirable behavior as a way of eliminating it.

facilitation   Enabling others to function effectively.

feedback   A special form of input that gives a system information on the effects of its output on other systems.

feeling   An intuitive sense of a situation or solution to a problem. Facts have not been sought. More of an emotional process than a cognitive one.

felt need   A need identified by a client.

feminist perspective   An approach related to redistribution of power that addresses discrimination; useful in working with women and minority groups.

field of practice   A system of policies, agencies, and services that focuses on a social problem, a disabling condition, a particular context, or a particular social system. A major organizing framework for the U.S. social welfare system.

focal system   The primary system on which the social work process focuses in the change activity.

formative evaluation   Evaluation that looks at the process of the work.

functional approach   A historic model of social work practice that places emphasis on the role and tasks of the social worker in the helping situation rather than on a client's deviance or illness.

Gemeinschaft   A characteristic of communities that demonstrates a sense of "we-ness" and informal functioning.

generalist practice   Practice in which the client and worker together assess the need in all of its complexity and develop a plan for responding to that need. A strategy is chosen from a repertoire of responses appropriate for work with individuals, families, groups, agencies, and communities. The unit of attention is chosen by considering the system needing to be changed. The plan is carried out and evaluated.

genogram   A pictorial assessment mechanism for showing intergenerational relationships and family characteristics.

Gesellschaft   A characteristic of communities in which individuals tend to relate through institutions and other formal structures.

goal   The overall, long-range expected outcome of an endeavor.

goal-attainment scaling   An evaluation technique that not only specifies goals but also specifies outcomes at five levels: expected, more desirable, most desirable, less than desirable, and least desirable.

good practice   Broadly defined as accepted practice in the field or setting or with a population, which is based on empirically based practice, practice experience, and the empowerment of clients.

group-building (group-maintenance) roles   Those roles that focus on the maintenance of the group as a system. The roles include encourager, harmonizer, or goal keeper.

group task roles   Those roles related to the accomplishment of the functions or tasks of the group. The roles may include initiator, coordinator, or clarifier.

holon   A system that is part of a larger system and is made up of several smaller systems. Often the system of focus.

homeostasis   Fixed balance in a system that allows some permeation of the system's boundary by ideas and individuals, yet maintains the capacity of the system's structure to remain stable.

human development perspective   A way of viewing human need that sees people as developing over the life cycle.

human diversity approach   A way of viewing persons in situations that considers culture, race, gender, and disabling conditions as they affect human functioning. It views human behavior as highly relative to the social situation in which persons function.

incongruity   A situation in which the interactions or transactions within an ecosystem are out of balance, resulting in unmet needs for the person and/or the environment.

indirect practice   Action taken with persons other than clients in order to help clients.

individual roles   Roles that satisfy individual need but detract from the work of the group. These can include the dominator, the special-interest pleader, and the blocker.

inductive learning   Moving from making observations of phenomena to searching for patterns that may lead to theory development. It means adopting an open-minded inquisitive approach, laying aside preconceived notions, and listening to the experiences of the client.

influence   General acts of producing an effect on another person, group, or organization through exercises of a personal or organizational capacity.

influentials   Persons in a community or an organization who have power or authority.

input   Matter, energy, or information that enters a system.

integrative practice   The effort to identify the commonalities of practice theory among casework, group work, and community organization.

interactional skill   The capacity of social workers to relate to both clients and significant others, both individuals and social systems, in such a manner as to be helpful and to support the work at hand.

interface   A point of contact between two systems where transactions occur.

intervention   Specific action by a worker in relation to human systems or processes in order to induce change. The action is guided by knowledge and professional values as well as by the skillfulness of the worker.

interventive repertoire   The package of actions, methods, techniques, and skills a particular social worker has developed for use in response to needs of individuals and social systems.

interview   The structure for operationalizing the interaction between a worker and a client.

knowledge   Picture of world and the place of humans in it. Ideas and beliefs about reality based on confirmable or probable evidence.

leadership   (in groups) The filling of a number of roles in a group, particularly those needed for group functioning.

life processes   The biological, social, psychological, and spiritual courses of individuals and social systems as they develop and function through the life span.

lifestyle   Manner in which an individual or family functions in meeting needs; in interactions with others; and in patterns of work, play, and rest.

locus of control   The source of an individual's motivation or drive for action or change. The major concern is whether it lies within the individual or within the environment.

mapping   A pictorial assessment mechanism that shows the relationship of subsystems to each other or the relationship of a system to other systems in its environment.

mediation strategy   A strategy in which a worker helps a client and a system in the immediate environment to reach out to each other and find a common concern or interest and to do the work necessary to bring about a desired change.

medical model   Used in medical field and often appropriated by social workers. Characterized by a process of study, diagnosis, and treatment.

moral code   Specification of what is considered to be right or wrong in terms of behavior.

multifinality   A situation when two systems start from similar conditions and reach different end states.

multiperson client system   A client system that is made up of more than one person such as a family, group, organization, or community.

multiperson helping system   A situation in which more than two persons are involved, such as a social worker working with a small group of clients or several workers (a team) working with a single client.

natural helpers   People who possess helping skills and exercise them in the context of mutual relationships, as opposed to professionals trained in certain helping skills who are not part of a client's immediate community.

natural helping systems   A client's friends, family, and coworkers. Those in an individual's informal environment to whom one turns in time of need.

naturalistic inquiry   An inductive learning process that begins with the position that one does not know what one does not know, which leaves one open to hearing the client's story without preconceived notions.

need   That which is necessary for either a person or a social system to function within reasonable expectations, given the situation that exists.

needs assessment   A process through which needs of a particular population or category of systems are determined.

negative entropy   The efficient use of energy by a system and the addition of energy to the system from the outside.

network   A loose association of systems. Not a social system but an entity that operates through mutual resource sharing.

networking   Development and maintenance of communication and ways of working together among people of diverse interests and orientations. One means of coordination.

norming   The process of setting norms, or expected ways of behaving.

objectives   Intermediate goals that must be reached in order to attain the ultimate goal.

openness   A quality of social systems that describes the capacity of the system to allow information and individuals to permeate the system boundaries easily.

opportunity seizing   A skill that involves use of a keen sense of when the time is right to develop a project or involve an individual or system in a change activity.

output   Matter, energy, or information that is produced by a system.

patient   An individual treated in a medical setting. Sometimes used in place of the term *client* in clinical social work.

person in environment (or person in situation)   The focus of the social work endeavor. The focus of the social worker is not only on the person or the environment but on the complex interaction of the two as that interaction affects both person and social situation.

philosophy of life   Beliefs about people and society and about human life, its purposes, and how it should be lived.

plan of action   The way or method for carrying out planned change in the social work endeavor. It is structured and specifies goals and objectives, units of attention, and strategy.

private troubles   Relates to the needs of individuals.

problem   (in social work) A social functioning situation in which need fulfillment of any of the persons or systems involved is blocked and in which the persons involved cannot by themselves remove the block to need fulfillment.

problem-oriented record   A four-point record containing a data base of pertinent information, a problem list, plans and goals, and follow-up notes (including outcomes).

problem-solving process   A tool used by social workers to solve problems in a rational manner. It proceeds through identifiable steps of interaction with clients. These steps include identification of the problem, statement of preliminary assumptions about the problem, selection and collection of information, analysis of information, development of a plan, implementation of the plan, and evaluation.

process   A recurrent patterning of a sequence of change over time in a particular direction.

process recording   Narrative report of all that happened during a client contact, including the worker's thinking and feeling about what happened.

profession   A group of people who carry out some societal task. These trained and educated people work from systematic theory, carry authority and community sanction, and have a code of ethics and a culture.

professional relationship   A relationship with an agreed-on purpose, a limited time frame, and in which the professional devotes self to the interest of the client.

psychosocial approach   See *Diagnostic approach.*

public issues   Relates to need from a societal perspective.

referral   The process by which a social worker enables a client to know and use another resource.

reframing   Stating a concern or a problem in a new way, from a different point of view.

relationship   Cohesive quality of the action system. Product of interaction between two persons.

reliability   The extent to which repeated measurement would yield the same results in evaluation.

role   The way the worker uses self in the specific helping situation.

scientific philanthropy   Systematic, careful investigation of evidence surrounding the need for service before acting on the need.

self-help groups   Voluntary groups in which members with common problems help each other.

significant others   Those persons in an individual's social network who have importance to, or impact on, the system being worked with.

single-subject design   A research method used when the *n* (number of subjects) is one. Comparisons are made from baseline data, with progress toward goals being measured.

single-system design   A research design in which a single system—individual, family, group, program, organization, or community—is measured over time.

skill   A complex organization of behavior directed toward a particular goal or activity.

small groups   Three or more persons who have something in common and who use face-to-face interaction to share that commonality and work to fulfill needs and solve common problems of their own or others.

social action   A change strategy that organizes people (often oppressed people) so as to bring pressure on societal institutions for change in power distribution.

social functioning   People coping with environmental demands.

social history   A form of assessment of individuals or families. It includes information (historical and current) needed for understanding and working with clients.

social support network analysis   Specification of the nature of an individual's or family's support network. Both pictorial and written depictions are used.

social system   A system composed of interrelated and interdependent parts (persons and subsystems).

social work process   A change process carried out with clients to meet needs in social functioning that clients cannot meet without help. It is conceptualized as study, assessment, planning, action, and termination.

sociogram   A pictorial assessment technique used with small groups to show the relationships between group members.

solution-based interventions   An approach that focuses on quickly finding a successful solution and empowering clients for change.

special populations   Refers to specific groups of people, such as women, members of a particular minority group, those with a particular disabling condition, and so on. These groups may need special consideration when providing services.

steady state   State of a system's functioning that provides a balance between stability and adaptive change.

strategy An overall approach to change in a situation. Includes defining roles and tasks of both worker and client.

strengths approach An approach to social work practice that emphasizes the strengths and capabilities of the client system and the resources within the client's natural environment.

summative evaluation Evaluation concerned with outcomes and effectiveness.

support The use of techniques that help clients feel better, stronger, and more comfortable in some immediate way.

task group A relatively formal and structured time-limited group of persons involved with or concerned about a particular problem who work together to reach a common goal.

tasks Steps necessary to achieve a goal.

team A group of persons, often representative of various professions, who work together toward common goals and plans of action to meet the needs of clients.

termination The last phase of the social work process when the emphasis is on disengagement, stabilization of change, and evaluation.

thinking Use of a cognitive process to sort out information or to engage in a problem-solving process.

throughput The processing of matter, energy, or information by a system from input to output.

transaction The exchange of matter, energy, or information among persons or systems within an ecosystem.

treatment Term used for action segment of the social work process. Very often used in clinical social work.

unit of attention The system or systems on which the change activity is focused; also called *focal system*.

validity The accuracy of information or data.

values What is held to be desirable and preferred. Guides for behavior.

Author Index

A

Abramson, Marcia, 423
Ackerman, Nathan, 393
Addams, Jane, 383
Adler, Alfred, 390
Aiger, Stephen, 214, 429
Alder, Catherine, 432
Alexander, Ernestina, 426
Alinsky, Saul, 384, 396, 434
Allen-Meares, Paula, 199, 429
Anderson, Joseph D., 433
Ankersmit, Edith, 145, 427
Aptekar, Herbert H., 421
Armstrong, John, 284, 432
Atherton, Charles R., 423
Attneave, Carolyn, 231, 430
Auslander, Brian, 361, 433
Auslander, Gail, 361, 433
Avila, Donald, 85, 425

B

Baer, Betty, 26, 422, 427
Bailey, Royston, 87, 425
Bales, Robert E., 433
Bartlett, Harriet, 13, 17, 25, 183, 422, 423, 428
Bean, Roy A., 424
Beatman, Frances, 393
Beck, Judith, 430
Bedell, Tina M., 424
Bell, Peter, 56, 424
Benne, Kenneth, 342, 433
Berg, Insoo Kim, 433
Berger, 422
Berlin, Sharon, 426, 432
Biddle, William W., 394
Biestek, Felix, 12, 142, 150, 422, 427
Bloom, Martin, 422, 432
Blundall, Joan, 102, 426
Boehm, Werner W., 422
Boettcher, Richard E., 431
Booth, Charlotte, 433
Borgotta, Edgar F., 433
Borum, Valerie, 57, 424
Boss, Pauline G., 427
Brager, George, 381, 434
Bramhall, Martha, 137, 427
Brammer, Lawrence M., 426, 427

Briar, Scott, 100, 422, 426
Bricker-Jenkins, Mary, 392, 424, 430
Brilhart, John K., 433
Brownlee, Ann, 152, 428
Bubolz, Margaret M., 427
Butler, J. P., 424
Buxton, Edward B., 428

C

Cameron, J.Donald, 381, 434
Caplan, Gerald, 391
Carkhuff, R. R., 428
Carroll, Charles, 434
Cartwright, Darwin, 433
Chapmen, Nancy J., 429
Chau, Kenneth L., 106, 426
Chen, Sheying, 44, 45, 424
Chess, Wayne A., 425
Cimmarusti, Rocco A., 433
Cloward, Richard, 384, 396, 434
Coady, Nick F., 144, 427
Cohen, Saul, 434
Collins, Alice, 231, 429, 434
Combs, Arthur, 85, 425
Compton, Beulah, 27, 85, 149, 243, 423, 425, 427, 430, 432, 432
Congress, Elaine P., 107, 424, 426
Cooper, Lynn B., 424
Cooperrider, David, 30, 423
Corcoran, Kevin, 290, 432
Cornett, Carlton, 79, 425
Cowger, Charles, 397
Cox, Fred M., 429, 433
Coyle, Grace, 422
Crawford, Dale, 153, 428
Croxton, Tom, 223, 429

D

Dane, Barbara Oberhofer, 125, 427
Delaney, Anita, 213, 429
Deloria, Vine, Jr., 64
deMoll, Lane, 431
Dewees, Marty, 44, 423, 424
Diller, Jerry V., 44, 424
Doherty, William J., 427
DuBois, Brenda L., 430
Dulaney, Diane D., 428

E

Ellis, Albert, 390, 430
Elman, R., 384, 434
Epstein, Laura, 290, 397, 432
Erikson, Erik, 6, 78–79, 416, 421
Erlich, John, 368, 372, 429, 432, 433
Evans, Jimmy, 56, 424
Evens, Wayne, 432
Ezell, Susan, 137, 427

F

Falicov, Celia Jaes, 61, 424
Farris, Buford E., 432
Federico, Ronald, 26, 422, 427
Feiner, Harriet A., 184, 428
Fellin, Phillip, 426
Ferris, Patricia, 430
Fischer, Joel, 290, 428, 432
Fletcher, Joseph F., 425
Foren, Robert, 87, 425
Fortune, Anne E., 296, 432
Fowler, James W., 7, 79, 421, 425
Fraley, Yvonne, 153, 428
Frazio, Rosemary T., 428
Freud, Sigmund, 390
Fried, Jane, 44, 424
Froland, Charles, 429

G

Galaway, Burt, 27, 85, 149, 423, 425, 427, 430, 432
Gambrill, Eileen, 423
Garbarino, James, 429
Gartner, Alan, 429
Garwick, Geoffrey, 432
Germain, Carel, 188, 268, 392, 421, 428, 431
Ghali, Sonia, 200, 429
Gibson, Gaudalupe, 431
Gidron, Benjamin, 232, 429
Gilchrist, Lewayne D., 12, 422
Gilligan, Carol, 7, 79, 421, 425
Ginsberg, Leon, 431
Gitterman, Alex, 188, 268, 428, 431
Glasser, William, 390
Golan, Naomi, 391
Gold, Nora, 110, 266, 426, 431
Goldberg, Gale, 429

Goldstein, Howard, 18, 20, 422
Gomez, Ernesto, 265, 431
Gonzales, Manny J., 424
Gordon, William E., 422
Gottlieb, N., 424
Greenwood, Ernest, 9–10, 421
Grinnel, Richard, 268, 431
Guba, Ergon, 291, 432
Guest, Geoffrey, 123, 427
Gulati, Padi, 123, 427
Gutheil, Irene, 270, 431
Gutierrez, Lorraine M., 421, 430
Gutkin, Terry, 45, 424

H

Haapala, David, 433
Hadakand, Mary T., 428
Haddock, Shelley A., 255, 430
Haley, Jay, 390
Hall, Edward T., 431
Hamilton, Gordon, 11, 421
Hare, Paul A., 433
Harmin, Merrill, 423
Harris, Oliver, 432
Hartford, Margaret E., 433
Hartman, Ann, 316, 425, 429, 432
Hartman, Carl, 144, 427
Hasenfeld, Yeheskel, 232, 429
Hess, Howard, 296, 432
Hess, Peg McCartt, 296, 432
Ho, M. K., 424
Hofstein, Sal, 33, 423
Hollis, Florence, 184, 244, 268, 428,
   430, 431
Homans, George, 433
Horejsi, Charles, 145, 427, 433
Horejsi, Gloria A., 433
Horwitz, John J., 434
Howe, Elizabeth, 9, 421
Hudson, Peter, 284, 432
Hunter, Floyd, 117, 426

I

Irey, Karen, 428
Itlleson, William H., 431

J

Jackson, Don, 390
Janzen, Curtis, 432
Johnson, David, 85, 425
Johnson, F. E., 427
Johnson, H. Wayne, 428, 429
Johnson, Louise, 118, 153, 422, 425,
   427, 428, 429, 430, 434
Johnson, Vanessa D., 56, 424
Jorgensen, James D., 434

K

Kadushin, Alfred, 422
Kagle, Jill Doner, 91, 423, 426
Kahn, Alfred J., 422
Kaiser, Clara, 395
Kaplan, Karen Orloff, 274, 431
Katz, Harriet, 184, 429
Katz, Sanford N., 423
Keith-Lucas, Alan, 423
Kelley, James, 430
Key, Michael, 284, 432
Kimboko, Priscilla J., 429
Kinney, Jill, 433
Kiresuk, Thomas J., 432
Kirk, Stuart A., 174–175, 428
Kirkland, Janet, 428
Kirst-Ashman, Karen, 425
Kisthardt, Walter, 397, 428
Klepinger, Brian W., 434
Kluckholm, Florence, 75, 77, 425
Knight, Carolyn, 430
Kohlberg, Lawrence, 7, 79, 421
Konopka, Gisela, 421, 422
Kopels, Sandra, 423
Kyte, Nancy, 268, 431

L

Laird, Joan, 316, 425, 429, 432
Landy, David, 102, 426
Lane, Bruce A., 199, 429
Lantz, Jim, 430
LaRossa, Ralph, 427
Lauffer, Armand, 427
Leigh, James W., 44, 163, 424, 428
Leighninger, Leslie, 9, 421
Levy, Charles, 23, 423, 431
Lewin, Kurt, 433
Lincoln, Yvonne, 291, 432
Linderman, Erich, 391
Litwak, Eugene, 117, 231, 273,
   426–427, 429, 431
Longres, John, 105, 425, 426
Lorentz, Elizabeth, 434
Lowe, Gary R., 421
Lowenberg, Frank M., 102, 426
Lu, Yuhwa, 44, 45, 424
Luckmann, 422
Lum, Doman, 44, 45, 162, 163, 424,
   428

M

MacDonald, Ginger, 426
MacPhee, David, 255, 430
MacRae, Robert, 381, 434
Maier, Henry, 341, 433
Maileck, Mildred, 429
Maluccio, Anthony, 86, 425, 427, 431
Marsh, Jeanne, 432
Marshall, Catherine A., 430

Martineza-Brawley, Emilia, 102, 426
Maslach, Christina, 137, 427
Maslow, Abraham, 6, 133, 191, 399,
   413, 421, 427, 429
Maton, Kenneth, 434
Matson, Floyd, 157, 428
Mattaini, Mark A., 174–175, 426, 428,
   430
McBroom, Elizabeth, 430
McCoy, Ruth, 424
McMaster, Gerald, 425
McPheeters, Harold, 213–214, 381,
   429, 430, 434
Mermelstein, Joanne, 153, 428
Meyer, Carol H., 421, 422, 426
Meyer, Henry, 273, 431
Middleman, Ruth R., 429, 430
Miley, Karla Krogsrud, 430
Miller, Henry, 100, 426
Miller, Jean Baker, 425, 427
Miller, Pamela, 223, 429
Minahan, Anne, 100, 298, 421, 422,
   423, 426, 432
Mizio, Emelicia, 213, 429
Molyneaux, Brian Leigh, 63, 425
Montagu, Ashley, 157, 428
Moore, Stephen T., 275, 432
Morales, Armando, 23, 25, 423
Morgan, Ralph, 135, 427
Mullen, Edward, 86, 425
Myers, Isabel Briggs, 425

N

Nee, Robert H., 422
Nelson, Judith, 244, 390, 430
Nicholas, Elizabeth, 430
Nichols, W., 44, 423
Norlin, Julia M., 425
Northen, Helen, 30, 423
Northway, Mary L., 433
Norton, Dolores, 43, 108, 114, 199,
   423, 426, 429
Nybell, Lynn, 427

O

Okum, Barbara, 44, 424
Okum, Marcia, 44, 424
O'Melia, Michael, 430
Orme, John, 432
Overbeiger, Carla, 427
Ozawa, Martha, 41, 423

P

Pancoast, Diane, 231, 429, 434
Papell, Catherine P., 422
Parad, Howard J., 391, 426
Parks, Sharon, 79, 425
Parsons, Ruth J., 236, 430

Patti, Rino, 371, 372, 433
Pawlak, Edward, 373, 434
Pearlingi, Bill, 296, 432
Perlman, Helen Harris, 12, 30, 148, 395, 422, 423, 426, 427, 431
Perls, Fritz, 393
Perry, Benjamin J., 424
Phillips, Helen, 395
Piaget, Jean, 6, 421
Pincus, Allen, 100, 298, 422, 423, 426, 432
Polemis, Bernice P., 426
Pollak, Otto, 393
Poplin, Dennis, 117, 427
Pray, Jackie E., 111, 426
Prigmore, Charles S., 423
Proshansky, Harold M., 431
Pruger, Robert, 135–136, 427
Purkey, William, 85, 425

R
Rapoport, Lydia, 27, 391, 423
Rapp, Charles, 428
Rapp, Richard, 397
Rappaport, Julian, 397
Raths, Lewis, 423
Reamer, Frederick G., 423
Reed, Beth, 427
Reed, William J., 422
Reid, P. Nelson, 421
Reid, William J., 290, 294, 397, 432
Reisch, Michael, 423
Resnick, Herman, 371, 372, 433
Reynolds, Diane, 144, 427
Rhodes, Sonya, 318, 433
Richmond, Mary, 10, 268, 421
Riessman, Frank, 429
Ripple, Lillian, 426
Rivas, Robert F., 433
Rivlin, Leanne G., 431
Roberts, Robert W., 422
Rochell, Cherie D., 296, 432
Rodwell, Mary K., 185, 428
Rogers, Carl, 252
Rokeach, Milton, 21, 422
Rose, Sheldon, 388
Rosenblatt, Aaron, 422
Ross, Murray, 30, 423
Rossi, Alice S., 425
Rothman, Beulah, 422
Rothman, Jack, 274, 368, 372, 382, 389, 422, 429, 432, 433
Rousseau, Lorraine, 153, 428
Rubin, Allen, 422
Ruckdeschel, Roy A., 432

Ryan, William, 423
Ryland, Gladys, 422

S
Saleeby, Dennis, 8, 397, 421, 423, 425
Sarason, Seymour B., 434
Satir, Virginia, 390
Scherz, Frances, 393
Schiele, Jerome H., 54, 56, 424
Schindler Zimmerman, Toni, 255, 430
Schinke, Steven P., 12, 422
Schulman, Eveline D., 428
Schumm, Walter, 427
Schwartz, William, 263, 264, 265, 395, 431, 433
Seabury, Brett, 157, 428, 431
Selby, Lois, 243, 430
Sheafor, Bradford, 23, 25, 423, 433
Sheats, Paul, 342, 433
Sherman, Sanford, 393
Shulman, Lawrence, 160, 264, 395, 428, 431
Shyne, Anne, 432
Simon, Barbara L., 125, 427
Simon, Sidney B., 423
Simons, Ronald, 214, 429
Siporin, Max, 18, 174, 213, 268, 422, 428, 431
Sodowsky, Gargi, 45, 424
Solomon, Barbara Bryant, 430
Soloshin, Henriette Etta, 433
Sommer, Robert, 431
Sontag, M. Suzanne, 427
Speck, Ross, 231, 429
Spergel, Irving, 431
Spiegal, John, 393
Spitzer, Kurt, 423
Srivasta, Suresh, 30, 423
Staub-Bernasconi, Silvia, 236, 430
Steinmetz, Suzanne K., 427
Strodtbeck, Fred, 75, 77, 425
Stuart, Richard, 388
Studt, Elliot, 217, 429
Sullivan, W. Patrick, 397, 428
Sundet, Paul, 153, 428
Sunley, Robert, 381, 434
Sykes, Pamela, 430
Szelenyi, Ivan, 231, 427, 429

T
Taffe, Richard, 45, 424
Taft, Jessie, 421
Talavera, Esther, 381, 434

Teare, Robert, 213–214, 381, 429, 430, 434
Teresa, Joseph, 368, 372, 433
Theodorson, Achilles, 423
Theodorson, George, 423
Thomas, Edwin, 388
Thomison, Ray, 388
Thyer, Bruce, 430
Tönnies, Ferdinand, 116, 426
Toseland, Ronald W., 433
Towle, Charlotte, 133, 191, 413, 421, 427, 429
Tracy, Elizabeth M., 110, 201, 426, 429
Tratzer, Clifford E., 425
Trecker, Harleigh, 422
Tropman, John E., 382, 429, 432, 433
Tropp, Emanual, 99, 426
Truax, C. B., 428
Turner, Francis J., 430

V
Van Den Bergh, Nan, 424
Vander Schie, Roger, 431
Vandiver, Susan T., 430
Vigilante, Florence Wexler, 429
Vinter, Robert, 247, 430

W
Walker, Lenore, 409
Walz, Thomas, 431
Warren, Roland, 117, 120, 427
Weick, Ann, 397, 428, 430
Welsh, Betty, 423
Werner, Harold, 390
Whittaker, James K., 12, 110, 201, 422, 426, 429
Willenberg, Georgina, 431
Williams, Robin, 423
Wilson, Gertrude, 422
Winkel, Gary H., 431
Wise, Steven, 45, 424
Wodarski, John, 388, 430

Y
Yanca, Stephen J., 430

Z
Zalba, Serapio, 264, 265, 431
Zander, Alvin, 433
Zastrow, Charles, 425
Zeff, Lawrence, 427
Zimmerman, Larry J., 63, 425
Zimmerman, Laura Rose, 421
Zivotosky, Ethyl, 428

Subject Index

Page numbers followed by f denote material in a figure. Page numbers followed by t denote material in a table.

A

AB design, 287

Acceptance
in group development, 358
in helping relationship, 149
principle of, 150
as support, 244

Accountability, 90–96
defined, 72, 435
effect of privacy and open-access laws, 94
for records, 90–94
use of computers and, 94–96

Acculturation, degree of, 56–57, 61

Action phase, in change process, 35–36

Actions. *See also* Direct practice actions; Indirect practice actions
in change process, 35–36
defined, 435
planning process and (*See* Plan of action)
principles in choosing, 229
principles in valuing diversity, 25
in social work process, 14

Action system, one-to-one, engagement of, 142–148, 435

Activist movement, 278

Activity(ies)
actions to structure group, 359
adversarial, 372
beliefs about, 76–77
collaborative, 372
defined, 435
with families, actions that use, 330
as interventive strategy, 246–249

Addiction, 400–403

Administrator, social worker as, 214

Adolescence, 241, 258, 416–419

Adoption services, 405–407

Adult daily living skills (ADLSs), 400

Adults, older, 41, 107–108

Adversarial activities, 372

Advice giving in helping relationship, 149–150

Advocacy
actions to change organizations, 276–277
case, 235, 381
cause, 235, 380–382
family, 381
skills, for social action organizing, 384

Advocate, social worker as, 214, 234–235, 381

African American language, 57

African Americans
addressing in interview, 160
diversity competence with, 54–59, 102, 109
strategies in planning process, 213

Afrocentric approach, 253–254

Afrocentricity, 54–58

Age, as diversity factor, 107–108
elderly people, 41, 107–108

Agencies, 125–132, 435. *See also* Organizations
boundary definition of, 127
clients seeking help from, 102
community support of, 126
as component of community, 217
in direct practice action, 233, 245
expectations concerning, 126, 127
as factor affecting plan of action, 217
field of practice of, 126
funding limitations, 131, 137
multiservice centers and, 273
networking at monthly meetings, 379–380
program planning, 369–370
schema for study of, 130t
structure and functioning of the system, 127–129
types of, 125–126

Agency collaborative, 278

Agency evaluation, 283

Aggressiveness, 238

Aging services, good practice in, 398–400

Agreement, 145, 223–224, 265

AIDS (acquired immunodeficiency syndrome), 24

Alcohol, 400–403

Alleviation, in group development, 358

American Association for Study of Groups, 12

American Association of Group Workers, 12

American Indians, 425. *See also* Native Americans

American Legion, 232–233

Analysis, 174
of information in assessment phase, 193–194
social support network analysis, 201

Answer-and-agree question, 166–167

Appreciative inquiry, 30

Areas of service, 398

Art of social work, 27

Asians, 106

Assertiveness, 257

Assertiveness training, 238

Assessment, 173–202
of activity as interventive strategy, 247–249
analysis of information, 193–194
as base for ecological/strengths approach, 13, 14
in case management, 274
in change process, 34–35
of changing from within, 370–371
characteristics of, 179–183
client system selection, 177–179
defined, 174, 435
from dual perspective, 199–200
with families, 313–319
identifying needs or concerns, 187–191
information selection and collection, 192–193

judgment, 183–186
mapping, 200–201
needs, 366–367
process of, 175–176
of resources and strengths in ecosystem, 191–192
with small groups, 338–349
social support network analysis in, 201
stages in, 186–194
transactional, 194, 199–201
Assessment document, 175–176
Assessment phase, in change process, 34–35
Assumptions, in assessment phase, 191, 192
Attitude, nonjudgmental, 150
Authority, of helping person, 86–88, 149
Authority stage, of group development, 344–345, 359

B
Backlash, 382
Backup system for computer, 96
Balance theory of coordination, 273
Bargaining strategy, 147, 213
Barriers to change, 267
Barrios, 62
Bedroom community, 118
Behavior
limiting, in groups, 358
measuring for quantitative evaluation, 284
Behavior changer, 214
Behavior therapy practice theory, 388–389
Being in becoming, 76–77
Belief system of helping person, 85–86
Best practices, 13, 205–206, 291, 435
Biracial families, 46, 311–312
Bisexual people, 46
Black English, 57
Blame, 309
Blaming the victim, 30, 31
Blended families, 310, 316, 435
Body language, in interviews, 165
Bond, 342–343, 435
Boundaries, of community, 116, 118
Boundary, of social system, 341, 435
Brief model, 250–251
Broker, social worker as, 214, 234, 435
BSW (bachelor of social work) degree, 10, 12
BSW social workers, status and role, 177, 337, 413

Bureaucracy
of agency, 127, 134–138
decision making traditions, 375
as formal system, 273
Bureaucratic skills, 135–136
Bureaucrat roles, 135
Bureau of Indian Affairs (BIA), 66, 151
Burnout, 137–138, 435

C
Capacity, of client, 109–110, 145
Caregiver, social worker as, 214
Case advocacy, 235, 276, 381, 435
Case conference, 435
Case evaluation, 283
Case examples
activity as interventive strategy, 249
advocacy role, 235–236
case management, 275
change-oriented case record, 92
community organizing, 384–385
community study, 124
crisis intervention, 242–243
employment at agency, first day of, 132–133
enabling approach with feedback, 239–240
environmental change, 271
group session summary, 360
influence and Hispanic culture, 268
interview stages, 161–162, 163, 165, 166, 167
knowledge of self, 81–83
needs of adolescent, 5–6
plan of action, 215
single-system evaluation design, 288–290
small group as social system, 345–349
social history of family, 319–325
social study of individual, 195–199
supportive action, 246
using knowledge, values, and skills with elderly client, 28–29
Case management, 435
as coordination approach, 274–275, 332
practice theory, 389–390
Casework, 389
Casework process, 30
Casework relationship, 12, 150–151
Casework Relationship, The (Biestek), 12
Catholics, 107
Cause, 435
Cause advocacy, 235, 380–382, 435
Cause-effect relationships, 11

Cause-function debate, 262, 435
Change. *See also* Change process
actions for, 227 (*See also* Direct practice actions; Indirect practice actions)
barriers to, 267
focus for clients, 99
resistance to, 267, 373
stabilization of, 300–301
of status, as life transition, 188–189
types to consider in planning process, 211
Change-from-within strategy, 370–373
Change-oriented record, 92
Change process. *See also* Change
in communities, 365, 382–385
enabling the family to use, 312–334
evaluation during phases of, 291–293
in organizations, 371–372
as part of life cycle, 33
phases of, 34–36
Charity Organization Society, 389
Chemical dependence, good practice in, 400–403
Chicanos, 265
Child abuse and neglect, 24, 107, 307
Child protective services (CPS), 403–404
Children. *See also* Families
adoption services, 405–407
in biracial families, 46, 311–312
from diverse cultures, and needs of, 189
as diversity group, 107
domestic violence and, 408
economic concerns, 41
foster care, 404–405
loved and accepted, 307, 329
of same-sex couples, 46, 259, 312
youth and delinquency services, 416–419
Child welfare, good practice in, 403–407
Child welfare cases, 332
Civil unions, 49
Clients, 98–112
becoming, 99–103
capacity of, 109–110
crisis determination, 110
cultural background of, 104
defined, 99–100, 436
diversity in, 101, 102, 105–109
empowerment of, 110, 297
enabling to use available resources, 230–236
expectations of, 101

family influence on, 307–308
help seeking, 102–103
knowledge and understanding of, 103–111
motivation of, 109–110
needs of, 100–101, 142, 398
nonclients, 148
nonvoluntary, 147
opportunity of, 109–110
in planning process, 204–205, 207, 219, 223–224
resistant, 147
role of, 103, 105, 219
self-determination (*See* Self-determination of client)
social history (*See* Social history)
strengths of, 110–111
stress in, 110
transactions between ecosystem and, 133–134
types of, 101, 177
vital roles of, 105
Client system
basing goals on strengths of, 209
in change process, 35
compared to target system, 100
defined, 303
selection of, in assessment, 177–179, 178t
Climate setting, in groups, 354
Climate-setting skills, in interviews, 163–165
Clinical evaluation, 284
Closed-ended questions, 166, 167
Closedness, 436
Clubhouses, 414
Code of Ethics (NASW), 10, 23–24, 89–90, 217, 228, 298, 365. *See also* Ethics, in social work
Cognitive approach, 237
Cognitive-behavioral approach, 237–238
Cognitive practice theory, 390
Cognitive skills, 26
Collaboration, 272, 436
Collaborative activities, 372
Collective identity, 58
Collectives, 262
Commitment, in helping relationship, 149
Common Base of Social Work Practice, The (Bartlett), 17
Common human needs, 6–9, 78–80, 80t
Communication
in action system, 155–157
barriers to effective, 157
difficulties with diverse cultures, 189

in environmental systems, 264, 269
gender differences in, 273
in groups, 343, 344
in helping relationship, 149
in teams, 375
Communication patterns and processes
of African Americans, 57
area of study, 53
of Hispanic/Latinos, 61
of Native Americans, 65
Communication theory, 390
Communicative-interactive theory, 390
Communities
agency as component of, 217
boundaries of, 116, 118
cause advocacy for social change, 380–382
defined, 116, 117–118, 436
diversity factors in planning process, 220–221
as factor affecting plan of action, 216–217
functions of, 117, 120
generalist social work practice with, 365
indirect practice actions to change, 277–279, 333
involvement of influentials, 378–379
needs assessment of resources, 366–367
networking for social change, 379–380
organizing for social change, 382–385
power structure in, 117, 378–379
program planning and resource development, 368–370
rural and urban, 116, 117–118
as social system, 115–125
study of, 119–124
Community benefits, 232, 436
Community organization, 12
models of practice, 277–278
political process and, 382–385
Community Organization: Theory, Principles, and Practice (Ross), 30
Community partnership, 278
Community planner, social worker as, 214
Community resources, 368–370
Community structures
of African-Americans, 58
area of study, 53
of Hispanic/Latinos, 62
of Native Americans, 65–66
Community system, 116

Community task force, 279
Community units, 116
Complementary resource pattern, 274
Complex systems, environmental, 264
Computer use, for recordkeeping, 91, 94–96, 131
Concerns
defined, 4, 436
in helping relationship, 149
identifying in assessment phase, 186, 187–191
social work as response to, 3–15
Confidentiality
code of ethics and, 24
ethical dilemma of, 89–90
in needs assessment, 367
principle of, 151
privacy and open-access laws, 94
record keeping and, 93, 95
Conflict, 436
in families, 328, 329
in groups, 343–344, 355–356
Conflict resolution, 328, 329, 355–356
Conflict strategy, 213
Confrontation, in interviews, 168
Congruity, 8, 436
Consciousness raising, 236–237, 257
Consensus strategy, 213
Consent, informed and written, 93–94
Conservative political climate, 382
Consultant, social worker as, 214, 361
Consultation, 436
Consultation model, with self-help groups, 361
Consultation task, 377
Consumer, 101
Content, 255
Continuing education, 290–291
Continuity of care, 275
Contract, 145, 223–224, 265, 436
Control experimental groups, 285–286
Cooperative task force, 278
Coordination, 436
balance theory of, 273
case management as, 274–275
of services, 272–275, 332
Coordination task, 377
Coordinator, social worker as, 214
Coping, 102, 242, 436
Coping patterns
of African Americans, 58
area of study, 53
of Hispanic/Latinos, 61
of Native Americans, 65
Coping-task approach, 244
Corrections system, 332, 418

Council on Social Work Education (CSWE), 26, 40
Counseling groups, 337, 351
Covenant approach, 223
Creative blending, 17, 27–28
Crisis, 436
  action in response to, 240–243
  determination and stress of client, 110
  in families, actions taken to resolve, 329
  situations, 189
Crisis groups, 242
Crisis intervention, 240, 242, 391
Crisis process, 241, 241f
CSWE (Council on Social Work Education), 26, 40
Cuba/Cubans, 60, 62
Culturagram, 107
Cultural competence, 40, 436. *See also* Diversity
Cultural identity of social workers, 44–45
Cultural patterns
  of African Americans, 55–57
  area of study, 52
  in communication, 155, 157
  of Hispanic/Latinos, 60–61
  of Native Americans, 64
Cultural roots, knowledge of, 77–78, 104, 317
Culture, dominant, 42, 105, 106, 108, 200
Curandero, 231
Current issues
  of Hispanic/Latinos, 62
  of Native Americans, 66

D
Data manager, social worker as, 214
Death, 296
Decision making
  in environmental change, 269
  ethical, 89–90
  in groups, 357
  in professional judgment, 184
  in teams, 375
Deductive learning, 45, 436
Degree of acculturation, 56–57, 61
Delinquency and youth services, good practice in, 416–419
Demographic trends, 40–41, 46
Demonstration strategy, 213
Denial, 299
Determinism, 184–185
Development
  and action selection, 229

of community resources, 368–370
of family system, 313, 317–318
of goals in groups, 357
of groups, 344–345, 358–359
Developmental needs, 78–80, 80t
Developmental stress, 240
Development perspective, human, 6–7
Diagnosis, 10, 174, 436
Diagnostic and Statistical Manual of Mental Disorders (DSM-IV), 416
Diagnostic approach, 11, 436
Directional change, 211
Direct practice, 436
Direct practice actions, 226–260
  defined, 227–228
  to empower and enable client systems, 236–240, 329
  enabling client systems to use resources, 230–236, 328
  to facilitate group development, 358–359
  to facilitate group discussion, 354–355
  to facilitate group formation, 352–354
  with families, 326–330
  for group interaction, 356–357
  influence as action, 266
  as mediation, 330
  to resolve conflict, 355–356
  in response to crisis, 240–243, 329
  with small groups, 351–360
  to structure group activities, 359
  supportive, 243–246, 329
  to use the change process, 328
  using activity as interventive strategy, 246–249, 330
  using other theories and models, 249–259, 330
Direct service groups, 337
Discrimination
  Afrocentric approach and, 253–254
  challenging social injustice, 365–366
  defined, 74
  economic oppression of African Americans, 57
  in gender diversity competence, 47–48
  generalist practice with families and, 311
  plan of action and, 205
  recognizing against self, 44
  understanding individual clients, 106–109
Discussion, in groups, 354–355, 357

Discussion-activity-discussion (DAD), 350, 351
Disengagement, 299–300
Disintegration stage, of group development, 345, 359
Dispossession, 63
Distortion, in communication, 155–156
Diversity. *See also* Cultural patterns; Diversity competent practice
  in action selection, 229
  in clients, 101, 102, 105–109
  communication and, 155, 157
  concept of, 40
  as factor in planning process, 212, 219–221
  factors in communities, 119
  of group members, 353, 355
  helping relationships, influences on, 151–153
  personal needs arising from, 79, 80t
  termination issues, 296
  understanding feelings, thinking, actions, 74
  use of dual perspective, 199–200
  valuing, 24–25
  in worker-client interactions, 143
Diversity competent practice, 39–68, 436
  with African Americans, 54–59
  in assessment phase, 175, 187, 188
  becoming diversity competent, 44–47
  development in social workers, 40–44
  with ethnic groups, 50–54
  in evaluation during change process, 291
  with families, 326–327, 333
  feminist practice and, 254–257
  with gays and lesbians, 49–50
  gender competence, 47–48
  with Hispanic/Latinos, 59–63
  with Native Americans, 63–67
  outline for developing, 41
  understanding clients, 105–109
  understanding environment, 115, 119
Divorce, 310, 316
Domestic violence, 407–410
Dominant culture, 42, 105, 106, 108, 200
Drug prevention groups, 338
Drugs, 400–403, 415
Dual perspective (Norton's), 43, 108, 114, 200–201, 437

E

Ecological perspective, 7–8, 12, 134, 437
Ecological practice theory, 392
Ecology, 8
Eco-map, 316
Economic hardship, 57, 62
Economy, and action selection, 229
Ecosystem
    defined, 114, 437
    identifying strengths and resources in assessment phase, 191–192
    person in environment as, 114–115
    of small groups, 339
    transaction between person and, 133–134
Ecosystems approach, 115
    in community organization change, 278
    mediation in, 263
Ecosystems perspective, 8, 31, 437
Ecosystems strengths approach, 437.
    See also Strengths approach
    in assessment, 175
    blending of ecosystems and strengths approach, 28
    in environmental change, 269
    with families, 311, 328
    with groups, 304
    interventions to change, 33, 36
    meeting client needs, 104
    in planning process, with managed care, 219
    in problem-solving process, 31–32
    social service agency in, 125
    in worker-client interaction, 141, 148, 163
Education, as support, 244
Educational Policy and Accreditation Standards (CSWE), 26
Education groups, 351
Elderly people, 41, 107–108
Emotional response, controlled, 150
Emotions. *See* Feelings
Empathy, 149, 164
Empirically based practice, 205–206, 291, 437
Empowerment, 437
    actions to empower families, 329
    of client, 110, 297
    in direct practice action, 236–239, 257
    need for, 6
    of populations at risk, 205
Enabling, 237–239, 329, 358, 437
Ending stage. *See* Termination

Energy
    exchange with matter and information in transactions, 133–134, 141, 194
    group functioning use of, 343
Engagement, in one-to-one action system, 142–148, 437
Entropy, 437
Environment, 113–139. *See also* Ecological perspective
    agency understanding, 125–132
    community as social system, 115–125
    family system in, 316
    person in, as ecosystem, 114–115
    of small groups, 341–342
    transactions between person and ecosystem, 133–134
    working in bureaucracy, 134–138
Environmental change, 211, 212, 268–271, 331–332
Environmental demands, 7, 437
Environmental manipulation, 268, 437
Environmental psychology, 269
Environmental systems, and interactions of individuals, 264
Environmental treatment, 268
Environmental unresponsiveness, 189
Equifinality, 437
Equilibrium, 437
Erikson's psychosocial stages, 6–7, 78–79, 416
Essential question, 163
Ethical decision making, 89–90
Ethical dilemma, 89–90, 137, 296, 331
Ethics, in social work, 23–24. *See also* *Code of Ethics* (NASW); Moral code; Values
Ethnic groups
    of clients, separating social class from culture, 105–106
    dual perspective of minority people, 200–201
    retention of culture, 257
    schema for studying, 50–54
    value conflicts in, 76
European invasion of Americas, 63–64
Evaluation, 281–293
    in change process, 36, 291–293
    as component of termination, 301–302
    defined, 282, 437
    with families, 333–334
    in group development, 358
    kinds of, 283–285

research techniques in, 285–291 (*See also* Research techniques in evaluation)
    with small groups, 360–361
    social worker's role as, 214
Evidence-based practices, 205–206, 291
Executive bureaucrats, 135
Experimental design, 285–286
Extended family, 231, 316
Extinction, 238, 437

F

Facilitation task, 377, 437
Fair, for networking, 379
Families. *See also* Children; Parenting
    bicultural, and gender competent practice, 257
    biracial or multiracial, 46, 311–312
    blended, 310, 316, 435
    cohesiveness of, 316
    crises in, 329
    cultural differences in, 104, 311–312
    diversity competence toward, 46
    extended, 231, 316
    as natural helping system, 231
    resources of, 328
    roles in, 46, 47, 310, 312, 317, 327
    same-sex partners, 46, 50, 312
    self-knowledge of background, 77–78
    social history, schema for development, 308, 313, 314–315t
    strengths and challenges of, 318–319
    subsystems, 312, 316
    support of social functioning of, 329
Families, generalist practice with, 306–335
    assessment phase with, 313–319
    change process with, 312–334
    direct practice actions with, 326–330
    evaluation phase with, 333–334
    indirect practice actions with, 326, 330–333
    as multiperson client system, 308–309
    planning phase with, 325–326
    termination phase with, 333–334
    types of, 310–312
Familismo, 60, 61
Family advocacy, 381
Family life, stages of, 318
Family patterns and structure
    of African Americans, 57
    area of study, 52–53
    of Hispanic/Latinos, 61
    knowledge of client's, 104
    of Native Americans, 64–65

Family preservation model, 332, 403
Family service agency, 125
Family tree (genogram), 77, 316, 317, 438
Federal Privacy Act (1974), 94
Feedback, 437
  in communication, 155–156
  in direct practice action, 239
  in families, 329
  in group discussion, 357
Feeling, thinking, acting system, 73–74, 114–115, 141, 227f
Feelings, 437
  purposeful expression of, 150
  in social work process, 13–14
  at termination and disengagement, 299–300
Felt need, 5, 437
Feminist groups, 108
Feminist perspective, 47–48, 437
Feminist practice, 254–258, 392–393
Field of practice, 126, 437
Field theory, 433
First Nations tribes, 60, 425. *See also* Native Americans
Floods, 76
Focal system, 211, 437
Focusing skills, in interviews, 167–169
Follow-up, in referral, 234
Formal structure of agencies, 129
Formal systems, 273, 380
Formative evaluation, 283, 437
Foster care, 404–405
Freudian psychotherapy, 390
Friendship networks, 231
Function
  in complex organization, 375–376
  of family system, 313, 316–317
  of small groups, 343–344
Functional approach, 11, 262, 438
Functional bureaucrats, 135
Functional stage, of group development, 345, 359
Funding limits, on agencies, 131, 137
Funding sources, needs assessment for, 366

G
Gays and lesbians
  direct practice action, 258–259
  diversity competence with, 49–50
  family diversity of, 46, 312
  understanding diversity of clients, 108–109
Gemeinschaft, 116, 438
Gender, effect on helping relationships, 152–153

Gender-based roles, 46, 47, 258–259
Gender differences in communication, 273
Gender diversity competence, 47–48, 255–257
Generalist approach, defined, 1
Generalist social worker, enabling client to use available resources, 230–236
Generalist social work practice
  choosing from possibilities of action, 228
  defined, 12, 13, 438
  with families (*See* Families, generalist practice with)
  good practices in, 398–419 (*See also* Good practices in social work)
  with groups (*See* Groups, generalist practice with)
  with organizations and communities, 364–386
Generalist Social Work Practice with Groups (Johnson & Yanca), 277
Genogram, 77, 316, 317, 438
Genuineness, 149, 164
Geographic community, 121–123
Gesellschaft, 116, 438
Gestalt therapy, 393
Gift giving, 296
Goal-attainment scaling, 287, 290, 438
Goals, 438
  in action selection, 229
  in case management, 275
  evaluation of, 282
  with families, 325–326
  in groups, 355, 357
  in organizations, 372
  in plan of action, 208–211
  in program planning, 368
Good judgment, 85, 136
Good practice, 438
Good practices in generalist social work practice, 206–208, 303–305, 398–419
  in aging services, 398–400
  in chemical dependence services, 400–403
  in child welfare, 403–407
  in domestic violence services, 407–410
  in health care settings, 410–411
  in mental health care, 411–416
  model for, 206–208
  research-based, 291
  in youth and delinquency services, 416–419
Governmental agencies, 125

Governmental task force, 278
Grassroots movement, 278, 369–370, 384
Grid, Social Network, 201
Group-building (group maintenance) roles, 342, 438
Group dynamics, 433
Group homes for delinquent boys, 342, 342f, 345–349
Group members
  involvement of, 356
  new, 354, 356–357
  selection of, 338–339, 352–353
  social workers as, 373–378
Groups. *See also* Small groups; Task groups
  activities of, 359
  bond in, 342–343
  conflict in, 343–344, 355–356
  conflict resolution in, 328, 329, 355–356
  crisis, 242
  defined, 337
  development of, 344–345, 358–359
  discussion in, 354–355, 357
  formation of, 352–354
  goals in, 355, 357
  interaction enhancement, 356–357
  leadership in, 342, 354–355, 376–377
  members in (*See* Group members)
  participation in, 374
  purpose of, 337–338
  role of social worker in, 373–378
  self-help, 232
  sociogram of, 342f
  starting new, 350–351
  structure of, 341–343
  support, 237
  types of, 337–338, 351
Groups, generalist practice with, 336–363
  assessment with small groups, 338–349
  direct practice actions with small groups, 351–360
  evaluation with small groups, 360–361
  planning with small groups, 350–351
  purpose of, 337–338
  self-help groups, 361–362
  termination with small groups, 360–361
Group sessions, 350–351, 360
Group task roles, 342, 438
Group work, 11–12

Growth and skill development groups, 337, 351
Guiding, in group development, 358
Guiding skills, in interviews, 167–169
Guilt, 188, 309

H
Hallucination, 184
Hard line information, 284–285
Healers, 231
Health care. *See* Managed care
Health care settings, good practice in, 410–411
Health care system, and funding limits on agencies, 131
Health Insurance Portability and Accountability Act (1996), 94
Helping person, 72, 84–89
Helping professional, 84
Helping relationship
    about, 149–151
    action in response to crises, 242
    natural system (*See* Natural helping system)
    needs of clients in, 142
    special influences on, 151–154
Help seeking, as client, 102–103
Heterosexuality, assumption in social work, 49–50
Hierarchy of needs, Maslow's, 6, 133, 191, 399, 413
Hispanic/Latinos
    addressing in interview, 160
    diversity competence with, 59–63
    natural helpers in community, 231
    understanding oppression of clients, 106
    value system of, 76
Historical considerations in diversity competence
    of African Americans, 55
    of Hispanic/Latinos, 59–60
    of Native Americans, 63–64
Historical perspective
    Eurocentric view of America, 107
    of social work knowledge, 10–13
Holon, 438
Homan's systems theory, 433
Homeostasis, 438
Homosexuals, 108–109. *See also* Gays and lesbians; Lesbians
Horizontal patterns, in communities, 117
Host agency setting, 125–126
Human development, and personal needs, 78–80, 80t

Human development perspective, 6–7, 438
Human Dialogue, The (Matson), 157
Human diversity. *See* Diversity
Human nature, beliefs about, 76–77
Human needs, 6–9, 78–80, 80t
Human transactions, interventions into, 32–34
Hunches, 187

I
Illness, 218
Immigration policy, 62, 106
In, as focal point for social work services, 115
Incongruity, 8, 438
Indian, American. *See* Native Americans
Indian Child Welfare Act (1978), 66
Indian Public Health Services, 66
Indigenous helpers or healers, 231
Indirect practice, 438
Indirect practice actions, 261–280
    to change organizations, 276–277, 332
    to change the community, 277–279, 333
    coordination of services, 272–275, 332
    defined, 228
    for environment change, 268–271, 331–332
    with families, 326, 330–333
    influence as action, 262, 265–268, 330–331
    as mediation, 263–265, 330
Individual, relationship to nature, 76
Individualization
    in action selection, 229
    of family members, 318
    principle of, 150, 185
Individualized rating scales (IRSs), 290
Individual psychology, 390
Individual roles, in groups, 342, 438
Inductive learning, 45, 162–163, 438
Influence, 262, 265–268
    defined, 266, 438
    ethical considerations with, 267, 331
    with families, actions that use, 330–331
    interpersonal, 376–377
    in political process, 382–384
Influentials, 438
    involving in needs assessment, 367
    involving in resource development, 369
    power structure of, 378–379
Informal probation, 418

Informal systems, 380
Information. *See also* Knowledge; Naturalistic inquiry
    in assessment phase, analysis of, 193–194
    in assessment phase, gathering, 179, 192–193
    collected about community, 119–124
    in evaluation during change process, 292
    exchange with matter and energy in transactions, 133–134, 141, 194
    gathered by human service agencies, 131–132
    hard line–soft line continuum, 284–285
    for needs assessment, 367
    use by group functioning, 343
Information and referral service, 274
Informed consent, 93
Innovation, in change in organizations, 372
Input, 438
In-service training for social workers, 372–373
Institutional community, 118
Instrumental values, 22
Insurance companies, 298
Insurance for health care, 131
Intake form, 175
Integrative practice, 12, 439
Integrative practice theory, 393–394
Interaction, of worker and client. *See* Social worker-client relationship; Worker-client interaction
Interactional process, 69–70
Interactional process analysis, 433
Interactional skill, 439
Interactive skills, 26
Interactive-transactional approach, 1
Interdependence, in action selection, 229
Interdisciplinary team, 374–376
Interface, 115, 439
Interference, in communication, 155
Interpersonal influence, 376–377
Interpreting, in group development, 358
Interpreting skills, in interviews, 167–169
Intervention
    as base for ecological/strengths approach, 13
    components of, 171
    crisis (*See* Crisis intervention)
    defined, 32, 439
    development of concept of, 11
    into human transactions, 32–34

Interventive action. *See* Intervention
Interventive repertoire, 25, 439
Interventive strategy, 244, 246–249
Interview, 439
in assessment phase, 176
as interactional tool, 157–169
in needs assessment, 367
preparing for, 159
skills used by worker during,
162–169
stages of, 159–162
I statements, 326, 327–328

J
Jim Crow system, 55, 57
Job bureaucrats, 135
Johnson-Yanca model, 12–13
Judgment, in assessment, 183–186

K
Kennedy, John F., 107
Kinship of African Americans, 56, 57
Knowledge, 17–21. *See also* Information; Self-knowledge
blending values, skills and, 27–28
choosing for social work education,
184–185
compared to values, 21
defined, 17–18, 439
enabling client to use available resources, 230
of individual client, 103–111
scientific, 18
sources of, 20–21
of system, by the influentials, 379
using with values and skills, 29–32,
42–44
Knowledge base
problems inherent in, 19
for social work, 10–13
of social workers, 182
Korean War, 106
Ku Klux Klan, 55
Kwanzaa, Nguzo Saba of, 56–58

L
Land and community use of, 116
Language. *See* Communication; Communication patterns and processes
Latino. *See* Hispanic/Latinos
Leadership, 342, 354–355, 376–377,
439
Leading question, 166
Legislative action, 382
Lesbians. *See* Gays and lesbians
Liberal arts knowledge base, 20
Licensing laws, 10

Life experiences, 78
*Life Model of Social Work Practice,
The* (Germain & Gitterman), 269
Life model theory, 392
Life processes, 439
Life-role approach, 244
Lifestyle, 74–75, 439
Life transitions, 188–189
Lions Club, 233
Listening skills, in interviews, 165–166
Living arrrangements
group homes for delinquent boys,
342, 342f, 345–349
residence of family, changing, 332
residential care, 416, 417, 418
settlement houses, 11, 381, 389
Locality development, 277, 394–395
Locus of control, 110, 439

M
Machismo, 60
Macropractice, 262, 277, 365–366
Managed care
bureaucracy of, 137
evaluation and termination, 287,
291, 298
as factor affecting plan of action,
217, 218–219
limits on length of service, 131, 158,
338
Management evaluation, 284
Mapping, 199f, 200–201, 439
Maps of community, 116
Maslow's hierarchy of needs, 6, 133,
191, 399, 413
Mass neighborhood, 117
Matter, energy, and information
exchange in transactions,
133–134, 141, 194
Maturity, 85
Maximum level of functioning, 275
Mediating practice theory, 395
Mediation, in conflict resolution, 356
Mediation strategy, 263–265, 269,
330, 439
Medicaid, 412
Medical model, 10, 439
Mental health, good practice in,
411–416
Mental health agencies, 131
Mental health care, and bureaucracy, 137
Mental illness, 101
Message, in communication, 155–157
Metropolitan areas, 117–118
Mexican-American War, 60, 106
Mexican descent, people of, 60, 62
Milford Conference, 11

Milieu therapy, 271
Minorities. *See* Ethnic groups
Mobile neighborhood, 117
Mobilizer, social worker as, 214
Models of social work practice theory,
388–398
behavior therapy, 388–389
case management, 389–390
cognitive (rational, reality), 390
communicative-interactive, 390
crisis intervention, 391
ecological (life model), 392
feminist practice, 392–393
Gestalt therapy, 393
integrative, 393–394
locality development, 394–395
mediating, 395
problem-solving, 395–396
social action, 396
social planning, 396–397
strengths perspective, 397
task, 397–398
Models with direct practice action
Afrocentric approach, 253–254
brief, 250–251
case management, 274
of community organization practice,
277–278
feminist practice, 254–258
for generalist practice in families,
330
for good practices in generalist
practice, 206–208
narrative approaches, 252–253
person-centered theory, 252
of practice, 213
solution-focused, 250–251
task-centered, 251–252
Moral code, 75–77, 439
Motivation, capacity, and opportunity
of client, 109–110, 145
MSW (master of social work) degree,
10
MSW social workers, role and status
of, 177, 337, 412
Multifinality, 439
Multiperson client system, 308–309, 439
Multiperson helping system, 72, 439
Multiperson systems, 303–305
Multiservice centers, 273
Multisystem model, 318
Muslims, 107
Mutual aid, 232, 361
Mutual goals, 326

N
Narrative approaches, 252–253

National Association of Social Workers
(NASW), 10, 12, 40 *Code of
Ethics,* 10, 23–24, 89–90, 217,
228, 298, 365
  publications of, 400, 407, 411,
  416, 419
National Coalition against Domestic
Violence, 409
National Domestic Violence Hotline,
409
Native Americans
  diversity competence with, 63–67
  gender influence on helping relationships, 153
  natural helping system in direct
  practice action, 231
  strategies in planning process, 213
  understanding oppression of clients,
  106
  use of term, 425
  value system of, 76, 184
Natural disasters, 76
Natural helpers, 231, 273, 380, 439
Natural helping system, 231–232, 273,
439
Naturalistic inquiry, 439. *See also*
  Information
  in assessment phase, 175, 193
  in direct practice action, 229,
  253, 256
  in evaluation during change
  process, 291–293
  with families, 327, 333
  in groups, 353
  in interviews, 163
  in planning process, 220
Needs, 3–15
  of clients, 100–101, 142
  common human, 6–9, 78–80, 80t
  defined, 4–5, 440
  of families, 328
  felt, 5, 437
  identifying in assessment phase,
  186, 187–191
  in life cycle, 33
  Maslow's hierarchy of, 6, 133, 191,
  399, 413
  professions as a response to, 9–10
  social functioning and, 13–14
  social work knowledge development,
  10–13
  Towle's elements of, 133, 191, 413
Needs assessment, of community
  resources, 366–367, 440
Needs-based record, 91
Negative entropy, 440
Negative feedback, 239

Negotiation stage, of group develop-
  ment, 345, 359
Neighborhoods, 117, 118
Network, 440
Networking, 231, 379–380, 440
Network therapy, 231
New records, 91
Nguzo Saba of Kwanzaa, 56–58
Nonjudgmental attitude, 150
Nonpossessive warmth, in interviews,
  164
Nonsexist orientation in practice, 254
Nonverbal communication, 155
Norming, 357, 440
Norton's dual perspective, 43, 108, 114,
  200–201, 437

O

Obama, Barack, 40, 54, 106
Objectives, in plan of action, 208–211,
  222, 440
Obligation, in helping relationship, 149
Observation skills, 165, 358
Older adults, 41, 107–108
One-to-one action system, formation
  and engagement of, 142–148
Ongoing groups, 360
Open-access laws, 94
Open-ended questions, 166, 167
Openness, 440
Opportunity, for client, 109–110, 145,
  151
Opportunity seizing, 379, 440
Oppression, 74, 106–109, 205. *See also*
  Discrimination
Organizational task force, 278
Organizations. *See also* Agencies
  actions to change, 276–277, 332
  actions to change community,
  277–279, 333
  change-from-within strategy, 370–373
  generalist social work practice with,
  365
  involvement of influentials, 378–379
  networking for social change,
  379–380
  program planning and resource
  development, 368–370
Orientation stage, of group development, 344, 359
Output, 440
Outreach worker, 214

P

Paperwork, 131–132, 175, 176. *See
  also* Records
Paraphrasing, in interviews, 168

Parenting. *See also* Families
  gender equity in families, 256
  positive reinforcement and feedback,
  239
  same-sex couples with children, 46,
  259
Participation
  in change in organizations, 372
  in groups, 374
  principle for making judgments in
  assessment, 185
Patient, 101, 440
Patriarchal system, 255, 327
People-changing agencies, 126
People-processing agencies, 126
People who are older, 40–41, 43,
  107–108
Personal functioning, 83–84
Personalismo, 60
Personal needs, 78–80, 80t
Person-centered theory, 252
Person in environment, 13, 31, 103, 440
Person in situation, 31, 440
Perspectives on social work practice, 1–2
Philosophy of life, 74–75, 440
Physical arrangement in environment,
  270–271, 354
Physically disabled, 107, 270
Planning, 203–225
  agreement between worker and
  client, 223–224
  in change process, 35
  client input in, 204–205, 207
  developing a plan, 204–205, 216
  empirically based practice, 205–206
  for evaluation, 283
  with families, 325–326
  good practices model, 206–208
  in group development, 358
  process of, 30, 222–223
  program planning, and resource
  development, 368–370
  as a skill, 204
  with small groups, 350–351
Planning phase, in change process, 35
Plan of action, 216–222, 440. *See also*
  Planning
  agency as factor affecting, 217
  case example of, 215
  client as factor affecting, 219
  community, as factor affecting,
  216–217
  components of, 208–216
  diversity as factor affecting, 219–221
  factors affecting, 216–222
  goals and objectives as component
  of, 208–211, 222

populations at risk as factor affecting, 219–221
social issue as factor affecting, 217–218
strategy as component of, 212–215
strengths and challenges of systems involved, 221–222
units of attention as component of, 211–212
worker as factor affecting, 218–219
Policy changes, in organizations, 277
Political process, 382–385
Populations at risk, in planning process, 219–221
Positive feedback, 239
Positive reinforcement, 238–239
Positive self-worth, 83
Poverty
  community and social justice, 123
  in diverse ethnic groups, 41, 55, 59, 62, 64, 65, 66
  historical view of, 11
  value conflicts and, 76
Power
  action to empower clients, 236–239
  in communities, 117
  discretionary, in bureaucracy, 135–136
  in helping relationship, 149
  sharing between worker and client, 257–258
Power/control model, of professions, 9–10
Power Equity Guide, 255
Power structure of influentials, 378–379
Power system of agencies, 129
Practice. *See* Social work practice
Practice actions. *See* Actions
Practice theory knowledge, 20
Practice wisdom, 18–19, 286
Prejudice. *See also* Discrimination
  challenging social injustice, 365–366
  of group members, 353
  understanding individual clients, 106–109
  in worker-client interactions, 152
Prevention groups, 338, 351
Primary systems, 273
Privacy. *See also* Confidentiality
  and open-access laws, 94
Private practice model, of professions, 9
Private sector, 11
Private troubles, 262, 440
Proactive advocacy, 276–277, 371
Probation services, 145, 418
Problem, defined in terms of need, 31, 440
Problem-focused approach, 221

Problem-oriented record, 91, 440
Problems, in knowledge base, 19
Problem-solving practice theory, 395–396
Problem-solving process, 30–32, 440
Process, 11, 13, 33, 255, 440. *See also* Social work process
Process model, of professions, 9–10
Process recording, 92–93, 440
Profession, as response to need, 9–10, 440
Professional development, 290–291
Professional expectations of agency, 127, 134
Professional relationship, 148–149, 441
Program evaluation, 283–284
Program planning. *See also* Planning and resource development, 368–370
Proposal for new group, 350
Protection, as support, 244
Proximate values, 22
Psychosocial approach. *See* Diagnostic approach
Psychosocial stages (Erikson's), 6–7, 78–79, 416
Public employment policy, 381
Public issues, 262, 441
Publicity campaign, in needs assessment, 367
Public model, of professions, 9
Public records, open access to, 94
Public sector agencies, 125
Public social policy, 382
Puerto Ricans, 60, 62, 200, 213
Purpose, in helping relationship, 149

Q

Qualitative evaluation, 284
Quantitative evaluation, 284
Quebec, Canada community, 123
Questioning skills, in interviews, 166–167
Question(s)
  collecting information, 192
  essential, 163
  types of, 166–167

R

Rapid-assessment instruments (RAIs), 290
Rating-ranking pattern, in groups, 342
Rational casework theory, 390
Rational-emotive psychotherapy, 390
Reactive advocacy, 276
Reality therapy, 390
Receiver, in communication, 155–156
Reciprocal goals, 326

Records
  about accountability, 90–94
  assessment document, 175–176
  computerized, 94–96
  open access to, 94
  paperwork required by agencies, 131–132
  reading for initial contact, 143
  types of, 90–92
Referral, 233–234, 274, 441
Reforms in social welfare, 131
Reframing, 441
Refusal of services, 298
Regents of the University of California, Tarasoff *v.*, 24
Regression, 299
Reinforcement, in families, 329
Relationships
  in action system, 148–154, 154f
  among people in communities, 116
  as base for ecological/strengths approach, 13
  change, in planning, 211
  defined, 148, 154, 441
  effect of gender on, 152–153
  in environmental change, 270, 271
  in families, actions to develop, 327–328
  in groups, 341, 358
  helping relationships, 149–151 (*See also* Helping relationship)
  of individual to nature, 76
  professional, 148–149
  sustaining, 211
Release of information, 233
Reliability, 291–292, 441
Religion. *See also* Spirituality
  in Hispanic/Latino culture, 60, 61
  homophobic attitudes and, 49
  prejudice and understanding clients, 107
Religious development, 79
Religious values, 22
Research, using in social work practice, 205–206
Research techniques in evaluation, 285–291
  goal-attainment scaling, 287, 290
  other forms, 290–291
  single-subject design, 286–287
  single-system design, 285–286, 288–290
Residence of family, changing, 332
Residential care, 416, 417, 418
Resistance to change, 267, 373
Resource development, and program planning, 368–370

Resources
community, and development,
368–370
enabling clients to use available,
230–236
enabling family to use available, 328
identifying in ecosystem in assessment phase, 191–192
in strengths approach, 8–9
Responding question, 166
Response, in communication, 155
Responsibility. *See also* Accountability
of family for situation, 309
of helping person, 86–88, 150–151
Risks, in changing organizations, 373
Role definition, in groups, 357
Role(s), 441
in agencies, 129
of BSW social workers, 177, 337,
413
of clients, 103, 105, 219
in families, 46, 47, 310, 312, 317, 327
individual, in groups, 342, 438
of MSW social workers, 177, 337,
412
of social worker, 213–214, 233,
234–235, 373–378
Role structure, 342
Room arrangements, 270
Rural areas, 116, 117–118, 153, 277,
414

S

Same-sex couples, 46, 258–259, 312
Same-sex marriage, 49
Schools, and diversity competence, 189
Science of social work, 27
Scientific knowledge, 18
Scientific philanthropy, 441
Scientific process, 30
Secondary agency setting, 125
Seeking help as client, 102–103
Self-blame, 237
Self-determination of client
and action selection, 229
in feminist practice, 256
influence and, 267
locus of control and, 110
principle of, 150–151
and social responsibility, 87–88
Self-directiveness of social workers,
136
Self-fulfilling prophecy, 210
Self-help groups, 232, 245, 361–362,
441
Self-interest of environmental systems,
264

Self-knowledge, 72–84
becoming diversity competent, 45–46
of family and cultural roots, 77–78,
317
life experiences, 78
lifestyle and philosophy of life,
74–75
moral code and value system, 75–77
and personal functioning, 83–84
and personal needs, 78–80, 80t
person as feeling, thinking, acting
system, 73–74, 73f
Self-worth, 83
Sender, in communication, 155–156
Service bureaucrats, 135
Service delivery systems, 145, 230–233
Services
coordination of, 272–275, 332
good practice to clients, 398
provision of, 69
refusal of, 298
short-term, 294
Settlement houses, 11, 381, 389
Sexual orientation, 49
Sexual preference, 49
Significant others, 141, 441
Silence, in interviews, 168
Single-parent families, 310
Single-subject design, 286–287, 441
Single-system design, 285–286,
288–290, 441
Situational intervention, 268
Skill development groups, 351
Skillfulness, 26
Skills, 25–27
advocacy, for social action organizing, 384
basic, 26
blending knowledge, values and,
27–28
climate-setting, 163–165
defined, 17, 25, 441
in environmental change, 269
focusing, guiding, interpreting,
167–169
of helping person, 88–89
inductive learning, 162–163
interviewing, by worker, 162–169
listening, 165–166
naturalistic inquiry, 163
observation, 165
planning, 204
questioning, 166–167
for social workers in coordination,
380
types of, 26

in understanding communities, 123
using with knowledge and values,
29–32, 42–44
Slavery, 55, 57
Small groups, 441. *See also* Groups
in agencies, 129
assessment with, 338–349, 340–341t
direct practice actions with, 351–360
ecosystem of, 339
environment of, 341–342
evaluation with, 360–361
family as, 308
membership in (*See* Group members)
planning with, 350–351
as social system, 339–349, 340–341t
termination with, 360–361
types of, 337–338
Small systems, 262
Soap problem-oriented records, 91
Social action, 441
changing social institutions, 381
model of community organization,
278
organizing for, 383–384
practice theory, 396
Social agency. *See* Agencies
*Social Casework: A Problem-Solving
Process* (Perlman), 12, 30
Social class, influence of, 105
Social Diagnosis (Richmond), 10–11
Social functioning, 13–14, 441
Social history, 441
about, 104–105
developing for strengths approach, 111
of family unit, 308, 313, 314–315t,
319–325
individual case example, 195–199
schema for development of, 179,
180–181t, 314–315t
Social issues, and planning, 217–218
Social justice, and macropractice,
365–366
Social Network Grid, 201
Social planning, 278, 396–397
Social policy, 218
Social role, 100
Social study. *See* Social history
Social support network analysis, 201,
441
Social system, 441. *See also* Groups
aspects of, 313
community as, 115–125
family as multiperson client system,
308–309
personal needs arising from, 79–80,
80t
small groups as, 339–349, 340–341t

Social systems theory, 7–8, 313
Social tasks, 217–218
Social work
  models of practice theory, 388–398
    (*See also* Models of social work
    practice theory)
  perspectives on, 1–2
  as response to concern/need, 3–15
  values in, 22–23
Social worker, 71–97
  accountability of, 72, 90–96
  developing community resources,
    368–370
  developing diversity competence,
    40–44
  ethical decision making, 89–90, 137
  feminist, 47–48
  as group member, 373–378
  as helping person, 72, 84–89
  identifying own cultural diversity,
    44–45
  knowledge of self, 72–84 (*See also*
    Self-knowledge)
  licensing of, 10
  in planning process with client,
    204–205, 207, 218–219, 223–224
  professional development of,
    290–291
  role in groups, 350–351
  roles of, 213–214, 233, 234–235
  termination by leaving an agency,
    294–295
  transactions between ecosystem and,
    133–134
Social worker-client relationship
  agreement or contract in, 223–224
  historical development of, 11
  interaction of worker and client (*See*
    Worker-client interaction)
  in termination process, 296
Social worker-nonclient relationships,
  148, 153–154
Social work practice
  empirically based practice, 205–206
  good practices in, 206–208
  models of, 388–398 (*See also* Mod-
    els of social work practice theory)
Social work practice theory, 388
Social work process, 13–14, 14f,
  171–172, 172f, 186, 441
Social Work with Groups (Northen), 30
Societal value system, 22
Sociobehavioral therapy, 388
Sociogram, 441
  of groups, 342, 342f
  mapping variation, 200
Soft line information, 284–285

Solution-based interventions, 441
Solution-focused model, 250–251
Spacial arrangement, in environment,
  270–271, 332
Spanish-American War, 60
Spanish language, 61
Specialist bureaucrats, 135
Special populations, 441
Specific behavioral change, 211
Spiritual development, 79
Spirituality. *See also* Religion
  of Native Americans, 64, 76
Spiritual values, 22
Stabilization of change, 300–301
Standard Metropolitan Statistical
  Area, 117
Statistical data, 366
Statistical methods, 285–286
Steady state, 343, 441
Stereotype, 74
Story-telling, 253
Strategic thinking, 204
Strategy, in planning, 212–215, 442
Strengths
  in client, 84, 99, 100, 104–105, 109,
    110–111
  of community and ecosystem, 116,
    120, 182, 183, 185
  of family, 312
  identifying in ecosystem, 33–35,
    191–192
  using knowledge and skills to see,
    18–19, 21, 25–26
Strengths approach. *See also* Ecosystems strengths approach
  blending of ecosystems and
    strengths approach, 28, 115
  client uniqueness and, 110–111
  defined, 8–9, 442
  in planning process, 209, 221–222
  in problem-solving process, 30–32
Strengths perspective practice theory,
  397
Stress
  as block to need fulfillment,
    188–189
  of client, 110
  developmental, 240
  in interviews, 165
  of managed care for social workers,
    137
Structure
  of family system, 313, 315–316
  of small groups, 341–343
Student, 101
Study of social agency, 130t
Substance abuse, 245, 311, 368, 400–403

Suicide, 258, 415
Summarizing, in interviews, 168
Summary record, 91–92
Summative evaluation, 283, 442
Supervision in bureaucracy, 136
Supplemental Security Income (SSI), 66
Support, 243–246, 442
  actions taken for social functioning
    of families, 329
  in group development, 358
Support groups, 245, 338, 351
Sustaining relationship, 211
Sustainment, and support, 244
Systemic transactions, 185
Systems theory, 433. *See also* Social
  systems

T
Taping, 93
Tarasoff *v.* Regents of the University of
  California, 24
Target system, 100
Task-achievement scaling (TAS), 290
Task-centered model, 251–252
Task-centered social work, 18
Task forces, in action to change
  community, 278–279
Task groups, 368, 370, 371, 378, 442
Task implementation process, in
  groups, 344
Task practice theory, 397–398
Tasks, 442
  in planning, 215
  of social work, 377–378
Teacher, social worker role as, 214
Teambuilding, 375
Teams, 374–376, 442
Teamwork, 272
Termination, 281–283, 293–302
  in change process, 36
  components of, 298–302
  defined, 282, 442
  disengagement as component of,
    299–300
  evaluation as component of,
    301–302
  with families, 333–334
  with individuals, 297–298
  kinds of, 293–297
  leaving an agency, 294–295
  planned, with individuals, 297–298
  with small groups, 360–361
  stabilization of change as component
    of, 300–301
  unplanned, 282, 294
Terminology and definitions, of client,
  101

Terrorist attack of 9/11/2001, 107
Theory. *See* Models of social work practice theory; Models with direct practice action
Theory and Practice of Social Casework, The (Hamilton), 11
Therapeutic alliance, 144
Therapy groups, 337
Thinking, 13–14, 442. *See also* Feeling, thinking, acting system
Throughput, 442
Time element in community, 116
Time factors in environmental change, 271, 331
Time-limited group, 360, 361
Time orientation, and value conflicts, 76
Time-series design, 285
Towle's elements of need, 133, 191, 413
Traditional neighborhood, 117
Trait-attribute model, of professions, 9
Transactional approach, 77
Transactional assessment, 194, 199–201
    dual perspective in, 199–200
    mapping in, 200–201
    social support network analysis in, 201
Transactions, 442
    interventions into, 32–34
    between person and ecosystem, 133–134
    in social work services, 115
Transgendered people, 46
Transmitter, in communication, 155
Treatment, 442
    history of, 11
Twelve-step programs, 402

U

Ultimate values, 22
Units of attention, 1
    client systems and, 177, 178t
    in community organization change, 278
    defined, 303, 442
    in families, 313, 326
    in planning, 211–212, 212–213
Unplanned termination, 282, 294
Urban communities, 116, 117–118, 277
U.S. Census Bureau, 117

V

Validation, 244, 329
Validity, 291, 442
Value conflicts, 76
Values, 21–25
    in assessment phase and decision making, 184
    attributes of communication, 164
    in being, 76–77
    blending knowledge, skills and, 27–28
    defined, 17, 21, 442
    of ethnic clients, 53–54
    held by social work profession, 22–23
    influence and, 266, 267
    of Nguzo Saba of Kwanzaa, 56
    in planning process, 208, 211
    right to have needs met, 365
    system of, 75–77
    types of, 22
    using with knowledge and skills, 29–32, 42–44
Value system, 75–77
Valuing diversity, 24–25
Vertical patterns, in communities, 117

Veterans Administration hospital, 127
Victims, 101, 407–410
Vietnam war, 106
Violence, domestic, 407–410
Violence or threat of, 256, 328
Vital roles, 105
Voluntary agencies, 125

W

Waiting list, 286
Welfare reform, 131
White flight, 58
Women
    domestic violence services, 407–410
    gender diversity competence, 47–48
    understanding diversity of clients, 108
Women's issues orientation in practice, 254
Women's movement, 108
Work, in mediative strategy, 265
Worker. *See* Social worker
Worker burnout, 137–138
Worker-client interaction, 140–170
    blocks to engagement, 146–147
    communication and, 155–157
    engagement of one-to-one action system, 142–148
    interview as interactional tool, 157–169
    relationship and, 148–154
    relationships in small groups, 341
World War II, 106
Written consent, 93–94

Y

You statements, 328
Youth and delinquency services, good practice in, 416–419

Photo Credits